The Lost Language of Symbolism

The LOST LANGUAGE of SYMBOLISM

AN ESSENTIAL GUIDE FOR RECOGNIZING AND INTERPRETING SYMBOLS OF THE GOSPEL

ALONZO L. GASKILL

FOREWORD BY JOSEPH FIELDING McCONKIE

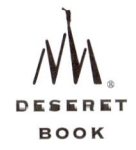

DESERET BOOK

SALT LAKE CITY, UTAH

© 2003 Alonzo L. Gaskill

All rights reserved. No part of this book may be reproduced in any form or by any means without permission in writing from the publisher, Deseret Book Company, P. O. Box 30178, Salt Lake City, Utah 84130. This work is not an official publication of The Church of Jesus Christ of Latter-day Saints. The views expressed herein are the responsibility of the author and do not necessarily represent the position of the Church or of Deseret Book Company.

DESERET BOOK is a registered trademark of Deseret Book Company.

Visit us at DeseretBook.com

Library of Congress Cataloging-in-Publication Data

Gaskill, Alonzo L.
    The lost language of symbolism : an essential guide for recognizing and interpreting symbols of the Gospel / Alonzo L. Gaskill.
      p.   cm.
    Includes bibliographical references and indexes.
    ISBN 978-1-57008-891-9 (alk. paper)
    1. Mormon Church—Sacred books.   2. Symbolism.   I. Title.

BX8622.G37 2003
246'.55—dc21   2002156486

Printed in the United States of America
Edwards Brothers Incorporated, Lillington, NC

20   19   18   17   16   15   14   13   12   11

With sincere gratitude, this book is dedicated to the members of the Menlo Park California Stake, who have taught me so much about what it means to truly live the law of consecration. Your actions have forever changed my life.

CONTENTS

Foreword ix
Preface xv
1. Why Symbols? 1
2. The Art of Interpreting Symbols 11
3. Body Parts As Symbols 27
4. Clothing As Symbols 61
5. Colors As Symbols 83
6. Numbers As Symbols 107
7. Directions As Symbols 149
8. People As Types 171
9. Names As Symbols 219
10. Animals As Symbols 243
11. Types and Symbols of Christ 269
12. Summary of the Symbols 307
Notes 325
Bibliography 407
Scripture Index 437
Subject Index 455

FOREWORD

Most Latter-day Saints are scripturally literate and do some scriptural reading and study. Yet virtually all of us could enhance our understanding and love of the scriptures by improving our fluency in the language of symbols. This is equally true of the temple. An increased understanding of the scriptures always brings with it a greater love and appreciation for everything that takes place in the temple. I was quite surprised by a comment a temple worker made to me the other day. He said, "People keep asking me questions about the symbolism of the temple. Since I don't understand it I just tell them it doesn't matter." This seemed to me almost like saying, "Since I do not appreciate good music I make it a point to discourage others from doing so." Or perhaps like the person who said to me, "I'm sorry, I cannot hear what you are saying without a hearing aid, and I don't like to wear my hearing aid."

Symbolism is a marvelously instructive and expressive language. It is a universal and timeless language. In the context of the gospel, symbolism bounds cultures to bind the saints of all gospel dispensations together. It partakes of the language of the heart and the language of the Spirit. It gives a fulness to our expression and understanding as it draws upon the eloquence of life's experiences and associations. It brings color and life to the spoken word and emotion and meaning to the world of visual expression.

As Alonzo Gaskill deftly points out in this work, the

language of symbolism embraces everything from the dust of the earth to the glories of the heavens. To miss what is being expressed or taught with symbols is like living in a world without sunsets or autumn leaves. It also makes you a first cousin to the fellow who could not read and refused to learn because he was getting along just fine without being able to do so.

Even a quick glance reveals how much more interesting our world is when we are conversant with the language of symbolism. For instance, it is my privilege, with many others, to hold the Melchizedek Priesthood. And why is it so called? What great lesson is to be found within its name? The name *Melchizedek* is created by combining two Hebrew words: the word "Melch," which means *king,* and the word "Zedek," which means *righteousness.* Thus Melchizedek means "king of righteousness" (Hebrews 7:2). The name is a constant reminder to me that it is my destiny to become a king and that the power and authority that is mine—the extent of my kingship or influence—exists only within the bounds of righteousness. Should I step outside the bounds of righteousness I am without power and authority.

I also note with interest that the Church is governed at all levels by a presidency of three. These presidencies are in similitude of the heavenly presidency of three, or the Godhead. A presidency's likeness to the Godhead clearly dictates the spirit and purpose of all that they do. The idea of counselors or a presidency also reminds us that no man is left to stand alone.

As we examine the government of the Church we also notice that its second leading quorum is the Quorum of the Twelve. Why twelve? Would not eleven do, or would thirteen be too many? It is significant that there were twelve tribes in Israel and the great promise made to them was that in the last days they would be restored to the greatness and glory of David's day. Thus the existence of a Quorum of the Twelve is a constant reminder that the Lord will make good on the promises he made with the ancients. This in turn reinforces our confidence that he will in like manner keep all of the promises he has made to us.

We obtain membership in the Church through the waters of baptism, a wonderfully expressive symbol. It signifies a new birth in which we, like the infant child, come forth surrounded by the elements of water, blood, and spirit. Enoch explained, "For by the water ye keep the commandment; by the Spirit ye are justified, and by the blood ye are sanctified" (Moses 6:60). Showing the versatility of symbols, Paul likened baptism to death, burial, and resurrection. That is, the old man of sin is laid to rest in a watery grave while the new man in Christ comes forth out of the water into a newness of life in the resurrection (Romans 6:4–7).

Recently my wife and I visited Nauvoo to see the new temple there. It was a breathtaking experience. The temple, built in the likeness of its predecessor, stands as a marvelous tribute to the Abrahamic faith of our pioneer forebears. Having laid their all upon the altar of the Lord, they had rightful claim to his blessings as they, like the children of Israel in ancient days, journeyed into an unknown wilderness. Surely the Lord was with them like a pillar of fire in the day and a cloud at night, for despite all the hardships that beset them, they established Zion, doing so in a land with its own likeness of the Sea of Galilee, the River Jordan, the Mount of Olives, the Dead Sea, and a forbidding desert. Surely there is more than coincidence in all the parallels between ancient Israel and her children in the last days.

When our progenitors came west, no physical structure more perfectly symbolized their faith than the Salt Lake Temple. The city itself takes its orientation from the ten-acre plot, known as Temple Square, on which it rests. At the southeast corner of Temple Square, surveyors established the Great Salt Lake base and meridian. This spot was used as the base reference point for survey work done in the region. In like manner, the temple stands at the heart of the Mormon cosmos. It is our spiritual "base and meridian," giving unity and direction to all that we do. Hugh Nibley calls the temple "a scale model of the universe" (Nibley, *Temple and Cosmos*, 15). From it we get our bearings and learn the way back to our heavenly home. In that journey, the temple is our compass, and it is fitting that on the west center tower of the Salt Lake Temple we find the Big Dipper chiseled in stone, pointing the way to the North Star so that we can fix our course.

The temple's most prominent architectural features are its towers. The taller, or eastern, towers represent the three presiding high priests of the Church, the First Presidency. The three western towers represent the Presiding Bishopric, who constitute the presidency of the Aaronic Priesthood and preside over the temporal affairs of the Church.

The gold-plated statue of the angel Moroni holding a trumpet to his lips crowns the highest pinnacle of the temple. It was Moroni who delivered to Joseph Smith the record from which the Book of Mormon was translated. His place on the pinnacle of many temples symbolizes the proclamation of the restored gospel to those of every nation, kindred, and tongue. As Matthew declared, God "shall send his angels with a great sound of a trumpet, and they shall gather together his elect from the four winds, from one end of heaven to the other" (Matthew 24:31).

Other notable symbolic features of the Salt Lake Temple include the granite stones from which the temple was built. They represent stability, steadfastness, and an enduring faith. They typify the everlasting covenants made within the walls of the temple. As with all temples, the chief cornerstone represents the Lord Jesus Christ. President Gordon B. Hinckley identified the other three cornerstones as the First Vision, the Book of Mormon, and the restoration of the priesthood with its keys and offices (Conference Report, October 1984, 67).

The greater symbolism, however, is found within the temple, where the saints of the Lord, according to scriptural promise, are endowed with power from on high. Here, for instructional purposes, I become Adam and my wife becomes

Eve. God then makes the same covenants with us that he made with our first parents and teaches us the same principles they were taught. This is a dramatic way of saying that the system and plan of salvation is the same for all the family of Adam. It is also a way of saying that in the eternal scheme of things we are as important as the ancients and thus can lay claim to the same blessings they have received.

Before Adam and Eve left the Garden of Eden, God taught them the law of sacrifice and clothed them in garments of protection. Symbolically those garments, made from the skins of animals, undoubtedly lambs, represented the protection that would be theirs from all the effects of the Fall. Those garments were to be a constant reminder that only in and through the blood of the Lamb of God could they find meaning and reason to all that they would suffer in the lone and dreary world into which they were now to go.

Thus we too are prepared for our journey in life, just as Adam and Eve were prepared. The physical hardships of our journey may not match those experienced by our pioneer progenitors, but the journey will be beset with many hazards and difficulties, and we too will have sufficient cause to call upon the powers of heaven to deliver us.

As Adam and Eve were married by the hand of the Lord in the "holy mountain of God" (Ezekiel 28:14) in an eternal union, so my sweetheart and I went to the temple to be married by that same authority. In this ceremony, symbolically, I became as Abraham and my wife became as Sarah, and we made the same covenant as our ancient counterparts. As they received the promise of a righteous posterity and of an endless seed, so did we.

Unlike the weddings of the world, in this sacred ceremony both husband and wife are clothed in purity, and both kneel to receive the blessings that will be theirs. And where is it that they kneel but at the altar, which in ancient days was the place of sacrifice, the place of covenant, the place of revelation, and the place of the divine presence.

So the story of Adam and Eve, a very real and personal story, becomes at the same time a universal story. It becomes the story of every man and woman who, like Adam and Eve, enter into the covenant of the Lord and then labor side by side to honor and keep that covenant.

These things and a host of others become more plain, clear, and meaningful to us as we learn the language of symbolism. Yet, well might we ask, as did Philip, "How can I [learn], except some man should guide me?" (Acts 8:31). To that end a master teacher, Alonzo Gaskill, has chosen to expand the walls of his classroom by taking pen in hand and sharing the fruits of countless hours of study in this work, *The Lost Language of Symbolism*. I expect that it will bless the lives of many Saints for many years to come.

JOSEPH FIELDING MCCONKIE

PREFACE

For several years I have felt a need in Latter-day Saint literature for a book that explains the origins and meanings of the rich symbolism found in the scriptures of The Church of Jesus Christ of Latter-day Saints and reflected in the worship practices of its holy temples. A number of LDS scholars have written on temple and scriptural symbolism,[1] and much of what is currently available is worth reading. I have been enlightened and inspired by their insights, as well as by those of various early church fathers and Catholic and Protestant scholars. This book is based on that foundation. My purpose is not to supplant any other work on scriptural symbolism, but simply to gather under one cover for easy reference the important symbolic categories that have been alluded to or expounded upon in hundreds of works over the centuries.

    This book has been difficult to write. My natural inclination was to take a wholly academic approach, but doing so would have limited the book's overall appeal and usefulness. So every effort has been made to present the material so as to engage the lay membership, my primary audience. (After all, the scholars of the Church will already be sufficiently aware of the symbols explored herein.) However, because this book is the result of extensive research, it retains a moderately academic flavor, particularly in its attempt to offer precise delineations, careful analyses, accurate interpretations, and responsible documentation of sources. One author counseled,

"Never read a book that you can comprehend in one reading, for a book that can be grasped in one reading was not worth that reading."[2] This book will not likely be grasped in just one reading; it covers too much ground for that. I certainly hope it is worth reading—and that it invites review and even rereading.

It should be understood, however, that this book is not designed to be an exhaustive treatise of symbols or scriptural passages with evident or potential symbolic intent.[3] A comprehensive study of symbolism would be volumes in length and, again, beyond the target audience. A famed chaplain of the U.S. Senate, Dr. Peter Marshall, penned the following words the day before he died: "Small deeds done are better than great deeds planned. We know that we cannot do everything. But [God] help us to do something."[4] Because the research and writing for this book could have gone on indefinitely given the nature of the subject, I decided to conclude my effort as a small deed done rather than risk the project's becoming nothing more than a great deed planned that never came to fruition. The reader is reminded that this book is only a primer. Its twofold purpose is to (1) open the eyes of those who feel frustrated when reading scripture or attending the temple because of their lack of understanding and insight, and (2) help satisfy the cravings of those who are curious about the meanings of things symbolic. Just as a gold mine yields its treasures only through the arduous toil and efforts of the miner, so it is with scripture and ritual: we must diligently dig if we are to discover the precious treasures embedded within the pages and practices of the restored gospel.[5] It is my hope that this book will serve as a valuable tool in that task, easing the way by showing how and where to dig.

I wish to thank those who reviewed this text and offered helpful editorial suggestions: Don Brugger, Elaine Cannon, Paul Damron, Anthony Celaya, Keith Fackrell, Lori Gaskill, Jan Nyholm, Lisa Mangum, Cory Maxwell, Doreen McKnight,

Susan Cannon McOmber, Robert Millet, Jay Parry, and David Phillips.

Finally, this book is not a publication of The Church of Jesus Christ of Latter-day Saints, nor does it necessarily represent the official position of the Church or the publisher. I bear sole responsibility for the content of this book.

1
WHY SYMBOLS?

OVER THE YEARS, some of my students have questioned the propriety of interpreting a passage of scripture symbolically when a literal interpretation might just as well be drawn. Although we must be careful not to read into a text unintended meanings, we should not be so literal that we overlook the symbolic dimension of scripture.[1] To reject in wholesale fashion symbolic, allegorical, or typological interpretations of scripture is naive.

There can be no question that symbolism in its various forms is intentionally present in scripture.[2] Indeed, symbolism is the very language of scripture.[3] To be unversed in symbolism is to be scripturally illiterate.[4] This is because, as the LDS Bible Dictionary states, "The scriptures are rich in symbolism and figurative expression."[5]

Commenting on this fact, one scholar wrote: "It is impossible to properly and fully interpret the symbols in Scripture without a proper understanding of the language of the symbol," for the scriptures "are written in the language of the symbol as well as the language of the type. . . . The whole of the Bible, from Genesis chapter 1 to Revelation chapter 22, abounds with . . . symbolism."[6]

Another commentator observed that "the whole outward creation . . . is so made as to represent spiritual things . . . ; thus almost everything that was said or done, that we have recorded in Scripture from Adam to Christ, was [a type] of Gospel things."[7] This is true not only of scripture but also of liturgy, or ritual, within the Church:

> Symbols are the language in which all gospel covenants and all ordinances of salvation have been revealed. From the time we are immersed in the waters of baptism to the time we kneel at the altar of the temple with the companion of our choice in the ordinance of eternal marriage, every covenant we make will be written in the language of symbolism.[8]

Let us not forget that the primary purpose of scripture is to bring people unto Christ and not simply to preserve a historical message.[9] Protestant theologians Gordon Fee and Douglas Stuart have argued, "You will not fully do justice to any individual narrative without recognizing its part within . . . Israel's history in the world . . . [and] the ultimate narrative of God's creation and his redemption of [the world]."[10] In the third century, Origen wrote, "You must be prepared to recognize that the narratives of Holy Scripture are 'figures,' and for that reason you must consider them in a spiritual rather than a carnal fashion, and thus grasp their purport. For, if you take them in a carnal manner, they . . . fail to nourish."[11]

For Philo of Alexandria, scripture, with God as its author, could not contain useless information or insignificant details. It was not to be understood solely on the basis of its literal meaning. Rather, the literal meaning was much like the husk on an ear of corn—it was to be peeled off to reveal the more important symbolic meaning.[12] Thomas Aquinas indicated that the literal sense referred to the meaning of words in the scriptures and that the spiritual sense referred to the meaning of things, events, or teachings of the scriptures.[13] One biblical scholar stated that the Mosaic laws and regulations were "offensive and ridiculous" if not seen in light of their "deeper symbolical meaning," with the intent of making Israel more like, and obedient to, her God.[14]

As interesting as the historical facts in scripture can be,

they are eclipsed by the spiritual messages. Astute readers should always be on the lookout for profound meanings.[15]

The scriptures themselves declare their symbolic nature, as the following sampling demonstrates. King Benjamin observed that Christ had given the people "many signs, and wonders, and types, and shadows . . . concerning his coming; . . . and yet they hardened their hearts, and understood not" (Mosiah 3:15). On numerous occasions Paul, Alma the Younger, Abinadi, and others testified that the law of Moses was a symbolic type of things to come (see Colossians 2:17; Hebrews 8:4–5; 10:1; Alma 25:15; Mosiah 16:14).

Indeed, Nephi joyfully declared, "Behold, my soul delighteth in proving unto my people the truth of the coming of Christ; for, for this end hath the law of Moses been given; and all things which have been given of God from the beginning of the world, unto man, are the typifying of him" (2 Nephi 11:4). Prophets such as Adam and Melchizedek are said to have been types of Christ (see 1 Corinthians 15:21–22; Romans 5:14; Hebrews 7; 8:1–3). Alma indicated that the Liahona was a symbol representing the words of Christ and that the brass serpent that Moses raised up in the wilderness foreshadowed Christ's power to save those who would exercise faith in Him (see Alma 33:19; 37:38–45). He also taught that ordination to the priesthood was symbolic of Christ (see Alma 13:14–18; see also Hebrews 9–10). Abinadi declared that even the actions of King Noah against him would have symbolic and typological significance (see Mosiah 13:10; Alma 25:10).

According to Paul, the Church, or body of Christ, was prefigured in the story of Israel (see 1 Corinthians 10:1); baptism was symbolically depicted in the parting of the Red Sea (see 1 Corinthians 10:1–2); Christ was the spiritual "meat and drink" that Israel partook of in the wilderness (see 1 Corinthians 10:3–4); Abraham's sons, Ishmael and Isaac, were types for the Old Law and the New (see Galatians 4:22–26); and the veiled face of Moses when he came down from Sinai symbolized how the Jews would not clearly see Jesus foretold in scripture (see 2 Corinthians 3:14–18).

Most importantly, the premortal Christ stated: "And behold, all things have their likeness, and all things are created and made to bear record of me, both things which are temporal, and things which are spiritual; things which are in the heavens above, and things which are on the earth, and things which are in the earth, and things which are under the earth, both above and beneath: all things bear record of me" (Moses 6:63). One Latter-day Saint specialist in the field of typology noted that some "seventy-five listings in the Topical Guide to the LDS edition of the King James Bible refer to 'types, shadows and similitudes.'"[16]

Mormonism has its own unique set of symbols that play a significant role in LDS life, literature, and liturgy. The iron rod symbolizes the word of God, or scripture (see 1 Nephi 8:19); the Liahona, the guidance of the Holy Spirit (see 1 Nephi 16:10; Alma 37:38–40). Handcarts and covered wagons conjure images of faith, courage, sacrifice, and endurance. Seagulls remind us of God's willingness to intervene in rather miraculous ways. The beehive has become a standard symbol for industry and work. The tree of life is equated with Christ, eternal life, the love of God, and the sweet joy of living the gospel (see 1 Nephi 8:10–12; 11:8–23; 15:21–22.). The initials *CTR* appear on rings worn by thousands of Latter-day Saints as a constant reminder to "choose the right." The "Mormon Tabernacle" generates thoughts of choral music and perhaps the architectural genius of the early pioneers. The infamous "great and spacious building"—representing the wisdom and pride of the world—can evoke images of the worldly corruption leading to destruction (see 1 Nephi 11:35–36).

Each of those symbols brings to mind very strong and well-established images for practicing Latter-day Saints. We simply cannot dismiss the significant role of symbolism in the scriptures of the restored gospel, nor can we overlook the influence of that unique symbolism[17] in the worship practices and very lives of Church members.

The scholarly world is united in the belief that the standard Christian approach to the Old Testament was typological.[18] This approach is evident in New Testament writings and heavily present in the writings of the Apologists of the second and third centuries.[19] Maurice Farbridge noted that "in the ancient East . . . symbolism permeated the whole life of the people."[20] One text on the history of biblical interpretation notes: "Without the typological method it would have been almost impossible for the early church to retain its grasp on the Old Testament. . . . The early church was intensely interested in the ways in which the life of Jesus was prefigured in the Old Testament."[21] This same text notes that Jesus went beyond contemporary Judaism and interpreted the prophecies of the Old Testament in reference to himself and the Christian church: "The idea that he regarded prophecy as somehow fulfilled in himself lies deep in the tradition."[22] Along similar lines, one LDS author has stated, "The Lord taught his disciples to look upon the contents of the scriptures and see things 'concerning himself.'"[23] Elsewhere we read:

> Jesus especially used symbolic language. It was God's secret code for veiling or revealing truth according to the attitude of the listener. He did this when He taught by the parabolic method. This is specially seen in Matthew 13 in the teaching on the Parables of the Kingdom. . . . The disciples realized it was "the language of the symbol." . . . They perceived by the interpretation of the parables that there was more to it than the natural, the literal and the material.[24]

Early Christian authors who believed that certain narrative events were symbolically interpreted in the New Testament still deemed those events historical. In their view, God inspired those involved in such events to live in a symbolically significant manner, and he also inspired the recorders of those events to emphasize the aspects that were later fulfilled in the New

Testament.[25] In other words, God is entirely able to saturate historical events with symbolic and typological meanings without mortal intervention or the distortion of historical facts.[26]

A further word regarding definitions is appropriate. Although it is necessary to distinguish between symbols, types, allegories, and so on when examining a passage of scripture, in this book the term *symbolism* has so far been used broadly to refer to any facet of symbolic meaning, such as discourse, action, or clothing. Standard definitions include "something that stands for or represents another thing[,] especially an object used to represent something abstract";[27] "a material object substituted for a moral or spiritual truth";[28] "a representation, visual or conceptual, of that which is unseen and invisible";[29] and "a token, pledge, [or] a sign by which one infers a thing."[30] One scholar wrote:

> The word "symbol" derives from the Greek word *súmbolon*, which means literally "something thrown together"; this word can be translated "token." Contracting parties would break a *súmbolon*, a bone or tally stick, into two pieces, then fit them together again later. Each piece would represent its owner; the halves "thrown together" represent two separated identities merging into one. Thus this concept of "symbol" (unity; separation; restoration) provides a model for love, the Atonement, separation and reunification, our original unity with God, our earthly separation, our eventual return to the divine presence and renewed perfect unity with God. Furthermore, this meaning of symbol shows that understanding any symbol requires the "throwing together" of an earthly, concrete dimension and a transcendent, spiritual dimension. Plato's idea that knowledge is remembrance (of a premortal existence) has relevance here.[31]

We might appropriately ask why the Lord and his prophets have chosen to use symbols when teaching or establishing modes of worship and ritual. Six possible reasons come to mind. First of all, to understand symbols requires persistent effort. Their use in the standard works and ordinances of the Church encourages participants to ponder the truths of the restored gospel and to seek the guidance and inspiration of the Holy Ghost. This attitude of prayerful searching and reflection is rewarded through the receipt of new discoveries, previously unknown insights, and a significantly deepened love for the scriptures and the temple.

Second, symbols are designed to protect that which is sacred by revealing truth and insight to those who are prepared and by concealing the same from the unworthy. Elder Bruce R. McConkie taught:

> Our Lord used *parables* on frequent occasions during his ministry to teach gospel truths. His purpose, however, in telling these short stories was *not* to present the truths of his gospel in plainness so that all his hearers would understand. Rather it was to phrase and hide the doctrine involved so that only the spiritually literate would understand it, while those whose understandings were darkened would remain in darkness. (Matt. 13:10–17; JST, Matt. 21:34.).[32]

A third reason why revealed religion is saturated in symbolism is that many symbols are timeless,[33] allowing many of them to translate well from language to language, culture to culture, and age to age. One scholar observed, "Some symbols are images of things common to all men, and therefore have a communicable power which is potentially unlimited."[34] For example, a lamb has a fairly universal association with innocence, gentleness, meekness, and purity.[35] Even more pervasive is the symbolic connotation of light. Blood, on the other hand, is technically "never a good sign"[36] and is traditionally associated cross-culturally with death, guilt, impurity, sin, the need for atonement, and so on.[37]

Fourth is the reality that symbols have a tremendous ability to influence the mind and create lasting impressions. Traditionally, once we have attached a specific meaning to a given symbol, any future encounter of that symbol will bring a resurgence of thoughts or feelings associated with the assigned meaning. Perhaps one of the most universal examples of this reality is found in the sign of the cross. Although the majority of the world's inhabitants (including Latter-day Saints) do not use the cross as a religious symbol, most people instantly associate it with Christianity, and nearly all Christians see it as a reminder of Christ's sacrifice on their behalf.

A fifth reason might be that symbols are multilayered, providing numerous levels of understanding contingent upon one's level of spiritual maturity or understanding. One commentator employs a helpful analogy to emphasize this point:

> Symbols are the language of feeling, and as such, it is not expected that everyone will perceive them in the same way. Like a beautifully cut diamond, they catch the light and then reflect its splendor in a variety of ways. As viewed at different times and from different positions, what is reflected will differ, yet the diamond and the light remain the same. Thus symbols, like words, gain richness in their variety of meanings and purposes, which range from revealing to concealing great gospel truths.[38]

Along the same lines, another scholar explains that symbols and types are

> but a "shadow of . . . [heavenly truths]"; and therefore, like all shadows, they give but an imperfect representation. . . . Most objects cast differently shaped shadows as the light falls upon them in various directions; . . . though the object is the same, the light is thrown upon it in different directions, and reveals shadows cast from opposite sides: so is it in the types [and symbols]. Sometimes in the same type [or symbol] we may find different sides of the truth represented.[39]

As a sixth and final point, those versed in religious symbolism will recognize that one of the great values of symbols is their ability to functionally teach abstract concepts. For example, bread as a symbol for Christ teaches well the abstract idea that Jesus must become part of our very beings if we are to be exalted in the celestial kingdom of God. Just as the bread we eat is digested and absorbed by our bodies, sustaining and strengthening us, so also Christ's gospel and teachings must become a part of us—written upon the tables of our hearts, to use a common scriptural metaphor—if they are to strengthen and sustain us eternally.

Sadly, for some members of the Church,

> symbolism is a dead language. The difficulties of interpretation and the barriers posed by scriptural language have discouraged some Saints from feasting upon the inspired word [or participating in the ordinances of the holy temple.] But those hungering for this greater substance have turned to the scriptures and commenced the struggle to learn the language of revelation. They have discovered that to be fluent in the language of the Spirit one must be fluent in the language of symbolism.[40]

The remainder of this book is dedicated to facilitating that understanding. It is my hope that readers who grasp the key aspects of scriptural symbolism outlined herein will be enabled to discover the deeper, more profound insights and truths that have eluded them, that they might more readily liken the scriptures unto themselves for their profit and learning (see 1 Nephi 19:23).

2

THE ART OF INTERPRETING SYMBOLS

In GENERAL TERMS THE WORD *hermeneutics* means "the art of understanding a text." In a more narrow sense, the word refers to the methods or techniques used to accurately interpret passages of scripture.[1] This chapter lays necessary groundwork to help us understand and apply sound methods of interpreting the many symbols in scriptures.

Our first order of business is to define useful technical terms and to note the subtle yet important distinctions between them. For ease of comparison, let's begin by briefly returning to the definition of *symbol*. Simply put, a symbol is something that represents another thing. It may be a material object that represents an abstract moral or spiritual truth, or it may be a visual or conceptual representation of that which is unseen. Put another way, a symbol is "an image that stands for something in addition to its literal meaning. It is more laden with meaning than simply the connotations of the straight image."[2]

An *image*, on the other hand, is any word or action that names a concrete thing. If an object or action can be pictured, it is an image. Images require two things from us as readers of scripture. First, we must experience the image as literally and in as fully a sensory way as possible. Second, we must be sensitive to the connotations or overtones of the image. For example, in light of the context in which it appears, is the image positive or negative?[3]

A *type* is a symbol that looks forward to an antitype, or

future fulfillment. The thing a type symbolizes always comes after the type; they are never concurrent. There is a major difference between symbols and types: a symbol represents something potentially concurrent with itself. For example, Jesus said of himself, "I am the bread of life" (John 6:35, 48) and "I am the light of the world" (John 8:12; 9:5). The bread and light that symbolized Jesus existed while he did. One commentator explained the distinction between symbols and types as follows:

> Symbols serve as signs of something they represent, without necessarily being similar in any respect, whereas types resemble in one or more ways the things they prefigure. . . . Types point forward in time; whereas symbols may not. A type always precedes historically its antitype, whereas a symbol may precede, exist concurrently with, or come after the thing which it symbolizes.[4]

Thus, a type can be defined as a "preordained representative relationship which certain persons, events, and institutions bear to corresponding persons, events, and institutions occurring at a later time in history."[5] There are basically five classes of types common in scripture.[6]

1. *Typical persons.* These are individuals whose lives illustrate some significant principle or truth related to the gospel and plan of salvation. The most significant and common occurrences of typical persons are found in the reality that all ancient prophets typify Christ, just as all modern prophets symbolize him.[7]

2. *Typical events.* These are historical events that possess an analogical or corresponding relationship to some later event. Examples include the wickedness and eventual destruction of Sodom and Gomorrah (see Genesis 19), typifying the state of the worldly at the second advent of Christ,[8] and God's judgment on faithless Israel as a typological warning to Christians not to engage in immorality (see 1 Corinthians 10:1–11).

3. *Typical institutions.* These are practices that prefigure later saving events. The quintessential model is the Mosaic

requirement of animal sacrifice, typifying the future atonement of the Lord Jesus Christ (see Moses 5:4–8; Genesis 22:8; Exodus 12:5; Numbers 9:12; John 1:29; 1 Corinthians 5:7; 2 Nephi 11:4).

4. *Typical offices.* These are offices that typify or symbolize Christ. This category is really a subset of typical persons. As we noted above, the prophetic office certainly falls into this category, but so also does the ancient office of high priest.[9]

5. *Typical actions.* These are personal actions that anticipate parallel manifestations of divine will. This category is exemplified by Isaiah's walking naked and barefoot for three years as a sign to Egypt and Ethiopia that Assyria would soon lead them away naked and barefoot (see Isaiah 20:2–4). Another example can be found in Hosea's marriage to the prostitute Gomer and his subsequent redemption of her after her infidelity, typifying the Lord's covenantal love for weak and ofttimes faithless Israel (see Hosea 1:2–3).

LITERARY DEVICES

Metaphors and *similes* are two of the most simple literary devices, yet they function much as symbols do. Scholars commonly use the term *symbol* interchangeably with *metaphor* and *simile.* A metaphor is an implied comparison (e.g., "I am the bread of life," "Ye are the light of the world"). Metaphors are not intended to be taken literally. As one author noted, "Christ is no more a piece of bread than Christians are photonemitters."[10] Similes also compare one thing to another, but they make the comparison explicit by using the formula *like* or *as* (e.g., "the kingdom of heaven is like . . ."). Simple as they are, metaphor and simile engage the reader's imagination as "bifocal utterances that require us to look at both the literal and figurative levels."[11]

According to the Gospel of Mark, Jesus' use of *parables* during his Galilean ministry was constant (see Mark 4:33–34). Parables are much less common in the Hebrew Bible (Old

Testament) than in the New Testament.[12] In simplistic terms, parables can be understood as extended similes. They are brief stories that employ familiar situations, events, characteristics, or elements in order to teach important spiritual truths.

In parables, as with many other forms of symbolism, it is important to distinguish between the interpretation and an application. "The only true interpretation is the meaning the parable conveyed, or was meant to convey, when first spoken. The application of a parable may vary in every age and circumstance. But if the original meaning is to be grasped, it is important to consider its context and setting."[13]

Whereas a parable is like an extended simile, an *allegory* "can be understood as an extended metaphor: the comparison is unexpressed, and the subject and the thing compared are intermingled. A parable generally proceeds by keeping the story and its application distinct from each other: usually the application follows the story. Allegories intermingle the story and its application so that an allegory carries its own interpretation within itself."[14] One additional difference between parables and allegories is the extent to which their details are symbolic. With allegories, often most of the details have significance and require interpretation. With parables, however, taking the interpretation too far will do damage to the parable and will no doubt confuse the recipient.[15] Some biblical scholars see typology as nothing more than a subdivision of allegory.[16]

A *motif* can be described as a recurring theme or "a structurally unified verbal whole."[17] For example, in literature and drama there is the common motif of conflict between good and evil. A symbolic motif can be defined as

> a pattern that appears in a written text.... Even though a single instance of such a pattern warrants the application of the term *motif*, it is more customary to apply the term to repeated instances of the same pattern.... The literary term currently in vogue to designate the recurrence of common ingredients in a story is *type scene*.... A motif is thus made up of a set of *conventions*—ingredients that recur so often in similar situations

that they become expectations in the minds of writers and readers alike.[18]

One LDS scholar has suggested that the key to understanding the Book of Mormon's typological unity is the recurring central motif of Lehi's dream of the tree of life:

> Ultimately, as in all Judeo-Christian figures of pilgrimage, [Lehi] goes through the wilderness of a fallen world toward a redeemed world abounding in the joy of God's loving presence. Call it quest or conversion, at bottom the pattern is a simple transformation: from dark and barren waste by means of the Word to a world fruitful and filled with light. And the transformation is enacted again and again in the Book of Mormon, at both the individual and communal levels.[19]

Finally, an *archetype* is an image or pattern that recurs throughout literature and, more particularly, life. Archetypes might be described as "the universal elements of human experience."[20] Archetypes are a universal language; we know what they mean simply by virtue of being human (e.g., health and sickness, pleasure and pain).[21] Although beliefs and customs differ greatly from time to time and place to place, archetypes are the fundamental experiences of life. They traditionally fall into one of three categories: either an image or symbol (such as the "great and spacious building" of 1 Nephi 11:35–36), a plot motif (such as the battle between good and evil), or a character type (such as an evil villain or a cherished hero).

The foregoing definitions adequately cover the variety of symbolism found in scripture. Additional categories and details could be multiplied but are beyond the scope of this book. For example, somewhat interchangeable are technical terms such as *analogy, comparison, emblem, figure, hallmark, insignia, model, seal, sign,* and *token*.

METHODS OF ANALYZING SCRIPTURE

Responsible and accurate scriptural interpretation can be complex and demanding. It is not enough to know the difference between the various kinds of symbolism. We must also know what to look for and what to analyze. Several types of analysis should be conducted when endeavoring to fully understand a scriptural text. They are as follows:

CONTEXTUAL ANALYSIS

Most of us know the frustration of having said something that was taken out of context, so the importance of contextual analysis should be immediately clear. Contextual analysis is seeing the words in a given verse in proper relation to a larger, informing context—be it the passage, the chapter, the book, the author's overall writings, or the standard work in which the verse is found. Relevant questions include, What was the general historical or cultural milieu in which this writer was speaking? What was the specific historical and cultural context? What was the author's ostensible purpose? What is the immediate context of the verses under consideration?

HISTORICAL AND CULTURAL ANALYSIS

We must consider the environment in which a given author wrote. Readers who overlook the setting, time, and culture in which a text was written are prone to misunderstand the author's intended meaning. Indeed, the meaning of a scriptural text cannot be ascertained with any degree of certainty without the interpreter first being aware of the historical-cultural context of the passage. As one text on biblical interpretation states:

> Biblical passages not only express a writer's train of thought but also reflect a way of life—one that in most ways differs radically from that of present-day readers. The literature and events recorded in the Bible originated thousands of years ago. Beyond reflecting ancient languages, cultures, and lifestyles, the biblical writers wrote their messages for people different from ourselves. Consequently, every time we study a Scripture text, we must be aware of these cross-cultural and epoch-spanning dimensions. . . . This is the basis of an important principle of hermeneutics: *The correct interpretation of a*

biblical passage will be consistent with the historical-cultural background of the passage.[22]

The same can be said not only of the Bible but of all scripture. One contemporary theologian wrote: "Understanding requires a conscious effort to overcome . . . historical distance. The interpreter must transpose himself or herself out of the present time frame to that of the past. Understanding is a *Nacherleben* (re-experience) of an original *Erlebnis* (experience)."[23]

Theological Analysis

Theological analysis, related to historical and cultural analysis, considers both the personal theology of the author and the theological understandings of the Church at the time the revelation was given.

Etymological, Lexical, and Syntactical Analysis

These approaches focus on the origin and definition of words employed by the author (etymology and lexicology) and the relationship of those words to one another (syntax). Such analyses help the student of scripture to recognize when an author intends his words to be understood literally, figuratively, or symbolically. Etymology will primarily be of use in biblical research, although in recent years some have applied it to the Book of Mormon and, to a lesser extent, to the facsimiles in the Pearl of Great Price. Following a key principle of hermeneutics, "interpreters must deliberately pursue what the original words of a passage meant at the time they were written in the context in which they occur. The meaning of the original words, not what ideas may occur to us when we read the passage, is the objective for word studies."[24]

Literary Analysis

Literary analysis is a broad categorization of a text into a genre of scriptural literature, such as law, narrative, poetry, exposition, apocalyptic, wisdom, and prophecy. Although perhaps less important than the aforementioned forms of analysis, the defining of literary form should not be ignored. Noting the dangers of interpreting and applying scripture without attention to genre, one author coined the phrase "genre mistake." An example of this lapse would be to turn "a narrative *description* into a *prescription* for us, as if this [narrative] were the legal genre."[25]

ANALYSIS OF APPLICABILITY

Although a potentially subjective practice, analyzing for application—that is, relating the text to our own time and, much more subjectively, to our personal needs and circumstance—is vital because the absence of application entirely misses the point of why divinely inspired texts have been preserved.[26] The role of scripture to instruct and inspire presupposes our need to, as Nephi said, "liken all scriptures unto us, that it might be for our profit and learning" (1 Nephi 19:23).

RULES OF RESPONSIBLE INTERPRETATION

We now turn our attention to the rules of hermeneutics, or scriptural interpretation. Biblical scholars traditionally hold that scriptural symbolism is not the result of prophets, apostles, or holy men applying a set of interpretive standards or rules when speaking or writing. Indeed, the Spirit itself determines the rules of symbolism—both in speaking or writing symbolically and in interpreting the same. Thus, Gerhard von Rad wrote of symbolic interpretation: "No pedagogical norm can or may be set up; it cannot be further regulated hermeneutically, but takes place in the freedom of the Holy Spirit."[27] Similarly, the University of Chicago's highly acclaimed professor of New Testament and early Christianity, Robert M. Grant, wrote: "I am not entirely certain that a detailed hermeneutical system is either possible or desirable."[28] Thus, as with all scripture study, the Spirit must be our guide. Symbols may teach, enlighten, and inspire in any number of ways, but our interpretations of scripture will be in harmony with the Spirit only to the degree that we are reliant upon and made recipients of its revelatory power.

The ultimate purpose of any imagery used by the Lord surely must be to cause an intellectual and spiritual reaction within the reader. It is meant to strengthen the impact of the truth. It is meant to illuminate our souls—to help us see and feel relationships more clearly. The full illumination can only come with witness of the Spirit. We must humbly seek that witness.[29]

There can be no question, then, that the following principles for ascertaining and elucidating symbols must, in the end, be subject to the dictates of the Spirit and the teachings of the prophets.[30]

1. *Rightly determine which elements of the verse under consideration are meant to be interpreted as symbols.* If the language of the verse makes no literal or actual sense, then it must be interpreted as having symbolic sense (e.g., Revelation 12:1–4; 13:1–2). Contrarily, the following saying has some credence: "If the sense of scripture makes common sense, then seek no other sense or you may fall into non-sense." However, if a verse does make literal or actual sense, the interpreter should still seek to determine (a) if the passage could be dualistic (i.e., have more than one meaning or application, as do some of Isaiah's prophecies) or (b) if another passage of scripture interprets or intimates that the passage in question is symbolic (see John 2:19; see also John 2:21; 1 Corinthians 3:17).

2. *Look beyond the symbol.* Symbols have denotations and connotations. A symbol's denotation is its actual, literal meaning, its face value and essential nature. The connotation is what our minds associate with the symbol, the images, ideas, and values the symbol stirs in us. The parables of Jesus are good examples of symbolism in which the denotation never changes but the connotation does, constantly evolving and taking on new dimensions over time and from person to person.

3. *Consider what the scriptures or modern prophets teach regarding the symbol.* The Prophet Joseph Smith taught, "Whenever God gives . . . an image, or beast, or figure of any kind, He

always holds Himself responsible to give a revelation or interpretation of the meaning thereof, otherwise we are not responsible or accountable for our belief in it."[31] Accordingly, the interpretation may be specifically explained in the passage in question (see Daniel 2:19, 31–34; Isaiah 5:1–7; Revelation 5:8) or in another passage (see Matthew 25:1–13, cross-referenced with D&C 45), or the Lord's modern prophets, seers, and revelators may have expounded on the passage, offering an interpretation beyond what ancient scripture gives.[32]

4. *Let the nature of the symbol help clarify its meaning.* Consider the moon as a symbol. Having no light of its own, the moon merely reflects the light of the sun. Thus when John speaks of a celestial woman (the Church) with the moon under her feet (see Revelation 12:1), it should be clear that the moon symbolizes a weak or greatly diminished portion of light. Much like the moon, nonrevealed religions reflect watered-down versions of the fulness, in this case the fulness of gospel truths. While those religions may be able to raise their faithful adherents to a terrestrial level (symbolized by the moon), they have not the power to bring them into the celestial kingdom (symbolized by the sun).[33]

5. *Watch for a consistency in use of particular symbols.* Because many symbols are used more than once in scripture, it is often helpful to compare every instance of them in order to better understand their significance. Even so, we must keep in mind that symbols can have multiple meanings. For example, water serves as a symbol for chaos and death but also for cleansing and sanctification. Moreover, some symbols possess both good and evil aspects. The lion, for example, symbolizes Jesus in Revelation 5:5 but Satan in 1 Peter 5:8.

6. *Study the meaning and origin of the idioms employed.* Idioms are verbal shortcuts whose meaning cannot be taken literally (e.g., "he was born with a silver spoon in his mouth"). Of course, understanding archaic idioms does not come naturally; it requires research into the remnants of a culture, society, and

people very much removed from modern recipients of the scriptural text.[34]

7. *Balance the interpretation of symbols with an overall knowledge of gospel teachings.* If your interpretation of a symbol or the passage in which a symbol appears contradicts what has been prophetically revealed about that symbol, you must assume that your private interpretation is wrong. All interpretation of scripture must be in harmony with what the Lord's prophets have revealed in scripture and in discourse. If your interpretations are not harmonious with revealed truth, they must be rejected.

8. *Use the footnotes, chapter headings, dictionary, and other study aids provided in the standard works of the Church.* The scriptures and the words of modern prophets should be our primary sources for answers to our questions about the scriptures. Most conveniently, the LDS edition of the Bible and the other standard works of the Church contain excellent study aids. For example, the chapter headings for Isaiah 13 and 14 indicate that Babylon is a symbol of the world, or the wicked. And in Jeremiah 23, footnote 5b indicates that the word *Branch* is a symbol for Christ.

9. *Be attentive to linguistic issues.* The Bible was written in Hebrew and Greek, the Book of Mormon in "reformed Egyptian." The English translation of the Book of Abraham evidences Egyptian influence, and even the Doctrine and Covenants employs a form of English somewhat removed from what is now common. Words translated from Hebrew or Greek into English and words read without regard to the English of Joseph Smith's day do not always carry the same meanings their original authors intended. For this reason, those who seek to better understand the scriptures and their symbolism need to be aware of linguistic issues. While not every member of the Church has the opportunity to study Greek and Hebrew, much can be learned from readily available aids, such as lexicons and dictionaries, that will allow a novice to be linguistically attentive to the text.[35]

10. *Don't get too caught up in determining authorial*

awareness. Certainly it is helpful when a prophet makes clear that the words he is speaking are intended to be understood either symbolically or dualistically. However, we should not forget that it is possible that the prophets did not always know that they were writing something saturated in symbolism; that is where God's intervention comes in. Thus when Moses recorded the life of Joseph of Egypt in such a way that it serves as a heavily detailed typological symbol of the life of Christ, it matters little whether Moses knew that the story he was recording was symbolic. What matters is that the detail is such that the symbolism is unmistakable and undeniable.[36]

PITFALLS TO AVOID

In all of this, certain dangers should be noted so that we will not be misled. Four such pitfalls are discussed below.

1. *Avoid reading into a scriptural symbol or passage something that the Lord or his prophet did not intend.* Of course, we can freely liken the scriptures to ourselves and allow them to stimulate our thinking along lines that may not be directly traceable to the authors' original intentions. Rather, the danger lies in misunderstanding important doctrines and truths, which will cloud our judgment and eventually lead us astray. In reading scripture, we must exercise great care, keeping ever in mind that

> the meaning of a text is the author's intended meaning, rather than the meanings we may wish to ascribe to his words. . . . Problems result when readers interpret statements in a mode other than the one intended by the author. As much distortion of the author's meaning results from interpreting a literal statement figuratively as from interpreting a figurative statement literally. . . . The words are to be interpreted according to the author's intention. If the author meant them to be interpreted literally, we err if we interpret them symbolically. If the author meant them to be interpreted symbolically, we err equally if we interpret them literally.[37]

This is not to imply that the authors of scripture always knew *all* of the implications of their written or preached words. Rather, this caution will help us not dismiss as figurative that which the Lord and his prophets intend to be understood literally, or vice versa. Elder Bruce R. McConkie noted:

> This is difficult to do; it requires considerable experience and discernment; and it surely rates as a three or a four [on a ten-point scale]. In general we are safer in taking things literally, although the scriptures abound in figurative matters. Literal occurrences include speaking with God face to face as a man speaketh with his friend (Ex. 33:11; Moses 7:4); that man was made in the image of God both physically and spiritually (Gen. 1:26–27; 5:1; James 3:9); the coming of Christ as the Only Begotten in the flesh (Moses 1:6, 17, 33; 2:1, 26–27; 3:18; 4:1; Jacob 4:5, 11; Alma 12:33–34; 13:5; D&C 20:21; 29:42; 49:5; 76:13, 25; John 3:16); the Lord Jesus himself dwelling in Enoch's Zion (Moses 7:16, 21, 69); his personal reign during the Millennium (Joel 3:17, 21; Zech. 2:10–13; Rev. 20:4; D&C 29:11; 43:29; 133:25); the resurrection of all men from the dead with corporeal bodies of flesh and bones (1 Cor. 15:21–22; Alma 11:40–41, 44; 42:23; Rev. 20:13); and so on.[38]

This caution is also intended to remind us that it is not our place to personally attribute modern meanings to ancient symbols.[39] Rather, it is our obligation to seek out their ancient meanings and then apply them appropriately. Whatever they meant for their ancient audiences should determine how we read and apply them in scripture or liturgy today.

2. *Avoid extremes.* Some argue that if the interpretation of a symbol is not given in the scriptures, any interpretation, commentary, or elaboration on our part is unwise, unsafe, and unauthorized. To give commentary, they argue, would be to clarify what the Lord has not.[40] However, if our interpretations of symbols are confined exclusively to what is given in the scriptures, then scriptural symbolism would be virtually worthless (because more often than not the scriptures do not explain the symbols they employ).[41] In another camp are those who hold

that it is appropriate to allegorize every story, event, and doctrine in the scriptures to the point that, when finished, there is nothing in all of holy writ that can be taken as literal or true. It must be remembered that the purpose of symbols is to teach more, not less. If a particular symbolic interpretation does nothing more than call into question the historicity of the recorded event, the interpretation is likely wrong and forced. On the other hand, if it simply adds another layer to the picture or an additional (but agreeable) insight, it may well be appropriate. Joseph Fielding McConkie wrote:

> One of the great injunctions of this dispensation is that we "deny not the spirit of revelation" (D&C 11:25). Surely the refusal to see or read beyond the literal rendering of a particular verse is to deny that spirit. The warning that those who seek to seal or close the canon of scripture will lose what little understanding they have (2 Nephi 28:30) is as true of chapters and verses as of the book itself. The principle [and warning] applies as much to the figurative or symbolic as it does the literal.[42]

Elsewhere we read, "We will miss a lot of what the Bible contains if we do not see and understand the literal and symbolic meanings of the Bible's images."[43] Again, if something is found to be symbolic, that does not negate the historicity of the event, person, or passage.[44]

3. *Be cautious not to limit a symbol.* As pointed out earlier, symbols can have multiple meanings. For example, a prophet can typify or symbolize a number of other people: Adam can be seen as typifying both the Father and the Son; aspects of Abraham's life echo events in the lives of the Father, the Son, and the Prophet Joseph Smith; and Moses' life prefigured the lives of Christ, Joseph Smith, and Brigham Young. In this regard, one biblical typologist noted that

> Biblical personages, events or things, while having full value on their own, also serve as patterns or "types" of other realities. . . . We must be very careful . . . and not assume that if something or someone appears to be a "type," it means there is no other

value or significance. Rather, the object, situation, or person becomes doubly significant, possessing value within the Biblical time and setting, but meaningful for the future as well.[45]

4. Keep in mind that symbols do not reveal new doctrines. In the October 1984 general conference, Elder Boyd K. Packer offered six points of conviction pertaining to recognizing basic doctrine and not being deceived. In the first of those six, he stated, "Instruction vital to our salvation is not hidden in an obscure verse or phrase in the scriptures. To the contrary, essential truths are repeated over and over again."[46] If your study reveals something not known elsewhere, your interpretation is amiss.[47] Doctrine is not revealed through symbols. It may be emphasized in symbols, but the doctrines are always first taught openly so that there is no misunderstanding.

Numerous scholars both inside and outside of the Church have emphasized that the most important key one can utilize in order to better understand scripture is to rely upon the companionship of the Spirit, which will "teach you all things, and bring all things to your remembrance" (John 14:26).

> The prophetic scriptures . . . can only be understood correctly in the Spirit from whom they originated. . . . If it is the Spirit of Jesus Christ who spoke through the prophets (1 Pet. 1:11), then the only appropriate exegesis is done in this Spirit (1 Cor. 2:10f.). If Jesus of Nazareth is "the one who was to come," if he is the goal of all [scriptural] history, then he is the focal point that gathers all the rays of light that issue from Scripture.[48]

3

BODY PARTS AS SYMBOLS

IF YOU HAVE EVER OBSERVED A PERSON communicating in one of the numerous dialects of sign language or, for that matter, ever had a discussion with someone who makes a lot of hand gestures while speaking, it should be evident that the various parts of the body and the ways we use them can be highly symbolic. For those who have been endowed in the holy temple, a reflective thought about the gifts promised in the initiatory ordinances and the manner in which those promises are conveyed is sufficient to provoke a confirming witness of this truth.

In everyday life we engage in symbolic behaviors of which we are typically unaware. The common practice in Western culture of greeting people by extending one's hand has been traced back to the ancient ritual of requesting a "token of recognition" from individuals encountered.[1] The very practice of bowing or kneeling in prayer is itself a standard symbol of submission, although it may be done without conscious intent or meaning.[2] Although we bathe frequently, primarily for hygienic reasons, the metaphor of washing or scrubbing one's body in order to remove physical impurity is itself a powerful metaphor of life.[3] The degree to which we primp after the cleansing is completed serves to establish that something beyond mere hygiene is involved in this frequent ritual.

In ancient Semitic culture the body and its various members held more meaning than they do in modern Western societies.[4] Each part of the body invoked a very strong connotation or idea. In the case of most symbolic parts of the body, the scriptural meaning was typically associated with, and discernible through, the primary function of the part. In the days of ancient scripture these symbols were well established, commonly understood, and frequently employed. Although some of them are utilized in Western culture today, the once-strong undertones of many have been lost.

We will now turn our attention to the various body parts and their standard symbolic meanings in ancient scripture.

ARM

In antiquity the arm invoked ideas of power or strength, both human (see 2 Nephi 4:34; 19:20; D&C 1:19) and divine (see Enos 1:13; D&C 3:8; 15:2).[5] Depending on the context, the image of an arm in scripture can represent power in good or evil circumstances. Common is the refrain, "The Lord hath made bare his holy arm in the eyes of all the nations" (Isaiah 52:10).

The outstretched arm is always a symbol of God's power being exercised, whether in creation (see Jeremiah 32:17), judgment (see Jeremiah 21:5; 1 Nephi 20:14; 2 Nephi 8:5; Mosiah 12:24; D&C 1:14), or deliverance of his people (see Deuteronomy 4:34; 26:8; Mosiah 29:20; D&C 133:67). When men, however, endeavor to show their strength, the symbol is frequently associated with "the arm of flesh" and always in opposition to the arm of God (see 2 Chronicles 32:8; 2 Nephi 4:34; Alma 17; D&C 1:19; 121:33). Occasionally the scriptures mention righteous men as God's emissaries on earth and in so doing state metaphorically that their arms symbolize God's arm (see D&C 35:13–14; 1 Nephi 22:10–11).

When a person's arms are folded during prayer, the primary symbolic implication is that of submission, and secondarily humility and reverence. Again, we may be unaware of such symbolic meanings in our personal prayers, but these traditions stem from a conscious effort on the part of the ancients, who were seemingly more aware than we are of the inherent power in such symbolic gestures. Also associated with prayer is the image of upraised arms (see Psalm 28:2; 134:1–2; 141:2; 1 Kings 8:22), which typically denotes supplication and reaching up to heaven with a desire to call down blessings.[6]

BLOOD

In scripture a number of standard ideas are associated with blood, including *life, humanity,* and *mortality* (see Genesis 9:4–5; Leviticus 17:11, 14; Deuteronomy 12:23), as well as *death* (see Genesis 9:6; Exodus 22:2–3; 1 Nephi 4:10; Mosiah 17:10; D&C 136:36), *impurity* or *guilt* (see Leviticus 12:5; 15:19, 25), and *sacrifice for sin* (see John 6:53–54; Hebrews 9:13–14; D&C 20:79; 27:2).[7] Typologists frequently assume that these are all separate and unrelated symbolic meanings. However, scripture does not always use blood as a symbol in such a way that we can necessarily narrow its figurative implications to one of the numerous aforementioned categories. Blood can, for example, represent both our sins and Christ's expiation of them via his self-sacrifice. Thus, in Alma 5 we read:

> I say unto you, ye will know at that day that ye cannot be saved; for there can no man be saved except his garments are washed white; yea, his garments must be purified until they are cleansed from all stain, through the *blood* of him of whom it has been spoken by our fathers, who should come to redeem his people from their sins. And now I ask of you, my brethren, how will any of you feel, if ye shall stand before the bar of God, having your garments stained with *blood* and all manner of filthiness? Behold, what will these things testify against you? (Alma 5:21–22; emphasis added.)

Here we read first of the cleansing and purifying power of Christ's blood, as brought to pass in his atoning sacrifice. Then we are warned of the potential stain that will be upon the garments of those whose lives were filled with filthiness, corruption, and sin. Twice this passage mentions blood. The first time it conjures up an image of atonement and cleansing. The second provokes thoughts of filthiness and sin. The symbol is the same, but the association is decidedly different.

One might wonder how a single symbol could link multiple concepts, such as life, sin, and atonement. It is curious that Adam and Eve, while sinless residents of Eden, had no blood in their bodies.[8] However, upon partaking of the fruit of the "tree of knowledge of good and evil," they transgressed God's laws and their bodies became fallen.[9] Thus blood, for the first time, entered their veins.[10] Some four millennia later Jesus entered the Garden of Gethsemane for the last time as a mortal. There he "learned vicariously . . . what it would have felt like to commit the sins He never committed." In that garden, the Sinless One took upon himself our sins so that we could become clean and sinless.[11] In the process, he shed his blood for us. During the Millennium and throughout eternity, when the fallen state of mankind is overcome through the atoning sacrifice of the Lord Jesus Christ, there will again be no blood in the veins of God's creations.[12] Jesus, the Son of God, condescended by coming to earth and taking upon himself a mortal, and thus fallen, body so that he might work out an atonement on behalf of all humanity, "worlds without end" (Moses 1:33).[13] His body was subject to all of the imperfections, temptations, and weaknesses that all mortal people are susceptible to.

While Christ suffered in Gethsemane, the burden of the sins of all humanity bore down on him with unfathomable intensity. During that incomprehensibly wrenching few hours,[14] he suffered in ways inconceivable: "We know that he lay prostrate upon the ground as the pains and agonies of an infinite burden caused him to tremble, and would that he might not drink the bitter cup."[15] Luke records, "And being in an agony, he prayed more earnestly; and he sweat as it were great drops of blood falling down to the ground" (JST, Luke 22:44). King Benjamin taught his people, "And lo, he shall suffer temptations, and pain of body, hunger, thirst, and fatigue, even more than man can suffer, except it be unto death; for behold, blood cometh from every pore, so great shall be his anguish for the wickedness and the abominations of his people" (Mosiah 3:7). Is it possible that one of the reasons blood must be shed in order for an atonement to be made[16] is that blood is a type for the fallen or mortal nature of man? As Adam and Eve possessed blood only by virtue of the Fall,[17] and as redeemed humanity will not have blood, so also our Savior, in atoning for the sins of all (thereby ridding the world of sin and death upon conditions of repentance), had the blood literally squeezed out of him. In this context, perhaps, blood is not a multiplicity of different shadows, but one complete symbol for the cycle of mortality, sins, and redemption. We each must find the strength to squeeze all that is fallen and ungodly from our being if we are to benefit fully from the Atonement and become exalted.[18]

BOSOM

In antiquity the bosom, or breast, was a standard symbol for an intimate, nonsexual relationship.[19] It implied the attainment of a favored status.[20] We see this meaning in the popular passage about the beggar Lazarus, who upon his death found himself in "Abraham's bosom," while the unnamed "rich man" found himself in hell (see Luke 16:19–31). The passage clearly indicates that Lazarus, through the way he lived his life and via the atonement of Christ, found himself in an intimate and favored relationship with God. The rich man, however, because of his self-centeredness and greed in mortality, at death found himself outside of "Abraham's bosom," or in other words, in an unfavorable relationship to God.

On a similar note, the city of Enoch was translated and taken up to heaven because of the righteousness of its residents. Of them we read, "And thou hast taken Zion to thine own bosom, from all thy creations" (Moses 7:31). Through their consistent obedience and love for the things of God, they attained to that favored status and intimacy with the divine that all people have been sent to earth to seek.

The bosom was also the place of security and protection.[21] This meaning may be implied in the apostle John's description of the Last Supper:

> For the child there is safety ("safe on my mother's breast" [Ps 22:9]), security ("Can a woman forget her nursing child?" [Is 49:15]) and consolation at the mother's breast. It may be that for the adult, the hug provides a similar comfort. Perhaps it is not stretching the imagination too much to see John's reclining on the breast of Jesus at the Last Supper in those terms (Jn 13:25, 21:20).[22]

BOWELS

The bowels, or intestines, carry several symbolic meanings in scripture. In the Bible the Hebrew and Greek words translated as "bowels" imply compassion, sympathy, love, or pity.[23] Thus the bowels are most often associated with one's feelings or emotions.[24]

> Exactly where in the body one locates the focal point of emotion is somewhat arbitrary. For modern speakers of English it is the heart. Our language is full of colorful expressions that employ and play with this idiom. For the biblical writers and their secular contemporaries, the so-called seat of emotions was the bowels. . . . It is easy to surmise why intense feelings were expressed by the image of the "inner parts." The image was probably born out of the physiological experience that often accompanies intense emotion. When one feels appalled by a terrible crime, for example, real nausea may accompany the emotion. Hence, we express our feelings by saying, "That makes me sick." It is understood that whether or not physical discomfort is truly experienced, the speaker is expressing emotional disgust.[25]

Sometimes in scripture, however, the bowels are linked with the loins and thus to reproduction, fertility, or one's offspring.[26] Additionally, on occasion the scriptures use the bowels as symbols for martyrdom, disease, or death.[27] Thus, statements such as "my bowels are filled with compassion" (3 Nephi 17:6; D&C 101:9) or "my son, which came forth of my bowels" (2 Samuel 16:11) have meaning beyond what the literal rendering might imply.

EARS

In the Judaeo-Christian tradition, ears are symbolic of receptivity and obedience.[28] They are often synonymous with the heart and mind because they represent what one listens or hearkens to, just as the heart and mind imply what one loves and focuses on.[29]

A person whose ears are said to be "open" is obedient (see Mosiah 2:9; 3 Nephi 11:5; D&C 33:1), while a person with "closed" ears is not hearkening to the counsels and commands of God (see Jeremiah 6:10; Matthew 13:15; Acts 28:27). People with "itching" ears (see 2 Timothy 4:3) are said to only be "favorably disposed" to what they have already "found agreeable."[30] God is always depicted as having open ears (see 2 Chronicles 6:40; 7:15; Psalm 34:15; 1 Peter 3:12).

Although visions are a reality, anciently and in modernity,[31] more often than not God speaks through the whisperings of the "still small voice" (1 Kings 19:12; 1 Nephi 17:45; D&C 85:6). The covenant people have always sought revelation primarily through the promptings of the Spirit or, metaphorically, "through the ear and hearing."[32]

In the scriptural recitation of the martyrdom of Stephen, we see a wonderfully illustrated example of the employment of this symbol. Prior to his stoning, Stephen proclaimed of his persecutors, "Ye stiffnecked and uncircumcised in heart and ears, ye do always resist the Holy Ghost: as your fathers did, so do ye" (Acts 7:51). Stephen's announcement greatly offended his antagonists. In Luke's words, "they were cut to the heart" (Acts 7:54). As if his condemnation were not enough, what happened next only added to the anger of the mob. Luke records that Stephen was privileged to see in vision the resurrected Lord, standing at the right hand of God. In response to his description of what he was viewing, Stephen's assailants "cried out with a loud voice, and stopped their ears, and ran upon him with one accord, and cast him out of the city, and stoned him" (Acts 7:55–58). Of this act of "stopping" their ears, one scholar wrote, "The physical gesture is wonderfully expressive of Stephen's charge that they are 'uncircumcised in ears'" (7:51). They do everything to keep from hearing the prophet's proclamation that Jesus is the one raised to the presence of God."[33] Of course, Stephen's declaration regarding his killers can only be understood metaphorically. One does not circumcise ears. Rather, as circumcision is a token or sign of the covenant,[34] this episode implies that Stephen's enemies were both closing their ears to what they knew to be true and also deliberately not hearkening unto the promises that they had made to their God as his covenant people.

Similarly, the prophet Ezekiel proclaimed that the Son of man "dwellest in the midst of a rebellious house, which have . . . ears to hear, and hear not: for they are a rebellious house" (Ezekiel 12:2). Zechariah indicated that the wicked of his day refused to hearken to God, but rather "stopped their ears, that they should not hear" (Zechariah 7:11). In like manner, Matthew recorded of his unbelieving contemporaries that their ears were "dull of hearing" (Matthew 13:15). In Proverbs we are wisely informed, "A wicked doer giveth heed to false lips; and a liar giveth ear to a naughty tongue" (Proverbs 17:4). In ancient Babylonian texts, mutilation was frequently spoken of as a punishment for crimes committed. The form of mutilation was traditionally symbolic of the offense committed. "As a mark of disobedience the ear was often cut off."[35] However, at the other extreme, Jesus said to his apostles, "Blessed are your . . . ears, for they hear" (Matthew 13:15, 16). And Job recorded, "He openeth also their ear to discipline, and commandeth that they return from iniquity" (Job 36:10).

In the aforementioned passages, the closing of the ears is

deemed as a negative type. It implied an attitude of disobedience and a lack of hearkening. However, in a slightly different usage of the figure, Isaiah shows when the closing of the ears is a good thing. In chapter 33 the prophet is asked who among the hypocritical can dwell, as God does, in everlasting burnings. In response, Isaiah indicates that only those who have developed the necessary attributes can attain that exalted state. Prominent among those attributes is a person's ability to stop "his ears from hearing of blood" (Isaiah 33:15) or, in other words, pay no heed to plans to shed blood or take life.[36]

In Leviticus 14 we read: "And the priest shall take some of the blood of the trespass offering, and the priest shall put it upon the tip of the right ear of him that is to be cleansed, and . . . of the oil that is in his hand shall the priest put upon the tip of the right ear of him that is to be cleansed" (Leviticus 14:14, 17). As blood often typifies atonement, and oil the guiding and sanctifying influence of the Holy Ghost, this passage indicates that the recipient of the priesthood ordinance should live his life in such a way as to ensure that all that he hears, and all to which he hearkens, is in accordance with the dictates of the Holy Spirit. Doing so will allow him to partake of the cleansing power and associated blessings of the Atonement.[37]

On the theme of eternal judgment, the wording of Doctrine and Covenants 88 is curious. Verse 104 reads:

> And this shall be the sound of his trump, saying to all people, both in heaven and in earth, and that are under the earth—for every ear shall hear it, and every knee shall bow, and every tongue shall confess, while they hear the sound of the trump, saying: Fear God, and give glory to him who sitteth upon the throne, forever and ever; for the hour of his judgment is come.

Certainly everyone will indeed eventually hear the truth. However, the imagery here seems to imply that at some point not only will all hear and know the truth (as the confessing tongue implies) but also that they will obey (as the knee bowed in submission suggests).

EYES

Anciently, eyes were a symbol for the receipt of light, knowledge, insight, and revelation (see D&C 77:4).[38] Multiple eyes on one being are usually interpreted as a symbol of omniscience, as is the concept of God's "all-searching" (2 Nephi 9:44; Mosiah 27:31) or "piercing" (Jacob 2:10) eye.[39] Thus John the Revelator was shown "four beasts full of eyes before and behind" (see Revelation 4:6–8). Of these "beasts" Doctrine and Covenants 77:4 records, "Their eyes are a representation of light and knowledge, that is, they are full of knowledge." One commentator added, "The beast, full of eyes before and behind, has the capability of seeing things to come (before), and things which have passed (behind)."[40] Ezekiel also sees a beast or being with many eyes (see Ezekiel 1:18). Of that creature residing near the throne of God, one source records: "These eyes probably represent the omniscience of the Spirit of God. When it is written that there are seven 'eyes,' it no doubt means that there is perfect vision and understanding on the part of this wonderful Person (see also Ezekiel 10:12)."[41]

To some degree, eyes are also a representation of our desires.[42] Thus Christ states: "The light of the body is the eye; if, therefore, thine eye be single, thy whole body shall be full of light. But if thine eye be evil, thy whole body shall be full of darkness. If, therefore, the light that is in thee be darkness, how great is that darkness!" (3 Nephi 13:22–23; Matthew 6:22–23). If we desire what God desires, our bodies and lives will be filled with light. If, on the other hand, we desire evil things, darkness (or a lack of light, knowledge, insight, and revelation) will be our lot. With every desire to protect his children, the Lord commands: "And if thy right eye offend thee, pluck it out, and cast it from thee: for it is profitable for thee that one of thy members should perish, and not that thy whole body should be cast into hell. And if thy right hand offend thee, cut it off, and cast it from thee: for it is profitable for thee that one of thy members should perish, and not that thy whole body should be cast into hell" (Matthew 5:29–30). Does the Lord mean this counsel to be taken literally? To do so would be to miss the point of the symbolism. The meaning of Christ's admonition is that if there is something around you that is causing you to stumble (e.g., television, your associates), get rid of it before it kills you spiritually. If something about your job makes it hard for you to keep the commandments, change jobs before it destroys your spirituality. If you are doing things that are detrimental to your spirituality, stop! The whole purpose of the commandments of God is to make it possible—and for that matter easier—for us to return to him. We're playing Russian roulette with our salvation if we don't "pluck out" the things that are detrimental to us.

On a related note, the Lord declared that "an eye single to the glory of God" qualifies missionaries for that work (D&C 4:5). They are to turn their attention from the world, to Christ only, because our eyes affect our hearts. Therefore, those called to the missionary work are told to let only those things enter their minds and hearts that will bring glory to God and bless the work in which they are engaged.[43]

FEET

Feet are employed symbolically at least three different ways in the scriptures. The most common use of feet is as a symbol of how we live and what path we choose to follow (see 1 Samuel 2:9; Job 12:5; Ephesians 6:15), whether it be an avenue of wickedness or one of righteousness.[44] They represent "one's personal direction, mission, or goal."[45] Examples of symbolically employing feet in this way are frequent. As a warning against following the paths of the wicked, the book of Proverbs counsels, "My son, walk not thou in the way with them; refrain thy foot from their path: For their feet run to evil, and make haste to shed blood" (Proverbs 1:15–16). Emphasizing the importance of repentance and having one's life in order, the Lord stated, "And I give unto you, who are the first laborers in this last kingdom, a commandment that you assemble yourselves together, and organize yourselves, and prepare yourselves, and sanctify yourselves; yea, purify your hearts, and cleanse your hands and your feet before me, that I may make you clean" (D&C 88:74). Regarding the importance of the scriptures in keeping us on the strait and narrow path, the Psalmist recorded, "Thy word is a lamp unto my feet, and a light unto my path" (Psalm 119:105).

A second way in which feet are symbolically employed is in relation to one's enemies. Occasionally a person is depicted as being under the feet of God or under another person (see 2 Samuel 22:10, 39; Romans 16:20; Mormon 5:6), implying that the person underneath is in subjection to, or under the control of, the person on top.[46] Consistent with this understanding, Christ proclaimed to the Nephites, "And ye shall tread down the wicked; for they shall be ashes under the soles of your feet" (3 Nephi 25:3), and to the Saints in these last days, "Their arm shall be my arm, and I will be their shield and their buckler; and I will gird up their loins, and they shall fight manfully for me; and their enemies shall be under their feet; and I will let fall the sword in their behalf, and by the fire of mine indignation will I preserve them" (D&C 35:14). Similarly, if a person is depicted as standing upon a piece of property (see Deuteronomy 2:5; 11:24; Joshua 1:3; Ether 6:12; D&C 59:3), this is a traditional sign that he or she possesses that land.[47] This may well explain the following passage from the book of Mosiah: "How beautiful upon the mountains are the feet of him that bringeth good tidings; that publisheth peace; that bringeth good tidings of good; that publisheth salvation; that saith unto Zion, Thy God reigneth" (Mosiah 12:21; see 15:15–18). Faithful gospel ministers will inherit the earth, an idea effectively conveyed by the image of their feet upon the mountaintops, the highest points of the earth.[48] Likewise, the act of falling down at the feet of another symbolizes subjection (see 1 Samuel 25:24; Acts 10:25; 3 Nephi 11:17–19; 17:10).[49] This meaning is clearly evident when Nephi records, "I looked, and I beheld the Son of God going forth among the children of men; and I saw many fall down at his feet and worship him" (1 Nephi 11:24).

Finally, the washing of feet in scripture is symbolic.[50] For example, the priests who worked in the Mosaic tabernacle were to wash their feet before entering therein (see Exodus 30:19–21), likely as a symbol of their need to be clean as they enter God's labor.[51] The symbolic message in this is no less applicable to priesthood holders today, and it carries profound meaning for the fifteen modern apostles who preside over the work of the last days. On a related note, at the Last Supper, Jesus washed the feet of the apostles (see John 13:5–14). In light of the fact that anciently the washing of the feet was an act to be performed by slaves and servants, this action by Christ is traditionally seen as a strong symbol of his humility and holy servitude. It is also a message about the level of meekness and servitude to which the followers of Christ must attain if they are to truly become like the Master.[52]

FOREHEAD

In the scriptures the infrequent symbol of the forehead represents what a person's thoughts dwell on and therefore what he loves or desires. For this reason the Lord metaphorically ordered Israel to place his commandments "as an emblem on [their] forehead" (i.e., in their minds) as a "memorial" forever (see Exodus 13:9, 16; NRSV, Deuteronomy 6:8; 11:18). For the same reason, the Mosaic high priest wore an engraved gold signet on his forehead that read "Holiness to the Lord" (see Exodus 28:36–38). This was a reminder that his thoughts should always be holy, with the result that his actions would follow suit. The prophet Jeremiah compared unrepentant Israel to the forehead of a prostitute: "Thou hadst a whore's forehead, thou refusedst to be ashamed" (Jeremiah 3:3). In other words, the covenant people in their state of apostasy were not even ashamed of their sinful thoughts or their sinful state.[53] The red mark placed by the Amlicites on their own foreheads, in fulfillment of prophecy, was a comparable act (see Alma 3:13–19). It too showed where their hearts were and that they truly loved the things of Satan rather than those of God. In the end their sinful cravings brought upon them the judgment of God.

The best-known symbolic use of the forehead in scripture is found in the book of Revelation. Many interpretations of this pericope miss the point of the text.[54] John records:

> And he causeth all, both small and great, rich and poor, free and bond, to receive a mark in their right hand, or in their foreheads: And that no man might buy or sell, save he that had the mark, or the name of the beast, or the number of his name. Here is wisdom. Let him that hath understanding count the number of the beast: for it is the number of a man; and his number is Six hundred threescore and six. And I looked, and, lo, a Lamb stood on the mount Sion, and with him an hundred forty and four thousand, having his Father's name written *in* their foreheads. (Revelation 13:16–14:1; emphasis added.)

The placement of the mark "on" or "in" the forehead and hand suggests that the Lord's concern here may be with what a person thinks and pursues. John speaks of those in spiritual Babylon as having Satan's name or mark in their foreheads. However, those in Zion, at the temple, having their calling and election made sure, are said to have God's name in their foreheads. The passage calls each follower of Christ to introspectively ask, What do I love and seek, and on what do I focus my attention? Is it the things of this world or the building up of the kingdom of God on the earth? Pursuing the latter leads to eternal life. Hence, the apostle James recommends, "Draw nigh to God . . . and purify your hearts, ye double minded" (James 4:8). In speaking of those with metaphorically "unclean" hearts as "double minded" sinners, James, too, utilizes the mind as a representation of one's desires.

Like John, Ezekiel also employed the forehead as a symbol for the desires of the righteous. Upon showing the prophet the withdrawal of the Lord's glory from the desecrated temple, God commanded Ezekiel to "go through the midst of the city, through the midst of Jerusalem, and set a mark upon the foreheads of the men that sigh and that cry for all the abominations that be done in the midst thereof" (Ezekiel 9:4). Precious few were found worthy to be marked as ones having pure desires, clean hearts, and righteous thoughts. Few cried out in abhorrence of the abominations that were happening around them.

If nothing more could be said than this, it would be sufficient to note that the desires of the heart—depicted by the forehead—determine the actions of the body. If in the end we are to be exalted, it will be based on how well we control our thoughts and on what we dwell on and truly desire.

HAIR

In the Bible are some seventy-three verses that refer to hair. More often than not, hair is a positive, albeit complex, symbol,[55] having numerous metaphorical or symbolic uses beyond its aesthetic value (see, for example, 2 Samuel 14:25–26; Song of Solomon 4:1; 5:11; 6:5). The overarching meaning of hair in the scriptures, however, is that of life.[56]

In ancient times, hair could signal either a person's health or lack thereof. The negative association is apparent in Leviticus 13–14, where we read of the priest examining people's hair in order to ascertain whether or not they have leprosy, which was itself a symbol for spiritual sickness.[57] Also negative was the image of tearing out one's hair as a sign of grief or devastation (see Ezra 9:3; Ezekiel 23:34; Jeremiah 7:29). On the other hand, King Nebuchadnezzar is described as being deranged, symbolized in part by his having grown his hair and nails out to an excessive length (see Daniel 4:33). When baldness is mentioned, it seems to be a negative sign—the opposite of the positive symbol of a full head of hair. A loss of hair represents a loss of life or quality of life.[58] Isaiah speaks of the Assyrian king and his armies as "the Lord's hired razor" (Isaiah 7:20) who would humiliate and dishonor their prisoners by "shaving them from head to toe."[59] He also foretold a time when the women of Judah would no longer have "well set hair" but instead would be bald (see Isaiah 3:24). Their loss of hair symbolizes that they have cause to mourn and repent. In this same spirit of mourning, the prophet Jeremiah saw in vision a people desolated, a vision that included an image of every head bald and every man's face shaved (see Jeremiah 48:37).

The minute nature of human hair is also symbolic. For example, our many hairs show that God is omnipotent and omniscient, because he will not allow a hair of our heads to be lost (see Alma 11:44; 40:23; D&C 29:25), for every hair of our head is numbered to him (see Matthew 10:30; D&C 84:116). Indeed, as a sign of his omnipotence, God is frequently said to protect every head of those who fight for Israel (see 1 Samuel 14:45; 2 Samuel 14:11; 1 Kings 1:52; Acts 27:34; D&C 9:14). God's protection of the hair implies an eternal protection of our spiritual life.[60]

The large number of hairs on the average head was also symbolic. For example, King David compared the myriad of hairs on his scalp to the innumerable trials he had in his life (see Psalm 40:12). And of his enemies he wrote, "They that hate me without a cause are more than the hairs of mine head" (Psalm 69:4).

The Apostle Paul considered long hair to be the norm for women of his day but degrading for his male contemporaries (see 1 Corinthians 11:14–15). However, those of Paul's time and earlier who took the vow of a Nazarite were required not to cut their hair, a symbol that they had been set apart and were striving to live a life of holiness (see Numbers 6:5, 18). Their lives, as the symbol of uncut hair suggested, was focused on God and the things of eternity rather than on the fleeting things of this life (such as physical appearance).⁶¹ One such Nazarite was Samson, whose hair was cut off by Delilah (see Judges 16:15–21). In this famous story, it appears that the hair symbolized Samson's commitment to God. As one scholar noted: "The hair itself was not the source of Samson's unique strength. This lay in his [vow] to the Lord [to be separate from the world], of which the unshorn locks were the symbol."⁶² When Samson slowly allowed himself to be pulled away from his unique status as a Nazarite—one set apart for God—he lost the companionship of God, which had given him his unique and unmatched strength (see Judges 16:20). Seemingly related to this is the following comment by one biblical scholar:

> It was believed that some part of a man's life resided in the hair, and that possession of hair from his head maintained a certain connection with him, even after his death. Before freeing a prisoner, the Arabs cut a portion of his hair, and retained it, as evidence that he had been in their power. Chalid B. al-Walid wore, in his military head-gear, hair from the head of Mohammed.⁶³

White or gray hair was most often a symbol of aging, wisdom, maturity, and honor (see Leviticus 19:32; Deuteronomy 32:25; Proverbs 20:29). Thus, resurrected beings are universally depicted as having white hair (see Daniel 7:9; Revelation 1:14; D&C 110:3).⁶⁴

HAND

The hand is traditionally a symbolic representation of our actions, or that which we choose to do or pursue.⁶⁵ It functions as a symbol of power, whether good or evil.⁶⁶ "The hand . . . is the corporeal manifestation of the inner state of the human being and . . . it expresses an attitude of mind."⁶⁷ Further:

> The hands are the essence of the individual. Hands communicate our attitudes and perform our deeds. They speak more eloquently than our words, since the actions of the hands come from the heart. Through hands come blessing and healing, or

bloodshed and deeds of wickedness. . . . If dirty hands represent past mistakes, clean hands represent contrition and a fresh start.[68]

The manner in which a hand is used deepens the symbolism. "The giving of the hand," for example, "showed that a relationship was established between two persons (2 Kings 10:15; Jeremiah 50:15; Ezekiel 17:18)."[69] To clasp another's hand was a sign of a "pledge" or an expression of "solidarity."[70] As we noted above, the hand is a symbol of power, probably because the Hebrew root for hand can mean either "power" and "strength," or it can mean literally one's "hand."[71] Hence, one source on biblical and Semitic symbols states, "By stretching out the hand towards a person . . . one symbolized the transference of power from one party to another."[72] On a related note, one dictionary of symbols suggests that "in esoteric doctrine, the position of the hand in relation to the body, and the arrangement of the fingers, convey certain precise symbolic notions."[73]

Because of this concept of hands possessing and transferring power, it is traditionally held that the laying on of hands "symbolizes the placing of God's hand or power upon the one so blessed (see D&C 36:1–2)."[74] The priesthood holder, after all, is a symbol of the divine.[75] "While the touch of the human hand conveys differing intentions and evokes a gamut of feelings, the gentle, firm gesture that is the laying on of hands intends the sense of imparted power."[76]

Besides symbolizing our willingness to sustain another or our entrance into a covenant, the raised right hand is understood to be "a sign of power and command."[77] When both hands are lifted, the action is a manifestation of "supplication to God, and of dependence on God (Exodus 17:12; 1 Timothy 2:8)."[78] One text records:

> Among the Indians of North America the figure of a human hand is used to denote supplication to the Master of Life or Great Spirit, and it stands in their system of picture-writing as the symbol of strength, power, and mastery, thence derived. "In the great number of instances which I have met

with of its being employed," says an American traveler, "both in the ceremonial observances of their dances and in their pictorial records, I do not recollect a single one in which this sacred character is not assigned to it. Their priests are usually drawn with outstretched and uplifted hands."[79]

When Jehovah asks, "Who shall ascend into the hill of the Lord? or who shall stand in his holy place? He that hath clean hands, and a pure heart" (Psalm 24:3–4; see Job 17:9; 2 Nephi 25:16; D&C 88:74), His meaning is clear. We must do (symbolized by hands) righteous acts and desire (symbolized by the heart) righteous things if we wish to regain the presence of the Lord. Worried about his own well-being, King David prayed, "Let not the . . . hand of the wicked remove me" (Psalm 36:11). He feared the wicked actions (hands) of other men, but believed in God's ability to deliver him.[80] Uzzah's putting his hand forth to "steady the ark" (2 Samuel 6:6) was a symbol of inappropriate deeds or actions in our lives, actions that bring upon us spiritual death.[81] Thus the Lord's command, "If thy right hand offend thee, cut it off, and cast it from thee: for it is profitable for thee that one of thy members should perish, and not that thy whole body should be cast into hell" (Matthew 5:30; 18:8; Mark 9:43), would have been helpful counsel for Uzzah. If our actions or pursuits are not in harmony with the will of the Lord and the covenants we have made, we should "cut them off" (i.e., cease and desist), lest our "whole body [soul?] should be cast into hell." For this reason the Lord stated, "No man, having put his hand to the plough, and looking back, is fit for the kingdom of God" (Luke 9:62). Once we have made the decision to engage in the work of the Lord, we must not look back. The world must be set aside. We must not seek to "plough" with "corrupt hands" (see Psalm 26:10–11).

HEAD

Whereas in Western culture the head would be a symbol for the thoughts of the person, this was less the case for the ancient Hebrews. For them, the heart was the seat of knowledge and thoughts.[82] Scripture does depict the head as controlling or governing the body, but the person's desires and thoughts were located elsewhere. As a symbol, the head represented three main ideas: the entirety of the person, the life of the person, and the source of governance or rulership.

When Jacob blessed his sons, he stated that "the blessings of [Jacob] . . . shall be on the head of Joseph" (Genesis 49:26). Solomon stated that "blessings are upon the head of the just" (Proverbs 10:6). Numerous times in the Doctrine and Covenants we read of blessings being placed or poured out upon the head of one individual or another (see D&C 39:8; 52:37; 107:83; 124:21, 57; 133:34). Each of these pronouncements is designed to emphasize the head as a symbol for the entire person.[83] For this reason, anointings and blessings are traditionally performed on a person's head (see Genesis 48:14; Exodus 29:7; Leviticus 8:12; 1 Samuel 10:1; Proverbs 10:6).[84] Similarly, as evidence of an all-encompassing grief or mourning, ancients would shave their heads (see Job 1:20), cover their heads (see 2 Samuel 15:30), or place dirt or ashes on their heads (see 2 Samuel 13:19; 15:32).[85]

Since the head was also a representation of the seat of one's life, the severed head was frequently employed in scripture as a representation of the "decisive defeat of the enemy."[86] Thus we are told that Christ will "crush" Satan's head (Genesis 3:15; Moses 4:21), symbolizing the eventual "utter defeat" of the adversary of all mankind.[87] David forewarned Goliath that he would cut off his head (see 1 Samuel 17:46). The Philistines took Saul's head and hung it in the temple of their god, Dagon (see 1 Chronicles 10:9–10). At the request of Herodias, Herod Antipas had John the Baptist beheaded (see Mark 6:24–28). Reluctantly, but at the command of the Lord, Nephi smote off the head of Laban, who had been seeking to thwart God's will (see 1 Nephi 4:17–18). And Coriantumr concluded his battle with Shiz by cutting off his head (see Ether 15:30).

As the head rules the body physically and gives it all that

it needs (such as food, oxygen, information, and so forth), time and again Christ is spoken of in scripture as the "head of the Church" (Ephesians 4:15; 5:23; Matthew 21:42; Mark 12:10; Luke 20:17; Acts 4:11; 1 Corinthians 11:3; Colossians 1:18; 2:10; 1 Peter 2:7; Jacob 4:17; Mosiah 5:8), who gives the Church all that it needs.[88] This same concept of governance stands behind the metaphor describing the leaders of armies and nations as the "head" (Alma 47:8; 49:10; 60:24). Additionally, if we learn to govern our head, which, in turn, will govern our own body, salvation is said to be sure.[89]

HEART

Although today we associate thought and memory with the brain, anciently these functions were, at least metaphorically, believed to take place in the heart—the seat of knowledge; the recipient of revelation, inspiration, and omniscience; and the location of the true inner man or woman (see 1 Chronicles 28:9; 29:18; Job 17:11; Psalm 33:11; Jeremiah 4:14; 23:20; Daniel 2:30; Mark 7:21; Mosiah 5:13; Alma 18:20; D&C 6:16; 33:1).

Symbolically speaking, revelations are given not just to the mind but to the heart (see D&C 8:2; Galatians 4:6), and the conversion they provoke is also in the heart (see D&C 58:5; Ephesians 1:17–23). It follows that if something is known by the Spirit or some truth has been revealed, it is to the heart that such knowledge comes and thereafter resides.[90] One Bible dictionary states:

> In more than three hundred cases where the word refers to the human heart it has a spiritual significance and refers to a person's relationship with God. . . . Paul explicitly declares the connection between the heart and God, saying that God's revelation bears witness to or within the human heart (Romans 2:14ff.). . . . Just as the heart or core of a person's being is the recipient of divine revelation, so it is the subject of the response, positive or negative, one makes to God. With the heart one believes (Romans 10:10), desires (1:24), obeys

(6:17), and performs the will of God (Ephesians 6:6). The redeemed heart is the dwelling place of Christ (3:17) and of His peace (Colossians 3:15) and love (Romans 5:5).[91]

The word *heart* is often used of such things as "personality and the intellect, memory, emotions, desires and will."[92] Thus the Lord told Noah that the thoughts of the hearts of almost all of the people then inhabiting the earth were "evil continually" (Genesis 6:5; Moses 8:22). The book of Hebrews declares that "the word of God is . . . a discerner of the thoughts and intents of the heart" (Hebrews 4:12). The Spirit is said to have convinced Zeezrom that Alma and Amulek "knew the thoughts and intents of his heart" (Alma 12:7).

Emphasizing the ancient belief that what we are is determined by our heart, Christ announced that "out of the heart proceed evil thoughts, murders, adulteries, fornications, thefts, false witness, [and] blasphemies" (Matthew 15:19). In ancient sources we read of hearts filled with pride (see 2 Chronicles 32:26; 1 Samuel 17:28), when today this same sin might be associated with a sin of the mind. Some hearts are said to be deluded or deceived (see Isaiah 44:20; Jeremiah 17:9). Again, today such attributes would be associated with mental transgressions. A heart not dedicated to God is frequently referred to in the scriptures as "uncircumcised" (Deuteronomy 10:16; Jeremiah 9:26; Romans 2:29). The prophet Ezekiel speaks of the transition from self-serving to God-fearing as going from a "heart of stone" to a "heart of flesh" (Ezekiel 11:19; see 18:31).

We are commanded to seek God with all our hearts (see Deuteronomy 4:29; 6:5; 1 Samuel 16:7), apparently meaning with all of our thoughts, desires, and focus. In the language of scripture, it is our heart that God does and will use to judge us fit or unfit for his kingdom: "For man looketh on the outward appearance, but the Lord looketh on the heart" (1 Samuel 16:7; see also Jeremiah 11:20; Hebrews 4:12; Mosiah 5:13; Alma 12:7; Moroni 7:9; D&C 33:1). The "pure in heart" are promised that they will "see God" (Matthew 5:8; 3 Nephi 12:8).

Anciently, the removal of a person's heart, whether through human sacrifice or the embalming of the deceased, was a symbol not simply of the loss of life but also of the removal of the soul and the potential omniscience of the departed.

HORNS

In scripture horns are used as symbols of power and strength, whether good or evil.[93] The Assyrians, Hittites, Egyptians, and Gauls all depicted their deities as having or wearing horns. Indeed, even the leaders of some of these ancient civilizations wore clothing adorned with horns to depict both their power and their divine nature.[94]

> In Hebrew literature the word "horn" is equivalent to power. "To break the horns" of a people signifies defeat, "to raise the horns" means pride, victory. Balaam described God as having horns like a wild ox (Numbers 23:22); whilst the tribe of Joseph is said to have horns like those of a unicorn, with which it will push people (Deuteronomy 33:17). In paintings Moses was represented with horns. This is usually explained by the passage in Exodus 34:29, where we are told that the skin of his face shone (literally, sent forth horns). The expression is taken here to mean "sent forth beams of light," but it has been suggested that there may be a textual error. . . . One can multiply this symbolism from the religions of many ancient peoples. It seems fairly certain that in many instances . . . the horn became a symbol of power because man noted how the horned animals made use of its horns as a destructive force.[95]

The image of horns as symbols of power is particularly common in the Bible. David sang, "The Lord is . . . the horn of my salvation" (Psalm 18:2; see 2 Samuel 22:3), implying that Jehovah had the power to save David and that none else could. The altars of the Mosaic tabernacle had four horns on them (see Exodus 27:2), one on each corner. "The horns of an altar . . . probably came to symbolize the power of that altar."[96] Thus an altar of sacrifice, adorned with horns, would highlight the power of the sacrifices performed thereon—or, more particularly, the power of the Great and Last Sacrifice typified by the symbolic offerings made thereon. Similarly, the four-horned altar of incense, or altar of prayer, symbolized the power of sincere, daily prayer to God. In the book of Revelation, John depicts the Lord as a lamb with seven horns (see Revelation 5:6), in an effort to highlight Christ's perfect omnipotence.[97] John also describes Satan and his beast as having ten horns (see Revelation 12:3; 13:1), representing the fact that they have only limited power.

> The horns seem to denote the dragon's all-pervasive false sovereignty. Horns symbolize power.... Ten represents the whole of a part but not the whole itself. Thus, the dragon has great power, but John shows that he does not have all power; some portion is lacking. This is not true of the Lamb whom John depicts with seven horns, the symbol of fulness (see Revelation 5:6). Thus, John's metaphors subtly show that the Lamb has all power and can overmaster the dragon.[98]

Paraphrasing the book of Micah, Christ promises the Nephites that through their faithfulness he will "make their horn iron" (3 Nephi 20:19), implying that they will be invincible.

Some sources associate horns with an outpouring of the Holy Ghost.[99] Anciently kings were usually anointed with oil that was carried in a horn (see 1 Samuel 16:13; 1 Kings 1:39; Psalm 92:10), implying that they should be directed by God's Spirit and would be empowered by it if they lived and served faithfully. From antiquity to the present, oil has served as a standard symbol for the Holy Ghost; thus its connection with horns and power seems appropriate.[100]

KNEES

Knees are most often used to signify the state of one person before another, either in submission or fear.[101] Thus when a certain leper came to Christ begging to be healed, he knelt down before Jesus to make his request (see Mark 1:40–45), apparently signifying his reverence for Christ and his awareness of his lower station and reliance on him. Indeed, to kneel before someone demonstrated obeisance and recognition of that person's superiority. The practice of kneeling has become a major part of most religious traditions.[102] For this reason, we understand, upon offering the dedicatory prayer of the newly completed temple, Solomon "stood before the altar of the Lord in the presence of all the congregation of Israel, and . . . kneeled down upon his knees . . . and spread forth his hands toward heaven" (2 Chronicles 6:12–13; see also 1 Kings 8:54). Solomon was stating his submission not to Israel but to God.

Failing or trembling knees depict fear or weakness. When King Belshazzar saw the mysterious hand write a message on the wall, the book of Daniel records, "his knees smote one against another" (see Daniel 5:1–6). And when Elijah called down fire from heaven to consume more than one hundred men, a captain of King Ahaziah's army dropped to his knees before the prophet and pleaded, "O man of God, I pray thee, let my life, and the life of these fifty thy servants, be precious in thy sight" (see 2 Kings 1:12–14). This was a clear manifestation of the man's fear of Elijah and his miraculous powers. Likewise, after Peter fished all night and caught nothing but then hauled in a nearly net-bursting load upon heeding Christ's simple command, the astonished fisherman dropped to his knees in acknowledgment of the Lord's powers (see Luke 5:1–9). Similarly, before the feet of Christ shall every knee bow and every tongue confess his Messianic role (see Romans 14:11; Mosiah 27:31; D&C 88:104).

LOINS

Although the loins can be defined as "the waist and lower torso," in scripture the word most often refers to the reproductive organs.[103] One of the primary symbolic meanings of the loins is offspring or reproduction and therefore, in an eternal sense, omnipresence (see 1 Kings 8:19; 2 Chronicles 6:9;

Jeremiah 13:11; Acts 2:30; 2 Nephi 3:4–21; Jacob 2:25; D&C 132:20; Moses 8:2).

The second symbolic connotation of this body part is that of preparedness, encapsulated in the phrase "gird up your loins."[104] This meant to tuck the loose ends of a robe or outer garment into the belt or sash fastened around the waist. By so doing, one was prepared to work and to make haste. Concerning the latter meaning, the Israelites, during the Passover feast, were to eat with their loins girded in the expectation that they might need to flee Egypt with minimal notice (see Exodus 12:11; 2 Kings 4:29; 9:1). Although this practice was thought to have typological implications, it was not symbolic on the very first Passover; rather, it was a manifestation of the tense circumstance in which that meal took place.

With more symbolic intent, the Apostle Paul's commission to the Saints to have their "loins girt about with truth" (Ephesians 6:14; see also Isaiah 5:27; 11:5; Luke 12:35; 1 Peter 1:13; D&C 27:15; 35:14; 36:8) was a call to spiritual activity and "an undergirding of *truth* in the sense of 'integrity,' 'truth in the inward being.'"[105]

NECK

In scripture the neck is most often associated with attitude or subjection.[106] Ancient texts frequently employ the outward posture of the neck as a symbol for the inward state of the heart. When someone is described as being "stiff-necked," the implication is that the person is prideful, obstinate, or disobedient. On a number of occasions this term is applied to the covenant people when they resist God's commands (see Exodus 32:9; 33:5; Nehemiah 9:29; Jeremiah 7:26; Acts 7:51; 2 Nephi 28:14; Jacob 2:13). Isaiah also speaks of the worldly as having "stretched forth necks" (Isaiah 3:16), evidencing their pride, self-centeredness, arrogance, and defiance.

The opposite extreme is the symbol of the bowed head, which is a depiction of humility, contrition, repentance, dependence, and mourning. In the Hebrew Bible this symbol is commonly coupled with the word "worshipped" (see Exodus 4:31; 1 Chronicles 29:20; 2 Chronicles 29:30; Nehemiah 8:6).

As a symbol of oppression or subjection, the neck is employed time and again in scripture. We read of those who are forced to serve against their will as having a "yoke" upon their necks (see Genesis 27:40; Deuteronomy 28:48; Jeremiah 27:8). Joshua instructs his army commanders to "put their feet upon" the necks of their captives as a form of humiliation and domination (see Joshua 10:24; Genesis 49:8). Job speaks metaphorically of trials as a collar (such as a slave's collar) around the neck (see Job 30:18; Jeremiah 27:2). Even the Savior notes that for those who harm children, it would be better for them to have a millstone tied to their necks and then be tossed into the sea (see Matthew 18:6; Mark 9:42; Luke 17:2).[107]

NOSE

The nose is a symbol for anger or temperament.[108] In parts of Europe one occasionally hears the colloquial phrase "You get up my nose," meaning "You're angering me." The symbol seems to have derived from the association of flared nostrils with anger: "Excited breathing, with distension of the nostrils when moved by indignation, led to the nose being used figuratively for anger."[109]

To a much lesser extent in scripture, the nose is a symbol for temperament or indignation.[110] When God is depicted as being angry, we read of smoke coming forth from his nostrils (see 2 Samuel 22:9; Job 41:20; Psalm 18:8).

The nose can also symbolize loathing or repugnance: God told ungrateful Israel that she would get so sick of quail that it would come out of her nose (see Numbers 11:20; see also 2 Samuel 10:6).

SHOULDERS

In the ancient Near East, people carried objects such as water pots or clothing on their shoulders (see Genesis 21:14; 24:45–46). The manual labor of those times required that one's shoulders be used for moving stones to create homes, temples, altars, and other structures (see Joshua 4:5; Judges 9:48). Shepherds carried lambs on their shoulders (see Luke 15:5). Oxen carried a yoke on their shoulders (see 1 Samuel 11:7; 14:14). It is easy to see how shoulders became a symbol for labor, burdens, and responsibilities.[111]

Jesus condemned the Pharisees for placing "heavy burdens" upon "men's shoulders" but not being willing to work themselves (see Matthew 23:1–4). Similarly, we read that the Jaredite Riplakish offended the Lord by placing "upon men's shoulders [that] which was grievous to be borne" (Ether 10:5).

In the book of Nehemiah we read of Israel's unwillingness to obey the Lord. Nehemiah employs a number of body metaphors to make his point. He states that Israel refused to obey the life-giving commandments of God but, rather, "withdrew the shoulder, and hardened their neck, and would not hear" (Nehemiah 9:29). Bible commentators note that the Israelites, who simply "would not put their shoulders to the work,"[112] are portrayed as a "stubborn ox . . . refusing to accept the yoke."[113] The turned shoulder implies an unwillingness to accept the responsibilities and burdens of the covenants into which they had entered. The hardened neck, as a sign of their pride and obstinacy, is coupled with the unhearing ears.

In the book of Deuteronomy we are told that Benjamin metaphorically rests between the shoulders of Yahweh (see Deuteronomy 33:12). "This picture indicates that God's people are protected and sheltered by the mighty power of God as the papoose is safe between the shoulders of the Indian mother in a secure resting place."[114]

In the Book of Mormon the Lord promises Alma and his people that he will "ease the burdens" that have been placed upon their shoulders by their persecutors (see Mosiah 24:13–14).

The Mosaic high priest, who typifies Christ,[115] has written on the breastplate, which is hung from his shoulders, the names of each of the tribes of Israel (see Exodus 28:12; 39:7), symbolizing the fact that Christ has taken us as his responsibility (see Abraham 3:27; 3 Nephi 9:22) and thus labors on our behalf, shouldering our burdens and weaknesses (see Alma 7:10–13). Isaiah prophetically declared, "For unto us a child is born, unto us a son is given: and the government shall be upon his shoulder: and his name shall be called Wonderful, Counsellor, The mighty God, The everlasting Father, The Prince of Peace." (Isaiah 9:6). The phrase "the government shall be upon his shoulder" is traditionally understood to be from one of two ceremonies. During the ancient Semitic wedding ceremony, the one performing the rite would remove the veil from the face of the bride, placing it on the shoulder of the groom, while reciting this line.[116] Also, as part of ancient royal vesting rites, a king who was being crowned and enthroned would receive upon his shoulders the "robe of regal authority" as an indication of his right to rule and reign.[117] Both of these images apply well to Christ and serve to highlight the burden, responsibility, and labor associated with the shoulders.

THROAT

Although not a common symbol in scripture, the throat represented power, and more specifically priesthood power, because of its association with the vocal cords and one's ability to command or speak. Moreover, the throat "corresponds to one's personal will and willpower or lack of it."[118] If one can speak, one has power. If one cannot speak, weakness prevails. God's "voice connotes his power" (see 2 Samuel 22:14; Job 37:2–5; Psalm 18:13; Isaiah 30:30), and "judgment is implicitly associated with His voice" (see Isaiah 30:31; John 5:25, 28; Hebrews 12:26).[119] God's throat symbolizes his omnipotence.

In this context Psalm 115 depicts powerless idols that cannot "utter a sound with their throats" (NIV, Psalm 115:7). Note the many symbolically employed body parts:

> Our God [Jehovah] is in the heavens: he hath done whatsoever he hath pleased.
> Their idols [the false gods of the heathens] are silver and gold, the work of men's hands.
> They have mouths, but they speak not [no power to command, no omnipotence]: eyes have they, but they see not [no knowledge, no omniscience]:
> They have ears, but they hear not [no ability to hear the prayers and petitions of those who pray to them]: noses have they, but they smell not [they cannot smell the offering made to them, nor do they have emotions, such as wrath, when their followers are disobedient]:
> They have hands, but they handle not [no works]: feet have they, but they walk not [no paths or pursuits]: neither speak they through their throat [again, no omnipotence or power].
> They that make them are like unto them; so is every one that trusteth in them [powerless]. (Psalm 115:3–8.)

Implied is the notion that Jehovah has all of these aforementioned attributes, including priesthood power, whereas the gods of the heathens have none and should not, therefore, be honored or worshipped.

In Proverbs a man who seeks political advancement is warned that, should he be summoned to eat with a ruler, he should "put a knife to [his] throat, if [he] be a man given to appetite" (Proverbs 23:2). The passage is interpreted variously, from "Make sure you use utensils when you eat so that you don't look like a pig"[120] to "If you eat in a gluttonous manner, you basically slit your throat regarding any promotion or advancement."[121] The basic message seems to be that the man will thwart his efforts to gain power and advancement if he appears overly eager and greedy.

When Satan entered into his secret combination with

Cain, Satan required an oath of him, saying, "Swear unto me by thy throat, and if thou tell it thou shalt die; . . . and this day I will deliver thy brother Abel into thine hands" (Moses 5:29).[122] In an identical act, Akish is said to have administered this oath and penalty unto those over whom he wished to rule and deceive:

> And it came to pass that Akish gathered in unto the house of Jared all his kinsfolk, and said unto them: Will ye swear unto me that ye will be faithful unto me in the thing which I shall desire of you? And it came to pass that they all sware unto him, by the God of heaven, and also by the heavens, and also by the earth, *and by their heads,* that whoso should vary from the assistance which Akish desired *should lose his head;* and whoso should divulge whatsoever thing Akish made known unto them, the same should lose his life. And it came to pass that thus they did agree with Akish. And Akish did administer unto them the oaths which were given by them of old who also sought power, which had been handed down even from Cain, who was a murderer from the beginning. (Ether 8:13–15; emphasis added.)

In the end, neither Satan nor Akish had the authority or ability to deliver that which they promised—power, as symbolized by the throat. Nevertheless, they promised it anyway. Not only were the false promises never realized, but the potential power offered by Christ to everyone (see D&C 84:38), including Cain and the Jaredites, was lost.

WINGS

Doctrine and Covenants 77 informs us that "wings are a representation of power, to move, to act, etc." (v. 4). This interpretation, along with that of protection, is standard in texts dealing with symbolism.[123] "The imagery of wings . . . is primarily figurative; in fact, references to the literal wings of birds are striking for their scarcity."[124]

Regarding the power to protect, we read of eagles catching their young on their wings (see Exodus 19:4; Deuteronomy

32:11) and a mother hen protecting her chicks (see Matthew 23:37; Luke 13:34). Christ's application of this last image to himself is suggestive not only of his parental instincts but also of his innate power and desire to ensure our security and protection. The motif of God's sheltering wings is commonplace in scripture, particularly in the Psalms (see Psalms 17:8; 36:7; 57:1; 63:7).

The prophet Jeremiah uses wings as an image of power swooping down upon Moab and Bozrah (see Jeremiah 48:40; 49:22). Isaiah develops a similar image regarding Judah (see Isaiah 8:8).

More often than not, ancient and modern iconography depicts heavenly beings as possessing wings.[125] This image is purely symbolic, however, for "an angel of God never has wings."[126] Readers who encounter a scriptural passage depicting beings as having wings must decide whether the symbol is one of power or protection (or possibly both) and whether the being possessing them is good or evil.

In the book of Revelation, John speaks of a particular set of "beasts" in the presence of God singing praises to him (see Revelation 4:8). John speaks of them as having many eyes (representing knowledge, perhaps omniscience) and wings (power to move and to act). It is curious that John highlights these heavenly creatures as having six wings. It is generally understood that in his apocalypse, John always uses numbers with intent. Thus, the question must be asked, Why do these angels in the presence of God have six wings? The answer is unclear in the text. However, the number six is a standard symbol for incompleteness or some deficit.[127] Knowing that these beings are in the presence of God and possess the knowledge that they do, we cannot see the employment of the number six here as a negative symbol. It may simply be a representation of their interim state as celestial heirs awaiting resurrection, which may explain the sense in which they are "incomplete."[128]

When Nephi states, "Upon the wings of his Spirit hath my body been carried away upon exceedingly high mountains"

(2 Nephi 4:25), he is speaking metaphorically about the power of the Holy Ghost. When scripture records that Christ arose from the grave with "healing in his wings" (Malachi 4:2; 2 Nephi 25:13; 3 Nephi 25:2), it is an image of his power over death and the blessing that awaits all people because of that power.

4
CLOTHING AS SYMBOLS

"THE TRANSFORMING EFFECT OF CLOTHES," one source informs us, "has always given them considerable emblematic power."[1] That clothing played a significant role in ancient society is particularly apparent in the Bible, which records how prophets used clothing metaphorically to make ethical exhortations, send theological messages, and indicate the status or character of significant figures.[2] The importance of apparel in scripture and ceremony can be physical, economic, social, moral, or spiritual.[3]

"Priestly clothing was intended to represent the garb of God and of the angels. . . . Dressing in special clothing in the temple denotes a change in role, from that of mortal to immortal, from ordinary human to priest or priestess, king or queen."[4] Donning sacred dress has long symbolized personal consecration and preparation for "spiritual duties" (see Exodus 29:1–9; 40:12–15; Leviticus 6:11; 16:1–4).[5] The priestly garments were held sacred, for when they wore out they were not to be discarded but had to be burned in the temple during Sukkoth.[6]

It has been said that scriptural and liturgical clothing can "protect, conceal, display or represent a person's current state and can be symbolic of moral and spiritual qualities."[7] This apparently applies to both man and God, because even Deity (see Daniel 7:9; Matthew 28:3; Revelation 19:13) and angels (see Revelation 6:11; 7:9; D&C 29:12; 109:76) are depicted as wearing clothing.[8]

Anciently, raiment was expensive and scarce, and thus very valuable. For this reason, the image of clothing wearing out (see Psalm 102:26; Isaiah 51:6, 8; Hebrews 1:11) or being eaten by moths (see Job 13:28; Proverbs 25:20; Isaiah 50:9; 51:8) was one of terror.[9] In contrast, preserved clothing conveyed a positive image. For example, reminding Israel of how blessed they had been, the Lord said, "I have led you forty years in the wilderness: your clothes are not waxen old upon you, and thy shoe is not waxen old upon thy foot" (Deuteronomy 29:5).

Obviously not all clothing, in scripture or in life, is symbolic. Yet even so, literal and figurative meanings are intertwined in nearly every category of clothing.[10] The primary design of this chapter is to remind us that the clothing we wear speaks as loudly about who we are, what we desire, and what we will become as does perhaps anything else. In the temple, clothing has as much to say and reveal as any other part of the ritual, if we are attentive to it. This chapter will examine clothing of symbolic import, primarily so we will be more apt to find significance in these articles next time we don them or read about them in scripture.

APRONS

Perhaps the most familiar and meaningful passages that mention the wearing of an apron pertain to Adam and Eve. The prophet Moses recorded, "And the eyes of them both were opened, and they knew that they were naked; and they sewed fig leaves together, and made themselves aprons" (Genesis 3:7; see Moses 4:13).[11]

Anciently, both aprons and figs symbolized fertility and reproduction.[12] "In ancient Semitic custom, young children ran about with a loose shirt or cloak. As they reached sexual maturity, they began to wear an 'apron' or loincloth. . . . [W]earing [an apron] represented adulthood."[13] It was not until the Fall that Adam and Eve were able to "multiply and replenish" the earth as they had been commanded (Moses 5:11). Upon placing themselves in a position to "be fruitful and multiply," Adam and Eve appropriately donned the very symbols of their newly received power. What are we to make of Adam and Eve's wearing aprons of fig leaves that, at the very least, symbolize "fertility" and "reproduction"?[14] In light of Elder Richard G. Scott's counsel that we should "learn from the lives of Adam and Eve," the whole episode seems highly significant and applicable.[15]

On several occasions, President Joseph Fielding Smith taught: "The Lord said to Adam, here is the tree of knowledge of good and evil. If you want to stay here then you cannot eat of that fruit. If you want to stay here then I forbid you to eat it. But you may act for yourself and you may eat of it if you want to. And if you eat it you will die."[16] Adam and Eve's choice was quite simple.

Option number one entailed God giving them the right to stay in Eden forever. They would never really have to work, for everything would be provided for them. They wouldn't really grow because they wouldn't be tried and tested by being placed in difficult circumstances. According to this option, Adam and Eve would be allowed to focus on the things they wanted. Of course, major drawbacks were (1) they would never become like God because of their lack of growth, and (2) none of their potential offspring would ever have a chance at becoming like God either, because Adam and Eve's choice would prevent them from having children.

Option number two, as President Smith read the account, entailed Adam and Eve's sacrificing their opportunity for guaranteed ease and pleasure so that others could be born and have a chance at godhood also. This option promised hard work, requisite sacrifice, and trials and tests that would stretch the first of the human family to the core. They would likely have to give up some worldly goals and aspirations in order to make it back to God. According to this option, they were assured that, no matter how good a life they lived, in the end they would still die. However, the very things that would make the mortal experience so hard would also enable Adam and Eve and all of their posterity to return to God and to become like him.

The two choices given to Adam and Eve in Eden are the very same choices given to every couple when they kneel at an altar in the temple and enter into the new and everlasting covenant of marriage. Their first option, if it can even be called such, is to be self-serving and to put off having children until they have done all they want to do and have obtained all they want to obtain. The second option is to forgo some of things they might want, and to ignore much of what the world tells them that they should and must have, in order that others can have a chance at mortality and exaltation. Adam and Eve's choice was really between having or not having a family. They chose the former, reflected in Lehi's words, "Adam fell that men might be" (2 Nephi 2:25).

Thus if nothing else can be seen in the fig-leaf aprons, this much is certain: Adam and Eve made the right choice. They were going to be "fruitful and multiply," having decided to put God's ultimate will before any potentially competing desires of their own—and at great cost and sacrifice on their part. Such is the commitment God asks of us.

In ancient times aprons also symbolized priesthood[17] and work.[18] It is likely that for this reason the high priest who served in the Mosaic tabernacle was required to wear an apron, or ephod (see Exodus 28).[19] He was engaged in the "work" of the Lord, a work requiring that he possess priesthood power. It seems clear that the Mosaic priest's apron was symbolically associated with the aprons of Adam and Eve:

> Adam and Eve, while in the garden, possessed two items of clothing that apparently held ritual meaning: the apron (Genesis 3:7) and the garment of skins (see Genesis 3:21). . . . No doubt [the apron] held some sort of ceremonial significance for the first couple. . . . It is quite likely that these vestments, belonging to Adam and Eve and obtained while in the garden, served as archetypes for later sacral vestments belonging to the Israelite temple system.[20]

ARMOR OF GOD

Both the Lord (see D&C 27:15–18) and the Apostle Paul (see Ephesians 6:11–17) commanded the Saints to "put on the whole armor of God" so they could fortify themselves against the work of Satan and be enabled to "withstand the evil day."

The "whole armor of God" consists of spiritual weapons employed by righteous individuals to assist them in their warfare "against principalities, against powers, against the rulers of the darkness of this world, against spiritual wickedness in high places" (Eph. 6:11–17; D&C 27:15–18). Referred to also as the "armour of light" (Rom. 13:12) and the "armour of righteousness" (2 Cor. 6:7; 2 Ne. 1:23), this protective armament includes the "breastplate of righteousness," the "shield of faith," the "helmet of salvation," and the "sword of the Spirit," as well as protection for the feet and loins. Paul explained, "For the weapons of our warfare are not carnal, but mighty through God to the pulling down of strong holds" (2 Cor. 10:4).[21]

Much has been written on this surprisingly vast subject.[22] Space constraints will allow only brief mention here of the symbolic meaning of each piece of armor. It will have to be left to the reader to seek out personal, detailed applications of the divine dictate to put on the whole armor of God.

In general terms, armor is a scriptural motif for "protection against evil."[23] Anciently "the proof of a warrior's prowess [was] in his successful return from battle."[24] In theological terms, the proof of a person's spiritual prowess lies in his or her ability to successfully regain God's presence at the conclusion of this earthly battle against Satan and sin. "Christians are to follow their victorious Christ by putting on spiritual armor and engaging in the battle where . . . victory [is found] in Christian virtues and the armaments of faith. . . . The helmet, shield and breastplate, or scaled armor, form a panoply of spiritual armor calling for individual attention."[25]

First of all, the followers of Christ are commissioned to "gird their loins with truth" (Ephesians 6:14; D&C 27:16). In scripture (e.g., Genesis 35:11; 1 Kings 8:19; 2 Chronicles 6:9; 2 Nephi 3:4; D&C 132:30) the loins symbolize procreative powers.[26] The metaphor implies that knowing truth will protect us from being deceived or from becoming morally unclean. "To overcome the lures and entrapments of wicked ones, we must know the truth and be able to instantly and firmly label evil, evil—not adult, sophisticated, mature, funny, or clever, but evil. . . . Truth that is internalized becomes the armor about the loins that protects one's virtue. The importance of chastity cannot be overstated."[27] The clear message is that, contrary to what the world encourages people to do, the followers of Christ are to guard against becoming morally unclean.

Next there is the "breastplate of righteousness" (Ephesians 6:14; D&C 27:16). It protects one's heart.[28] The heart, as noted earlier, is a symbol of our desires and thoughts, of who we truly are inside.[29] Thus in 1 Thessalonians 5:8 Paul speaks of the "breastplate of faith and love." The heart implies what we truly love and exercise faith in. One LDS commentator suggested that wearing the "breastplate of righteousness" ensured that we would be "pure in heart."[30] President Harold B. Lee wrote:

> The righteous man, although far superior to his fellows who are not, is humble and does not parade his righteousness to be seen of men but conceals his virtues as he would modestly conceal his nudity. The righteous man strives for self-improvement knowing that he has daily need of repentance for his misdeeds or his neglect. He is not so much concerned about what he can get but more about how much he can give to others, knowing that along that course only can he find true happiness. He endeavors to make each day his masterpiece so that at night's close he can witness in his soul and to his God that whatever has come to his hand that day, he has done to the best of his ability. His body is not dissipated and weakened by the burdens imposed by the demands of riotous living; his judgment is not rendered faulty by the follies of youth; he is clear of vision, keen of intellect, and strong of body. The breastplate of

righteousness has given him "the strength of ten—because his heart is clean."³¹

Righteous Saints will also have their feet "shod with the preparation of the gospel of peace" (Ephesians 6:15; D&C 27:16). The *Doctrine and Covenants Encyclopedia* asserts:

> What may appear to be the most insignificant components of a soldier's battle gear are his shoes. Yet, without adequate shoes to bear up the weight of the body, all the armament and weaponry will lose their effectiveness. Thus, the Lord suggested that part of our spiritual armament should be the spiritual sandals with which our feet are shod. Such shoes are called "the preparation of the gospel of peace."³²

Feet are symbols of the path we choose to follow, the direction we choose to go in our lives.³³ Those who walk the "strait and narrow path" (1 Nephi 8:20; 2 Nephi 31:18–19) have clearly "shod their feet with the preparation of the gospel of peace."

The Greek of Ephesians 6:15 can also accurately be rendered as "having one's feet shod with the *stability* or *solidity* of the gospel of peace."³⁴ The former interpretation of the Greek text—"shod with the *preparation* of the gospel of peace"—implies that we must "prepare for future service and future conflicts by studying the scriptures, listening to the words of our inspired leaders, and applying all of these true teachings and principles in our lives."³⁵ The alternative interpretation indicates that the gospel is sound, trustworthy, and safe and that it will give us sure footing in life if we rely upon it instead of our own wisdom or the teachings of the world. Indeed, the gospel is the only source of peace and stability in a world of conflict, moral turpitude, and shifting values.³⁶

The "shield of faith" serves to deflect the "darts of the wicked" and "quench" the flames on the burning arrows of temptation that are shot at us (Ephesians 6:16; D&C 27:17). "The shield was so basic to a soldier's outfit that 'shield and spear' or 'shield and sword' symbolized a warrior trained and ready for battle (Judges 5:8; 1 Chronicles 5:18; 12:8, 24), and the image of uncovering the shield signified preparation for battle (Isaiah 22:6; cross-reference Jeremiah 51:11)."[37]

The shield is a symbol of faith. If we have faith in the Lord Jesus Christ, we will be protected from spiritual death. We will be able to deflect the harmful assaults and quench the burning temptations sent our way. "I can't think of any more powerful weapons," President Harold B. Lee stated, "than faith and a knowledge of the scriptures in the which are contained the Word of God. One so armored and one so prepared with those weapons is prepared to go out against the enemy [and] is more to be feared than the enemies of the light."[38]

The "helmet of salvation" reminds us of a good military helmet that protects the head, especially the brain, eyes, and ears. Likewise, the spiritual helmet provides salvation because it protects our minds from dwelling on, our eyes from seeing, our ears from hearing, and our mouths from partaking of inappropriate things that pollute our hearts and spirits. This seemingly small device actually protects the whole body because it determines and controls what is allowed to enter the body through the key senses of sight, sound, and taste. For those who take full advantage of such vital protection, salvation is almost assured.

The Lord's description of the last piece of armor—"the sword of the Spirit"—is slightly different than the Apostle Paul's. Whereas Paul speaks of this sword as being "the word of God" (Ephesians 6:17), the Lord says that his children should take "the sword of my Spirit, which I will pour out upon you, and my word which I reveal unto you" (D&C 27:18). Christ implies that, through his Spirit and his word (which he reveals through the Spirit), the Saints will be equipped for the battle and will be "caught up" when he comes (D&C 27:18).

Swords are standard symbols for the words of God, including his commandments, covenants, revelations, and so on.[39] Thus Paul's phrasing does not imply a drastically different image than that of Christ's. In both cases, it appears that the implication is that the scriptures, covenants, and teachings of the living prophets, combined with the constant companionship of the Holy Ghost, will ensure our ability to return victorious from the raging spiritual battle of mortal life. "In this conflict the defenders must be well versed in the scriptures and be in touch with the Spirit of revelation."[40] Although many protections have been suggested, the only "weapons," per se, are the scriptures, covenants, teachings of the living prophets, testimony, and the companionship of the Holy Ghost. Set any one of those aside and we eventually will be spiritually wounded.

BOWS

Implied but never explicitly mentioned in scripture, bows are symbols worthy of note (see Exodus 29:9; Leviticus 8:7).[41] President John Taylor is said to have taught that making a bow knot represents "the marriage covenant between man and wife."[42] Similarly, one British typologist indicated that bows on clothing were a symbol of the combination of the "masculine and feminine"[43]—the bride and the Bridegroom. In some Eastern cultures, the tying of a bow knot was a marriage custom that symbolized the binding of the two people, hence the old cliché "tying the knot."[44]

One source indicates that bows were "once a sacred symbol, and signified the concealment or secrecy surrounding sacred mysteries."[45] On the surface, this insight might seem unrelated. However, on a deeper level it may well be in harmony with the aforementioned definition of bows.

CAPS AND HATS

In the scriptures, men are often described as wearing hats, or "miters," particularly in association with temple service (see Exodus 28:4, 37, 39; 29:6; 39:28, 31; Leviticus 8:9; 16:4; Zechariah 3:3–5). Hats, caps, crowns, and the like represent authority, victory, wisdom and power.[46] Anciently, the covered head was a symbol of nobility and freedom.[47]

We also read of political rulers wearing hats or crowns as

symbols of their authority and political power (see, for example, 2 Samuel 12:30; 2 Kings 11:12; Esther 2:17). However, the crown is also employed as a symbol for the reward that awaits the righteous (see 2 Timothy 4:8; James 1:12; Revelation 2:10; 3:11; D&C 20:14), implying that in the next life they will enjoy authority and power.[48]

The Mosaic high priest wore simultaneously a miter and crown (see Leviticus 8:9) because his life typified Christ, the eternal king, who possesses both authority and power. The caps or bonnets worn by the priests that worked in the Mosaic tabernacle (see Exodus 39:28) were made of white linen and, according to one Jewish scholar, were flat on top.[49]

GARMENTS/COATS OF SKIN/BREECHES

It is widely accepted that priests who served in the temples of the Judaeo-Christian tradition wore special undergarments known as "linen breeches."[50]

The prophet Ezekiel spoke of these articles of clothing, both in relation to ancient temple work and modern temple worship. He foresaw the "linen garments," the "linen bonnets upon their heads," and the "linen breeches upon their loins" to be worn by priests in the latter-day temple in Jerusalem (see Ezekiel 44:17–18).[51] This linen apparel recalled the garments of skin that God made for Adam and Eve in Eden. In fact, "according to Jewish tradition, the earliest priestly clothes were the garments of skin provided to Adam and Eve after the fall."[52]

The prophet Moses recorded, "Unto Adam also and to his wife did the Lord God make coats of skins, and clothed them" (Genesis 3:21; see Moses 4:27). These "coats" are likely related to clothing that the endowed in our day wear and represent, in part, the glory possessed by God, Christ, and all exalted beings. Early Jewish sources strongly support this interpretation of the symbolic connotations of the sacred priestly garments. For example, while in the Garden of Eden, and prior to their fall, Adam and Eve are said to have worn "garments of light" akin to the glory and light that radiated from the Father.[53] When they partook of the fruit of the tree of knowledge of good and evil, God stripped them of those garments of light and made coats of skins for them as a replacement.[54] According to a leading scholar of Jewish studies, "God killed certain animals in order to furnish Adam and Eve with clothes."[55] They "received their garments [of skin] from God after the fall . . . and [Adam's] descendants wore them as priestly garments at the time of the offering of the sacrifices. Furthermore they . . . [are said to have had] supernatural qualities."[56]

On a related note, the book of Hebrews teaches that the veil of the temple represents the flesh of Jesus Christ (see Hebrews 10:19–22). This being the case, when in the temple we ceremonially act out our ascent back to God, at the final stages of the endowment a person representing our Savior stands between us and the Father. Jesus Christ is, of course, our Mediator, or go-between (see 1 Timothy 2:5; 2 Nephi 2:27). Since it is Christ through whom we communicate with our Father (both at the veil and in prayer)—and through whom we enter the celestial kingdom—then it is also Christ who is symbolized by the sacred clothing we receive at the conclusion of the temple initiatory ceremonies.[57] This clothing represents the crucified flesh of Christ and should be received with a covenant and reminder to always live in accordance with what that newly procured covering represents. This should give new meaning to the idea of taking upon ourselves the name (see 2 Nephi 31:13; Mosiah 5:8) or image (see Alma 5:19; 1 John 3:1–3) of Christ.

Thus, the "coats of skins" made for Adam and Eve, the "linen breeches" of the priests of old, and some of the temple clothing of the Latter-day Saints represent the flesh of Christ and the purity and glory that he and his Father possess through their supernal righteousness. And just as Adam and Eve received these earthly tokens to remind them of the heavenly reality until they could return and reclaim the light they had lost through the Fall, endowed Saints are privileged to wear a temporary covering symbolic of the reward that awaits the faithful.[58]

The concept of having clean, white, and unsoiled garments is found everywhere in scripture (see Revelation 3:4–5; Alma 5:21, 24; D&C 135:5). The implication of unspotted garments is that the wearers have achieved what they were sent to this earth to do. Through covenants, obedience, repentance, and the atonement, they have worked their way back to a state that will enable them to regain the metaphorical garments of light that were lost as a result of the Fall.

ROBES

There are numerous references in the scriptures to people wearing robes, particularly in relation to service in the temple. "In . . . priestly tradition, special outerwear depicted power."[59] The British typologist J. C. Cooper indicated that robes are standard symbols for "the power of heaven" (priesthood power) and that the wearer is to be viewed as the "earthly representative" of God.[60] One expert in biblical clothing noted that some traditions in the Old and New Testaments "portray the outer garment of special persons as conveying power."[61]

Obviously, not every reference to an outer garment or robe should be construed as being laden with symbolic overtones of power or priesthood. Wicked or righteous, priesthood holder or not, few in antiquity did not wear such robes. However, in many cases in scripture the robe of a prophet or priest is highlighted as evidence of his priesthood power.

In 1 Kings we read, "So [Elijah] departed thence, and found Elisha the son of Shaphat, who was plowing with twelve yoke of oxen before him, and he with the twelfth: and Elijah passed by him, and cast his mantle upon him" (19:19). This transferring of Elijah's mantel, or robe, symbolizes the transference of authority or power.[62] Note the presence of the number twelve, which is itself a symbol for power and priesthood.[63] Some time later, after Elisha received this initial call, we read, "Elijah took his mantel, and wrapped it together, and smote the waters, and they were divided hither and thither, so that they two went over on dry ground" (2 Kings 2:8). By God's authorization and power (symbolized by the mantle), Elijah is able to divide the waters.

Recorded in 1 Samuel is an interaction between Saul and Samuel that highlights the symbolic implications of a robe.

> And Samuel said unto Saul, I will not return with thee: for thou hast rejected the word of the Lord, and the Lord hath rejected thee from being king over Israel. And as Samuel turned about to go away, he laid hold upon the skirt of his mantle, and it rent. And Samuel said unto him, The Lord hath rent the kingdom of Israel from thee this day, and hath given it to a neighbour of thine, that is better than thou. (1 Samuel 15:26–28; see also 24:4–20.)

Unrighteous Saul is depicted as grabbing and ripping the hem of Samuel's robe. Samuel's response to Saul is that, just as Saul's actions caused the rending of Samuel's robe, so also his other unrighteous actions have caused the rending of his kingdom and the loss of his crown to David. Thus, here again, the robe represented power.

The book of Isaiah records that the Lord's servants will declare, "He hath clothed me with the garments of salvation, he hath covered me with the robe of righteousness" (Isaiah 61:10). Commentators frequently see this as a reference to clothing donned in the temple. For example, one text states, "These garments . . . suggest the garments and robes of the priesthood, as found in the temple."[64] Another text records, "The 'garments of salvation' . . . may mean the garment of the Priesthood . . . [and] the robes of righteousness . . . could mean the holy robes of the temple."[65] Perhaps. But it may be more to Isaiah's point to see the "robe of righteousness" as the eschatological[66] gift of power and enduring priesthood promised to all who enter and keep sacred covenants in the house of the Lord.

Such appears to be the way in which John utilizes the symbol (see Revelation 6:11; 7:9; 19:8).

Jesus' coat "without seam" (John 19:23) is frequently seen as having been typified by the robe of the Mosaic high priest (see Exodus 39:27), which was also said to be seamless.[67] John's emphasis on this article of clothing serves to highlight Jesus' power and the fact that Jesus is the Great High Priest.

SACKCLOTH

Sackcloth was a coarse, dark cloth made of goat or camel hair. It was typically worn by mourners as a symbol of their grief, humiliation, repentance, or dismay.[68] When Jacob heard that his son Joseph had been killed, he rent his clothes and put on sackcloth "and mourned for his son many days" (Genesis 37:34).[69] When Mordecai heard that Haman had convinced the king to exterminate the Jews, he "rent his clothes, and put on sackcloth with ashes, and went out into the midst of the city, and cried with a loud and a bitter cry" (Esther 4:1). When King Hezekiah was told by his cabinet ministers about the threats and blasphemies of the Assyrians and the effect that this had on his people, he tore his clothes, put on sackcloth, and then went to the temple (see Isaiah 37:1).

SASHES

The Old Testament records that the Mosaic priests were to wear a sash around their waists when working in the tabernacle (see Exodus 29:9; Leviticus 8:7).[70] This sash, or belt, was worn outside the robe, with the ends hanging down.[71] It was apparently "tied in an ample bow or loop."[72] In certain periods and regions the wearing of a sash symbolized chastity, virginity, or fidelity.[73]

SHOES/SANDALS/SLIPPERS/FOOTWEAR

Shoes have basically three symbolic connotations in scripture and temple worship: enslavement and poverty, entrance into a hallowed place, and covenant making.

Because in ancient times clothing was expensive and wardrobes were limited, it was the poor and the enslaved who were most often depicted as barefoot.[74] Keeping prisoners and slaves barefoot made it difficult for them to escape. When Isaiah and Micah wished to prophetically warn the people of pending enslavement, they went about naked and shoeless (see Isaiah 20:2–4; Micah 1:8). David walked barefoot as a symbol of the temporary captivity of his kingdom at the hands of Absalom (see 2 Samuel 15:30). To be barefoot and then receive shoes again served as a symbol of reinstatement or the regaining of one's social standing (see Ezekiel 16:10; 2 Chronicles 28:15; Luke 15:22).

Bare feet also symbolized a person's "inner state, serving as an image of spiritual poverty,"[75] while the wearing of shoes "denote[d] liberty and freedom since the slave went barefoot."[76] In Exodus 12:11 the Israelites are commanded to eat the Passover with their shoes on. The Passover typified the Atonement, and just as the feast was part of the process that would free Israel from Egyptian bondage, the atonement of Jesus Christ frees us from spiritual bondage. Metaphorically speaking, if we utilize the atonement of Christ, "our feet are shod."

Being barefoot could also symbolize entrance into a holy place.[77] One typologist noted that "putting off shoes on entering a holy place represents leaving earthly contact outside . . . and [divesting] oneself of vice."[78] Another source states: "Shoes are necessary only on the earth because of the filth of the ground. By removing them, we symbolically leave the world outside the Lord's sanctuary. Muslims and others remove their shoes when entering mosques and other holy places (in Islam, one may not pray with one's feet shod). The Japanese and some other peoples even remove their shoes upon entering a house."[79] For this reason, upon approaching the burning bush, Moses is told, "Draw not nigh hither: put off thy shoes from off thy feet, for the place whereon thou standest is holy ground" (Exodus 3:5). Similarly, when Joshua had a heavenly visitation in Jericho he was told, "Loose thy shoe from off thy foot; for the place whereon thou standest is holy" (Joshua 5:15). One commentary records, "the divinity of the messenger is indicated by his instructions to Joshua, which, like those that Moses had been given at the burning bush, were to show reverence because the place had become holy."[80]

Finally, removing their shoes as part of the covenant making process was common in ancient Semitic societies (see Ruth 4:1–8). A man would remove his shoes to acknowledge that he was willingly divesting himself of some possession he once had a right to (often property), in anticipation of gaining something better through fulfilling his part of the covenant.[81] So, for example, when Adam and Eve willingly partook of the fruit of the tree of knowledge of good and evil, they divested themselves of Eden (with its ease and luxury) in hopes of gaining the celestial kingdom. Likewise, we symbolically divest ourselves of our inheritance in premortal life (our "first estate") so that we can live in the "lone and dreary world"—all in hopes of one day gaining the celestial kingdom.

SWADDLING CLOTHES

In the Gospel of Luke we read, "[Mary] brought forth her firstborn son, and wrapped him in swaddling clothes, and laid him in a manger; because there was no room for them in the inn" (Luke 2:7). Swaddling clothes were strips of cloth tied together so as to enwrap an individual much as we would wrap a wound with a gauze bandage.[82] Indeed, the Hebrew word of which "swaddling" is the English translation denotes cloths used in the binding of broken limbs (see Ezekiel 30:21).[83] The significance of this symbol, as it relates to Christ's ministry of healing the spiritually broken, seems obvious (see Ezekiel 34:15–16; D&C 138:42).

The distinguished Catholic biblical scholar Raymond Brown noted that Luke "is careful to report that Jesus was swaddled and laid in a manger because of the lack of space at the lodgings. The precise picture that he wishes to convey is not clear; but the details about the swaddling and the manger are repeated later (see vv. 12, 16) and must be of significance. Most of the popular reflection on vs. 7, however, misses Luke's purpose."[84]

The use of swaddling clothes invokes two images. First of all, there is the representation of parental care and compassion. These bands provided the child with warmth, protection from the extremities, and a sense of security.[85] As this pertains to Christ, certainly the Father was ever watching over his Firstborn Son. However, in the end, it is Christ who warms, protects, and offers security to us. It is Christ to whom numerous maternal emblems are applied (see Luke 13:34; 3 Nephi 10:6; D&C 10:65). It is Christ who is the father of our salvation and who entered Gethsemane that he might "know according to the flesh how to succor his people according to their infirmities" (see Alma 7:10–13). Numerous commentators, ancient and modern, have seen significance in the Savior's first bit of clothing. For example, Gregory Thaumaturgus, a third-century Alexandrian Father and student of Origen, wrote: "She wrapped in swaddling-clothes Him who is covered with light as with a garment (Psalm 104:2). She wrapped in swaddling-clothes Him who made every creature. . . . She wrapped Him in swaddling-clothes who binds the whole creation fast with His word."[86] The Presbyterian commentator Matthew Henry wrote, "He was wrapped in cloths, as other children are when they are new-born, as if he could be bound, or needed to be kept straight."[87]

A second but equally important symbolic connotation is that the strips of cloth seem reminiscent of the clothing of the deceased, such as mummies. Luke's emphasis on the fact that Christ was wrapped in these strips (commonplace in the world of a physician) may have been for the sake of emphasizing the fact that this child was born to die. "The bonds uniting life with death, where man is concerned, are represented by swaddling clothes (echoed by the bandages that swaddle a corpse)."[88]

VEILS

The veil has many symbolic associations, depending on the cultural or liturgical context surrounding its use. Contrary to modern attitudes, the veiled face can convey a strongly positive image in scripture.[89] Three significant uses of the veiled face are discussed below.

In many cultures, veils symbolize chastity personified. They indicate that a person is modest and filled with virtue,[90] implying a "renunciation of the world."[91] For example, some Islamic and Jewish women veil themselves to keep men from being distracted, this being a symbol of the fallen and weak condition of men rather than women.[92] We read that, in an apparent display of modesty, Rebekah "lifted up her eyes, and when she saw Isaac . . . she took a veil and covered herself" (JST, Genesis 24:69–70).

An additional symbolic meaning of the veiled face, which sometimes strikes people as offensive, is that of submission to righteously held and exercised authority.[93] The offense likely comes from the fact that some cultures have abused this model and allowed men to exercise a form of "unrighteous dominion" (see D&C 121:36–37, 39, 41–44). However, this symbol should provoke no resentment if understood properly.[94] Still, as an example of how readily the metaphor is missed, note the following passage from the writings of the Apostle Paul: "Wives, submit[95] yourselves unto your own husbands, as unto the Lord. For the husband is the head of the wife, even as Christ is the head of the church: and he is the Savior of the body. Therefore, as the church is subject unto Christ, so let the wives be to their own husbands in every thing. Husbands, love your wives, even as Christ also loved the church, and gave himself for it" (Ephesians 5:22–25). The fact that many men do not act like Christ can make this symbol and Paul's counsel hard to accept. Additionally, many women do not perceive righteous priesthood holders as symbols for and representatives of God and

Christ, so in this context the symbol of a veiled face becomes a source of agitation.

Some suggest that Paul's comments came during a time when some parts of the world afforded women fewer opportunities and rights than those men enjoyed. Actually, Paul makes it clear that women in the Church had tremendous rights, actively participating in worship services and perhaps even occasionally moving "beyond self-control in the new social freedom of the Early Church."[96] Thus Paul's message in Ephesians 5:22–25 is likely not appropriately understood as an issue of cultural dictates alone.

Note Paul's emphasis in Ephesians 5. He indicates that a wife's "subjection" to her husband is a symbol for the bride (Church) subjecting herself (male and female) to the Bridegroom, who is Christ.

> The relation between a god and his people was represented as one of marriage. . . . Thus, in the Old Testament Jahveh is frequently imagined as the husband of Israel. . . . Hosea, for example, thinks of Israel as an unfaithful wife who is still beloved by her husband and is forgiven and restored. Paul takes up the Old Testament idea and conceives of the relation between the Church and Christ as one of marriage. . . . The book of Revelation culminates in the glowing description of the Church as the Bride of Christ, and . . . the submission of a wife to her husband is in some way to represent the obedience which the Church owes to Christ.[97]

Additionally, verse 21 makes it clear that what Paul is about to say in the subsequent verses applies "not only to wives, children, and slaves, but also to husbands, fathers, and masters."[98] The bride of Christ, his Church, is to live in subjection to the Bridegroom and Savior.

It is in this context that we should understand at least part of the symbolism of the veil. Anciently, the veil carried very strong connotations of blindness, unbelief, a lack of faith, obscured sight, the concealment of certain aspects of truth and deity, and so on. To be veiled implied a "pre-enlightened state" and ignorance of certain bits of "hidden or esoteric knowledge."[99] Clearly, this understanding of the veiled face is not a statement about the spiritual ignorance of women. On the contrary, it is a statement about the spiritual blindness of all mankind, including those in the Church—covenant Israel. Thus "Paul reinterprets and spiritualizes this veil to represent the Jewish inability to understand the Scriptures correctly."[100] Similarly, Isaiah scholar Edward Young noted that God depicts the bride of Christ as veiled because she is spiritually blind and ignorant aside from her relationship with the Lord.[101] Leland Ryken, an expert on biblical imagery, wrote: "As an image of concealment, the veil also has the negative meaning of a mind that is cut off from the truth. Paul pictured the unbelieving mind as having a veil over it (2 Corinthians 3:12–16) and the gospel as being veiled to people who disbelieve it (2 Corinthians 4:3)."[102]

There is an interesting linguistic connection between the veil worn over the face and the veil of the temple and Mosaic tabernacle. This association is made in nearly every Bible dictionary. That being the case, the meaning of the veiled face may be understood by examining the meaning of veiled space. Both suggest something hidden or unseen, God being hidden by the veil over his abode and the veil over the face of the person trying to view him.[103]

None of this is to imply that there is no distinction between men and women, husbands and wives, fathers and mothers. They have different divinely given roles. Rather, the point of this discussion is simply to emphasize the fact that any offense caused by the symbol of the veiled face likely stems from a misunderstanding of the emblem. When serving as a sign for spiritually limited vision, the veil over the face of a woman stands as a symbol of the condition of all of God's children. They do not see as clearly as the Lord or his prophets.

One other symbolic connotation behind the scriptural employment of facial veils seems important here. From the Apostle Paul we read that a woman "ought . . . to have power on her head because of the angels" (1 Corinthians 11:10). The Revised Standard Version translates the verse as "The woman should have a veil on her head."[104] The Greek, however, would be more accurately rendered as "The woman should have Authority on her head."[105]

This is a passage that confuses scholars; there is no consensus in the literature on the subject as to its meaning. Some commentators and translators believe that the verse is implying that women should always be in subjection to men.[106] However, the Greek does not support this reading of the verse. Leon Morris notes, "When anyone is said 'to have authority' it does not mean that the person is set under someone." Rather, it means that the person is one of those who are authorized and empowered. "Far from being a symbol of the woman's subjection to man, therefore, her head-covering is what Paul calls it—authority: in prayer and prophecy she, like the man, is [acting] under the authority of God."[107] In the writings of Ambrosiaster, we are informed that "the veil signifies power."[108] One commentator suggested that the phrase "because of the angels" meant that the angels would not recognize the "authority" of the Corinthian women when they participated in the ordinance of prayer if they did not choose to come attired as God had commanded them.

> It was the practice in some ancient Near Eastern societies for priestesses to have their heads covered "like a bride" when they were invested with the robes of their office. . . . The Apostle Paul, in speaking of the "ordinances" that he had delivered unto the Saints, directed that when women prayed and prophesied, they were to have their heads *covered* (see 1 Corinthians 11:2–13). The Joseph Smith Translation of this epistle brings verse 10 into line with the rest of the passage by changing *power* to *covering*—"For this cause ought the woman to have *a covering* on her head because of the angels." It should be noted that the word translated in verse 5 and 13 as "uncovered" is *akatakaluptos* and means "unveiled" . . . and the word translated in verse 6 as "covered" is *katakalupto* and means "to

cover wholly, i.e. *veil."* . . . The word "power" in verse 10 may have also been mistranslated because of the fact that in Aramaic the roots of the words *power* and *veil* are spelled the same. It is therefore of great interest to note that there are several ancient manuscripts of verse 10 that contain the word *veil* instead of *power.* . . .

When all of these possible changes are taken into consideration, Paul's teachings on women's veils are brought into sharper focus. It is clear that Paul's words reflect a firmly established church practice, as there are a great many early Christian artworks that depict women with upraised hands in prayer and wearing white robes with white veils upon their heads. . . . It is known from historical records that some of the early Christians wore veils when they participated in ceremonies of initiation. . . .

But why were early Christian women required to wear veils during prayer (speaking with God) and while exercising the gift of prophecy (speaking for God)? . . . Paul, in his comments, explained that women wore their veil *"because of the angels"* (1 Corinthians 11:10). . . . Paul implied on one occasion that the activities of the Saints were seen or witnessed by "God, and the Lord Jesus Christ, and the elect *angels"* (1 Timothy 5:21). According to Joseph Smith, all of the ordinances of the gospel constitute *signs* to God and his *angels,* and unless they are carried out in the divinely prescribed manner, mortals cannot receive the blessings that are attached to them.[109]

In this light it seems quite possible that a veiled face, in certain contexts, can represent an authority or power that is divinely recognized.

5
COLORS AS SYMBOLS

ALTHOUGH COLOR SYMBOLISM is often overlooked, it is one of the most universal of all types of imagery.[1] Colors carry tremendous significance and potential impact in liturgy and scripture. Indeed, for many people a pictorial representation of an idea—especially one with definite color associations—produces a much better and longer-lasting effect than does a verbal description of the same idea.[2]

Experts have shown that colors, beyond their theological significance, can influence the perceiver in both physiological and psychological ways.

> The use of colour in modern psychiatry to treat mental disorders reflects the belief that colour can influence the psyche directly and profoundly. . . . Colour is one of the areas in daily life in which symbolism is most readily apparent. This is because colours have an immediate impact on our emotions, possessing the power to arouse or to tranquillize, to gladden or to depress. Psychologists suggest that the effects of colours on the mind derive from their associations with the natural world (blue sky, red blood, gold sun and so on).[3]

It is traditionally held that colors have had a place of importance from the earliest of times and that their significance and meaning have been relatively the same for every people.[4] The fact that the most common scriptural colors are white, black, purple, red, blue, gold, and silver[5] may in part be due to linguistic issues rather than to symbolic value. Biblical Hebrew did not have the highly developed color vocabulary that exists today in English or in other modern Indo-European languages. In antiquity most Hebrew color words were descriptive of the color's origin rather than its shade. Consequently, for ancient Hebrews a person clothed in purple was not primarily seen as beautiful, but rather as a person of royalty or wealth, since purple dyes were costly and rare. Similarly, a person in sackcloth was not principally perceived as ugly or poorly dressed, but as a beggar or mourner.[6]

> The ancient Hebrews experienced color primarily through nature; colors suggested to them elements of the physical world. Blue was the color of the sky, green the color of grass and plants, red the color of blood, white the color of wool and snow. . . . The Hebrew vocabulary for color was quite limited, with only three distinct color words and essentially no words for painting, the visual arts or the concept of color and hue.[7]

This same source indicates that colors are symbolic in scripture because of their repeated use in certain contexts in ancient culture. Thus, from a modern perspective, the colors red and green are associated with Christmas because of their repeated use in Christian culture, but not because of any necessarily inherent connection with the significance or celebration of Christmas. Similarly, colors employed symbolically in scripture convey meanings reflecting their primary association with elements of nature and their use within the culture in which the text is found.[8]

As to the validity of colors as symbols, one biblical scholar noted that God placed them in scripture and attributed "symbolic significance" to them.[9] Another wrote:

> Those who have made any study of the types will not doubt that there was a meaning in the colours. . . . Where God told [Israel and her prophet] to use blue, and purple, and scarlet, there was some significance in those shades; and green and yellow would not have answered the same purpose. . . . We may be sure that there was some teaching in them; and that it is well

for us to search, with the help of . . . Scriptures and the guidance of the Holy Spirit, into [God's] object in thus making use of them.[10]

We will now look briefly at some of the most commonly employed colors.

BLACK

Black is the traditional color of grief, sorrow, and mourning. It carries with it overtones of foreboding and an association with negativity, sin, evil, and death. Images of judgment, primordial darkness, corruption, destruction, and sadness are also attached to the color black. Finally, scripture frequently employs black as a symbol for death by famine, plague, and pestilence.[11]

> Black has almost inescapable symbolism as the colour of negative forces and unhappy events. It stands for the darkness of death, ignorance, despair, sorrow and evil (whose Prince of Darkness is Satan), . . . and for ominous augury. In superstition—and in modern English idiom—black is synonymous with disaster: black cats, black days, black spots, black marks, blackballing. As the colour of mourning, it dramatizes loss and absence.[12]

Whereas light is traditionally associated with God, Christ, and the divine,[13] darkness and blackness connote the exact opposite. The very physics of black implies Luciferic associations, for black has been said to absorb all colors and thus bury the light.[14] Darkness is the absence of light.[15] Satan desires nothing more than to "bury the light" so that none of God's children have access to it (see D&C 93:39). His very abode is known as "outer darkness."[16]

The contrast between light and dark is as strong as any symbolic use of color in scripture, the temple, or secular literature.[17] It is perhaps the best possible representation of the continuing struggle that exists between the kingdom of God and that of the devil. In the Gospel of John this contrast of light and darkness is a major motif, with Jesus portrayed as the "light of the world" (see John 8:12; 9:5) who disperses the darkness of divine judgment.[18] John is not the only scriptural figure to draw on this emblem. In Alma 38:9, and again in Doctrine and Covenants 10:70 and 11:28, Christ is depicted as the light that is given to a darkened world.

Drawing on the vivid, contrasting imagery of light and dark, Alma depicts those who do not believe as being in darkness, while those who have faith in God are characterized as being filled with light. Thus he says of King Lamoni that the "power of God" had cast away the "dark veil of unbelief" over his mind (Alma 19:6).

Speaking not simply of those who disbelieve but also of those who desire and propagate wickedness, Nephi states: "And wo unto them that seek deep to hide their counsel from the Lord! And their works are in the dark; and they say: Who seeth us, and who knoweth us? . . . But behold, I will show unto them, saith the Lord of Hosts, that I know all their works" (2 Nephi 27:27). Similarly, Isaiah states of those who promulgate evil and darkness, "Woe unto them that call evil good, and good evil; that put darkness for light, and light for darkness; that put bitter for sweet, and sweet for bitter!" (Isaiah 5:20). In the Book of Mormon we read of the darkening of a person's countenance because of sins committed (see 1 Nephi 13:15; 2 Nephi 5:21; 30:6; Jacob 3:9; Alma 19:6; 26:3; Mormon 5:15).[19]

Black is a standard scriptural symbol of divine judgment. This is why God, the Great Judge of all, is occasionally described as dwelling in darkness rather than light (see Exodus 20:21; Psalms 97:2; 104:2). One biblical scholar wrote:

> It is often associated with the threatening presence of God in dark times of divine judgement upon sin and evil. Throughout the Old Testament, images of the coming of God in judgement are painted in hues of black. In anger God parts the heavens and comes down with dark clouds under his feet; he is covered in darkness when he shoots his arrows (Psalm

18:9, 11). The day of the Lord, a day of judgment for sin, is described by prophets as "a day of darkness and gloom, a day of clouds and blackness" (Zephaniah 1:15; Joel 2:2). The Gospels report that when Jesus died on the cross, bearing God's judgment on sin, darkness fell over the whole land (Matthew 27:45; Mark 15:33; Luke 23:44). . . . In about a quarter of its uses, [black] clearly accompanies God's judgment.[20]

On several occasions, biblical prophets symbolically employ the color black when speaking of God's sending plagues, famine, or death as a punishment for sins (see Lamentations 4:8; Jeremiah 8:21; Revelation 6:5). The black horses mentioned in both the book of Zechariah (6:2, 6) and the book of Revelation (6:5–6) stand as a forewarning of evil and an associated punishment that would shortly come.[21] Professor Richard Draper has written:

> At the command of the living creature, "Come and see" (v. 5), the third horse thunders forth, its blackness symbolic of death, especially by plague, famine, pestilence. The engine of want drove the third millennium. Even the Lord's people knew the gnawing of hunger. Abraham's brother, Haran, died of starvation, and the famine forced the prophet himself to move into Canaan and eventually into Egypt to survive (see Abr. 1:29–30; 2:2–15). The same held true for Jacob and his sons (see Gen. 41–44). Vast movement marked the whole era from 2,000 to 1,200 B.C. It is called the *Volkswanderungenzeit*, the time of the people's wandering—an era of mass migrations when peoples collided against peoples. Strife and war resulted, and tumult ruled the day. The rider holds a scale on which to make weight, and a voice hocks his wares: "A measure of wheat flour for a denarius, and three measures of barley meal for a denarius" (v. 6, AT). A measure, Greek *choinix*, was equal to about a U.S. quart. The silver denarius, or "penny" in the KJV, was the daily wage for a common laborer (see Matt. 20:2). Ordinarily, a denarius would buy between ten and sixteen quarts of wheat flour or twice that of barley meal. Here, under famine conditions, a day's work supplied only enough flour to keep a person alive for one day, or enough meal for three.[22]

The book of Job (30:30) and the book of Lamentations (4:8; 5:10) speak of skin being turned black as sign of judgment. Jude speaks of false teachers as the eventual recipients of the "blackest darkness" (Jude 1:13). Doctrine and Covenants 109 indicates that Israel's dispersion and state of spiritual darkness were results of disobedience to covenants, which caused the pouring out of God's judgment (see D&C 109:61).

Perhaps the most common idea cross-culturally associated with black is that of an omen of impending evil. In the Book of Mormon, Lehi noted that the Lord had shown him in a dream "a dark and dreary wilderness," which he understood to be a sign of the dangers to spirituality present on the path that his sons Laman and Lemuel chose to tread (see 1 Nephi 8:4).

Curiously, those who conspired to take the life of the Prophet Joseph Smith had painted themselves black so as not to be recognized (see D&C 135:1). Perhaps they saw themselves as the instruments of God's wrath or judgment upon the Mormons. Ironically, however, their blackened faces also effectively symbolized the reality that they were filled with darkness and sin (see D&C 88:67) and served as omens of the wrath and judgment of God that their actions would bring upon themselves.

In Western culture it is commonplace to see attendees at funerals dressed in black. This practice stems from the occasional scriptural association of black with the act of bereavement or mourning. It is for this same reason that clerics in a number of Christian denominations dress in black, as a symbol of their mourning the death of Christ.[23]

Chapter 6 of Revelation speaks of the opening of the sixth seal, which is to be followed by the sun becoming "black as sackcloth" (v. 12). Sackcloth, which was "made of the hair of black goats and was a fabric dark in color,"[24] "symbolizes mourning and its connection with darkening the sun implies that all God's creations are in mourning over the wickedness of the world."[25] Jeremiah metaphorically employs the color black when expressing his feelings of affliction, sadness, and grief (see

Jeremiah 4:27–29; 8:21; 14:2), as does Job (see Job 30:28, 30).[26] Malachi laments, "Ye have said, It is vain to serve God: and what profit is it that we have kept his ordinance, and that we have walked mournfully before the Lord of hosts?" (Malachi 3:14). A more accurate rendering of the Hebrew would be "we have walked *in black* before the Lord,"[27] which emphasizes the strong connection between black and those who are in a state of mourning.

BLUE

Anciently, the color blue was most often associated with the godly, spiritual, or heavenly nature of a thing.[28] When someone or something was depicted as blue or was adorned in blue, it implied that the person or thing had a heavenly or celestial nature or origin or was divinely appointed.[29] Thus the robe of the Mosaic high priest, worn over his inner garment, was required to be entirely blue. This emphasized the fact that his authority was of heavenly origin and his life was the typifying of God and Christ.[30] Similarly, one of the dominant colors of the Mosaic tabernacle was blue (see Exodus 26:1, 31, 36), likely because the temple serves both as an earthy abode for heavenly beings and also as an earthly prototype of the heavenly city.[31] Even God's throne was described as being blue in color (see Ezekiel 1:26),[32] implying that it exists in heaven and that he who is seated thereon is of a heavenly or divine nature. One commentator indicated that perhaps the purpose of the blue on the tabernacle was to "remind Israel that though they were traveling on earth, their destination was heaven."[33]

In Mexico, Egypt, and Chaldea, blue was worn during mourning as a token of the felicity which the soul, freed from the trammels of matter, was enjoying in the celestial regions. Egyptian mummies are frequently found shrouded in a network of blue beads. In order to signify their exalted and heavenly character the Gods were frequently painted blue. The term "blue-blooded" may have originated from this cause, and up to the time of the Spanish conquest of Mexico, those natives who offered themselves as propitiatory sacrifices to their Deity smeared their bodies with blue paint.[34]

Occasionally, blue is associated with the "idea of revelation and its source," namely because of its tendency to remind us of the sky or the heavens—from which revelation flows.[35] One authority noted, "To the Christian, blue is the colour . . . [that] denotes faith, compassion and the waters of baptism,"[36] the color of the water reminding us of the God who instituted the ordinance for the salvation of his children. The color has been called by some a "constant reminder" of Israel's covenantal obligation to always conform to God's will. It carries with it feelings of rest and peace, symbolic of the fact that true rest and peace are enjoyed by men only as they place their lives in accordance with the will of those who dwell in the heavens above.[37]

In the book of Numbers, Moses was commanded to put a man to death for breaking the Sabbath (see 15:35). As a direct result of this, God commanded the children of Israel to place a ribbon of blue on their garments as a constant reminder that they were to obey "the message from heaven, and not live by their own ideas."[38] In Esther 8:15 we read that Mordecai, who acted as the messenger of God's will to Esther, was dressed in blue and white robes. Although the color blue potentially could be misunderstood as a symbol of Persian royalty, its employment here would specifically remind Israel that Mordecai had functioned as God's instrument and had carried out God's purposes and plan.[39] On the other hand, in Ezekiel 23:6 we are told that the Assyrians clothed themselves in blue, in all likelihood to "give a religious touch to their evils" and to imply that they were a "godly people." In so doing they hoped to deceive Israel and gain their confidence.[40]

BRASS

Although metals, such as gold, silver, and brass, are only secondarily colors, because the "color" of these metals carries symbolic connotations, several sources have included gold, silver, and brass among the symbolic colors rather than creating a separate category of symbolic metals.[41]

Brass, or copper, is generally taken to represent judgment; for brass is that which can stand fire. "His feet were like unto fine brass, as if they burned in a furnace" (Rev. 1:15). In the Tabernacle it surrounded everything, and was the basis for the whole; for all the outer court stood upon brazen sockets. The altar of burnt-offering and the laver were made of brass, and each of these connected with the thought of judgment.[42]

When Moses raised the brazen serpent upon the pole in an attempt to destroy the effects of the fiery flying serpents, the Christ-centered typology was deepened through the employment of brass, for Christ will be the judge of all mankind (see John 5:22).[43] Similarly, in Daniel 10:6 and Revelation 1:15 (see also 2:18) Christ is described as having feet of brass. In both cases it appears that the message, beyond the image of strength, stability, and permanence, is that Christ's life was such that he could serve as the perfect judge because he lived the perfect life.[44]

The Book of Mormon mentions time and again the "plates of brass." Perhaps it is more than coincidental that Laban was condemned and *judged* deserving of death by the Lord because of his unwillingness to give up the plates of *brass* (see 1 Nephi 3:12). Similarly, Nephi indicates that the Lord would preserve those plates so that they would be had by "all nations, kindreds, tongues, and people" (see 1 Nephi 4:8–18; 5:18–19) and so that by these same plates—or more particularly, the record that in part originated with those plates—the world would be judged as either accepting of God and his plan or as rejecting God's prophets because of the foolishness of the traditions of their fathers.

GOLD

Like brass, gold is a metal as well as a color with symbolic meanings intertwined in and conveyed by both characteristics.

For Latter-day Saints, gold has very strong connotations by virtue of its association with the sun and thus the celestial kingdom and eternal glory.

First of all, there are the more obvious meanings—gold as a symbol of wealth, temporal power, or worldliness.[45] Nephi frequently mentions gold as part of the substantial wealth that his family walked away from when father Lehi was commanded by the Lord to flee Jerusalem (see 1 Nephi 2:4, 11). In Isaiah 13:12 and 2 Nephi 23:12, the Lord promises that he can "make a man more precious than fine gold." So, as valuable as gold is as a temporal or monetary commodity, God can make those who follow him more valuable, even of infinite eternal worth.

> Gold adorns, but Christ adorns much greater. Gold buys one's way into earthly places but Christ brings one into the throne room of heaven. Gold meets the requirements of this life but Christ equips for the eternal life. Gold settles quarrels between men but Christ settles the quarrel between God and man. Gold saves the life from many discomforts, but Christ saves the life from eternal loss.[46]

Gold also symbolizes the celestial, divine, or godly nature of a thing. Commentators make this connection partly because gold is pure, incorruptible, precious, and glorious.[47] The Apostle Paul established an ancient connection between gold and things celestial when he stated: "There are also celestial bodies, and bodies terrestrial: but the glory of the celestial is one, and the glory of the terrestrial is another. There is one glory of the sun, and another glory of the moon, and another glory of the stars" (1 Corinthians 15:40–41).[48] Joseph Fielding McConkie wrote, "Gold is the color of the sun; it represents divine power, the splendor of enlightenment; radiance, and glory. Because of its great value, and its radiance, gold is known to us as the possession of kings and great kingdoms. It is a symbol common to scriptural descriptions of God and the heavenly kingdom."[49] Additionally, in antiquity gold occasionally functioned as a symbol for wisdom—an appropriate symbol for heavenly things and beings.[50]

As a representation of the divine, it is fitting that gold metal was found throughout the Mosaic tabernacle and in Israel's temples, not simply because they functioned as God's house but, more particularly, because these earthly edifices, like those today, were to remind people of God, teach them of God, and in time bring them to God.[51] As one small example of this, the ark of the covenant, which symbolized God,[52] was covered in gold (see Exodus 25:10–13, 17–18). Scripture speaks of God's desire to refine the Saints as one would refine gold (see Job 23:10; Proverbs 17:3; 27:21; 3 Nephi 24:3). The dross of sin must be removed from our lives if we are to become celestial beings. Once we are purified, we will be prepared to dwell in God's presence, where the streets are said to be paved with gold and those who reside with God wear crowns of gold (see Revelation 4:4; 21:21).

In their testimony about having seen the plates from which the Prophet Joseph Smith translated the Book of Mormon, the Eight Witnesses stated, "The plates . . . have the appearance of gold"—indeed, for they are of God and contain that which one must know and do to return to Him.

GREEN

Green is a standard symbol of life.[53] In light of its scriptural association with everlasting life, it also signifies hope.[54] The Egyptians placed "greenstone" amulets in their tombs as a sign of eternal youth and that which is "everlasting, evergreen, fresh, young, and immortal."[55] They spoke of God as "The Great Green One" because he possesses eternal life and is able to bestow it.[56] One authority of Semitic symbolism noted that "Green, as the colour of plants—growths to which people look forward in winter—symbolized hope and resurrection. . . . Hammurabi tells us that he 'bedecked the grave of Malkat with green,' the colour of resurrection."[57]

Job says of the vain that "his branch shall not be green" (Job 15:32; see also Psalm 37:1–2), or as one commentator interpreted it, "There shall be no *scion* [i.e., descendants] from his roots; all his posterity shall fail."[58] Another interpretation is "The man who is deceived and is not true to God's Word, and is not really linked up with God, will not prosper, and shall not be productive in his life."[59] Without a doubt, the man who rejects God will be less productive than he would otherwise be. Additionally, the absence of the color green ("his branch shall not be green") implies that the vain man has forfeited his exaltation, which explains his loss of posterity.[60]

Jehovah is said to lead those who accept him as their Shepherd to "lie down in green pastures" (Psalm 23:2). Taken in its most literal sense, this passage would seem to refer to pens that were constructed where the flock might be safe all night. These were enclosures "where [the flocks] had grass and provender to eat."[61] However, it is evident from verse 1 that this psalm is to be understood metaphorically, because "the Lord" is stated to be the Shepherd of the Psalmist. The song is not speaking of literal sheep, but rather the followers of Christ. The Hebrew verb in verses 2 and 3 implies a future event (e.g., "he will make it possible for me to lie down in green pastures"),[62] perhaps suggesting a post-resurrectional event, as does the Psalmist's comment, "I will dwell in the house of the Lord for ever" (Psalm 23:6).[63] Thus the use of the color green here appropriately foreshadows the future reward of eternal life in the kingdom of God. Elsewhere the Psalmist states that the righteous person who has made God his strength will be like a "green olive tree in the house of God" (Psalm 52:8; see also Jeremiah 11:16–17; 17:7–8; Hosea 14:8). Again, the connotation is of one who has inherited eternal life.[64]

In Revelation 6:8 we read, "And I looked, and behold a pale horse: and his name that sat on him was Death." The Greek word translated "pale" in the King James Version is literally a "sickly pale green."[65]

> Green is . . . a generally positive symbol. . . . Green is universally associated with plant life and by extension with spring renewal, youth, freshness, fertility and hope. . . . Many traditions make a distinction between dark green [as a symbol of life] and the pale greenish tinge of death. . . . Perhaps this stems from the fact that green is not the skin-colour of healthy normality.[66]

While staggering under the weight of his cross, Christ prophetically uttered, "Daughters of Jerusalem, weep not for me, but weep for yourselves, and for your children. . . . For if they do these things in a green tree, what shall be done in the dry?" (Luke 23:28, 31). In other words, "If Israel's oppressors could do what was then in process of [being done] to the 'Green Tree,' who bore the leafage of freedom and truth and offered the priceless fruit of life eternal, what would the powers of evil not do to the withered branches and dried trunk of apostate Judaism?"[67] Joseph Fielding McConkie noted, "Trees [represent] men: green trees the righteous, dry trees the wicked."[68] Thus, in reference to the martyrdom of the Prophet Joseph and his brother Hyrum, John Taylor penned, "If the fire can scathe a green tree for the glory of God, how easy it will burn up the dry trees to purify the vineyard of corruption" (D&C 135:6).

> Laborers are again called to labor in the Church and in the world for the salvation of men. They are going out to prune the vineyard for the last time. And the branches that bear no fruit—whether in the Church or in the world—shall soon be burned. The burning of the earth both is and includes the burning of the vineyard. . . . The wicked and ungodly, in and out of the Church, shall be consumed in the fires. And "if the fire can scathe a green tree for the glory of God," our scripture says with reference to that which befalls even the righteous, "how easy it will burn up the dry trees to purify the vineyard of corruption" (D&C 135:6).[69]

In both passages, the color green serves as an indicator of

righteousness and the promise of eternal life, whereas the dry, brown tree stands as a symbol of judgment and damnation.

PURPLE

To the ancients the color purple provoked images of wealth, power, royalty, majesty, and the like.[70] In biblical times colored textiles were produced from natural dyes that were rare and therefore very expensive. Purple dye was made by combining the secretions of two species of molluscs, a process that was not only costly but also difficult.[71] Only the wealthy, such as rulers, royalty, or those of high rank, could afford to decorate their homes and palaces with brightly colored fabrics—purple being one of the rarest of colors.[72] Indeed, because of the color's consistent association with power, affluence, honor, and dignity, the children of Byzantine emperors were traditionally born in a room with purple drapes, hence the phrase "born in the purple."[73]

One of the dominant colors on the Mosaic tabernacle was purple (see Exodus 26:1, 31, 36). All of the aforementioned definitions of this color seem to apply to this portable temple in the wilderness. One dictionary of biblical imagery explains: "In ancient culture [the color purple] suggested wealth and royalty. . . . Blue, purple, and scarlet colored the tabernacle of ancient Israel, suggesting that Yahweh was the wealthy and powerful God-King, who brought an impoverished people out of slavery in Egypt to make them a mighty nation."[74] The presence of this color on the tabernacle and the robes of the high priest potentially served to remind Israel that "they were of the royal or heavenly family. It was also a reminder of the wealth of blessings that awaited righteous heirs."[75]

In the book of Esther (6:8; 8:15), Mordecai is described as receiving a purple or "royal" robe from the king, signifying his new position as "prime minister."[76] As one commentator wrote, "To wear a robe that the king had worn and ride a horse that the king had ridden was the highest mark of honor that could be shown to a subject."[77] As implied by the purple robe, Mordecai had become royalty, second only in rank to the king.[78]

In the book of Daniel, King Belshazzar offered a reward to anyone who could interpret the writing on the wall (see NIV, Daniel 5:7, 16). As was the Oriental tradition,[79] he promised extravagant honors to the person who could give an interpretation, saying, "Who ever reads this writing and tells me what it means will be clothed in purple and have a gold chain placed around his neck, and he will be made the third highest ruler in the kingdom" (v. 7). Daniel was brought to the king and successfully interpreted the writing. For doing so, he received the aforementioned purple robe and the position of high authority in the government, which the robe symbolized (see v. 29).

In John 19 we read of the cardinal act of sacrilege in all of recorded history. One commentator on the passage wrote, "In order to insult [Christ] and show their hatred they clothed Him in mockery with the royal garments. Thus they exposed the wickedness of their hearts."[80] The Gospel of John informs us, "The soldiers platted a crown of thorns, and put it on his head, and they put on him a purple robe, and said, Hail, King of the Jews! and they smote him with their hands" (John 19:2–3). This is perhaps the clearest example in scripture of the strong associations of the color purple and royalty. The crown of thorns pressed into Christ's trembling brow was an effort to depict the crown of a king or the laurel wreath commonly worn by emperors of the day.[81] The purple robe was an emblem of the imperial office. The chants of "Hail, King!" mimicked the standard greeting given the emperor, "*Ave Caesar.*"[82]

Typologists suggest that in this passage purple represents Christ's "Kingly glory, especially as Son of Man, over the whole world"[83] and that the color was "symbolic of spiritual development."[84] Both are correct. Christ was and is "King of the whole world" and the most "spiritually developed" of all mankind (see Abraham 3:19). The Romans employed all of the right symbols but were seemingly oblivious to the truth.

It is apropos that this next and final example should follow the last one and come at the hands of John the Beloved. Clearly referring to the "great and abominable church" (see 1 Nephi 13), the prophetic apostle recorded that he saw "the great whore that sitteth upon many waters . . . arrayed in purple and . . . decked with gold and precious stones and pearls, having a golden cup in her hand full of abominations and filthiness of her fornication: And upon her forehead was a name written, MYSTERY, BABYLON THE GREAT, THE MOTHER OF HARLOTS AND ABOMINATIONS OF THE EARTH" (Revelation 17:1–5). One scholar notes how the symbolism in this passage reveals the deceptive nature of this priestess-harlot:

> The harlot drinks from a golden cup filled with abominations and corruption (cf. Jer. 7–8). This stands in contrast to the golden chalice held by the Levitical high priest and used in the temple for making a wine offering to God. But this is not the only imitation of holy things that John associates with the woman. Purple and scarlet comprise her clothing. These colors, along with white and blue, dominate the fabric of the veils and interior of the temple as well as the vestments of the high priest. Further, the high priest wore a miter. Engraven upon a golden plate fastened to it were the words "Holiness to the Lord," identifying the priest as the Lord's own. The whore also wears an inscription upon her brow proclaiming her threefold status as "MYSTERY, BABYLON THE GREAT, THE MOTHER OF HARLOTS AND ABOMINATIONS OF THE EARTH" (v. 5, KJV). . . . Through these images, John paints the picture of a priestess-harlot standing as a counterfeit high priest.[85]

Another commentator stated, "The royal color on this woman represents [the fact that she] seeks to be king of kings, and lord of lords in the place of our Lord Jesus Christ."[86] Ironically, or perhaps better put, tragically, the Roman soldiers mocked Jesus as a false king, and the world worships Babylon as its true king! Thus Isaiah warned:

> Wo unto them that call evil good, and good evil, that put darkness for light, and light for darkness, that put bitter for sweet, and sweet for bitter! . . . Therefore, as the fire devoureth

the stubble, and the flame consumeth the chaff, their root shall be rottenness, and their blossoms shall go up as dust; because they have cast away the law of the Lord of Hosts, and despised the word of the Holy One of Israel. (2 Nephi 15:20, 24)

RED/SCARLET

Most often in scripture the colors red and scarlet represent sin or the blood of Christ that was shed because of sin.[87] Red is occasionally associated with both life and death, resurrection and evil. However, as noted in chapter 3, these are not contradictory images, but images that are intertwined and closely associated with Christ's atonement—making red an essentially negative symbol.[88] Thus red can represent life and death since it is the "life of the body" (Genesis 9:4) and to shed blood is to take life. It serves well as a symbol for evil and sin because it reminds us of Christ's blood that had to be shed because of the evils mankind has committed. "In some respects . . . Christ's shed blood could be seen metaphorically as the shedding of mortality and sin, and his complete victory over them both (see John 16:33; Mosiah 15:8; Mormon 7:5–7)."[89] When Christ overcame sin in Gethsemane, it was blood that oozed out of him (see Luke 22:44; Mosiah 3:7) as though sin, too, had entirely left his being through that most painful means of payment. Finally, blood is associated with resurrection because of its connection with life—resurrection bringing to pass the eternal life of all. Indeed, in some early societies, red was so closely linked to the concept of life that the bodies of the deceased were painted red to ensure their resurrection and eternal life.[90]

The colors red (see Revelation 6:4; 12:3–4; Zechariah 6:2) and scarlet (Joshua 2:18, 21) are also employed scripturally as symbols for war, bloodshed, and violent death.[91] Both colors appear quite frequently, and in symbolic context, throughout the standard works of the Church. What follows is but a sampling of the many passages in which red or scarlet is used as a symbol for sin, evil, blood, death, war, life, or resurrection.

In scripture scarlet is most often associated with the Old Testament tabernacle. It is found extensively in Moses' portable temple (see Exodus 25:4; 26:1). It appears on the clothing of the high priest (see Exodus 28:33; 29:19–21, 32–33), who represented Christ (see Hebrews 3:1; 5:10) and who, multiple times each day, offered blood sacrifices in anticipation of Christ's atonement. In part, the high priest's clothing reminds us that Christ will return to earth in red apparel as a symbol of the blood he shed on our behalf (see Isaiah 63:1–3; JST, Luke 22:44; Revelation 19:11–13; D&C 19:18; 133:46–51). Elder Neal A. Maxwell noted:

> Knowing as we do that before the scourging and crucifixion Jesus bled at every pore in Gethsemane, how red His raiment must have been then, how crimson His cloak!
>
> No wonder that, in one of His appearances—when He comes in power and glory—Christ will come in red attire (D&C 133:48), thereby not only signifying the winepress of wrath but also bringing to our remembrance how He suffered, for each of us, in Gethsemane and on Calvary![92]

Although the tabernacle's curtains and roof were dyed in red and scarlet (see Exodus 26:1, 14), only one piece of its furniture was required to be covered with scarlet when carried from place to place—the "table of shewbread" (Numbers 4:8). Apparently this was because its emblems (bread and wine) typified the slain body of Christ, as represented in the ordinance of the sacrament and the red cloth that was required to be draped over it.[93]

On Yom Kippur, the Day of Atonement, the high priest led the scapegoat, which bore the sins of the nation, into the wilderness (see Leviticus 16:8–10, 26).

> A ribbon of [scarlet], representing the sins of Israel, was tied round the neck of the scapegoat on the Day of Atonement before it was driven into the wilderness to its death. It became

indirectly associated with harlotry and the deep sins of ungodly conduct. (See Isaiah 1:18; Psalm 51:7.) The color stands in contrast to the white robes of the redeemed and of the gown of the bride of the Lamb (see Revelation 19:8).[94]

When a Levitical priest performed the required Mosaic ceremony to cleanse a leper, he placed blood on the afflicted person's right earlobe, right thumb, and the big toe of the right foot. In each instance the blood represented the atonement of Christ, as well as Israel's need to hearken to his commands and follow his example (see Leviticus 14).[95] The blood symbolically employed in this ceremony functions as a reminder of Israel's need to live in such a way that the atoning blood of Christ can sanctify them, thus fulfilling Isaiah's words "though your sins be as scarlet, they shall be as white as snow" (Isaiah 1:18). The visual contrast between scarlet and white found in that verse expresses the transition from guilt to purity worked by God's forgiveness. The biblical association of the color scarlet with sin continues in the imagery of modern literature, for instance in Nathaniel Hawthorne's novel *The Scarlet Letter*.[96]

The book of Genesis records the rivalry between the brothers Esau and Jacob. As the story goes, in the process of time Esau sold his birthright to Jacob for a bowl of pottage (see 25:34). Because the notion of birthright aptly symbolizes the promises of exaltation and a man's right to preside over his posterity in the eternities,[97] it is appropriate that the Genesis account highlights the fact that when Esau was born "[he] came out red" (Genesis 25:25). His sinful choice to sell his birthright—typifying the sin of selling one's soul and eternal inheritance for the transitory pleasures of this flesh—was effectively depicted by his reddish color.[98]

As we noted previously, John the Revelator informs us that the great and abominable church clothed herself in purple in an apparent effort to usurp the position of royalty rightfully belonging to Christ and, by so doing, hoped to deceive us into following and worshipping her.[99] However, in Revelation

17:4 we are also told that alongside her purple garments she draped scarlet or red raiment.

Anciently, the high priest functioned as a divinely appointed type for Christ. Serving in this capacity, on the Day of Atonement he would don white clothing and then enter the Holy of Holies, only to exit with his beautiful white garments splattered with blood.[100] By so doing the high priest symbolically indicated that a sacrifice had been made on behalf of Israel. As a representation of Christ, his garments were soiled with blood so that Israel's garments could be clean and white.[101] It appears that the great and abominable church's choice to clothe herself in scarlet apparel was an attempt to get us to worship her and place our trust in her power to save—in her power to atone on our behalf. She mimics the high priest, and thus Christ, and the blood-red apparel she sports is only a further act of misdirection. She is deserving of the symbolic color, but not because of her power to save. On the contrary, she deserves to be arrayed in red because she is guilty of much sin, murder, and violence, including having been party to the shedding of the blood of the very Son of God.

In sum, red and scarlet are employed in scripture through many alarming images, including: blood (see 2 Kings 3:22), garments sprinkled with blood (see Isaiah 63:2), sacrificial animals typifying Christ (see Numbers 19:2), bad omens (see Zechariah 1:8; 6:2), diseases symbolizing sin (see Leviticus 13:19; 14:37), the bloodshed of war (see Zechariah 6:2; Revelation 6:4; 12:3), the conscious choice to live a wicked life (see Alma 3:13–19), and Satan (see Revelation 12:3–4).

SILVER

Silver falls into the same category as brass or gold. It is a metal that is occasionally used for the symbolic connotations suggested by both its value and color. One typologist explained that silver symbolized redemption and that the tabernacle, which stood on sockets of silver, was to be understood as the place of redemption.[102] Along the same line, other scholars have noted that "silver, like gold, is of great value and hence is associated with Christ. Traditionally, it is associated with the idea of a Reconciler, Savior, and Redeemer."[103]

In relation to the Mosaic tabernacle's use of silver (see Exodus 36:24), one theologian wrote: "In the sandy desert [of the Exodus], as well as in this wicked world, the sinner needs a sure foundation, a safe resting place. These sockets perhaps weighed one hundred pounds each. The board therefore rested on a solid foundation in the sand. . . . We do not read of silver being in heaven. No one in heaven needs to be redeemed."[104] It appears, then, that silver, as it pertains to the temple, signifies the source of redemption via saving ordinances performed under proper priesthood authority. Another source associates silver with the receipt of revelation and spiritual insight,[105] which is another purpose of the temple. Indeed, the temple serves well as that "safe resting place" from this fallen and chaotic world, pointing our minds and our hearts to that "Sure Foundation," which is Christ (see 1 Corinthians 3:11; Jacob 4:16–17).

In Doctrine and Covenants 128 we read that the Lord "is like a refiner's fire, and like fuller's soap," and that at his coming he will "sit as a refiner and purifier of silver" to "purify the sons of Levi, and purge them" as a refiner purifies silver (v. 24). Appropriately, "silver is thought to carry the idea of moral purity."[106] Through our earthly tests, trials, and experience, God seeks to purify us and thereby strengthen us so that we might abide the day of his coming and be fit to dwell in his presence.

WHITE

White is the most common scriptural color, finding a prominent place in scripture and liturgy both inside and outside of the Church. Even in the secular world, white carries stronger connotations than any other color—black being a distant second.[107]

Theologically, the color is associated with the concepts of purity, righteousness, holiness, innocence, victory, light, and revelation.[108] Beyond these standard ideas, white is also occasionally equated with happiness, virginity, the presence of the Holy Ghost, and spiritual dedication or mastery.[109]

> Inevitably, white, the absolute colour of light, became a symbol of purity, truth, innocence and the sacred or divine. . . . White is the positive side of the black-white antithesis in all symbol systems. It is also the colour of initiation, the novice, neophyte or candidate (the Latin word for which means "shining white") and of rites of passage, including baptism, confirmation, marriage.[110]

On the Day of Atonement the high priest would dress all in white to emphasize that he was acting by "divine investiture of authority" as a type for Christ, who is pure and victorious over sin and death (see Leviticus 16; Exodus 28:6). Because of Christ's atonement, prepared from the foundations of the world, Isaiah could proclaim, "Though your sins be as scarlet, they shall be as white as snow" (Isaiah 1:18).

The courtyard of the Mosaic tabernacle was surrounded by a wall of white linen (see Exodus 27:9), symbolic of that which took place within its walls and suggestive of what those who entered should be. This white barricade strongly implied the necessary separation that must exist between the things of God (including his covenant people) and the harmful things of this world.

The faithful members of Christ's true church are depicted as wearing white garments (see Revelation 3:4; 19:8),[111] as are those who entirely overcome the world (see Revelation 3:4–5; 6:11; 7:14).[112] Angels are almost exclusively depicted as being clothed in white (see Matthew 28:3; Mark 16:5; John 20:12; Acts 1:10; 1 Nephi 8:5; 14:19). It is through the atoning blood of Christ that their raiment is said to have become clean and white (see Alma 13:11). White is the "color of heaven's garments and symbolizes a dazzling purity that dispels the darkness of divine wrath (Isaiah 1:18; Daniel 7:9; Mark 16:5; Revelation 3:4)."[113] Of course, it is only those who overcome this world through Christ who are allowed to partake of the fruit of the tree of life (see Revelation 2:7). That fruit has been described as being white and "desirable to make one happy" (1 Nephi 8:10–11) and thus symbolizes not only what is requisite to regain God's presence but also what will be felt by those who so obtain.

The apostle John indicates that those who are exalted will receive a white stone upon which is written a new name (see Revelation 2:17; D&C 130:10). He also speaks of righteous Saints as riding upon white horses (see Revelation 6:2; 19:14). Indeed, Christ is seen on a white horse, descending in a white cloud, and seated on a throne of white (see Revelation 14:14; 19:11–14; 20:11). Of the events that took place on the Mount of Transfiguration, we read that Jesus' "face did shine as the sun, and his raiment was white as the light" (Matthew 17:2).

> White is used in biblical imagery as the contrasting opposite to black and darkness.... It is often used to describe the radiance of light in contrast to the darkness of divine wrath on evil and sin. For instance, in contrast to the image of God wrapped in darkness and descending to earth in judgment (e.g., Psalm 18:7–11), Jesus is clothed in robes "as white as light" (Matthew 17:2, New International Version; Mark 9:3; Luke 9:29).[114]

Finally, in words that recall the experience on the Mount of Transfiguration, the Book of Mormon speaks of the countenances of the righteous as being white (see 1 Nephi 13:15; 2 Nephi 5:21; Alma 19:6; 26:3), which may expand the meaning behind the scriptural declaration that the missionary field is "white, and ready to harvest" (John 4:35; D&C 4:4). Both ideas seem to imply a people who are striving for purity and who seek light, truth, and the companionship of God's Spirit.

6
NUMBERS AS SYMBOLS

NUMBERS, OF COURSE, are nothing more than symbols, as is any form of writing. The term *numerology* is derived from the Latin *numerus* (meaning "a number") and *logy* (a "science" or "study"). Thus numerology means "the science or study of numbers" or "the investigation of the nature and purpose of . . . numbers" as found in the scriptures or life.[1] One expert on numbers and their historical development wrote, "Numbers do not just express arithmetical quantities, but are endowed with ideas and forces that are sometimes benign and sometimes malign, flowing under the surface of mortal things like an underground river."[2] Indeed, it is the assertion of this chapter that numbers in scripture frequently mean more than what is suggested at face value.

All ancient societies and many in modernity have attached great importance to numbers.[3] Beyond their mathematical value, numbers can express complex ideas with utmost succinctness. The Hebrews, Greeks, Romans, Babylonians, Egyptians, Aramaeans, Gnostics, and Christians all used numbers in this way, as symbols for ideas in their speaking, writing, and teaching.[4]

Moses, who is traditionally believed to have authored the oldest biblical books now extant, used numbers as symbols, as did his contemporaries. While the use of number symbols was common in ancient Israel[5] they were used as colloquial literary tools much earlier than the Mosaic dispensation.[6]

During the age of Hammurabi [2,000 B.C.] and following, a rather large quantity of literary productions appeared which did employ some numbers in a symbolic manner.... In the old Babylonian version of "The Epic of Gilgamesh" there seems to be a regular employment of 7 in a symbolic manner.... The literature of Ugarit... is replete with examples of this phenomenon.... [However] it was not until the age of Pythagoras (sixth cent. B.C.) that number symbolism received systematic treatment.[7]

The intertestamental period saw significant development in the use of number symbolism. Apocalyptic writings, which were commonplace in that era, employed symbolic numbers with considerable freedom.[8] Likewise, many of the church fathers saw symbolic significance in the numbers of the Bible. Augustine's "stamp of approval" on number symbolism in scripture solidified their legitimacy within the Christian church.[9]

Symbolic numbers were also a prominent feature of the talmudic, cabalistic, and midrashic literature of the Jews. Indeed, from the cabalistic era onward (beginning no later than the twelfth century A.D.), there was a preoccupation with the idea of "mystical numbers" in Jewish and Christian philosophy.[10]

Regardless of the evidence supporting the idea that this practice has a long and diverse history, it is to be expected that some people question the validity of attaching symbolic value to numbers in scripture. Curiously, numbers raise more eyebrows than other symbolic categories do. In all probability, this is because too many people inaccurately associate "numerology" with practices such as fortune telling, the reading of tarot cards, or reliance upon horoscopes. As one source notes, "Statistics of the Bible, like the calculations of the Great Pyramid of Egypt, have a fatal attraction for cranks and crackpots—and even for wise men in their less guarded moments."[11]

Some people who doubt the validity of numbers as symbols dismiss out of hand the possibility of divine intervention as the source for these symbols in scripture. They argue that numbers are the language of man, not of God.[12] Yet time and again scholars have rebutted the naive suggestion that numerology is nothing more than cultural. Indeed, some scholars point to the statistical improbability that men could be responsible for the cross-culturally consistent use of numbers and the tendency of scriptural authors to use certain words and phrases a symbolically significant number of times. As one scholar stated, the biblical authors were clearly ignorant of how many times they had used a given word or phrase, and must simply have been "moved by the Holy Ghost."[13] Simply put, the theory that numbers are used in a calculated and symbolic manner in recorded revelation is based on the premise that the author of scripture is God.[14]

If the truth be told, there is a strong and overwhelming consensus among scholars that the existence and use of numbers in scripture and ancient culture is too frequent, detailed, and consistent to be attributed to men.[15] One expert in Semitic and biblical symbolism wrote, "A study of ancient Oriental Literatures is bound to lead us to the conclusion that there were some numbers at least which occur very frequently and were never intended to be taken in their literal sense by those who made use of them."[16] Another argued, "The subject of Biblical numerology touches, in one way or another, every area in Biblical studies. The subject is vitally connected with the overall field of theology and more specifically with the prophetic doctrines of the Bible. . . . Compare, for example, the important role numbers play in the books of Daniel, Ezekiel and Revelation."[17] Augustine (A.D. 354–430), in his treatise on Christian doctrine, laid down a number of rules for exposition of scripture. His rules included the idea that "there is a significance in biblical numbers."[18] By the Middle Ages, it had become normative for biblical scholars to acknowledge that to misunderstand biblical numerology was to misinterpret the Bible.[19]

Historical sources are unclear as to the specific date and location of the origins of numerology.[20] Some trace it back to the Sumerians.[21] Others insist that the priestly scribes of Egypt are the source.[22] Most commonly the credit for the systemizing of numbers as symbols goes to Pythagoras, who is frequently referred to as "the father of the symbolism of numbers." However, scholars generally agree that he was really an heir of a science that had its origins much earlier.[23] One scholar notes: "Why certain numbers became laden with symbolic meaning is unknown; in most cases this arose in prehistoric times and is now lost to us. Interestingly there is a general consistency across cultures to the meaning of certain numbers."[24] We have records from Egypt (3,400 B.C.) and Mesopotamia (3,000 B.C.) that establish the use of numbers for the purpose of tabulating.[25] However, the earliest appearance of the symbolic use of numbers has been dated somewhere around 2,000 B.C.[26]

The symbolic use of numbers in scripture can be broken down into four basic categories or approaches.

1. *Numbers with standard meanings.* Anciently, and almost cross-culturally, most numbers had an assigned symbolic meaning. So when people heard or read the number seven, for example, they were reminded of ideas such as fulness and completion. Similarly, in modern Western culture, the number thirteen evokes images of bad luck and superstition.

2. *The multiplication of numbers.* This is the practice of using the multiples of symbolic numbers to heighten the emphasis of the symbol. For example, the apostle John applies the number 144,000—a multiple of twelve (representing priesthood)—to those who have made their calling and election sure (see Revelation 7:4–8). Of the multiplication of the number twelve, one commentator wrote:

> The number 144,000 is a symbolic series of multiples. . . . The number 12 represents priesthood, it is then multiplied by itself to come up with 144, symbolizing an even greater priesthood power and magnitude, and finally it is multiplied by 1,000 signifying multitudes, which express the idea that this power which the 144,000 possess is an overwhelming priesthood power. . . . Anytime multiples of a number are used in the Revelation it is to symbolically expand the powers and strength

of the things being described, whether they are beasts, armies, or servants of God.[27]

3. *Repetition of words, names, or phrases.* This is the practice of using a certain word, name, title, or phrase a significant or symbolic number of times in a book or passage, without drawing attention to the fact that this has been done. As an example, one text states of Christ:

> He was the stone which the builders rejected, yet seven times it is declared that it is now become the Head of the corner. Again, twenty-one times, or three times seven, is He spoken of as being at the right hand of God,—the perfection of exaltation. [In the biblical text] He is declared seven times to be a High Priest after the order of Melchizedek, thus proclaiming the perfection and abiding character of His work of intercession for His people. . . . In the book of Revelation, where the number seven predominates, the Name of names, Jesus, is repeated just seven times, Jesus Christ a like number, and Lord twenty-one times, or three times seven, all symbolical of His intrinsic perfection.[28]

4. *Gematria.* The word *gematria* means literally "reckoning by numbers."[29] In most ancient societies, letters and numbers were used interchangeably,[30] and each letter of an alphabet had a numerical value. Technically speaking, gematria is a mode of interpretation in which the numerical values are substituted for each letter in a word. By so doing, a word's numerical value could be determined and compared for potential relationships with other words possessing the same numerical value.[31]

As an example, many people have assumed that John's use of the number 666 in the book of Revelation is an instance of gematria (see Revelation 13:18). In the hopes of determining who the anti-Christ is, scholars and others have expended a great deal of energy over the centuries to find personal names that also have a numerical value of 666.[32]

When numbers are used in a calculated and symbolic

manner, they support the premise that God is the author of the scriptures.

> Many writers . . . attribute symbolic numbers to the direct revelation of God. . . . A larger group of scholars . . . contends that symbolic or significant numbers were in use before the writing of the Old Testament and were a common literary device of scribes from Babylon, Egypt, etc. Within this group of scholars there is division of opinion as to the specific origin of symbolic numbers. Some attribute their origin to the fact that certain numbers have special or unique factors involved in their coefficients. This view is generally disregarded. . . . Another proposal is that the universe exhibits certain numerological phenomena which had its origin in God. Man, according to this view, was influenced by this numerical phenomena and symbolism of numbers was the result.[33]

Before turning to an examination of individual numbers with symbolic significance, a couple of questions should be asked. First of all, how is one to know if a number is intended symbolically rather than literally? One source suggests, "The only valid method of ascertaining the symbolical meaning and usage of . . . numbers, names, and colours in the Scriptures, is by an ample collation and study of the passages where they occur."[34] In other words, it requires effort and study. The text continues, "The determination of possible numerical values . . . must be derived from the context in which the expression occurs."[35]

The second question is simply this: Why should one care about the presence of symbolic numbers in scripture? The answer is obvious. If scriptures actually do employ numbers with symbolic intent, to overlook their meaning is to miss the point of the text. As John Davis wrote, "A careful study of these numeric patterns . . . will give the student insights into Scriptures which he could get in no other way."[36]

ONE

One is a very common number in scripture,[37] although more often than not it is intended literally rather than figuratively.

When employed as a symbol, it most often represents unity.[38] That unity can apply to the Godhead,[39] the Church,[40] a group of people,[41] and so on.

As a symbol for God, one numerologist noted, the number one is "indivisible, and not made up of other numbers, [and] is therefore independent of all others, and is the source of all others. So [it is] with the Deity."[42] Another wrote: "Two words are made use of in the Old Testament Scriptures for 'one'; *yacheed*, which signifies 'only one,' and *echad*, meaning 'one of others.' . . . *Yacheed* is never used of God. Always the word is *echad*, one of others, signifying not an absolute unity, but a compound unity, three in one."[43] The implication of the Hebrew, then, is that God is "one" with those with whom he serves in the Godhead. They are perfectly united; they are not "alone."[44] For this reason the Shema[45] states, "Hear, O Israel: The Lord our God is one Lord" (Deuteronomy 6:4).

Pertaining to the oneness of the Church, the Apostle Paul states that the members are "one body" (see Ephesians 4:4–6). Similarly, "the Lord called his people ZION, because they were of one heart and one mind" (Moses 7:18; see D&C 38:27).[46] The two sticks of Ezekiel are also said to be "one in [our] hand" (Ezekiel 37:17).

Applicable to all married couples is this command to Adam and Eve: "Therefore shall a man leave his father and his mother, and shall cleave unto his wife: and they shall be one flesh" (Genesis 2:24; Abraham 5:18).

Prior to the incident at the Tower of Babel, Moses speaks of the oneness of language and speech that prevailed throughout the earth (see Genesis 11:1, 6–7). Under Joshua the armies of Israel were said to fight "with one accord" (Joshua 9:2). Nephi makes an interesting comment when he notes that, in order to fulfill God's promise to scatter the house of Israel throughout the earth, the Nephites needed to "be led with one accord into the land of promise" (1 Nephi 10:13).

There are too many examples to list. Suffice it to say that

in each case the idea is that two or more people or things are united into a "oneness" that constitutes a "spiritual unity."

TWO

The number two has a dualistic meaning in scripture. Its first symbolic connotation is that of opposition, separation, or good versus bad.[47] Its second meaning pertains to the law of witnesses and the canonical necessity to sustain a charge.[48]

Of two as a symbol of division or separation, note several examples. In the Book of Mormon we are told there are "two churches only; the one is the church of the Lamb of God, and the other is the church of the devil; wherefore, whoso belongeth not to the church of the Lamb of God belongeth to that great church, which is the mother of abominations; and she is the whore of all the earth" (1 Nephi 14:10). Elsewhere we read of similar two-part divisions—of the sheep and goats (see Matthew 25:31–33), wheat and tares (see Matthew 13:24–30), light and darkness (see Genesis 1:4), and the breakup of the kingdom of Solomon (see 1 Kings 11:9–13). All are symbolic of the division, opposition, and enmity that have existed since at least as early as the war in heaven.[49]

There are numerous examples of the one good and the other bad (or marred) in scripture. Jeremiah speaks of the potter's two vessels, one marred and one good (see Jeremiah 18:1–4). There are the two covenants or laws (i.e., the law of Moses and the fulness of the gospel of Jesus Christ), the former of which the book of Hebrews refers to as "decaying" and "faulty" (see Hebrews 8:6–13; 10:9, 16, 17). God's first and fallen creation (see Genesis 3) will be replaced by a new heaven and earth (see Revelation 21–22), just as the "first Adam" who fell has been replaced by the "second Adam" who raises all from the Fall (see 1 Corinthians 15:45–50).

As an additional image imbedded in the number two, there is the frequent mention in scripture of the need for two or three witnesses in order to sustain a charge against any accused man (see Deuteronomy 17:6; 19:15; Matthew 18:16; John 8:17–18; 2 Corinthians 13:1; 1 Timothy 5:19; Hebrews 10:28; D&C 6:28; 128:3). Similarly, the Twelve and the Seventy were spoken of as going out in twos (see Mark 6:7; Luke 10:1), as do missionaries in this last dispensation (see D&C 42:6). In the Old World, God offered two testaments of the sacred and divine origins and meanings of his word (i.e., the Old and the New Testaments). The New World has also brought forth two witnesses: the Book of Mormon and the Doctrine and Covenants. Citing Matthew 22:40, one commentator stated that the keeping or not keeping of two cardinal commandments will stand as a witness of the worthiness of all the children of God.[50] Another wrote, "Generally, . . . two speaks of fullness of testimony, either for good or for evil."[51]

There is an additional layer to the number two that is much less common than the other meanings just covered. It is the image of "reproduction," "life force," or "creative power." The symbol is employed in the creation and preservation of the two sexes (see Genesis 1:27; 7:2).[52]

THREE

Next to the number seven, three is the most common symbolic number employed in scripture.[53] It occurs more than 450 times in the Bible alone.[54] One commentator wrote, "An examination of [passages exhibiting the triadic formula] is bound to lead to the conclusion that the number 'three' is not used literally, but rhetorically."[55]

Whereas the number one reminds us of unity, including that which exists between the Father, Son, and Holy Ghost, the number three emphasizes the distinct and separate nature of the three members of the Godhead. More than any other number, three symbolizes God.[56] When the number is used in scripture, it frequently serves to emphasize divine involvement, backing, or influence.[57]

It appears significant, then, that Jesus served a three-year mortal ministry in which key events involved the number three: he was tempted three times by Satan (see Luke 4); he raised three people from the dead (see Matthew 9:18; Luke 7:12–15; John 11); he took three disciples, who represented the Godhead, into the garden of Gethsemane with him;[58] he was crucified at the third hour; on Golgotha were three crosses; darkness reigned for some three hours while he was on the cross; his body lay for three days in a tomb. The repetitive presence of the number three in relation to the Atonement implies that God was behind this most sacred of events.

Other examples of this same use of the number three include the following: Three times God spoke to the Nephites before they recognized his voice (3 Nephi 11:1–7), as was the case with Samuel and Eli (see 1 Samuel 3). Like Adam and Eve, Abraham received three heavenly messengers (see Genesis 18:3). Three times God showed Peter the vision of the descending sheet so that he would know to send the gospel to the Gentiles (see Acts 10). Jonah was three days in the belly of the "great fish" until he repented. Elijah poured water on his burnt offering three times (see 1 Kings 18:34) and stretched himself over a dead child three times in an effort to raise the boy from the dead (see 1 Kings 17:21). In each case, the number three serves to emphasize the idea that God is the one speaking or performing the miraculous act.

Under the law of Moses, the number three was prevalent. The tabernacle was marked by this number, having an outer court (telestial), a Holy Place (terrestrial), and a Holy of Holies (celestial). The brazen sea, or laver, held three thousand baths and was compassed by a line of thirty cubits on which were three hundred knops (see 1 Kings 7:23–24, 26). "'Three measures of meal' formed the great meal offering; because it set forth the perfection of Christ's perfect and divine nature."[59] The great feasts were three (see Deuteronomy 16:16), for which the Israelites were commanded to come to Jerusalem (see Exodus 23:17). "The complete separation of Israel is shown in *'the three days' journey* into the wilderness' (Exodus 5:3)."[60] Three-year-old animals were prized for special sacrifices.⁶¹ That the number three was so frequently employed in temple worship underscores the idea that the temple and its ordinances are the typifying or symbolizing of God.

The attributes of deity are traditionally divided into three: omniscience, omnipresence, and omnipotence. There are three kingdoms of glory: telestial, terrestrial, and celestial. Time, pertaining only to man, is divided into past, present, and future. "Oriental speculation tended to group all things under three heads."⁶²

THREE AND ONE-HALF

The number three and one-half is sometimes given in scripture as "a time and times and the dividing of time" (Daniel 7:25; 12:7), or 1,260 (see Revelation 12:6).⁶³ Being half of seven, its meaning is that which is "arrested midway in its normal course."⁶⁴

John the Revelator speaks of two "witnesses," or prophets, who will prophesy in the streets of Jerusalem for forty-two months,⁶⁵ or in other words, three and one-half years (see Revelation 11:3–14). Suddenly, and in the midst of their ministry, they will be slain. Satan will appear to have "arrested" their work while in course. However, God will ensure that Lucifer does not win. After their bodies lay unburied in the street for three and one-half days, they will be resurrected, "arresting" Satan's work "in its normal course."

Daniel spoke of a "beast"⁶⁶ that would "devour the whole earth" and "tread it down and break it in pieces" (see Daniel 7:21–25). This "beast" would "speak great words against the most High" and "wear out the saints," to some degree prevailing against them. It would "think to change times and laws" and would seemingly have power to do so "until a time and times and the dividing of time" (i.e., for three and one-half years). Again, the utilization of the number three and one-half indicates that, although the accomplishments of this heinous, corrupt, and immoral movement will not be insignificant, they will not last. In the end, God, his Church, and the Saints will prevail.

Related to this concept of limited power is the fraction one-third. Of it, one scholar wrote, "One-third symbolically [shows] that their bounds have been set. They can go only so far. The fraction one-third is used by a number of the prophets in association with what is called 'remnant theology,' the remnant being the unaffected part. We see this in Ezekiel 5:1–5 . . . [and] again in Ezekiel 5:12 and in Zechariah 13:8–9."[67] When this fraction is utilized toward a particular individual or event, the suggestion is that they have a limited degree of power or influence.[68]

In Revelation, chapter 8, John sees fire and desolation poured out upon the earth during the seventh seal but preceding the Second Coming (see vv. 7–12). In this outpouring he views a "third part" of the trees and green grass burned up, a "third part" of the sea turned to blood, a "third part" of the creatures in the sea and boats on the sea being destroyed, a "third part" of all water becoming bitter and undrinkable, and a "third part" of the sun, moon, and stars darkened. All of this, though catastrophic, still sends the message that not "everything" is destroyed. God yet exhibits a degree of mercy by limiting the power or influence of the disasters John was shown in his vision.

When John speaks of the war in heaven, his description of Lucifer's activities is slightly different from the typical interpretation in Latter-day Saint circles. He states that the devil drew away a "third part" of the hosts of heaven with him (see Revelation 12:4; D&C 29:36–38). The distinction between "one-third" and a "third part" may seem subtle, yet it is real. The fraction one-third implies 33 ⅓ percent, whereas the phrase "third part" implies a numerically undetermined segment of the population who symbolize the fact that Satan's power over the premortal spirits was limited.[69] Thus, the numerology in the passage implies that we have no knowledge of the fraction or percentage of the Father's children who followed the adversary. All we know is that Satan had a limited influence over those in the presence of God.

FOUR

The number four symbolizes geographic completeness or totality.[70] In other words, if the number four is associated with an event or thing, the indication is that it will affect the entire earth and all its inhabitants. One source informs us:

> The number *four* always has reference to all that is *created*. It is emphatically the *number of Creation*. . . . The *fourth* day saw the *material creation* finished (for on the *fifth* and *sixth* days it was only the *furnishing* and *peopling* of the earth with living creatures). . . .
>
> Four is the number of the great elements—earth, air, fire, and water. Four are the regions of the earth—north, south, east, and west. . . . Four are the seasons of the year—spring, summer, autumn, and winter. . . . In Gen. ii. 10, 11, the one river of Paradise was parted and became into *four* heads. . . . It is the first *square* number also, and therefore it marks a kind of *completeness* as well, which we have called *material completeness*.[71]

There are many examples of the utilization of the number four in scripture, each with a consistent message of geographic totality.

As noted above, the river that flows forth from Eden and parts into four different directions implies that the issuance of Eden influences or affects all of the earth (see Genesis 2:10–14; Moses 3:10; Abraham 5:10). Perhaps the number four in this episode was meant to imply that all of the earth, prior to the Fall, was in a paradisiacal condition. Or perhaps the image is associated with Eden as the first temple.[72] If the latter is the case, then the water flowing forth from Eden in four directions is mirrored by John's vision of the river flowing out from under the throne of God in the heavenly Jerusalem (see Revelation 22:1–2; Zechariah 14:8) and implies that it is the Spirit and its revelations that come from Eden (and the temple), flowing to all the world (see John 7:37–39).[73] Or perhaps the use of the number four in this episode is a symbol for the idea that chaos (via the Fall) went forth from Eden unto all the world.[74] Moses certainly uses water as such a symbol.[75]

The prophet Isaiah speaks of an ensign, representative of the restored gospel and its accompanying light (see D&C 45:9; 115:4–5), that would be raised up in the last days to gather the dispersed of Judah from the "four corners of the earth" (Isaiah 11:12). The number four implies not only the location of the dispersed but also for whom the gospel and its teachings have been restored.

Zechariah 2:6 speaks of the lost tribes as being spread "abroad as the four winds of the heaven." Despite popular theories that attempt to pinpoint their physical location, Zechariah's use of the number four indicates that they are spread throughout the entire earth.[76]

When Ezekiel sees his vision of the resurrection of the dead (Ezekiel 37:9), he speaks of the event in association with "the four winds," representative of the fact that the Resurrection will be universal. One wonders if John's discussion of the crucifixion of Christ and the dividing of his possessions into four lots was somehow also intended to convey a geographic symbolism. Could John have been hinting at the idea that Christ was giving his life and all that he had for the salvation of *all* (no. 4) mankind?

In the parable of the sower (Matthew 13) there are four kinds of soil, apparently representing all the peoples of the earth and their attitude or receptiveness to the gospel of Jesus Christ.

FIVE

Although the number five is not common in scriptural symbolism, two ideas are associated with it: God's grace[77] and man in his fallen state.[78] Contextual clues help to clarify which idea is meant.

Regarding the symbol of God's grace being poured out, one commentator noted that the Mosaic dispensation, including its tabernacle, had the number five stamped all over it.[79] "Five sacrifices [were required]—a heifer, a goat, a ram, a dove, and a pigeon (Gen. xv. 9)."[80] If these sacrifices were performed with faith, and as the typifying of their Messiah, Israel had reason to believe that they would be the recipients of God's grace. The portable temple in which these sacrifices were to be performed "had *five* as its all-pervading number; nearly every measurement was a multiple of *five*."[81] It, too, was a source of God's grace, just as temples and temple work are today.

Samuel the Lamanite prophesied to the people that in five years the ultimate grace of God would be manifest in the birth of the Messiah (see Helaman 14:2).

One commentator asserts that in the parable of the ten virgins (Matthew 25:1–13) the number five is a symbol for both God's grace and the nature of fallen man.[82] In this model the five wise virgins who have oil in their lamps, or testimonies, and righteousness in their hearts[83] would be a representation of the grace of God. The five unwise virgins, of course, represent those who, in the spirit of fallen man as an "enemy" to God (Mosiah 3:19), have not prepared themselves for the coming of Christ.

As another example of the potentially combined symbols of grace and fallen humanity, David chose five stones for his sling as he prepared to battle Goliath (see 1 Samuel 17:40). This likely serves to emphasize the fact that David approached the task relying upon the grace of God to see him through (see 1 Samuel 17:46).[84] Indeed, keeping in mind the symbolic meaning of the number one, the very fact that David slew Goliath with only one stone serves to emphasize *God's intervention* (no. 1), which evidenced David's receipt of divine *grace* (no. 5).[85]

The book of Helaman records how Nephi prophesied that the chief judge had been murdered by his brother as part of a continuing Gadianton struggle for the judgment-seat (see 8:27). Immediately, five men went to the seat of the chief judge to test Nephi's words, to see "whether this man be a prophet [of] God" (9:2). In accordance with the secondary symbolic implications of the number five, these men stated that they did not believe Nephi was really a prophet and that they would believe only if that was proven to them (see v. 2), thus exhibiting characteristics of fallen men in their approach to revelation. Upon finding the chief judge dead, they believed that Nephi was a true prophet but were later arrested for the murder along with Nephi (see vv. 4–5, 8–9, 19). By the grace of God they were freed. Ultimately, many people were converted by the testimony of these five "doubting Thomases" and the words of Nephi (see v. 39).

SIX

The number six is a very uncommon number in scriptural numerology. Its meaning is deficit, imperfection, or failure to attain completeness.[86] It can also symbolize "opposition to and independence of God."[87] One numerologist reasons that since six falls short of the numerical perfection found in the number seven, it symbolizes incompleteness in the sense of representing man without Christ.[88] He also sees six as representing a manifestation of evil.[89] Illustrating the primary definition, "Abraham's six intercessions for Sodom (Gen. xviii.) marked man's imperfection in prayer, which falls short of that of the Divine Intercessor."[90]

Note that the armor of God, as described by the Lord and the Apostle Paul, consists of six pieces: the girdle, breastplate, sandals, shield, helmet, and sword (see Ephesians 6:14–18; D&C 27:16–18). The context clearly rules out the primary symbolic implications of the number six. But if the number is intended to be symbolic, perhaps it is seen as a manifestation of evil: the six pieces of armor protect mortals from the evils that can rob them of eternal life.

Time, which pertains only to man, has the number six "stamped" upon its imperfect measurements. For example, a day consists of twenty-four hours (4 x 6). There are twelve hours in a day (6 x 2) and twelve in a night (6 x 2). There are twelve months in a year (6 x 2). An hour consists of sixty minutes (6 x 10). And a minute contains sixty seconds (6 x 10). All is seemingly related to the temporal, imperfect nature of time.[91]

The concept of six as a representation of spiritual deficit, imperfection, man without Christ, and evil seems entirely appropriate as an epitaph for the Nephites, who, within a six-year period "turned from their righteousness, like the dog to his vomit, or like the sow to her wallowing in the mire" (3 Nephi 7:8).

Curiously, Goliath was said to be six cubits and six inches tall (see 1 Samuel 17:4). He is described as wearing six pieces of armor (1 Samuel 17:5–7), of which was a spear whose head weighed six hundred shekels of iron (1 Samuel 17:7). The man was, no doubt, the height of "opposition to and independence of God"[92] and served well as the proverbial "manifestation of evil."[93]

In the second chapter of John, the apostle records the first miracle of the Savior's earthly ministry—the turning of water to wine at the wedding at Cana. Central to the story are six stone jars, traditionally used for the ceremonial washings of the law of Moses. The difference in quality and desirability between the old wine (provided by the host of the wedding) and the new wine (which Jesus made) has been compared to the two laws, the law of Moses being less desirable than the fulness of the gospel of Jesus Christ. The six pots have frequently been compared to the imperfection of the law of Moses, which would shortly be fulfilled in Christ, whose law is more desirable.[94] "This 'Judaic' water becomes wine . . . In place of the water of Judaism, Jesus now offers wine, the wine of the age of salvation. Indeed, the old has been transformed into the new so that there is no longer any place for the old."[95]

SEVEN

Seven is the most common of all symbolic numbers.[96] It is employed more frequently, and with more consistency, than any other number, theologically or culturally.[97] In fact, there are so many references to the number seven in scripture and Semitic literature that one scholar suggested this is proof that something symbolic is intended.[98] This same source suggested that it would take nothing short of a miracle to chronicle and explain all of the references to the number seven in the Bible, let alone in Judaeo-Christian ritual and extracanonical religious texts.[99]

Seven symbolizes fulness,[100] completion,[101] entirety or totality,[102] and spiritual perfection.[103] As a rule, multiples of seven carry the same spiritual or symbolic significance.[104] Etymologically, seven is connected with the Hebrew words for "full," "satisfied," or "complete."[105] According to one text:

> In the Hebrew, seven is *shevah*. It is from the root *savah*, to be full or satisfied, have enough of. Hence, the meaning of the word "seven" is dominated by this root, for on the seventh day God rested from the work of Creation. It was full and complete, and good and perfect. Nothing could be added to it or taken from it without marring it. . . . Seven means . . . according to its etymology, that which is spiritually complete or satisfying.[106]

Another source states, "The root of the Hebrew word for seven *(sheva)* is identical to the Hebrew verb that means 'to take an oath,' thus connecting the word *seven* to covenants and covenant making."[107]

The following is but a minute sampling of the hundreds of scriptural references to the number seven as a symbol. A thorough exegetical study of the number seven in scripture would produce a text hundreds of pages long. Constraints on space will allow only a few examples.

In all four accounts of the creation we are informed that the great work of organizing this earth and its inhabitants to a state of completion, or perfection, took seven days or periods.[108] Additionally, there are seven days in a whole week, both models implying "a complete period or cycle."[109]

Enoch was said to be "the seventh from Adam" (Jude

1:14). This is likely not a coincidence, because Enoch is the prophetic model of perfection. One scholar noted that the Hebrew phrase "the seventh from Adam" totals eighty-four (or 7 x 12) in gematria. This may be an innuendo regarding Enoch's *complete* or *perfect* (no. 7) *priesthood power* (no. 12).[110]

Noah was said to have taken seven of every kind of clean beast onto the ark (see Genesis 7:2). As chapter 10 of this books suggests, the number seven, when used in relation to animals, represents the idea that they were positive or clean symbols. It suggests that they were symbolic of people who had learned to keep and live the commandments of God fully.

In a most chivalrous act, youthful Jacob worked seven years for Rachel but was tricked into marrying Leah. So Jacob worked another seven years for Rachel, implying the totality or fulness of his love for her (see Genesis 29).

In Pharaoh's dream, as interpreted by Joseph, it was foretold that Egypt would encounter seven years of plenty followed by seven years of famine, a symbolic warning of Egypt's initial perfect state of plenty followed by a fulness of famine (see Genesis 41).

In Exodus, chapter twelve, Israel was commanded to remove all leaven from their homes for a period of seven days (see 12:15, 19). Leaven was a symbol for sin and corruption.[111] In this episode the number seven suggests that all sin and corruption must be entirely removed from one's life. The Atonement (symbolized by the Passover) was the vehicle by which that took place.

Although a number of features in the Mosaic tabernacle had numerical significance, the seven branches of the candlestick placed between the Holy Place and the Holy of Holies seems particularly significant (see Exodus 25:31–32). It was the only light in that windowless chamber and thus served as the source of light or direction to pass from the outer (telestial) court to the Holy of Holies (or equivalent of the celestial room). As a symbol for the Holy Ghost,[112] the seven branches serve to highlight the perfect nature of that gift.

The law of Moses required that a leper be sprinkled seven times in order to be fully cleansed (see Leviticus 14). Lepers were symbols for those who are spiritually unclean, spiritually dying because of their sins, just as a leper is one who is physically dying because of disease.[113] Spiritual death is overcome through *full* or *complete* (no. 7) repentance.

One commentator recorded: "On the great Day of Atonement the blood was sprinkled 'on the mercy-seat eastward' . . . seven times . . . because this was the perfect testimony for the *people* that the atonement for their sins was accomplished" (see Leviticus 16:14). Additionally, "the day of atonement was [celebrated] in the seventh month."[114]

The Israelites under Joshua exercised "full" faith and obedience by marching for seven days around Jericho, encompassing it seven times on the seventh day—after which the city walls collapsed, making their victory "complete" (see Joshua 6:2–4, 15).

In the book of Proverbs we read, "For a just man falleth seven times, and riseth up again: but the wicked shall fall into mischief" (24:16). The use of seven here is a clear effort to highlight the degree to which the man is just and the totality of his dedication to the cause. He always gets up again no matter how often he proverbially falls.

There is a curious comment in the book of Isaiah, offered here *only* by way of conjecture and in light of the consistent symbolic connotations of the number seven. We read, "And in that day seven women shall take hold of one man, saying, We will eat our own bread, and wear our own apparel: only let us be called by thy name, to take away our reproach" (4:1). The Hebrew versions of the Old Testament always place this verse as the last verse of chapter 3.[115] Most commentators also place it in the context of chapter 3 rather than in chapter 4.[116] If the Hebrew placement is correct, then the context changes from millennial to pre-millennial.[117] Current editions of the Book of Mormon place the verse in a millennial context. However, the current chapter and verse breakdown was not part of the original manuscript.[118] If one examines the printer's manuscript of the Book of Mormon, the verse comes in the middle of a rather lengthy run-on sentence that connects chapters 3 and 4 of Isaiah.[119] Thus the original text of the Book of Mormon, as well as the Joseph Smith Translation, offers no help in determining what the context of the verse is.

If one assumes that the Hebrew is correct, then the passage seems to be highlighting very worldly women in a premillennial era who will do anything physically to attract men. If the context is the Millennium, then a literal reading of the verse would suggest a possible restoration of plural marriage. However, noting Isaiah's employment of the symbolic number seven, an alternate millennial reading may be drawn. As a possible suggestion, note the following rendering of the verse: "In the Millennium seven women [the entire Church?] will lay hold of one man [Christ?] and say to him, We will eat our own bread and wear our own clothes: but let us be called after thy name [through covenants, also associated with the number seven] that we might have our shame removed."[120]

Delilah cut off seven locks of Samson's hair. In so doing, she left him completely destitute of strength (see Judges 16:15–21).

Matthew records Christ's command to forgive not seven times but seventy times seven (see Matthew 18:21–22). Christ's point is not that we should forgive 490 times, after which forgiveness is no longer required. On the contrary, his point is that we must forgive all men completely, every time we have reason to be offended.

While nailed to the cross, Christ is said to have made seven significant statements (see Matthew 27:46; Luke 23:34, 43, 46; John 19:25–28, 30).

The book of Revelation informs us that once John wrote down his vision, he sent it to seven branches of the Church in Asia (see 1:4). The number seven here serves as a symbol for the fact that John's vision was for the whole Church.[121] Similarly, when John speaks of the "seven seals," we understand that he means the entire history of the world (see 5:1, 5–6). One source indicates, "In the Book of the Revelation of Jesus Christ, *seven* seems to be the predominating number, not only used as a numeral, but in the occurrences of the important words:—'Jesus' occurs 14 times (2 x 7) (*seven* times alone, and *seven* times with 'Christ'). 'Lord' [in the RSV] occurs 21 times (3 x 7). 'Spirit,' 14 times."[122] The list of these "sevens" and multiples of seven in the book of Revelation is extensive. Biblical scholar E. W. Bullinger chronicles several pages of words or things mentioned seven times (or some multiple of seven) in the book of Revelation.[123]

In the days of Alma, the city of Zarahemla had "seven churches in the land" (Mosiah 25:23). However, because the members were all so united, the record states, "Notwithstanding there being many churches they were all one church" (v. 22). Thus these seven branches of the Church served as a symbol for the whole Church, "even the church of God" (v. 22).

In symbolic terms, Ammon's slaying of seven marauding Lamanites constituted a complete or utter defeat of King Lamoni's enemies and potentially reflected Ammon's omnipotence in the eyes of Lamoni (see Alma 18:16).

One scholar noted that the number seven seems to be ingrained in the reproductive process. He noted that with the human species, the gestation period is 280 days, or 7 times 40. Since seven means full or complete, and forty represents mourning and trial, the combination of the two represents full or complete mourning. It will be remembered that upon her fall in Eden, Mother Eve was told, "I will greatly multiply thy sorrow and thy conception; in sorrow thou shalt bring forth children" (Genesis 3:16; Moses 4:22). Thus in sorrow—multiplied sorrow—women bring forth children. The pain and suffering that accompany labor and childbirth, coupled with the very real possibility of death from the experience, certainly brings cause for mourning. Clearly, the penalties of the Fall as pertaining to Eve have been passed on to all women in the form typified by the significant length of the gestation period. "Thus the number *seven* is stamped upon physiology. . . . May we not expect to find the same phenomena in the greatest of all God's works, viz., His Word?"[124]

EIGHT

The number eight is associated with the concepts of resurrection,[125] new beginnings,[126] rebirth,[127] and baptism.[128] Because of its association with resurrection, it is sometimes also seen as the number of Christ. Additionally, some commentators call the number eight the sign of superabundance.[129]

The Apostle Paul associated baptism with the symbol of resurrection rather than cleansing. He stated:

> Know ye not, that so many of us as were baptized into Jesus Christ were baptized into his death? Therefore we are buried with him by baptism into death: that like as Christ was raised up from the dead by the glory of the Father, even so we also should walk in newness of life. For if we have been planted together in the likeness of his death, we shall be also in the likeness of his resurrection. (Romans 6:3–5.)

In reference to this passage, one numerologist wrote, "Christ rose from the dead on 'the *first* day of the week,' that was of necessity the *eighth* day."[130] Since, for all of those born in the covenant, baptism is to be performed at the age of eight (see D&C 68:27), the connection between the symbols of baptism, resurrection, Christ, and the number eight are natural and appropriate. Indeed, the reason the number eight is utilized as a symbol for Christ, resurrection, baptism, new beginnings, and so on is that they are all intricately related ideas.

Continuing this theme, it is noteworthy that only eight humans survived the deluge of Noah's day. In 1 Peter 3:18–21 we read:

> For Christ also hath once suffered for sins, the just for the unjust, that he might bring us to God, being put to death in the flesh, but quickened by the Spirit: By which also he went and

preached unto the spirits in prison; which sometime were disobedient, when once the longsuffering of God waited in the days of Noah, while the ark was a preparing, wherein few, that is, eight souls were saved by water. The like figure whereunto even baptism doth also now save us (not the putting away of the filth of the flesh, but the answer of a good conscience toward God,) by the resurrection of Jesus Christ.

A number of commentaries note that Peter's declaration is clearly a symbolic reference to the saving powers of baptism.[131] Just as Noah and his family were "saved by water," those who accept Christ and his revealed ordinances—including baptism—are also "saved by water." Reference is made in the passage to the symbolic number eight, baptism, Christ, and, by default, a new order of things—as Noah and his family witnessed the destruction of all and began anew the human family.

According to the law of Moses, circumcision was to be performed on the eighth day (see Genesis 17:12). As a foreshadowing of the ordinance of baptism, that time frame served as a reminder to Israel that their children were not accountable until their eighth year (see JST, Genesis 17:4–20).

Aaron and his sons were consecrated on the eighth day, after waiting "at the door of the tabernacle of the congregation day and night seven days" (Leviticus 8:35; 9:1). The number eight here is likely a symbol, both of their new beginning as consecrated priests and also of their typification of Christ, whose number is eight.[132] Indeed, E. W. Bullinger noted, "Eight is the dominical number, for everywhere it has to do with the LORD. It is the number of His name, Jesus," which totals 888 in Greek gematria.[133] He indicates that "other Dominical Names of Jesus are also marked by gematria and stamped with the number eight as a factor."[134]

Regarding eight as a number for both Christ and resurrection, one commentator offers an interesting insight: In the Bible "the risen Christ was seen by 512 persons. And 512 is the cube of 8 (8^3). The number of the disciples gathered in the upper room (Acts i. 15) was 120 (8 x 15)."[135]

One pioneer LDS typologist, Lenet Hadley Read, pointed out that "the beginning of God's new kingdom of glory" will be the "eighth age" and at the conclusion of the Resurrection.[136] She added, "The age of Latter-day Saint baptism . . . fits perfectly into [the] pattern: Circumcision, eighth day; baptism, eighth year; Christ's resurrection, eighth day; the beginning of God's new kingdom of glory, eighth age. Each time period signifies becoming a member of God's covenanted people and (for those faithful to the covenant) entrance into God's glory."[137]

The number eight may have symbolic value in the Book of Mormon as well. For example, the Jaredites prepared eight barges so that they could cross the waters and obtain the promised land (see Ether 3:1). This crossing has been compared by one LDS author to the ordinance of baptism as a step on the voyage to the celestial promised land.[138] In 1 Nephi we read that Nephi and his family spent eight years in the wilderness before embarking on their journey to the new land (see 1 Nephi 17:4). Eight here seems symbolic of the concept of new beginnings. We read further that Alma and his new converts traveled "eight days' journey into the wilderness" to escape King Noah and his men (Mosiah 23:3). Not coincidentally, one of the early symbols of their newfound faith was their participation in the ordinance of baptism, after which they began new lives in Christ (see Mosiah 18).

NINE

The number nine is occasionally used symbolically in scripture. When employed, it carries the meaning of judgment, finality, or completion.[139] One commentator wrote:

> Nine is . . . the number of finality or judgment, for judgment is committed unto Jesus as "the Son of Man" (John v. 27; Acts xvii. 31). It marks the completeness, the end and issue of all things as to man—the judgment of man and all his works. It is a factor of 666, which is 9 x 74. The gematria of the word "Dan," which means a judge, is 54 (9 x 6). . . . The sieges of Jerusalem have been 27 in number, or three times *nine*, and they

are stamped with the number of Divine completeness [or Divine involvement] (3) and the number of judgment (9).... The signification of the number *nine* is *judgment*, especially divine judgment, and the conclusion of the whole matter so far as man is concerned. But *nine* is the square of three, and *three* is the number of Divine perfection, as well as the number peculiar to the Holy Spirit. It is not surprising, therefore, to find that this number denotes *finality* in divine things.[140]

The judgments of God, as given in the book of Haggai, are enumerated in nine particulars, with drought being sent upon the land, mountains, corn, new wine, oil, produce of the earth, men, cattle, and the labors of all hands (see 1:11). This is a grand example of judgments being poured out.

Jesus healed ten lepers, but only one came back to acknowledge and thank him. Then asked Jesus, "Where are the nine?" (Luke 17:17). The numerology suggests they will be judged for their ingratitude.

TEN

The number ten denotes "all of a part."[141] In other words, it is a whole or complete unit existing within a greater whole. For example, the Ten Commandments did not comprise all of God's commandments to ancient Israel. Rather, as Philo of Alexandria indicated, the Decalogue contained only a "kernel of the entire Torah." Judaism acknowledges some 613 precepts or commandments in the Torah. It is worth noting that the "talmudic-midrashic sources never speak of the Decalogue as containing the entire Torah."[142] It contains a complete unit of the law of Moses but not the whole law.[143]

Members of the Church are expected to pay 10 percent of their increase as a tithe to the Lord. That amount is not all of their income, nor, ideally, all of their sacrifice. Nevertheless, a tithe is a complete unit within the greater whole of the fulness of the gospel of Jesus Christ and the law of consecration.[144]

Using Moses as his emissary, God warned Pharaoh to let the children of Israel go free, lest Egypt be plagued grievously.

Pharaoh refused to submit, so God poured out a set of ten plagues that softened Pharaoh's heart sufficiently long to enable Israel to flee Egypt (see Exodus 7–10). God did not unleash the fulness of his wrath, but rather a whole portion of it sufficient to accomplish his will in that particular circumstance.[145]

Ten tribes of the house of Israel have been described as lost. They certainly are not all of covenant Israel, but they do form a distinct and separate unit within Israel's body and eschatology.[146]

Ammaron approached Mormon regarding the plates when the latter was but ten years old. However, this was but one stage, portion, or unit of Mormon's life that would be dedicated in some respect to the plates (see Mormon 1:2–4; 2:17–18; 6:6).

According to one source, the number ten is the root of the decimal numerical system specifically because of the fact that it anciently carried the connotation of "all of a part."[147] Another source indicates, "The Hebrew word for 'ten' . . . is to be connected with the Arabic word for 'kinsman' or 'tribe,' or 'collection.'"[148] This would certainly relate to the notion that ten symbolizes "a whole part, but not the whole itself." Indeed, the number ten is frequently associated with complete cycles, series, or units.[149]

ELEVEN

There are few examples of the number eleven in scripture. It symbolizes sin, transgression, peril, conflict, disorder, imperfection, and disintegration.[150] Thus Jacob's eleven sons get rid of a twelfth child, Joseph, and in so doing signal "the disintegration and disorganization in Jacob's family" through conflict and sin.[151]

The sinful puppet king of Judah, Jehoiakim, reigned amid conflict, disorder, and controversy some eleven years before dying in office (see Jeremiah 36:30).[152] Similarly, King Zedekiah, the son of Josiah, reigned for some eleven years, after which he was attacked by Nebuchadnezzar, forced to watch the slaying of most of his children, and then had his eyes put out (see 2 Kings 25:7).

One text on numerology noted that "from Horeb to Kadesh-Barnea, that journey fraught with such great disaster to the people of Israel, was an eleven days' journey (Deut. 1:2). It was short of the land of promise, and of the complete administration of God's laws, by one day."[153]

Judas's betrayal left the Quorum of the Twelve with only an imperfect eleven members, necessitating a reorganization at a very difficult time in the Church's history.

TWELVE

The number twelve is a symbol for priesthood, including its power and right to govern.[154] Examples of this in scripture and the temple are legion.

In Matthew 10:1–4 we are told that Jesus called twelve Apostles and gave them the priesthood. When he appeared to the Nephites, Jesus again called twelve men as ministers to the people and gave them "power and authority to baptize" (3 Nephi 12:1).[155] In the dispensation of the fulness of times, the Lord has again called and commissioned twelve Apostles to further his work (see D&C 18:27). The number twelve in relation to the Apostles suggests that they are the epitome of priesthood authority and governance.[156]

The baptismal font (or laver) in temples, both ancient (see 1 Kings 7:23–26; 2 Chronicles 4:3–5) and modern,[157] rests upon the back of twelve oxen facing the four cardinal directions. This signifies the fact that this is a *priesthood* ordinance (no. 12) necessary for *all* (no. 4) who wish to enter the celestial kingdom. The oxen also represent the twelve tribes of Israel, who were scattered to the four corners of the earth—and who must be gathered from the four corners of the earth through the ordinance of baptism.

Jesus' comment to his disciples that he could pray to his Father and thereby have "more than twelve legions of angels"

(Matthew 26:53) to help him may have been a suggestion that through priesthood keys, including the ministry of angels (see D&C 13), Jesus could have divine intervention were such the will and intent of the Father. However, in deference to his foreordained call to lay down his life on behalf of all, he did not exercise that priesthood power that was rightfully his.

In an effort to highlight the power by which the miracle of healing can occur, Mark employs the number of priesthood when he recounts Jesus' healing of the woman who had an "issue of blood" some twelve years (see Mark 5:25–34) and his raising from the dead the twelve-year-old daughter of Jairus (see Mark 5:35–43).

John the Revelator saw a woman, symbolic of the Church, who had upon her head a crown of twelve stars (see Revelation 12:1). Symbolically, the image depicted the twelve apostles with priesthood authority who direct the work and preside over Christ's Church.

In that same vision, John was shown the celestial kingdom, which he described as having twelve gates or entrances (see Revelation 21:12–14, 21). Symbolic of priesthood, the presence of twelve here reminds us that in order to gain entrance into the celestial world, we need the ordinances of the priesthood and associated covenants.[158]

The number twelve appears over and over again in relation to priesthood holders, the temple, the covenant people who have received the necessary priesthood ordinances, and the celestial kingdom. Hence there are twelve tribes, twelve stones on the breastplate of the high priest, twelve foundations and gates into the heavenly city, twelve priesthood-holding patriarchs from Seth to Noah, and another twelve from Shem to Jacob.[159]

Because the number twelve symbolizes priesthood, multiples of twelve are traditionally understood to be a symbol for the fulness of the priesthood, or making one's calling and election sure.[160] Thus one commentary notes, "Anytime the number twelve is multiplied by another number, it symbolizes an increase in power and covenant responsibility."[161]

So in Revelation 7 we read, "And I heard the number of them which were sealed: and there were sealed an hundred and forty and four thousand of all the tribes of the children of Israel" (v. 4). Of these 144,000 individuals, "we are to understand that those who are sealed are high priests, ordained unto the holy order of God, to administer the everlasting gospel; for they are they who are ordained out of every nation, kindred, tongue, and people, by the angels to whom is given power over the nations of the earth, to bring as many as will come to the church of the Firstborn" (D&C 77:11). Contrary to the teachings of some churches, this number is not intended to be taken literally.[162] Rather, it serves to highlight the necessity of priesthood and priesthood ordinances (e.g., "twelve thousand" of each tribe). It emphasizes the fact that those who partake of the ordinances required by the Lord, and then keep the covenants associated therewith, shall become members of the Church of the Firstborn and have their calling and election made sure. This is available to all of God's children, not a predetermined, limited number. Of this verse, one commentator wrote:

> Twelve represents the priesthood. Biblical people squared a number to amplify its symbolic meaning. Thus, 144 suggests a fulness of priesthood authority. But John is not satisfied with that. He gives the image a superlative quality by multiplying 1,000, representing completeness. In this way he shows the strength and breadth of the priesthood in the latter days, in this dispensation that is, indeed, the dispensation of the fulness of times. During this period that complete priesthood authority will operate.[163]

THIRTEEN

The number thirteen seldom appears in scripture and is infrequently treated in commentaries. In light of its modern Western connotations, it is not surprising that anciently the number represented apostasy and an evil or ill omen.[164] "Every occurrence of the number *thirteen*, and likewise *every multiple* of it, stamps that with which it stands in connection with *rebellion, apostasy, defection, corruption, disintegration, revolution, or some kindred idea."*[165]

For this reason, in Genesis 14:4 we read, "Twelve years they served Chedorlaomer, and in the thirteenth year they rebelled." Similarly, Ishmael "was *thirteen* years old when Abraham circumcised him and admitted him into the covenant to which he was a stranger in heart, and which ended in his rebellion and rejection."[166]

Likewise, the destruction of the city of Jericho was stamped with the number thirteen. Joshua's armies were said to have circled Jericho once each day for six days, and seven times on the seventh day, making thirteen times in all. At the conclusion of this "ill omen," the walls of Jericho fell (see Joshua 6; Hebrews 11:30).

It was in the thirteenth year of the reign of Josiah that Jeremiah began to prophesy against the apostasy of Judah (see Jeremiah 1:2; 25:3). King Solomon spent thirteen years building his own house (see 1 Kings 7:1), which was full of apostasy (see 11:4). But he spent only seven years building the Lord's house (see 6:38).

FORTY

Some commentators interpret this number as simply meaning "a lengthy period of time."[167] As it is applied to years, it is certainly that. However, the symbolism in the number goes beyond this simple definition. In scripture, the number represents a period of trial, testing, probation, or mourning.[168]

In the days of Noah it is said to have rained some forty days and forty nights (see Genesis 7:12). This cleansing of the earth, both literal and symbolic, gave God and Noah reason to mourn (see Moses 7:27–38; 8:22–30). One typologist added that Noah's faith was tested and found to be all that it should be.[169]

Israel's sojourn in the wilderness lasted forty years. Because they had exhibited lack of faith when they initially fled Egypt, God required that they be tested forty years; then he called another generation to receive the promised land, instead of those who had come out of Egypt under Moses (see Numbers 14:20–23).

In accordance with the law of Moses, no more than forty lashes could be imposed on an offender (see Deuteronomy 25:3). The number forty here is likely symbolic of both the mourning that will come to those who sin and refuse to repent, and possibly that trials and tests have their limits. The Lord gave the inhabitants of the city of Nineveh forty days to repent, or they would be "overthrown" (Jonah 3:4).

Moses was on Mount Sinai forty days while the children of Israel were being tested by Jehovah. They failed miserably because, lacking faith in the true God, they chose to create the golden calf as an image of their god (see Exodus 24:18). After the episode with the idol, Moses again went up upon the mount for an additional forty days (see Deuteronomy 9:18, 25).

One text offers this interesting observation: "According to the reckoning in our Bibles, Christ was born into the world about the four-thousandth year, or fortieth century. Forty, we have seen, is the symbol of probation. So after a full period of the world's probation under law, Jesus Christ was born into the world to usher in grace."[170]

Jesus fasted for forty days and then was tempted prior to beginning his official earthly ministry.[171] As evidence of his commitment to the Father and his divine plan, Christ passed the trials and tests put to him (see JST, Matthew 4:1–11).

Jesus spent forty days after his resurrection (see Acts 1:3) teaching his disciples and initiating them into the higher ordinances of the fulness of the gospel.[172]

Perhaps it is not coincidental that it took a total of forty years to build the Salt Lake Temple.[173]

FORTY-TWO

See the section titled "Three and One-Half."

SIX HUNDRED AND SIXTY-SIX
See the section titled "Gematria."

ONE THOUSAND
This number serves mainly to magnify or embellish that with which it is associated. One authority on the book of Revelation indicated that the number one thousand evokes images of "power, strength, and magnitude. Anytime it occurs, by itself or as a multiple of another number, it symbolizes greatness and vastness."[174] Another wrote that it symbolizes "superlative greatness."[175] One historian of numbers specified that it traditionally represents a "multitude" or that which is "incalculable."[176] Thus, this number may be used in scripture without literal intent, but rather in an effort to highlight an event or numerical symbol with which it is associated.

A similar principle is behind the concept of "ten thousands." An excellent example of this usage occurs in the Book of Mormon when Mormon records the details of the great and final battle between the Nephites and Lamanites at Cumorah. Mormon notes that each of the Nephite leaders had "fallen with his ten thousand" (Mormon 6:10, 12–15). One source records: "'Ten thousands' is an ancient way of saying 'great numbers.' . . . Ten thousand times ten thousand, and thousands of thousands" [literally 100 million] . . . may signify a great, indefinite number."[177]

GEMATRIA
As stated previously, the word *gematria* simply means "to reckon by numbers."[178] One source notes: "Most ancient people did not have a separate numbering system and alphabet, so letters also served as numbers [and vice versa]. Generally the first nine letters of the alphabet stood for numbers one through nine, the next nine for numbers ten through ninety, and so on."[179] It was common for people to associate a certain numerical value with every letter of the alphabet. Thus every name

had a number that was arrived at by adding together the value of each of its letters.[180] "Gematria provides a method of converting words into numbers."[181] In English the name Alonzo would be broken down as follows:

A	L	O	N	Z	O
1	30	60	50	800	60

The numbers, once added together, would give the name Alonzo a numerical equivalent of 1,001. This would then serve as the "number of Alonzo" and would be compared to other words with the same numerical value. Those who practiced gematria believed they would learn more about a person or thing that was "numbered" in this way.

Numerous ancient cultures, including the Hebrews, Babylonians, and Greeks, used letters and numbers interchangeably and applied the principles of gematria,[182] although the practice reached its height of popularity in Jewish talmudic and cabalistic texts.[183] One historian wrote, "The Jewish *gematria*,[184] the Greek *isopsephy*,[184] and the Muslim *khisab al jumal*[185] ('calculating the total') . . . are of common occurrence in Rabbinic literature, especially the Talmud and the Midrash."[186] Even the early Christian church fathers were profoundly influenced by gematria, so much so that they made it part of their apologetic (or defense of the church).[187]

There are a number of approaches to gematria.[188] One ancient Hebrew manuscript in the Bodleian Library at Oxford University (designated Manuscript Hebrew 1822) lists more than seventy different systems.[189] Our focus here will be on the most commonly practiced form, which is the numerical value of one word (the sum of the numerical value of all its letters) compared to a word of equal value. The following are but a handful of the many examples that could be given.

THIRTEEN

The Hebrew word for "love" (*ahavah*) and the Hebrew word for "one" (*ekhad*) both total 13. Zion's love for one another is what makes them "one" and what makes them like God (see 2 Nephi 26:29–32; Moses 7:18). Significantly, if you combine the totals for love (13) and one (13) you get 26, which is the number of the name of God (Yahweh). This is evidence that becoming a Zion people guarantees that they will become as God is.[190]

Twenty-six

The name Adam has a numerical total of 45. The name Eve totals 19 in gematria. The numerical difference between the two is 26, which happens to be the number for Yahweh, implying, perhaps, that it is God, and God only, that can make man and woman one.[191] In Genesis 1:26, God says: "Let us make man in our image." There are 26 generations that separate Adam and Moses. Similarly, 26 descendants are listed in the genealogy of Shem.[192]

Thirty

In the Gospel of Matthew we read, "Then Judas, which had betrayed him, when he saw that he was condemned, repented himself, and brought again the thirty pieces of silver to the chief priests and elders" (Matthew 27:3). One biblical scholar conjectured, "The fact that the consonants of his [Judas's] name *(Yhwdh)* give in Hebrew the numerical value of thirty may have contributed to [Matthew's] count of thirty pieces of silver."[193]

Three Hundred and Eighteen

One of the most widely acknowledged examples of biblical gematria is found in the fourteenth chapter of Genesis:

> And when Abram heard that his brother [actually nephew] was taken captive, he armed his trained servants, born in his own house, *three hundred and eighteen,* and pursued them unto Dan. And he divided himself against them, he and his servants, by night, and smote them, and pursued them unto Hobah, which is on the left hand of Damascus [or North of

Syria]. And he brought back all the goods, and also brought again his brother [or nephew] Lot, and his goods, and the women also, and the people. (Genesis 14:14–16; emphasis added.)

Thus, in an attempt to free Lot, Abraham brings together some 318 of the servants who were born in his house (i.e., not purchased servants, but rather the offspring of Abraham's servants), employing them on this rescue mission.

However, Jewish Midrash on this passage claims that Abraham had only one helper—Eliezer, Abraham's chief servant (see Genesis 15:2; 24:2).[194] In gematria the name Eliezer totals 318, the exact number of the servants whom Abraham is said to have enlisted in freeing Lot. Therefore, most exegetes versed in gematria assume that the symbolic message of the passage is that Eliezer and Abraham successfully freed Lot without the assistance of others.

In the opinion of this author, those relying on the gematria of the passage for a correct interpretation need to take one last step before their exegesis can be complete. The Hebrew name Eliezer means "God is my help."[195] True, the number 318 points one's mind to Eliezer. However, it seems that Moses' purpose for employing gematria in this passage (if he indeed intended on doing such) would have been to draw men unto Christ, not to Eliezer. Thus the utilization of the number 318 would likely be for the purpose of drawing one's attention to the phrase "God is my help" (as encapsulated in the name Eliezer). In light of this, the passage should be understood as symbolically emphasizing that Abraham did have only one helper in freeing his nephew—not Eliezer, but God! For this reason, Melchizedek is said to have told Abraham, "And blessed be the most high *God, which hath delivered thine enemies into thy hand*" (Genesis 14:20; emphasis added).

In light of the gematria of the passage, Abraham's success in freeing Lot is directly attributed to God's intervention, and not to any mortal help that he received. Such is the case with any success we have in mortality. God should always receive the credit (see D&C 59:21).

Support for this interpretation of the 318 men as a symbol for Christ is found in the General Epistle of Barnabas. The Apostle Paul's missionary companion argued that a breakdown of the number 318 would show that the 300 equals the letter T and refers to the cross of Christ, and the numbers 10 and 8 are a representation of the name of Jesus, being the first two letters in the Greek version of the name. Thus, for Barnabas, the message is that the atonement of Christ was the salvation of Lot.[196]

Three Hundred and Fifty-eight

One of this author's favorite examples of gematria appears in the book of Numbers, where we read, "And Moses made a serpent of brass, and put it upon a pole, and it came to pass, that if a serpent had bitten any man, when he beheld the serpent of brass, he lived" (Numbers 21:9; see also Helaman 8:13–15; Alma 33:19–20).

This brass serpent is traditionally understood by Christian commentators to be a symbol for Christ, who, if we look upon him in faith, can heal us from our spiritual (and physical) sicknesses.[197] In the book of Helaman we read: "Yea, did [Moses] not bear record that the Son of God should come? And as he lifted up the brazen serpent in the wilderness, even so shall he be lifted up who should come. And as many as should look upon that serpent should live, even so as many as should look upon the Son of God with faith, having a contrite spirit, might live, even unto that life which is eternal" (8:14–15). Alma 33:19–20 records:

> Behold, [Christ] was spoken of by Moses; yea, and behold a type was raised up in the wilderness, that whosoever would look upon it might live. And many did look and live.
>
> But few understood the meaning of those things, and this because of the hardness of their hearts. But there were many who were so hardened that they would not look, therefore they perished. Now the reason they would not look is because they did not believe that it would heal them.

The Hebrew word for Messiah *(mashiyakh)* totals 358 in gematria. Not coincidentally, the Hebrew word for serpent *(nakhash)* has the same numerical value.[198] Thus by the gematria employed in Numbers 21, it is confirmed that the serpent lifted up by Moses upon his staff was indeed a type for the Savior, Jesus Christ.

SIX HUNDRED AND SIXTY-SIX

The passage most commonly associated with gematria, by scholars and laymen alike, is found in the thirteenth chapter of the book of Revelation.[199] Of the anti-Christ, John writes: "Here is wisdom. Let him that hath understanding count the number of the beast: for it is the number of a man; and his number is Six hundred threescore and six" (Revelation 13:18).[200]

Interpretations of the number 666 are legion. The list of examples below are but a sampling of the many names that total 666 and have been associated with the mark of the beast.

The name of the Roman emperor Titus totals 666 in Greek and 616 in Latin.[201] Either way his name seems to qualify him for candidacy. However, although the Greek *Teitan* could refer to Emperor Titus, he was never a persecutor of the Christians, so perhaps the name has reference to "the Titans."[202]

Caligula, known for his oppression of the Jews and for calling himself a god, has a name that totals 616 when written in Greek. Adolf Deissmann suggested that the title "Caesar God" could appropriately be applied to Caligula, for in Greek that title also totals 616.[203]

The Emperor Diocletian, who led a persecution against the Christians at the beginning of the fourth century, has a name that, if written out in Greek *(Diocles Augustus)*, totals 666.[204]

The most commonly accepted interpretation of 666 is the Roman emperor Nero. When his name is written out as "Nero Caesar" (in Hebrew letters), it totals 666.[205] Also, if Nero's name is written in Latin it totals 616.[206] Thus either way he can qualify as the anti-Christ.

Napoleon, if written in Greek, totals 666, as does the name of Islam's founder, Mohammed.[207] If one employs a less common form of gematria (e.g., A = 100, B = 101, C = 102, and so on), even the name of Hitler totals 666 (H = 107, I = 108, T = 119, L = 111, E = 104, R = 117).[208]

During the Protestant Reformation it was common to see in the number 666 some reference to the Catholic church. Thus the Greek word *Lateinos,* which totals 666, was interpreted as a reference to the "Roman Empire" or the "Roman church."[209] The phrase "the Latin Kingdom," if written in Greek, gives a sum of 666, as did the title "Italian church."[210] The Latin phrases *Vicarius Generalis Dei In Terris* or *Vicarius Filii Dei* (supposedly inscribed on the Papal coronation tiara) have also been said to total 666, as does the Greek word *Papeiskos* (which has been used for "Pope").[211] One source suggests that the Reformation's association of the number 666 with the Pope and the Catholic church was a direct result of Catholics claiming that Martin Luther was the anti-Christ:

> At the time of the Wars of Religion, a Catholic mystic called Petrus Bungus, in a work published in 1584–1585 at Bergamon, claimed to have demonstrated that the German reformer [Martin] Luther was none other than the Anti-Christ since his name, in Roman numerals [LVTHERNVC], gives the number 666. But the disciples of Luther, who considered the Church of Rome as the direct heir of the Empire of the Caesars, lost no time in responding. They took the Roman numerals contained in the phrase VICARIUS FILII DEI ("Vicar of the Son of God") which is on the papal tiara, and drew the conclusion that one might expect. [The title totals] 666.[212]

Not only does the name Luther (when written in Roman numerals) total 666, but the word *Saxon* (also used by Catholics in reference to Luther), when written in Greek, totals 666.[213]

The King James translation of Revelation 13:18 includes the phrase "[666] is the number of a man." This rendering of the Greek implies that John is saying that 666 is the number of a specific person. Such an interpretation seems to support the foregoing explanations of the mark of the beast. However, the New International Version, as well as a number of commentaries on the passage, render the Greek to read "it is man's number."[214] The traditional interpretation of this rendering is that 666 is the number of mankind, or a normal earthly number that requires no "supernatural wisdom to understand it."[215] This latter rendering and interpretation of the Greek finds some support in John's previous comments that the "mark" is something that will be accepted by all men who wish to buy or sell more than they wish to follow the commandments of God (see Revelation 13:16–17).[216] This interpretation has also provoked a number of explanations of the gematria of the number 666, including the following.

The Greek word *primasius* has a numeric total of 666 and comes from the verb *apneisthai*, which means "to deny" or to be "apostate."[217] Those who take upon them the mark of the beast are certainly denying Christ and apostatizing from the faith. Similarly, the Hebrew phrase "you shall turn aside" totals 666 and also seems to highlight the actions of those who turn from God to follow Satan's agent.[218] "Primeval abyss," if spelled out in Hebrew, totals 666.[219]

Other Greek words or phrases, such as *kakos* (meaning "the evil leader") or *amnos adikos* (meaning "the evil lamb"), total 666 and seem to have some potential application to the passage in question.[220]

As the evidence presented suggests, "by a little careful manipulation, any name in some form or other, in Hebrew, Greek, or Latin, could be made by *Gematria* to yield 666."[221] The exercise seems futile. Indeed, the assumption that the mark of the beast is an example of apocalyptic gematria may in itself be flawed. One scholar noted,

> Nowhere does John use gematria as a method. Everywhere, however, he gives symbolic significance to numbers

(e.g., seven churches, seals, trumpets, and bowls; twenty-four elders; 144,000 sealed; 144 cubits for the New Jerusalem, etc.). ... What John seems to be asking for ... is divine discernment and not mathematical ingenuity! Believers need to penetrate the deception of the beast. John's reference to [the beast's] number will help them to recognize the true character and identity.[222]

Even though commentators commonly associate 666 with gematria, a secondary interpretation of the number seems, to this author, more credible. It centers around the idea that the number six is a standard symbol for imperfection.[223]

In Revelation, chapters 12–14, Satan and his two counselors try to usurp the role of the Godhead.[224] One scholar noted that "the 'Satanic Trinity' . . . parodies but falls short of duplicating the characteristics of his counterpart in the 'Holy Trinity' (e.g., by mimicking the crucifixion [13:3] or working signs and wonders [13:13])."[225]

There is a common suggestion that John's utilization of 666 is an effort to compare the anti-Christ with the true Christ.[226] One Protestant author suggested that the mark of the beast may simply be a "continuation of the contrast with Christ of v. 11. The number of the name 'Jesus' in [Greek] is 888; and, according to this interpretation, the meaning is that the beast falls as far short of 'seven' (i.e., perfection and holiness) as Jesus goes beyond it."[227] Another source records:

> The number 666 is the heaping up of the number 6. [Paul] Minear adds, "Because of its contrast with 7 we may be content with an interpretation which sees in 666 an allusion to incompleteness, to the demonic parody in the perfection of 7, to the deceptiveness of the almost-perfect, [or] to the idolatrous blasphemy exemplified by false worshipers." . . . This interpretation of 666 as a symbolic number referring to the unholy trinity of evil or to the human imperfect imitation of God rather than a cipher of a name . . . has been held by a long line of conservative commentators.[228]

It seems fairly certain that the meaning of the mark of the beast is not to be found in gematria. Rather, it appears to be centralized in the concepts of *imperfection* (no. 6), bodily representation (the hand as a symbol for what one pursues, and the head for what one dwells on or thinks about), and the love of mammon (John indicates that people will take the mark so that they can "buy and sell"; see Revelation 13:16–17).

Unlike traditional numerology, which is a relatively well established "science," gematria has its dangers.[229] There is the problem of not taking the interpretation as far as one should and thus misunderstanding the message (as in the case of our discussion of Genesis 14:14). But the fact that it is clearly a very subjective practice (as is evidenced by our discussion of Revelation 13:18) also poses some dangers. As curious as the study of gematria is, it seems of little value in understanding the meaning of scripture, ancient or modern. Indeed, it runs counter to President Boyd K. Packer's teaching that "instruction vital to our salvation is not hidden in an obscure verse or phrase in the scriptures. To the contrary, essential truths are repeated over and over again."[230]

Numerology in general, although traditionally acknowledged by scholars as present and symbolically employed in scripture, was not utilized for the sake of saturating a text with hidden meanings.[233] On the contrary, it was a commonly employed and understood symbolic approach that only seems mysterious or esoteric to modern Western cultures. For Semitic peoples, ancient and modern, the device served as a clear and common teaching tool that, for the most part, has ceased to function for many modern readers of scripture. This being the case, ideas intended to be conveyed by scriptural authors who employed numerology are being entirely missed because modern Christians are not versed in this branch of symbolism.

7
DIRECTIONS AS SYMBOLS

From earliest antiquity, the four cardinal directions have held an important place in most eastern cultures.[1] This is likely because there is an innate human need, both spiritually and psychologically, for security and stability. Direction and orientation allow us to know where we stand in relation to our life, the universe, and God's plan and provides a sense of security and control. The Hebrews, Akkadians, Sumerians, and Egyptians employed north, south, east, and west with religious meaning. "Orientation plays its due part in rites and ceremonies all over the world, particularly in those to do with the founding of temples and cities."[2] For obvious reasons, the cardinal points of the compass continue to figure prominently in the burial ceremonies and customs in most cultures.[3]

Typically, the heavenly bodies were the basis of man's proper orientation with the universe. When relying on astronomy as the basis of directions, most Semitic peoples used the rising of the sun as their primary point of reference.[4] Although ancient Near Eastern peoples used the four points of the compass (see Genesis 13:14; 28:14; Deuteronomy 3:27; Luke 13:29; compare Isaiah 11:12; Ezekiel 37:9), because the sun rose in the east and served as their principal means of gaining bearings, that direction was preeminent in Semitic cultures. The other directions were often reckoned and described according to their relationship to east.[5]

In part, our sense of direction and orientation may stem from our physical bodies:

> The notion of orientation . . . plays a powerful part in the symbolic organization of space. The human anatomy itself, . . . in distinguishing between the front and the back thereby designates two corresponding points of orientation. The natural position of the arms and shoulders completes this quadrangular scheme—a symbolic pattern which, interpreted according to strictly anthropological and empirical criteria, would perhaps provide us with the key to the original conception of orientation.[6]

Islam teaches that one's orientation is the "materialization of intent."[7] In other words, a person's intent or heart can, to some degree, be known by the things that person orients himself or herself toward, by the symbolic direction that person chooses to face. Many of the passages examined below serve to substantiate this idea.

Before attempting to interpret directions in scripture, we need to bear a couple of points in mind. First of all, the direction mentioned in a verse is often the key to understanding the essential message of the verse. One who naively glosses over specified directions will miss much of import in scriptural texts. One scholar observed: "In Scripture, God attributed symbolic significance to directions. Therefore, many times, beyond the geographical or physical, there is some spiritual and symbolic significance to be discovered. Such may be seen specified or implied."[8] Second, although directions are often symbolic, they must, as with all symbols, be carefully considered in their context and in light of the dictates of the Spirit. Whereas a direction in one passage may be laden with symbolic meaning and suggestions of authorial intent, in another passage that same direction may well be meant quite literally.

EAST

East is the direction most often employed in the standard works of the Church. Anciently it was the direction that represented God.⁹ If something came from the east it was representative of the idea that it was of God, sent by God, or godly in nature.¹⁰ Both blessings and punishments were believed to have been sent from the east (i.e., from God).¹¹ People from the east were often respected for their wisdom and perceived as being messengers of God.¹²

East was the primary direction of orientation for most of the ancient Near Eastern world,¹³ meaning that east was the direction a person faced in order to get his or her orientation.¹⁴ The very words *orient* and *orientation* actually point to the east.¹⁵ Ancient maps down through the Middle Ages typically placed east at the top. In biblical Hebrew, the root *qdm* is the most common word-group meaning "east." It literally referred to what was before or in front of oneself.

The Hebrew words *kawdeem, kaydmaw, kidmaw, kadmonee, kehdem,* and *kadmone* all can have the meaning "east," "eastward," or "eastern." The other common word for east is *mizrawkh,* which means "the place of sunrise."¹⁶ Thus, just as the original meaning behind our English word *east* was literally "light resplendent," in biblical Hebrew the phrase "the rising sun" was one of the ways to indicate the direction east.¹⁷ Similarly, in the New Testament, the Greek word rendered "east" also means "sunrise."¹⁸

One significant use of east as a symbolic direction appears in the account of the Fall of Adam and Eve, a point sometimes misunderstood by non-LDS commentators.¹⁹ Moses recorded: "Therefore the Lord God . . . drove out the man; and he placed at the east of the garden of Eden Cherubims, and a flaming sword which turned every way, to keep the way of the tree of life" (Genesis 3:23–24; see Alma 12:21; 42:2; Moses 4:31). When Adam and Eve partook of the fruit of the tree of knowledge of good and evil, they were driven out of Eden in an eastward direction. For most of Christendom this is evidence of God's displeasure with the first of the human race. As Elder Talmage noted: "It has become a common practice with mankind to heap reproaches upon the progenitors of the family, and to picture the supposedly blessed state in which we would be living but for the fall; whereas our first parents are entitled to our deepest gratitude for their legacy to posterity—the means of winning title to glory, exaltation, and eternal lives."[20]

The eastward movement of Adam and Eve following their expulsion from Eden should not be overlooked. Its presence in the text ensures that the student of scripture will perceive the Fall as the positive and divinely foreordained event that it was. As one text records:

> Eastward in Eden the Lord planted a garden—containing both the tree of life and the tree of the knowledge of good and evil—where he placed Adam and Eve (see Gen. 2:8). As a result of the Fall, they were expelled to the east from the garden, and the Lord placed cherubim and a flaming sword to prevent their reentering the garden in their fallen state to partake of the tree of life. In biblical Hebrew, one oriented oneself by facing east. Thus, the movement into mortality, away from God's presence, was a movement forward—to the east.[21]

If something moves eastward, it is symbolically moving "toward God." Thus the Fall was not a tragedy wherein all was lost and thrown into chaos as a result of Adam and Eve's transgression. On the contrary, their expulsion from Eden began their mortal journey along the only path that would prepare them for eternal glory; it was a movement toward God in the truest sense.[22]

Numerous passages of scripture depict those striving to do God's will as moving in an eastward direction. Jacob headed east and in so doing found Rachel and Leah, through whom the nation of Israel was born (see Genesis 29). Similarly, of Enoch we read: "And it came to pass, as I journeyed from the land of Cainan, by the sea east, I beheld a vision; and lo, the heavens I saw, and the Lord spake with me" (Moses 6:42). Thus Enoch, who like Jacob traveled toward the east, was the recipient of a great experience with God.[23]

Anciently, people from the east were typically seen as the

people of God. Nephi recorded the redemption of Israel in the following words: "Sing, O heavens; and be joyful, O earth; for the feet of those who are in the east shall be established; and break forth into singing, O mountains; for they shall be smitten no more; for the Lord hath comforted his people, and will have mercy upon his afflicted" (1 Nephi 21:13; see Isaiah 49:13). Those of the east—God's covenant people—shall have reason to rejoice, as will the righteous of all the earth. The Saints shall no longer be persecuted, and God's extended mercy will be recognized by all of the righteous.

Matthew records that soon after the birth of Christ there appeared in Jerusalem "wise men from the east" who sought to worship the Christ child (see Matthew 2:1–2). The fact that they were Spirit-directed and heaven-sent seems substantiated, not only by their prophetic dream to avoid returning to Herod (see v. 12) but also by their eastern origin.[24]

In Alma 2 we read that when the Nephites (in the east) were attacked by the Amlicites (from the west), God intervened and the Nephites conquered. Elsewhere, Alma speaks of the great city of Gideon as being in the east (see Alma 6:7). The righteous Saints in Gideon, it will be recalled, received of Alma "a profound prophetic oracle regarding the birth of Jesus and the atonement he would make."[25]

Because east was also associated with God's glory, influence, and wrath, many passages of scripture employ the direction in reference to dramatic events that are to be understood as a manifestation of God's hand. So, for example, John the Revelator notes: "And I saw another angel ascending from the east" (Revelation 7:2). This angel was one of the many who held the title of Elias (see D&C 77:9). Symbolically he hailed from the east (i.e., God's presence) and thus was to be perceived as divine, both in his origin and his mission.

The infamous east wind carries such negative connotations that few associate it with the divine, as will be seen in the following examples. However, anciently it was perceived as the instrument of God's wrath.[26] Indeed, the prophet Hosea actually called it "the wind of the Lord" (Hosea 13:15). Of it, one commentator wrote:

> The east wind was the wind coming from the desert regions of Syria and Arabia. . . . It comes in a season marked by low humidity, high winds, and extremely hot weather. . . . This east wind can be called "the wind of Yahweh," for he controls it. He uses the east wind as an instrument of his judgment. It was a strong east wind that drove back the waters of the Red Sea and permitted the Hebrews to cross on dry ground.[27]

Not only did Israel attribute the parting of the Red Sea to this divinely sent zephyr (see Exodus 14:21), but it was also the stated source of the plague of locusts that annoyed Pharaoh's kingdom during the ministry of Moses (see Exodus 10:13). In an effort to reprove Jonah, the Lord is said to have "prepared" a strong east wind to send upon him (see Jonah 4:8–11). In his rebuke of King Noah and his people, Abinadi prophetically warned that the Lord would "send forth hail among them, and it shall smite them; and they shall also be smitten with the east wind; and insects shall pester their land also, and devour their grain" (Mosiah 12:6). King Limhi cited the Lord's promise, "If my people shall sow filthiness they shall reap the east wind, which bringeth immediate destruction" (Mosiah 7:31). Isaiah indicated that through the east wind the iniquities of the house of Jacob would be purged (see Isaiah 27:7–9). Jeremiah similarly states, "I will scatter them as with an east wind before the enemy" (Jeremiah 18:17). And Job's parable regarding the unrighteous includes the warning that the east wind would carry the wicked away, and storms would "hurl" them out of their place (see Job 27:21).

Because east is the direction that symbolizes God's abode, when Israel became so saturated in sin that God's glory had to withdraw from her, scripture indicates that it was toward the east that God moved (see Ezekiel 11:22–23). The loss of God's Spirit always spells calamity for those who call themselves his covenant people.[28] However, equally as ominous and foreboding are the effects of the withdrawal of God's protecting hand from the world in general. John the Revelator recorded, "And the sixth angel poured out his vial upon the great river Euphrates; and the water thereof was dried up, that the way of the kings of the east might be prepared" (Revelation 16:12).

> There is an irony in the sixth plague. On at least two other occasions, waters were dried up in the service of God's people: the first time was the Red Sea (see Ex. 14:21); and the second, the Jordan River (Josh. 3:14–17). This time the dry waters allow horror to sweep the land. But the engines of destruction are in reality the tool of the Almighty. "I, the Lord, am angry with the wicked," he proclaims, and "I am holding my Spirit from the inhabitants of the earth. I have sworn in my wrath, and decreed wars upon the face of the earth, and the wicked shall slay the wicked, and fear shall come upon every man; and the saints also shall hardly escape" (D&C 63:32–34).[29]

The use of east as a symbol for Yahweh's glory is found in the book of Ezekiel. The prophet informs his audience that, upon Israel's repentance and subsequent restoration by God, Jehovah's Spirit returned to the covenant people from an eastward direction, filling the holy temple with God's glory (see Ezekiel 43:2–5). Thus we see east not only as a symbol of God's wrath but also as an emblem of his offered deliverance.[30]

Isaiah declares: "Arise, shine; for thy light is come, and the glory of the Lord is risen upon thee. For, behold, the darkness shall cover the earth, and gross darkness the people: but the Lord shall arise upon thee, and his glory shall be seen upon thee. And the Gentiles shall come to thy light, and kings to the brightness of thy rising" (Isaiah 60:1–3). The Psalmist proclaims, "Unto the upright there ariseth light in the darkness: he is gracious, and full of compassion, and righteous" (Psalm 112:4). The sending forth of God's glory like the dawn that breaks forth from the east, or as the sun which sheds light on all the inhabitants of the earth, is a symbol of "light, truth, and Christ."[31] Regarding ancient temples, one author noted:

> It should not go unnoticed that the gate was always to be located on the east side of the tabernacle. The first of the sun's rays would always point themselves to it. This heavenly light would thus reveal the beauty of the multicolored gate as the light of heaven reveals Christ as "the way, the truth, and the life" and the only way that men may approach the Father (John 14:6). . . . As the direction of the dawn and the rising sun, [east] becomes a symbol of light, truth, and Christ. The orientation of the East Gate of the Temple at Jerusalem was such that on the days of the spring and fall equinoxes the first rays of the rising sun, heralding the advent of the glory of God, could penetrate into the Holy of Holies. Joseph Smith said that the coming of the Son of Man will be as the light of the morning coming out of the east.[32]

On more than one occasion, Ezekiel spoke of the Messiah as entering his temple from the east (see Ezekiel 43:1–2, 4; see also 10:19).

The Prophet Joseph Smith repeatedly discoursed on the well-established figure of the rising of the sun as a symbol of the second advent of Christ.[33] Similarly, one popular Bible dictionary records, "Jesus likened the certainty and the suddenness of his return with lightning flashing from east to the west (Matt. 24:27)"—perhaps a symbol of Christ's appearance to the righteous (east) and the wicked (west) or his coming from the presence of God (east) to those of this fallen world (west).[34] Doctrine and Covenants 43 rightly asks, "For . . . what will ye say when . . . the lightnings shall streak forth from the east unto the west, and shall utter forth their voices unto all that live, and make the ears of all tingle that hear, saying these words—Repent ye, for the great day of the Lord is come?" (D&C 43:21–22). When Christ returns, will we be found among those "of the east" or among them "of the west"?

SOUTH

In Hebrew, one word commonly rendered "south" means literally "right" or "right hand."[35] Another word frequently translated as "south" means to face east—or in other words to face God.[36] In both cases the connotation derives from the fact that when we face east, south is at our right (or covenant) hand. Because of this, the direction south symbolically reminds many commentators of the covenant. In scripture this direction is occasionally associated with the divine.[37]

Curiously, one of the New Testament Greek words translated as "south" is traditionally used in speaking of the pouring of liquid,[38] a downpour of rain,[39] or the bringing of moisture.[40] Thus, appropriately, one author wrote that this direction symbolized a "place of refreshment."[41] It is a word that, in its most literal sense, is related to the heavens or the heavenly.[42]

Thus, in general terms, when the direction south is used symbolically it should provoke thoughts of a renewal, an outpouring, refreshment, covenant, conservatism, and proper choice.[43]

Having said this, outside of being applied as one of the four cardinal directions, south is neither a strong nor a commonly employed symbol in scripture. There are, nevertheless, a few canonical examples worth noting.

When Moses gave Israel the law he received upon Sinai from the hand of Jehovah, he told God's covenant people: "The Lord came from Sinai. . . . From his right hand went a fiery law for them" (Deuteronomy 33:2). Although less evident in the King James Version than in the Hebrew, it was from Jehovah's right (or covenant) hand that his law was given. The Hebrew word *yawmeen*, here translated as "right," can also denote "south."

Abraham was commanded of God to leave Haran, the home of his nativity, and travel south so that God might enter into a covenant with him (see Genesis 12:1–9). Indeed, we are told that "he went on his journey from the south even to

Bethel" (Genesis 13:3)—*Bethel* meaning "house of God." Similarly, when Lehi took his family into the wilderness (in hopes of obtaining the promised land), the Lord initially led them in "nearly a south-southeast direction" (1 Nephi 16:13).

Perhaps coincidental is the mention of south in the story of David and Jonathan (see 1 Samuel 20:41). At their last mortal meeting, David arose from his hiding place to the south and bowed himself three times to the earth "in order to acknowledge Jonathan's covenant superiority."[44]

When the lost tribes of Israel return from symbolic north, they are metaphorically headed south or toward God's covenant and true church, where they will receive an outpouring of God's Spirit, revelation, direction, and renewal. Indeed, the gathering of Israel is first and foremost realized when people come to a knowledge of the restored gospel and learn their true identity as children of God, at which point they gather to God's kingdom by accepting and entering into covenants.

In Psalm 126 we are told of a past redemption of Zion. Whether this refers to her liberation from the Babylonian exile or to some other restoration is unclear from the passage.[45] What is clear, however, is that this past redemption remained a vivid memory for the Psalmist, for he requests that God again renew Israel: "Turn again our captivity, O Lord, as the streams in the south" (v. 4). This request is for nothing less than a "gift from heaven."[46] "Sudden bounty has its perfect illustration here, since few places are more arid than *the Negeb,* and few transformations more dramatic than that of a dry gully into a torrent. Such can be the effect of a downpour, which can also turn the surrounding desert into a place of grass and flowers overnight."[47] The Psalmist thus symbolically represents the heavenly moisture that God can pour out upon those who have faith in his covenants. God can cause Zion to blossom when he sends his divine influence, as represented by the requested downpour.

The Song of Solomon describes a fountain of living water that nourishes the gardens, which are a metaphorical representation of the female lover (see 4:15–16). Typologists see the combined employment of water and the direction south in this passage as a symbol of the "blessed influences of God"[48] upon the church.

> Christian expositors explained the fountain as Holy Scripture or the Church as the expounder of Scripture. As a fountain of gardens it irrigates the local churches and all holy souls. It is also a well because of its depth and hidden mysteries. The living waters flow from the perennial source of Divine wisdom, unlike the teaching of heretics stored in broken cisterns hewn by human hand (Jer 2:13), and the waters are virtually identical with the source (Ps 36:8; John 4:14).... It was noted that the fountain deepens to a well and the well turns to streams, denoting the continual increase and advance of God's grace in the Church and in the soul, as Wisdom's canal grew to a river and the river to a sea ([Wisdom of ben Sira] 24:30–31), or as the stream from the Temple (Ezek 47:1–12). The devout soul is also a perennial fountain, ever renewed by God, ever bubbling forth with love for Him and expanding in love for its neighbor; it is also a well containing the deep grace and knowledge of the Holy Spirit, sufficient to supply itself and pour forth for others.[49]

In Jeremiah 13 the nation of Judah is given a strong rebuke by the Lord for allowing herself to become corrupted by pagan religious influence. Five warnings are offered in the hopes of turning her from the path of destruction (see Jeremiah 13:1–11, 12–14, 15–17, 18–19, 20–27). In the fourth of these warnings, Jeremiah rebukes Judah's king and queen mother for their contemptuous response to his prophetic message. He informs them of the captivity and exile that are about to befall their nation for their unwillingness to keep their covenants with God. In verse 19 Jeremiah prophetically declares: "The cities of the south shall be shut up, and none shall open them: Judah shall be carried away captive all of it, it shall be wholly carried away captive." With south as a symbol for the covenant, the prophet states that those who should have kept their promises to God have not and thus find themselves under siege.[50]

It may be more than coincidental that the Lord commands Ezekiel to preach against the south (see Ezekiel 20:45–49),[51] quite possibly referring to those of the covenant who would be burned if they did not repent. Although the King James Version has Ezekiel employing the direction south some five times in as many verses, the original Hebrew uses three different words all rendered "south." Of those three, only one means literally "south." The other two are figurative and carry the connotations of "right hand," thus supporting a symbolic reading of the verses.[52]

Finally, there is a very curious episode recorded in the book of Ether that appears to employ directions in a highly symbolic fashion—although it can and should be read literally as well. In Ether 8–15 we read of the fall of the great Jaredite nation. As is so often the case in the Book of Mormon, this tragedy began with secret combinations and materialism and ended with a war that nearly destroyed an entire race. Chapter 9 speaks of poisonous serpents that, among other things, caused the livestock to move into the region southward. These serpents remained between the land northward and the land southward, trapping the majority of the livestock or food and apparently a small group of people in the land of the south (see vv. 31–33).

This was a time of great wickedness among the people (see v. 34). As a repercussion, a great drought came upon the land wherein no rain fell to water the ground and crops and relieve the people's thirst. This condition lasted until the inhabitants of the region repented of their sins, at which point the rains came and the snakes died (see vv. 30, 35; 10:19). When the snakes began to die, numerous people from the north country were able to have contact with those few in the south, where, significantly, all of the food or game had existed in such plenitude.

As strange as this episode may seem, when each of its major elements is examined from the perspective of potential symbolic implications, a significant message emerges. Admittedly, it is impossible to state with certainty what the intention of the author was. Even so, the symbolism of south as a land of refreshment works harmoniously with other symbols in the same context, yielding instructive applications that might otherwise be missed.

For example, although serpents as symbols can carry both positive and negative connotations,[53] poisonous serpents typically conjure up images of the latter. Symbolically speaking, they remind us of Satan and his teachings, buffetings, temptations, and pitfalls.[54] That the serpents were in the land northward is compatible with the connotations of symbolic north: darkness, catastrophe, and calamity.

Metaphorically, rain is frequently associated with outpourings of the Holy Ghost, revelation, blessings, heavenly influences, sanctification, God's grace, and so on (see John 7:37–39; Deuteronomy 11:11; 32:2; Ezekiel 36:25–26; John 3:5; 1 John 5:6–8).[55] The fact that the direction south can function as a symbol for the covenant (or facing God), and that the word in Greek means "to bring rain" or an outpouring of "moisture," suggests a probable relationship between two of the potential symbols in Ether's account: rain and the land southward.

Food and game, as depicted in Ether 8–11, can serve as figurative representations of that which sustains life, functioning similarly to the symbol of Jesus as the "bread of life" (John 6:35; Revelation 2:17; Alma 5:34). The game or livestock in Ether seem to fill this emblematic role. They preserve the life of those in the land southward. They were needed for the preservation of the life of those in the land northward. They symbolize the bounties, blessings, ordinances, and covenants of the gospel of Jesus Christ—which are all necessary to sustaining our spiritual life.[56]

NORTH

Whereas Western cultures traditionally use north as the direction of orientation, ancient Semitic cultures oriented themselves toward the east. Consequently, as mentioned before, ancient maps, even through the Middle Ages, commonly placed the east, rather than north, at the top.[57]

Biblical Hebrew had two major words that were frequently translated as "north": *tsawfone* is defined in lexicons as meaning "dark," "hidden," or "gloomy";[58] and *semole* means literally "left hand" (or, by implication, "non-covenant").[59] An additional Hebrew word that was occasionally rendered "north," *mezawreh*, means "scatterer."[60]

Of the direction north, one commentator stated that it conjures up "ominous imagery."[61] Another wrote that "the ancients regarded the north as the seat of gloom and darkness."[62] In accordance with the linguistic connotations of the word, anciently the direction north provoked symbolic images of coldness, darkness, obscurity, the land of the dead, night, the region of Lucifer and powers of evil, barbarianism, apostasy, and the judgment of God.[63] One typologist noted that in some Christian traditions, the reading of the gospel "from the north end of the altar represents the Church's work to convert the heathen."[64]

It is possible that the geographic positioning of Israel added to this symbolic perception of north. With the sea on her west and the desert on her east, the only directions that a massive invasion could come from would be either south (from Egypt) or north (from Assyria, Babylon, Damascus, Media, Persia, and so on).[65]

When we face east, north is at the left hand and south at the right. Thus left, like north, carries the connotation of "dark" or "apostate" and may have added to the "ominous imagery" associated with that direction.[66] In fact, *north* and *left* are sometimes interchangeable words in scripture.[67] Indeed, our English word *sinister* actually derives from a Latin term that means "on the left side."[68] Throughout Semitic and Mediterranean cultures, the left side or north was the direction that characteristically signified "catastrophe and calamity."[69] One commentator stated that turning to the left symbolized making a wrong choice.[70]

When it is said that the lost tribes will return from the north, the implied meaning is that they will come out of darkness and apostasy and enter into the covenant.[71] Although many in the Church believe that the lost tribes will literally return from the north, this scriptural declaration should not be taken as a statement about their physical location.[72] Numerous passages in the Old Testament, New Testament, and Doctrine and Covenants indicate that they are scattered as leaven throughout the entire earth (see, for example, Deuteronomy 30:3; Amos 9:9; Zechariah 7:14; Luke 21:24; Jeremiah 30:3; Jacob 5:30; D&C 45:24–25). Thus the term *north* is commonly applied to Gentile nations even when their actual geographical location indicates otherwise.[73]

Examples of this symbolic employment of the word *north* are legion, with more instances occurring in the writings of Jeremiah than in those of any other prophet. Time and again this prophet spoke of judgment, gathering, and invasion as all coming from the north (see Jeremiah 1:13–15; 3:12, 18; 4:6; 6:1, 22; 10:22; 13:20; 16:15; 23:8; 25:9, 26; 31:8). Several of the many scriptural references to north as a negative symbol follow.

Isaiah speaks of the king of Babylon—and by inference Lucifer—as desiring to exalt himself as the gods (see Isaiah 14:12–13 or 2 Nephi 24:12–13): "How art thou fallen from heaven, O Lucifer, son of the morning! How art thou cut down to the ground, which did weaken the nations! For thou hast said in thy heart; I will ascend into heaven, I will exalt my throne above the stars of God; I will sit also upon the mount of the congregation, in the sides of the north." The "mount of the congregation" in the "north" had reference to Mount Zaphon (whose location is unknown),[74] where the Canaanite gods were said to assemble in council.⁷⁵ The message is one of both self-aggrandizement and darkness or apostasy.

Scriptural references to north are commonly associated with the invasion of nations by foreign barbarians (see Jeremiah 1:13–15; 4:6; 6:1, 22; 10:22; 16:15; 25:9; Isaiah 14:31; Ezekiel 26:7; Zechariah 6:6, 8).⁷⁶ Apart from Egypt, most invaders of Israel were from the north. Thus, the eschatological (i.e., last days) attack of Israel by Gog of Magog is said to originate from the north (see Ezekiel 38:6, 15; 39:2). Gog is a composite of Israel's "northern" enemies.⁷⁷ Anciently, even Babylon was accosted by those hailing from the north (see Jeremiah 50:9; Zechariah 2:6). Daniel spoke of a despicable king of the north (see Daniel 11:21–45).

Just as invaders come from the north, so can God's judgment. God is said to have stretched out his hand against the north and destroyed Assyria (see Zephaniah 2:12; Ezekiel 39:2–4; Isaiah 10:5–16; 14:31; 2 Nephi 24:31). Zechariah records that the righteous are to leave the "northern climes" before the area is judged (Zechariah 2:6–9). Symbolically speaking, the righteous need to flee Babylon lest they too suffer God's wrath, which will inevitably be poured out upon the wicked. Jeremiah spoke of the Lord sending his judgments upon Jerusalem in the form of evil from the north:

> Then the Lord said unto me, Out of the north an evil shall break forth upon all the inhabitants of the land. For, lo, I will call all the families of the kingdoms of the north, saith the Lord; and they shall come, and they shall set every one his throne at the entering of the gates of Jerusalem, and against all the walls thereof round about, and against all the cities of Judah. And I will utter my judgments against them touching all their wickedness, who have forsaken me, and have burned incense unto other gods, and worshiped the works of their own hands. (Jeremiah 1:14–16.)

The Book of Mormon frequently associates the direction north with wicked or non-covenant people and their activities (see Mosiah 10:5–8; 11:13–14; Alma 8:6–10; Helaman 1:22–23; Ether 1:1; 13:11). For example, the final chapter of the book of Alma makes note of "the deaths of Pahoran, Moroni, Helaman, and his brother Shiblon, marking the end of this era of righteous Nephite control of Zarahemla."[78] Then, as a seemingly symbolic note to emphasize the transition from righteousness to apostasy and wickedness, Alma 63:5 informs us that Hagoth built ships to transport people to the north. He was never heard from again.[79]

The Doctrine and Covenants occasionally invokes north as a symbol related to the gathering of Israel and the return of the lost tribes (see D&C 110:11; 133:26–32).

In the Pearl of Great Price, Enoch is shown in vision many wicked cities to which he is to cry repentance (see Moses 7:5–12). At the very beginning of the vision he is instructed to turn to the north. Indeed, the only direction associated with all of these cities is that of north, as though to emphasize their wicked or apostate status (see Moses 7:6–8).

North and left are synonymous. In Genesis 48 we read of the blessing that Jacob pronounced on Ephraim and Manasseh. In the process of giving that blessing, Jacob deliberately crossed his arms and put his left hand on Manasseh, the firstborn (see vv. 13–14). Joseph, Manasseh's father and Jacob's son, objected to Jacob's action because, under normal circumstances, the right, or covenant, hand should have been placed on the elder son, Manasseh. The placement of the left hand on Manasseh implied a non-chosen status. Joseph clearly understood the symbolism but was confused because, as far as he knew, Manasseh was entitled to be blessed according to his firstborn status.[80]

One commentator wrote: "The left side is usually the sinister, dark, illegitimate . . . aspect. . . . In Christianity at the Judgment the sheep are on the right hand and the goats on the left and in crucifixion scenes the good thief is depicted as on the right hand of Christ and the bad thief to the left."[81]

In Ecclesiastes 10:2 we read, "A wise man's heart is at his

right hand; but a fool's heart at his left." In reference to this, one commentator explained: "Since the heart of man is universally found on the left side of the chest, and not on the right side, the lesson to be learned is that all men are fools in the sight of God while in their natural state."[82] The commentator's explanation may be a bit simplistic. However, in general terms it is true that "the natural man is an enemy to God" (Mosiah 3:19) and that not to yield to the enticings of the Holy Spirit is to act the part of the fool. More to the point, however, is the connection of the symbols left and north, for Ecclesiastes' Preacher's words might be more literally rendered "A wise man's heart [or desire] is in the covenant; but a fool's heart [desire] is in darkness."

Finally, it is said that following their expulsion from Eden, Adam and Eve lived north of the Garden of Eden in a place known to Latter-day Saints as Adam-ondi-Ahman (or "the valley of God, where Adam dwelt").[83] The northern direction placed emphasis on the fact that Adam and Eve were in a fallen state and needed to regain God's presence and favor through entering into and keeping sacred covenants.

WEST

Regarding the symbolic direction west, one scholar noted that it "is the most ominous of the four directions" employed in the biblical text.[84] It has traditionally carried very negative connotations. Standard associations include something to be discarded, something irrelevant, something lacking in priority and not requiring attention, the cessation of human activity, that which is foreign and thus undesirable, sorrow, chaos, evil, darkness, the kingdom of the devil, the dying of the sun, and death itself.[85] Although the word *west* is occasionally associated with seemingly common-place things—the setting of the sun, the closing of the day, the end of a situation or experience, that which is behind or to the rear, toward the sea, and so on[86]—when taken in the context of the overall symbol, even these connotations provoke negative images.

The directions west and north generate ideas very similar to each other. Both are essentially negative symbols and share concepts such as that which is dark or foreign and undesirable. Occasionally the two emblems are coupled together in scripture (see Joshua 8:13; Isaiah 49:12; 1 Nephi 21:12; Alma 2:36–37).

Additionally, the word *west* is frequently used interchangeably with *sea* or *seaward* in many translations of the Hebrew Bible.[87] One scholar wrote: "The usual word for west [in Hebrew means] 'sea,' referring to the Mediterranean Sea, Palestine's western border."[88]

In Hebrew, the concept of the setting sun provided one of the common phrases for the westward direction. In addition to *mawbo,* the Hebrew words for west include *maharawb* (which means literally "the place of the sunset," or by implication "evening") and *akharone* (meaning literally to "come after or behind," or by implication to "have west behind you"). This last Hebrew word emphasizes the fact that Hebrews used their bodies to determine orientation. Thus when they faced east, west was the direction behind them; and if they were in Israel, west would be the location of the western or Mediterranean Sea, also known as the Great Sea.[89]

In order to show that God's influence, power, and eye are everywhere, the Psalmist employs a merisum[90] whose words suggest the all-encompassing span "from east to west." This is apparent if we remember that east is associated with things heavenly and west with "the dark and benighted dominion of Sheol."[91] The language of the Psalmist includes these images: "If I ascend up into heaven [east], . . . if I make my bed in hell [west], . . . if I take the wings of the morning [east], and dwell in the uttermost parts of the sea [west] . . ." (Psalm 139:8–10). Combining the symbols of east and west to convey totality or completeness is common in scripture (see Psalms 75:6; 103:12; 107:3). A related comparison of the rising and setting sun, although capable of implying completeness, also serves well as a symbol of the heavenly versus the worldly.

We read of the rising sun as a symbol for the second advent of Christ. Matthew records: "For as the light of the morning cometh out of the east, and shineth even unto the west, and covereth the whole earth; so shall also the coming of the Son of man be" (JST, Matthew 24:27; see also Psalm 113:3; Isaiah 45:6; 59:19; Malachi 1:11; Mark 13:29; Joseph Smith—Matthew 1:26). Similarly, the Prophet Joseph Smith taught: "The dawning of the morning makes its appearance in the east and moves along gradualy [sic]. . . . The comeing [sic] of the Son of Man [shall] be . . . small at its first appearance and gradually [become] larger untill [sic] every eye shall see it."[92]

Employing the directional symbols of east and west in relation to Christ's coming implies that Christ shall be seen by the righteous (east) and the wicked (west). Thus one scholar noted, "In contrast to the joyous response of life to the light of the rising sun, darkness and the cessation of human activity result when the sun sets in the west. . . . The west is the place where the sun ceases to provide its light."[93] Such will certainly be the case when Christ returns. Those who have dedicated their lives and hearts to God (east) shall have reason to rejoice. Yet those who have loved and propagated chaos, evil, darkness, and the kingdom of the devil (west) shall experience the "cessation" of their wicked lives.

As noted above, the word *west* is sometimes associated with "the end of a situation or an experience."[94] The experience that has come to an end (for those in the west) is that of an evil mortal existence. As one typologist noted: "Ceremonies concerned with death and resurrection stress the East as sunrise and life and the West as sunset and death. . . . The western direction is universally associated with dying [and] sorrow."[95] Such is the lot of those whom the scriptures metaphorically place in the west. Likewise, Jerome noted that it is a symbol for the abode of the devil. Thus the east symbolizes the kingdom of Christ and the west, aptly, the kingdom of the devil.[96]

In a fascinating Old Testament story we are told that Moses' successor, Joshua, persuaded the Lord to lengthen the duration of the sun's light so that the Israelites could defeat their enemies. Commentators are not in agreement as to what exactly happened in this episode. Some read the Hebrew as implying that the sun actually ceased to shine.[97] Some understand the text as implying that just as the sun was about to go down, Joshua offered his prayer and the light continued until the battle was won.[98] Others suggest that the sun was just rising in the east when the prayer was offered and that Joshua requested that it remain there so that Israel's enemies to the west would be facing into the blinding sun both when they were attacked and during most of the battle.[99] The important factor in this episode is the reality that the sun—itself a symbol of Christ—came out of the east (i.e., came from God's presence) in support of Israel and to the defeat of her enemies in the west.

In a similar vein, frequently in scripture we find the symbolic direction west associated with the enemies of the righteous. Isaiah speaks of the uncircumcised Philistines as dwelling west of Israel (see Isaiah 11:14). Alma records that the sin-laden Lamanites and the Amlicites fled westward (chaos and darkness) and northward (darkness and apostasy) in order to escape the Nephite army (see Alma 2:35–38). Later in that same record we learn that, after preaching to the Saints in Gideon, Alma returned to his home in Zarahemla to rest for a season. But in the commencement of the tenth year of the reign of the judges, he then traveled west to the land of Melek, where he preached and converted many humble people who had been in darkness regarding the truths of the gospel (see Alma 8:3–5). From Melek, Alma headed north to the apostate people of Ammonihah. The record indicates that they would not repent nor accept his message, and so in accordance with the prophecies (and the typology), the city was destroyed (see Alma 8–10).

Isaiah speaks of the gathering of Israel out of the apostate world: "And then, O house of Israel, behold, these shall come from far; and lo, these from the north and from the west; and these from the land of Sinim" (1 Nephi 21:12; Isaiah 49:12). In the most literal terms the passage supports the idea that Israel is scattered throughout the earth (see Deuteronomy 30:3; Jeremiah 30:3; Amos 9:9; Zechariah 7:14; Luke 21:24; Jacob 5:30; D&C 45:24–25). However, symbolically speaking, Isaiah employs only two directions: north and west. The implication is that Israel will be brought out of her state of apostasy, chaos, and darkness into the covenants of the Lord.[100]

The book of Genesis records that those who built the Tower of Babel first moved westward to a "plain in the land of Shinar." There they built their pseudo-temple (see Genesis 11:2–4).

Just as those in the west are perceived as "the enemy," the book of Judges records that the Israelite tribes conquered Canaan by entering the land in a westward movement, because they were spiritual enemies to the people of Canaan (see Judges 11:18).[101] Similarly, Alma recorded that Captain Moroni and the Nephite armies hid from their enemies in the valley on the west side of the river Sidon (see Alma 43:27).

In summary, because of the significant nature of directions in most ancient cultures, those who study scripture or attend the temple need to be conscious of the ancient meanings attached to them. Otherwise, the intended message of the prophets as given in scripture and the divinely revealed rituals as presented in the temple will be misunderstood.

8
PEOPLE AS TYPES

THE PEOPLE MENTIONED in the standard works of the Church are historical realities. God's hand was manifest in their lives, the evidence of which is seen in the narratives pertaining to them. When men such as Jacob's son Joseph are known to be detailed types or symbols for a greater reality,[1] this does not imply that they and their experiences are anything less than historical. But because God can inspire people and be actively involved in their lives, the exemplary persons recorded in scripture were receptive to the Spirit of God and were moved to live in ways harmonious with what they came to typify. Similarly, the writers of scripture were moved by that same spirit to include in their records events that would best emphasize the typological significance of those figures.

One typologist noted that "there is no such thing as a perfect type."[2] Typology is not the same as allegory. Similar to what is true for Jesus' parables, if one takes typology too far it will break down; the comparisons will not hold up. Whereas allegories are usually symbolic in almost every aspect, types simply present a few major comparisons. Pressing to find symbolic meaning in every aspect of the life of a typological figure is to strain the type beyond its limits and to miss its true value and meaning.[3]

Below are several examples of how people serve as types of various gospel realities. This list is by no means exhaustive, and the parallels drawn between certain figures and their antitypes are merely a sampling that should be sufficient to open the eyes of the reader to a common pattern in scripture. Although chapter 11 will deal with Christocentric symbols, the comparative tables that follow also focus on people as types for Christ. The tables also examine people as types for the Church, unnamed people as types, and named people as non-Christocentric types.

TYPES FOR CHRIST

ABEL	CHRIST
Abel was a shepherd (Moses 5:17).	Christ is the Good Shepherd (John 10:11).
Abel offered an acceptable offering, which consisted of a first-year male lamb without blemish (Moses 5:20).	Christ's offering was accepted by God and was typified in the law of Moses by the slaying of a first-year male lamb without blemish.[4]
Abel's offering involved the shedding of blood (Moses 5:20).	Christ's offering involved the shedding of his own blood (Moroni 5:2).
In making his offering, Abel was opposed by his brother Cain (Moses 5:21).	In making his offering and atonement, Christ was opposed by his brother Lucifer (Abraham 3:27–28).[5]
Abel walked in holiness before God (Moses 5:26).	Jesus walked in holiness before God the Father (2 Nephi 31:7; 3 Nephi 11:7).
Abel was slain by his brother while he labored in the field (Moses 5:32).	Jesus was slain by his brother (i.e., Satan caused him to be slain) while he labored at his mission in the field (or vineyard or earth).[6]

According to Philo of Alexandria, the name Abel means "referring to God."[7] A more traditional rendering of this Hebrew name is "transitory" or "fading away."[8] Such seems appropriate in light of Abel's abbreviated life. One Jewish source records, "After a while, Eve bore [another] son, whom she named Hebel, because, she said, he was born but to die."[9] "Hebel" is the transliteration of the Hebrew name "Abel."

Jesus is the Son of God whose life and teachings "refer" or point us to God the Father (John 14:6). Additionally, Jesus was "born but to die."

ABRAHAM	CHRIST
Abraham was known as the father of the faithful (Genesis 15:6; D&C 138:41).	Christ is the spiritual father of all of the faithful (Romans 4:11; Mosiah 5:7).
Before Abraham's birth, the king's astrologers foretold the coming of one whose right it would be to rule. In an attempt to prevent this, the king ordered the slaughter of all newborn babies.[10]	Before Christ's birth, the prophets foretold the coming of one whose right it would be to rule. In an attempt to prevent this, the king ordered the slaughter of all newborn babies (JST, Matthew 2:1–6, 16).
All nations of the earth were blessed through Abraham (Abraham 2:9).	All nations of the earth have been and will be blessed through Christ (Acts 4:12).
Abraham was a mediator between God and man (Genesis 18:20–33).	Christ is the great intercessor or mediator between God and man (1 Timothy 2:5).

Abraham sought the salvation of others (Genesis 14; 18).	Christ sought the salvation of others (Hebrews 9:28).
Abraham cleansed the house of his father, Terah, of idols.[11]	Jesus cleansed his Father's house, the temple, of money changers and merchants (John 2:12–16).
Believers are known as the "seed of Abraham" (Galatians 3:29).	Believers in Christ become his seed, his children (Mosiah 5:7).
Upon death, the faithful are said to go to "Abraham's bosom" (Luke 16:22).	When they die, the faithful are said to be taken to the bosom of Christ (D&C 38:4).
Abraham was offered by his father as a sacrifice (Facsimile 1).	Submitting to the will of the Father, Christ offered himself as a sacrifice for sin (John 3:16).
In Abraham's greatest hour of darkness, God sent an angel to comfort and help him (Abraham 1:15).	In Christ's greatest hour of darkness, God the Father sent an angel to comfort and help him (Luke 22:43).
Abraham received the land of his father (Canaan) as a "promised land" and inheritance, which he willingly shared not only with his offspring but with all who accepted the gospel (Genesis 11:31; 17:18; Abraham 2:15).	Jesus received the land he and his Father created (this earth) as a "promised land" and inheritance (when celestialized), which he willingly shares (as a "joint heir") with all who accept and live the gospel.[12]

People As Types

ADAM	CHRIST
Adam was physically the firstborn of God the Father (Moses 3:7).	Christ was the Firstborn spirit of God the Father (Colossians 1:15).
Adam was created in the Father's image (Genesis 1:27).	Christ was created in the Father's image (Hebrews 1:3).
Adam was foreordained to his earthly mission (Abraham 3:22–23).	Christ was foreordained to his earthly mission (Abraham 3:22–23).
Adam was the head of the human family (D&C 107:55).	Christ is the spiritual head of the family of God (Ephesians 4:15).
In the Garden of Eden, Adam was a sinless man who, for the benefit of others, chose to take upon himself mortality (and, therefore, sin), and in so doing died (2 Nephi 2:25).	Christ was a sinless man who chose, for the benefit of others, to take upon himself the sins of mortal man, and then gave up his life (Mosiah 26:23).
Adam provided all mankind with an opportunity for mortal birth and thus eternal life (2 Nephi 2:25).	Jesus provides all mankind with the opportunity for spiritual rebirth and eternal life (1 John 5:1).
Adam ruled on earth in its paradisiacal splendor (Eden).	Christ will rule on the earth when it returns to its paradisiacal splendor (during the Millennium).
Adam is the "first Adam" (1 Corinthians 15:45).	Christ is the "last Adam" (1 Corinthians 15:45).
Adam's name in the premortal life, Michael, means "who is like unto Jehovah."[13]	Christ, the premortal Jehovah, is "like unto God" (Abraham 3:24).
According to ancient legend, while Adam was making a sacrifice, Satan smote him in his side, causing blood and water to flow out.[14]	While Jesus was making his sacrifice on our behalf, Satan caused that he be smitten in his side, causing water and blood to flow out (John 19:34).

DAVID	CHRIST
David was a faithful shepherd (1 Samuel 16:11).	Christ is the Good Shepherd (John 10:14).
David was anointed king long before he received the kingship (1 Samuel 16:13).	Christ was anointed King long before he entered mortality (1 Peter 1:20).
David defeated Goliath and put the enemies of Israel to flight (1 Samuel 17:49–50).	Christ has defeated all "Goliaths" for us, putting our enemies to flight if we will accept him (Philippians 4:13; Moroni 9:26; 10:23).
Without provocation, David was opposed by Saul (1 Samuel 18:11–12).	Christ and his servants are always opposed by those whose allegiance is to another kingdom (2 Nephi 2:11; JS–H 1:20).
David conquered the Jebusites and gave Israel Jerusalem, where the temple would be built (2 Kings 5:6–9).	The Lord conquers the world and gives his church Jerusalem (old and new) in which to build his temple (1 Corinthians 15:25–27; 3 Nephi 20:22).
David extended Israel's borders to where God had promised Abraham they would reach (2 Samuel 8).	Today the "borders" of the Lord's kingdom are expanding as promised by the Lord (Exodus 34:24).
God established a covenant with David regarding the receipt of an eternal kingdom (2 Samuel 7:12–16).	God established a covenant with Christ regarding his receipt of an eternal kingdom (Psalm 2:7–8).

ENOCH	CHRIST
The true church was called "the church of Enoch" (D&C 76:67).	The true church is called after the name of Christ (D&C 115:4).
Enoch's name means "dedicated to Jehovah."[15]	Christ was dedicated to God the Father (John 5:19; 8:28).
In later Jewish mysticism, Enoch was identified with "Little Yahweh," or the angel closest to God.[16]	Jesus is Yahweh, the angel closest to God (Abraham 3:2, 19).
Enoch and his people will return to the earth during the millennial Zion (Moses 7:62–63).	Christ and his people will return to usher in the millennial era (D&C 45:44).
Enoch was the seventh man from Adam (Jude 1:14), the number seven symbolizing divine completion or rest (indicating that Enoch and his people symbolized the peaceful millennial dispensation).	Christ provides the divine completion and rest we all seek, for he will reign over all during the millennial dispensation, when all the earth will know the Lord.

ISAAC	CHRIST
Isaac was the birthright son of a righteous father (Genesis 21).	Christ is the birthright Son of a righteous Heavenly Father (D&C 93:21).
Isaac's birth required a miracle (Genesis 11:30; 17:15–22).	Christ's birth required a miracle (Luke 1:26–38).
Isaac was offered as a sacrifice by his father prior to his thirty-seventh year of life.[17]	Jesus was offered up according to the will of the Father apparently sometime during his thirty-fourth year of life.

The journey to the place of Isaac's sacrifice took three days (Genesis 22:4).	The journey to Christ's sacrifice—from his baptism in Jordan to his crucifixion on Golgotha—took three years.
The attempted sacrifice of Isaac took place on Mount Moriah (Genesis 22:2).	The same group of hills commonly called Mount Moriah was the site of Solomon's temple and Jesus' crucifixion (Mark 15:22).
Isaac carried the wood on which he would be placed up to the top of Mount Moriah (Genesis 22:6).	Jesus carried the wooden cross on which he would be placed to the hill where he would be crucified (John 19:17).
As part of the sacrifice, Isaac was bound to the wood (Genesis 22:9).	Jesus was crucified, being nailed to a wooden cross (Luke 23:33).
An angel ministered to Isaac during his hour of sacrifice (Genesis 22:11).	An angel ministered to Jesus during his hour of sacrifice (Luke 22:43).
Isaac willingly went to his place of sacrifice trusting his father's judgment and decision.[18]	Jesus willingly went to his place of sacrifice trusting in his Father's judgment and plan (Moses 4:2; Abraham 3:27).
A ram was provided in place of Isaac so that he would not have to die (Genesis 22:13).	Christ is the scapegoat for Isaac and all mankind, having died in our stead (Romans 5:8; Revelation 5:6).
The ram that died in Isaac's place had the top of its head caught in some thorn bushes (Genesis 22:13).[19]	Christ, who died in part on Isaac's behalf, had a crown of thorns placed upon his head (Matthew 27:29).

People As Types

JACOB	CHRIST
Jacob's name was changed by God to Israel (Genesis 32:28).	God changed Jesus' name from his premortal title, Jehovah, to his mortal name and title, Jesus the Christ.
The name Israel means "a prince with God" or "ruling with God."[20]	Jesus is the prince of God who rules with God.[21]
Jacob was informed that he would have power with God and men and would prevail (Genesis 32:28).	Jesus certainly has power with God and men and prevails in all things (1 Corinthians 15:27–28).
Jacob was loved by God before he was born (Romans 9:10–13).	Christ was loved by God prior to his birth into mortality (John 3:16; D&C 76:25).
Jacob was said to be "a plain man" (Genesis 25:27).	Isaiah spoke of Christ as one who would have "no form nor comeliness" and would be void of "beauty that we should desire him" (Isaiah 53:2).
Jacob would have a brother who would sell his birthright for temporal attainment (Genesis 25:29–34).	Jesus' brother Lucifer sold his position of authority for worldly power (2 Nephi 24:12–14; D&C 76:25–27).
Jacob overcame his brother (Genesis 27:37–40).	Jesus overcame Satan and will make it possible for all of us to do the same (D&C 88:112–15).
Jacob was promised that his descendants and followers would be stronger than the followers of his brother (Genesis 25:23).	Jesus' followers are stronger than Satan and his minions, and the devil has no power over the followers of Christ, except that which they give him.[22]
Jacob's brother sought to kill him (Genesis 27:41).	Lucifer sought to take the life of Christ.[23]

JOSEPH OF EGYPT[24]	CHRIST
Joseph's name was changed from Joseph to Zaphnath-paaneah (Genesis 41:45).	Christ's name was changed from his premortal title, Jehovah, to his mortal name-title, Jesus the Christ.
Zaphnath-paaneah means, among other things, "savior of the world," "the giver of the nourishment of life," and "revealer of a secret."[25]	Each of Joseph's name-titles finds direct application in the life and ministry of the Savior, Jesus Christ.
Joseph was a shepherd (Genesis 37:2).	Christ is the Good Shepherd (John 10:14).
Joseph was his father's chosen and dearly loved son (Genesis 37:3).	Christ is God the Father's chosen and beloved Son (Mark 1:11).
Joseph was clothed in authority and power by his father (Genesis 37:3).	Christ has been clothed in power and authority by his Father (JST, Matthew 7:37).
Joseph was a seer or revelator (Genesis 37:5–10).	Christ is a seer and revelator (Matthew 24).
Joseph was fully obedient to the will of his father, responding to his call by saying, "Here am I" (Genesis 37:13).	Christ is fully obedient to the will of his Father, responding to his call by saying, "Here am I" (Abraham 3:27).
Joseph was promised future sovereignty (Genesis 37:7).	Christ was promised future sovereignty (Revelation 11:15).
Joseph was betrayed by his brother Judah (Genesis 37:26).[26]	Christ was betrayed by a brother in the gospel, Judas (Matthew 10:4).

Joseph was cast into a pit (Genesis 37:24).	Christ was cast into a spiritual pit (Isaiah 24:22).
Joseph was sold for the price of a slave (Genesis 37:26–28).	Christ was sold for the price of a slave (Matthew 26:15).
Joseph refused to give in to temptation (Genesis 39).	Christ refused to give in to temptation (Matthew 4:1–11).
Joseph was falsely accused (Genesis 39:16–19).	Christ was falsely accused by the Sanhedrin (JST, Matthew 26:59).
Joseph was thirty when he began his mission (Genesis 41:46).	Jesus was thirty when he began his earthly ministry (Luke 3:23).
Joseph served as a savior for his people (Genesis 45:5, 7).	Christ is the Savior of all people (1 Nephi 10:4).
Joseph was initially unrecognized by his brethren (Genesis 45).	Christ was unrecognized by his people (the Jews) at his first advent (Acts 13:27).
Joseph was recognized and accepted by his people only the second time they met (Genesis 45).	Christ will be universally recognized by his people (the Jews) only at his second advent (D&C 45:51–53).
All bowed to Joseph (Genesis 43:26–28).	All will bow to Christ (D&C 76:110).

JOSEPH SMITH[27]	CHRIST
Joseph's name means "he shall add."[28] The prophet added much to what the world understands about God, his plan, and what we must do in order to return to him.	Christ restored the gospel in the meridian of time, adding much to what the world then understood about God, his plan, and what one must do in order to return to him.

Joseph was said to be "great like unto Moses" (2 Nephi 3:9).	Christ was said to be "like unto Moses" (3 Nephi 20:23).
Joseph was of humble beginnings (JS–H 1:46).	Christ was of humble beginnings (Luke 2:7).
Joseph was betrayed by those who professed to be his friends and most intimate disciples.[29]	Christ was betrayed by one who professed to be his friend and intimate disciple (Luke 22:48).
Joseph was falsely accused and heavily persecuted by both the religious leaders of his day and mobocrats (D&C 127:2; 135; JS–H 1:1).	Christ was falsely accused and heavily persecuted by both the religious leaders of his day and others (Matthew 26:59–60; Mark 14:55–59).
Joseph called twelve apostles to assist him in the work of the Lord.[30]	Christ called twelve apostles to assist him in his work (Matthew 10:1–4).
Joseph willingly went as a "lamb to the slaughter," dying as a martyr (D&C 135).	Christ willingly went like a "lamb to the slaughter," dying as a martyr (Isaiah 53:7).
Joseph restored the ordinances necessary for the atonement's efficacy (D&C 135:3).	Christ provided the atonement necessary for the efficacy of the ordinances.
Joseph lived a comparatively short life.[31]	Christ lived a comparatively short life.[32]
Joseph was a prophet and a "savior on mount Zion" (Obadiah 1:21).[33]	Christ was a prophet and the Savior of all (Matthew 21:46; John 6:14).
Joseph restored the Church in the fulness of times.	Christ restored the Church in the meridian of time.

People As Types

JOSHUA	CHRIST
Joshua was a successful leader in battle (Exodus 17:9–10, 13).	Christ was a successful leader in the battle against Satan and sin (Revelation 3:21).
Joshua's name was changed from Oshea to Joshua (Numbers 13:16).[34]	Christ's premortal name, Jehovah, was changed to his mortal name/title, Jesus the Christ.
The Hebrew name Joshua is the equivalent of the Greek name Jesus.[35]	The Greek name Jesus is the equivalent of the Hebrew name Joshua.[36]
Joshua acted as a guide to show Israel the way from their wilderness wanderings to the promised land.[37]	Christ acted as a guide to show covenant Israel the way out of the world and home to the promised land of the celestial kingdom (John 14:6).
According to Jewish legend, Joshua radiated a glory or light (much as Moses did when he came down from Sinai), but it did not attain its full intensity until he crossed over the Jordan and entered the promised land.[38]	Jesus radiated a glory or light, but it was not until he was resurrected that he attained the full intensity of his glory and exalted status (Matthew 5:48; 2 Corinthians 4:6; D&C 6:21; compare 3 Nephi 12:48).

MELCHIZEDEK	CHRIST
Little is known about Melchizedek's early life.	Little is known about Christ's early life.
Melchizedek manifested gifts of the Spirit in his youth (JST, Genesis 14:26).	Christ manifested gifts of the Spirit in his youth (JST, Luke 2:41–52).[39]

Melchizedek bore the title "King of Righteousness," which Jews associate with their Messiah.[40]	Christ is the "King of Righteousness" and the Messiah.
Melchizedek offered the Lord's Supper (Genesis 14:18–20; JST, Genesis 14:17–20).	Christ offered the Lord's Supper as the fulfillment of the paschal feast (Matthew 26:26–28).
Scripture associates Melchizedek with Christ (Psalm 110:4; Hebrews 7:14–16).	Scripture associates Christ with Melchizedek (Psalm 110:4; Hebrews 7:14–16).
Melchizedek was used by Paul to prove that salvation is not found in the law of Moses (Hebrews 7).	Salvation does not come through the law of Moses, but in and through his holy name (Mosiah 13:32).
Melchizedek preached repentance to those around him (Alma 13:18).	Jesus preached repentance to all who would hear him (Matthew 4:17; D&C 18:22; 19:15–20).
Melchizedek administered ordinances for the remission of sins (JST, Genesis 14:17; Alma 13:16).	Jesus administered ordinances for the remission of sins (JST, John 4:1–3).
The priesthood is called after Melchizedek's name (D&C 107:3–4).	The priesthood used to be called after Christ's name, even the "Holy Priesthood, after the order of the Son of God" (D&C 107:3–4).
Melchizedek reigned "under his father" (Alma 13:18).	Christ reigns "under his Father" (John 5:19).
Melchizedek was king of Jerusalem (Genesis 14:18; Psalm 76:2).	By right Christ should have been King of the Jews and Jerusalem (Matthew 1–2; 5:35).

Melchizedek was said to have had miraculous powers (JST, Genesis 14:26).	Christ has miraculous powers.[41]
Melchizedek was called the "king of heaven" by his people (JST, Genesis 14:34–36).	Christ is the King of Heaven and acknowledged as such by his people (2 Nephi 10:14; Alma 5:50).
Melchizedek was known as the "Prince of Peace" (JST, Genesis 14:33; Hebrews 7:1–2; Alma 13:18).	Christ is the "Prince of Peace" (Isaiah 9:6; John 14:27; 2 Nephi 19:6).
It was said of Melchizedek that no high priest was greater (Alma 13:19).	Christ is the Great High Priest (Hebrews 3:1; 9:11).
Melchizedek ordained to the priesthood the prophet who would succeed him (D&C 84:14).	Christ ordained to the priesthood the prophet who would succeed him (Matthew 10:1–2).
Melchizedek overcame the world (JST, Genesis 14:33–34).	Christ overcame the world (John 16:33).

MOSES[42]	CHRIST
To Moses the Lord said, "Thou art in the similitude of mine Only Begotten" (Moses 1:6).	Jesus is the Only Begotten of the Father in the flesh (John 1:14).
Moses was one of the noble and great ones (D&C 138:38, 41; Abraham 3:22).	Christ is the noble and great One (Abraham 3:3, 19).
Moses was foreordained to his calling.[43]	Christ was foreordained to his calling (Abraham 3:27).

Moses was known by name generations before his birth, as were the details of his mortal ministry (JST, Genesis 50:29–35).	Christ was known by name generations before his birth, as were the details of his mortal ministry (Mosiah 3:5–10).
Ancient legends state that at Moses' birth the whole house was filled with light.[44]	At Jesus' birth a bright light filled the sky, leading the magi to the place of his nativity (Matthew 2:1–2).
As an infant, Moses' life was threatened by an evil king (Exodus 1).	As an infant, Christ's life was threatened by an evil king (Matthew 2).
Moses was rejected when he first came to Israel (Exodus 2:13–14).	Christ was rejected when he first came as a mortal to covenant Israel (Matthew 21:42–46).
Moses went into the wilderness for a time to be with God, where he was ministered to by angels (JST, Galatians 3:19).	Christ went into the wilderness for a time to be with God, where he was ministered to by angels (Mark 1:13).
Moses fasted for forty days and nights (Deuteronomy 9:18).	Christ fasted for forty days and nights (Matthew 4:2).
Moses was confronted by Satan, who told him to worship him (Moses 1:12–23).	Christ was confronted by Satan, who desired that Jesus worship him (Matthew 4:1–10).
Moses was carried by the Spirit to a high mountain where he was transfigured and shown the destiny of the earth (Moses 1:1, 8, 11).	Christ was carried by the Spirit to a high mountain where he was transfigured and shown "all the kingdoms of the world and the glory of them" (JST, Matthew 4:8).

Moses began his ministry by performing miracles (Exodus 4; 7–12).	Christ began his ministry by performing miracles (John 2:1–11).
Moses had control over the elements, such as water (Exodus 7; 14; 15:20–27; 17).	Christ has control over the elements, such as water (Matthew 14:25–32; John 2).
Moses fed his followers with bread from heaven (Exodus 16; Deuteronomy 8:3).	Christ fed his followers bread; at the same time, he was that "bread" from heaven (Matthew 14–15; Mark 6; Luke 9; John 6:35).
Isaiah referred to Moses as the shepherd of Israel (Isaiah 63:11).[45]	Jesus is the Good Shepherd (John 10:11).
Moses left Egypt and in so doing fulfilled prophecy (JST, Genesis 50:29).	Jesus left Egypt and in so doing fulfilled prophecy (Matthew 2:15).
Moses was a liberator for Israel (Exodus 13:3; 1 Nephi 17:24; Moses 1:26).	Christ was *the* Liberator of Israel (Exodus 13:3).
Moses was the mediator of the covenant and a lawgiver (Exodus 32:32).	Christ was *the* Mediator of the Covenant and *the* Giver of the Divine Law (1 Timothy 2:5; D&C 88:21).
Moses sought to make an atonement for Israel's sins (Exodus 32:30–32).	Christ personally atoned for Israel's sins—and the sins of all mankind (Alma 34:8).
Moses went atop a mountain and brought down a "new law" (Exodus 20–24; 31–34).	Christ went atop a mountain and brought forth a "new law" (Matthew 5–7).
Moses was a judge in Israel (Exodus 18).	Christ is to be the judge of all (John 5:22).

Moses was noted for his meekness (Numbers 12:3).	Christ was noted for his meekness (Matthew 11:29).
Moses restored the Church in his day.	Christ restored the Church in his day.
As part of the structure of the Church in his day, Moses instituted two bodies of ecclesiastics: one of twelve men and another of seventy (Exodus 24:9–11; Numbers 7; 11; Joshua 9:15).	As part of the structure of the Church in his day, Christ instituted two bodies of ecclesiastics: one of twelve men and another of seventy (Matthew 10:1–4; Luke 10:1).
From the top of a mountain, Moses sent his disciples forward into a new promised land (Deuteronomy 3:25–28).	From the top of a mountain, Christ sent his disciples forward to prepare God's children to receive the celestial promised land (Matthew 28:16–20).
Moses spoke prophetically regarding the destiny of Israel (Deuteronomy 33).	Christ spoke prophetically regarding the destiny of Israel (Matthew 24; JS–M 1).
At the end of his mortal ministry, Moses ascended into heaven in a cloud.[46]	At the conclusion of his mortal ministry, Christ ascended into heaven in a cloud (Acts 1:9).
The second time Moses came to Israel, he was accepted by them as their liberator (Exodus 15:1–19).	When Christ returns, he will be accepted by a remnant of Israel as the spiritual liberator that he is (Zechariah 13:6; 14:1–5).
Although his name in Hebrew is traditionally believed to mean "drawn" or to "draw out," his name in Egyptian is understood to mean "son"[47] or "savior."[48]	Jesus is the Son of God and Savior of all mankind—"worlds without end."[49]

NOAH[50]	CHRIST
Noah's name means "rest" or "repose" (Genesis 5:29).	Christ is the only one who can truly provide us with rest (Matthew 11:28–29; Luke 10:5–6; Hebrews 4).
Noah was said to be "just" and "perfect" (Moses 8:27).	Christ was in all things just and perfect (Mosiah 3:18; 3 Nephi 12:48).
In direct relation to Noah's ministry, the earth was cleansed of wickedness and renewed for the righteous to inhabit (Genesis 6–9).	In direct relation to Christ's ministry, the earth will be cleansed of wickedness and renewed for the righteous to inhabit (1 Nephi 22:15–31; Articles of Faith 1:10).
As a major part of his ministry, Noah cried repentance to the people, but most did not heed his warning.[51]	As a major part of his ministry, Christ cried repentance to the people, but most did not heed his warning (Matthew 4:17; Luke 13:1–5; John 7:5).
Noah's efforts saved both man and beast (Genesis 7:1–4).	Christ's sacrifice saves both man and beast.[52]
Noah, who was the premortal Gabriel, announced the coming of Christ (Luke 1:26–38).	Jesus, who was the premortal Jehovah, announced the coming of Noah (Moses 8:1–3).
Because of mankind's sinfulness, a penalty of death was sent to cover the earth. However, Noah, one chosen from before the foundations of this earth was sent to preserve the faithful (Genesis 6–7; D&C 138:41; Abraham 3:22–23).	Because of mankind's sinfulness, a penalty of spiritual death would cover the earth. However, Christ, the One chosen from before the foundations of this earth was sent to preserve the faithful (1 Peter 1:19–21; Alma 44:4).

The pattern for the means of salvation of the righteous (the ark) would originate in heaven and would offer protection to those who obeyed, by lifting them up above the earth (Genesis 6:15–16; 7:17).	The pattern for the means of salvation of the righteous (Christ) would originate in heaven and would offer protection to those who obeyed, by lifting them up above the earth (Testimony of the Three Witnesses; John 6:42; 1 Thessalonians 4:17).
The ark was lifted up upon the water (Genesis 7:17–18).	Christ was lifted up upon the cross (Ether 4:1).
Noah was tried or tested through some forty days and forty nights of rain (Genesis 7:4).	Christ was tried or tested during some forty days and forty nights of fasting in the desert (Matthew 4:1–11).
Noah was the head of a dispensation.[53]	Christ was the head of a dispensation.[54]

SETH	CHRIST
His name means "substitute" or "appointed."[55]	Jesus was the substitute for us all, appointed to die on our behalf.[56]
Seth ruled in glory with his father (Moses 6:3–4).	Jesus rules in glory with his Father in Heaven (Revelation 11:15).
Adam, who was a type for God the Father, was Seth's father (Genesis 4:25).	Jesus is the Son of God (Mark 1:1).

PEOPLE AS TYPES FOR THE CHURCH

In the fifth chapter of Ephesians, the Apostle Paul compares the ideal relationship of a faithful husband and wife to the relationship that exists between Christ (the Bridegroom) and his church (the bride). That same symbolism is employed by John in the final chapters of the book of Revelation. The lives of many scriptural figures mirror the model of Christ's relationship with his church. First, however, the following is a singular example of how the scriptures draw upon this metaphor in an effort to establish this symbolic model.

THE NEW JERUSALEM AS A BRIDE	THE EXALTED OF CHRIST'S CHURCH
The New Jerusalem, or bride of the Lamb, is clothed in fine linen, bright and pure (Revelation 19:7–9).	The Saints must be spiritually pure and clean and have their garments "bright and pure"—having cleansed them through the blood of the Lamb (Alma 13:10–11; 34:36).
If the bride does not keep her covenants, she will find herself divorced from her groom (Revelation 18:23).	If the Saints do not keep their covenants, they will not be with Christ in the eternities. Indeed, they will remain single and separate from God and from their earthly spouses (1 Corinthians 6:9–10; D&C 132:7).
An invitation is extended to people to come and be part of the marriage supper (Matthew 22:1–10; Luke 14:12–24).	All mankind receive an invitation to follow Christ and by so doing dwell with him in his kingdom (Alma 5:33, 62; D&C 20:59).

All those who come to the wedding feast must wear the requisite garment, as dictated by the King (Matthew 22:1–14).	All those who wish to make God's kingdom their eternal abode must also accept and wear the requisite garment, as dictated by the heavenly King.[57]
The New Jerusalem is depicted as a bride leaving her former place of residence to move into her new home (Revelation 21:2).	The Saints worthy of exaltation shall leave behind the telestial and temporary to inherit a celestialized and eternal abode (D&C 88:25–27).
The bride enters her home through one of twelve[58] gates or doorways—at which there stands an angelic guard (Revelation 21).	Those who enter the celestial kingdom will do so by participating in the ordinances of the temple and keeping the covenants associated therewith.[59]
Traditionally, as part of the wedding, there is a reception and the partaking of refreshments (Luke 14:12–14; Revelation 2:7; 22:1–2, 17; 2 Nephi 13:10).	The celestial Saints shall partake of the fruit of the tree of life in that they shall dwell eternally in the presence of God and Christ (Mosiah 2:41).

Examples of scriptural couples whose marriage has been seen as a symbol for Christ's union with his bride include Abraham and Sarah, Adam and Eve, Boaz and Ruth, Isaac and Rebekah, Jacob and Rachel, and Lehi and Sariah.[60] Rebekah's willingness to answer a call to marry Isaac makes her a type for faithful covenant Israel, the bride of Christ.

REBEKAH	THE BRIDE OF CHRIST
Rebekah was worthy of her bridegroom (Isaac) through living a Christlike life filled with service and charity (Genesis 24:12–28).	Christ, our Bridegroom, has told us, "If any man will do his will, he shall know of the doctrine, whether it be of God, or whether I speak of myself" (John 7:17).
Rebekah knew a bit about her bridegroom but had never met him when she committed to marry him (Genesis 24).	We know only a little of Christ when we (as his bride) commit to enter into a covenant relationship with him.
A mortal man taught Rebekah about her prospective bridegroom, and she felt the Spirit and believed (Genesis 24).	Mortal men (prophets) reveal Christ to us, and we can feel the Spirit and know that their testimony is true (Acts 10:38–48).
Before ever meeting her bridegroom, Rebekah was blessed by him (Genesis 24:22).	Before we ever meet Christ, we partake of the blessings he freely sends us (Mosiah 4:16–26).
Rather than being forced, Rebekah chose to enter into a covenant relationship with Isaac in advance of meeting him (Genesis 24:58).	We must choose of ourselves to enter into a covenant relationship with the Bridegroom (Christ) in advance of our meeting him.
Rebekah's covenant relationship with Isaac brought her posterity and the receipt of all that Isaac had. Indeed, it brought her all of the blessings of Abraham, Isaac, and Jacob.	Our covenant relationship with Christ, if we are faithful to it, will bring us innumerable posterity and an inheritance of all that he possesses (Romans 8:17). Indeed, it will bring upon us all of the blessings of Abraham, Isaac, and Jacob. It will bring us our exaltation.

Serving as the antithesis of the positive bride typology is the unfaithful spouse as an established symbol for the covenant people in a state of apostasy or rebellion. Thus the scriptures occasionally employ the symbol of the harlot as a representation of God's covenant people leaving their covenantal obligations and following after other gods. The story of Hosea and Gomer is perhaps the best-known and most detailed scriptural example of this symbol.

HOSEA AND GOMER[61]	CHRIST AND HIS CHURCH
Hosea means "Jehovah is help," "deliverance," or "salvation."[62]	Christ is our only means of deliverance or salvation (Acts 4:10–12).
Hosea was given a divine injunction by God to take a woman to wife (Hosea 1:2).	By divine injunction from the Father, Christ has entered into a covenant relationship with Israel (Isaiah 54:5; Jeremiah 3:14; Mormon 5:14).
According to God's command, Hosea married Gomer (Hosea 1:2).	Christ has entered into a covenant with Israel that is frequently described in terms of a marriage relationship.
Hosea's wife, Gomer, was a harlot (Hosea 1:2).[63]	Israel (the bride) is unfaithful to Christ (the Bridegroom) as a harlot is unfaithful (Jeremiah 3:6–8; Ezekiel 16).
After marrying Hosea and having children by him, Gomer decided to leave him and return to her former life of immorality (Hosea 2).	Time and again the covenant people have left the world to enter into a covenant with God only to turn from those covenants, entering into apostasy and necessitating a restoration.[64]

Hosea was pained at the sins of his bride and pleaded for her return (Hosea 2).	Christ is pained at Israel's apostate actions and pleads that she repent and return to him (Helaman 13:11; 3 Nephi 9:13; 10:6).
Hosea and Gomer had three children whom the Lord commanded be named Jezreel (meaning "God will disperse or scatter"[65]), Loruhamah (meaning "not having obtained mercy"[66]), and Loammi (meaning "not my people"[67]).	Because of wickedness, idolatry and apostasy, the covenant people have often been dispersed or scattered, lost God's mercy, and been stripped of their status as God's "covenant people."
Gomer suffered for her infidelity (Hosea 2:2–13).	Destruction, bondage, and suffering are the promises given to those who forsake the Lord for other gods (Hosea 4).
Gomer came back to Hosea, and he accepted her again as his wife (Hosea 3:1–3).	Israel repeatedly apostatizes and then comes back, but Christ is ever waiting to accept her as his bride (Hoses 3:4–5).

Some seven times in the Old Testament alone, God speaks of covenant Israel as "prostituting" herself before other gods.[68] Israel is also depicted as a prostitute when she seeks out mediums and spiritualists rather than calling upon God in prayer (see Leviticus 20:6), when she relies on her own military power or on alliances with other nations instead of trusting in God for protection (see Ezekiel 23:5–6; Nahum 3:1–4), and when she places her trust in temporal things rather than in God (see Isaiah 1:21–23). The metaphor of the unfaithful bride as a symbol of the covenant people in a state of apostasy is a common image in scripture. The following model is related to this recurring theme of apostasy.

ESAU AND JACOB[69]	JUDAISM AND CHRISTIANITY
Esau represented ancient Israel, the law of Moses, and Judaism in its apostate form.	Jacob represented the new covenant that Christ would give in the form of Christianity.
By New Testament times, the "firstborn" (law of Moses) had become the stronger "nation" (or religion), just as God had told Rebekah it would (Genesis 25:23).	In New Testament times, the "secondborn" (Christianity) was a weaker "nation" (religion) than the apostate form of Judaism then prevalent.
Jacob supplanted or replaced Esau as the possessor of the birthright or chosen status (Genesis 25:34; 27:27–29).	The fulness of the gospel (Christianity) replaced the law of Moses as the "chosen" fountain of revealed religion (Matthew 5:17).
Esau lost his birthright or chosen status because he loved the things of this world more than he loved his right to spiritual blessings (Genesis 25:29–34).	Ancient Israel lost their birthright or chosen status because they loved the things of this world more than their right to spiritual blessings through their Messiah.
Jacob came to Isaac in a form that Isaac did not recognize (Genesis 27:6–33).	Christ came to the Jews in a form that they did not recognize.[70]
Jacob came to Isaac disguised in goatskin (Genesis 27:11–23).	Christ is our scapegoat and is the Lamb of God (John 1:29; 1 Nephi 10:10).

Jacob offered his father "savory" meat, bread, and wine (Genesis 27:17, 25).	Christ made an offering to his Father of the True Bread (the Bread of Life)—his crucified flesh—and the wine of his blood (John 6).
Because of his offerings, Jacob received exaltation over his brother (Genesis 27:18–33).	Because of his offering, Christ secured for himself exaltation over all nations and peoples (John 3:31; Ephesians 4:10; 1 Nephi 11:6).
Jacob's posterity became his joint heirs, inheriting all that God had given him (Genesis 35:12).	Christ's spiritual posterity will also be joint heirs with him (Romans 8:17).
Esau despised his birthright and willingly gave it up (Genesis 25:29–34).	Ancient Israel despised their Messiah and the birthright that he offered them (Isaiah 53:3).
Esau was angry at Jacob and sought to take his life (Genesis 27:41).	The Jews were angry at Christ and sought to kill both him and his followers (Acts 5:30; 1 Thessalonians 2:14).
Jacob had to flee into the wilderness in order to preserve himself (Genesis 27:41–46).	John the Revelator depicts the restored gospel in the meridian of time as fleeing "into the wilderness" (Revelation 12:6) so that it could be preserved from Satan and the apostasy.[71]
Esau and Jacob were eventually reunited (Genesis 33).	The two covenant peoples—Jews and Christians—will eventually be reunited in Christ (D&C 45:51–53).

UNNAMED PEOPLE AS TYPES

SYMBOL	INTERPRETATION
An adulterer (Proverbs 30:20; Isaiah 57:3–12; Jeremiah 3:6–11; Matthew 12:39; 16:4; Mark 8:38; James 4:4; Mosiah 1:13).	Like the harlot symbol, this represents one who is unfaithful to God and covenants by worshipping idols of *any* kind.
A baby (Leviticus 14; Hebrews 5:12; 1 Peter 2:2).	One who is immature in the gospel, a new convert to the faith, or one recently "born again."
Children (Mark 10:15; Luke 18:17; 1 John 2:12–14; 3 Nephi 9:22; 11:37–38; D&C 99:3).	One who stands innocent before God and is pure and humble, having been forgiven.
The daughter(s) of Zion.[72]	The city of Jerusalem and its inhabitants. This title is often used in the context of a call to repentance.
A hireling (Job 7:1–2; 14:6; Isaiah 16:14; 21:16; John 10:12–13).	One who is uncommitted or has inappropriate motivations.
A leper (Leviticus 13–14; 2 Kings 15; 2 Chronicles 26; Matthew 8:1–4; 10:7–8; Mark 1:40–45; Luke 17:11–19).	Those in a state of sinfulness.
A virgin (Leviticus 21:10–15; Isaiah 7:14; 62:5; Jeremiah 31:4; Matthew 1:23; Luke 1:27; 1 Corinthians 7:34; 2 Corinthians 11:2–3; 1 Nephi 11; 2 Nephi 17:14; Alma 7:10).	One who is pure, undefiled by the world, faithful to covenants, and acceptable to the Lord. This image is the antithesis of the whore or harlot symbol.

NAMED PEOPLE AS NON-CHRISTOCENTRIC TYPES

AARON	OLIVER COWDERY
Aaron was divinely appointed to serve as a spokesman for the prophet Moses (Exodus 4:10–17).	Oliver was divinely appointed to serve as a spokesman for the Prophet Joseph Smith (D&C 28:1–4).
Aaron served as a second witness to the words of the prophet Moses (Exodus 4:29–31).	Oliver served as a second witness to the words of the Prophet Joseph Smith (D&C 6:28).
Aaron was privileged to see Christ in vision (Exodus 24:9–10).	Oliver was privileged to see Christ in vision (D&C 110:1–4).
Aaron was the first in his dispensation to be ordained to the Aaronic Priesthood (Exodus 39–40).[73]	Oliver was the first in his dispensation to be ordained to the Aaronic Priesthood (D&C 13; JS–H 1:68–71).
Aaron faltered when he made the golden calf (Exodus 32:1–6, 21–25).	Oliver faltered and was excommunicated on 12 April 1838.[74]
Aaron repented of his apostate actions and died in full fellowship.[75]	Oliver repented of his apostate actions and died in full fellowship.[76]
Aaron had delegated to him power and authority (Exodus 4:16; 40).	Oliver had the "gift of Aaron," which was a delegated power and authority (D&C 8:6–9).
Aaron was given a rod that both he and Moses used in the performance of miracles (Exodus 7:9, 19; 8:5, 16; Numbers 20:8).	Oliver is said to have received a rod or staff with which he would bring to pass miracles.[77]

ADAM	GOD THE FATHER
Adam was the earthly father of all mankind.	God is the Heavenly Father of the spirits of all mankind (Acts 17:28–29).
Adam had a righteous and obedient son (Abel).	God had a righteous and obedient Son (Jesus).
Adam had a rebellious son (Cain) who became perdition (Moses 5:24).	God had a rebellious son (Lucifer) who became perdition (D&C 76:26).
Adam's righteous son Abel was murdered by his evil brother, Cain (Genesis 4:8).	God's righteous Son, Jesus, was caused to be murdered by his evil brother, Lucifer (John 17:12).
Adam's son Seth looked just like his father (D&C 107:43).	God's firstborn Son, Jesus, looked just like his Father in Heaven (Hebrews 1:3).[78]

ABRAHAM	GOD THE FATHER
Abraham's birth name, Abram, means "exalted father."[79]	God the Father is an exalted man.[80]
The name Abraham means "father of a multitude."[81]	God the Father is the literal father of a multitude of spirit offspring (Acts 17:28–29; Hebrews 12:9).
Abraham offered up as a sacrifice his only son begotten through his wife, Sarah (Genesis 21:1–3; 22).	God the Father offered up as a sacrifice for sins his Only Begotten Son in the flesh, Jesus (John 3:16).
Abraham offered his son as a sacrifice when Isaac was in his thirties.[82]	God's Son, Jesus, was approximately thirty-three years old when he gave his life on our behalf.[83]

Abraham offered Isaac on Mount Moriah (Genesis 22:2).	The same group of hills commonly called Mount Moriah was the site on which Jesus, Son of the Father, offered himself as a ransom for the sins of the world (Mark 15:22).
The name of Abraham's son Isaac has traditionally been interpreted as meaning "to laugh." However, some biblical scholars reject that rendering of the Hebrew and insist that it means "to rejoice" or, more literally, "El [or God] rejoices" over him.[84]	God's Only Begotten Son in the flesh, Jesus, gives us cause to rejoice, and without question the Father rejoices because of what Christ has done.
Abraham, as the father of Isaac, found this obligatory sacrifice very painful, though of saving necessity.[85]	God the Father, as Christ's Father, found this obligatory sacrifice very painful, though of saving necessity.[86]

ABRAHAM[87]	JOSEPH OF EGYPT (AND MOSES)
There was a famine in the land (Genesis 12:10).	There was a famine in the land (Genesis 41:54).
"When he drew near to go into Egypt . . ." (Genesis 12:11).	"When they came toward the land of Goshen . . ." (Genesis 46:28).
"He said to Sarai his wife . . ." (Genesis 12:11).	"Joseph said to his brothers . . ." (Genesis 46:31).
"And it shall come to pass when the Egyptians see you, they will say . . ." (Genesis 12:12).	"And it shall come to pass when Pharaoh calls you, he will say . . ." (Genesis 46:33).

Abraham tells Sarai what she should say to the Egyptians (Genesis 12:15).	Joseph tells his brothers what they should say to Pharaoh (Genesis 46:34).
"... that it might be well with me on account of you" (Genesis 12:13).	"... that you might dwell in the land of Goshen" (Genesis 46:34).
"And the officers of Pharaoh saw her and declared it to Pharaoh" (Genesis 12:15).	"And Joseph came and declared to Pharaoh..." (Genesis 47:1).
"And the wife was taken into the house of Pharaoh" (Genesis 12:15).	"And Pharaoh said... settle your father and brothers in the best part of the land" (Genesis 47:5–6).
"And Abraham acquired sheep and cattle" (Genesis 12:16).	"Put them in charge of my livestock" (Genesis 47:6). "They acquired property and were fruitful and increased greatly" (Genesis 47:27).
"And the Lord struck Pharaoh with great plagues" (Genesis 12:17).	"One more plague I will bring against Pharaoh" (Exodus 11:1).
"And Pharaoh called Abram and said..." (Genesis 12:18).	"And Pharaoh called Moses and Aaron and said..." (Exodus 12:31).
Take your wife and go (Genesis 12:19).	Take your people and go (Exodus 12:31–32).
The Egyptians sent them away (Genesis 12:20).	The Egyptians sent them away (Exodus 12:33).
"And Abram went up from Egypt" (Genesis 13:1).	"And the sons of Israel traveled from" Egypt (Exodus 12:33).

"And Lot went with him" (Genesis 13:1).	"And also a great mixed multitude went with him" (Exodus 12:38).
"And Abram was very rich with livestock, silver, and gold" (Genesis 13:2).	"And they had very much livestock" (Exodus 12:38) and "silver and gold" (v. 35).
Abraham worshipped God for bringing him up out of Egypt (Genesis 13:4).	The children of Israel worshipped God for bringing them up out of Egypt (Exodus 15).

ABRAHAM[88]	JOSEPH SMITH
Abraham was foreordained to his prophetic calling (Abraham 3:22–23).	Joseph was foreordained to his prophetic calling (D&C 127:2).[89]
As one reared without the priesthood in his home, Abraham was chosen by God to be a recipient of that divine authority (D&C 84:14; Abraham 2:9–11).	As one reared without the priesthood in his home, Joseph was chosen by God to be a recipient of that divine authority (D&C 13; 128:20).
Abraham was a mighty preacher of the gospel (Genesis 18–19; Facsimile 3).	Joseph was a mighty preacher of the gospel.[90]
Abraham encountered formidable opposition (Abraham 1:5–17; Facsimile 1).	Joseph encountered formidable opposition (D&C 127:1–3).
Abraham spoke face to face with divine messengers and with God himself (Genesis 18; Abraham 2:6).	Joseph spoke face to face with divine messengers and with God himself (D&C 13; 110; JS–H 1:16–17).

Abraham was in possession of and employed a Urim and Thummim (Abraham 3:1–4).	Joseph was in possession of and employed a Urim and Thummim (JS–H 1:35, 62).
Abraham translated Egyptian records (Facsimile 3).	Joseph translated ancient Egyptian records.[91]
Abraham wrote scripture.[92]	Joseph wrote scripture.[93]
Abraham founded an influential community of believers dedicated to God.[94]	Joseph founded an influential community of Saints dedicated to God.[95]
Abraham is believed to have been fourteen years old when he petitioned God to know where to find the truth in the apostate world in which he lived.[96]	Joseph was fourteen years old when he petitioned God to know where to find the truth in the apostate world in which he lived (JS–H 1:16–17).
Abraham is known for introducing the Abrahamic covenant even though it did not originate with him (Genesis 15).	Joseph is known for introducing the Abrahamic covenant even though it did not originate with him (D&C 132).
Abraham was the first of three prophets in his immediate family: Abraham, Isaac, and Jacob.	Joseph was the first of three prophets and Church presidents in his family: Joseph Smith Jr., Joseph F. Smith, and Joseph Fielding Smith.
Abraham practiced the principle of plural marriage (Genesis 16:1–4; 25:1).	Joseph practiced the principle of plural marriage (D&C 132:1–55).

ENOCH	JOSEPH SMITH
Enoch built the city of Zion (Moses 7:19).	Joseph built numerous Zion communities in various cities of the United States.[97]
Enoch gathered the righteous together out of the wicked world that surrounded them (Moses 7:20–21).	Joseph gathered the righteous together out of the wicked world that surrounded them.
Enoch taught his people to live the law of consecration (Moses 7:18).	Joseph taught his people to live the law of consecration (D&C 6:6; 11:6; 12:6; 14:6; 42:32–39).
Enoch means "dedicated to Jehovah."[98]	Joseph's willingness to give his life for the gospel is evidence of his dedication to Jehovah. Joseph was also called "Enoch" in early editions of the Doctrine and Covenants (D&C 78:1, 4, 9).
Enoch was a visionary man (Moses 7:20–21, 23–24).	Joseph was a visionary man (D&C 76; 110; 128; JS–H 1:24, 30–32).
Enoch had great priesthood power (Moses 7:13).	Joseph had great priesthood power.[99]
Enoch believed in and upheld a theocratic government.[100]	Joseph taught of and sought to establish a theocracy.[101]
Enoch saw in vision Satan and the influence he would have over the world (Moses 7:24–26).	Joseph both saw in vision and experienced firsthand Lucifer and his power (D&C 76:25–29; JS–H 1:15).
Enoch's teachings were such that many of his people were enabled to see God and have their calling and election made sure (Moses 7:69).[102]	Joseph's teachings were such that many of his people were enabled to see God and have their calling and election made sure (D&C 76:14, 23; 110:2).[103]

JOHN THE BAPTIST[104]	JOSEPH SMITH
The New Testament describes John as one who was rough and unsophisticated, hailing from the wilderness (Matthew 3:1–4).	Joseph was said to be rough and unsophisticated, coming from the wilderness (farm).[105]
John raised a voice of warning as the "Elias" (or forerunner) who was sent by God to prepare the way before the Savior's first coming (JST, Mark 9:3; JST, John 1:21–28; D&C 27:7).	Joseph raised a voice of warning as the "Elias" (or forerunner) who was sent by God to prepare the way before the Savior's second coming (JST, John 1:21–28).
John's preaching focused heavily on requisite repentance and the restoration of the gospel (Matthew 3:2).	Joseph's message focused heavily on requisite repentance and the restoration of the fulness of the gospel (D&C 19; 128:17).
John died as a martyr because of what he preached (Mark 6:14–18).	Joseph died as a martyr because of the message he preached.[106]
Upon John's death, his head was severed from his body (Matthew 14:8; Mark 6:25).	It is claimed that, upon Joseph's death, some tried to sever his head.[107]

JOSEPH OF EGYPT[108]	JOSEPH SMITH
Joseph's name has been interpreted as meaning "the Lord addeth," "he will add," "increaser," "he who gathers," "he who causes to return," and "God gathereth."[109]	Joseph Smith not only possessed this name, he exemplified its meaning. He added much to Christianity's knowledge of God and his plan, and he was also sent to gather the elect of the house of Israel in the last days.

Joseph was of humble beginnings, e.g., Joseph began his Egyptian career as a slave (Genesis 37:28, 36; 39:1, 20).	Joseph Smith was of humble beginnings (JS–H 1:46).
Joseph had visions in his youth (Genesis 37:5–10).	Joseph Smith had visions in his youth (JS–H 1:16, 30, 44, 46, 49).
Joseph was hated for his visionary gifts (Genesis 37:4, 8, 11, 18–20).	Joseph Smith was hated for his visionary gifts (JS–H 1:25).
Joseph was falsely accused (Genesis 39:7–20).	Joseph Smith was falsely accused (D&C 122).
Joseph acted generously toward those who betrayed him (Genesis 42–46).	Joseph Smith treated generously those who betrayed him.[110]
Joseph was imprisoned for something he had not done (Genesis 39:7–20).	Joseph Smith was imprisoned numerous times for things he had not done.[111]
Joseph knew intimately what it was like to be imprisoned in a pit (Genesis 37:24).	In a proverbial sense Joseph Smith knew what it was like to be in a "pit" much of his life (D&C 122:7).
Joseph prophesied much of the future (Genesis 37:5–11; 40–41).	Joseph Smith prophesied much of the future.[112]
Joseph knew the pains of being separated from his family and friends (Genesis 42:24; 43:30; 45:14; 46:29).	Joseph Smith knew the pains of being separated from his family and friends (D&C 122:6).
Joseph was amazingly resilient amid adversity (Genesis 37–46).	Joseph Smith was amazingly resilient amid adversity.[113]

MORMON[114]	JOSEPH SMITH
Mormon was a "sober child" and "quick to observe" (Mormon 1:2).	Joseph was "a remarkably quiet, well-disposed child."[115]
Mormon was a "pure descendant of Lehi" and thus from Joseph of Egypt (1 Nephi 5:14; 2 Nephi 3:4; 3 Nephi 5:20).	Joseph was "a descendent of Joseph of Egypt" (2 Nephi 3:11, 15).
Mormon was named after his father (Mormon 1:5).	Joseph was named after his father (2 Nephi 3:15).[116]
Mormon was seen in vision by his ancestors (1 Nephi 12:14–19).	Joseph was seen in vision by his ancestors (2 Nephi 3:5).
Mormon was carried by his father into the land southward (Mormon 1:6).	Joseph went south with his father, from Vermont to New York (JS–H 1:3).
At fifteen years of age, Mormon was visited by God (Mormon 1:15).	In his fifteenth year, Joseph was visited by God (JS–H 1:7, 16).
Mormon was instructed by older prophets regarding his mission and role in the Church and kingdom of God (Mormon 1:2–4).	Joseph was instructed by ancient prophets regarding his mission and role in the Church and kingdom of God (JS–H 1:27–54).[117]
Mormon was ministered to by heavenly messengers (Mormon 8:10–11).	Joseph was ministered to by heavenly messengers (JS–H 1:29–35)[118]
Mormon was a man of large stature (Mormon 2:1).	Joseph was a man of large stature.[119]
Mormon was commanded to go to the hill Shim to dig up the plates (Mormon 1:3–4).	Joseph was commanded to go to the hill Cumorah to dig up the plates (JS–H 1:51).

Mormon did not remove all of the plates from the hill (Mormon 1:4).	Joseph did not remove all of the plates from the hill.[120]
In his twenty-fourth year, Mormon began recording on the plates what he had seen (Mormon 1:3–4).	In his twenty-fourth year, Joseph began translating what was on the plates (JS–H 1:66–67).
Mormon gathered his people into one body, at the hill Cumorah, to try to escape persecution (Mormon 6).	Joseph gathered his people into one body—eventually in Illinois—to try to escape persecution.
Mormon sealed his testimony with his blood (Mormon 8:3).	Joseph sealed his testimony with his blood (D&C 135:1; 136:39).
Mormon's charisma made him a natural leader; he served as captain of the Nephite army for some fifty-eight years (Mormon 2).	Joseph's charisma made him a natural leader; he served as lieutenant general of the Nauvoo Legion (*History of the Church*, 4:296).
Mormon gave a poignant farewell address prior to his death (Mormon 6:17).	Joseph gave a powerful farewell address prior to his death.[121]
In the face of evil against him, Mormon maintained charity and forgiveness (Mormon 2:18; Moroni 9:3–6).	In the face of evil against him, Joseph maintained charity and forgiveness.[122]
From the time he was called, Mormon never ceased to labor in the gospel cause (Moroni 9:6).	From the time he was called, Joseph never ceased labor in the gospel cause.[123]
Unlike some (such as King David), Mormon was faithful his entire life.[124]	Unlike many of his associates, Joseph was faithful his entire life (D&C 135:3).

Mormon's calling and election was made sure while he was in the flesh (Mormon 2:19).	Joseph's calling and election was made sure while he was in the flesh (D&C 132:49).
Mormon saw the end of a great civilization and the beginning of a great apostasy.	Joseph saw the end of the Great Apostasy and the beginning of a great civilization (Zion).
As the author and abridger of the Book of Mormon, Mormon led a life focused on preparing the stick of Joseph so the world might know that Jesus is the Christ.	As the translator of the Book of Mormon, Joseph led a life focused on preparing the stick of Joseph so the world might know that Jesus is the Christ.

MOSES	BRIGHAM YOUNG
Moses was converted to the gospel as an adult (Exodus 3).[125]	Brigham was converted to the gospel as an adult.[126]
Moses was a political leader stripped of his governmental authority by corrupt political officials.[127]	Brigham was a political leader stripped of his governmental authority by corrupt political officials.[128]
Moses had to leave Egypt because of a combination of negative public opinion and the corrupt government (Exodus 2:14–15).	Brigham and his people were chased out of Nauvoo by a combination of negative public opinion and the corrupt government.[129]
Moses fled into the desert (Exodus 2:15; 3:1).	Brigham and his people fled into the desert.[130]
Moses had a vision of the earth's inhabitants from the beginning of the world to its end (Moses 1:8).	Brigham had a vision of the earth's inhabitants from the beginning of the world to its end.[131]

Moses	Brigham
Moses was the prophet who succeeded Joseph of old.	Brigham was the prophet who succeeded Joseph Smith.
Moses led an exodus to the promised land.	Brigham led an exodus to a promised land.
Moses established captains over the Israelites (Exodus 18).	Brigham established captains over the Mormon pioneers (D&C 136).
Moses, by the command of God, built a tabernacle in which were administered the ordinances requisite for covenant Israel (D&C 124:38).	Brigham, by the command of God, built temples in which are administered the ordinances requisite for covenant Israel.[132]
Moses is believed to have practiced the law of plural marriage.[133]	Brigham was commanded by God to practice plural marriage.
Moses led the Church for approximately forty years.[134]	Brigham presided over the Twelve and then the Church for nearly forty years.[135]

MOSES[136]	JOSEPH SMITH
Moses was mighty in writing but not in speaking.[137]	Joseph was mighty in writing but not in speaking (2 Nephi 3:17).[138]
Moses saw and spoke with Jehovah (Exodus 33).[139]	Joseph saw and spoke with Jehovah (JS–H 1:16–20).
The Lord gave Moses a spokesman in Aaron (Exodus 4:10–17).	The Lord gave Joseph a spokesman in Sidney Rigdon (2 Nephi 3:18; D&C 100:9–11).
Moses depended largely on his brother Aaron (Exodus 4:10–17).	Joseph depended largely on his brother Hyrum (D&C 135:3).

Moses held the keys of the gathering of Israel (D&C 110:11).	Joseph received the keys of the gathering of Israel from Moses (D&C 110:11).
Moses was given the name Moses by the daughter of the pharaoh (Exodus 2:10).	Brigham Young referred to Joseph as a modern "Moses."[140]
Moses led ancient Israel on an exodus out of Egypt (Exodus 14).	Joseph led modern Israel on an exodus from New York, Ohio, and Missouri.[141]
Moses saw the land of promise but was not permitted to enter it (Deuteronomy 34:1–4).	Joseph prophetically saw that the Saints would enter the Salt Lake Valley but was not permitted to enter it.[142]
Moses introduced a new and higher law to ancient Israel, who had been living in apostasy.[143]	Joseph introduced a new and higher law to modern Israel, who had been living in apostasy.[144]
Moses performed miracles through the power of God (Exodus 4; 7–12; 14).	Joseph performed miracles through the power of God.[145]
Moses encountered opposition from friends and enemies (Exodus 2:15; Numbers 12:1; 16:1–3).	Joseph encountered opposition from friends and enemies (D&C 121–122).
Moses was the head of his dispensation.[146]	Joseph was the head of the dispensation of the fulness of times.[147]

NEPHI[148]	JOSEPH SMITH
Nephi was young when visited by the Lord (1 Nephi 2:16).	Joseph was only fourteen years old when the Lord first appeared to him (JS–H 1:7, 16–17).
Nephi was large in stature (1 Nephi 2:16).	Joseph was large in stature.[149]
Nephi was entrusted with plates that God deemed highly sacred (1 Nephi 1:17; 5).	Joseph was entrusted with plates that God deemed highly sacred (JS–H 1:59).
Nephi was called by the Lord to be both the spiritual and temporal leader of his people (1 Nephi 3:29; 2 Nephi 5:19).	Joseph was called by the Lord to be both the spiritual and temporal leader of his people (D&C 1:38; 21:5).[150]
Nephi gave important doctrinal discourses to his people (1 Nephi 6; 15; 19; 22; 2 Nephi 5; 11; 25–33).	Joseph gave important doctrinal discourses to his people.[151]
Nephi bore witness of the divinity of Christ (1 Nephi 19:8; 2 Nephi 11:2; 25; 26:1).	Joseph bore witness of the divinity of Christ (D&C 76:22–23; 110:2; JS–H 1:23–25).

PAUL[152]	JOSEPH SMITH
Paul's given name at birth was Saul, but his name was later changed to Paul (Acts 13:9).	On several occasions the Prophet Joseph noted that he "felt like Paul" (D&C 127:2; JS–H 1:24).
Paul had a "first vision" (Acts 26:12–23).	Joseph had a "first vision" (JS–H 1:16–25).
Paul delayed telling others the details regarding what he saw in his vision of Christ.[153]	Joseph delayed telling others the details regarding what he saw in his vision of Christ.[154]
There exist several accounts of Paul's vision, but the most detailed version was given last (Acts 26:9–20).	There exist several accounts of Joseph's First Vision, but the most detailed account came after several others were recorded.[155]
Paul had more than one vision of the resurrected Lord (Acts 18:9–10; 22:17–21; 23:11; 2 Corinthians 12:1–4).	Joseph had more than one vision of the resurrected Lord (D&C 76:22–24; 110:1–10; 137:1–3).
Paul gave insightful doctrinal instruction.[156]	Joseph gave insightful doctrinal instruction.[157]
Paul was considered a "blasphemer" and anti-Jewish by his contemporaries.[158]	Joseph was considered a "blasphemer" and non-Christian by his contemporaries.[159]
Paul had a vision of the three degrees of glory (1 Corinthians 15).	Joseph had a vision of the three degrees of glory (D&C 76).

Paul sacrificed beyond measure for the work to which he was called, including enduring a great deal of persecution and temporal impoverishment (2 Corinthians 11:24–28).	Joseph sacrificed beyond measure for the work to which he was called, including enduring frequent persecution and financial impoverishment.[160]
Paul bore a powerful testimony of the truthfulness of the gospel until the day of his martyrdom (Acts 28:23).	Joseph bore a powerful testimony of the truthfulness of the gospel until the day of his martyrdom.[161]
Paul anticipated his martyrdom (2 Timothy 4:6).	Joseph anticipated his martyrdom (D&C 5:22; 6:29–30).
Paul was beheaded.[162]	Mobocrats attempted to behead Joseph.[163]

CAIN	LUCIFER
Cain was a "tiller of the ground" (Moses 5:17). The earth is a standard type for things temporal, worldly, and temporary.[164]	Lucifer's works are of a temporal, worldly, and fleeting nature.
Cain loved Satan and his ways more than he loved God and his ways, probably because Satan seeks power for himself by oppressing others for eternity, whereas God gives his power to as many as will have it (Moses 5:18).	Satan loves himself and desires to be empowered over all mankind throughout all eternity.

Cain's offering was unacceptable because it was not sacrificial and did not involve the shedding of blood (Moses 5:19–21).	Lucifer's offering required no sacrifice of us or him and didn't require the shedding of blood by a Savior, all contrary to God's plan.
Cain was angry that his offering was rejected (Moses 5:21).	When the Father rejected Lucifer's conditional offer to function as the Savior, Lucifer became violently angry and "kept not his first estate" (Abraham 3:28).
Cain's countenance fell (Moses 5:21).	Satan fell (D&C 76:26).
Cain was called perdition (Moses 5:24).	The devil is called perdition and is the father of the sons of perdition (John 17:12; D&C 76:26).
Cain rejected the Father and his counsel (Moses 5:25).	Lucifer rejected the Father's counsel and plan in the premortal life.
Cain would not listen to his father, Adam, nor to his brother Abel (Moses 5:12–13, 26).	Lucifer did not listen to his Father in Heaven nor to his Elder Brother Jesus Christ.
Cain's parents mourned over him and those who followed him (Moses 5:27).	Father and Mother in Heaven surely mourned the loss of Lucifer and his followers.
Cain slew his brother, thus sealing his own fate and destroying his own work (Moses 5:32–36).	Satan "slew" his brother Jesus, thus destroying his own work (for it brought to pass the Atonement).

Cain convinced many of his brothers and sisters to follow him (Moses 5:27–28, 41).	A third part of the hosts of heaven followed Lucifer (Revelation 12:3–4).
Cain became a fugitive and vagabond on the earth (Moses 5:37).	The devil wanders the earth as a fugitive and a vagabond.
Cain accused someone else for his evils (Moses 5:38).	Satan proclaimed that he was only doing that which had been done in other worlds.[165]
Cain was cast out of the presence of the Lord forever (Moses 5:39, 41).	Satan was permanently cast out of God's presence for his rebellion (Revelation 12:9).
Cain is said to be the father or mastermind of much wickedness (Moses 5:24, 31, 51).	The devil is the father of lies and the mastermind behind all wickedness (2 Nephi 9:9).
Cain was not to be killed by men but only by God (Moses 5:40).	No man can destroy Satan. Only God has this power over him.[166]
Cain was given an external, physical mark by which he could be recognized (Moses 5:40).	D&C 129 indicates that Lucifer too received an external mark: The lack of a physical body allows him to be detected and recognized.

9
NAMES AS SYMBOLS

In modern Western culture, more often than not, names are selected based on current societal trends or on how good a given name sounds with the newborn's surname. True, some people select "family names" in order to honor someone from a previous generation. Yet the average parent today does not see the meaning and value in the names of his or her ancient counterparts.[1] Indeed, one text notes, "When contrasted with their general devaluation in the modern West, the significance of naming and the wide attestation of renaming and the giving of hidden names in the ancient world is astonishing."[2] Elsewhere we read:

> It is a standard view today that names, as well as concrete or abstract terms, are no more than a *flatus vocis*, a mere sound. This tendency to reduce language to whimsical convention without concern for more profound origins may be symptomatic of the secularization of men and even the trivialization of life itself. At any rate, it reflects a diminishing of the religious consciousness that some names were thought anciently to be of divine origin.[3]

The giving of a name was once a sacred, significant, and meaningful experience. And the invoking of one's name—or the name of another—also held a great deal of significance in ancient societies. The use of a person's name in regard to something implied ownership, possession, or responsibility. In this way, when a person enters into the covenant of baptism, and in so doing takes upon himself or herself the name of Christ, that person belongs to Christ.[4] "The phrase 'in [so-and-so's] name' can indicate status (Mt. 10:41–42; Mk. 9:41), impersonation (Mt. 24:5), responsibility (Esth. 2:22; Eph. 5:20) or purpose (Ps. 118:26; Mt. 18:20). Usually, however, it claims delegated authority."[5]

In the esoteric ordinances of many ancient societies, there was a belief that if one were in possession of a secret name, that name would need to be guarded with the utmost care. For another to discover your secret or esoteric name would, it was believed, give the discoverer power over you.[6]

In most civilizations of the past, a very high value was placed upon having one's name live on after one's death (see Genesis 48:16; Numbers 27:4; Deuteronomy 25:6–7; Ruth 4:10; 1 Samuel 24:21; 2 Samuel 14:7; 18:18; Psalm 41:5; Ecclesiastes 6:4; Isaiah 56:5). Similarly, scripture promised the wicked that their names would "rot," be "blotted out," or not have "honor" associated with them (see Genesis 11:4, 8; Deuteronomy 25:10; Job 18:17; Psalm 34:16; 49:11–12; 83:4; Proverbs 10:7; Isaiah 14:22; 65:15; Zephaniah 1:4; Mosiah 1:12; 5:11; 26:36; Alma 1:24; 5:57; 6:3; Moroni 6:7; D&C 20:83).

In ancient scripture, names were generally given in order to indicate something about the nature,[7] character,[8] experience,[9] or function of the person,[10] place, or nation named.[11] It was common in antiquity for a name to capture the essence or experience of a person.[12] Thus, in Hebrew society parents would often choose a name either in the hope the child would live up to the connotations of the name[13] or because of some circumstance or event surrounding his or her birth.[14] Rachel named her son Benoni ("son of my sorrow") because her labor was so hard that in the end it cost her her life (Genesis 35:18). Hannah named her boy Samuel ("heard of God") because she believed the boy to be an answer to her prayers (1 Samuel 1:20). Hagar named her child Ishmael ("the Lord hears") because an angel commanded her to do so as a token of the fact that God had heard, and would continue to hear, her in her afflictions (see Genesis 16:11). Upon hearing the tragic news that her husband had been killed, her nation had been defeated, the ark of the covenant had been captured, and her father-in-law had suddenly passed away, Phinehas's pregnant wife went into labor and delivered a son whom she named, just before she died, Ichabod ("no glory" or "the glory has departed") in recognition of what had taken place in her life and nation (see 1 Samuel 4:21). Rachel named her firstborn son Joseph ("he shall add" or "increase") as a sign of her faith that God was not yet finished blessing her (see Genesis 30:24).[15]

A frequent occurrence in scripture is the practice of renaming an individual at some stage in his or her life:

> Formal renamings register a change in personality and signal a new phase of one's life. Abram, Sarai, and Oshea have their names replaced (Gen 17:5, 15; Num 13:16); Naomi in her sorrow thinks that she should (Ruth 1:20). Jacob, Gideon, and Solomon are given supplementary names, Israel, Jerubbaal, Jedediah—nicknames, in the old sense. So also, in the NT, are James and John (Boanerges), Simon (Cephas/Peter), the Cypriot Joseph (Barnabas) and Thomas/Didymus (Aramaic and Greek for "twin"; his true name was Judas, according to patristic tradition).... Daniel's new name, Beltesshazzar, contains the name of the god Bel (Dan 4:8).[16]

New names or titles are relatively common in modern times also. Depending on their cultural background, people may receive them at birth, at baptism, upon ordination, upon making certain temple covenants, and in some cases upon marriage. Each of these events signals a new stage in one's life, and so does the accompanying name. One dictionary of scriptural names indicates that each of those names has meaning—so much so that sometimes when people's nature changed, God changed their names also.[17] Elsewhere we read, "If naming constituted the giving of an identity, the giving of a new name gave a new identity to the recipient, and was frequently associated with an important transition in the recipient's life."[18]

Just as the names of people were highly significant in antiquity, so also were the names that the ancients assigned to their cities. Place names often commemorate events in history. For example, the name Babel ("confusion") was bestowed in commemoration of the confusion of the languages resulting from the building of the pseudo-temple known as the Tower of Babel (see Genesis 11:9). Genesis 32:30 records that Jacob named the place where he received a heavenly visitation Peniel ("the face of God"). After the barges had been prepared, Mahonri Moriancumer is said to have ascended a mountain that the "pilgrims" had named Shelem. *Zebach Shelem* is said to be Hebrew for "thank offering," suggesting that this mount had been set apart for sacred purposes (see Leviticus 7:12, 15; 22:27).[19] In recording that the Nephites drove the Lamanites into a northern land called Hermounts— a land "infested by wild and ravenous beasts" (Alma 2:37)— the Book of Mormon may reflect the adoption of an Egyptian name with that very meaning: Hermonthis, the god "of wild places" and "wild things." Bethlehem ("house of bread") was, appropriately so, the name of the city in which Jesus, the "Bread of Life," was born. It should be clear that, along with personal names, place names should not be ignored when reading scripture.[20]

Before we turn our attention to examples of other symbolic names in scripture, it should be noted that there are more than seventeen hundred references to the word *name* and its inflected forms in the standard works of the Church. Additionally, well over three thousand different people are mentioned by name in the scriptures, let alone the many references to places with symbolic names. Space constraints will not permit our listing here all of the names with symbolic connotations. An exhaustive dictionary of scriptural names would fill volumes. Thus we will consider here only a few examples from each letter of the alphabet. The primary design of this chapter is to alert the reader to the significance of scriptural names and to encourage further study of their meanings. Although the

LDS Bible Dictionary defines many biblical names,[21] the serious student would do well to invest in one or two Bible dictionaries, name dictionaries, or Hebrew and Greek lexicons in order to have on hand more complete resources for interpreting scriptural names.[22]

SYMBOLIC NAMES IN SCRIPTURE

Abel

This Hebrew name is traditionally understood to mean "transitory" or "fading away."[23] Such seems appropriate in light of Abel's abbreviated life. Louis Ginzberg wrote, "After a while, Eve bore [another] son, whom she named Hebel, because, she said, he was born but to die."[24] "Hebel" is the English transliteration of the Hebrew name "Abel."

Aha

This Egyptian name means "warrior."[25] Thus we see it appropriately utilized as the name of one of the Book of Mormon's Nephite generals (Alma 16:5).

Ammon

This Egyptian name, in its various forms (Ammon, Amon, Ahman, Amen), is very common in ancient texts. Hugh Nibley noted the following: "There are more Ammon names and Amon compounds than anything else because actually in the time of Lehi *Amon* was the god of the empire. It was the one time when God filled the earth. Amon filled the earth with the Egyptian Empire. They claimed everything, but always in the name of *Amon*. We have the marvelous sermons of Wenamun, the Egyptian ambassador to the court of Biblos. He was on business there when he talked about 'Amon who rules all the seas and rules all nations.' We have songs in which we refer to Adam-ondi-Ahman and Amon as an epithet for God. Actually, it means 'the one who is not known, the secret one whom we can't name, whose name is not known to us.'"[26]

Balaam

This Hebrew name means "destruction of the people." It was the title of the infamously disobedient priesthood holder of Numbers 22–24, who ignored the council of the Lord (see Numbers 22:12, 20–35) and sought to help Israel's enemies in the hope of acquiring temporal gain. The result of his actions was the apostasy of Israel (see Numbers 31:16; Revelation 2:14).

Barabbas

This Greek name means literally the "son of a father," but by implication it means "son of *a* man." Matthew 27:18–26 tells us that Barabbas was the prisoner the Jews chose over Jesus to be released at the annual Passover pardon by the governor. The name *Barabbas* seems significant in the book of Matthew for two reasons. First, in the most ancient manuscripts of the New Testament, we learn that both Barabbas and Christ had the same personal name: Jesus Barabbas and Jesus the Christ.[27] Second, Pilate's declaration seems prophetic and revealing: "Therefore when they were gathered together, Pilate said unto them, Whom will ye that I release unto you? [Jesus] Barabbas [Jesus the 'son of a father' or 'son of *a* man'] or Jesus [the 'Son of Man'] which is called Christ?" (Matthew 27:17). They chose the "son of *a* man"—a mere mortal—and commanded that "the Son of Man" (Moses 6:57)—a God in mortal form—be put to death!

Beelzebub

This Greek and Ugaritic name is traditionally understood to mean "Baal, the Prince," which was the title of the chief god of Ekron[28] (a city on the border between the Israelites and the Philistines). Over time Beelzebub became the name of the "chief of demons" in early Jewish demonology. Thus, by applying the name to Jesus (see Matthew 10:25; 12:24), it appears that the Pharisees were simply implying that if Christ did in reality have power to "cast out demons," the source of that power was either the false god Baal or the chief of Lucifer's hosts.

CAESAR

This Greek surname of Julius Caesar was adopted by Octavius Augustus and his successors. It was eventually appropriated by the Roman emperors as part of their title. It means "one cut out." This is very curious in light of the fact that in New Testament times it was the title and office of Caesar that the masses appeared to be so concerned with showing respect to, over and above their true King (see Luke 23:2; John 19:12, 15). Yet Caesar and his successors are dead—"cut out," as it were—and Christ lives![29]

CHEMISH

Of this Book of Mormon name, Hugh Nibley has written: "Chemish is the same as the Latin *Quintus*. It means *the fifth*, either the fifth son, or the fifth in line of succession. Is he fifth? He looks more like sixth. If you have Jacob, Enos, Jarom, Omni, and Amaron, that would make him the sixth. Unless it is after Jacob. Who knows? Anyway it is a perfectly good Semitic name which means *the fifth*. It's a common proper name too."[30] Chemish may have been the fifth son of Omni.

CLAUDIUS

This Greek name means "lame," and appropriately so, for Claudius was the name of the fourth Roman emperor, who weakly reigned from about A.D. 41–54. He was chosen to govern mainly through the pull of Herod Agrippa the First. During Claudius's reign there were devastating famines arising from unfavorable harvests (see Acts 11:28–30). Eventually, he was provoked by the tumult of the Jews in Rome to expel them from the city (see Acts 18:2). After a weak and foolish reign, the "lame" emperor was poisoned by his fourth wife.

DANIEL

This Hebrew name means "God is my judge." It seems quite appropriate in light of the fact that one of the chief themes of the book of Daniel is his judgment and condemnation for breaking the corrupt laws of man. Daniel stands as the epitome of one who truly believed that men should fear only God (see Ecclesiastes 12:13) and not other men (see D&C 122:9).

Delilah

This was the Hebrew name of the Philistine mistress of Samson who betrayed him by revealing the secret of his great strength. The name means "feeble," "weak," or "delicate." Delilah cut off Samson's hair and by so doing enfeebled or weakened him.

Deseret

This is the Egyptian word for "Holy Land." It means literally "red land" because the land of Egypt was red rock country.[31] Perhaps the presence of the bees on the Jaredites' ships (see Ether 2:3) was a statement about where they perceived themselves as going (i.e., to a promised or holy land).

Elijah

This Hebrew name means "my God is Jehovah." Because Elijah was the prophet over the Church during his day, his name does not seem unusual or extraordinary. However, in the famous contest between Elijah and the priests of Baal (see 1 Kings 18), Elijah engages the priests in an effort to establish that his God (Jehovah) is the true God, one who is "awake," attentive to his children, and omnipotent, unlike their god, Baal (1 Kings 18:27). The underlying theme of the encounter is encapsulated in the name of the prophet, "my God is Jehovah."

Enos

This Hebrew name means "the man," or "human being."[32] In the Bible, Enos was the son of Seth, who was the son of Adam. Hugh Nibley noted: "Enos means exactly the same thing as Adam. It means human being or man. In Hebrew today if you call a person a human being, you can either say *ben Adam*, son of Adam, or *ben enosh*, which is the same as Enoch."[33] In the Genesis account, Enos serves as the third

Adam per se. There is his grandfather, Adam (which means "man"), then his father, Seth (which means "a substitute," "successor" for Adam, or "double Adam"), and then Enos (which means "the man," "man again," or "Adam").[34]

ESTHER

This name, which is likely either Persian or Babylonian in origin, most often is interpreted as meaning "star."[35] However, on occasion it is also taken to mean "she that is hidden."[36] Both names seem appropriate for the heroine of the Jewish people. It was the fact that her true identity remained hidden that allowed her to become the star of her people, and their deliverer from the plots of wicked Haman.

FELIX

The Greek version of this Latin name means "delusive" or "deceptive."[37] Felix's life exemplified this. He was the Roman procurator of Judea appointed by the emperor Claudius in A.D. 53. He ruled the province in a cruel and immoral manner. Indeed, he had persuaded his third wife, Drusilla, the daughter of Herod Agrippa I, to leave her husband and marry him. During his tenure as procurator there was frequent trouble and sedition. While he had a very sound understanding of the gospel (Acts 24:22) and a strong and repetitive desire to speak with Paul about it, he nevertheless kept Paul in prison for some two years, in hopes of extorting money from him (Acts 24:26–27).[38]

FESTUS

The name of this procurator of Judea meant "joyful" or "prosperous." Festus would have seemed like a breath of fresh air to the residents of Judea when compared with his predecessor (Felix) and successor (Albinus).[39]

FORTUNATUS

This Latin name means "blessed" or "lucky." Fortunatus was a friend of the Apostle Paul. Along with Stephanas and

Achaicus, he visited Paul in Ephesus (see 1 Corinthians 16:17). His name had become a very popular one in Paul's day, traditionally given to freedmen or slaves who had gained their autonomy or at least some degree of privileged status in a household; hence they were called "lucky" or "blessed."[40] It is assumed that this is the case with this Corinthian Christian.

GAMALIEL

The Greek version of this name means "God is the one who brings recompense." He was the tutor of Saul prior to his conversion and call as an apostle, and he is the Pharisee who prevented the Sanhedrin from taking the lives of the Twelve by proclaiming, "Refrain from these men, and let them alone: for if this counsel or this work be of men, it will come to nought: But if it be of God, ye cannot overthrow it; lest haply ye be found even to fight against God" (Acts 5:38–39). Gamaliel's name highlights his teaching: God is in charge. Let him decide who should be rewarded and who should be punished.

GIDEON

The name *Gideon* means "hewer" or "one who cuts down." One dictionary of scriptural names also interprets the name as "great warrior."[41] The name applies well to the Gideon of Judges 7 and the Gideon of Mosiah 19. Both men were warriors and are spoken of in relationship to their swords with which they "hewed" or "cut down" their enemies.

GIDDIANHI

The name *Giddianhi* means "the Lord is my life."[42] This is ironic because Giddianhi was the leader of the Gadianton robbers, who were anything but followers of the Lord (see 3 Nephi 3–4). Curiously, Giddianhi boasted that his people were in the right: in his letter to Lachoneus, the governor of the land, Giddianhi berated the Nephites and their governor for their wickedness (see 3:10). Even Lachoneus is said to have been "astonished" at the bizarre accusation, as though Giddianhi really believed that the Gadianton robbers were model citizens and the Nephites were the epitome of evil (see 3:11).

HAGAR

As the Egyptian slave of Sarah, Abraham's wife, this second wife of the patriarch ran away when she had a falling out with Sarah (see Genesis 16:6). Her name, which means "flight" or "to flee," thus foreshadows her eventual departure from her master's residence.

HELAMAN

The Egyptian version of this name is well known. It means one who has the "countenance of Amon [or God]."[43] The Hebrew version of the same name apparently means "an army."[44] Both names suit Helaman, the eldest son of Alma, who served as prophet and leader of the Nephite host. The Egyptian version of the name seems quite applicable to Helaman's son Helaman, who also sought righteousness and justice during his tenure as chief judge.

HYRUM

This name, belonging to the brother of the Prophet Joseph, means "my brother is exalted."[45] Joseph Fielding McConkie wrote: "What more appropriate name could have been given to the man who was destined to go with Joseph to Carthage and seal his testimony with his blood? So the testimony of the Restoration has been sealed on this dispensation with the blood of two prophets who, according to the ancient tradition, bore the right names."[46]

IMMANUEL

It is well known that this name means "God with us" or "with us is God." In a Messianic prophecy, Isaiah indicated that a virgin would conceive and call her child's name Immanuel (see Isaiah 7:14). No better name could be given to the Christ child in an effort to describe who he was. It is noteworthy that

Jehovah, Jesus himself, gives this revelation to Isaiah regarding His future identity and assigned name-title.[47]

ISAAC

This Hebrew name has traditionally been interpreted as meaning "laughing" or "to laugh"[48] and has been assumed to be a play on words, highlighting the response of both Abraham and Sarah to the news that in their advanced years they would have a baby (see Genesis 17:17; 18:12).[49] However, the linguistic evidence suggests that the name *Isaac*, like that of Jacob or Ishmael, is likely an abbreviated form of a prefixing verb and a divine name. If that is the case, then the name would actually mean something akin to "God smiles" or "God favors."[50] Such an interpretation highlights the fact that Isaac is the fulfillment of the covenant that God made with Abraham, for it is in the context of God reiterating His promise to fulfill this covenant that He commands Abraham to name the child Isaac (Genesis 17:19).[51]

ISRAEL

The covenant people were called by this name in part because they were the descendants of Jacob, whose name God changed to Israel. The name means several interrelated things, including "ruling with God," "soldier of God," "God will rule [them]," and "he will be a prince with God."[52] Each interpretation of the name serves to highlight the role of the covenant people as those who allow God to rule them and who strive to serve him, and in so doing have the promise that they will eventually rule and reign under him.

JARED

This was the name of the brother of the prophet Mahonri Moriancumer. It means "he that descends" or "he that goes down." Jared, along with his brother, built barges in which they and their families would cross the great deep—literally descending into the deep "as a whale in the midst of the sea" (Ether 2:24) or as one who had been "swallowed up in the depths of the sea" (Ether 2:25). One source notes: "Jared, whose name in Hebrew means 'to go down,' was one of those sent forth when the tower fell. Like Adam and many before and many after, Jared embarked on a new beginning."[53]

Jesus

This is one name we could not properly ignore here. It means "Jehovah (or Yahweh) saves." It is the Greek version of the Hebrew *Jehoshua* or *Joshua*, which means the same thing. As a child, Jesus would have gone by the Hebrew version of the name. The significance of Christ's being called by this name is evident.

Joseph

This name means "he shall add."[54] Could there be a better description of the mission and ministry of the Prophet Joseph Smith, who added much to what the world understands about God, His plan, and what we must do in order to return to Him? Of course to a lesser extent the name is also applicable to Joseph of Egypt, who added both to the knowledge of the king and people of Egypt, and also to their temporal security. Significantly, in response to all Joseph had done for Egypt, Pharoah changed the prophet's name to Zaphnath-paaneah (Genesis 41:45). This new name/title meant, among other things, "Savior of the world," "the giver of the nourishment of life," and "revealer of a secret."[55]

Korihor

This Book of Mormon anti-Christ worked to destroy testimonies of Christ in the city of Zarahemla (see Alma 30). His name means "in the presence of Horus," suggesting that the name is Egyptian.[56] Horus is often seen as the Egyptian deity paralleling Christ.[57] The significance of Korihor's name is unclear. If it is intended to be suggestive of Christ, rather than the false god Horus, then the name foreshadows Korihor's confession that he "always knew that there was a God" (Alma 30:52) who could hear his every lie—even though outwardly he denied his existence. However, it is more likely that the name *Korihor* indicates a false Christ or anti-Christ who serves as a representative of his false god.

Kareah

This Hebrew name means "bald." The figure to which it is attached was a sixth-century B.C. army commander (see Jeremiah 40–42). Kareah was not a highly significant figure in scripture. However, his name is a prime example of how many ancients were physically described by the names they bore.

Kemuel

Three different men are recorded in the Old Testament as bearing this name: Abraham's nephew (see Genesis 22:21), the leader of the tribe of Ephraim in the days of Moses (see Numbers 34:24), and the head of the tribe of Levi during the reign of King David (see 1 Chronicles 27:17). The name means "raised of God" or "reared by God" and may imply God's intervention in their lives, whether through giving them the gospel or preserving them through trials.

Laban

This name means "white" and, by implication, "to be clean." The Book of Mormon Laban was the antithesis of this, although we must assume his parents named him this in the hope that he would live up to his namesake.[58]

Lemuel

The name of this younger brother of Laman means "devoted to God" or "for God," likely reflecting his parents' hope that he would be a righteous son, devoted to God. Thus Lehi proclaimed to his wayward son, "O that thou mightest be like unto this valley, firm and steadfast, and immovable in keeping the commandments of the Lord!" (1 Nephi 2:10).

Lucifer

A perfect companion to names like Laban and Lemuel, Lucifer means "light bearer" or "shining one." It is traditionally held that attributing such a title to the devil (which means "slanderer") was the result of premortal valiance. Elder Bruce R. McConkie wrote, "He was one of the early born spirit children of the Father. . . . Satan [which means 'adversary'] held a position of power and authority in [the] pre-existence (D&C 76:25–27; Isaiah 14:12–20)."[59]

MORMON

This ancient name has been said to mean "more good."[60] If such is the case, then the prophet who bore it certainly lived up to his namesake. Such is the commission of each and every Latter-day Saint once they take upon themselves the name of Christ and, along with it, the nickname "Mormon."

MOSES

In his *Legends of the Jews*, Ginzberg indicates that Moses' Hebrew birth name was Melkiel, which means "God is my King."[61] It is said that, upon drawing him out of the waters of the Nile, the daughter of the pharaoh gave him the name *Moses*, which is traditionally interpreted to mean "drawn" or "to draw out" (see Exodus 2:10). The name *Moses*, in Egyptian, however, apparently means "son"[62] or "savior."[63] All three of these titles and interpretations seem highly applicable to one or more stages of the great prophet's life.

MULEK

This was the name of one of the sons of King Zedekiah (see Helaman 6:10). He was a prince by birth, and his name literally means "little king."[64] A derivative of that same name, Melek, was given to the land west of the river Sidon (see Alma 8:3). Of it Reynolds and Sjodahl wrote: "No reason is given why it was so called, but its meaning is evident. It was *the king's land*. The ancient Phoenician word for king is spelled letter for letter the same as in the Book of Mormon (Melek), and the Hebrew word is almost identical."[65]

Nephi

The Egyptian name *Nephi* is said to mean "my Lord is God."[66] Of this name, Elder George Reynolds wrote:

> From very ancient times the Egyptians believed that all who died had to have their acts upon earth scrutinized by a council of inquisitors, before they could be proclaimed fit to enter the eternal abodes of bliss and stand in the presence of the god Osiris, the chief lord of the land of the departed. One of the names given to this god, expressive of his attributes, was Nephi or Dnephi (the D being silent . . .), or the good, and the chief city dedicated to him was called N-ph, translated into Hebrew as Noph, in which form it appears in Hosea, Isaiah and Jeremiah. Its modern English name is Memphis.[67]

Nimrod

Nimrod was a "mighty hunter against the Lord" who built the Tower of Babel, perhaps the first pagan temple, in an attempt to contact heaven without making and keeping covenants. His name means "rebellious," and such he was.[68]

Noah

This name means "rest" or "comfort." That is exactly what the Lord brought, through the flood, to this world, which had been so burdened by the weight of the sins and evils of its inhabitants that it literally groaned and mourned its lot (see Moses 7:49). We can only wonder whether King Zeniff named his son Noah (see Mosiah 7:9) in the hope that he would live up to both the name and the prophet who had previously held it.

Obadiah

The prophet Obadiah, apparently a contemporary of the prophet Jeremiah, was said to "fear the Lord greatly" (1 Kings 18:3). As the fourth of the twelve "minor" prophets, his name means "a servant of the Lord" or "a worshipper of Jehovah," a name appropriate for any prophet of God.

Og

This king of Bashan has a unique name that appears to be descriptive of his physical attributes. His name means one who has a "long neck." Og was apparently a very large man, for his bed was said to be about six feet wide and thirteen and a half feet long (see Deuteronomy 3:11). Indeed, in this same passage he is actually referred to as a "giant."

Omni

It is interesting that Omni should be one of the men chosen to preserve and write upon the plates, for he describes himself as "a wicked man" who had not "kept the statutes and the commandments of the Lord as [he] ought to have done" (Omni 1:2). It is unclear if Omni was truly wicked or if he was simply humble and ashamed of his weaknesses. (Both Paul [see Romans 7:24] and Nephi [see 2 Nephi 4:17] spoke of themselves as "wretched" men who should have been able to overcome the flesh but had not. Yet we would hardly consider either of them to have been wicked.) Omni's name, which means "belonging to Amon [or God]," implies righteousness rather than wickedness.[69] Nibley speaks of him as "the heroic Omni, who fought gallantly to preserve his people."[70] Thus, he may have simply been a "card-carrying member" of this fraternity of penitent prophets.

Paanchi

This name has been called "the one indisputable Egyptian name in the Book of Mormon."[71] It was unknown at the time Joseph translated the Book of Mormon and has been established as the name of "a very important person in Egyptian history, just before Lehi's day."[72] The name is Egyptian and means "Amon [or God] is my life."[73] The name is far from fitting, in light of the fact that Paanchi led a ferocious rebellion against the people and his own brother Pahoran II, drawing away many followers in the process (see Helaman 1:7–9). Once again, this may be an example of a name bestowed at birth in the hope that the child would live up to it. If this be the case, Paanchi failed miserably.

PAUL

Paul's Jewish name was Saul, which means "the one asked for, [or] requested."[74] The meaning of this name may be underscored in the book of Acts when Ananias did not want to heal Saul because of all of the terrible things he had done to the Christians, and the Lord told Ananias, "Go thy way: for he is a *chosen vessel unto me*, to bear my name before the Gentiles, and kings, and the children of Israel" (Acts 9:15; emphasis added). What is somewhat less clear is the intent of the Greco-Roman name, *Paul*, which means "little" or "small." This name may have been given to him in connection with his citizenship in the Roman city of Tarsus, where Paul was born and reared. However, why, upon commencement of his missionary labors, Saul only refers to himself as Paul is never explicitly stated within the text. Sidney B. Sperry suggested that the switch from Saul to Paul may have been nothing more than an effort to use his Roman name when dealing with Gentiles, a name that just happened to mean "little."[75] Similarly, even though the popular assumption is that Saul changed his name to Paul at his conversion, biblical scholars traditionally hold that Paul had both names from his youth and likely used whichever name suited a given interaction (i.e., Jew or Gentile).[76] Another possible explanation regarding the meaning of the name Paul would be its emphasis on the Apostle's humility (see 2 Corinthians 12:7; Colossians 3:12).[77]

PHARAOH

This title applied to the kings of Egypt means "Son of the sun" or "mouth of the sun," the sun being a reference to the Egyptian god Ra. Thus the name-title *Pharaoh* implies that the king of Egypt is the "son of God," but also the "spokesman for deity" or the "mouthpiece of God." One source records: "There was a close interdependence between Ra and the Egyptian kings. The kings claimed not only relationship with the sun but also identity. Thus a Pharaoh was the son of the sun, and also the incarnation of it. Ra was the sun and the king was Ra."[78]

QUARTUS

This Latin name means "fourth." Quartus bears the only personal name beginning with the letter Q in the standard works of the Church. He apparently received the name because he was the fourth child born into his family. Indeed, some commentators believe that Tertius (the "third") and Quartus, who are mentioned alongside each other in Romans 16:23, might have been brothers.[79]

RABBANAH

In the eighteenth chapter of Alma, King Lamoni is called by the Aramaic title *Rabbanah*. The Book of Mormon indicates that this name means "powerful or great king" (Alma 18:13). Of this title, Hugh Nibley stated:

> It means "a great one, a great king, a great person, a great wise man." But it means "a person of utter preeminence" with the *nah* ending. With the *nah*, it means "our lord." *Rab* is great, and Rabannah would be "our great one." Notice that these people were Ishmaelites, which is important. That's why they didn't use the Hebrew term for "great king," which would be Melek. You get Meleks (kings) all through the Book of the Mormon—Amalickiah, Mulek, etc. But here it's Rabannah, which is what the Ishmaelites would say. We are told that these people are descendants of Ishmael in this particular community, so they would say Rabannah, "great king."[80]

REBEKAH

She was the mother of Esau and Jacob. Her name means "ensnarer" or "one with a noose," quite possibly in reference to the trickery she employed on her husband Isaac, in order to transfer the birthright from Esau to Jacob (see Genesis 27). However, the name may also be a wordplay on the Hebrew word for cattle, thereby making it analogous to several other female names in the patriarchal narratives, such as *Rachel* ("ewe lamb") or *Leah* ("cow").[81]

RIPLAKISH

This man was the son of the Jaredite king Shez. When Riplakish became king, he ruled in wickedness (see Ether 10:4–7). Of his name, Hugh Nibley wrote: "Riplakish—there's a good archaic name, 'lord of Lakish.' There are at least five ancient cities named that. In fact the oldest city in Mesopotamia is supposed to have been called Lakish."[82]

SARAI

This was the name of Abram's wife before the Lord commanded the patriarch, "Thou shalt not call her name Sarai, but Sarah shall her name be" (Genesis 17:15). *Sarai* means "contentious" and "quarrelsome," or as one commentator put it, "my ruler."[83] As she progressed, the Lord saw need for a change. Sarai's new name was the Hebrew *Sarah,* which means "princess" or "noblewoman." Elder George Reynolds wrote: "It is a name of extreme beauty and force. Its roots are in Sara, a princess, and *Jahor Iah,* Jehovah, thus meaning a princess of Jehovah; a most fitting name for the mother of a multitude of nations."[84]

SHEREM

Sherem was one of the Book of Mormon's infamous anti-Christs (see Jacob 7). His name means "snub-nosed" or "pug-nosed." This name may have been given to him as an infant because of his physical appearance. However, those familiar with the Jacob-Sherem debate will concur that "snub-nosed" is the ideal epithet for this sophist.[85]

STEPHEN

This great Christian martyr had a name befitting the event for which we all know him. In Acts 7:55–56 we read of Stephen's martyrdom at the hands of the Sanhedrin, specifically for his testimony of Jesus as the fulfillment of the law of Moses.

His name, meaning "wreath" or "crown,"[86] is suggestive of a laurel victory wreath and, more particularly, the crown of eternal life earned by this great Christian martyr.

TERTULLUS

He was the attorney who, on behalf of the Jews, prosecuted Paul (see Acts 24:1–2). Of the charges for which Paul was being arraigned, one scholar wrote: "Tertullus' statement of the charges shifts their originally religious nature (Acts 21:28; 23:29) to one of sedition. Paul is a public troublemaker, a threat to the peace of the empire. Tertullus' prosecution plays on one of the governor's fears in troubled Judea."[87] Luke depicts Tertullus as a dishonest and manipulative lawyer who knows how to play his audience in order to get what he wants. Hence his name, meaning "liar" or "impostor," is fitting.

THEUDAS

He was the leader of an unsuccessful Jewish rebellion in the region of Judea sometime in the first century of the common era. Rabbi Gamaliel cites Theudas's movement, and its collapse, as support for his argument that the Sanhedrin should leave the Christians alone and let God decide if their movement prospers or dies (see Acts 5:34–39). Of Theudas, Josephus recorded, "A certain magician, whose name was Theudas, persuaded a great part of the people to take their effects with them, and follow him to the river Jordan; for he told them he was a prophet, and that he would, by his own command, divide the river, and afford them an easy passage over it; and many were deluded by his words."[88] Not surprisingly, Theudas's name means "false teacher."[89]

TIMOTHY

He was a missionary companion and for many years a trusted emissary of the Apostle Paul. Paul speaks of Timothy as his "beloved and faithful child in the Lord" (NRSV, 1 Corinthians 4:17; see 1 Timothy 1:2). His name means one who "honors God" or is "valued by God."

ULAM

In the book of Chronicles he is described as the first of two sons born to Sheresh (see 1 Chronicles 7:16). His name means simply "firstborn" and "leader." Curiously, his father's name, Sheresh, means the "'root' of the family union," or in other words, the source of the family.[90]

URIAH

The name *Uriah* means "Jehovah is my light." There are several individuals in scripture with this name. Uriah the Hittite was exceedingly loyal to the ark of the covenant, his king, and his military commander (see 2 Samuel 11:11). The priest Uriah was chosen by the prophet Isaiah to be one of two men to stand as a witness to Isaiah's prophecy (see Isaiah 8:2). Uriah the prophet was put to death for preaching against the wicked inhabitants of his city (see Jeremiah 26:20–23).[91] While publicly reading the law, Ezra had standing with him a man named Uriah (see Nehemiah 8:4). What little we know of these men suggests that their name, Uriah ("Jehovah is my light"), represents the way they lived.

UZZIA

He was one of King David's chief military officers and is listed among the sixteen Reubenites in the king's military elite (see 1 Chronicles 11:44). His name means "my strength is Jehovah."

VAJEZATHA

This young man was one of the ten sons of Haman who were hanged with the former Persian prime minister (see Esther 9:5–10). Although the Hebrew name *Vajezatha* is thought to mean "strong as the wind," the list of names of the sons of Haman, as given in the Septuagint, do not agree with the Masoretic text. The Greek names are believed to be the more accurate, and they derive from an Iranian etymology. Thus the Iranian name translated Vajezatha in the King James Version is believed to mean "given from the best one" or "descended from the best."[92] If this be the case, then self-inflated Haman clearly chose the boy's name!

VANIAH

With a group of exiles, Vaniah returned to Jerusalem (at the time of Zerubbabel and Ezra) to rebuild the temple. This name means "we were oppressed," which describes the conditions of the Jewish people during their many years in captivity.

VASHTI

She was the queen of the Persian Empire from about 485–465 B.C. Her husband, King Ahasuerus, requested her to appear at the royal banquet in order to show the attendees her unsurpassed beauty. She refused, and for so doing she was removed from her throne. This act opened the way for Esther's enthronement and the deliverance of the Jewish people. The name *Vashti* is Persian and means "the best" or the "beloved and desired one," likely highlighting her tremendous physical beauty.[93]

ZORAM

This is an Aramaic name that means "a welcome [and] strong, refreshing rain."[94] Again from Hugh Nibley we read: "Zoram was a servant of Laban. He was drafted by Lehi's family, by Nephi especially. Being a servant of Laban, the military governor of Jerusalem, he would not be an Israelite because you can't enslave or make a servant of an Israelite. The name Zoram is again one of those desert names. It's from the eastern half of Manasseh. It means a welcome, refreshing, powerful rain."[95] Nibley's suggestion that Zoram is a desert name may well explain why Zoram's parents gave it to him. If they were used to the arid conditions of the desert, a strong rainstorm would be a coveted and highly welcomed godsend. Zoram's birth may have come as a similar blessing. Perhaps his mother had been barren for a time. Perhaps the family had been blessed with only daughters. A number of unexplained events could have provoked the comparison that exists in Zoram's name.

God indicated that He knew Moses by name (see Exodus 33:17; 3:4). Christ, the Good Shepherd, calls his sheep "by name" (see John 10:3; 2 Timothy 2:19). For the Lord to call King David (see 1 Samuel 16:3), the prophet Isaiah (see Isaiah 49:1), the Twelve Apostles (see Luke 6:13), and even Cyrus (see Isaiah 45:3–4) by name meant divine selection for some revealed task. Moses informs us that the names of the twelve tribes were worn on the high priest's garments as "a memorial before the Lord continually" (see Exodus 28:9–12, 21, 29). Those who inherit the celestial kingdom are said to be in possession of a "white stone" on which is written "a new name . . . which no man knoweth save he that receiveth it. The new name is the key word" (D&C 130:11). In the Book of Mormon, King Benjamin warns:

> I would that ye should remember to retain the name [of Christ] written always in your hearts, that ye are not found on the left hand of God, but that ye hear and know the voice by which ye shall be called, and also, the name by which he shall call you. . . . And again, doth a man take an ass which belongeth to his neighbor, and keep him? I say unto you, Nay; he will not even suffer that he shall feed among his flocks, but will drive him away, and cast him out. I say unto you, that even so shall it be among you if ye know not the name by which ye are called. (Mosiah 5:12, 14; see D&C 18:25.)

As in antiquity, and also today (and apparently throughout eternity), names are significant and empowering. They can serve as a warning, motivator, key word, and more—but only if the recipient is attentive and aware.

10
ANIMALS AS SYMBOLS

FROM THE EARLIEST TIMES, animals have been employed as symbols. Shortly after they were expelled from Eden, Adam and Eve engaged in animal sacrifices in accordance with God's command:

> And [God] gave unto them commandments, that they should worship the Lord their God; and should offer the firstlings of their flocks for an offering unto the Lord. And Adam was obedient unto the commandments of the Lord. And after many days, an angel of the Lord appeared unto Adam, saying, Why dost thou offer sacrifices unto the Lord? And Adam said unto him, I know not, save the Lord commanded me. And then the angel spake, saying, This thing is a similitude of the sacrifice of the Only Begotten of the Father, which is full of grace and truth; Wherefore, thou shalt do all that thou doest, in the name of the Son. And thou shalt repent, and call upon God, in the name of the Son for evermore. (JST, Genesis 4:5–8.)[1]

Through an angel sent directly from the presence of God, Adam learned that the animals he had sacrificed were symbols for Christ and his vicarious atonement on behalf of fallen man.

In intertestamental, New Testament, patristic, and rabbinic literature, animals are commonly represented as symbols for humans and their attributes. One New Testament example of this is found in Luke's recitation of Peter's vision of the descending sheet (see Acts 10). In light of this divine manifestation to the chief apostle of the meridian Church, it is evident that over the centuries covenant Israel had lost its focus on the primary meaning of animal symbolism. In this vision Peter was commanded to partake of animals that, under the law of Moses, were deemed unclean. He immediately refused, stating that he had "never eaten any thing that [was] common or unclean" (Acts 10:14). The voice in the vision then spoke three times to Peter in a spirit of rebuke, commanding him, "What God hath cleansed, that call not thou common" (Acts 10:15). From this the apostle understood that the unclean animals in the vision symbolized non-Jews and that it was the Lord's will that he take the gospel to the Gentile nations.[2] The Petrine revelation (see Acts 10:9–48), as it is called, serves well to emphasize the New Testament church's understanding of both the kosher law as primarily metaphorical in intent and, more particularly, animals as symbols of men and their attributes.[3]

Most often in scripture, animals fall into one of two categories: animals are deemed either "clean" and acceptable to God or "unclean" and taboo for man. Although this concept of uncleanliness as it pertains to animals is typically associated with the introduction of the law of Moses, it should not be overlooked that, in reality, such a distinction was introduced by God much earlier than the Mosaic dispensation. To Noah, for example, God commanded that both clean and unclean animals be taken onto the ark, the clean by sevens and the unclean by twos (see Genesis 7:1–2).

In this and other instances, the Hebrew word used in the biblical text for animal uncleanliness is *tawmay*.[4] Contrary to English connotations of the term *unclean*, this Hebrew word implies ceremonial or ritualistic uncleanliness rather than physical dirt or filth.[5] The word is used in scripture as a metaphor for immoral or unethical behaviors.[6] Thus God's dictate to Noah to distinguish between animals that were clean and those that were unclean clearly implies that something symbolic was intended (see Genesis 7:2).

Later, when Moses received the "kosher" law from Jehovah

(see Leviticus 11; Deuteronomy 14), this same language of spiritual or symbolic uncleanliness was used. Therefore God's condemnation of certain animals as dietarily unclean was a statement about what these animals symbolized and not necessarily—as so many have assumed—a statement about how healthful they were as food.[7]

No one source gives us a comprehensive, detailed explanation of what each animal represented to the ancients. However, a fairly defined composite picture can be drawn by comparing and contrasting ancient sources such as the writings of Barnabas, Aristeas, Aristobulus, Philo of Alexandria, and Origen. Additionally, texts such as the *Leviticus Rabbah*, Ginzberg's *Legends of the Jews*, the *Gospel of Philip*, and *Fourth Maccabees* illuminate one's understanding of this symbolic principle and its wide acceptance in antiquity.[8]

In very general terms, the aforementioned sources define the ancient symbolic meanings of animals as follows:

1. *Clean animals.* These are traditionally a symbol for Jesus and his followers. They represent those who pore over the words of God time and again (i.e., "chew the cud") until the teachings found in the scriptures become a part of their very being. They are a token of people who are more surefooted (i.e., "cloven hoofed") because of their gospel grounding and thus less likely to slip into transgressions. Included in this symbolic category would be any animal that both chews the cud and "parts the hoof": oxen, sheep, lambs, and goats.

2. *Creeping things.* Chameleons, for example, and other creatures found in the same category of "creeping things" (see Leviticus 11:29–31), were apparently understood in antiquity as representing people who were deceptive or misrepresentative. Some ancient sources also associate this class of animals with the sinful practice of gluttony. The weasel, mouse, tortoise, ferret, lizard, snail, and mole are all included in this symbolic category.

3. *Dogs.* Like pigs (see below), dogs are symbols for hypocrisy. They represent people who, time and again, cycle

through the pattern of feigned repentance and a return to past sins (see Proverbs 26:11).

4. *Eagles or vultures.* These represent people who prey upon the weakness of others to get personal gain. They do not work for their maintenance but rely on someone else's work or misfortunes to provide for their needs. Ravens, owls, hawks, swans, pelicans, storks, and bats all fall into this symbolic category.

5. *Fish without scales or fins.* These are a symbol for people who do not "swim" with the mainstream of the Church and its teachings, lifestyle, beliefs, and so on. They are ever endeavoring to chart a new path or explore the dark and uncharted waters of morality, ethics, or the "mysteries." Thus they subject themselves and any who follow them to a greater degree of temptation and a heightened potential for apostasy or deception. Fish in this category would include the lamprey, cuttlefish, and polypus.

6. *Locusts or grasshoppers.* Anciently these represented members of the Church who had overcome or risen above this world and its telestial temptations, cravings, and lifestyles.

7. *Rabbits.* In antiquity as it is today, rabbits represent immorality, adultery, fornication, and so on. From the "Playboy bunny" to the colloquial phrase "They're multiplying like rabbits," these animals have a well-established symbolic connotation. This category of symbolism also includes camels.

8. *Swine.* These are symbols for people who call upon or remember their God only in times of need, but when their life is going well they forget their Maker. They are an example of the quintessential hypocrite.

So what is the application in all of this? What does this have to do with the life of a Latter-day Saint Christian living in the twenty-first century? The following examples represent an attempt at a modern application of the ancient symbolic understanding.

There are many who profess to have testimonies of Christ and the restored gospel but who, although active and outwardly pious, are as the "whited sepulchers" Jesus condemned (see Matthew 23:27). It is the tendency of some to put on sanctimonious airs in public while in reality they are like the *chameleon* or *snail* that anciently symbolized people who were deceptive and anxious to present a false image. Many of these "unclean" people actually deceive themselves into thinking they are righteous when in fact they are not. Others may perceive them to be righteous by their outward actions without knowing their hearts or true desires.

There are those within and without the Church who use the gospel as a vehicle to get personal gain. Their goal is money, and the Church becomes the means to an end for them. In their business dealings with their fellowmen, they act as the *birds of prey*, taking every possible advantage at the expense of others. Like the *vulture*, when they are successful at obtaining their carrion, they may mistakenly consider themselves blessed and chosen of the Lord because of their "hard work" and resulting wealth. They seldom consider those who have been harmed in the process or the negative example they have set.

On the other hand, people who justify ignoring the prophetic counsel of the divinely appointed leaders of Christ's restored church would well be symbolized by a *cuttlefish* or *lamprey* (i.e., *fish without fins or scales*), because they are avoiding the mainstream of righteousness in exchange for the uncharted waters of rebellion.

Latter-day Saint youth who, with or without the permission of parents, begin dating before the age of sixteen increase the likelihood that they will eventually become as the symbolic *camel*, *hare*, or *weasel*, steeped in immorality and heartache. If, on the other hand, they heed the rules of spiritual *kashrut* (i.e., living a spiritually "kosher" or righteous life), they will remember the dangers such actions pose, and they will be much less likely to fall into the snare of immorality.

Many professing to be devout Christians, Jews, Moslems, and so on nevertheless act as *swine*, calling out to God when in need but forgetting him in their actions, words, and thoughts when all is going as they wish in their personal lives.

Only by avoiding the unclean, by being "spiritually kosher," can one learn to overcome the defects and weaknesses inherent in the character of fallen man. Indeed, it is this innate weakness that makes us different from God. If we are clean and right before God, our salvation is sure. However, this can happen only as we make a conscious choice to seek to walk in his footsteps and enjoy spiritual health. If, on the other hand, we choose to set aside the counsel and guidance of the scriptures, the prophets, and the Savior, we will surely find ourselves very unhealthy indeed, even partakers of spiritual death. The parting words of Moroni echo the entire theme of this chapter and the whole proposition of scripturally employed animal symbolism: "And again I would exhort you that ye would come unto Christ, and lay hold upon every good gift, and touch not the evil gift, nor the unclean thing" (Moroni 10:30). We must not allow ourselves to slide into spiritual uncleanliness, nor can we afford to associate too closely with those who choose a life of uncleanliness.

The remainder of this chapter will examine the implications of this form of symbolism for the study of scripture. We will look at an example or two from the most common animal symbols. As with many categories of symbolism, some scriptural authors utilize this category and others do not. One must of course use judgment and discretion and follow the dictates of the Spirit in order to insure an orthodox reading of the standard works.

BIRDS OF PREY

In biblical times, scavenger birds and birds of prey signified individuals who would "sit idle" and then "devour the flesh of others," by which they prove "themselves pests [to all]."[9] Birds such as the eagle, raven, hawk, vulture, or owl are to remind us of people who do not know "how to procure food for themselves by [their own] labor and sweat, but [rather] seize on that of others."[10] They present an appearance of "simplicity" and innocence, placing their potential victims at ease, just as the stereotypical used car salesman or ambulance-chasing lawyer.[11] Most birds of prey symbolize the human scavenger by their habit of gaining from the weaknesses and misfortunes of others. This is a very common symbol in scripture.

An example of this symbolism is seen in the words of Moses: "The Lord shall bring a nation against thee from far, from the end of the earth, as swift as the eagle flieth; a nation whose tongue thou shalt not understand" (Deuteronomy 28:49). The surrounding context of this passage deals with the blessings promised to Israel through obedience and with the curses of which she is assured if she disobeys God (see vv. 53–57, 64–65). One of the prophesied curses was that Israel would be overrun and scattered among all nations. "The aim of the sermon is to contrast two alternatives: the rejected option of serving Yahweh willingly, out of love and gratitude; and the imminent alternative, forced servitude to conquering aliens,"[12] symbolized by an attacking eagle.

Paul's missionary companion Barnabas described eagles as figures of men who "seize on that of others," watching that they might "plunder" their victims so as to not have to work. They prove themselves a nuisance to all those with whom they interact because of their wicked designs.[13] The actions of the eagle are so like the actions of men who prey upon the weaknesses of others that a better type would be hard to find. Indeed, the Hebrew seems to make no effort to distinguish between an eagle and a vulture. This serves to further emphasize the mental picture Moses was creating.[14]

In light of this theme, the warning to Israel is clear (see Deuteronomy 28:49). Through disobedience they will be overrun and scattered by men who are nothing more than scavengers. In other words, Israel's enemies will prey upon her weaknesses that, incidentally, the Lord offers to replace with strengths if she will obey (see Deuteronomy 28:1–14). If she does not, however, her foes will swoop down upon her as an eagle or vulture upon its prey. One biblical scholar noted: "Behind the cumulative horrors of the siege portrayal is an understanding of Yahweh as the cohesive force who keeps humanity human. When the grace-full restraints of covenant presence and covenant relation are removed [through Israel's disobedience], cities become jungle and 'humanity' preys on 'humanity.'"[15]

In Deuteronomy 28, Hosea 8:1, Jeremiah 48:40, and Jeremiah 49:22 the enemy is shown as a scavenger "swooping" down on its prey, intending to "plunder and destroy."[16]

CAMELS

Matthew records Christ's stinging rebuke of the Pharisees: "Ye blind guides, which strain at a gnat, and swallow a camel" (Matthew 23:24).

This condemnation of Pharisaism was leveled in a discourse condemning outward appearances of piety (see Matthew 23:1–36). The Pharisees overemphasized the letter of the law while entirely ignoring the spirit of the law. Jesus denounced them for paying tithing on every small seed and every blade of grass while neglecting important principles such as mercy. Their distorted observance of the law of tithing with its rabbinic origins had been attributed by them to Moses as an oral tradition received by him on Sinai. Pharisaic tradition claimed that when Jehovah appeared to Moses on the mount and revealed the Torah (law), he also gave the prophet an "oral torah," or oral law that expounded upon the law of Moses. However, it was this so-called oral Torah—created by men, not by God—that Jesus saw as the great corrupter of Judaism and of Jehovah's Sinai revelation.

Referring to the distinction between the true law and its Pharisaic counterfeit, Jesus denounced the Pharisees as unclean, the very thing they believed others to be. He linked them with camels, while associating those upon whom they condescendingly looked with gnats. As the Pharisees were straining to swat or reprove the unclean gnat, a representation of small transgressions or infractions of the law of Moses, they were themselves swallowing a camel. The camel was an emblem of immorality and spiritual adultery, sins for which Jesus had earlier accused the Jewish leadership (see Matthew 12:38–39).[17]

The Pharisees were committing far greater sins than the people they condemned. The major ethical sin of the Pharisees was a neglect of justice, mercy, and faith.[18] Yet the camel implies that their sins were not simply ethical but moral also. What is a minor infraction of the law of tithing when contrasted with adultery? The Pharisees appear to have been ethically impoverished and morally destitute.

But what of the gnat? The restriction in Leviticus and Deuteronomy regarding the eating of insects is unusual because it concentrates more on what may be eaten than on what should not be eaten. Perhaps this is the reason Barnabas, Philo, and others are silent in their commentaries regarding the gnat and its symbolic meaning. Philo does, however, provide us with an explanation of what the locust symbolizes and, since it is clean, we can likely determine why the gnat is unclean, as the two insects were anciently classed, respectively, as positive and negative symbols from the same category.

According to Philo, the locust is a type for those who are able to "spring up from the earth and all low things"[19]—specifically sin and temptations—and in so doing, not be dragged down as are the spiritually weak. Philo says they take "heaven in exchange for the earth, and immortality in exchange for destruction."[20] The gnat, therefore, is likely a symbol for those who do not have this inner strength and resolve in the face of temptations. Gnats are those who succumb to temptation. Philo suggests that insects opposite to the locust are "small minded."[21] Significantly, the Hebrew *sherets* (or *shérec*) is a broader term than the English translation "insects" indicates. "Swarming things" or "swarmers" expresses its meaning more aptly.[22] One scholar suggested that the gnat's symbolic meaning is disclosed in its dual methods of movement, which are crawling and flying.[23]

Whether we call it teeming, trailing, creeping, crawling or swarming, it is an indeterminate form of movement. Since the main animal categories are defined by their typical movement, "swarming" which is not a mode of propulsion proper to any particular element, cuts across the basic classification. Swarming things are neither fish, flesh nor fowl. . . . There is no order in them. Recall what the Prophecy of Habakkuk says about this form of life: " . . . crawling things have no ruler" (I, v. 14).[24]

Thus the gnat is seen as typifying those who have no real direction in their lives and who vacillate when it comes to their commitments to God. They are tossed to and fro by the whims and trends of society and by their varying inclinations from day to day. Unlike locusts, who have strength to rise above such ambiguity, the gnats are much like those taken advantage of by birds of prey.

The Joseph Smith Translation of the verse quoted earlier is illuminating: "Ye blind guides, who strain at a gnat, and swallow a camel; who make yourselves appear unto men that ye would not commit the least sin, and yet ye yourselves transgress the whole law" (JST, Matthew 23:21). The last portion of the verse seems in keeping with what Jesus had taught time and time again regarding the Pharisees. They were hypocrites who were continually committing sins that were much more grave than anything committed by those whom they condescendingly condemned. They were constantly rebuking others for small, petty infractions of the law of Moses or, more particularly, the embellished and uninspired "oral law." Yet while condemning others of smaller infractions, they were guilty of heinous sins including adultery and murder.

Commentators seem united in their recognition that Jesus wanted his followers to see his reference to a gnat and a camel as an allusion to two unclean animals. In other words, it is not coincidental that Jesus uses a gnat and a camel, nor is it simply a message about the size of the creatures.[25]

The message regarding hypocrisy was manifestly expressed in the text. However, an application of the types serves to bring into focus not just the physical difference in seriousness of the two sins noted but also the spiritual differences suggested by the physiological distinctions that are shown. If credence can be placed in the ancients' interpretation of the camel, we must understand that Jesus was highlighting the adulterous nature of his hearers.

Alma pointed out that sexual sins—of which the Pharisees were guilty—are "an abomination in the sight of the Lord; yea, most abominable above all sins save it be the shedding of innocent blood" (Alma 39:5). The murder of Jesus, for which the Pharisees became guilty only a short time later, became the apex of their evil ministry, they having then committed the two most heinous of transgressions.

FISH

The books of Leviticus and Deuteronomy give us our most comprehensive list of clean and unclean animals. However, neither of these books condemns specific fish. Rather, the only categorization of fish offered in the scriptures is a distinction between fish with fins and scales, which are considered clean, and those with neither fins nor scales, which are unclean. Thus although ancient extracanonical sources provide definitions of the symbolic meaning of fish, these definitions are somewhat moot when examining scripture, as they speak only generally about fish, making interpretations of given passages nearly impossible.

In intertestamental, New Testament, patristic, and rabbinic literature, fish carried both positive and negative symbolic connotations. Sometimes they were types for faithful Israel and other times they were figurative representations of fertility gods of the underworld.[26] When used in the former sense, they could be very broad symbols typifying, among other things, religious rebirth, baptism, hope, Christ, resurrection, faith, or spirituality.[27]

Fins and scales themselves were highly symbolic and were often used in the ancient world to suggest ideas of stability, self-control, or power to avoid being swept away either by strong water currents or social trends.[28] The absence of fins or scales on a fish suggested a pleasure-loving attitude. Those without fins or scales well represented a man or woman whose actions, desires, and associations sink to the very depths where things are dark and murky.[29] Of fish without scales or fins, one ancient commentator on the Bible wrote that they "float in the deep, not swimming [on the surface] like the rest." They make their "abode in the mud," we are told. The commentator speaks of fish like the lamprey, which do not swim with the school but on their own in the dark. We are informed that they are condemned by the law and, as noted previously, serve as symbols of individuals who do not go with the mainstream of thought, doctrine, and morality within the Church. Instead, they chart their own course in "muddy waters" where danger is imminent. "Blessed is the man who hath not walked in the counsel of the ungodly, even as the fishes [referred to] go in darkness to the depths [of the sea]."[30]

In most scriptural passages, we are left to speculate whether a given reference to a fish or fishes is speaking of clean or unclean specimens. There are at least forty-five references to "fish" in the standard works of the Church. In virtually every passage, it is nearly impossible to determine the kind of fish to which reference is made. However, in light of the above, we offer this one passage as evidence of the symbolic nature of fish in scripture and ancient thought.

> Again, the kingdom of heaven is like unto a net, that was cast into the sea, and gathered of every kind: which, when it was full, they drew to shore, and sat down, and gathered the good into vessels, but cast the bad away. So shall it be at the end of the world: the angels shall come forth, and sever the wicked from among the just, and shall cast them into the furnace of

fire: there shall be wailing and gnashing of teeth. (Matthew 13:47–50.)

In the case of this passage, the specific kind of fish represented is unknown. However, Jesus made a distinction between "good" and "bad" fish. Regarding the bad fish, some commentators see in the Greek a clear reference to Leviticus 11:10 and *tawmay* creatures.[31] Even English translations of the text seem to imply a distinction between two types of people within the covenantal group or Church. Just as the law of Moses distinguished between those animals that were ceremonially and ritualistically clean or unclean, the Master makes a similar distinction between people in the covenant who are faithful as contrasted with those who are not. Both kinds join the Church.[32] Elder McConkie wrote:

> Some are repentant and worthy and will be put in vessels; others are swept along by the tides of social pressure. Some are drawn in by the tight net of business necessity and economic advantage; yet others join with the saints to inherit property, marry selected persons, or gain political preferment. And all such shall be cast away with the wicked to be burned. There are many reasons for coming into the earthly kingdom of heaven.[33]

In the passage at hand, a distinction is clearly being made between those who come into the covenant for proper reasons and those who come in for the improper purpose of getting some kind of personal, temporal, or social gain. Do we see in those fish the symbol of those who swim in "the deep, not swimming [on the surface] like the rest, but make their abode in the mud which lies at the bottom" of the sea? Does this parable depict people who are "ungodly to the end and are condemned to death"?[34] Certainly the answer to both questions must be yes![35] It is the ungodly attributes and intents of these individuals that will cause them to be "cast away with the wicked to be burned." The Doctrine and Covenants states: "And every corruptible thing, both of man, or of the beasts of the field, or of the fowls of the heavens, or *of the fish of the sea,* that dwells upon all the face of the earth, shall be consumed" at Christ's coming (101:24; emphasis added).[36]

The bad fish of Matthew 13, representing those who are not faithful to the truth, are tossed to and fro by the dictates of the world because of the absence of metaphorical fins and scales. These are they who "enter in not by the door" (John 10:1) or who avoid the "strait and narrow path" (Matthew 7:13–14; Luke 13:24). Jesus was clear that some would try to gain entrance into his kingdom through methods other than those that he had specified. He said, "Verily, verily, I say unto you, he that entereth not by the door into the sheepfold, but climbeth up some other way, the same is a thief and a robber" (John 10:1). He also spoke of the lifestyle required for entrance into that kingdom: "Enter ye in at the strait gate: for wide is the gate, and broad is the way, that leadeth to destruction, and many there be which go in thereat: Because strait is the gate, and narrow is the way, which leadeth unto life, and few there be that find it" (Matthew 7:13–14; see 22:1–14).

A decision to seek "alternate paths" places one under the symbolic category of both the bad fish of Matthew 13:48 and the fish "without fins and scales" of Deuteronomy 14 and Leviticus 11. It removes one from the safety and shelter of God's influence and at the same time opens one up to the strong societal currents that are sweeping many away to destruction. Using another metaphor, one source wisely counseled, "Don't climb to the extreme branches of the tree, for there is danger of falling: cling close to the trunk."[37]

OXEN, SHEEP, LAMBS, AND GOATS

In the scriptures oxen, sheep, lambs, and goats are almost always positive symbols. Each is clean according to the law of Moses. According to ancient commentators, these animals symbolize the types of people and activities appropriate for the house of Israel, God's covenant people. As might be expected when dealing exclusively with kosher animals, there are similarities in the standard symbolic meanings of each of these four animals.

Oxen are established types for Israel and represent power, patience, and sacrifice, as well as Christ or deity.[38] Bulls also suggest images of royalty, divinity, power, sacrifice, atonement, and Jehovah.[39]

Sheep invoke images of Christ, the faithful, timidity, gentleness, sincerity, compassion, discipleship, and apostleship.[40] Lambs can also connote innocence, meekness, purity, patience, humility, Christ, and the Church. They can also suggest rebirth, resurrection, martyrdom, sacrifice, and obedience to God's will.[41]

Goats, on the other hand, can be either positive or negative symbols. They can represent Satan, sinners, lust, lasciviousness, evil, stubbornness, blame, and the damned.[42] Or, as positive symbols, they are similar to sheep or lambs because they can represent determination, self-discipline, deity, order, and cautiousness, as well as Christ burdened with the sins of mankind.[43]

There are minor differences in the symbolic representation of these various animals, although they generally represent a singular standard type.

Moses declared that the reason these animals were clean and acceptable was that they chewed the cud and had cloven hooves (see Leviticus 11:3; Deuteronomy 14:6). Cud chewing, as mentioned previously, was a symbol for those who meditated again and again upon the words of Christ, who continually studied and pondered the scriptures and teachings of the prophets, looking for increased understanding of the divine will.[44] Paul's missionary companion Barnabas wrote that cud chewing symbolized pondering and acknowledging one's God and one's dependence upon him.[45]

Philo of Alexandria indicated that the cloven hoof symbolized that everything has its opposite and that there are always two paths, one leading to vice and the other to virtue.[46]

According to the Old Testament, animals with multiple toes were unclean. They symbolized people who believe there are many roads leading back to God, none being preferential.[47] The solid hoof, on the other hand, symbolized those who taught relativism, implying there was no bad or good, all being equal, dependent only upon personal philosophy.[48] Anciently the parted hoof implied eternal opposition or, in other words, living in the world and yet looking forward to the world to come.[49] One modern source states: "Cloven-hoofed animals which part their hooves symbolise that all our actions must betray proper ethical distinction and be directed toward righteousness."[50] Oxen, sheep, lambs, and goats each fall into the clean category of "cud chewing" and "hoof-cleaving."

In light of the hundreds of passages that employ this symbol, isolating a single pericope as an illustration of this symbolic principle is very difficult. Although what follows is, in all probability, not the best example, it seems adequate to make our point.

> Thou shalt not see thy brother's ox or sheep go astray, and hide thyself from them: thou shalt in any case bring them again unto thy brother.... Thou shalt not see thy brother's ass or his ox fall down by the way, and hide thyself from them: thou shalt surely help him to lift them up again.... Thou shalt not plow with an ox and an ass together. (Deuteronomy 22:1, 4, 10.)

This selection of verses from Deuteronomy 22 is an example of a passage that, although teaching the importance of ethics and uprightness, according to the symbolic imagery, certainly implies that something more is involved. Verse 10 is a powerful image regarding interfaith marriages and associations.[51] According to Philo, the instruction about growing two kinds of crops in the same field or mixing two kinds of cloth in the same garment (see vv. 9, 11) is designed to teach that "our people ought not to be anxious for marriages with foreigners."[52] Thus, as a kosher animal, the ox represents stalwart members of the Church or the house of Israel. The ass typifies non-covenant, perhaps even apostate, neighbors of Israel.[53] The Apostle Paul gave this instruction:

> Be ye not unequally yoked together with unbelievers: for what fellowship hath righteousness with unrighteousness? and what communion hath light with darkness?
>
> And what concord hath Christ with Belial? or what part hath he that believeth with an infidel? And what agreement hath the temple of God with idols? for ye are the temple of the living God; as God hath said, I will dwell in them, and walk in them; and I will be their God, and they shall be my people. Wherefore come out from among them, and be ye separate, saith the Lord, and touch not the unclean thing; and I will receive you. (2 Corinthians 6:14–17.)[54]

The warning in Deuteronomy 22:10, coupled with Pauline and extracanonical explanations of the passage, provides additional insight into the other two verses cited in our selection from Deuteronomy.

Deuteronomy 22:1 warns that, if our brother's sheep or ox, both of which are clean animals, should go astray, we must seek to bring them back to him. Perhaps "going astray" stands as a metaphor for inactivity or apostasy. When any of the Father's children are in such a state, we have an obligation to bring them back to "our brother," even Jesus Christ. After all, we are "our brother's keeper" (Genesis 4:9).[55] As covenant Israel, we are the "watchmen" assigned to "give them warning" (see Ezekiel 3:17–19; 33:3–6).

Correspondingly, Moses stated in Deuteronomy 22:4 that if we see our brother's ass or ox fall down by the way, we should not hide but endeavor to "lift him up again." It does not matter if it is an ass, meaning a less-active member or nonmember, or an ox, meaning an active member of the Church. We are to help all in their times of physical or spiritual need. All are children of God, who is no respecter of persons.[56] The Father and Son desire the well-being and salvation of all, and Christ has atoned for the sins of all humankind on conditions of repentance. We are commissioned to help God's children to repent and come unto Christ.

SWINE

As noted above, swine were seen anciently as standard figures for hypocrisy, gluttony, and self-centeredness.[57] They represented those who called upon God only if they needed something. Ancient peoples of the East who understood the emblematic nature of animals held this to be the message behind the symbolic use of the pig.

There are three New Testament passages in particular, offered as parables, teachings, or experiences of Jesus, that include pigs (see Matthew 7:6; Mark 5:1–13; Luke 15:11–32). Each of them seems to utilize swine with symbolic intent. We will begin with an examination of the parable of the prodigal son.

> And he said, A certain man had two sons: And the younger of them said to his father, Father, give me the portion of goods that falleth to me. And he divided unto them his living.
>
> And not many days after the young son gathered all together, and took his journey into a far country, and there wasted his substance with riotous living. And when he had spent all, there arose a mighty famine in the land; and he began to be in want. And he went and joined himself to a citizen of that country; and he sent him into his fields to feed swine. And he would fain have filled his belly with husks that the swine did eat: and no man gave unto him.
>
> And when he came to himself, he said, How many hired servants of my father's have bread enough and to spare, and I perish with hunger! I will arise and go to my father, and will say unto him, Father, I have sinned against heaven, and before thee, and am no more worthy to be called thy son: make me as one of thy hired servants. And he arose, and came to his father. (Luke 15:11–20.)

Anciently, Jews who kept swine were cursed and looked upon as outcasts, much like those in some Islamic countries today.[58] Frederic W. Farrar noted: "Jews detested swine so much, that they would speak of a pig euphemistically as *dabhar acheer*, 'another thing,'"[59] and commonly would say "Cursed be the man who would breed swine."[60] The Moslems also have a history of avoiding the word *pig*, preferring to call them "the black one."[61] Symbolically, "to eat swine was to become a Gentile and [be] outside of the covenant (Leviticus 11:7; Isaiah 65:4; 66:17)."[62] As will be recalled, the prodigal in his downward fall eventually stooped to tending swine.[63]

The established typology suggests that since the younger son chose to participate in this action, he had indeed hit rock bottom. He was now associated with heathens ("swine") and had accepted their ways. He was a friend of those who thought they could do without God. He had become like them in every way. As one commentator pointed out, the very act of approaching his father to request his inheritance before his father's death serves as a symbol of the "man's desire to be independent of God (Genesis iii.5), of his desire to take the ordering of his life into his own hands, believing that he can be a fountain of blessedness to himself."[64] Indeed, St. Augustine indicated that the boy's choice to go to a "far country" was itself a symbol for his choice to forget God.[65]

The scriptural text informs us that it was this absolutely miserable state of affairs, being reduced to eating husks unfit for human consumption, that caused the prodigal to return to his father looking for relief from his pain-filled existence.[66] This action is exactly what swine typify. They are images of those who call upon God only because they have hit bottom. However, when their bellies are full (i.e., their lives are going well), they acknowledge not their master. In this parable the younger of the two sons epitomizes this, and the swine in the episode serve to highlight his hypocrisy—at the very least when he left home, and quite possibly when he first thought of the benefits of returning to his father's house.[67]

Pertinently, the Lord has declared, "In nothing doth man offend God, or against none is his wrath kindled, save those who confess not his hand in all things, and obey not his commandments" (D&C 59:21). In light of the established symbolism, the swine in this passage are intended to emphasize the spiritual state of the prodigal and to cause the reader to ponder his or her need for a conscious decision to live as God commands or forfeit eternal life. With this interpretation, the prodigal son well represents a life of feigned prayer, whereas Christ is the definitive model of a sincere and saving relationship with God. Of Christ, Elder Jeffrey R. Holland wrote: "He seemed always to be praying. Unlike us, He needed no crisis, no discouraging shift in events to direct His hopes heavenward. He was already instinctively, longingly looking that way."[68] The parable warns us not to be like swine or those who associate with them.

In another gospel account we read:

> And they came over unto the other side of the sea, into the country of the Gadarenes. And when he was come out of the ship, immediately there met him out of the tombs a man with an unclean spirit, who had his dwelling among the tombs; and no man could bind him, no, not with chains: because that he had been often bound with fetters and chains, and the chains had been plucked asunder by him, and the fetters broken in pieces: neither could any man tame him. And always, night and day, he was in the mountains, and in the tombs, crying, and cutting himself with stones.
>
> But when he saw Jesus afar off, he ran and worshiped him, and cried with a loud voice, and said, What have I to do with thee, Jesus, thou Son of the most high God? I adjure thee by God, that thou torment me not. For he said unto him, Come out of the man, thou unclean spirit.
>
> And he asked him, What is thy name? And he answered, saying, My name is Legion: for we are many. And he besought him much that he would not send them away out of the country.
>
> Now there was there nigh unto the mountains a great herd of swine feeding. And all the devils besought him, saying, send us into the swine, that we may enter into them. And henceforth Jesus gave them leave. And the unclean spirits went out, and entered into the swine: and the herd ran violently

down a steep place into the sea, (they were about two thousand;) and were choked in the sea. (Mark 5:1–13; see Matthew 8:28–32; Luke 8:26–33.)

Of the highly symbolic and kosher-related nature of this fascinating story, one theologian wrote:

> This healing is in Gentile country. The story is set in the territory of one of the Hellenistic towns of Decapolis (5:20) on the southeastern shore of Lake Tiberius (the Sea of Galilee). The incident is preceded by a crossing of the sea (4:34–41) and followed by a notice of the return crossing (5:21).... [Notice] the interest of the text in the fact that this is Gentile country, "opposite Galilee," as Luke 8:26 specifies. Nothing about it is kosher; everything is unclean: the spirit(s), the tombs, the pigs, the territory.[69]

Somehow this unnamed victim was possessed by "Legion," that is, many evil spirits.[70] Surely the man himself bears at least some responsibility for the tragedy. If not, wouldn't we all be subject to demonic possession? Regarding the devil and his influence over us, the Prophet Joseph taught:

> We came to this earth that we might have a body and present it pure before God in the Celestial Kingdom. The great principle of happiness consists in having a body. The Devil has no body, and herein is his punishment. He is pleased when he can obtain the tabernacle of man and when cast out by the Savior he asked to go into the herd of swine showing that he would prefer a swine[']s body to having none. All beings who have bodies have power over those who have not. The devil has no power over us only as we permit him; the moment we revolt at anything which comes from God the Devil takes power.[71]

The man was possessed of unclean spirits apparently because of his disobedience to the commandments of God. Was he disobedient to all of the commandments? Such is unlikely and hardly necessary for the demonic possession that followed.[72] All this man needed to do was to willfully rebel against commandments he knew he should obey, and he would lose his right to the companionship of the Holy Ghost and potentially open himself up to the devil's influence. Adam Clarke wrote, "How little is the *power* or *malice* of any of them to be dreaded by those who have God for their portion and protector!"[73]

This interesting episode also supports the ancient belief that swine are those who neglect to regularly commune with their Father in Heaven. The passage may well show the baneful results upon individuals who neglect their responsibilities toward prayer. As such, contemplation of these verses "inevitably . . . moves from exegesis to theology."[74]

A poignant correlation to all of this is found in 2 Nephi: "For if ye would hearken unto the Spirit which teacheth a man to pray ye would know that ye must pray; for the evil spirit teacheth not a man to pray, but teacheth him that he must not pray" (32:8). Salvation can come only through remembering God and Christ, and through a prayerful relationship with them. To forget to pray is to sin and eventually to be damned. In this particular episode, the animal symbolism suggests that this man had become lax in calling upon or acknowledging God in his daily activities. He had thereby exposed himself to the adversary.

Realizing they would be obligated to leave the body they had been inhabiting, the evil spirits requested they be sent into a herd of swine so they could possess the swines' bodies instead. Symbolically, these swine also represent those who choose to ignore opportunities to develop a spiritual relationship with God.

The end result for the herd of swine was that they charged down a steep hill and plunged into the sea and drowned. Why, one might ask, would Jesus permit innocent pigs to be attacked by evil spirits and killed? The Catholic theologian Joseph Fitzmyer offers this comment:

> This is a strange story. It has always raised questions and problems that strain the imagination: Is Jesus not presented here as cruel to animals? How could he have caused the owner

of the pigs such a financial loss—obviously they were not keeping two thousand pigs for display? What was a herd of two thousand swine doing in an area into which Jews like Jesus would go? How could swine be so energetic to stampede over the miles that separated them from the slope and the lake? . . . Obviously, such questions miss the point of the gospel-story itself, being recounted for a symbolic and religious purpose.[75]

Aware that something symbolic may be intended, we must give careful attention to the various elements that Mark's version of this incident provides.

In the biblical text, water carries both the connotation of cleansing and also of chaos. "The sea," *The New Jerome Biblical Commentary* informs us, is "a common symbol for chaos and death."[76] Similarly, one biblical scholar indicated that there is a likely correlation between the calming of the sea and the healing of the man possessed by many demons.[77] "If a raging sea is a threat, demonic force is much worse."[78] The fact that these swine drown as they rush headlong into the sea discloses the symbolic meaning of this action: chaos, spiritual death, and eventual damnation are the result of a spiritually feigned life.

The man who was originally possessed was freed from his spiritual illness through faith in the Son of God. Had he not made such a change, his fate would be that symbolized by the final action of the herd of swine. The destruction of the swine by their demonic captors was a type for the demons' desire to destroy the soul of the very man they had previously possessed—indeed, their desire to destroy the souls of all men.[79] One commentator wrote: "Here is an emblem of the final impenitence and ruin into which the *swinish sinners*, the habitually *impure*, more commonly fall than other sinners. Christ permits the demons to do that in the *swine* . . . to show us what rage they would exercise on us if left to their own liberty and malice."[80]

An interesting account in the history of the Church provides a modern example of how the truths revealed by the swine symbol find application in the lives of postbiblical Saints.

Newel Knight, a resident of Colesville, New York, had a rather strange and unexplained fear of praying vocally that continued for an extended period of time. To the Prophet Joseph he committed that he would "take up his cross, and pray vocally" during a 9 June 1830 gathering of the Saints. However, when the time came, Knight excused himself.

According to Brother Knight, he postponed praying until the next morning when he retired to the woods. He made several attempts to pray out loud but claimed that he was unable, feeling that, in refusing to pray in the presence of others, he had not done his duty. He recorded in his journal that he began to feel uneasy and continued to feel worse, both mentally and physically, until he reached his home with a physical appearance that was such that his wife felt alarmed.

At Newel's request she quickly sent for the Prophet. By the time Joseph arrived, Knight was suffering greatly and acting very strange. His sight was blurred, his limbs were distorted and twisted, and he had a general appearance that was difficult to explain. He recorded that finally he was "caught off the floor of the apartment, and tossed about most fearfully."

News of the happening quickly spread, and a crowd of neighbors and friends gathered around his home. After several minutes of this scene, Joseph was able to get hold of Knight's hand, at which point Newel immediately spoke and requested that Joseph cast the devil out. Responding to his plea, the Prophet said: "If you know that I can, it shall be done." The devil was immediately rebuked and commanded, in the name of Jesus Christ, to leave. At that moment Brother Knight spoke out, saying that he saw the devil leave and then vanish from his sight.

The scene immediately changed. As soon as the devil had departed from him, those present said that Knight's countenance became natural and his bodily distortions ceased. The Spirit of the Lord descended upon him. Knight recorded that immediately the "visions of eternity were opened" to his view.[81]

Newel Knight's experience is remarkably similar to that of

the man possessed with "Legion." Significantly, Knight acknowledged that his condition was the result of his unwillingness to call upon God in prayer. It was his hearkening to the "evil spirit, [which] teacheth . . . a man . . . that he must not pray" (2 Nephi 32:8) that provoked this episode with false spirits.

None of this is to suggest that failure to pray automatically results in demonic possession. It does, however, clearly suggest what kind of spirit influences those who do not desire to pray. There can be no question about the result of hearkening to that spirit over an extended period of time, as illustrated by Newel Knight's experience and, perhaps, by that of the man possessed by "Legion." Whether a person is possessed by Satan or duped by his servants makes little difference. The reality is that neglecting private prayer increases the likelihood of either. A hypocritical calling upon God only in times of need will not do. We would do well to heed the counsel of the Doctrine and Covenants: "Pray always, that you may come off conqueror; yea, that you may conquer Satan, and that you may escape the hands of the servants of Satan that do uphold his work" (D&C 10:5).

What has been offered in this chapter is necessarily a small overview of an enormous tapestry interwoven with threads of animal symbolism.[82] There are many, many scriptural passages that employ this particular genre of scriptural symbolism.

11

TYPES AND SYMBOLS OF CHRIST

IT WOULD BE INAPPROPRIATE for a book on scriptural symbolism not to dedicate at least a portion to a discussion of symbols of Christ. Yet to attempt to delineate the types and symbols of Christ in a single chapter of a book such as this is probably equally inappropriate, particularly in light of scriptural declarations from the Book of Mormon. For example, Nephi wrote: "Behold, my soul delighteth in proving unto my people the truth of the coming of Christ; for, for this end hath the law of Moses been given; and *all things* which have been given of God from the beginning of the world, unto man, are the typifying of him" (2 Nephi 11:4; emphasis added).[1] Of this verse, Elder Jeffrey R. Holland noted, "Nephi testified that 'all things . . . are the typifying of [Christ].' The literary evidence of that is seen throughout the holy scriptures."[2]

Nephi's brother Jacob recorded: "And I said unto [Sherem]: Believest thou the scriptures? And he said, Yea. And I said unto him: Then ye do not understand them; for they truly testify of Christ. Behold, I say unto you that none of the prophets have written, nor prophesied, save they have spoken concerning this Christ" (Jacob 7:10–11). Alma informed Korihor that "all things denote there is a God; yea, even the earth, and all things that are upon the face of it, yea, and its motion, yea, and also all the planets which move in their regular form do witness that there is a Supreme Creator" (Alma 30:44). And in the Book of Moses, the Lord stated: "Behold, all things have their likeness,

269

and all things are created and made to bear record of me, both things which are temporal, and things which are spiritual; things which are in the heavens above, and things which are on the earth, and things which are in the earth, and things which are under the earth, both above and beneath: all things bear record of me" (Moses 6:63).

From these prophetic utterances it appears that (1) all things given by God symbolize or typify Christ, (2) all prophets have prophesied and testified of Christ, and (3) potentially all things can remind us of Christ. Indeed, one commentator remarked: "The red line of [Christ's] blood runs all through the Old Testament, and . . . thus we are constantly reminded of the shed blood, without which there is not remission."[3]

In scripture are many well-established and frequently taught types for Christ. Volumes have been written on Abraham's sacrifice of Isaac, the Passover meal of Exodus 12, and the life and mission of Joseph who was sold into Egypt—all as types or symbols for the Only Begotten of the Father. However, it is not the purpose of this text to revisit here many of those symbols that have been so frequently discussed.[4]

Rather, this chapter's aim is to delineate categories of Christocentric symbols and types. In the spirit of Alma's comment that all things denote there is a God (see Alma 30:44), we will examine the following Christocentric symbolic classes:

- People as types for Christ
- Animals as symbols of Christ
- Events as types for Christ
- Objects that symbolize Christ
- Actions that symbolize Christ
- Names as symbols or reminders of Christ
- Places or locations as types or symbols of Christ
- Food as a symbol of Christ
- The temple and Christ

Because of constraints on the length of this text, only one or two examples from each category will be given, even though many examples could be drawn from scripture, for, as the above list indicates, *all things* truly testify of Christ.

PEOPLE AS TYPES FOR CHRIST

It is a well-established fact that every prophet spoken of in scripture stands as a type for the Savior, Jesus Christ. Latter-day Saint commentators and other Christian commentators alike acknowledge this.[5] In addition, LDS commentators have noted strong parallels between the life and ministry of the Prophet Joseph Smith and that of Jesus Christ.[6] For that matter, every man who holds the priesthood of God and exercises that authority in righteousness functions in that capacity as a symbol of the Savior, Jesus Christ.[7]

When Latter-day Saints read the story of Cain and Abel in the Book of Moses, they are often led to ask why Cain's offering was rejected by the Lord. As important as the question is, the typology represented in the episode is of greater pertinence and may answer that question. Note some of the significant elements of the story.

Abel was by occupation a shepherd, while Cain was a "tiller of the ground," a farmer (Moses 5:17). Cain killed Abel because he wanted power and also access to his brother's flocks (see v. 33). Upon the death of his brother, Cain convinced a number of his siblings to follow him to a land called Nod, away from the Church and their parents (see vv. 7–28, 41).[8] Upon hearing of the death of their one son, the vicious crime of another of their children, and the apostasy of a multitude of their other offspring, Adam and Eve mourned greatly over their losses (see v. 27).

This tragic story is a detailed symbol for the conflict between Jesus and Lucifer, beginning in the premortal world and continuing throughout the temporal existence of this earth. Cain typifies Lucifer, and Abel represents Christ. (The following tables appeared in chapter 8; but they are reproduced here to provide a clear comparison.)

CAIN	LUCIFER
Cain was a "tiller of the ground" (Moses 5:17). The earth is a standard type for things temporal, worldly, and temporary.[9]	Lucifer's works are of a temporal, worldly, and fleeting nature.
Cain loved Satan and his ways more than he loved God and his ways, probably because Satan seeks power for himself by oppressing others for eternity, whereas God gives his power to as many as will have it (Moses 5:18).	Satan loves himself and desires to be empowered over all mankind throughout all eternity.
Cain's offering was unacceptable because it was not sacrificial and did not involve the shedding of blood (Moses 5:19–21).	Lucifer's offering required no sacrifice of us or him and did not require the shedding of blood by a Savior, all contrary to God's plan.
Cain was angry that his offering was rejected (Moses 5:21).	When the Father rejected Lucifer's conditional offer to function as the Savior, Lucifer became violently angry and "kept not his first estate" (Abraham 3:28).
Cain's countenance fell (Moses 5:21).	Satan fell (D&C 76:26).
Cain was called perdition (Moses 5:24).	The devil is called perdition and is the father of the sons of perdition (John 17:12; D&C 76:26).

Cain rejected the Father and his counsel (Moses 5:25).	Lucifer rejected the Father's counsel and plan in the premortal life.
Cain would not listen to his father, Adam, nor to his brother Abel (Moses 5:12–13, 26).	Lucifer did not listen to his Father in Heaven nor to his Elder Brother Jesus Christ.
Cain's parents mourned over him and those who followed him (Moses 5:27).	Father and Mother in Heaven surely mourned the loss of Lucifer and his followers.
Cain slew his brother, thus sealing his own fate and destroying his own work (Moses 5:32–36).	Satan "slew" his brother Jesus, thus destroying his own work (for it brought to pass the Atonement).
Cain convinced many of his brothers and sisters to follow him (Moses 5:27–28, 41).	A third part of the hosts of heaven followed Lucifer (Revelation 12:3–4).
Cain became a fugitive and vagabond on the earth (Moses 5:37).	The devil wanders the earth as a fugitive and a vagabond.
Cain accused someone else for his evils (Moses 5:38).	Satan proclaimed that he was only doing that which had been done in other worlds.[10]
Cain was cast out of the presence of the Lord forever (Moses 5:39, 41).	Satan was permanently cast out of God's presence for his rebellion (Revelation 12:9).
Cain is said to be the father or mastermind of much wickedness (Moses 5:24, 31, 51).	The devil is the father of lies and the mastermind behind all wickedness (2 Nephi 9:9).
Cain was not to be killed by men but only by God (Moses 5:40).	No man can destroy Satan. Only God has this power over him.[11]

Cain was given an external, physical mark by which he could be recognized (Moses 5:40).	D&C 129 indicates that Lucifer too received an external mark: The lack of a physical body allows him to be detected and recognized.

ABEL	CHRIST
Abel was a shepherd (Moses 5:17).	Christ is the Good Shepherd (John 10:11).
Abel offered an acceptable offering, which consisted of a first-year male lamb without blemish (Moses 5:20).	Christ's offering was accepted by God and was typified in the law of Moses by the slaying of a first-year male lamb without blemish.[15]
Abel's offering involved the shedding of blood (Moses 5:20).	Christ's offering involved the shedding of his own blood (Moroni 5:2).
In making his offering, Abel was opposed by his brother Cain (Moses 5:21).	In making his offering and atonement, Christ was opposed by his brother Lucifer (Abraham 3:27–28).[16]
Abel walked in holiness before God (Moses 5:26).	Jesus walked in holiness before God the Father (2 Nephi 31:7; 3 Nephi 11:7).
Abel was slain by his brother while he labored in the field (Moses 5:32).	Jesus was slain by his brother (i.e., Satan caused him to be slain) while he labored at his mission in the field (or vineyard or earth).[17]

According to Philo of Alexandria, the name Abel means "referring to God."[12] A more traditional rendering of this Hebrew name is "transitory" or "fading away."[13] Such seems appropriate in light of Abel's abbreviated life. One Jewish source records, "After a while, Eve bore [another] son, whom she named Hebel, because, she said, he was born but to die."[14] ("Hebel" is the transliteration of the Hebrew name "Abel.")

Jesus is the Son of God whose life and teachings "refer" or point us to God the Father (John 14:6). Additionally, Jesus was "born but to die."

Of this undeniable set of parallels, one scholar unacquainted with the added insights of the Pearl of Great Price wrote:

> In the New Testament . . . appears . . . the wrestling of the Two Sons of God—Messiah and Lucifer, Jesus and Satan, . . . Christ and Anti-Christ, the Risen Lord and the Man of Sin. . . . Abel, the good shepherd who makes an acceptable sacrifice, and who is then put to death, clearly can be thought of as a *type* of the Shepherd-Priest who is also the Lamb of God: in the same way Cain can be thought of as [representing] . . . Satan.[18]

Thus in the story of Cain and Abel, a passage seemingly unrelated to the Father's plan of salvation and the Savior's atoning sacrifice, we find great detail and meaning. Once the typology is understood, the meaning seems apparent. Clearly the grand council in heaven, the Atonement, and the plan of salvation are represented by the story of Cain's rejection and martyrdom of his brother Abel.

ANIMALS AS TYPES OR SYMBOLS OF CHRIST

In Matthew 24 we read, "For wheresoever the carcase is, there will the eagles be gathered together" (Matthew 24:28; see Luke 17:37). Scholars seldom agree on the meaning of this verse. They are commonly divided on what or whom the carcass and eagles symbolize.[19]

The rendering of the verse in the Joseph Smith Translation helps us to better understand its meaning: "And now I show unto you a parable. Behold, wheresoever the carcass is, there will the eagles be gathered together; so likewise shall mine elect be gathered from the four quarters of the earth" (JST, Matthew 24:28). Thus this parable or proverb is clearly about the gathering of Israel in the last days.

Most LDS commentators conjecture that the carcass is the restored Church.[20] On the other hand, in the second century A.D. Iranaeus indicated that the carcass was a type for Christ to whom God's children would gather prior to the Second Coming.[21] Similarly, in the sixteenth century the famed Protestant reformer John Calvin wrote that this verse portrayed God's children (the vultures) gathering to feed on Christ (the carcass).[22] Actually, the depiction of Israel as a bird was a common one in Jewish rabbinic sources.[23] Whether the carcass is actually the Church or Christ is of little consequence, since the Church is provided as the vehicle by which we come unto Christ. Indeed, time and again in scripture the Church is called the "body of Christ" (Romans 12:5; 1 Corinthians 10:17; 12:27; Colossians 1:18).

The main problem with the passage in question and with these fairly ancient explanations of its meaning is that they all associate Christ and those who are trying to follow him with unclean animals. Jesus is almost always associated with clean, or "kosher," animals in scripture. It seems strange that Matthew and Luke would use unclean animals to represent Israel's accepting the gospel and coming unto Christ. However, the uncleanliness of the carcass is actually necessary for understanding the intended type.

Nearly every Christian denomination accepts as foundational the fact that Christ, having taken upon himself the sins of the world, in a sense became unclean on our behalf. Emphasizing Christ's intimate knowledge of our personal suffering and experience, Stephen E. Robinson wrote:

> In experiencing both our punishment and our guilt, Jesus learned vicariously through the Atonement what it would have felt like to commit the sins he never committed. Thus, in a sense it would be correct to say that while Jesus committed no sins, he has been guilty of them all and knows intimately and personally their awful weight. Through us, by bearing our guilt, the sinless One experienced the full horror of human sinfulness, not merely the sins of one life, but all lives—the sins of the world. Thus through his vicarious Atonement, Jesus knows more than anyone about the dark side of being human. Even in that he is preeminent among us. At one point in his vicarious agony, Jesus cried out, "My God, my God, why hast thou forsaken me?" (Matt. 27:46.) Is it possible that the Heavenly Father had really forsaken him? Could God have abandoned him in this most sacred and terrible hour? Yes, indeed. For Christ had become guilty of the sins of the world, guilty in our place. What happens to the rest of us when we are guilty of sin? The Spirit of God withdraws from us, the heavens turn to brass, and we are left alone to stew in our guilt until we repent. In Gethsemane the best among us vicariously became the worst among us and suffered the very depths of hell. And as one who was guilty, the Savior experienced for the first time in his life the loss of the Spirit of God and of communion with his Father.[24]

According to the law of Moses, a clean animal that dies becomes unclean. Therefore, Christ is appropriately typified by the carcass, which is technically unclean—but not through its own fault. It was through his willingness to lay down his life that he became unclean on our behalf and through which we may become clean, as he is.

Speaking symbolically, the vultures gather to the body of a slain sheep or goat to partake of its flesh, which both cleanses and nourishes them.[25] In this scripture, this partaking of the flesh of the slain Christ is an apparent allusion to the sacrament (see John 6:53–58; see also Matthew 26:26–28; Mark 14:22–24; Luke 22:19–20).

As mentioned in chapter 10 of this work, in ancient times eagles and vultures were symbols for people who, like scavengers, relied upon the merits and work of others for their maintenance, food, security, and so on.[26] We, of course, are reliant upon Christ for our eternal maintenance and are not capable of completely earning that which he provides for us. We, in a sense, scavenge his works that we might be saved. He became unclean so that we may become clean. As we partake of his broken flesh, we are sustained and cleansed by his sacrifice and thus prepared to abide the day of his coming.

EVENTS AS TYPES FOR CHRIST

Were one to ask evangelical Christians, "Where did the atonement of Jesus Christ take place?" most would reply, "On Golgotha or Calvary." If that same question were posed to members of The Church of Jesus Christ of Latter-day Saints, the majority would reply, "In Gethsemane." Latter-day Saints don't reject the cross, but they don't usually speak much about it either.

A number of years ago I heard one Christian scholar give an Easter talk in which he indicated that the resurrection was not the thing that one should focus on at Easter. "It's a given," he said. "It's going to happen to everyone, no matter what you do." He stated that what was important was the part Christ had done for us that was within our power to accept or deny. In a way, he is right, but we need to remember that although the resurrection will certainly happen to all, the glory, power, and nature of one's resurrected body is entirely determined by his or her love and commitment to Christ and his gospel. If we are blessed with the right to live in the celestial kingdom, we will have a celestial body. But if we are worthy of only a telestial or terrestrial inheritance, our bodies will reflect that. We have a great deal of influence over what happens to us in the resurrection.[27]

By definition, the atonement of Jesus Christ included the Savior's experiences in Gethsemane, on Golgotha, and at the garden tomb. Christ's suffering for sin, his death, and his resurrection are *all* part of the atonement—and are necessarily connected. If the atonement had stopped before the cross, I suppose that we would all be exactly as we were before we came here—safe and saved in the presence of God, but without bodies.

Related to this is a powerful statement by Elder Bruce R. McConkie. He wrote: "All of the anguish, all of the sorrow, and all of the suffering of Gethsemane recurred during the final three hours on the cross, the hours when darkness covered the land. Truly there was no sorrow like unto his sorrow, and no anguish and pain like unto that which bore in with such intensity upon him."[28] Similarly, Elder James E. Talmage observed: "'*Eloi, Eloi, lama sabachthani? which is, being interpreted, My God, my God, why hast thou forsaken me?*' What mind of man can fathom the significance of that awful cry? It seems that in addition to the fearful suffering incident to crucifixion, the agony of Gethsemane had recurred, intensified beyond human power to endure."[29]

The scriptures disclose that at the height of Christ's suffering on our behalf, a very dramatic and significant thing happened. The Gospel of Mark records: "And Jesus cried with a loud voice, and gave up the ghost. And the veil of the temple was rent in twain from the top to the bottom. And when the centurion, which stood over against him, saw that he so cried out and gave up the ghost, he said, Truly this man was the Son of God" (Mark 15:37–39; see Matthew 27:51; Luke 23:45). Of the significance of this event, one commentator noted:

> *The rending of the vail* of the temple at the moment that our Lord gave up the ghost was the conclusion of the Old Testament types. The vail which had hitherto hung between the Holy Place and the [Holy of Holies] had been to "divide" between the two (Exod. xxvi.33), and teaches us that the Incarnation [or birth] of our Lord, which is typified by the vail, could not of itself bring us to God. It was the rending of that vail that opened the way. Now we may by faith boldly enter into God's presence.[30]

The commentator's point is simply that it wasn't enough that Jesus was born. He had to die in order that we might pass through the veil and regain God's presence. Similarly, as noted previously, it was not enough for Jesus to experience Gethsemane. Without laying down his life and taking it up again, the atonement would not have had the power to save us. Hence the rending of the veil is a type for the death of Jesus the Christ.[31]

OBJECTS THAT SYMBOLIZE CHRIST

In the seventeenth chapter of the book of Numbers we read:

> And the Lord spake unto Moses, saying, Speak unto the children of Israel, and take of every one of them a rod according to the house of their fathers . . . [and] write thou every man's name upon his rod. And thou shalt write Aaron's name upon the rod of Levi. . . .
>
> And thou shalt lay them up in the tabernacle. . . . And it shall come to pass, that the man's rod, whom I shall choose, shall blossom. . . . And Moses laid up the rods before the Lord in the tabernacle of witness. . . . And it came to pass, that on the morrow Moses went into the tabernacle of witness; and, behold, the rod of Aaron for the house of Levi was budded, and brought forth buds, and bloomed blossoms, and yielded almonds. And Moses brought out all the rods from before the Lord unto all the children of Israel: and they looked, and took every man his rod. And the Lord said unto Moses, Bring

Aaron's rod again before the testimony, to be kept for a token against the rebels; and thou shalt quite take away their murmurings from me, that they die not. And Moses did so: as the Lord commanded him, so did he. (Numbers 17:1–11.)

The blooming of the staff was for the purpose of designating which tribe would have the authority to officiate in the office of priest, serving the Lord in his tabernacle.[32] By establishing this in a miraculous way, there was to be no doubt in the minds of the people whom God had chosen and who really had the power to save them—by officiating on their behalf in the holy temple.

In this episode we are told of twelve dead sticks, all of which were put forth before the Lord in his tabernacle. Although there were twelve tribes from which God was choosing, the presence of the number twelve in this passage may well have a dual meaning, for, as noted earlier,[33] in antiquity the number twelve was commonly associated with priesthood.[34] Its placement here may indicate not simply that the Lord would extend a call to one of the twelve tribes, but more particularly that the call would be to officiate in the ordinances of the priesthood.

Of these twelve dead pieces of wood left in the temple, one of them came back to life and brought forth fruit.[35] Typologically speaking, there is great significance in this:

> In Numbers xvii we have a beautiful type of the resurrection of the Lord Jesus Christ, in *the budding of Aaron's rod*. The twelve rods were laid up before the Lord. All were equally dead, and there was no sign of life in them; but when the morning came a wondrous miracle had taken place—one rod, that on which was inscribed the name of Aaron, had become full of life: buds and blossom and fruit had all appeared. No eye saw the change take place; but when Moses came in the morning there was abundant evidence of life, reminding us of that morning when the women came to the sepulcher at the rising of the sun, and found that He whom they sought was not dead but was risen.[36]

After the rod came back to life, Moses brought it before the tribes of Israel and it was shown to the people. Having examined the budded rod, they then stood as witnesses of the miracle.

> And so we read in Acts that our risen Lord "showed Himself alive after His passion, by many infallible proofs." "Him God raised up the third day, and showed Him openly—not to all the people, but unto witnesses chosen before God." . . . Aaron's rod was caused to bud, to prove that he was God's chosen one; and Jesus Christ our Lord was "declared to be the son of God . . . by the resurrection from the dead" (Rom. i.4). There could be no doubt that He was accepted by God, since He raised Him from the dead. After the rod had been shown to the people, it was laid up in the presence of the Lord; and so when God had raised Christ from the dead, "He was seen many days of them which came up with Him from Galilee to Jerusalem," and then "sat down on the right hand of the majesty on high."[37]

The one sure sign that separates Jesus from all of the great moralists and thinkers of his day, or any other time in the history of the world, is that sacred event attested to by so many—his resurrection from the dead. While all others who have claimed divinity are dead, He lives! Thus, as Paul states, it is "by the resurrection from the dead" that Jesus is "declared to be the Son of God" (Romans 1:4).

ACTIONS THAT SYMBOLIZE CHRIST

Related to the message of the budding rod is another Old Testament story found in the second book of Kings.

> So he [Elisha] went with them. And when they came to Jordan, they cut down wood. But as one was felling a beam, the axe head fell into the water: and he cried, and said, Alas, master! for it was borrowed. And the man of God said, Where fell it? And he shewed him the place. And he cut down a stick, and cast it in thither; and the iron did swim. Therefore said he, Take it up to thee. And he put out his hand, and took it. (2 Kings 6:4–7.)

Although this was without question a miraculous occurrence, curiously most biblical commentaries downplay the significance of the event.³⁸ Many conjecture that the message here is little more than a statement about the prophet's concern for the individual in distress.³⁹ Indeed, one commentator wrote: "The story has no particular merit or significance apart from the fact that it emphasizes the supernatural power which the man of God possesses."⁴⁰

Reemphasizing the words of two of Lehi's sons, the reader is reminded that "all things . . . are the typifying of" Christ (2 Nephi 11:4) and that "none of the prophets have written, nor prophesied, save they have spoken concerning this Christ" (Jacob 7:11). Therefore, let's consider another possible interpretation of this passage, one that is more supportive of these statements from the Book of Mormon and more consistent with the purpose of scripture.

First of all, the Hebrew translated as "it was borrowed" is acknowledged by scholars to mean literally that it was "begged [for] or prayed for."⁴¹ So the issue may not have been that something that did not belong to the man had been lost. Rather, the concern was probably that something he had prayed for, longed for, and finally received appeared to have been lost.

Additionally, the loss of the axe head in the water is significant. As noted previously, water has two standard symbolic meanings in scripture. At times it represents the Holy Ghost, cleansing, and life (see, for example, John 7:37–39; Numbers 8:7; Exodus 17:6). And other times it symbolizes chaos, death, and the grave (see Genesis 7; Mark 5:13; Revelation 8:10–11; 11:6).⁴²

From a Christocentric typological perspective, note the following elements of this curious story:

For much of his life a certain man had prayed for and sought for something that he deemed precious, even sacred.

The man finally obtained that which he had been so earnestly seeking.

While the man was working to build a new house, that

thing so valued by him—and necessary for the completion of the house—was lost.

The cherished item fell into the water, and the man knew exactly where, although he could no longer see it.

By an act of the priesthood, the axe head was raised up and restored to the builders of the house.

Unfortunately, the potential typological interpretation of this miracle escapes most people. In this story it appears that we have an illustration of what Christ did by going down into the proverbial "waters of death" and then rising again. As one commentator put it, "That which was lost and sunken was raised and restored."[43]

Jesus came to rebuild God's house (the Church), which was at that time in a state of apostasy.

Many, like Simeon in the temple, had sought the coming of the Messiah for many years—including through personal fervent prayer (see Luke 2:25–35).

Numerous individuals, including some of the disciples of Jesus, saw his death as a loss of that which they had so earnestly sought.

Some felt that the house they had begun to build, namely the restored gospel in the meridian of time, would never be completed, because Christ had died.

However, by an act of the priesthood, Jesus was raised from his grave.[44]

And much like Christ's statement to his disciples shortly after his resurrection, "Handle me, and see; for a spirit hath not flesh and bones, as ye see me have" (Luke 24:39), so also the man who thought the axe head was lost is told, "Take it up to thee. And he put out his hand, and took it" (2 Kings 6:7).

NAMES AS SYMBOLS OR REMINDERS OF CHRIST

Because chapter 9 dealt with the ancient practice of employing symbolic names, the discussion here will be brief. However, in the context of this chapter it is worth emphasizing that in antiquity names were highly symbolic and very significant—both in their imagery and in their meaning in the lives of the people.

In practice the ancients would strive to live up to their namesake.[45] People's names either captured their essence or gave them a goal to strive for in their pursuit of perfection.[46] This is particularly the case in relation to theophoric names (names including part of the name of God), which served as reminders of Christ, his attributes, and the obligation of the name's recipient to be as Christ is.

Israelite theophoric names are those that begin or end with some form of *Yah* or *El*. They are compound words composed of either a noun, pronoun, adjective, or verb combined with a name of God.[47] When given to people, they "represent declarations about or expressions of petition to the deity mentioned in the name."[48]

The most common name of God found in Israelite theophoric personal names is a form of *YHWH* (Yahweh or Jehovah), the Tetragrammaton.[49] Because the ancient Jews considered it blasphemy to write or speak the name of God, *YHWH* never occurs in a name in its full form, but it does appear in several standardized forms, such as *ja, ya, yo,* and *yahu*. The second most common divine name used in personal names is *El*.[50]

In some cases in scripture, parents gave their children theophoric names. In other instances, God himself dictated the name to the parents of the newborn child. In either case the purpose appears to be basically the same: the sanctification of the name's recipient. One biblical scholar noted, "The very fact that so many of the names in ancient Semitic societies, including the Israelites, were of a theophoric nature demonstrates a strong disposition toward the role of the divine in the lives of these people."[51] Supporting this is the fact that a number of Christians who were on trial (because of their Christian affiliations) at Caesarea in A.D. 309 actually bewildered their judges because they had renounced their birth names, which were in so many cases pagan theophoric names. In place of their former namesakes, they had chosen names to identify with their new faith, such as Eli*jah* (meaning "my God is Jehovah") and Samu*el* (which means "appointed by God").⁵²

What follows is only a sampling of the numerous theophoric names in scripture.⁵³ In many cases, if we are attentive to theophoric roots in scriptural names, we will see a correlation between the names of many individuals and their life's events or attributes. In the examples below, the root *El* appears in boldface type, and different forms of the root *Yah* appear in italic type.

BETHEL ("HOUSE OF GOD")

It was at Beth**el** that Jacob received his endowment (see Genesis 28:10–19)⁵⁴ and Abraham worshipped the Lord (see Genesis 12:8). King Saul met three prophets "going up to God to Beth**el**" (1 Samuel 10:3); and Elijah and Elisha traveled to Beth**el**, where they met the "sons of the prophets" (2 Kings 2:2–3). The name reminds us that we, too, must turn to the Lord's house (both the Church and the temple) if we are to inherit God's kingdom.

DANIEL ("GOD IS MY JUDGE")

One of the chief themes of the book of Dani**el** is the unjust judgment of Dani**el** for breaking the corrupt laws of men (see Daniel 1; 3; 6). Dani**el** placed the laws of God above the laws of men and firmly believed that God would be his judge. This namesake reminds us not to fear what man can do to us (see Psalm 118:6; Moroni 8:16; D&C 122:9), but rather place our trust in God, who is the only one who has a right to judge (see Psalm 50:6).

ELEAZAR ("GOD IS MY HELP")

Eleazar was Abraham's chief servant, who helped him to free Lot. In Hebrew gematria, **El**eazar totals 318, the exact number of servants that are said to have helped Abraham free Lot (see Genesis 14:14). Thus commentators traditionally believe that **El**eazar, rather than 318 servants, was Abraham's helper. However, the meaning of the name **El**eazar implies that it was God who really helped Abraham free Lot. We are reminded by this name that it is God to whom we should turn for help in our times of need (see Psalm 46:1; Isaiah 41:13).

E**LIJAH** ("Y**AHWEH IS MY** G**OD**")

Eli*jah* confronted the priests of Baal in an effort to prove to them that their god was nothing, whereas Yahweh (Jehovah) has all power, for which men should worship him (see 1 Kings 18). **El**i*jah*'s name and life remind us that Jehovah is the only true God.

E**LISHA** ("G**OD SHALL SAVE**")

The scriptures paint **El**isha as a soul who is ever engaged in acts of service, kindness, and mercy. His miracles, as helps to those in need, form the major part of his recorded work. Each saving act on his part typified something Christ has done or will do for us, and each emphasized what his name means—God will save![55]

E**ZEKIEL** ("G**OD WILL STRENGTHEN**")

Ezeki**el**'s name seems appropriate, both in light of the strength he would need from God in order to fulfill his mission of speaking judgment against Jerusalem and the nation (see Ezekiel 1–24) and in light of the fact that he saw in vision some of the miraculous things God would, in his strength, do for those who loved him (see Ezekiel 25–48). Thus the name stands as a constant reminder that it is in God only that we will find the strength to fulfill our mortal missions and overcome this world (see 2 Nephi 22:2; Alma 26:11–12).

G**ABRIEL** ("G**OD IS STRONG**")

In light of his announcement to a barren couple (see Luke 1:11–19) and a virgin (see Luke 1:26–38), who both would have a child, it seems appropriate that Gabri**el**'s name brings to mind the reassuring refrain "God is strong" and to him nothing is impossible (see Matthew 19:26; Mark 9:23).

Hezekiah ("My strength is Yahweh")

This man was the king of Judah and a great political and religious reformer who, among other things, suppressed idolatry among his people, reconstituted the temple ordinances and services, worked closely with the prophet Isa*iah* to reform both the Church and the state, refused to pay tribute to the wicked Assyrians, and led his people back from Assyrian captivity. His was a life and career that emphasized God's strength and the importance of relying upon Jehovah rather than on mankind. Thus, like the theophoric names Ezekiel and Gabriel, Hezek*iah*'s name emphasizes the omnipotence of God and his Christ.

Immanuel ("God is with us")

Nephi (see 2 Nephi 17:14; 18:8), Isa*iah* (see Isaiah 7:14; 8:8), and the Prophet Joseph Smith (see D&C 128:22) all used this name as a title referring to the mortal Messiah. Jesus was, as John testified, "God" (John 1:1).

Isaiah ("Yahweh is salvation")

Perhaps the chief message in the book of Isa*iah* is that of salvation, temporal and spiritual, being found only in God. Reliance upon any source other than Jehovah will in the end bring disappointment and ruin. Thus, as Isa*iah* over and over again warned Israel to ally themselves with God rather than with wickedness or "mighty" nations, his name served to emphasize his main message, both to those in antiquity and to those of us living in modernity.

Ishmael ("God hears")

Abraham's son Ishma*el* is, in part, a fulfillment of God's promise to Abraham that his descendants would be as innumerable as the sands of the sea. Ishma*el*'s birth was a sign that God truly had heard Abraham's pleas. The pleas of Ishma*el*'s mother, Hagar, for God to preserve her life and Ishma*el*'s, were also heard (see Genesis 16:7–12; 17:20). In the Book of Mormon we are informed that the Lord "heard" the desire of Lehi's sons to have companions and therefore commanded Lehi to send his sons to Ishmael to receive his daughters to wife (see 1 Nephi 7:1–5). In this vein the Ishmael of the Book of Mormon truly was an answer to prayer, and evidence that God does see our needs and hear our petitions (see Psalm 4:1; Mosiah 9:18; 23:10).

ISRAEL ("GOD CONTENDS" OR "GOD WILL PREVAIL")

Anciently Israel were God's covenant people, and thus the name has been defined as meaning a "true believer in Christ."[56] If God's covenant people trusted in him and relied upon him, they had the guarantee that he would contend on their behalf and in the end they, through him, would prevail. Isaiah's constant message to Israel was to quit trusting in their own strength or that of their political allies. Rather, they should trust in Jehovah and know that he would contend and prevail on their behalf. Such is also the message to modern covenant Israel (see D&C 1:19; 84:116).

JEREMIAH ("YAHWEH RAISES UP" OR "JEHOVAH APPOINTS")

Jeremiah was a prophet raised up by God to condemn the unrepentant and warn of the scattering that would befall the inhabitants of Jerusalem if they did not change their ways. This ancient name should stand as a reminder that "every man who has a calling to minister to the inhabitants of the world was ordained to that very purpose in the Grand Council of heaven before this world was."[57] God raises up those whom he needs to bring to pass his work.

JOEL ("YAHWEH IS GOD")

Joel was the messenger of God's wrath upon unrepentant Judah. A severe plague of drought accompanied by locusts was sent, which was only to be lifted if the people turned to God and repented (see Joel 1). Like the name Elijah, the name Joel stands as a reminder that there is only one God. To deny that truth, or to be disobedient to what one knows to be God's will, is to provoke his displeasure (see Mosiah 1:17; D&C 101:90).

Joshua ("Yahweh saves")

As with all prophets, *Joshua* was a type for Christ. His given name at birth was Oshea ("God saves"). However, because this prophet would typify Christ, God commanded Moses to change Oshea's name to "*Joshua*" (see Numbers 13:16), which is the Hebrew equivalent of the Greek name Jesus. Jesus or Yahweh, whom *Joshua* typifies, is the Savior of all (see Acts 4:12).

Nehem*iah* ("Yahweh comforts")

Nehem*iah* received a royal commission from Artaxerxes to rebuild the walls of Jerusalem amid great opposition. Jehovah's comfort seems present in the life of Nehem*iah*, both in his commission and in his overcoming opposition to his appointed task. The name also reminds us that only in Christ will we truly find peace and comfort (see Isaiah 51:3; Zechariah 1:17; 2 Corinthians 1:3–4; Alma 31:31–32).

Peniel ("Face of God" or "to behold God's face")

Peniel was a city in eastern Palestine, on the Jabbok River. It was there that Jacob saw God face to face and, in commemoration of that blessed theophany, renamed the city. We, too, are commissioned to seek God's face (see 1 Chronicles 16:11; 2 Chronicles 7:14; Psalm 105:4; D&C 101:38). Jacob's experience reminds us of the results of such a quest.

Samuel ("Heard of God")

Samuel's barren mother, Hannah, named her boy this because she had fervently petitioned the Lord for a son, whom she committed to dedicate to the Lord should she be blessed to receive offspring (see 1 Samuel 1). As with Hannah and Hagar, so also with us: God always hears (see Psalm 4:1; Mosiah 9:18; 23:10).

Zacharias ("Yahweh is renowned")

There are two significant events in the life of this New Testament priest that correlate with his name. First, there was the miraculous birth of his son John (see Luke 1). Luke's description of the event makes it clear that the vision and accompanying miracle caused the already reverential Zachar*ias* to hold God in high acclaim. Additional evidence of these feelings of appreciation is found in the second name-related event: the martyrdom of Zachar*ias* (see Matthew 23:35; Luke 11:51). The priest, true to the vision and commission he had received in the Lord's house, gave his life in celebration of Jehovah's will, over his own temporal preservation. The name reminds us to always hold God in renown—even above our own lives.[58]

Although there are many theophoric names in the standard works, the above sampling should be sufficient to establish the fact that even the names of numerous scriptural figures can remind us of Christ, what he desires of us, and what he promises us.

PLACES OR LOCATIONS AS SYMBOLS OF CHRIST

Those who are converts to The Church of Jesus Christ of Latter-day Saints will likely remember the first time they heard of Kolob. As one born outside of the Church, my introduction to that term occurred while I was a freshman in college. One antagonist of the Church, endeavoring to demean, inaccurately reported that although "the LDS God rarely leaves his planet," he occasionally journeys to Earth "from the star base Kolob."[59] The Abrahamic account does imply that Kolob is the planet or star nearest to the "throne of God" (Abraham 3:3, 9). However, nowhere in scripture is it stated that God *lives* on Kolob.

The notion that Kolob is a type for the Savior, Jesus Christ, is not new.[60] However, aside from the temple, Kolob is perhaps the best example in the standard works of a physical location that is designed to typify the Messiah.

It should be noted that a Christocentric reading of Abraham 3 is the only interpretation of the passage that renders the text beneficial to the pursuit of exaltation. To read Abraham's description of Kolob as solely a statement about astronomy is to miss the point of all scripture, that is, to bring all people unto Christ.

Recognizing the relationship between Kolob and Christ and between the stars and the spirits gives purpose to this revelation. A revelation on astronomy pales in importance to a revelation setting forth the order and nature of the kingdom of God. Abraham was the head of a dispensation, the man through whom all peoples of the earth in that day were to receive the saving principles of the gospel. One cannot reject a prophet—let alone the prophet chosen to stand at the head of one's dispensation—and expect to stand approved of God. The message and the messenger are inseparable; one cannot have the one without the other. When the Lord said to Abraham, "I show these things unto thee before ye go into Egypt, that ye may declare all these words" (v. 15), did the Lord have in mind that Abraham be a visiting professor of astronomy, or a witness of Christ? Surely it is of lesser importance what the Egyptians knew about the revolutions of planets if they had no idea of how they are to receive a remission of sins or become citizens in the kingdom of God. Yet, as is often the case, the great difficulty in missionary work is simply getting people to listen to the message. And what better way to captivate the attention of the Egyptians than to first teach them of Kolob and the stars, and then having done so to say, "Now, behind all that I have taught you about heavenly bodies there stands an even greater truth, a truth through which you become the inheritors of endless blessings—this is the truth about God and his eternal plan for the salvation of all his children."[61]

Abraham himself draws the comparison between Kolob and Christ when he states that just as one star is greater than another, so it is with the spirits of all mankind (see Abraham 3:16–19). The following table identifies major parallels between Kolob and the Savior.

KOLOB	CHRIST
The name of "the great one" is Kolob because it is near unto God (Abraham 3:3, 16).[62]	Jesus is the Great One because of his nearness to God.
Kolob is the star or planet nearest to the throne of God (Abraham 3:2; Facsimile 2, fig. 1).	Jesus is nearest to God in attributes and relation (Hebrews 1:3; 2 Corinthians 4:4; D&C 76:25).
Kolob exists in God's time (Abraham 3:4).	Jesus is certainly on God's time.
Kolob is "after the manner" of, or in the likeness of, the Lord (Abraham 3:4, 24).	Jesus is in the likeness of the Father (Hebrews 1:3).
Kolob is the "first creation" (Abraham 3:2; Facsimile 2, fig. 1).	Jesus is the Firstborn of the Father (D&C 93:21).
Kolob is first in government (Facsimile 2, fig. 1) and governs all that belongs to this same order (Abraham 3:3).	Jesus is the first to govern, and it is he who governs all (Isaiah 9:6; Revelation 17:14; D&C 41:1).
Kolob holds the key of power (Facsimile 2, fig. 2).	In the kingdom of God, Jesus holds the keys, which he has delegated to men on earth (Daniel 7:9–14; D&C 132:45).
There are many "great ones" near Kolob that also govern under it (Abraham 3:2–3).	Jesus had many great rulers around him whom he has authorized to rule in his stead here on the earth (D&C 138:53–55).

Kolob is the source of light for all other stars and planets (Facsimile 2, fig. 5).	Jesus is the source from which radiates all light (D&C 88:6–13).
Kolob is the greatest of all the Kokaubeam (stars) because it is nearest to God (Abraham 3:16).	Jesus is the greatest of all the pre-earth spirits, being described as "like unto God" (Abraham 3:24).
Abraham learned about Kolob through the use of a Urim and Thummim (Abraham 3:1).	The phrase "Urim and Thummim" means "lights and perfections" in Hebrew and appropriately symbolizes Jesus. But *Urim* begins with the first letter of the Hebrew alphabet, *aleph*. And *Thummim* begins with the last letter of the Hebrew alphabet, *tav*. This also reminds us of Jesus, who is the "First and the Last," the "Beginning and the End."

FOOD AS A SYMBOL OF CHRIST

This is a common enough motif in scripture and worship that it should not be new to practicing Latter-day Saints. Perhaps the best-known example of a food that typifies Christ would be the bread utilized by Christians throughout the world when commemorating the sacrifice of Christ through partaking of the sacrament. In John 6 we are told that Christ adopted bread as a symbol of himself. Indeed, Christ declared:

> Our fathers did eat manna in the desert; as it is written, He gave them bread from heaven to eat. . . . Verily, verily, I say unto you, Moses gave you not that bread from heaven; but my Father giveth you the true bread from heaven. For the bread of God is he which cometh down from heaven, and giveth life

unto the world. . . . And Jesus said unto them, I am the bread of life: he that cometh to me shall never hunger; and he that believeth on me shall never thirst. (John 6:31–35.)

Thus Christ not only proclaims himself the "Bread of Life," but also acknowledges that the manna sent by himself as Jehovah to preserve the lives of ancient Israel (during their wilderness trek) was a type or symbol of his life-sustaining flesh. Note some of the following parallels between Jesus and Israel's manna:

MANNA	JESUS
Manna is a form of bread.	Jesus was the "Bread of Life" (John 6:35) who came from Bethlehem (which means the "house of bread").
Manna appeared miraculously from heaven, as supplied by God (Exodus 16; Deuteronomy 8:3).	Jesus was born into mortality in a most miraculous manner, having been sent by God. His second advent will be no less miraculous.
Manna sustained the life of ancient Israel for some forty years—forty being the standard Hebrew number representing trials or tests.	Jesus sustains us both physically and spiritually throughout this life and into the life to come. Only he can enable us to endure life's trials.
Manna is a Hebrew word meaning "What is this?"	Matthew records that of Christ the question was asked, "Who is this?" (Matthew 21:10).
Manna was said to taste sweet like honey (Exodus 16:31).	Not only are the words of Christ sweet to those who love God, but so also are the life, teachings and ministry of the *Logos*, the actual Word of God (John 1:1).

If Israel did not gather their manna before the Sabbath, it would be too late to do so once the Sabbath came (Exodus 16:22–30).	When Christ returns for the Sabbath of the earth's temporal existence (the Millennium), those who have not gathered of his heaven-sent nourishment prior to his arrival will ever remain unfilled (Matthew 25:1–13; Alma 34:33–34).[63]

THE TEMPLE AND CHRIST

President Gordon B. Hinckley has said:

> Each of our temples has on its face the statement "Holiness to the Lord," to which I should like to add the injunction, "Keep His house holy!" . . . I remind you of the absolute obligation to not discuss outside the temple that which occurs within the temple. Sacred matters deserve sacred consideration. We are under obligation, binding and serious, to not use temple language or speak of temple matters outside.[64]

Outside of the holy temple, a spirit of restraint and discretion must necessarily accompany any discussion of temple ordinances, covenants, and worship practices. Such is our intent.

Nevertheless, one point should be understood by those examining this book. Were nothing more to be said, this much must be known: the temple is saturated in symbols of Christ. The language employed, the clothing donned, the covenants entered into, and endowments (or "gifts") received therein are *all* about the Savior, without which there could be no salvation. We simply cannot discuss each of these ideas here. Rather, we will focus on two other aspects of the endowment: the expulsion from the Garden of Eden and the appearance of the three messengers.

Expulsion from the Garden of Eden

In Moses 4 we read, "So I drove out the man, and I placed at the east of the Garden of Eden, cherubim and a flaming sword, which turned every way to keep the way of the tree of life" (Moses 4:31; see also Genesis 3:24). As noted previously, in biblical Hebrew one oriented oneself by facing the east. Thus the movement of Adam and Eve into mortality, and seemingly away from God's presence, was a movement forward—toward God.[65] Rather than a negative event, Adam and Eve's fall was progression in the truest sense.

At the point that the first of the human family were removed from the Garden of Eden, Jehovah placed "cherubim and a flaming sword" to guard the way of the tree of life (Alma 12:21; 42:2; Moses 4:31). The Lord did this to keep Adam and Eve safe. It was to keep them from partaking of the tree of life in their fallen state, which would cause them to "live forever in their sins."[66]

Cherubim, of course, are angels. However, there is some controversy surrounding the placement of cherubim instead of seraphim at the gate of Eden. Drawing on Doctrine and Covenants 38:1, Elder Bruce R. McConkie indicated that seraphs include the unembodied spirits of the premortal existence, but it is unknown if they also included angels in any other physiological state.[67] Scholars invariably emphasize that seraphs are depicted as having six wings.[68] Since the number six is a standard symbol for something that has fallen short of, or has yet to attain perfection, the association of that number with seraphs may be intended to imply that these angels are either premortal spirits or postmortal nonresurrected spirits that have yet to attain perfection and exaltation.[69]

Of cherubs, typologist Patrick Fairbairn indicated that they are the angels who have become like God and dwell in his presence in eternity.[70] One theological dictionary noted that the Hebrew word for *cherub* is likely related to the idea of an "intercessor."[71] Dictionaries, religious and secular alike, often define cherubs as "celestial beings."[72] Joseph Fielding McConkie wrote that cherubs are placed to ensure that the "holiness of God is not violated by those in transgression or those who have not complied with the proper rituals."[73]

It should be firmly understood that the Church has no official doctrine as to whether there are any resurrected seraphs or unembodied cherubs, nor is the linguistic evidence sufficient to settle the issue. Additionally, it does not make any difference in the interpretation of the typology. Oscar W. McConkie Jr. rightly noted that "none of the standard works sets forth either the identity or job description of [cherubs]."[74] The point is simply that the placement of cherubs in Eden rather than seraphs *may* indicate that something symbolic is intended, for if seraphs are unembodied spirits and if cherubs *are* indeed resurrected beings, then the placement of cherubs may suggest that any return to Eden or God's presence would be in the future (i.e., in a resurrected state).[75]

What is the meaning of the tree of life? The symbolism involved may furnish clues. Trees have several standard symbolic meanings. Green trees often represent the righteous, whereas dry trees can symbolize the wicked.[76] M. Catherine Thomas noted that "most often in scripture . . . the tree is an anthropomorphic symbol. A tree serves well as such a symbol because it has, after all, limbs, a circulatory system, the bearing of fruit, and so forth. Specifically, scriptural trees stand . . . for Christ and his attributes."[77] Elsewhere we read, "In ancient times, sacred trees . . . were [representative of the] attributes of the gods."[78] Susan Easton Black wrote: "The tree of life is connected with the cross, the two having somewhat the same significance. Both relate to the resurrection, eternal life, the Lord, and the 'Love of God.' . . . Before the crucifixion of Christ, the *tree of life* symbol was used extensively. After the crucifixion the cross seems to have replaced it to a degree."[79] When Nephi wished to know the meaning of the tree that his father saw in his dream (1 Nephi 11:9–24), the angel showed him a vision of the birth of Christ. The angel then said to Nephi, "Behold the

Lamb of God, yea, even the Son of the Eternal Father! Knowest thou the meaning of the tree which thy father saw?" (1 Nephi 11:21). To this Nephi responded, "It is the love of God" (1 Nephi 11:22). Jesus is the "love of God" (John 3:16) and the "tree of life."

Note that it was acceptable for Adam and Eve to partake of the tree of life as long as they were keeping the commandments, just as it was permissible for them to partake of Jesus' glory so long as they were obeying the commandments.[80] So the question must be asked, after Adam and Eve partook of the fruit of the tree of knowledge of good and evil, why did God place the cherubs with flaming swords to guard the way? As noted, it was to prevent Adam and Eve from partaking of the fruit of the tree of life while they were under the curse of sin. Further, it was to protect Adam and Eve from the direct presence of Christ while they were in their fallen state. But the placement of cherubs has a meaning that is symbolic as well as literal.

Flames likely conjure up images of sanctification or purging. However, there are numerous connotations associated with this relatively popular symbol. Flames are a manifestation of the godly or celestial nature of a thing.[81] They represent holiness, illumination, inspiration, enlightenment, and purification.[82] As for swords, standard symbolic interpretations include the word of God, meaning covenants, commandments, teachings, and so on.[83] Swords symbolize discernment[84] and that which separates.[85]

Curiously, there appears to be a linguistic connection between these two seemingly separate and unrelated symbols. The early twentieth-century linguist and typologist Harold Bayley wrote:

> The symbolism of the sword as the *word* of God is enshrined in the word *Sword*, i.e. *se-word* or *is-word* [meaning] the Fire or Light of the *Word*. The Anglo-Saxon for a sword was *seax* [which meant] "the Fire of the great Fire." Similarly the Italian *spada* resolves into *sepada* [which translates] the Fire of the Shining Father, and the German *sabel* into Fire of Bel.[86]

Thus it appears that in the flaming sword we have a symbol of the celestial and divinely revealed words, commands, or covenants used to discern, protect, and separate the righteous from the disobedient. The cherubs with flaming swords in the Genesis and Moses accounts serve as a representation of those beings who will test us concerning the things we were to learn in this life in order to enter the presence of God. As noted previously, President Brigham Young once stated:

> Your endowment is, to receive all those ordinances in the house of the Lord, which are necessary for you, after you have departed this life, to enable you to walk back to the presence of the Father, passing the angels who stand as sentinels, being enabled to give them the key words, the signs and tokens, pertaining to the holy Priesthood, and gain your eternal exaltation in spite of earth and hell.[87]

Similarly, in section 132 of the Doctrine and Covenants we are told that if we keep the covenants we make in relation to eternal marriage, we will "pass by the angels, and the gods, which are set there, to [our] exaltation and glory in all things, as hath been sealed upon [our] heads" (D&C 132:19).

The placement of these sentinels in front of the tree of life indicates our need for the ordinances and covenants of the temple in order to regain the presence of the Father and the Son—Jesus himself being the tree of life!

Peter, James, and John

In ancient extracanonical religious literature, particularly apocalyptic literature, there was a common theme of three messengers being sent from God to selected mortals. Because the number three represents that which is of God, comes from God, or is authorized by God, the appearance of three messengers suggests where they came from and whom they represented.

As an example of this common motif in reference to Satan, "The Apocalypse of Daniel" states: "Three men will go forth and will condemn him as a liar and a deceiver. And these three men, two from heaven [the resurrected Peter and

James?], and one from the earth [the translated John?]" will expose him as the "Anti-Christ" and encourage all mankind to worship "Christ or Lord."[88] Similarly, President Wilford Woodruff told of how he was accosted by Satanic influences while serving a mission in London and that, in response to his prayer, "the door opened and three messengers entered, and the room was filled with light equal to the blazing of the sun at mid-day. Those messengers were all dressed in robes of immortal beings. Who they were I do not know."[89]

Numerous extracanonical sources speak of the visitation of three messengers to Adam and Eve. These three angels were later to live on the earth as ordinary mortals and prophets.[90] A number of scholars have provided prime examples. For instance, Hugh Nibley noted that "the Mandaean literature will tell you that the messengers that came to instruct Adam and Eve were the apostles who later became the pillars of the Chuch (Peter, James and John)."[91] Similarly, S. Kent Brown wrote:

> According to the Apocalypse of Adam [chapters 2 and 3] . . . Adam's recovery of the knowledge of both his premortal existence and what was to happen in future ages of the earth was . . . learned from three messengers who revealed to him the history of the world from beginning to end. Adam then transmitted those secrets to his son Seth, who was said to transmit them to "his seed," that is, only to worthy initiates.[92]

Cyrus Gordon, an acclaimed historian and philologist, indicated that there was a peculiar preoccupation in early Hebrew epics with "triads of officers," both mortal and heavenly in origin.[93]

On more than one occasion I have been asked, "How it is possible that Peter, James, and John could have had physical contact with Adam and Eve when the Resurrection had yet to take place and these three had yet to be born into mortality?"[94] It appears that the answer to that question has yet to be revealed. However, such a question may actually miss the point. There is likely something symbolic and highly instructive happening in these accounts of three messengers that should not be glossed over.

Peter, James, and John, whether appearing to Adam and Eve or serving as the head of the postresurrection Church in the meridian of time, are symbols of something much greater than themselves, namely, the Godhead. Elder Matthias F. Cowley wrote:

> The offices of this priesthood consist of the First Presidency, a quorum of three, bearing the holy apostleship, and as the organization of the Church on earth typifies the heavenly, these three symbolize the Father, Son and Holy Ghost, and hold the keys of authority over all departments of the Church, on all matters, spiritual and temporal, even as the Godhead is the great ruling power of the universe, the heavens and the earth and all that in them is.[95]

Peter, James and John, then, stand as symbols for the Godhead—as do all subsequent First Presidencies. Whether these three brethren, or any set of tripartite messengers, had physical contact with Adam and Eve (or any other Old Testament figure) makes no difference. What is of importance is what they brought and whom they represented.

On a related note, Satan, in an effort to deceive, appeared in the form of an "angel of light" to the Prophet Joseph Smith and Oliver Cowdery.[96] It was immediately after this Luciferic encounter that Peter, James, and John restored the Melchizedek Priesthood. Of this experience the Prophet wrote: "And again, what do we hear? . . . The voice of Michael on the banks of the Susquehanna, detecting the devil when he appeared as an angel of light! The voice of Peter, James, and John in the wilderness . . . on the Susquehanna river, declaring themselves as possessing the keys of the kingdom, and of the dispensation of the fulness of times" (D&C 128:20). Regarding the setting of the appearance of Lucifer, Adam [Michael], and then Peter, James, and John, we read:

> At Coalsville [sic], he and Oliver were under arrest on

charge of deceiving the people. . . . His attorney told the court that he wanted to see Mr. Smith alone [for] a few moments. When alone Mr. Reid said that there was a mob in front of the house. . . . Hoisting the window, Joseph and Oliver went to the woods [a few rods away], it being night. . . . They traveled until Oliver was exhausted and Joseph almost carried him through mud and water. They traveled all night and just at the break of day Oliver gave out entirely and exclaimed "Oh Lord! How long Brother Joseph have we got to endure this thing." Brother Joseph said that at that very time Peter, James and John came to them and ordained them to the Apostleship. They had 16 or 17 miles to travel to get back to Mr. Hales (his father-in-law) and Oliver did not complain anymore of fatigue.[97]

Lucifer tried to deceive Joseph and Oliver in their frightened and exhausted state by giving them a false revelation. At that very moment Adam appeared and cast Satan out. He then introduced Peter, James, and John as the messengers that Joseph and Oliver should give heed to. Joseph and Oliver were then ordained to the Melchizedek Priesthood. The placement of this event in section 128 of the Doctrine and Covenants, immediately preceding section 129 on the discernment of spirits, is likely not coincidental.

Joseph indicated that whenever "the Keys" have been brought from heaven, "they are revealed . . . by Adam's authority."[98] Indeed, one LDS scholar wrote, "According to Joseph Smith, if Adam did not personally reveal the ordinances, he would send messengers who would teach his posterity the endowment counsels that would lead them in the way of life and salvation."[99]

The typology behind this whole story is significant in understanding how Peter, James, and John symbolize the Godhead. Recalling Elder Cowley's comment about all First Presidencies representing the Father, Son, and Holy Ghost, note the following elements of comparison.

In section 130 of the Doctrine and Covenant we read, "The Father has a body of flesh and bones as tangible as man's;

the Son also; but the Holy Ghost has not a body of flesh and bones, but is a personage of Spirit. Were it not so, the Holy Ghost could not dwell in us" (D&C 130:22). The Father and Son have physical, resurrected bodies. The Holy Ghost, on the other hand, has a nonphysical, nonresurrected body. When they appeared to the Prophet Joseph, Peter and James were resurrected beings with physical bodies like unto the Father and the Son. John, on the other hand, had a nonresurrected translated body (see John 21:21–23; D&C 7:3), which continues to be the case.

James and John of Zebedee were brothers (see Matthew 26:37), just as Jesus and the Holy Ghost are brothers.[100] "Zebedee," their surname, means literally "endowment or gift from God."[101] Jesus is unquestionably a gift from God (see John 3:16), as is the Holy Ghost (see D&C 20:43). Curiously, just as the Holy Spirit's name remains unknown to us, in his Gospel, John refers to himself by titles such as "the disciple whom Jesus loved" (John 13:23) or "another disciple" (John 18:15), rather than using the first person. By so doing, John has confused some scholars as to the identity of this "other" disciple,[102] and like the Holy Ghost, he stands unnamed.

Finally, it is James we associate with the responsibility of teaching and leading prayers in the house of the Lord. In that ordinance he sets a pattern for us to follow. Luke records that Jesus did a similar thing: "And it came to pass that, as he was *praying in a certain place,* when he ceased, one of his disciples said unto him, Lord, teach us to pray" (Luke 11:1; emphasis added). This is followed by a version of the Lord's Prayer. One scholar has argued convincingly that the Lord's Prayer, which is part of the Sermon on the Mount, is itself a temple text.[103] Regarding the temple-oriented nature of Christ's prayer, Elder Bruce R. McConkie wrote: "Jesus himself 'was praying in a certain place.' Prayers may be offered in all places and at all times, but we are dealing here with a particular prayer. . . . Clearly it was a prayer in marked contrast to those customarily offered by the Jews in general. . . . Jesus now [taught] the true order of prayer ... [as] he had done ... in Galilee."[104] Just as anciently Jesus taught his disciples the "true order of prayer," so also in modernity James (as a type for Jesus) teaches this same ordinance to Adam and Eve and thus to all latter-day disciples.

The following chart provides a summary of the parallels between Peter, James, and John and the Godhead.

PETER	JAMES	JOHN
A type for or symbol of God the Father.	A type for or symbol of Jesus the Christ.	A type for or symbol of the Holy Ghost.
A resurrected being with a glorified and perfected body.	A resurrected being with a glorified and perfected body.	The only one of the three with a nonresurrected body, as is the Holy Ghost.
The presiding figure holding and exercising all of the keys.	A brother of John, just as Jesus is a brother of the Holy Ghost.	A brother of James, just as the Holy Ghost is a brother of Jesus.
	His surname means "gift from God," just as Jesus was the ultimate Gift from God.	His surname means "gift from God," just as the Holy Ghost is a gift to us from God.
	In the temple he leads us in prayer, just as Jesus taught his disciples how to properly pray.	In his Gospel, John leaves himself unnamed. The name of the Holy Ghost is also unknown.

The Christocentric nature of the endowment, as shown in these pages, helps us to better understand both what happened in Eden and what we must do in order to return to dwell in God's presence. The Father has revealed commandments, covenants, and ordinances that we are responsible to enter into, obey, and participate in during our sojourn here upon earth. We are taught that Adam and Eve received these requisite principles and powers at the hands of Peter, James, and John. In the last days they have been restored through the Prophet Joseph Smith and are administered under the direction of his successors. Just as Peter, James, and John were types for the Father, Son, and Holy Ghost, we must necessarily see the President of the Church and his two counselors as respective types for the Father, Son, and Holy Spirit. Such is the spirit and teaching behind the Lord's declaration, "Whether by mine own voice or by the voice of my servants, it is the same" (D&C 1:38). If we heed the counsel of the First Presidency as we would the counsel of the heavenly First Presidency, we will indeed regain the presence of the Father and Son and partake of eternal life with them in the celestial kingdom of God. If we do not heed them, we have no such hope.

In the spirit of the teachings of this chapter, we conclude with the words of Elder Bruce R. McConkie:

> If we had sufficient insight, we would see in every . . . rite that is part of revealed religion, in every performance commanded by God, in all things Deity gives his people, something that typifies the eternal ministry of the Eternal Christ. . . . It is wholesome and proper to look for similitudes of Christ everywhere and use them repeatedly in keeping him and his laws uppermost in our minds.[105]

12

SUMMARY OF THE SYMBOLS

THE FOLLOWING TABLES take inventory of many major symbols as they are explained in standard dictionaries and encyclopedias of symbolism and are further illustrated in this book. This chapter provides only brief summaries for the reader's convenience. Detailed definitions of these symbols, along with examples of how they are commonly employed in scripture, are found in the preceding chapters of this book.

ANIMALS	
Ass	Representative of noncovenant peoples.
Bull	Symbolic of royalty, kingship, and protection. A standard symbol for Jehovah and his dependability and strength.
Calf/Cow	Symbolized God in Greek, Hebrew, and Egyptian cultures.
Camel/Hare	Representative of immorality.
Chameleon	A symbol for deceptive people. Some ancient sources also associate chameleons with the sinful practice of gluttony. The weasel, mouse, tortoise, ferret, lizard, snail, and mole are all included in this symbolic category.

Clean animals	Figures of Christ and his followers. Clean animals represent people who pore over the words of God (i.e., "chew the cud") until those truths become part of their very being. They represent people who are more sure-footed (i.e., "cloven-hoofed") because of their gospel grounding and thus are less likely to slip into transgressions. Included in this symbolic category is any animal that chews the cud and "parts the hoof": oxen, sheep, lambs, and goats.
Cormorant	A type for people who succumb to insatiable and unquenchable desires, who are enslaved by passions.
Divided hoof	A symbol for having faith in God and steadily pursuing a course in accordance with the commandments and will of God. Also an image of distinguishing between right and wrong, with the view to choose the right and avoid the opposite.
Divided hoof without ruminating	A representation of people who are heretical because they profess a faith in God but do not meditate upon his words, whether ancient or modern.
Dog	A symbol for hypocrisy, representing men who repeatedly cycle through the pattern of feigned repentance and a return to past sins. Dogs in Semitic cultures were linked with evil forces and were often depicted as the devil's companion or an enemy of God.
Donkey	In Egypt a symbol for the god of evil. In numerous Hebrew writings the donkey symbolized the devil, evil, harm, and non-covenant people.

Summary of the Symbols

Dove	A symbol of the Holy Ghost, peace, purity, purification, the house of Israel, and constancy.
Dragon/the Serpent	A multifaceted symbol of evil, chaos, darkness, heresy, adversity, and destruction. The Latin and Greek words for "snake" and "dragon" are interchangeable.
Eagle	Sometimes a positive symbol, occasionally even representative of God or Christ. In the Hebrew Bible, however, the eagle can represent people who prey upon the weakness of others to get personal gain. Such do not work for their maintenance but rely on other people's efforts or misfortunes to provide for their needs. Ravens, owls, hawks, swans, pelicans, storks, and bats are all part of this symbolic category.
Fish with fins and scales	Potentially symbols for faithful Israel, rebirth, baptism, the invisible presence of Christ, self-control, and the hope of God.
Fish without fins and scales	Fins and scales keep fish from being swept away by strong currents. Fish so endowed symbolize self-control. Fish that do not have fins or scales tend to swim near the bottom and not with the school, thereby symbolizing people who do not "swim" with the mainstream of the Church but instead endeavor to chart a new path or explore the dark waters of immorality, unethical behavior, and the "mysteries." Those who follow them risk a greater degree of temptation and a heightened potential for apostasy or deception.

Goat	In Judaeo-Christian tradition, goats are alternately sacred and accursed. Apart from their evil connotations (e.g., Satan, the damned, sinners, lust), they can symbolize Christ burdened with our sins.
Grasshopper	Represents Church members who have overcome or risen above this world and its telestial temptations, cravings, and lifestyle.
Hare/Camel	Carries well-established symbolic connotations of immorality, adultery, fornication, and so on. This category of symbolism includes camels.
Hawk	Symbolizes people who prey on the weakness of others to get personal gain. Such do not work for their maintenance but rely on other people's work or misfortunes to provide for their needs. Eagles, ravens, owls, vultures, swans, pelicans, storks, and bats are all part of this symbolic category.
Hyena	A symbol for immorality.
Lamb	Representative of Christ and his followers; also gentleness, innocence, meekness, purity, humility, and the surrender of personal will.
Lamprey	Symbolic of members who take exception to the norms of the Church, who gravitate toward alternate paths, seedy places, and dark things. Anciently, this fish symbolized people who were altogether ungodly. See "Fish without fins or scales" above.
Locusts	Represents members of the Church who have overcome this world and its telestial temptations, cravings, and lifestyle.

Owl	Denotes scavengers who seek gain via the work and misfortunes of others; associated with darkness, death, evil, ingratitude, desolation, and mourning. The ancients held owls to be an omen for evil and impending death. See "Vulture" below.
Ox	Represents members of Christ's church, particularly when coupled with an ass; also denotes obedience, sacrifice, strength of character, and deity. Oxen served as a symbol for the Messiah under the Mosaic sacrificial system.
Pig/Swine	A symbol of those who call upon or remember their God only in times of need, but when their life is going well, they forget their Maker; also symbolic of the quintessential hypocrite and of greed, gluttony, and unbridled passions.
Rabbit	Represents immorality, adultery, fornication, and so on. This category of symbolism includes camels.
Ram	A representation of Christ, resurrection, protection, and sacrifice.
Raven	A scavenger bird symbolizing evil, mortification, corruption, sin, wandering, unrest, uncleanliness, carrion, impurity, destruction, deceit, and death. See "Vulture" below.
Rumination	To "chew the cud," or ruminate, was a symbol in ancient societies for meditating day and night on the words of God and being adorned with good works.

Ruminating but not parting the hoof	A symbol for members of the Church who have the words of God but do not heed them.
Serpent/Snake	Sometimes refers to the Messiah and resurrection but can also represent the devil, temptation, evil, and sin.
Sheep	A typification of Christ and his followers; symbolizes gentleness, innocence, meekness, purity, humility, and surrendering personal will.
Snail	A symbol of deceit, laziness, and sin.
Undivided hoof	A figure of those who struggle to distinguish between good and evil; for early Christians a symbol for not being well grounded in the gospel or pursuing a course leading back to God.
Vulture	Represents those who prey on the weakness of others to get personal gain. Such do not work for their maintenance but rely on other people's efforts or misfortunes to provide for their needs. Ravens, eagles, owls, hawks, swans, pelicans, storks, and bats are part of this symbolic category.
Weasel	A symbol for people who are deceptive or misrepresentative.
Wolf	A representation of evil, the devil, craftiness, heresy, bloodthirstiness, or the dark side of one's personality.

BODY PARTS

Arm	A symbol for power or strength, both human and divine. When folded, arms symbolize submission; when upraised, they connote prayer.
Blood	A multifaceted symbol for life, humanity, mortality, sin, impurity, sacrifice, and death.
Bosom/Breast	A figure for favored status or the nonsexual intimacy of a relationship; also represents a place of security, protection, or nurturing.
Bowels	Symbolize compassion, feelings, or emotion; also occasionally associated with the loins and thus with reproduction or fertility.
Ear	A symbol for a person's receptivity and obedience, what we choose to hearken to or obey.
Eye	A representation of light, knowledge, insight, and revelation; can also represent what we desire or long for. Multiple eyes symbolize omniscience or godliness.
Foot	A figure for how we live and what path we choose to follow. Feet also represent having power over someone (i.e., those under our feet are in subjection to us).
Forehead	A symbol for what we think about, love, or desire; secondarily a symbol for thoughts, which in antiquity were associated with the heart.
Hair	This symbol, although complex, was traditionally associated with life and health, both spiritual and physical.

Hand	A figure of our actions or pursuits. Clasped hands symbolized solidarity or covenantal relationship, while the placement of one's hand on another's was traditionally a symbol for the conferral or transfer of power or authority.
Head	A representation of that which governs the body. When crowned, it was a symbol for authority, royalty, or ruling power; also an emblem of the entirety of the person.
Heart	A symbol for the seat of knowledge, receipt of revelation, omniscience, true inner man, and so on.
Horn	A symbol for power or strength, both good and bad.
Knee	A representation of the state of one person in relation to another (e.g., bowed knees represent submission).
Loins	The primary symbol for offspring, reproductive powers, and omnipresence. A secondary meaning is preparedness.
Neck	An outward symbol of the state of our heart. When bowed, the neck is a symbol of humility, submission, or mourning. When stiff or erect, the neck is a symbol of pride, obstinacy, or disobedience.
Nose	A figurative representation of anger or temperament.
Shoulder	A symbol for labor, burdens, and responsibilities.

Throat	As related to our voice, the throat represented power and omnipotence, and more specifically priesthood power or the ability and right to command.
Wing	A symbol for a being's power to move and to act.

COLORS

Black	The traditional color of grief, sorrow, and mourning. Also carries overtones of foreboding, negativity, sin, evil, death, judgment, corruption, darkness, and destruction.
Blue	Most often a symbol of godliness, spirituality, and the heavenly nature of a thing.
Brass	A symbol of judgment.
Brown	In contrast with green, brown represents judgment, damnation, and death.
Gold	A representation of wealth, temporal power, and worldliness; also implies the celestial, divine, or godly nature of a thing.
Green	A standard symbol for life, including eternal life.
Pale Green	An image of impending death.
Purple	Among the ancients, this color invoked images of wealth, power, royalty, and majesty.
Red/Scarlet	Both colors represent a host of interrelated ideas, including sin, blood, atonement, war, violence, and death.
Silver	A symbol for redemption and moral purity.

White	Symbolizes purity, righteousness, holiness, innocence, victory, light, and revelation; also occasionally associated with happiness and the Spirit.

CLOTHING

Apron	A symbol with many applications, including fertility, reproduction, priesthood, and work.
Armor of God	A scriptural motif for the sources of protection that God has provided us and by which we can resist evil and ensure our exaltation.
Bows	A representation of the marriage covenant between man and wife and thus between God and his church.
Breastplate of righteousness	A symbol for controlling our thoughts and desires.
Breeches	An emblem of the glory that God, Christ, and all celestial resurrected beings possess. According to the Apostle Paul, it is also a symbol for the flesh of Christ.
Cap/Crown/Hat	A figurative representation of authority, victory, wisdom, and power.
Coat of skins	See "Garments" below.
Footwear	See "Shoes/Sandals/Slippers" below.
Garments	An emblem of the glory that God, Christ, and all celestial resurrected beings possess. According to the Apostle Paul, it is also a symbol for the flesh of Christ.
Girdle of truth	A symbol for using truth to not be deceived by the temptations and traps associated with immodesty and immorality.

Summary of the Symbols

Helmet of salvation	A symbol of the importance of controlling and limiting what enters our body, heart, mind, and being. Figuratively, the helmet suggests that salvation will be had only if we protect our eyes, mind, ears, and mouth from things forbidden by God.
Robes	An image of priesthood power.
Sackcloth	Traditionally worn by mourners as a token of their grief, humiliation, repentance, or dismay.
Sashes	In certain periods, the wearing of a sash symbolized chastity, virginity, or faithfulness.
Shield of faith	A symbol of protection from spiritual death through our ability to deflect temptations and evil assaults through faith in the Lord Jesus Christ.
Shoes/Sandals/ Slippers	Can represent enslavement and poverty when absent, and entrance into a hallowed place when removed (though the removal of shoes can also suggest a covenant in which one party gives up a place of residence in the hope of inheriting a better one). Having our feet shod "with the preparation of the gospel of peace" implies that the gospel is sound, trustworthy, and safe, giving those who rely on it a sure footing or stability in life.
Swaddling clothes	Symbolic of parental care and compassion, and also impending death.
Sword of the Spirit	A representation of the reality that the scriptures, covenants, and teachings of the living prophets, combined with the constant companionship of the Holy Ghost, will ensure our safe return from the spiritual battle that currently rages.

Veils	Three significant symbolic connotations of a veiled face are chastity, virtue, and modesty; submission, obedience, or commitment; and divinely recognized authority or power possessed by the veiled person.

DIRECTIONS

East	Traditionally associated with the presence of God or his influence. To face east was to face God. To move eastward was to move toward him. An attack from the east symbolized receipt of the wrath of God.
North	Its literal meaning in Hebrew is "dark," "hidden," "gloomy," and "left-handed" (i.e., "noncovenant"); thus it is a very negative symbol representative of apostasy.
South	In Hebrew it is associated with the covenant or covenant making because when we face east, south is at our right hand. In Greek, south is associated with that which is from heaven, such as heaven-sent refreshment or revelation.
West	A very negative symbol associated with sorrow, chaos, undesirability, evil, darkness, the kingdom of the devil, and death.

NUMBERS

⅓ or ⅔ part	A symbol for the idea that bounds have been set and power is limited.
1	A token of unity between the members of the Godhead, the Church, or any specified group. It can also symbolize God as the origin of all things.
2	As a layered symbol, it implies opposition, separation, and good versus evil. In Hebrew it represents the life force, creative power, and the combination of male and female. Under the law of Moses, it related to the canonical necessity of two witnesses in order to sustain a charge against someone.
3	A symbol of the Godhead and divine involvement, backing, or influence. For this reason, it is heavily associated with the atonement of Christ (e.g., Golgotha's three crosses, three hours of darkness, three days in the tomb).
3½	Being half of seven, it symbolizes something that has been arrested midway in normal course.
4	This number implies geographic fulness or totality, the earth, and the universality of divine acts.
5	Evokes images of divine grace and man in a fallen or mortal state.
6	A negative symbol conveying the idea of deficit, imperfection, or failure to attain completeness.

7	The most common of all symbolic numbers, it represents fulness, completion, wholeness, spiritual perfection, and totality. In Egypt it symbolized eternal life.
8	A symbol of resurrection, new beginnings, rebirth, baptism, and Christ.
9	This symbol evokes images of judgment, finality, and completion (in a negative sense).
10	Denotes "all of a part," or a whole or complete unit existing within a greater whole.
11	A rare symbol for sin, transgression, peril, conflict, disorder, imperfection, and disintegration.
12	Representative of priesthood, including its power and right to govern.
13	Rare in scripture, it foreshadows apostasy and is an evil omen.
24	As with any multiple of twelve, it symbolizes fulness of priesthood or making one's calling and election sure.
40	Suggests a period of trial, testing, probation, or mourning.
42	Carries the same connotation as 3½ and 1,260: arrested midway in normal course.
144	As with any multiple of twelve, it symbolizes fulness of the priesthood or making our calling and election sure.
666	With six as the symbol of imperfection, the triple repetition of the number six is commonly seen as a "trinity of imperfection," symbolic of Satan, the great and abominable church, and the anti-Christ—all imperfect and all setting themselves up as divine.

888	Represents Christ.
1,000	A symbol for completion. When associated with another number, it serves to magnify the symbolic meaning of the other number.
1,260	Carries the same connotation as 3½ and 42: arrested midway in normal course.
144,000	As with any multiple of twelve, it symbolizes fulness of the priesthood or making one's calling and election sure.

OTHER SYMBOLS

Ark of the covenant	A symbol for the presence or manifestation of God and also for the church of God. Because the ark was both wood and gold, many commentators see it as a symbol for the two natures of Christ—mortal and divine.
Bride/Woman	The Church of Jesus Christ or covenant Israel (includes males and females).
Bridegroom	The Messiah, Jesus the Christ.
Budding rod	The resurrected Christ, priesthood authority, divine investiture of authority.
Cherubs	Angels that stand as sentinels or guards, protecting us from the presence and glory of God until through covenants we are prepared to be received again into the presence of God.
Figs	Ancient symbols for fertility, reproduction, or the covenant people. Because early Jewish legend held that the tree of knowledge of good and evil was a fig tree, some commentators associate figs with sin and the fall of man.

Flaming swords	Symbolize the celestial and divinely revealed words, commands, or covenants used to discern, protect, and separate the righteous from the disobedient. Also represent those things we are to learn in this life in order to enter the presence of God.
Font/Baptistry	A symbol for the death, burial, and resurrection of Christ. Thus, represents not only Christ's atonement for us, but our need to allow the "natural man" within us to die if we are to gain access to Christ's sacrifice. The font mirrors the death of our sins and our effort to be born again.
Incense	A symbol meaning that the prayers of the Saints ascend to God.
Kolob	This star "nearest unto the throne of God" is a detailed type for Christ.
Leaven	Traditionally representative of infiltration, scattering, or dispersion. When used positively, leaven symbolizes the growth of the Church permeating the world. When used negatively, it illustrates the scattering or dispersion of the Saints as a punishment for wickedness or disobedience.
Manna	This heaven-sent sustenance symbolizes Christ, the "Bread of Life."
Mountain	An image of the temple or house of the Lord; also representative of revelation, inspiration, separation from the world, and so on.
Name	A symbol for a person's personality, character, nature, authority, or status. To be in possession of another person's esoteric name implied that one held power over the named person.

Summary of the Symbols

Olive oil	A symbol for the Holy Ghost and its influence and thus associated with revelation, inspiration, consecration, healing, and the Atonement.
People	For detailed information on individual people whose lives were typologically significant, see the tables in chapter 8.
Salt	A symbol of covenant making and sacrifice. Salt also represents purity and preservation from corruption.
Sun	A symbol for the Son of God and the glory of things celestial or divine in nature. A daily reminder of the second coming of Christ.
Tree of life	A symbol for the Savior and the blessings associated with his life, ministry, gospel, and atonement. As Christ is the source of immortality, so also the tree was said to be the source of that same blessing for Adam and Eve. In addition, dry trees represent the wicked and green trees the righteous.
Water	In scripture, water can symbolize two very different concepts: (1) cleansing, sanctification, revelation, and the Holy Spirit; and (2) chaos, death, and the grave.

NOTES

NOTES TO PREFACE

1. See, for example, Barber, *Celestial Symbols*; Brown, *Gate of Heaven*; Brown and Smith, *Symbols in Stone*; Charles, *Endowed from on High*; Compton, "Symbolism," 3:1428–30; Draper, *Opening the Seven Seals*; Holland, "Souls, Symbols, and Sacraments"; Holzapfel and Seely, *My Father's House*; Lund, "Understanding Scriptural Symbols"; McConkie, "The Bible—A Sealed Book"; McConkie, *Gospel Symbolism*; McConkie and Parry, *Guide to Scriptural Symbols*; Parry and Parry, *Understanding the Book of Revelation*; Read, *Unveiling Biblical Prophecy*; Smith, *Book of Revelation*; and Wilcox, *House of Glory*, 27.
2. See Wilcox, *House of Glory*, 27.
3. A comment by a noted biblical scholar is apropos here: "It would be blasphemy to suppose that such a work could be complete; for it would assume that the wonders of this mine could be exhausted, and that its treasures could be all explored" (Bullinger, *Number in Scripture*, vi).
4. Dixon, *Senate Prayers of Peter Marshall*, 95. Dr. Marshall wrote these words on Wednesday, 26 January 1949, with the intention of offering them as part of his Thursday morning prayer on the floor of the U.S. Senate. However, he passed away later that evening. The prayer was read the next morning by Dr. Clarence W. Cranford, on behalf of Dr. Marshall.
5. My source for the gold mine analogy is Johnston, *Numbers in the Bible*, 110. "'It is the glory of God to conceal a thing: but the honor of kings is to search out a matter' (Proverbs 25:2). In searching out the secrets of the word of God, we are doing not only a royal, but an honorable work" (Bullinger, *Number in Scripture*, 20).

NOTES TO CHAPTER 1: WHY SYMBOLS?

1. There is a crucial distinction between *exegesis* (applying the principles of hermeneutics, or biblical interpretation, to arrive at the original writer's intended meaning, that is, the actual meaning) and *eisegesis* (reading into a text a meaning that the author likely did not intend). Although Latter-day

Saints often accuse other religions of eisegesis, lay members of the Church are all too frequently guilty of this themselves. Eisegesis is sometimes referred to as "prooftexting" or, in other words, interpreting a verse without due attention to the context in which it is found. For a helpful primer on hermeneutics, see Virkler, *Hermeneutics*, 16, 18, 73, 84.

2. I use the generic term *symbolism* to refer not only to symbols but also to types, allegories, parables, and, to a lesser extent, similes, metaphors, and proverbs.

3. See Ryken, Wilhoit, and Longman, *How to Read the Bible as Literature*, 173; and McConkie, *Gospel Symbolism*, 1, 6.

4. The same could be said of those who make no effort to understand the cultural backgrounds of scripture. The result is most assuredly misunderstanding passages that are culturally conditioned. In this regard, books such as Gower's *New Manners and Customs of Bible Times* and Mackie's *Bible Manners and Customs* are most helpful.

5. LDS Bible Dictionary, s.v. "symbolism," 777–78.

6. Conner, *Interpreting the Symbols and Types*, 1, 3.

7. Edwards, *Images or Shadows*, 63.

8. McConkie and Parry, *Guide to Scriptural Symbols*. See McConkie, *Mormon Doctrine*, 773. Elsewhere Joseph Fielding McConkie has written: "There are few if any stories in the scriptures that do not cast a shadow, that are not types or illustrations of greater principles or events. Virtually every passage of scripture is layered with meaning, and its full interpretation need not be limited to our present understanding. . . . For us to begin to see those countless types and shadows, the endless symbolic representations of Christ, is for us to be ever assured of the reality of his gospel and the blessings enjoyed by those who choose to live it" (*Gospel Symbolism*, 249).

9. See Virkler, *Hermeneutics*, 140–45, 184–85. Gilbert Cope put it this way: The purpose of the Bible is to change and sanctify the "human destiny" (*Symbolism in the Bible and the Church*, 11). See Childs, *Old Testament Theology*, 89; Edwards, *Images or Shadows*, 63, 77; and Goppelt, *Typos*, 48–50.

10. Fee and Stuart, *How to Read the Bible*, 80.

11. Origen, "Homily on Leviticus," 32. "By the beginning of the eighteenth century, an array of Deists and Freethinkers, supported by a scholarship which could not be scorned, suddenly appeared on the scene with the contention that if biblical rhetoric were really to be read in a straightforward, honest fashion, it would prove the Bible to be a book like any other book, like Homer or Virgil." Thus, there must be a typological or deeper symbolic message embedded in the text. "The bizarre rites of the Mosaic law . . . were to be 'opened,' and the doctrines, which were 'invisible,' extracted from them, like the meat from a nut" (Edwards, *Images or Shadows*, 10, 11).

12. Philo's statement to this effect is cited in Davidson, *Typology in Scripture*,

21 note 1. Nephi declared, "I did liken all scriptures unto us, that it might be for our profit and learning" (1 Nephi 19:23). Origen wrote, "For, with respect to holy Scripture, our opinion is that the whole of it has a 'spiritual,' but not the whole a 'bodily' meaning, because the bodily meaning is in many places proved to be impossible" ("De Principiis," 4:369). This corresponds with the Qur'an's proclamation that "God disdains not to use the similitude of [all] things" (Sura 2:26)—including the gnat (the lowest of things), as well as the highest of His creations (see also Sura 22:73; 29:41).

13. Quoted in Davidson, *Typology in Scripture*, 26–27.
14. Goppelt, *Typological Interpretation*, 46.
15. Goppelt directs this counsel to exegetes (see ibid., 57). He also states, "By means of symbolical interpretation a deeper meaning and an intrinsic reason is sought for legal regulations and customs that outwardly seem arbitrary or curious" (ibid., 31). This approach invites "a more profound interpretation of the Old Testament" and motivates the earnest reader to "search for meaning beyond the literal grammatical-historical explanation" (ibid., 7).
16. Read, *Unveiling Biblical Prophecy*, 10.
17. One LDS scholar commented, "More connected to Hebrew traditions than most Christian churches and at the same time eschewing many traditional Christian symbols, LDS symbolism is unique among modern religions" (Compton, "Symbolism," 3:1428).
18. See Althaus, *Theology of Martin Luther*, 96; Childs, *Old Testament Theology*, 85; Terence Fretheim, *Interpreting Biblical Texts*, 121; Goppelt, *Typological Interpretation*, 4, 198, 200; Grant and Tracy, *Short History of the Interpretation of the Bible*, 9, 36; and Lategan, "Hermeneutics," 3:150.
19. Richard Davidson noted that "the Apologists of the second and early third centuries—especially Justin Martyr (d. 165), Tertullian (ca. 160–220), and Irenaeus (ca. 140–202)—made copious use of typology" (Davidson, *Typology in Scripture*, 20. See Cope, *Symbolism in the Bible*, 28, 30; Edwards, *Images or Shadows*, 44–45, 49, 129–30; Farrar, *History of Interpretation*, 156; Goppelt, *Typological Interpretation*, 9; and von Rad, "Typological Interpretation of the Old Testament," 27).
20. Farbridge, *Studies in Biblical and Semitic Symbolism*, 5, 53. J. H. Krutz indicated that a "wide-spread predominance of symbolism in all that concerned the worship of God" prevailed in Old Testament times (*Sacrificial Worship of the Old Testament*, 27). Indeed, an unlimited number of types and symbols fulfilled in the antitypes of the New Testament exist in the Old Testament text. For more discussion, see Davidson, *Typology in Scripture*, 108 note 1; von Rad, *Old Testament Theology*, 2:282–83, 319–429; and Hasel, *Old Testament Theology*, 2:363.
21. Grant and Tracy, *Interpretation of the Bible*, 33. There is a "continuity between Jesus and [Paul]. This continuity is evident in the attitudes of Jesus and of Paul towards the interpretation of the Old Testament. . . . Paul, who lives after the death and resurrection of Jesus, is able to discover

many messianic allusions. . . . He does not deny the reality of the Old Testament history. . . . His exegesis is Christocentric. To him Jesus is the promised Messiah, and not only the passages which explicitly foretell his coming, but the scriptures as a whole, are full of references to him. . . . Paul believes that unless the Old Testament writer had Christ in mind, his expressions would be meaningless. . . . For Christians the Old Testament is not a self-sufficient book. Its message is not complete. It looks forward beyond its own time to the coming of one who we believe came in Jesus" (ibid., 17, 18, 19, 20, 25–26).
22. Ibid., 11.
23. Lee, "Truly All Things Testify of Him," 99.
24. Conner, *Interpreting the Symbols and Types*, 4–5.
25. See ibid., 5, 12; Grunfeld, *Jewish Dietary Laws*, 1:25; and Goppelt, *Typological Interpretation*, xvi, 48–50, 201–2.
26. One controversial aspect of contemporary biblical interpretation involves the degree to which one should take scripture literally or figuratively. Conservative Christians have been condescendingly referred to as "wooden-headed literalists," whereas theologically liberal Christians tend to see events such as the Fall, the Deluge, or the life of Job as nonhistorical metaphors, allegories, or symbols (see Virkler, *Hermeneutics*, 27). But, as three scholars note, "it is not a matter of making things up but of 'packaging' them—in other words, of selectivity and arrangement. . . . There can be no doubt that the writers of the Bible carefully selected and arranged their material. The result is that the accounts we find in the Bible are more highly structured than real life is ordinarily felt to be, with the result that we see things more clearly in the Bible than we usually do in real life" (Ryken, Wilhoit, and Longman, *Dictionary of Biblical Imagery*, xvi–xvii). Elsewhere we read that in the New Testament Jesus "regards the events of the Old Testament times as real events. . . . And yet they are more than historical events. They have direct relevance to the times in which Jesus stands" (Grant and Tracy, *Interpretation of the Bible*, 9). Appropriately, Ryken, Wilhoit, and Longman ask, "Do literary conventions mean that the Bible is fictional? It is fair to ask at this point how all this talk about literary conventions relates to the question of the historicity or fictionality of the Bible. The answer, in brief, is that the presence of conventions and literary artifice in the Bible does not by itself say anything at all about historicity or fictionality" (Ryken, Wilhoit, and Longman, *Dictionary of Biblical Imagery*, xvi).
27. McKechnie, *Webster's New Twentieth Century Dictionary*, s.v. "symbol," 1847.
28. Bullinger, *Figures of Speech*, 769.
29. Buttrick, "Symbol," 4:472.
30. McKechnie, *Webster's New Twentieth Century Dictionary*, s.v. "symbol," 1847.
31. Compton, "Symbolism," 3:1428; see Conner, *Interpreting the Symbols and Types*, 5. Compton's reference to the writings of Plato is found in *Meno*,

81c–d, where Meno asks Socrates, "What do you mean when you say that we don't learn anything, but that what we call learning is recollection?"
32. McConkie, *Mormon Doctrine*, 553.
33. See McConkie, *Gospel Symbolism*, 1.
34. Frye, *Anatomy of Criticism*, 99.
35. See Bayley, *Lost Language of Symbolism*, 1:96–97; 2:309; Cooper, *Encyclopaedia of Traditional Symbols*, 94–95; Ryken, Wilhoit, and Longman, *Dictionary of Biblical Imagery*, 484; Tresidder, *Symbols and Their Meanings*, 60; and Wilson, *Dictionary of Bible Types*, 248.
36. Ryken, Wilhoit, and Longman, *Dictionary of Biblical Imagery*, 99.
37. See Farbridge, *Biblical and Semitic Symbolism*, 231; Ryken, Wilhoit, and Longman, *Dictionary of Biblical Imagery*, 99–101; and Wilson, *Dictionary of Bible Types*, 44–46. Some dictionaries and encyclopedias of symbolism place a seemingly positive spin on blood as a symbol. However, when blood is seen as a potentially positive token (via its connection with covenant making, sacrifice, or life), it is often still negative because of its tie to the penalties associated with covenant breaking, the bloodshedding sacrifice of Christ on our behalf, and the Fall of man, the latter bringing death and sin into the world.
38. McConkie, *Gospel Symbolism*, ix.
39. Habershon, *Study of the Types*, 22.
40. See McConkie, *Gospel Symbolism*, ix.

NOTES TO CHAPTER 2: THE ART OF INTERPRETING SYMBOLS

1. See Lategan, "Hermeneutics," 3:149.
2. Ryken, Wilhoit, and Longman, *Dictionary of Biblical Imagery*, xiv.
3. See ibid., xiii–xiv.
4. Virkler, *Hermeneutics*, 184–85. "A Symbol [is] a 'timeless figurative representation,' and a type [is] a 'figure or adumbration of that which is to come.' Symbols are objects expressing general truth, while types express relationships between historical facts. However, this distinction is blurred . . . and even traditional typologists tend to visualize symbols and types together as virtually synonymous" (101–2).
5. Ibid., 184.
6. See ibid., 188–89.
7. For examples of prophetic lives typifying the Messiah, see chapter 8 herein. See also Fairbairn, *Typology of Scripture*, 1:73–74, 114, 122, 125; Habershon, *Study of the Types*, 122–34, 165–74; McConkie, *His Name Shall Be Joseph*, 78–79; and McConkie, *Gospel Symbolism*, 146–60.
8. See Maxwell, *Look Back at Sodom*; and Roberts, *New Witnesses for God*, 1:365.
9. See Leviticus 21:16–24; and *Old Testament: Genesis–2 Samuel*, 187–88.

10. Virkler, *Hermeneutics*, 158.
11. Ryken, Wilhoit, and Longman, *Dictionary of Biblical Imagery*, xiv.
12. Examples from the Old Testament include 2 Samuel 12:1–4, where Nathan prophetically alludes to David's adultery and murder by telling a parable, and Ecclesiastes 9:13–16, which records a parable given to teach the lesson that wisdom is better than physical strength, even if society disregards it.
13. LDS Bible Dictionary, s.v. "parables," 740–41. "The text only has a single meaning, . . . that which was intended by the writer" (Danielou, *The Bible and the Liturgy*, 242). Gilbert Cope argues: "We have to distinguish between, on the one hand, a narrative (or saying) which is deliberately and consciously composed to have two meanings—a literal sense and a second or allegorical sense, and, on the other hand, a narrative (or saying) which is capable of being '*allegorized*'—i.e., a narrative which was originally intended to be a straightforward account of what was believed to have happened (or to have been said), but which can subsequently be interpreted as referring to something else as well. . . . These varieties of allegorization, in the main, were used to relate the Old Testament to the New Testament—the content of the Old Testament deriving its full and proper meaning from what is recounted in the New Testament by the process of 'back-interpretation.' Hence the saying: 'The New is concealed in the Old—the Old is revealed in the New'" (*Symbolism in the Bible*, 18–19). As noted in chapter 1 herein, the presence of symbolic material in a narrative does not necessarily affect the likelihood of the event's historicity.
14. See Virkler, *Hermeneutics*, 159.
15. Good examples may be found in the parables of the unjust judge (Luke 18:1–9) and of the friend at midnight (Luke 11:5–10). In both of these parables we see a male figure who, if taken as a representation of God the Father, completely distorts the intended message.
16. The *sensus mysticus*, or "allegory[,] is generally defined as the search for a more profound meaning hidden beneath the shell of the literal sense. Typology . . . becomes a subdivision of allegory. . . . [T]ypology was an attempt to identify the features in sacred history and in the characteristic elements of Mosaic worship that are preparatory for a comprehensive picture of the life and ministry of Jesus" (Goppelt, *Typos*, 9). Many typologists acknowledge that the distinction between typology and allegory may be more contrived than real. The historical correspondence often said to set the two apart is not always clear or evident in typology, and it is sometimes present in allegory (see Barr, "Biblical Theology," 103–48; Davidson, *Typology in Scripture*, 96, 100–101; and Jewett, "Concerning the Allegorical Interpretation of Scripture," 1–20).
17. Jorgensen, "The Dark Way to the Tree," 220.
18. Ryken, Wilhoit, and Longman, *Dictionary of Biblical Imagery*, xv.
19. Jorgensen, "Typological Unity," 222.
20. Ryken, Wilhoit, and Longman, *Dictionary of Biblical Imagery*, xvii.

21. A more narrow archetype might be one that is recognized by all who are active members of the Church or, even more esoteric, one that is known exclusively by those who have received an endowment in the temple.
22. Ibid., 172.
23. Lategan, "Hermeneutics," 149.
24. Klein, Blomberg, and Hubbard, *Introduction to Biblical Interpretation*, 184–85; emphasis removed.
25. Greidanus, *Preaching Christ from the Old Testament*, 36.
26. See Virkler, *Hermeneutics*, 76–77, 94; and Klein, Bloomberg, and Hubbard, *Introduction to Biblical Interpretation*, 155.
27. von Rad, "Typological Interpretation of the Old Testament," 38. See Goppelt, *Typological Interpretation*, 201–2. Gilbert Cope added, "The application of scientific techniques of literary, historical and textual criticism to the Scriptures themselves" has only "further complicated" man's attempt at understanding the Bible's efforts to sanctify and direct the "human destiny" (*Symbolism in the Bible*, 11).
28. Grant and Tracy, *Short History of the Interpretation of the Bible*, 134.
29. See Read, *Unveiling Biblical Prophecy*, 11–12. See also McConkie, *Mormon Doctrine*, 553. The introduction to a book on biblical imagery states: "Bible dictionaries and commentaries commonly err in . . . [that] some resources channel all their energies into uncovering the original context of an image, making sure that we get the literal picture but never asking what feelings or meanings are elicited by the image. Images call for interpretation, and to leave biblical imagery uninterpreted is a great waste. The images of the Bible exist to *tell* us something about the godly life, something they will not do if they are allowed to remain as physical phenomena only. In short, a common failing of commentaries and dictionaries is that they do not adequately speak to the issue of *significance* (what an image signifies by way of meaning)" (Ryken, Wilhoit, and Longman, *Dictionary of Biblical Imagery*, xiv–xv).
30. In part I have drawn on the hermeneutical suggestions of Elder Bruce R. McConkie, "The Bible—A Sealed Book"; Conner, *Interpreting the Symbols and Types*, 12–15; and Lund, "Understanding Scriptural Symbols," 23–27.
31. *Teachings of the Prophet Joseph Smith*, 291.
32. Examples of the latter would be Elder Russell M. Nelson's explanation of John 20, as given in the April 1993 general conference (in Conference Report, 40), and the teachings of Joseph Smith, which are saturated with clarifications of scripture.
33. See D&C 76:70, 75–78, and surrounding context on the kingdoms of glory likened to the sun and moon. Regarding the importance of understanding the nature of a symbol, one scholar wrote: "The significance of a symbol is based upon the literal or actual nature and characteristics of that which is being used as a symbol. A symbol is meant to represent something essentially different from itself. The link between that which is

used as a symbol and that which is symbolized is the characteristic common to both" (Conner, *Interpreting the Symbols and Types*, 13).
34. It is worth noting the distinction between figurative and symbolic words (see Virkler, *Hermeneutics*, 27). For example, speaking literally, one might say, "A crown, sparkling with jewels, was placed on the king's head." Speaking figuratively, an angry father might say to his son, "If you do that once more, I'll crown you!" Yet with symbolic intent the apostle John penned the following: "A great and wondrous sign appeared in heaven: a woman clothed with the sun, with the moon under her feet and a crown of twelve stars on her head" (Revelation 12:1).
35. Of knowing and utilizing Hebrew and Greek, Elder Bruce R. McConkie stated: "There is certainly no objection to this, but it does have some hazards. Joseph Smith and some of our early Brethren studied Hebrew. When a knowledge of ancient languages is used properly—as a means of gaining inspiration about particular passages—it merits a rating of, say, one or one and two-tenths. Improperly used, as an end in itself, its value sinks off the scale to a minus five or a minus ten, depending upon the attitude and spiritual outlook of the user. Those who turn to the original tongues for their doctrinal knowledge have a tendency to rely on scholars rather than prophets for scriptural interpretations. This is perilous; it is a sad thing to be numbered with the wise and the learned who know more than the Lord" (*Doctrines of the Restoration*, 284–85). Nevertheless, it should be remembered that Elder McConkie himself frequently offered insights from the Hebrew or Greek. What seems important is that we regard such training as supplemental (rather than primary) and then acquire the skills or tools necessary to utilize it as needed. There are numerous helps available, ranging from the less academic, such as James Strong's *Exhaustive Concordance of the Bible* or W. E. Vine's *An Expository Dictionary of New Testament Words*, to the more scholarly, like Johannes Botterweck and Helener Ringgren's *Theological Dictionary of the Old Testament*, Gerhard Kittel's *Theological Dictionary of the New Testament*, Francis Brown's *Brown-Driver-Briggs Hebrew and English Lexicon*, Joseph Thayer's *Greek-English Lexicon of the New Testament*, and W. Robertson Nicoll's *The Expositor's Greek Testament*. Many have found the facsimile edition of *Noah Webster's First Edition* [1828] *of An American Dictionary of the English Language* helpful in understanding what the Prophet Joseph Smith intended in his translation of the Book of Mormon and in the revelations recorded in the Doctrine and Covenants.
36. See McConkie, *Gospel Symbolism*, x. See chapter 8 of this work for the typology of Joseph of Egypt.
37. Virkler, *Hermeneutics*, 76, 28; emphasis removed.
38. McConkie, *Doctrines of the Restoration*, 287–88.
39. Admittedly, we do not approach scripture *tabula rasa* (i.e., with an intellectually "blank slate"). Thus, it can be difficult to set aside preconceived notions of what a symbol means. Martin Heidegger developed "his concept of the hermeneutical circle. To begin with, interpretation never starts

with a clean slate. The interpreter brings a certain pre-understanding to the process. This pre-understanding is challenged when new possibilities for existence are exposed through the event of understanding, which leads to a modification or revision of the interpreter's self-understanding. Finally, the modified understanding becomes the new pre-understanding in the next phase of the process" (Lategan, "Hermeneutics," 149). This process is successful only if we are willing to set aside our preconceived notions.

40. Many who specialize in biblical studies find the fact that allegory and typology soared during the period when the Greeks had influence over the Jews and Christians as sufficient reason to reject those approaches to interpreting scripture. Their position is that any typological, symbolic, or allegorical interpretation is simply a holdover from the days of Philo and the patristic fathers, including the influence that Egyptian allegory had on them, and therefore has no place in today's historical-critical environment. Overall, this is a weak argument because the typological and symbolic approaches were well under way at least by the time of Isaiah (see Alsup, "Typology," 6:684).

41. "There are occasional uses of figurative imagery, such as Ezekiel's 'wheels' (see Ezek. 1:15–21), for which the Lord has not yet given us the interpretation. But for the most part, we do have the keys for understanding the symbolic imagery used by the Lord and his prophets" (Lund, "Understanding Scriptural Symbols," 23). "Interpretation is essential to discerning the will of God" (Lategan, "Hermeneutics," 150).

42. McConkie, *Gospel Symbolism*, x.

43. Ryken, Wilhoit, and Longman, *Dictionary of Biblical Imagery*, xiii. A major difference between those of the house of Israel in Jerusalem and their New World counterparts was that the Nephites knew the meanings of types while the main branch of the house of Israel in the Old World was left in darkness because of hardheartedness (see Mosiah 3:15; 13:30–32).

44. "Figural interpretation is not figurative, not merely allegorical, for both figure and fulfillment, both type and antitype, . . . both 'sign and what it signifies' are regarded as fully historical. When Jesus cites Jonah or Moses' brazen serpent as figures of himself, when Paul cites Adam as a type for Christ, when Jacob in the Book of Mormon cites Abraham's sacrifice as 'a similitude of God and his Only Begotten Son'—none of them denies the historicity of the event or person thus given the added dimension of figural meaning (see Matt. 12:40; John 3:14; Rom. 5:14; Jac. 4:5)" (Jorgensen, "Typological Unity," 221).

45. Read, *Unveiling Biblical Prophecy*, 13, 15; emphasis removed. Remember the injunctions to "liken all scriptures unto us" (1 Nephi 19:23) and to "deny not the spirit of revelation" (D&C 11:25). The famous typologist Jonathan Edwards said that we should ask of each biblical event and experience, "What is God saying to me?" (*Images or Shadows*, 4, 98–99). Much of scripture is traditionally believed to have multiple fulfillment: "Prophecies are not always limited in their intent to events within the

range of understanding of those to whom they were first addressed. . . . Their fulfillment may go well beyond the understanding of the prophet by whom they were spoken" (McConkie, *Gospel Symbolism*, 243, 245).

46. Packer, in Conference Report, October 1984, 81–82. "The answer is simple, and appropriately it is given in the scriptures: 'Truth embraceth truth' (D&C 88:40). Interpretations in full harmony with truths already revealed are currency backed by the gold of heaven. Conversely, any doctrine relying on the interpretations of a parable, allegory, or symbol must be rejected. Let us state it thus—we do not deduce doctrine from parables; we do not concoct it from allegories; we do not wring it out of symbolic interpretations. But when that doctrine has already been revealed, when it has been clearly stated in the scriptures and by living prophets, then responsible interpretations of parables, allegories, or symbols that sustain the revelation already given are smiled upon by the heavens and may properly wear the label of divine truth. Thus, our gospel understanding must always come first. Before we can understand the symbol, we must understand the truth it is to convey" (McConkie, *Gospel Symbolism*, x–xi; see 243, 248).

47. Joseph Fielding McConkie wisely noted: "Beyond the obvious announcement that truth is always in harmony with itself, there are no rules or guarantees of infallibility. Our interpretation of the scriptures becomes a measure of our honesty, wisdom, and maturity" (*Gospel Symbolism*, 247). Actually, the caution regarding the folly of trying to discover "new doctrines" in symbols may serve well as a rule or safety net that will keep the student of symbols from going astray.

48. Goppelt, *Typological Interpretation*, 58. See Davidson, *Typology in Scripture*, 64; von Rad, "Typological Interpretation," 38; and Eichrodt, *Old Testament Hermeneutics*, 231, 243–44.

NOTES TO CHAPTER 3: BODY PARTS AS SYMBOLS

1. Compton, "Whole Token," 1–81. See Compton, "Handclasp and Embrace as Tokens of Recognition," 1:611–42; Nibley, "On the Sacred and the Symbolic," 557–59; Farbridge, *Studies in Biblical and Semitic Symbolism*, 274–75; and Brown, *Gate of Heaven*, 48 note 37, 135, 154 note 109, 156 note 130–32, 236 note 19.

2. See Farbridge, *Biblical and Semitic Symbolism*, 276; Ryken, Wilhoit, and Longman, *Dictionary of Biblical Imagery*, 483; Conner, *Interpreting the Symbols and Types*, 151; and Wilson, *Dictionary of Bible Types*, 245.

3. "The sacramental meaning of washing goes far beyond the removal of physical uncleanliness" (Ryken, Wilhoit, and Longman, *Dictionary of Biblical Imagery*, 927). See Farbridge, *Biblical and Semitic Symbolism*, 225, 273, 275; Conner, *Interpreting the Symbols and Types*, 178; and Wilson, *Dictionary of Bible Types*, 450–51.

4. One scholar noted that, for the ancients, the "'body' is much more than a

mere physical instrument (like, e.g., the stomach); it always belongs either to Christ or to other powers (e.g., to sin and death . . .)" (Schweizer, "Body," 1:769).

5. See Ryken, Wilhoit, and Longman, *Dictionary of Biblical Imagery*, 43; Julien, *Mammoth Dictionary of Symbols*, 27; McConkie and Parry, *Guide to Scriptural Symbols*, 15; Conner, *Interpreting the Symbols and Types*, 24, 127; and Wilson, *Dictionary of Bible Types*, 18.

6. See Cooper, *Encyclopaedia of Traditional Symbols*, 15; Julien, *Dictionary of Symbols*, 28; Brown, *Gate of Heaven*, 124–25; Farbridge, *Biblical and Semitic Symbolism*, 275; and Ryken, Wilhoit, and Longman, *Dictionary of Biblical Imagery*, 660.

7. See Farbridge, *Biblical and Semitic Symbolism*, 228; Cooper, *Encyclopaedia of Traditional Symbols*, 22; Ryken, Wilhoit, and Longman, *Dictionary of Biblical Imagery*, 100; Ricoeur, *Symbolism of Evil*, 36; McConkie and Parry, *Guide to Scriptural Symbols*, 22; Fairbairn, *Typology of Scripture*, 1:182–83; and McConkie, *Gospel Symbolism*, 253.

8. See Smith, *Answers to Gospel Questions*, 3:101, and Kimball, *Teachings of Spencer W. Kimball*, 44.

9. See Young, *Discourses of Brigham Young*, 103; and Pratt, in *Journal of Discourses*, 3:344.

10. See LDS Bible Dictionary, s.v. "Fall of Adam," 670.

11. Robinson, *Believing Christ*, 118–19.

12. See McConkie, *Millennial Messiah*, 654, 658.

13. See McConkie, *Mormon Doctrine*, 65, 642; and Romney, "Jesus Christ: Lord of the Universe," 46–49.

14. See McConkie, *Mortal Messiah*, 4:124.

15. See McConkie, *New Witness for the Articles of Faith*, xiii.

16. See Durham, *Gospel Kingdom*, 116; and Taylor, *Mediation and Atonement*, 149.

17. The Hebrew root from which the name *Adam* comes means literally "to show blood" (see Brown, Driver, and Briggs, *Hebrew and English Lexicon*, 10).

18. In chapter 5 of this work the concept of blood as it relates to the symbolic color red is addressed.

19. See McConkie, *Gospel Symbolism*, 254; and McConkie and Parry, *Guide to Scriptural Symbols*, 24.

20. See Wilson, *Dictionary of Bible Types*, 52; and Conner, *Interpreting the Symbols and Types*, 131. In some cultures the symbols of the breast or bosom also carried the connotation of being nurtured or fed, albeit this is not the conventional symbolic meaning in the scriptures. See Cooper, *Encyclopaedia of Traditional Symbols*, 25; and Todeschi, *Encyclopedia of Symbols*, 49.

21. See Ryken, Wilhoit, and Longman, *Dictionary of Biblical Imagery*, 118.

22. Ibid., 119.

23. See Thayer, *Thayer's Greek-English Lexicon*, 585; and Brown, Driver, and Briggs, *Hebrew and English Lexicon*, 589, 933.
24. See Cooper, *Encyclopaedia of Traditional Symbols*, 88; and McConkie and Parry, *Guide to Scriptural Symbols*, 24. See also 1 Kings 3:26; Job 30:27; Psalm 22:14; Song of Solomon 5:4; Isaiah 16:11; 63:15; Jeremiah 4:19; 31:20; Lamentations 1:20; 2:11; Ezekiel 7:19; 2 Corinthians 6:12; Philippians 1:8; 2:1; Colossians 3:12; Philemon 1:7, 20; 1 John 3:17; Mosiah 15:9; Alma 7:12; 26:37; 34:15; 3 Nephi 17:6–7; D&C 85:7; 101:9; 121:3–4, 45; Moses 7:41.
25. Ryken, Wilhoit, and Longman, *Dictionary of Biblical Imagery*, 424–25.
26. See McConkie and Parry, *Guide to Scriptural Symbols*, 24. See also Genesis 15:4; 25:23; 2 Samuel 7:12; 16:11; 2 Chronicles 32:21; Psalm 71:6; Isaiah 48:19; 49:1; Philemon 1:12; 1 Nephi 20:19; 21:1.
27. See Hall, *Dictionary of Subjects and Symbols in Art*, 52. See also Numbers 5:22; 2 Samuel 20:10; 2 Chronicles 21:15–19; Job 20:14; Acts 1:18.
28. See Wilson, *Dictionary of Bible Types*, 131–32; Julien, *Dictionary of Symbols*, 127; and Todeschi, *Encyclopedia of Symbols*, 95.
29. See Ryken, Wilhoit, and Longman, *Dictionary of Biblical Imagery*, 223.
30. Johnson, *First and Second Letters to Timothy*, 429; and Ryken, Wilhoit, and Longman, *Dictionary of Biblical Imagery*, 223.
31. See Packer, *Things of the Soul*, 56.
32. Ryken, Wilhoit, and Longman, *Dictionary of Biblical Imagery*, 223.
33. Harrington, *Acts of the Apostles*, 140. See Marshall, *Acts*, 149.
34. See McConkie, *Mormon Doctrine*, 142.
35. Farbridge, *Biblical and Semitic Symbolism*, 276.
36. See Young, *Book of Isaiah*, 2:419; and Parry, Parry, and Peterson *Understanding Isaiah*, 304.
37. Hugh Nibley offers an interesting insight into this ritual. He wrote, "The willingness of the candidate to sacrifice his own life is symbolized by the blood on the right thumb and right earlobe, where the blood would be if the throat had been cut" (*Temple and Cosmos*, 58).
38. See Conner, *Interpreting the Symbols and Types*, 17; McConkie, *Gospel Symbolism*, 259; Cooper, *Encyclopaedia of Traditional Symbols*, 62; Todeschi, *Encyclopedia of Symbols*, 101; and Ryken, Wilhoit, and Longman, *Dictionary of Biblical Imagery*, 255.
39. See Farbridge, *Biblical and Semitic Symbolism*, 266; Wilson, *Dictionary of Bible Types*, 140; Cooper, *Encyclopaedia of Traditional Symbols*, 62; Bayley, *Lost Language of Symbolism*, 1:84; and Cirlot, *Dictionary of Symbols*, 243.
40. Smith, *Book of Revelation*, 48.
41. Wilson, *Dictionary of Bible Types*, 140.
42. See ibid., 140–41. It is perhaps for this reason that Julien interprets the eyes as a symbol of one's "moral conscience" (Julien, *Dictionary of Symbols*, 144).
43. See Wilson, *Dictionary of Bible Types*, 141.

Notes to Chapter 3: Body Parts 337

44. See ibid., 147–49; Ryken, Wilhoit, and Longman, *Dictionary of Biblical Imagery*, 280; Conner, *Interpreting the Symbols and Types*, 141; and McConkie, *Gospel Symbolism*, 97.
45. Todeschi, *Encyclopedia of Symbols*, 106.
46. When individuals are depicted as trampling underfoot the teachings or commandments of God (see 1 Nephi 19:7; Alma 5:53; 60:33), this does not imply that they have power over those commands or teachings but, rather, that they disrespect them and refuse to place their lives in subjection to them. However, the time will come when such people *will* be in subjection.
47. See Ryken, Wilhoit, and Longman, *Dictionary of Biblical Imagery*, 280.
48. This is not to downplay the temple implications of the mountain in this passage.
49. See Wilson, *Dictionary of Bible Types*, 150; Ryken, Wilhoit, and Longman, *Dictionary of Biblical Imagery*, 280; and Cooper, *Encyclopaedia of Traditional Symbols*, 66.
50. See Wilson, *Dictionary of Bible Types*, 147–50; Ryken, Wilhoit, and Longman, *Dictionary of Biblical Imagery*, 280. See also D&C 88:139.
51. See McConkie, *Gospel Symbolism*, 105.
52. See Tresidder, *Symbols and Their Meanings*, 17.
53. See Wilson, *Dictionary of Bible Types*, 175.
54. See the discussion of the numeral 666 in chapter 6 of this work.
55. See Ryken, Wilhoit, and Longman, *Dictionary of Biblical Imagery*, 359.
56. See Farbridge, *Biblical and Semitic Symbolism*, 233, 236.
57. See Habershon, *Study of the Types*, 79–82; and Fairbairn, *Typology of Scripture*, 2:360–65.
58. See Farbridge, *Biblical and Semitic Symbolism*, 233–39.
59. Parry, Parry, and Peterson, *Understanding Isaiah*, 78.
60. Farbridge, *Biblical and Semitic Symbolism*, 233–39.
61. See Hamlin, *At Risk in the Promised Land*, 138; and Ryken, Wilhoit, and Longman, *Dictionary of Biblical Imagery*, 360.
62. Cundall, "Judges," 178. Maurice Farbridge wrote: "Samson's physical strength was ascribed to the spirit of God. When his hair was cut his superior strength left him. In other words the bond of union by which he was consecrated was broken" (*Biblical and Semitic Symbolism*, 236).
63. Ewing, "Hair," 360.
64. There seems to be no reason to assume that all resurrected beings do in reality have white hair. The fact that they always appear to have such when they are seen by mortals highlights two potential factors: (1) they are pure, holy, spiritually mature, and victorious, as the color white suggests; and (2) they radiate such a strong, concentrated glory and light that the mortal eye seems incapable of seeing them in detail as we do other things confined to this fallen earth.

65. See Julien, *Dictionary of Symbols*, 191; and Todeschi, *Encyclopedia of Symbols*, 128. Hands can also evoke images of strength, providence, authority, or blessings (see McConkie, *Gospel Symbolism*, 261; and Cirlot, *Dictionary of Symbols*, 137).
66. See Farbridge, *Biblical and Semitic Symbolism*, 274–75; Conner, *Interpreting the Symbols and Types*, 147; McConkie, *Gospel Symbolism*, 261; and Cirlot, *Dictionary of Symbols*, 137. In many religious traditions, the right hand is the "hand of power" and is associated with "rectitude," whereas the left hand often has negative connotations, such as "deviousness" (see Cooper, *Encyclopaedia of Traditional Symbols*, 78; Cirlot, *Dictionary of Symbols*, 137–38; Fontana, *Secret Language of Symbols*, 128; Tresidder, *Symbols and Their Meanings*, 22; and Janzen, *Abraham and All the Families of the Earth*, 185).
67. Cirlot, *Dictionary of Symbols*, 137.
68. Ryken, Wilhoit, and Longman, *Dictionary of Biblical Imagery*, 362.
69. Farbridge, *Biblical and Semitic Symbolism*, 275. See McConkie, *Gospel Symbolism*, 262; and Todeschi, *Encyclopedia of Symbols*, 128.
70. Cooper, *Encyclopaedia of Traditional Symbols*, 78; and Cirlot, *Dictionary of Symbols*, 137. The British typologist and linguist Harold Bayley wrote that, when clasped, "the hand was obviously an expression of concord" (*Lost Language of Symbolism*, 2:331).
71. See Brown, Driver, and Briggs, *Hebrew and English Lexicon*, 388, 1094; Tresidder, *Symbols and Their Meanings*, 22; and McConkie, *Gospel Symbolism*, 261. Harold Bayley noted: "The words *palm*, meaning a tree, and *palm*, the inner part of the hand, are identical, and may have originated from the same root because of the similitude between a palm leaf and the outspread fingers of the human hand.... The word *hand* (Anglo-Saxon *hond*) resolves ultimately into 'immutable, resplendent one,' and may be equated etymologically and symbolically with the *Hound* of Heaven and the *Hind* of the Dawn.

"The French word *main*, a hand, is the same as our *main*, meaning *chief* or *principal*. The Latin *manus* is 'sole light,' and the Greek *chier* is the 'Great Fire'" (*Lost Language of Symbolism*, 2:340).
72. Farbridge, *Biblical and Semitic Symbolism*, 274–75.
73. Cirlot, *Dictionary of Symbols*, 137.
74. McConkie, *Gospel Symbolism*, 261–62. "The hand of God is divine power; transmission of spirit; protection; justice" (Cooper, *Encyclopaedia of Traditional Symbols*, 78).
75. See Ballif, "Melchizedek Priesthood," 2:883.
76. Ryken, Wilhoit, and Longman, *Dictionary of Biblical Imagery*, 362.
77. Julien, *Dictionary of Symbols*, 189.
78. Wilson, *Dictionary of Bible Types*, 209. See Cooper, *Encyclopaedia of Traditional Symbols*, 78.
79. Bayley, *Lost Language of Symbolism*, 2:334.
80. See McEachern, *Psalms*, 59.

Notes to Chapter 3: Body Parts 339

81. See Habershon, *Study of the Types,* 69. Apparently Uzzah was the typifying of those who seek to counsel the Brethren on how they should run the Church.
82. See Myers, *Eerdmans Bible Dictionary,* 470; McKenzie, *Dictionary of the Bible,* 343; Emmet, "Head," 368; and Palmer, "Head," 508.
83. See Wilson, *Dictionary of Bible Types,* 214; and Ryken, Wilhoit, and Longman, *Dictionary of Biblical Imagery,* 367.
84. See Ryken, Wilhoit, and Longman, *Dictionary of Biblical Imagery,* 367.
85. See ibid.
86. Ibid. See Unger, *Unger's Bible Dictionary,* 461.
87. Wilson, *Dictionary of Bible Types,* 214.
88. See McConkie, *Gospel Symbolism,* 262. See also Cooper, *Encyclopaedia of Traditional Symbols,* 81; Wilson, *Dictionary of Bible Types,* 216; and McKenzie, *Dictionary of the Bible,* 343.
89. The "helmet of salvation" is "essential to the believer's successful resistance of the attacks of the hostile principalities and powers" (Ryken, Wilhoit, and Longman, *Dictionary of Biblical Imagery,* 367; see Isaiah 59:17; 1 Thessalonians 5:8; Ephesians 6:17).
90. See McConkie, *Gospel Symbolism,* 262; Myers, *Eerdmans Bible Dictionary,* 471; and McKenzie, *Dictionary of the Bible,* 344.
91. Myers, *Eerdmans Bible Dictionary,* 471.
92. Ryken, Wilhoit, and Longman, *Dictionary of Biblical Imagery,* 368. See Wilson, *Dictionary of Bible Types,* 219; Conner, *Interpreting the Symbols and Types,* 148; and Myers, *Eerdmans Bible Dictionary,* 471.
93. See Wilson, *Dictionary of Bible Types,* 231; Conner, *Interpreting the Symbols and Types,* 25, 1149; McConkie, *Gospel Symbolism,* 103, 262; Cooper, *Encyclopaedia of Traditional Symbols,* 84; Ryken, Wilhoit, and Longman, *Dictionary of Biblical Imagery,* 400.
94. See Farbridge, *Biblical and Semitic Symbolism,* 191–92.
95. Ibid. See Ryken, Wilhoit, and Longman, *Dictionary of Biblical Imagery,* 400.
96. Ryken, Wilhoit, and Longman, *Dictionary of Biblical Imagery,* 400.
97. The Joseph Smith Translation changes this to "twelve horns," representing priesthood power.
98. Draper, *Opening the Seven Seals,* 132. From about the eleventh century onward it was common to depict Satan as having horns, symbolic of his claim to be in possession of power. See Russell, *Lucifer,* 211.
99. See Bayley, *Lost Language of Symbolism,* 1:119.
100. See McConkie, *Gospel Symbolism,* 97; Holzapfel and Seely, *My Father's House,* 32.
101. See Ryken, Wilhoit, and Longman, *Dictionary of Biblical Imagery,* 483.
102. See Farbridge, *Biblical and Semitic Symbolism,* 276.
103. Myers, *Eerdmans Bible Dictionary,* 660.
104. Conner, *Interpreting the Symbols and Types,* 153.

105. Foulkes, *Ephesians*, 181. See Wood, "Ephesians," 11:87.
106. See Conner, *Interpreting the Symbols and Types*, 157; Wilson, *Dictionary of Bible Types*, 292; Banwell, "Neck," 874; and Ryken, Wilhoit, and Longman, *Dictionary of Biblical Imagery*, 591.
107. For discussion of a related symbol, see the section titled "Throat" in this chapter.
108. See Douglass, *New Bible Dictionary*, 895.
109. Ewing, "Nose, Nostrils," 701. See McKenzie, *Dictionary of the Bible*, 620.
110. The biblical image of leading one around by a hook or ring in the nose, although mentioned frequently in scripture, is not an example of the nose being employed as a symbol. Slaves were commonly subjected to this practice (see 2 Kings 19:28; 2 Chronicles 33:11). The focus of this image, however, is not the nose but the ring or hook and the accompanying bondage.
111. See Conner, *Interpreting the Symbols and Types*, 168.
112. Yamauchi, "Ezra, Nehemiah," 4:694.
113. Bowman and Gilkey, "The Book of Ezra and the Book of Nehemiah," 3:754.
114. Wilson, *Dictionary of Bible Types*, 365. See Thompson, *Commentaries: Deuteronomy*, 311–12.
115. See Habershon, *Study of the Types*, 25; and McConkie, *Gospel Symbolism*, 262.
116. See Gower, *New Manners and Customs of Bible Times*, 17, 66.
117. Parry, Parry, and Peterson, *Understanding Isaiah*, 96.
118. Todeschi, *Encyclopedia of Symbols*, 259–60.
119. Ryken, Wilhoit, and Longman, *Dictionary of Biblical Imagery*, 918. See Wilson, *Dictionary of Bible Types*, 449.
120. Scott, *Ecclesiastes*, 139.
121. Ross, "Proverbs," 5:1068.
122. Of this verse, Nibley stated: "In verse 29 they are starting to take their oaths and covenants, which are the same as those in the temple. Therefore, he says, we mustn't let Adam find out about this, because he will know what it is. . . . Adam must not know about this for he would immediately denounce and discredit it as phony, because that's what it was. They were establishing this as the real rites in the world" (*Teachings of the Book of Mormon*, 3:247). Elsewhere he noted: "Cain did all this and kept it secret so that Adam wouldn't find out that he was copying and corrupting the whole thing. So here it comes out again. . . . In Moses 5:29 we read about the oaths they made to each other. . . . By their oaths they have foresworn themselves. They were false oaths. ' . . . They have brought upon themselves death; and a hell I have prepared for them, if they repent not [and this is a decree which has gone out of my own mouth]'" (*Ancient Documents and the Pearl of Great Price*, lecture 22, 2).
123. See Wilson, *Dictionary of Bible Types*, 465; McConkie, *Gospel Symbolism*,

Notes to Chapter 4: Clothing 341

275; Cooper, *Encyclopaedia of Traditional Symbols*, 193; Conner, *Interpreting the Symbols and Types*, 181; and Cirlot, *Dictionary of Symbols*, 374.
124. Ryken, Wilhoit, and Longman, *Dictionary of Biblical Imagery*, 954.
125. See Hall, *Dictionary of Subjects and Symbols in Art*, 342.
126. Smith, *Teachings of the Prophet Joseph Smith*, 162.
127. See Draper, *Opening the Seven Seals*, 121; Bullinger, *Number in Scripture*, 123, 150; and Smith, *Book of Revelation*, 288.
128. It could also be an effort by the Revelator to compare these beings with God, although such an interpretation would seem to stand in contradiction with D&C 84:38. Possibly they are beings worthy of the celestial kingdom but not of exaltation, in which case they would be ministering angels throughout eternity (see D&C 132:17).

NOTES TO CHAPTER 4: CLOTHING AS SYMBOLS

1. Tresidder, *Symbols and Their Meanings*, 134.
2. See Edwards, "Dress and Ornamentation," 2:232.
3. See Ryken, Wilhoit, and Longman, *Dictionary of Biblical Imagery*, 317. See also Edwards, "Dress and Ornamentation," 2:232.
4. Tvedtnes, "Priestly Clothing in Bible Times," 665, 666. Elsewhere we read, "The fact that God Himself revealed the pattern for these vestments should alert us to the possibility that they imitate the clothing that is worn by heavenly beings. And indeed, there is some evidence to support this view. A post-biblical Jewish commentary on the book of Exodus explains that the high priest's garments were like those worn by the Lord. And one extrabiblical source also describes an angel wearing eight garments, alluding to those worn by the earthly high priest. With this connection between the heavens and the earth, it is little wonder that they were called 'holy garments' (Exodus 28:2, 4; 31:10; Leviticus 16:4)" (Brown, *Gate of Heaven*, 81).
5. Ryken, Wilhoit, and Longman, *Dictionary of Biblical Imagery*, 319. In Cyril of Jerusalem's second lecture on the ordinances, he states that "immediately upon entering you removed your street clothes. And that was the image of putting off the old man and his works . . . the former man corrupted as he was by the desire for false (deceptive) things; and may that garment, once put off, never be put on again" (see lecture 2, part 2, in Nibley, *Message of the Joseph Smith Papyri*, 280).
6. See Tvedtnes, "Priestly Clothing in Bible Times," 665.
7. Ryken, Wilhoit, and Longman, *Dictionary of Biblical Imagery*, 317. From a Latter-day Saint perspective, "liturgical" clothing is that which is worn during the performance of certain ordinances, such as baptism or the various temple ordinances.
8. See ibid.
9. See ibid., 318.

10. See ibid. Even fabric, like wool and linen, had symbolic importance. Only priests, for example, were allowed to mix the two (Leviticus 19:19; Deuteronomy 22:11).
11. The Hebrew here translated "apron" is a word more often rendered "girdle," and only sometimes "apron."
12. See Julian, *Mammoth Dictionary of Symbols*, 23–24; Cooper, *Encyclopaedia of Traditional Symbols*, 14; McConkie and Parry, *Guide to Scriptural Symbols*, 49; Bayley, *Lost Language of Symbolism*, 2:248; and Meyers, "Apron," 1:319.
13. Meyers, "Apron," 1:319.
14. This author uses "at the very least" because, without question, some symbols, including those employed in the temple, have multiple meanings (see Wilcox, *House of Glory*, 25). This seems to be the case with the fig leaf aprons of Adam and Eve. Symbolic meanings of figs and aprons, beyond fertility and reproduction, include the following: To be naked means to be innocent or exposed (see Wilson, *Dictionary of Bible Types*, 17, 289). To "cover one's nakedness" means to endeavor to make excuses for one's actions; something aptly depicted in the temple endowment (see Ryken, Wilhoit, and Longman, *Dictionary of Biblical Imagery*, 320; and Charles, *Endowed from on High*, 59). Elder James E. Talmage associated figs with the covenant people (*Jesus the Christ*, 443; see Cooper, *Encyclopaedia of Traditional Symbols*, 66). When Adam and Eve, in accordance with God's will, provoke the Fall, they became the first of God's covenant people, and for that reason their aprons of fig leaves became a symbol of the covenant. Curiously, Jewish legend held that the "forbidden fruit" was the fig (see Ginzberg, *Legends of the Jews*, 1:75, 96–97; 5:97, 98, 122; see also *Books of Adam and Eve*, 20:5). When Satan told Adam and Eve to cover their nakedness with fig leaves, he was really tricking them into guaranteeing that their transgression would be discovered, but this act became a symbol of righteousness instead. As one LDS source states: "By sewing fig leaves together and making aprons for themselves, Adam and Eve covered their nakedness (Moses 4:13). In so covering themselves with leaves, they became trees, as it were." Trees that are green represent righteous men and women (McConkie and Parry, *Guide to Scriptural Symbols*, 15, 103–4).
15. Scott, in Conference Report, October 1996, 100.
16. Smith, "Fall—Atonement—Resurrection—Sacrament," 124. See Smith, *Answers to Gospel Questions*, 4:81.
17. See Conner, *Interpreting the Symbols and Types*, 141; and Unger, *Unger's Bible Dictionary*, 317.
18. See Julien, *Mammoth Dictionary of Symbols*, 23–24; and Cooper, *Encyclopaedia of Traditional Symbols*, 14. The symbol of "work" also seems applicable to Adam and Eve, in that their choice to eat of the fruit was a choice to give up ease for a life of sacrifice and work.
19. Although there is not absolute agreement in the scholarly community, an ephod is traditionally believed to have been an apron (see McKenzie, *Dictionary of the Bible*, 241; Myers, *Eerdmans Bible Dictionary*, 342; and Brown, *Gate of Heaven*, 85–86).

20. Parry, "Garden of Eden," 145.
21. McConkie and Parry, *Guide to Scriptural Symbols*, 16.
22. See, for example, Hartshorn, *Put on the Whole Armor of God*; Lee, "Feet Shod with the Preparation of the Gospel of Peace," 2–7; Lee, *Stand Ye in Holy Places*, 323–40; and Ryken, Wilhoit, and Longman, *Dictionary of Biblical Imagery*, 44–47.
23. See McConkie, *Gospel Symbolism*, 252; Conner, *Interpreting the Symbols and Types*, 127; McConkie and Parry, *Guide to Scriptural Symbols*, 16; Todeschi, *Encyclopedia of Symbolism*, 28; Cooper, *Encyclopaedia of Traditional Symbols*, 15; and Ryken, Wilhoit, and Longman, *Dictionary of Biblical Imagery*, 44.
24. Ryken, Wilhoit, and Longman, *Dictionary of Biblical Imagery*, 44.
25. Ibid.
26. See Lee, "Feet Shod with the Preparation of the Gospel of Peace," 2; Lee, *Stand Ye in Holy Places*, 330; Unger, *Unger's Bible Dictionary*, 664; and Myers, *Eerdmans Bible Dictionary*, 660. Sometimes the loins are also associated with strength in a generic sense. However, this is not necessarily a separate symbol (see Conner, *Interpreting the Symbols and Types*, 153; and Wilson, *Dictionary of Bible Types*, 265).
27. Hartshorn, *Put on the Whole Armor of God*, 27, 28, 29.
28. See McConkie and Parry, *Guide to Scriptural Symbols*, 26; and Ryken, Wilhoit, and Longman, *Dictionary of Biblical Imagery*, 46.
29. See chapter 3 of this text.
30. Hartshorn, *Put on the Whole Armor of God*, 31.
31. Lee, *Stand Ye in Holy Places*, 332–33.
32. Brewster, *Doctrine and Covenants Encyclopedia*, 180. See Hartshorn, *Put on the Whole Armor of God*, 43.
33. See chapter 3 of this text.
34. Barth, *Ephesians 4–6*, 798; Nicoll, *Expositor's Greek Testament*, 3:386; and E. F. Scott, *Epistles of Paul*, 252–53.
35. Hartshorn, *Put on the Whole Armor of God*, 49–50. Hartshorn adds the Lord's counsel to Hyrum Smith, "Seek not to declare my word, but first seek to obtain my word, and then shall your tongue be loosed; then, if you desire, you shall have my Spirit and my word, yea, the power of God unto the convincing of men" (D&C 11:21, cited in ibid., 48).
36. Hoyt Brewster Jr. wrote: "The 'gospel of peace' is the plan of life which the Savior gave to us, his teachings and ordinances which, if obeyed, bring unspeakable joy and peace to our minds (John 14:27; 1 Ne. 8:10–12; Hel. 5:44; D&C 6:23). If the world would accept and live these teachings and ordinances, peace would reign supreme on the earth (see 4 Ne. 1:15–17)" (*Doctrine and Covenants Encyclopedia*, 180). Marcus Barth indicated, "Paul speaks here of the equipment provided by God which makes Christians able to 'stand' and 'resist.' They can say, 'We shall not be moved.' (Cross-reference Psalm 121:3: 'He will not let your foot be moved.')" (*Ephesians 4–6*, 799).

37. Ryken, Wilhoit, and Longman, *Dictionary of Biblical Imagery*, 45.
38. Lee, "Feet Shod with the Preparation of the Gospel of Peace," 7. Leon Hartshorn noted: "How appropriate that faith is the spiritual shield that is a vital part of our armor. The shield of faith is the part of the armor that is out in front, pushing forward, quenching the flaming arrows of the wicked so they do not wound us or destroy us spiritually" (*Put on the Whole Armor of God*, 54). Another commentator wrote, "A living faith in the God and Father of our Lord Jesus Christ is a sure protection from the assaults of the Evil One in the most vital warfare of all" (Ryken, Wilhoit, and Longman, *Dictionary of Biblical Imagery*, 46).
39. See Barth, *Ephesians 4–6*, 800; McConkie and Parry, *Guide to Scriptural Symbols*, 102; McConkie, *Gospel Symbolism*, 272–73; Cirlot, *Dictionary of Symbols*, 324; D&C 6:2; Hebrews 4:12; 1 Nephi 21:2; Ephesians 6:17; D&C 27:18; and Revelation 1:16; 19:15.
40. Smith and Sjodahl, *Doctrine and Covenants Commentary*, 138.
41. Matthew Brown notes that the sashes worn by the priests in Moses' day were "tied in an ample bow or loop" (*Gate of Heaven*, 84).
42. S. B. Roundy, "Record Book."
43. Cooper, *Encyclopaedia of Traditional Symbols*, 24. Like bow knots, Cooper indicates that knots in general are symbols of "continuity; connection; a covenant [or] a link" (ibid., 92). See Cirlot, *Dictionary of Symbols*, 191–92; Todeschi, *Encyclopedia of Symbolism*, 155; Fontana, *Secret Language of Symbolism*, 75; and Hall, *Dictionary of Subjects and Symbols in Art*, 184.
44. Tresidder, *Symbols and Their Meanings*, 36, 152; and Todeschi, *Encyclopedia of Symbolism*, 155.
45. Julien, *Mammoth Dictionary of Symbols*, 226.
46. See McConkie, *Gospel Symbolism*, 257; Conner, *Interpreting the Symbols and Types*, 137; Cooper, *Encyclopaedia of Traditional Symbols*, 80, 106; and Tresidder, *Symbols and Their Meanings*, 134–35.
47. See Cooper, *Encyclopaedia of Traditional Symbols*, 29, 80.
48. See Ryken, Wilhoit, and Longman, *Dictionary of Biblical Imagery*, 186. "Quite often in both the [New Testament] and [Old Testament], crowns are symbols of God's blessings on His people" (ibid., 185).
49. See Sarna, *JPS Torah Commentary*, 185. Hugh Nibley indicated that the flat, tasseled, mortarboard caps associated with academic commencement exercises are simply a spinoff of the temple clothing. Of the tassel that is attached to a commencement hat, hanging to one side, Nibley states, it is "the emergent flame of the fully enlightened" ("Commencement Speech," 1, 2; see Nibley, "Christian Envy of the Temple," 391–434). Similarly, Harold Bayley noted that ribbons or tassels attached to caps symbolized the resplendent light of God (see *Lost Language of Symbolism*, 2:64).
50. Edwards, "Dress and Ornamentation," 2:234. See Hyatt, "Dress," 223; and Brown, *Gate of Heaven*, 81.
51. Tvedtnes, "Priestly Clothing," 663–64.
52. Ibid., 649.

53. Ginzberg, *Legends of the Jews*, 5:97, and note 69. See Tvedtnes, "Priestly Clothing," 651–52.
54. See Ginzberg, *Legends of the Jews*, 1:79; 5:103–4. See Tvedtnes, "Priestly Clothing," 651–52. The two Hebrew words for "light" and "skin" differ in but the initial letters, and are pronounced alike in modern Hebrew. This explains why some traditions have the garments of Adam and Eve made of light, others have them made of skin (see Tvedtnes, "Priestly Clothing," 651).
55. Ginzberg, *Legends of the Jews*, 5:104 note 93. See McConkie, *Gospel Symbolism*, 202; and Tvedtnes, "Priestly Clothing," 649–50.
56. Ginzberg, *Legends of the Jews*, 5:103 note 93.
57. Blake Ostler wrote: "It should be noted that the ancient garment bore the same tokens as the veil of the temple at Jerusalem. . . . Many ancient texts confuse the garment with the veil of the temple, such as Ambrose of Milano's *Tractate of the Mysteries* or the *Hebrew Book of Enoch* where the 'garment' and 'veil' are used interchangeably" ("Clothed Upon," 35). "Linen fabric possesses several symbolic aspects that are relevant. . . . The fine linen worn by heavenly beings is described as 'clean and white' or 'pure and white' and is therefore an appropriate symbol of worthiness or righteousness (see Revelation 3:4–5; 15:6; 19:8). Since linen is not the product of an animal that is subject unto death, or 'corruption' as it is called, it is also a fitting symbol of immortality, which is also called 'incorruption' (see 1 Corinthians 15:52–54)" (Brown, *Gate of Heaven*, 81–82).
58. The temple, its ordinances, and clothing, are but earthly vehicles to get us back to the celestial kingdom or presence of God. One non-LDS commentator indicated that certain articles of temple clothing symbolized "being shielded or protected" (Todeschi, *Encyclopedia of Symbolism*, 27). Once we return to the Father many of these earthly vehicles will likely be done away with or will be replaced by the heavenly things which they represented (Revelation 21:22). Perhaps this explains why Joseph stated of Moroni, when he appeared (on Sept. 21, 1823): "I could discover that he had no other clothing on but this robe, as it was open, so that I could see into his bosom" (JS–H 1:31). Joseph describes Moroni as wearing a garment of light that was "lighter than at noonday" (JS–H 1:30). But there is no mention of the earthly "coat of skins" that fallen men are required by covenant to wear. In the *Nag Hammadi's* "Dialogue of the Savior," Judas and Matthew are recorded as having said to Christ, "We [want] to understand the sort of garments we are to be [clothed] with [when] we depart the decay of the [flesh]." To this the Lord replied, "Not with these transitory garments are you to clothe yourselves." Jesus added, "You will clothe yourselves in light and enter the bridal chamber" ("Dialogue of the Savior," 143:84–85; 138:50; brackets in original).
59. Edwards, "Dress and Ornamentation," 2:233. See Bromiley, *International Standard Bible Encyclopedia*, 4:204.
60. Cooper, *Encyclopaedia of Traditional Symbols*, 140.
61. Edwards, "Dress and Ornamentation," 2:233, 236.

62. See Rasmussen, *Latter-day Commentary on the Old Testament*, 295.
63. See chapter 6 of this work; Draper, *Opening the Seven Seals*, 24, 46, 56, 83; Parry and Parry, *Understanding the Book of Revelation*, 295; and Smith, *Book of Revelation*, 288–89.
64. Parry, Parry, and Peterson, *Understanding Isaiah*, 547. See Marshall, "Garments," 2:535.
65. Skousen, *Isaiah Speaks to Modern Times*, 728.
66. *Eschatology* refers to the last days or end-times.
67. See Brown, *Gospel According to John, XIII–XXI*, 920–21.
68. See McConkie, *Gospel Symbolism*, 270; Conner, *Interpreting the Symbols and Types*, 164; and Ryken, Wilhoit, and Longman, *Dictionary of Biblical Imagery*, 318.
69. Frequently associated with the wearing of sackcloth is the symbolic practice of rending or tearing the garments when people are grieving. For example, we read that Reuben tore his clothes when he returned to the pit and found Joseph missing (Genesis 37:29), and Ezra was said to have rent his garments when he learned about the Israelites' intermarriage (Ezra 9:3).
70. See Edwards, "Dress and Ornamentation," 2:234.
71. See Hyatt, "Dress," 223; and Edwards, "Dress and Ornamentation," 2:234.
72. Brown, *Gate of Heaven*, 84.
73. See Edwards, "Dress and Ornamentation," 2:237; Tresidder, *Symbols and Their Meanings*, 134; and Henry, *Catholic Customs and Symbols*, 69–70. For additional information regarding the symbolism of sashes or belts, see "Bows" in this chapter.
74. See Ryken, Wilhoit, and Longman, *Dictionary of Biblical Imagery*, 318; and Edwards, "Dress and Ornamentation," 2:234.
75. Ryken, Wilhoit, and Longman, *Dictionary of Biblical Imagery*, 74.
76. Cooper, *Encyclopaedia of Traditional Symbols*, 152.
77. See Edwards, "Dress and Ornamentation," 2:234; and Unger, *Unger's Bible Dictionary*, 125.
78. Cooper, *Encyclopaedia of Traditional Symbols*, 152.
79. Tvedtnes, "Priestly Clothing," 671.
80. Rasmussen, *Latter-day Saint Commentary on the Old Testament*, 197.
81. See Farbridge, *Studies in Biblical and Semitic Symbolism*, 9, 224; Unger, *Unger's Bible Dictionary*, 1020–21; Myers, *Eerdmans Bible Dictionary*, 911–12; and Edwards, "Dress and Ornamentation," 2:234.
82. See Ryken, Wilhoit, and Longman, *Dictionary of Biblical Imagery*, 831.
83. See Efird, "Swaddling," 1002.
84. Brown, *Birth of the Messiah*, 418.
85. See Ryken, Wilhoit, and Longman, *Dictionary of Biblical Imagery*, 831. "In Ezekiel 16:1–5, Jerusalem is symbolically described as a heathen child who

Notes to Chapter 4: Clothing   347

was neglected from birth till God rescued and cared for her. She had not been given the usual postnatal care and so was not wrapped with strips of cloth (Ezekiel 16:4)" (Liefeld, "Luke," 8:846).
86. Thaumaturgus, "Four Homilies," 6:60, 65.
87. Church, NIV Matthew Henry Commentary (New Testament), 218. Henry is not alone in the assumption that "swaddling clothes" were the common covering of most newborns of the era. However, the acclaimed biblical scholar Joseph Fitzmyer questions this. He queries, if swaddling clothes were so common, why is this a sign to the shepherds who would seek out the child? (see Fitzmyer, Gospel According to Luke I–IX, 410).
88. Cirlot, Dictionary of Symbols, 183.
89. See Ryken, Wilhoit, and Longman, Dictionary of Biblical Imagery, 911.
90. See Hall, Dictionary of Subjects, 318; Ryken, Wilhoit, and Longman, Dictionary of Biblical Imagery, 911; and McConkie, Gospel Symbolism, 274.
91. Cooper, Encyclopaedia of Traditional Symbols, 184.
92. See Orr and Walther, 1 Corinthians, 261; Zepp, Muslim Primer, 176–77; Glassé, Concise Encyclopedia of Islam, 413; Kertzer and Hoffman, What Is a Jew? 91; and de Lange, Judaism, 32–33. Women in modern Eastern cultures are traditionally veiled. In secular Western wedding ceremonies women also commonly wear a veil. These utilizations of veils appear to be distorted adaptations of temple clothing, coupled with the widely understood symbolism of chastity and virtue.
93. See Cooper, Encyclopaedia of Traditional Symbols, 184; and McConkie, Gospel Symbolism, 274.
94. For example, the emphasis is on "righteously held and exercised authority." What woman should be offended by being an equal partner (1 Corinthians 11:11) with a male (holding a different but not more important role) who honors his priesthood (D&C 121:36) and bears accountability before God for what happens in his home and family (D&C 68:25; 84:33–41)? If he is doing these things, what fear would a woman have in following him, except if her desires and goals were contrary to the will of the Lord!
95. Actually, the Greek word translated "submit" does not mean to "give in" or "blindly obey." One scholar noted that the verb never implies "servile submissiveness" or the "elimination or breaking of the human will." Rather, it is a "voluntary" sustaining of the spouse (Barth, Ephesians 4–6, 609). Another wrote, "'cooperate' is a loose translation, but that is the working concept that Paul asks of all Saints—cooperation with Church and civil leaders, and cooperation of wives with the family leadership of their husbands" (Anderson, Understanding Paul, 353).
96. Anderson, Understanding Paul, 111 (see 350–55); Orr and Walther, 1 Corinthians, 262–63; and "The Gospel of Bartholomew," 49–50.
97. Scott, Epistles of Paul to the Colossians, to Philemon, and to the Ephesians, 236–37. See Nicoll, Expositor's Greek Testament, 3:366.
98. Barth, Ephesians 4–6, 609. See Nicoll, Expositor's Greek Testament, 3:365.
99. See Wilson, Dictionary of Bible Types, 444; Conner, Interpreting the Symbols

and Types, 177; Cirlot, *Dictionary of Symbols*, 359; Todeschi, *Encyclopedia of Symbolism*, 274; and Cooper, *Encyclopaedia of Traditional Symbols*, 184.
100. Myers, *Eerdmans Bible Dictionary*, 1036.
101. See Young, *Book of Isaiah*, 2:194–95.
102. Ryken, Wilhoit, and Longman, *Dictionary of Biblical Imagery*, 911.
103. See Wilson, *Dictionary of Bible Types*, 444; Isaiah 25:7; 2 Corinthians 3:14; and Hebrews 6:19.
104. See JST, 1 Corinthians 11:10.
105. The NIV, NRSV, Jerusalem Bible, and New World Translation also render the Greek word translated "power" in the KJV and "veil" in the RSV as "authority."
106. For example, the Moffatt translation of this verse reads, "In view of the angels, woman has to wear a symbol of subjection on her head." See Dummelow, *Commentary on the Holy Bible*, 910.
107. Morris, *1 Corinthians*, 152. Perhaps this has something to do with Kevin Todeschi's claim that woman veiled stands as a symbol of "intuitive abilities" (*Encyclopedia of Symbolism*, 275).
108. See Bray, *Ancient Christian Commentary on Scripture*, 108. "Ambrosiaster" was the name given by Erasmus to the author of a work once thought to have been composed by the fourth century Ambrose of Milan.
109. Brown, *Gate of Heaven*, 157–58.

NOTES TO CHAPTER 5: COLORS AS SYMBOLS

1. See Cirlot, *Dictionary of Symbols*, 52.
2. See Farbridge, *Studies in Biblical and Semitic Symbolism*, 4.
3. Fontana, *Secret Language of Symbols*, 52, 66.
4. See Julien, *Mammoth Dictionary of Symbols*, 77. See also Farbridge, *Studies in Biblical and Semitic Symbolism*, 277. The European typologist, Ada Habershon, wrote: "The meanings of the colours are not clearly stated; so that with regard to some of them there is a slight difference of opinion" (*Study of the Types*, 95). Habershon is correct that, in some cases, the specific meaning is unclear from scripture alone. However, extracanonical sources coupled with scripture have left us with a reasonably clear understanding of their ancient meanings. Regarding the "difference of opinion" that supposedly exists, it would be more accurate to call it a distinction in how wide or broad one scholar's interpretation of a color is when compared to another. In other words, there is a strong consistency among biblical scholars in their interpretation of the meaning of colors, but some see facets that others do not. Contradictions are not present, but breadth and depth of interpretation vary.
5. See McConkie and Parry, *Guide to Scriptural Symbols*, 33. See also McConkie, *Gospel Symbolism*, 256.
6. See Cole, "Colours," 244.

Notes to Chapter 5: Colors 349

7. Ryken, Wilhoit, and Longman, *Dictionary of Biblical Imagery*, 157–58.
8. See ibid., 158.
9. Conner, *Interpreting the Symbols and Types*, 10.
10. Habershon, *Study of the Types*, 95, 97.
11. See Rest, *Our Christian Symbols*, 47; Cooper, *Encyclopaedia of Traditional Symbols*, 39; McConkie and Parry, *Guide to Scriptural Symbols*, 33; McConkie, *Gospel Symbolism*, 257; Ryken, Wilhoit, and Longman, *Dictionary of Biblical Imagery*, 97; Todeschi, *Encyclopedia of Symbolism*, 71; Bayley, *Lost Language of Symbolism*, 1:213; Fontana, *Secret Language of Symbols*, 67; Smith, *Book of Revelation*, 289; and Parry and Parry, *Understanding the Book of Revelation*, 80.
12. Tresidder, *Symbols and Their Meanings*, 157.
13. See Cooper, *Encyclopaedia of Traditional Symbols*, 96; and Conner, *Interpreting the Symbols and Types*, 153.
14. See Farbridge, *Studies in Biblical and Semitic Symbolism*, 278.
15. See Ryken, Wilhoit, and Longman, *Dictionary of Biblical Imagery*, 97.
16. Smith, *Doctrines of Salvation*, 1:87.
17. See Widtsoe, *Rational Theology*, 83–85.
18. See Ryken, Wilhoit, and Longman, *Dictionary of Biblical Imagery*, 98.
19. Of the Book of Mormon, Hugh Nibley stated: "It starts out by saying, 'I, Nephi.' You notice it is an autobiography, 'I, Nephi.' Now, at this time the only style of writing was autobiographical. Everybody wrote autobiographies, and there's a great autobiographical literature in Egyptian. There are some famous autobiographies, and we will refer to some because they are so very close to the Book of Mormon. They take place in Palestine, even at this time. Well, I just picked up one from de Buck's *Reading Book* (p. 73–74). It's called *The Autobiography of Kai*. He lived a short time before Nephi. He was an important man, and he gave his titles. He started out by saying, 'I, Kai, was the son of a man who was *nehet* and *saa* [who was worthy and wise].' And Nephi started out saying, 'I, Nephi, having been born of goodly parents.' Then Kai goes on to talk about himself here. Incidentally, I notice he referred to himself down here as *hedj-her* (white of countenance), *nefer bit* (excellent of character), *peha-het* (clean of body and in moral habits). And he shunned everything that was *senket*. The word is very interesting. It means 'black of countenance,' and it also means 'greed or anything that is evil.' Notice, in the Book of Mormon, that peculiar thing: 'a white and delightsome people' and 'a dark and loathsome people.' It doesn't refer to skin color at all, but there's a lot about race in the Book of Mormon. That comes in here already; we can see that. But here, you notice he used those peculiar terms. He was *hedj-her*. He has a picture of a white face (white of countenance). And he was clean of body, and he eschewed *senket* (what is greedy or what is dark of countenance)" (*Teachings of the Book of Mormon*, vol. 1, lecture 2, 1). See Nibley, *Lehi in the Desert, World of the Jaredites, There Were Jaredites*, 73–74; Nibley, *Since*

Cumorah, 216–18; Turner, "The Lamanite Mark," 133–57; and Reynolds and Sjodahl, *Commentary on the Book of Mormon*, 1:278.
20. Ryken, Wilhoit, and Longman, *Dictionary of Biblical Imagery*, 158–59.
21. See Wilson, *Dictionary of Bible Types*, 42.
22. Draper, *Opening the Seven Seals*, 65–66.
23. See McBrien, *Encyclopedia of Catholicism*, 185; and Henry, *Catholic Customs and Symbols*, 78–79.
24. Ford, *Revelation*, 100.
25. Parry and Parry, *Understanding the Book of Revelation*, 87. See 2 Samuel 3:31; 21:10; 1 Kings 20:31–32; 21:27; 2 Kings 6:30; 19:1–2; 1 Chronicles 21:16; Esther 4:1–4; Job 16:15; Psalm 30:11; 35:13; Mosiah 11:25; and D&C 133:69.
26. See Unger, *Unger's Bible Dictionary*, 212, 214; see also Lundbom, *Jeremiah 1–20*, 533–34, 693, 695, 698.
27. Hill, *Malachi*, 333–34; and Baldwin, *Haggai, Zechariah, Malachi*, 248.
28. See Cooper, *Encyclopaedia of Traditional Symbols*, 40; and Habershon, *Study of the Types*, 95.
29. See Conner, *Interpreting the Symbols and Types*, 61. In Catholic and Eastern Orthodox iconography the Virgin Mary and Christ are often shown wearing blue in an attempt to emphasize both their nature and the origin of their callings (see Tresidder, *Symbols and Their Meanings*, 157; and Wheeler, *His Face*, 14, 16, 26, 44–45, 51, 59, 62–63, 70, 110, 120).
30. See McConkie, *Gospel Symbolism*, 111. "Blue, the color of the sky, . . . [suggests] the boundary between God and his people and [symbolizes] his majesty. . . . Blue was the dominant color of the vestments of ancient Israel's high priest (Exo. 28). The high priest wore an outer garment of solid blue over the white robe of the priesthood. He was the boundary between the human and divine realms, moving in both as he ministered in the Holy of Holies" (Ryken, Wilhoit, and Longman, *Dictionary of Biblical Imagery*, 158).
31. "It is clear that the tent that Moses had built is a copy of the heavenly tent in accordance with the ancient religious principle, 'like is like.' The similarity in form between the earthly dwelling of the God and its heavenly prototype brings about the presence of the deity. In Israel, of course, the presence of Yahweh was subject to a number of conditions, yet the principle of 'like is like' seems imperative here, too. It is clear that the tent that Moses had built is a copy of the heavenly tent in accordance with the ancient religious principle, 'like is like'" (Goff, "Boats, Beginnings, and Repetitions," 72). The color blue also adorned Solomon's temple (2 Chronicles 2:7).
32. The Hebrew speaks of lapis lazuli, the well-known precious stone of the ancient Near East, which was bluish in color (see Alexander, "Ezekiel," 6:760 note 26). While the Masoretic text suggests that the throne of God is sapphire or blue, the Septuagint indicates that it is the pavement under the throne that is bluish. The Septuagint translation of the verse may have been influenced by Exodus 24:10, which reads, "and there was under his

Notes to Chapter 5: Colors

feet as it were a paved work of a sapphire stone" (see Greenberg, *Ezekiel 1–20*, 50). The Masoretic rendering of the verse is preferred over the Septuagint.

33. Wilson, *Dictionary of Bible Types*, 46.
34. Bayley, *Lost Language of Symbolism*, 1:212. Bayley explained, "The expression 'blue-blooded' probably originated from the symbolic idea that the Divine blood was blue, and that the nearer one's kinship to the Divine, the bluer the blood; hence the more perfect the *aristocracy*" (ibid., 2:79).
35. "Blue, representing the colour of an unclouded sky, symbolized revelation (Exod. 24:10). 'In Biblical symbolism there is associated with the colour the idea of the blue sky, and with the blue sky the idea of the godhead coming forth from its mysterious dwelling in the unseen world, and graciously condescending to the creature.' Delitzsch has shown that in various parts of the world blue is regarded as symbolizing loyalty and truth. In India a loyal man is described as unchangeable as the indigo flower. Blue was the first of the colours used for the curtains of the sanctuary, and the Israelites were commanded to have a ribbon of blue fringe in the edge of their garments in order to remind them of Jehovah (Num. 15:38)" (Farbridge, *Studies in Biblical and Semitic Symbolism*, 278). See Unger, *Unger's Bible Dictionary*, 213–14; McConkie and Parry, *Guide to Scriptural Symbols*, 33; and McConkie, *Gospel Symbolism*, 257.
36. Fontana, *Secret Language of Symbols*, 66.
37. See McConkie, *Gospel Symbolism*, 102.
38. Wilson, *Dictionary of Bible Types*, 47. See Levine, *Numbers 1–20*, 400.
39. See Wilson, *Dictionary of Bible Types*, 47. See also Whitcomb, *Esther*, 107.
40. Wilson, *Dictionary of Bible Types*, 47. The traditional interpretation of this verse is that the blue robes mesmerized Israel, because she perceived them as symbols for Assyria's wealth and power. However, Ezekiel 23:7 makes it clear that Israel did more than engage in a political alliance with Assyria. We are specifically told that the Israelites were taken in by the Assyrians, and the result was the acceptance of and engagement in idolatrous practices.
41. See Habershon, *Study of the Types*, 97; McConkie, *Gospel Symbolism*, 257; Cooper, *Encyclopedia of Traditional Symbols*, 40; McConkie and Parry, *Guide to Scriptural Symbols*, 33; and Fontana, *Secret Language of Symbols*, 66.
42. Habershon, *Study of the Types*, 97. See Wilson, *Dictionary of Bible Types*, 56–57.
43. See our discussion of the "brass serpent" as a symbol for Christ, in chapter 6 of this work.
44. See Morris, *Revelation*, 70; Wilson, *Dictionary of Bible Types*, 58; and Ford, *Revelation*, 383.
45. See Smith, *Book of Revelation*, 289.
46. Wilson, *Dictionary of Bible Types*, 197–98.
47. See Cooper, *Encyclopaedia of Traditional Symbols*, 40; Tresidder, *Symbols and Their Meanings*, 158; McConkie, *Gospel Symbolism*, 261; Rest, *Our*

Christian Symbols, 47; and Parry and Parry, Understanding the Book of Revelation, 222, 295.

48. "The colour of the sun, gold is the symbol of majesty and of the divine principle expressed through matter. For the Egyptians, it was linked with Ra, the sun god. . . . The ancient Greeks saw gold as the symbol of . . . immortality" (Fontana, Secret Language of Symbols, 66).

49. McConkie, Gospel Symbolism, 257. See McConkie and Parry, Guide to Scriptural Symbols, 33.

50. See Bayley, Lost Language of Symbolism, 1:154; 2:314. Gold was a symbol for "spiritual truth. . . . Something invaluable. . . . [It] may be associated with royalty [and] could correspond to money or riches (though usually riches of the soul)" (Todeschi, Encyclopedia of Symbolism, 71–72).

51. See Habershon, Study of the Types, 97; and McConkie, Gospel Symbolism, 105.

52. See McConkie, Gospel Symbolism, 69.

53. See Fontana, Secret Language of Symbols, 67; Smith, Book of Revelation, 289; Draper, Opening the Seven Seals, 45; Parry and Parry, Understanding the Book of Revelation, 58; and McConkie and Parry, Guide to Scriptural Symbols, 62.

54. Rest, Our Christian Symbols, 47.

55. Bayley, Lost Language of Symbolism, 1:158.

56. Ibid., 1:216. Similarly, in the book of Revelation "the act of praise focuses on the life-giving principle in God. The Revelator's frequent reference to the color green has underscored this idea" (Draper, Opening the Seven Seals, 50).

57. Farbridge, Studies in Biblical and Semitic Symbolism, 278.

58. Clarke, Holy Bible with a Commentary and Critical Notes, 3:79.

59. Wilson, Dictionary of Bible Types, 203.

60. Only those in the highest degree of the celestial kingdom will have "eternal increase" or offspring (see D&C 132:16–17; McConkie, Millennial Messiah, 707; and Adams, "Eternal Progression," 2:466).

61. Clarke, Holy Bible with a Commentary and Critical Notes, 3:297.

62. Dahood, Psalms I, 1–50, 146.

63. Dahood interprets the meaning of the Psalm as "After a peaceful life under the guidance and protection of Yahweh, the psalmist looks forward to eternal happiness in God's celestial abode" (ibid., 148–49).

64. One scholar noted that the olive is one of the longest-living trees. Its use here, and the placement of the tree in the "house of God" or temple-sanctuary, where none can tamper with it or uproot it, all imply the eternal nature of the scene being depicted (see Kidner, Psalms 1–72, 196).

65. Draper, Opening the Seven Seals, 67. See Thayer, Thayer's Greek-English Lexicon, 669; and Ford, Revelation, 99.

66. Tresidder, Symbols and Their Meanings, 158–59.

67. McConkie, Mortal Messiah, 4:215 note 2.

68. McConkie, *Gospel Symbolism*, 274. See Cooper, *Encyclopaedia of Traditional Symbols*, 178.
69. McConkie, *Millennial Messiah*, 530.
70. See Cooper, *Encyclopaedia of Traditional Symbols*, 40; Tresidder, *Symbols and Their Meanings*, 159; Farbridge, *Studies in Biblical and Semitic Symbolism*, 278; Todeschi, *Encyclopedia of Symbolism*, 73; Smith, *Book of Revelation*, 289; Parry and Parry, *Understanding the Book of Revelation*, 221; Conner, *Interpreting the Symbols and Types*, 61; Myers, *Eerdmans Bible Dictionary*, 227; Unger, *Unger's Bible Dictionary*, 213–14; McConkie and Parry, *Guide to Scriptural Symbols*, 33; McConkie, *Gospel Symbolism*, 106, 257; Ryken, Wilhoit, and Longman, *Dictionary of Biblical Imagery*, 158; and Rest, *Our Christian Symbols*, 46.
71. See Tresidder, *Symbols and Their Meanings*, 159; and Brown, *Gospel According to John*, XIII-XXI, 875.
72. See Ryken, Wilhoit, and Longman, *Dictionary of Biblical Imagery*, 158.
73. Tresidder, *Symbols and Their Meanings*, 159.
74. Ryken, Wilhoit, and Longman, *Dictionary of Biblical Imagery*, 158.
75. McConkie, *Gospel Symbolism*, 102.
76. See Baldwin, *Esther*, 98; Coggins and Re'emi, *Israel among the Nations*, 134; and Whitcomb, *Esther*, 107–8.
77. Breneman, *Ezra, Nehemiah, Esther*, 345.
78. See Baldwin, *Esther*, 98.
79. See Hart and Di Lella, *Book of Daniel*, 188.
80. Wilson, *Dictionary of Bible Types*, 327.
81. See Brown, *Gospel According to John*, XIII-XXI, 874–75.
82. See ibid., 875.
83. Habershon, *Study of the Types*, 95–96.
84. Todeschi, *Encyclopedia of Symbolism*, 73.
85. Draper, *Opening the Seven Seals*, 188.
86. Wilson, *Dictionary of Bible Types*, 327–28. See Ryken, Wilhoit, and Longman, *Dictionary of Biblical Imagery*, 158.
87. See Cooper, *Encyclopaedia of Traditional Symbols*, 41. "Some think that ... scarlet refers to suffering" (Habershon, *Study of the Types*, 95). "To the Christian, it denotes Christ's passion" (Fontana, *Secret Language of Symbols*, 66).
88. Even if red is used to imply a positive reality, such as resurrection or atonement, it remains at its core a negative symbol, in that suffering and death had to be encountered by Christ so that we might reap the positive benefits of His pain while avoiding the negative repercussions of our own actions. Hence, in many instances the colors red and scarlet symbolize the blood spilt by the Savior during his atoning sacrifice (Revelation 19:13, D&C 133:48; Isaiah 63:2; Numbers 19:2), and thereby function as constant reminders of our need for Christ's intervention (see McConkie and

Parry, *Guide to Scriptural Symbols*, 33, 92). See also McConkie, *Gospel Symbolism*, 102, 106, 257.
89. Brown and Smith, *Symbols in Stone*, 30.
90. See Tresidder, *Symbols and Their Meanings*, 156.
91. See Conner, *Interpreting the Symbols and Types*, 61; Smith, *Book of Revelation*, 289; Todeschi, *Encyclopedia of Symbolism*, 73; Rest, *Our Christian Symbols*, 47; Parry and Parry, *Understanding the Book of Revelation*, 79–80, 153; Myers, *Eerdmans Bible Dictionary*, 227; Farbridge, *Studies in Biblical and Semitic Symbolism*, 278; and Draper, *Opening the Seven Seals*, 64, 132, 187, 212.
92. Maxwell, *Not My Will, But Thine*, 53.
93. See Habershon, *Study of the Types*, 96.
94. Draper, *Opening the Seven Seals*, 187. See Habershon, *Study of the Types*, 96.
95. See chapter 3 of this work; and Nibley, *Temple and Cosmos*, 58.
96. See Ryken, Wilhoit, and Longman, *Dictionary of Biblical Imagery*, 158.
97. See Hebrews 12:16; Wilson, *Dictionary of Bible Types*, 41; and Ryken, Wilhoit, and Longman, *Dictionary of Biblical Imagery*, 97.
98. Note that, upon selling his birthright, Esau's name was changed to Edom, which means "red" (Genesis 25:30).
99. See Parry and Parry, *Understanding the Book of Revelation*, 222.
100. See Holzapfel and Seely, *My Father's House*, 62.
101. See Nibley, *Teachings of the Book of Mormon*, vol. 2, lecture 45, pp. 6, 14; and Nibley, *Approaching Zion*, 563.
102. See Habershon, *Study of the Types*, 97. See also Wilson, *Dictionary of Bible Types*, 371.
103. McConkie and Parry, *Guide to Scriptural Symbols*, 33. See McConkie, *Gospel Symbolism*, 257.
104. Wilson, *Dictionary of Bible Types*, 371.
105. See Todeschi, *Encyclopedia of Symbolism*, 73.
106. McConkie, *Gospel Symbolism*, 105.
107. In explaining the symbolic differences between black (evil, death, sin, and *mourning*) and white (purity, righteousness, holiness, light, and *happiness*), one Catholic commentator shared the following: "It is told of a certain minister that . . . was explaining once to a class of Sunday School children the symbolism of white. It expresses joy and happiness, he said, and the bride at a wedding is thus clothed because her wedding-day is the happiest of her life. 'Why,' asked a small boy, 'do all the men at a wedding wear black?'" (Henry, *Catholic Customs and Symbols*, 80–81).
108. See Conner, *Interpreting the Symbols and Types*, 61; Bayley, *Lost Language of Symbolism*, 2:38; Farbridge, *Studies in Biblical and Semitic Symbolism*, 278; Smith, *Book of Revelation*, 289; Myers, *Eerdmans Bible Dictionary*, 227; Unger, *Unger's Bible Dictionary*, 212–14; McConkie and Parry, *Guide to*

Scriptural Symbols, 33; McConkie, Gospel Symbolism, 105, 256–57; and Parry and Parry, Understanding the Book of Revelation, 59, 278.

109. See Todeschi, Encyclopedia of Symbolism, 73; Henry, Catholic Customs and Symbols, 80–81; Fontana, Secret Language of Symbols, 67; and Rest, Our Christian Symbols, 46.

110. Tresidder, Symbols and Their Meanings, 156. It should be noted that on very rare occasions white functions as a negative sign. In the secular world it is a sign of aging and gray hair. In certain parts of the world it provokes images of winter, coldness, and the accompanying death of plant life. More than a dozen times in the book of Leviticus, white is noted as the color of leprosy (see Ryken, Wilhoit, and Longman, Dictionary of Biblical Imagery, 944).

111. "The great whore was arrayed in showy, expensive, worldly clothing [see Revelation 17:4], but the bride of Christ is wearing simple clothing, which symbolizes 'the righteousness of saints' [see also Revelation 15:6]. The linen is white because it was 'washed . . . in the blood of the Lamb' [Revelation 7:14], meaning that the Saints are sanctified through the atonement of Christ" (Parry and Parry, Understanding the Book of Revelation, 252).

112. The white clothing "is a statement of triumph of the spirit over the flesh, of good over evil" (McConkie and Parry, Guide to Scriptural Symbols, 33; and McConkie, Gospel Symbolism, 256–57). "Among the Greeks and Romans, white symbolized victory—those 'clothed in white raiment' are those who have overcome the world (Revelation 3:5)" (Parry and Parry, Understanding the Book of Revelation, 59). See Revelation 6:2; Zechariah 6:3.

113. Ryken, Wilhoit, and Longman, Dictionary of Biblical Imagery, 159.

114. Ibid. Regarding the recurring dictate that we must wash our garments white in the blood of the Lamb (1 Nephi 12:10–11; Alma 13:11; 34:36; Ether 13:10), Hugh Nibley has written: "Since when can anyone be washed white in blood? The rationale expressed in these documents is that if you mix all colors together, you have a garment that is perfectly white, meaning that it can take any color. If you combine all colors, all experience, all knowledge, you will get (if there is any light at all) white. Of course if you turn off the light, all will be black. But it is the light, and the garment of white, in which all colors of the spectrum are contained" (Temple and Cosmos, 123).

NOTES TO CHAPTER 6: NUMBERS AS SYMBOLS

1. See Davis, Biblical Numerology, 18.
2. Ifrah, Universal History of Numbers, 214.
3. See Julien, Mammoth Dictionary of Symbols, 293.
4. See Davis, Biblical Numerology, 109; and Smith, Dictionary of the Bible, 456.
5. See Friberg, "Numbers and Counting," 4:1139. "Near Eastern literature,

not just Hebrew, reveals a fondness for using numbers to communicate ideas" (Draper, *Opening the Seven Seals*, 23).

6. See Davis, *Biblical Numerology*, 124.

7. Ibid., 107. "One of [the] distinguishing features . . . [of] the [21st century B.C.] *Epic of Gilgamesh* . . . is the tendency to use numbers as a literary tool" (Friberg, "Numbers and Counting," 4:1143).

8. Numbers such as 3, 4, 7, 10, and 12 occur repetitively in intertestamental writings. Similarly, the Qumran literature frequently employs the number 7 and its multiples (see Davis, *Biblical Numerology*, 109).

9. Ibid., 113.

10. See Bennett, "Number," 703; and Davis, *Biblical Numerology*, 115, 128, 131.

11. J. B. Segal, "Numerals in the Old Testament," 10:2. Fed up with such condescending remarks, Robert Johnston wrote, "Try it, gentlemen! Learn how God has mocked all your philosophy with the mere enumeration of 1, 2, 3!" (*Numbers in the Bible*, 41).

12. John Davis noted that some scholars simply refuse to acknowledge that there is "number symbolism" in any form in the Bible (see *Biblical Numerology*, 91, 103, 104, 115; see also Rust and Parry, "Book of Mormon Literature," 1:184). Admittedly, some societies have taken their use and interpretation of numbers far beyond the initial, divinely inspired concept. Yet, as with apostate forms of Christianity, God inspired the beginnings and then men corrupted these for their own reasons and uses (see Nibley, *World and the Prophets*, 68; and Ifrah, *Universal History of Numbers*, 258–59).

13. Bullinger, *Number in Scripture*, 44, 45; see 20–47, 234. See also Sabiers, *Astounding New Discoveries*, 7, 8, 9, 11, 13.

14. See Davis, *Biblical Numerology*, 125; see also 104–5; and Conner, *Interpreting the Symbols and Types*, 9. "When we see a number used not by chance, but by design; not as haphazard, but with significance; then we see not merely so many works and words, but the Living God working and speaking" (Bullinger, *Number in Scripture*, 2; see Johnston, *Numbers in the Bible*, 26).

15. See Davis, *Biblical Numerology*, 103, 116; Unger, *Unger's Bible Dictionary*, 799; Smith, *New Bible Dictionary*, 263; Watch Tower Bible and Tract Society of Pennsylvania, *Aid to Bible Understanding*, 1233; Friberg, "Numbers and Counting," 4:1145; Gower, *New Manners and Customs of Bible Times*, 300; Johnston, *Numbers in the Bible*, 34; McKenzie, *Dictionary of the Bible*, 620–21; Farbridge, *Studies in Biblical and Semitic Symbolism*, 87; and Drinkard, "Numbers," 711.

16. Farbridge, *Studies in Biblical and Semitic Symbolism*, 88.

17. Davis, *Biblical Numerology*, 17 note 6.

18. Virkler, *Hermeneutics*, 61.

19. See Davis, *Biblical Numerology*, 128, 132.

20. See ibid., 105, 125. One source conjectured, "In various primitive Asiatic

Notes to Chapter 6: Numbers   357

languages, if a man wished to say 'five' he would make use of the same word as when he wished to say 'hand,' and in all probability when he said 'five' his mental conception was really that of a hand consisting of five outstretched fingers" (Farbridge, *Studies in Biblical and Semitic Symbolism*, 88).

21. See Davis, *Biblical Numerology*, 106–7.
22. See ibid., 106.
23. See Farbridge, *Studies in Biblical and Semitic Symbolism*, 144; Davis, *Biblical Numerology*, 126, 128; and Rector, *No More Strangers*, 3:105.
24. Draper, *Opening the Seven Seals*, 23.
25. See Davis, *Biblical Numerology*, 29.
26. See ibid., 106. These dates are somewhat misleading, in that they do not take into account the fact that, written documents aside, God appears to use numerology in the creation (Genesis 2:2–3), as does Moses in his record of that and other events (Genesis 4:15; 7:2–4).
27. Smith, *Book of Revelation*, 72.
28. Johnston, *Numbers in the Bible*, 95, 97.
29. Bennett, "Number," 703.
30. See Davis, *Biblical Numerology*, 126, 140; and Draper, *Opening the Seven Seals*, 149.
31. "Gematria, a Hebraized form of the Greek *geometria*, . . . consisted in indicating a word by means of the number which would be obtained by adding together the numerical values of the consonants of the word" (Bennett, "Number," 703).
32. See our discussion of the number 666 in the Gematria section at the end of this chapter.
33. Davis, *Biblical Numerology*, 104–5. See Bullinger, *Number in Scripture*, 2; and Johnston, *Numbers in the Bible*, 26.
34. Davis, *Biblical Numerology*, 120.
35. Ibid., 104–5.
36. Ibid., 125.
37. There are 2,536 references to the number one in the standard works. Additionally, there are some 731 references to the word *first*.
38. See Bullinger, *Number in Scripture*, 24, 50, 51; Cirlot, *Dictionary of Symbols*, 232; Julien, *Mammoth Dictionary of Symbols*, 304; Todeschi, *Encyclopedia of Symbolism*, 185; Cooper, *Encyclopaedia of Traditional Symbols*, 113–14; and Davis, *Biblical Numerology*, 122–23.
39. See Ifrah, *Universal History of Numbers*, 499; Bennett, "Number," 703; Bullinger, *Number in Scripture*, 50; Johnston, *Numbers in the Bible*, 43–44; Julien, *Mammoth Dictionary of Symbols*, 304; Todeschi, *Encyclopedia of Symbolism*, 185; and Cooper, *Encyclopaedia of Traditional Symbols*, 113–14.
40. See Johnston, *Numbers in the Bible*, 15; and Bullinger, *Number in Scripture*, 59, 199.
41. See Bullinger, *Number in Scripture*, 56.

42. Ibid., 50.
43. Johnston, *Numbers in the Bible*, 43–44.
44. Bennett, "Number," 703; and Davis, *Biblical Numerology*, 122–23. Because all things originate with God, Mick Smith argues that the number one symbolizes "the beginning of all things" (*Book of Revelation*, 288). Other authors have proposed a similar idea (see Julien, *Mammoth Dictionary of Symbols*, 304; Todeschi, *Encyclopedia of Symbolism*, 185; and Cooper, *Encyclopaedia of Traditional Symbols*, 113–14).
45. The Shema is the most famous of Jewish prayers. "In the evening and the morning the *Shema* is . . . recited: this group of three passages from the Torah begins with the words 'Hear O Israel, the Lord is our God, the Lord is One,' which have come to be regarded as a basic affirmation of Jewish faith. Generations of Jews have striven to die with these words on their lips, and two of the three passages are copied on the *mezuzah*, the small parchment scroll which is fixed, usually in an ornamental case, to the doorposts of Jewish homes: they also figure among the passages of Torah which are contained in the *tefillin* or phylacteries, little boxes which are worn during the weekday morning service on the forehead and on the upper arm, next to the heart" (de Lange, *Judaism*, 39).
46. Like the Godhead, the oneness of the membership of the Church is, of course, a "spiritual unity" (Cirlot, *Dictionary of Symbols*, 232).
47. See Cooper, *Encyclopaedia of Traditional Symbols*, 114; Ifrah, *Universal History of Numbers*, 499; Johnston, *Numbers in the Bible*, 49; and Todeschi, *Encyclopedia of Symbolism*, 185. One source indicated that this symbolic connotation of "division," "opposition," "enmity," or "difference" is the result of the fact that two is the first number that can be divided by another (Bullinger, *Number in Scripture*, 92).
48. See Draper, *Opening the Seven Seals*, 120; and Bennett, "Number," 703.
49. See Bullinger, *Number in Scripture*, 97.
50. See ibid., 105.
51. Johnston, *Numbers in the Bible*, 49; see 52, 53.
52. See Ifrah, *Universal History of Numbers*, 499.
53. See Johnston, *Numbers in the Bible*, 55.
54. Davis, *Biblical Numerology*, 121.
55. Farbridge, *Studies in Biblical and Semitic Symbolism*, 99–100.
56. See Davis, *Biblical Numerology*, 121, 123; Todeschi, *Encyclopedia of Symbolism*, 185; Fontana, *Secret Language of Symbols*, 64; Cooper, *Encyclopaedia of Traditional Symbols*, 114; Bennett, "Number," 703; Bullinger, *Number in Scripture*, 107–8, 122–23; Smith, *Book of Revelation*, 288; Johnston, *Numbers in the Bible*, 39–40; Farbridge, *Studies in Biblical and Semitic Symbolism*, 99–100; Rest, *Our Christian Symbols*, 17–18; 60–61; Cirlot, *Dictionary of Symbols*, 232; and Julien, *Mammoth Dictionary of Symbols*, 448.
57. See Bullinger, *Number in Scripture*, 107; Davis, *Biblical Numerology*, 123; Cirlot, *Dictionary of Symbols*, 232; and Johnston, *Numbers in the Bible*, 55.

58. For a discussion of Peter, James, and John as types for the Father, Son, and Holy Ghost, see chapter 11 of this work.
59. Bullinger, *Number in Scripture*, 109.
60. Ibid., 112.
61. Drinkard, "Numbers," 712.
62. Farbridge, *Studies in Biblical and Semitic Symbolism*, 144. Even prayer seems to fall under this category: praying three times a day (Daniel 6:10; Psalm 55:17) and using patterns of three in prayer (Isaiah 6:3; Revelation 4:8; 2 Nephi 16:3). In the priestly benediction, the name of God was thrice repeated (Numbers 6:24–26).
63. See Parry and Parry, *Understanding the Book of Revelation*, 137, 155.
64. Draper, *Opening the Seven Seals*, 121, 138. See Parry and Parry, *Understanding the Book of Revelation*, 138.
65. Commentators generally agree that 3½, 42, and 1,260 are equivalent numeric symbols (see Daniel 7:25; 9:27; 12:7; Revelation 11:2–3, 6, 9, 11; 12:5, 14; 13:5). "The number forty-two often signifies the period when righteousness is cut short and the wicked dominate. . . . The number forty-two is manifest scripturally in several ways, each of which equals three and one-half. . . . Forty-two months, or three and one-half, or 1,260, belong to the wicked and apparently signify their work; the number three and one-half may mean that the work of righteousness is cut short. That number is one-half of seven, the number of perfection and completion, which belongs to God and his Saints. . . . One-half of seven, or three and one-half, represents an incomplete covenant (religious systems that appear to be spiritual and possess power but do not) or the broken covenant (apostate conditions). . . . The number forty-two may not indicate an actual number of months or other specific period of time but may instead symbolize a general, prolonged, but ultimately limited, time of wickedness" (Parry and Parry, *Understanding the Book of Revelation*, 137–38, 168). Of the number 42, one scholar has noted, "It is the result of six multiplied by seven, i.e., 'perfection missing the mark'" (Ford, *Revelation*, 170; see also Bullinger, *Number in Scripture*, 268; and Smith, *Book of Revelation*, 108).
66. According to the Prophet Joseph Smith, this "beast" was a representation of "the Kingdoms of the world the inhabitants whereof were beastly and abominable characters, they were murderous, corrupt, carnivourous and brutal in their dispositions." It represented "those kingdoms who had degenerated and become corrupt—the Kingdoms of the world" (*Words of Joseph Smith*, 184).
67. Draper, *Opening the Seven Seals*, 95–96.
68. See ibid., 108; and Parry and Parry, *Understanding the Book of Revelation*, 110.
69. If one were to read the verse with any degree of literalness the conjecture might be made that the "third part" were one of three groups in the premortal world; the great and noble ones, the general populace of spirits, and the apostates that followed Lucifer. However, in this author's

opinion, nothing in the text requires such a reading. Indeed, to take the phrase "third part" literally may miss John's point.

70. See Draper, *Opening the Seven Seals*, 24, 77, 94; Smith, *Book of Revelation*, 288; Johnston, *Numbers in the Bible*, 61; Farbridge, *Studies in Biblical and Semitic Symbolism*, 115; Rest, *Our Christian Symbols*, 61; Ifrah, *Universal History of Numbers*, 499; Cirlot, *Dictionary of Symbols*, 232; Julien, *Mammoth Dictionary of Symbols*, 167; Todeschi, *Encyclopedia of Symbolism*, 186; Fontana, *Secret Language of Symbols*, 64; Davis, *Biblical Numerology*, 122–23; Cooper, *Encyclopaedia of Traditional Symbols*, 115; Bennett, "Number," 703; Smith, *New Bible Dictionary*, 263; and Myers and Myers, *Haggai, Zechariah 1–8*, 317.

71. Bullinger, *Number in Scripture*, 123–24.

72. See Parry, "Garden of Eden," 133. One scholar noted, "If the Garden of Eden is an image of divine provision, it is paradoxically also a place of human labor" (Ryken, Wilhoit, and Longman, *Dictionary of Biblical Imagery*, 316). Such is the case with the temple also.

73. See Johnston, *Numbers in the Bible*, 63.

74. In a similar vein, in Revelation 14:20 John employs the number 1,600, a multiple of 4. "Symbolically, the number is the square of four, denoting geographical completeness, multiplied by the square of ten, the number denoting all of a part. Taken together, the number suggests that God's judgment actually involves all John's world, not just those who are around Jerusalem, and that all those who belong to that portion outside the protecting power of God will be affected" (Draper, *Opening the Seven Seals*, 164).

75. See Kselman and Barre, "Psalms," 541. Fitzmyer notes that "*abyssos* can denote . . . the abode of the dead (see Ps 107:26; Rom 10:7) or the final prison of Satan and the demons (Rev 20:3). It is used often in the LXX . . . [as] the symbol of chaos and disorder" (*Gospel According to Luke I–IX*, 739 note 31). C. S. Mann indicates that the sea represents the "place of final punishment for demons" (*Mark*, 278–79). Edwin Firmage indicated that the sea was a symbol for the "repository of impurity" ("Zoology," 6:1132). See also Williamson, *Mark*, 104; Clarke, *Holy Bible with a Commentary and Critical Notes*, 5:420; Freyne, "Sea of Galilee," 2:900; Morris, *Luke*, 171; and Liefeld, "Luke," 8:913.

76. For a detailed explanation of the location of the lost tribes and the symbolism surrounding their return from the land of the north, see "North" in chapter 7 of this work.

77. See Bullinger, *Number in Scripture*, 135–37; Johnston, *Numbers in the Bible*, 63; Ifrah, *Universal History of Numbers*, 499; Davis, *Biblical Numerology*, 122; and Conner, *Interpreting the Symbols and Types*, 53.

78. See Cirlot, *Dictionary of Symbols*, 233; Todeschi, *Encyclopedia of Symbolism*, 186; Cooper, *Encyclopaedia of Traditional Symbols*, 116; and Tressider, *Symbols and Their Meanings*, 166–67.

79. See Bullinger, *Number in Scripture*, 136.

Notes to Chapter 6: Numbers

80. Ibid.
81. Ibid., 140. "The outer court was 100 cubits long and 50 cubits wide. On either side were 20 pillars, and along each end were 10 pillars, or 60 in all; that is 5 x 12, or grace in governmental display before the world. . . .

"The pillars that held up the curtains were 5 cubits apart and 5 cubits high, and the whole of the outer curtain was divided into squares of 25 cubits (5 x 5). . . . 5 x 5 was also the measure of the brazen altar of burnt offering. . . .

"True, this brazen altar was only 3 cubits high, but this tells us that the provision was Divine in its origin, that atonement emanates solely from God.

"The *building* itself was 10 cubits high, 10 cubits wide, and 30 cubits long. Its length was divided into two unequal parts, the Holy Place being 20 cubits long; and the Holy of Holies 10 cubits, being therefore a perfect cube of 10 cubits. It was formed of forty-eight boards, twenty on either side, and eight at the end, the front being formed of a curtain hung on five pillars. These forty-eight boards (3×4^2) are significant of the nation as before God in the fulness of privilege on the earth (4 x 12). The twenty boards on each side were held together by *five* bars passing through rings which were attached to them.

"The *curtains* which covered the Tabernacle structure were four in number. The first was made of ten curtains. . . . They were hung *five* on each side, probably sewn together to form one large sheet (20 x 28); the two sheets coupled together by loops, and fifty (5 x 10) taches of gold. The second covering was . . . 30 cubits long and four wide. . . . The *third* was of rams' skins dyed red, . . . of which the dimensions are not given.

"The Entrance Veils were three in number. The *first* was 'the gate of the court,' 20 cubits wide and 5 high, hung on 5 pillars. The *second* was 'the door of the Tabernacle,' 10 cubits wide and 10 high, hung . . . on 5 pillars. The *third* was the 'beautiful vail,' also 10 cubits square, which divided the Holy Place from the Holy of Holies. One feature of these three vails is remarkable. The dimensions of the vail of the court and those of the Tabernacle were different, but yet the *area* was the same. The former was 20 cubits by 5 = 100 cubits; the latter were 10 cubits by 10, equaling 100 cubits also. . . .

"The *Gematria* of Hebrews ix., which gives an account of the Tabernacle, yields the number *five* as a factor" (Bullinger, *Number in Scripture*, 142–43).

82. See Johnston, *Numbers in the Bible*, 65.
83. Of the five wise virgins' refusal to share their oil, we read: "This was not selfishness or unkindness. The kind of oil that is needed to illuminate the way and light up the darkness is not shareable. How can one share obedience to the principle of tithing; a mind at peace from righteous living; an accumulation of knowledge? How can one share faith or testimony? How can one share attitudes or chastity, or the experience of a mission? How can one share temple privileges? Each must obtain that kind of oil

for himself" (Kimball, *Faith Precedes the Miracle*, 255–56). "Every man must light his own lamp with the oil of righteousness which he buys at the market of obedience" (McConkie, *Mortal Messiah*, 3:468).

84. It is also possible that the number five in the story was a reminder that, while Goliath seemed intimidating and indestructible, he was nothing more than a man.

85. See Bullinger, *Number in Scripture*, 138.

86. See Draper, *Opening the Seven Seals*, 121; Bullinger, *Number in Scripture*, 123, 150; Smith, *Book of Revelation*, 288; and Johnston, *Numbers in the Bible*, 67.

87. Bullinger, *Number in Scripture*, 123, 150.

88. See Johnston, *Numbers in the Bible*, 67.

89. Ibid.

90. Bullinger, *Number in Scripture*, 151.

91. See ibid., 150–51.

92. Ibid., 123, 150.

93. Johnston, *Numbers in the Bible*, 67.

94. See Morris, *Gospel According to John*, 160–61; Pryor, *John*, 15–16; Ellis, *Genius of John*, 42; and Richardson, *Gospel According to St. John*, 55–56.

95. Pryor, *John*, 16.

96. See Johnston, *Numbers in the Bible*, 71; and Todeschi, *Encyclopedia of Symbolism*, 186. The number appears over fifty times in the book of the Revelation alone. Its symbolic connotations are also found with similar meanings in the Egyptian, Assyrian, and Persian religions (see Bennett, "Number," 703).

97. See Bullinger, *Number in Scripture*, 158; and Davis, *Biblical Numerology*, 118.

98. See Farbridge, *Studies in Biblical and Semitic Symbolism*, 120.

99. See ibid., 119.

100. See McConkie, *Gospel Symbolism*, 199; and Davis, *Biblical Numerology*, 122, 123.

101. See Davis, *Biblical Numerology*, 118, 122–23; Drinkard, "Numbers," 711; Cooper, *Encyclopaedia of Traditional Symbols*, 117; Cirlot, *Dictionary of Symbols*, 233, 295; Julien, *Mammoth Dictionary of Symbols*, 373; McConkie and Parry, *Guide to Scriptural Symbols*, 99; McConkie, *Gospel Symbolism*, 199; and Parry and Parry, *Understanding the Book of Revelation*, 14, 27.

102. See Draper, *Opening the Seven Seals*, 24; Cooper, *Encyclopaedia of Traditional Symbols*, 117; and Julien, *Mammoth Dictionary of Symbols*, 373.

103. See Bullinger, *Number in Scripture*, 23, 107; Draper, *Opening the Seven Seals*, 138; Johnston, *Numbers in the Bible*, 40; Rest, *Our Christian Symbols*, 61; Todeschi, *Encyclopedia of Symbolism*, 186; McConkie, *Gospel Symbolism*, 199; Davis, *Biblical Numerology*, 122; and Smith, *Book of Revelation*, 288.

104. See Bullinger, *Number in Scripture*, 194. "When the number seven is insufficient to express the complete thought required, then multiples of seven are used" (Farbridge, *Studies in Biblical and Semitic Symbolism*, 126).
105. See Farbridge, *Studies in Biblical and Semitic Symbolism*, 136–38.
106. Bullinger, *Number in Scripture*, 167–68, 196; emphasis removed. "Some lexical or bilingual texts translate '7' (but also '40' and '50') with . . . a word meaning 'totality'" (Friberg, "Numbers and Counting," 4:1144).
107. McConkie and Parry, *Guide to Scriptural Symbols*, 99. See Davis, *Biblical Numerology*, 122; and McKenzie, *Dictionary of the Bible*, 621.
108. "The first statement as to the original Creation in Gen.i.1 [in Hebrew] consists of 7 words, and 28 letters (4 x 7)" (Bullinger, *Number in Scripture*, 168).
109. Cirlot, *Dictionary of Symbols*, 233.
110. See Bullinger, *Number in Scripture*, 194.
111. See McConkie, *Gospel Symbolism*, 265; Conner, *Interpreting the Symbols and Types*, 152; and Habershon, *Study of the Types*, 98–99.
112. See McConkie, *Gospel Symbolism*, 107; and Fairbairn, *Typology of Scripture*, 2:325.
113. See Ryken, Wilhoit, and Longman, *Dictionary of Biblical Imagery*, 507; and Wilson, *Dictionary of Bible Types*, 257.
114. Bullinger, *Number in Scripture*, 171, 181. "In regard to 7, the ritual arrangements found in the Pentateuch would alone warrant the conclusion that this number was regarded as in some sense sacred" (Muirhead, "Numbers," 2:92).
115. It should be acknowledged, however, that chapterization and versification of the biblical text were not given by the prophets, but are arrangements of the text made many years after the revelation was first recorded. Additionally, although the current JST also places Isaiah 4:1 in chapter 3, that change was not made by Joseph Smith, but rather by the RLDS church in 1866 (apparently because of their anti-plural marriage platform) (see Nyman, "Contribution of the JST," 122).
116. For example: Brewster, *Isaiah Plain and Simple*, 35; Grogan, "Isaiah," 6:44; Jensen and Irwin, "Isaiah 1–39," 233; Keil and Delitzsch, *Prophecies of Isaiah*, 1:150; Motyer, *Isaiah*, 57–58; Nyman, "Contribution of the JST," 122; Parry, Parry, and Peterson, *Understanding Isaiah*, 44–45; Peake, *Commentary on the Bible*, 439; Rasmussen, *Latter-day Saint Commentary on the Old Testament*, 506; Roth, *Isaiah*, 36–37; Skousen, *Isaiah Speaks to Modern Times*, 170; and Young, *Book of Isaiah*, 1:170–72.
117. The premillennial chapter 3 speaks of the worldly and apostate conditions of a people steeped in disobedience. The millennial chapter 4 refers to a beautiful and glorious branch of the Lord that is obedient to His dictates, and thus has joy. If the KJV Isaiah 4:1 belongs in the context of the millennium, it seems curious that, taken literally, the women in 4.1 have little reason to rejoice. They have been left husbandless and childless. Elder Bruce R. McConkie, who also placed this verse in Isaiah 4:1, attempted

to resolve this issue by suggesting that it foreshadowed a potential millennial restoration of plural marriage (see *Millennial Messiah*, 655). One other commentator on the plural marriage interpretation stated, "The actual text of the verse does . . . place the practice of plural marriage in a negative light" (Donaldson, *Restoration Study Bible*, 1:186 note 1).

118. "In 1879, President John Taylor assigned Orson Pratt to prepare a new edition which would include a redivision of chapters (increasing the number from 114 to 239) [and] reversification" (Horton, "Book of Mormon—Transmission from Translator to Printed Text," 240).

119. That section, found in what then would be 2 Nephi, chapter 8, reads, " . . . & her gates shall lament and mou{r}n and she shall be desolat[e] and shall sit upon the ground and in that day seven women shall take hold of one man saying we will eat our own bread and wear our own apparel only let us be called by thy {m̲ na}me to t(+)ake away our reproach in th{a}t day shall the branch of the Lord be bea{u}tiful and glorious the fruit [o]f the earth and excellent and comely to them that are escaped of Israel" (Skousen, *Printer's Manuscript of the Book of Mormon*, 1:190).

120. The earliest known commentary on the book of Revelation was penned somewhere around A.D. 270 by Victorinus—a bishop of the Church, who suffered martyrdom in A.D. 304. Victorinus wrote the following: "We read also that this typical number [7] is announced by the Holy Spirit by the mouth of Isaiah: 'Of seven women which took hold of one man.' [Isaiah 4:1] The one man is Christ, not born of seed; but the seven women are seven churches, receiving His bread, and clothed with his apparel, who ask that their reproach should be taken away, only that His name should be called upon them. The bread is the Holy Spirit, which nourishes to eternal life, promised to them, that is, by faith. And His garments wherewith they desire to be clothed are the glory of immortality, of which Paul the apostle says: 'For this corruptible must put on incorruption, and this mortal must put on mortality.' [1 Corinthians 15:53] Moreover, they ask that their reproach may be taken away—that is, that they may be cleansed from their sins: for the reproach is . . . sin which is taken away in baptism, and they begin to be called Christian men, which is, 'Let thy name be called upon us'" (see "Commentary on the Apocalypse,". 7:345–46).

121. "Revelation 1:4 [mentions] 'seven churches in Asia.' There is no doubt as to the literal nature of this number for seven churches did indeed exist in Asia at that time. But the fact that there were more than seven in Asia at that time indicates that the writer is using the number symbolically or ideally. Hieropolis and Colossae were both located in the province of Asia (Col. 1:2; 4:13, 15–16), but are not dealt with in Revelation" (Davis, *Biblical Numerology*, 111).

122. Bullinger, *Number in Scripture*, 32.

123. See ibid., 32–34. "Now the wonderful fact is that we have in the genealogy of Luke iii exactly 77 names, with GOD at the one end, and JESUS at the other. This is indeed stamping it with the number of *spiritual* perfection. . . . The genealogy in Matthew . . . is so arranged that it contains 42

Notes to Chapter 6: Numbers 365

generations, or SIX *sevens* (6 x 7). . . . . JESUS, the birth name of His humiliation as *Man*, is composed of *six* letters [in Greek]; while Christ, His Divine title as the Anointed of God, is composed of *seven* letters [in Greek]" (Ibid., 160–61).

124. See ibid., 10, 19.

125. See Cooper, *Encyclopaedia of Traditional Symbols*, 118; Johnston, *Numbers in the Bible*, 75; Julien, *Mammoth Dictionary of Symbols*, 135; Bullinger, *Number in Scripture*, 200; and Davis, *Biblical Numerology*, 122.

126. See Johnston, *Numbers in the Bible*, 75; Cirlot, *Dictionary of Symbols*, 233; Julien, *Mammoth Dictionary of Symbols*, 135; and Bullinger, *Number in Scripture*, 196, 200.

127. See Julien, *Mammoth Dictionary of Symbols*, 135.

128. See Cirlot, *Dictionary of Symbols*, 233; and McConkie and Parry, *Guide to Scriptural Symbols*, 46. "According to Clement of Alexandria, Christ placed those whom he gave a second life under the sign of 8" (Julien, *Mammoth Dictionary of Symbols*, 135).

129. "In Hebrew the number eight is Sh'moneh, from the root Shah'meyn, 'to make fat,' 'cover with fat,' 'to super-abound.' . . . Eight denotes that which is superabundant or satiating" (Bullinger, *Number in Scripture*, 196). See Draper, *Opening the Seven Seals*, 121; and Smith, *Book of Revelation*, 144.

130. Bullinger, *Number in Scripture*, 200.

131. See Elliott, *1 Peter*, 673; and Reicke, *Epistles of James, Peter and Jude*, 113–14.

132. Of the dimensions of the tabernacles in which they would serve, Bullinger noted: "*Eight* is the first *cubic* number, the cube of *two*, 2 x 2 x 2. . . . The significance of the *cube* is seen in the fact that the 'Holy of Holies,' both in the Tabernacle and in the Temple, were *cubes*. In the Tabernacle it was a *cube* of 10 cubits. In the Temple it was a cube of 20 cubits. In Rev. xx the New Jerusalem is to be a cube of 12,000 furlongs" (*Number in Scripture*, 201).

133. See ibid., 203. "The Sibylline Oracles 1:342–44 give the number of the name of the Savior in Greek as 888 (I=10, A=8, S=200, O=70, Y=400, S=200)" (Draper, *Opening the Seven Seals*, 273 note 29). "In the Hebrew alphabet this is the sacred number of Jesus" (Cooper, *Encyclopaedia of Traditional Symbols*, 120).

134. Bullinger, *Number in Scripture*, 204. Bullinger points out that, if spelled out in Greek gematria, "Christ" totals 1,480 (8 x 185); "Lord" totals 800 (8 x 100); "Our Lord" totals 1,768 (8 x 221); "Savior" totals 1,408 (8^2 x 32); "Emmanuel" totals 25,600 (8^3 x 50); "Messiah" totals 656 (8 x 82); "Son" totals 880 (8 x 110). Additionally, in gematria "the names of the Lord's people are multiples of eight" in most cases (see ibid., 203, 204, 205–7).

135. Ibid., 233.

136. Read, *Unveiling Biblical Prophecy*, 24–25.

137. Ibid., 25.

138. See Valletta, "Jared and His Brother," 304, 318.

139. See Bullinger, *Number in Scripture*, 207, 213, 235; and Davis, *Biblical Numerology*, 122.
140. Bullinger, *Number in Scripture*, 235, 236, 242. Another source states, "This is the last of those single numerals known as digits, beyond which we have merely combinations of those previous digits. It, therefore, marks the end. It is the number of finality or judgment" (Johnston, *Numbers in the Bible*, 77).
141. Draper, *Opening the Seven Seals*, 123–24, 132, 164; and Parry and Parry, *Understanding the Book of Revelation*, 229.
142. Ginzberg, *Legends of the Jews*, 6:50 note 258.
143. See Farbridge, *Studies in Biblical and Semitic Symbolism*, 141; McKenzie, *Dictionary of the Bible*, 621; and Bullinger, *Number in Scripture*, 243.
144. See Farbridge, *Studies in Biblical and Semitic Symbolism*, 141; and Bennett, "Number," 703.
145. See Farbridge, *Studies in Biblical and Semitic Symbolism*, 141. "The ten plagues were representative of the complete circle of God's judgments on Egypt" (Bullinger, *Number in Scripture*, 244).
146. *Eschatology* is the study of the last days.
147. McKenzie, *Dictionary of the Bible*, 621. Ten seems to play a similar role in the system of measurement employed in the Book of Mormon (see 2 Nephi 15:10; Mormon 6).
148. Farbridge, *Studies in Biblical and Semitic Symbolism*, 144.
149. See Cirlot, *Dictionary of Symbols*, 234; Julien, *Mammoth Dictionary of Symbols*, 446; Todeschi, *Encyclopedia of Symbolism*, 186; Bullinger, *Number in Scripture*, 239, 243; and Davis, *Biblical Numerology*, 122.
150. See Cooper, *Encyclopaedia of Traditional Symbols*, 120; Johnston, *Numbers in the Bible*, 81; Cirlot, *Dictionary of Symbols*, 234; and Bullinger, *Number in Scripture*, 251.
151. See Bullinger, *Number in Scripture*, 251.
152. See Comay, *Who's Who in the Old Testament*, 190; and Bullinger, *Number in Scripture*, 251.
153. Johnston, *Numbers in the Bible*, 81.
154. See Draper, *Opening the Seven Seals*, 24, 46, 56, 83; Parry and Parry, *Understanding the Book of Revelation*, 295; Bullinger, *Number in Scripture*, 2–3, 107; Smith, *Book of Revelation*, 288–89; Johnston, *Numbers in the Bible*, 39, 83; and Davis, *Biblical Numerology*, 122.
155. The Nephite Twelve, although referred to as "disciples," were ordained "Apostles" (see Smith, *Gospel Doctrine*, 190; Smith, *Doctrines of Salvation*, 3:157–59; and Widtsoe, *Priesthood and Church Government*, 22).
156. Whether related or not, it is curious that Jesus was twelve years old when he was found "in the temple, sitting in the midst of the doctors, and they were hearing him, and asking him questions" (JST, Luke 2:46).
157. See Talmage, *House of the Lord*, 155; and Brown, *Symbols in Stone*, 94–96.
158. Thus, President Brigham Young stated, "Your endowment is, to receive all

those ordinances in the house of the Lord, which are necessary for you, after you have departed this life, to enable you to walk back to the presence of the Father, passing the angels who stand as sentinels, being enabled to give them the key words, the signs and tokens, pertaining to the holy Priesthood, and gain your eternal exaltation in spite of earth and hell" (*Discourses of Brigham Young,* 416).

159. See Bullinger, *Number in Scripture,* 253.
160. See Smith, *Book of Revelation,* 48; and Draper, *Opening the Seven Seals,* 46–47, 83, 156.
161. Smith, *Book of Revelation,* 288–89.
162. See, for example, these publications of the Watch Tower Bible and Tract Society of Pennsylvania: *You Can Live Forever in Paradise on Earth,* 124–26; and *Revelation,* 19, 116–17. "Certain numbers appear often in the Bible in an illustrative, figurative or symbolic sense, and in such cases an understanding of their significance is vital to an understanding of the text." This is apparently denied as it pertains to the number 144,000 (see Watch Tower Bible and Tract Society of Pennsylvania, *Aid to Bible Understanding,* 1233).
163. Draper, *Opening the Seven Seals,* 83.
164. See Bullinger, *Number in Scripture,* 41 note 8, 205–6.
165. Ibid., 205.
166. Ibid.
167. Drinkard, "Numbers," 712; and Smith, *Book of Revelation,* 289.
168. See Davis, *Biblical Numerology,* 121 note 79, 122; Cooper, *Encyclopaedia of Traditional Symbols,* 120; Bullinger, *Number in Scripture,* 266; Johnston, *Numbers in the Bible,* 85; Farbridge, *Studies in Biblical and Semitic Symbolism,* 144–45, 155–56; and Todeschi, *Encyclopedia of Symbolism,* 187.
169. See Wilson, *Dictionary of Bible Types,* 177.
170. Johnston, *Numbers in the Bible,* 100. This "law" cannot be referential to the law of Moses, as it was not in effect the entire 4,000 years prior to Christ's birth. However, a probationary period, requiring sacrifices in similitude of the anticipated coming of the Messiah, did last for the entire 4,000-year span.
171. Elijah is also described as fasting forty days (see 1 Kings 19:8).
172. See Nibley, "Forty-day Mission of Christ," 10–44.
173. See Berrett, "Endowment Houses," 2:456.
174. Smith, *Book of Revelation,* 289.
175. Draper, *Opening the Seven Seals,* 24.
176. Ifrah, *Universal History of Numbers,* 499.
177. Parry and Parry, *Understanding the Book of Revelation,* 16, 72–73.
178. Bennett, "Number," 703.
179. Draper, *Opening the Seven Seals,* 149. See Bennett, "Number," 702; Unger, *Unger's Bible Dictionary,* 799; and Ifrah, *Universal History of Numbers,* 215,

216, 217, 219–22. Although it is uncertain, it is quite possible that this mode of numeric symbolism initially served as a mnemonic device in the ages before printing.
180. See Farbridge, *Studies in Biblical and Semitic Symbolism*, 93; and Davis, *Biblical Numerology*, 126 note 6, 128, 131.
181. Locks, *Spice of Torah*, 1. "Once the letters of an alphabet have numerical values, the way is open to . . . take the values of the letters of a word or phrase and make a number from these. Then this number may furnish an interpretation of the word, or another word with the same or a related numerical value may do so" (Ifrah, *Universal History of Numbers*, 252–53).
182. See Davis, *Biblical Numerology*, 126, 140; Ifrah, *Universal History of Numbers*, 214; Farbridge, *Studies in Biblical and Semitic Symbolism*, 95; Unger, *Unger's Bible Dictionary*, 799; Myers, *Eerdmans Bible Dictionary*, 768–69; and Vaner, "Christian Use of Jewish Numerology," 52.
183. See Drinkard, "Numbers," 712.
184. "Isopsephy consists of determining the numerical value of a word or a group of letters, and relating it to another word by means of this value" (Ifrah, *Universal History of Numbers*, 256).
185. "The numerical evaluation of names was also used in times of war by Muslim soothsayers, under the name of *khisab al nim*, to predict which side would win" (Ifrah, *Universal History of Numbers*, 261).
186. Ifrah, *Universal History of Numbers*, 252–53.
187. See Davis, *Biblical Numerology*, 128.
188. Aside from the most common form, secondary models include the following: (a) Squaring the numerical equivalents of letters (e.g., 5 becomes 25, 6 becomes 36, 10 becomes 100), (b) Spelling out each letter of a word (e.g., A in Hebrew would be written out as "Aleph," B as "Beyth") and then calculating its numerical value, (c) Substituting the last letter of the alphabet for the first (e.g., Z replaces A, Y replaces B, X replaces C) and then taking the new numerical total and comparing it with other words (see Isaacs, *Jewish Book of Numbers*, 181–85).
189. See Ifrah, *Universal History of Numbers*, 254.
190. See ibid.
191. See Friberg, "Numbers and Counting," 4:1145; and Ifrah, *Universal History of Numbers*, 254.
192. See Ifrah, *Universal History of Numbers*, 254.
193. Brown, *Death of the Messiah*, 2:1395.
194. See Cardwell, "Fish on the Fire: John 21:9," 12; McEleney, "153 Great Fishes (John 21:11)," 414 note 13; Birch, "Number," 3:560–61; Virkler, *Hermeneutics*, 51; Pope, "Number, Numbering, Numbers," 3:566; Drinkard, "Numbers," 712; Bennett, "Number," 703; Davis, *Biblical Numerology*, 142–43; and Dantzig, *Number, Language of Science*, 39.
195. See Smith and Cornwall, *Exhaustive Dictionary of Bible Names*, 66.

Notes to Chapter 6: Numbers 369

196. See "General Epistle of Barnabas," 1:142–43. See also Ifrah, *Universal History of Numbers*, 257; and McConkie, *Gospel Symbolism*, 223.
197. "This passage might well be unknown to many Christians except for the reference to it in John 3:14–15, which compares the lifting up of the Son of Man to Moses' lifting up of the serpent in the wilderness. The comparison is followed immediately by John 3:16, probably the best-known Bible verse in world Christianity" (Sakenfeld, *Journeying with God*, 118). "Men dying in sin are saved by the dead body of a man suspended on the cross. Just as physical contact was impossible between those bitten by snakes and the copper snake, so sinners are unable to touch the life-giving body of Christ. Yet in both situations the sufferers must appropriate God's healing power themselves: by looking at the copper snake or 'believing in the Son of Man' (John 3:15)" (Wenham, *Numbers*, 158).
198. See Johnson, "Revelation," 12:533; Barclay, "Great Themes of the New Testament," 295; Pope, "Number, Numbering, Numbers," 3:566; Fontana, *Secret Language of Symbols*, 152; Davis, *Biblical Numerology*, 143; and Ifrah, *Universal History of Numbers*, 253.
199. One scholar wrote, "'Gematria' is the obvious method of solving the meanings underlying the apocalyptic numbers 616 and 666" (Farbridge, *Studies in Biblical and Semitic Symbolism*, 95). See Irenaeus, "Against Heresies" (30:1–3), 1:558–59; Victorinus, "Commentary on the Apocalypse of the Blessed John," 7:356; Pope, "Number, Numbering, Numbers," 3:566; Barclay, "Great Themes of the New Testament," 292–96; Birch, "Number," 3:561; McEleney, "153 Great Fishes (John 21:11)," 413; Owen, "One Hundred and Fifty Three Fishes," 52–53; Romeo, "Gematria and John 21:11," 263; and Drinkard, "Numbers," 712.
200. Some early manuscripts have 616 instead of 666, but the latter number is believed to be correct. See Irenaeus, "Against Heresies" (30:1–3), 1:558; McEleney, "153 Great Fishes (John 21:11)," 413; and Birch, "Number," 3:561.
201. See Victorinus, "Commentary on the Apocalypse of the Blessed John," 7:356; Irenaeus, "Against Heresies," 1:559; Barclay, "Great Themes of the New Testament," 295–96; Pope, "Number, Numbering, Numbers," 3:566; and Davis, *Biblical Numerology*, 145.
202. Barclay, "Great Themes of the New Testament," 295–96.
203. See Cruse, *Eusebius' Ecclesiastical History*, 40–41; Barclay, "Great Themes of the New Testament," 296; Pope, "Number, Numbering, Numbers," 3:566; and Hocking, *Coming World Leader*, 211.
204. See Barclay, "Great Themes of the New Testament," 296; and Ifrah, *Universal History of Numbers*, 260.
205. See Owen, "One Hundred and Fifty Three Fishes," 52–53; McEleney, "153 Great Fishes (John 21:11)," 413; Birch, "Number," 3:561; Barclay, "Great Themes of the New Testament," 296; Pope, "Number, Numbering, Numbers," 3:566; Hocking, *Coming World Leader*, 211; and Davis, *Biblical Numerology*, 144.
206. See McEleney, "153 Great Fishes (John 21:11)," 413; Birch, "Number,"

3:561; Barclay, "Great Themes of the New Testament," 296; Pope, "Number, Numbering, Numbers," 3:566; and Ifrah, *Universal History of Numbers*, 260.
207. See Barclay, "Great Themes of the New Testament," 296.
208. See ibid.; and Hocking, *Coming World Leader*, 211.
209. See Barclay, "Great Themes of the New Testament," 296; Pope, "Number, Numbering, Numbers," 3:566; Ifrah, *Universal History of Numbers*, 260; Davis, *Biblical Numerology*, 144; and Irenaeus, "Against Heresies," 1:559.
210. See Barclay, "Great Themes of the New Testament," 296; and Clarke, *Holy Bible with a Commentary and Critical Notes*, 6:1026.
211. See Barclay, "Great Themes of the New Testament," 296; and Ifrah, *Universal History of Numbers*, 260–61. The name of Pope Leo X has also been associated with the number 666 (see Davis, *Biblical Numerology*, 145). Regarding the claim that the Pope's coronation crown bears an inscription totaling 666, Barry Bickmore has written: "A missionary companion once gave me an old typescript copy of an 'expose' in which it was revealed that the pope's tiara is inscribed with one of his official titles, *Vicarius Filii Dei* (Vicar of the Son of God). If you add up the Roman numerals in the title, it adds up to . . . 666! However, the pope has no such official title, and, in fact, his tiara bears no inscription. His real title, *Vicarius Christi* (Vicar of Christ), only adds up (with a disappointing thud) to 214" ("Clearing Up Misconceptions," 198–99).
212. Ifrah, *Universal History of Numbers*, 260–61. See Davis, *Biblical Numerology*, 128, 132, 145; and Barclay, "Great Themes of the New Testament," 296.
213. Barclay, "Great Themes of the New Testament," 296.
214. See Johnson, "Revelation," 12:535; Morris, *Revelation*, 168; Bray, *Revelation Decoded*, chapter 14, page 3; and Church, *NIV Matthew Henry Commentary* (New Testament), 798.
215. Ford, *Revelation*, 215. See Morris, *Revelation*, 168; Church, *NIV Matthew Henry Commentary* (New Testament), 798; Parry and Parry, *Understanding the Book of Revelation*, 176; and Nicoll, *Expositor's Greek Testament*, 5:434.
216. Curiously, the Hebrew phrase "you shall sell" totals 666 (see Locks, *Spice of Torah*, 266).
217. See Barclay, "Great Themes of the New Testament," 296.
218. See Locks, *Spice of Torah*, 266.
219. See Pope, "Number, Numbering, Numbers," 3:566.
220. See Barclay, "Great Themes of the New Testament," 296.
221. Bennett, "Number," 704. See Davis, *Biblical Numerology*, 146–47; and Vaner, "Christian Use of Jewish Numerology," 55.
222. Johnson, "Revelation," 12:534. Johnson accurately notes that there is no evidence in the book of Revelation, or, for that matter, in any of John's writings, that supports the notion that John employed gematria.
223. Parry and Parry, *Understanding the Book of Revelation*, 176; Smith, *Book of*

Notes to Chapter 7: Directions

Revelation, 289. One source notes that the number nine is a factor of 666 (being 9 x 74). Nine represents judgment, which shall surely come to all who figuratively acquire the mark of the beast (see Bullinger, *Number in Scripture,* 235).

224. See Draper, *Opening the Seven Seals,* 150–51; Johnson, "Revelation," 12:535; Bullinger, *Number in Scripture,* 282–84; and Cirlot, *Dictionary of Symbols,* 235.

225. Klein, Blomberg, and Hubbard, *Introduction to Biblical Interpretation,* 373. One source speaks of Lucifer, the Great and Abominable Church, and the Anti-Christ as "a trinity of imperfection" (Draper, *Opening the Seven Seals,* 151).

226. See Barclay, "Great Themes of the New Testament," 295; Bullinger, *Number in Scripture,* 282–86; Cirlot, *Dictionary of Symbols,* 235; Draper, *Opening the Seven Seals,* 150–51; and Johnson, "Revelation," 12:535.

227. Dummelow, *Commentary on the Holy Bible,* 1084.

228. Johnson, "Revelation," 12:535.

229. This is not to imply that standard numerology isn't without dangers. Some have gone far overboard in their interpretation or application of numbers. For example, in a discussion about gematria, E. W. Bullinger offers a list of 12 "Canaanite names" which he indicates, if added together, come to a numerical total of 3,211. However, Bullinger points out that $3,211 = 13^2 \times 19$. Thus, Canaanites are really symbolized by the number thirteen, and hence symbolize apostasy (see *Number in Scripture,* 205–6, 209).

230. Packer, in Conference Report, October 1984, 81.

231. Ryken, Wilhoit, and Longman, *Dictionary of Biblical Imagery,* 599–600.

NOTES TO CHAPTER 7: DIRECTIONS AS SYMBOLS

1. See Drinkard, "Direction and Orientation," 2:204.
2. Cirlot, *Dictionary of Symbols,* 245.
3. See Cooper, *Encyclopaedia of Traditional Symbols,* 51.
4. See Drinkard, "Direction and Orientation," 2:204.
5. Myers, *Eerdmans Bible Dictionary,* 1054.
6. Cirlot, *Dictionary of Symbols,* 245.
7. Ibid., 245.
8. Conner, *Interpreting the Symbols and Types,* 63; see 11.
9. See Cirlot, *Dictionary of Symbols,* 245.
10. See Cooper, *Encyclopaedia of Traditional Symbols,* 59; Drinkard, "East," 2:248; McConkie and Parry, *Guide to Scriptural Symbols,* 44; Myers, *Eerdmans Bible Dictionary,* 300; and Ryken, Wilhoit, and Longman, *Dictionary of Biblical Imagery,* 225.
11. See Drinkard, "East," 2:248; and Ryken, Wilhoit, and Longman, *Dictionary of Biblical Imagery,* 225.

12. See Drinkard, "East," 2:248; Drinkard, "Direction and Orientation," 2:204; and Myers, Eerdmans Bible Dictionary, 299.
13. See Drinkard, "East," 2:248; and Ryken, Wilhoit, and Longman, Dictionary of Biblical Imagery, 225.
14. See Drinkard, "Direction and Orientation," 2:204.
15. See Drinkard, "East," 2:248; and Ryken, Wilhoit, and Longman, Dictionary of Biblical Imagery, 225.
16. See Drinkard, "East," 2:248.
17. See Bayley, Lost Language of Symbolism, 2:45. See also Cooper, Encyclopaedia of Traditional Symbols, 59; Drinkard, "East," 2:248; McConkie and Parry, Guide to Scriptural Symbols, 44; Myers, Eerdmans Bible Dictionary, 299; and Todeschi, Encyclopedia of Symbolism, 96.
18. See Myers, Eerdmans Bible Dictionary, 299.
19. See Ryken, Wilhoit, and Longman, Dictionary of Biblical Imagery, 225. Ryken's bias, that the fall of Adam and Eve was a sinful mistake on the part of our first parents, has colored his reading of the symbolic meaning of east in scripture.
20. Talmage, Articles of Faith, 70.
21. Holzapfel and Seely, My Father's House, 17.
22. As an appendage to this argument, see our discussion in chapter 4 regarding Adam and Eve's fig leaf aprons.
23. "In verse 41, the fact is pointed out that Enoch's home was 'the land of Cainan.' This land is not the same country that was known as 'the land of Canaan' in the Old Testament record and Palestine in the New Testament. The land of Cainan was given that name by Adam's grandson, Enos.... It seems... that Enos moved from the home of his fathers and located near 'the sea east;' therefore, the land of Cainan—his new home—probably was located somewhere in what today is known as the eastern United States" (Hunter, Pearl of Great Price Commentary, 179–80).
24. See Drinkard, "East," 2:248; and Myers, Eerdmans Bible Dictionary, 299.
25. Millet, "Alma 2," 1:34.
26. See Drinkard, "East," 2:248; and Myers, Eerdmans Bible Dictionary, 300.
27. Drinkard, "East," 2:248.
28. See Ryken, Wilhoit, and Longman, Dictionary of Biblical Imagery, 225.
29. Draper, Opening the Seven Seals, 178. See Parry and Parry, Understanding the Book of Revelation, 207.
30. See Myers, Eerdmans Bible Dictionary, 299.
31. McConkie and Parry, Guide to Scriptural Symbols, 44.
32. McConkie, Gospel Symbolism, 102–3, 258. See the discussion below of east and west as combined symbols at the second coming of Christ.
33. See Smith, History of the Church of Jesus Christ of Latter-day Saints, 5:336–37; Smith, Words of Joseph Smith, 180, 181; and Smith, Teachings of the Prophet Joseph Smith, 287.

Notes to Chapter 7: Directions

34. Myers, *Eerdmans Bible Dictionary*, 299. See Todeschi, *Encyclopedia of Symbolism*, 96.
35. See Drinkard, "South," 6:171; Unger, *Bible Dictionary*, 1041; Myers, *Eerdmans Bible Dictionary*, 965; and Dahood, *Psalms III*, 288.
36. See Brown, Driver, and Briggs, *Hebrew and English Lexicon*, 412. See also Drinkard, "East," 2:248.
37. See Drinkard, "South," 6:171. For example, see Habakkuk 3:3; Deuteronomy 33:2; Judges 5:4.
38. See Thayer, *Greek-English Lexicon*, 378–79; and Vine, *New Testament Words*, 3:195.
39. See Strong, *Exhaustive Concordance of the Bible*, "Dictionary of the Greek Testament," #3047. See also Thayer, *Greek-English Lexicon*, 378–79.
40. See Unger, *Bible Dictionary*, 1041.
41. Conner, *Interpreting the Symbols and Types*, 63.
42. See Thayer, *Greek-English Lexicon*, 378–79. See Acts 27:12 as an example of the employment of this Greek noun.
43. See Todeschi, *Encyclopedia of Symbolism*, 87.
44. Youngblood, "1 and 2 Samuel," 3:725.
45. See Dahood, *Psalms III*, 217.
46. Kidner, *Psalms 73–150*, 439.
47. Ibid., 439–40.
48. Wilson, *Dictionary of Bible Types*, 384.
49. Pope, *Song of Songs*, 497–98.
50. See Lundbom, *Jeremiah 1–20*, 682–83.
51. This pericope is found at the beginning of Ezekiel 21 in the Hebrew.
52. See Taylor, *Ezekiel*, 160.
53. See Skinner, "Savior, Satan, and Serpent," 359–84.
54. See Ryken, Wilhoit, and Longman, *Dictionary of Biblical Imagery*, 773–74; Cooper, *Encyclopaedia of Traditional Symbols*, 150; Julien, *Mammoth Dictionary of Symbols*, 383; Hall, *Dictionary of Subjects and Symbols in Art*, 285; and Todeschi, *Encyclopedia of Symbolism*, 239.
55. See McConkie, *Gospel Symbolism*, 268; Cooper, *Encyclopaedia of Traditional Symbols*, 188–89, 136; Ryken, Wilhoit, and Longman, *Dictionary of Biblical Imagery*, 694; Wilson, *Dictionary of Bible Types*, 332–33; Julien, *Mammoth Dictionary of Symbols*, 343–45; Todeschi, *Encyclopedia of Symbolism*, 214, 281–82; and Fontana, *Secret Language of Symbols*, 113.
56. A detailed symbolic interpretation of Ether 8–15 might be that those in the "south" (covenant) had what those in the "north" (outside of the covenant or Church) needed: "food" or "game" (the saving teachings, covenants, and blessings of the gospel of Jesus Christ). The "snakes" (Lucifer's temptations, teachings, buffeting, false perceptions of others, and condescending attitudes) kept both groups away from each other. Only via repentance on the part of both parties could the heavens be opened and the "rains"

(revelations, sanctification, blessings, heavenly influences, and Holy Spirit) be poured out upon all.

57. Ryken, Wilhoit, and Longman, *Dictionary of Biblical Imagery*, 225.
58. See Brown, Driver, and Briggs, *Hebrew and English Lexicon*, 860; Drinkard, "North," 4:1135; and Strong, *Exhaustive Concordance of the Bible*, "Dictionary of the Hebrew Bible," #6828.
59. See Drinkard, "North," 4:1135; and Myers, *Eerdmans Bible Dictionary*, 768.
60. See Job 37:9; and Myers, *Eerdmans Bible Dictionary*, 768.
61. Ryken, Wilhoit, and Longman, *Dictionary of Biblical Imagery*, 597.
62. Unger, *Bible Dictionary*, 798.
63. See Cooper, *Encyclopaedia of Traditional Symbols*, 112; and Conner, *Interpreting the Symbols and Types*, 63.
64. Cooper, *Encyclopaedia of Traditional Symbols*, 112. North can have positive connotations, albeit infrequently. "In Mediterranean latitudes the northern circumpolar stars never set but remain forever in the sky, unlike those stars that rise nightly only to set in the west. These far northern stars, picturesquely designated 'the imperishable stars' in ancient Egyptian because they never set, became a picture of immortality and eternity in the ancient Near East" (Ryken, Wilhoit, and Longman, *Dictionary of Biblical Imagery*, 596). In Ugaritic and Canaanite mythology the holy mountain used by Baal and other gods was in the north. Closely related to this are the references to God's abode in the far north (Isaiah 14:13); God's appearance to Job out of the north (Job 37:22); and Ezekiel's chariot theophany which appeared from the north (Ezekiel 1:4) (see Drinkard, "North," 4:1136).
65. See Drinkard, "North," 4:1136; and Myers, *Eerdmans Bible Dictionary*, 768.
66. Ryken, Wilhoit, and Longman, *Dictionary of Biblical Imagery*, 597.
67. For examples of passages in which left is substituted for north, see Genesis 14:15; Joshua 19:27; Ezekiel 16:46.
68. See Ryken, Wilhoit, and Longman, *Dictionary of Biblical Imagery*, 500; and Janzen, *Abraham and All the Families of the Earth*, 185.
69. Ryken, Wilhoit, and Longman, *Dictionary of Biblical Imagery*, 597.
70. See Todeschi, *Encyclopedia of Symbolism*, 87, 159.
71. In Isaiah 43:6, Jeremiah 3:18; 16:15; 23:8; 31:8, and Zechariah 2:6, north is employed as the symbol for Jehovah gathering Israel back to him from their apostate condition (see McKenzie, *Dictionary of the Bible*, 620; and McCurdy, "North Country, Land of the North," 701).
72. Theories on their whereabouts are legion. Among the more popular theories are the following: scattered throughout the northern portion of the earth; living in a body in some northern unexplored region of the earth; dwelling under a hollow northern polar cap or in a northern subterranean cavern; on a secondary small planet that is attached to the earth at the north pole (by a narrow neck of land); on the north star (see Widtsoe, *Evidences and Reconciliations*, 405–6; Roberts, *Outlines in Ecclesiastical History*, 402; and Brough, *Lost Tribes*, 39–92).

73. See Ryken, Wilhoit, and Longman, *Dictionary of Biblical Imagery*, 597. For examples of this, see Jeremiah 46:20, 24; 47:2; 50:3, 9, 41–43; 51:48; Ezekiel 26:7.
74. See Brown and North, "Biblical Geography," 1180.
75. See Motyer, *Isaiah*, 120; and Myers, *Eerdmans Bible Dictionary*, 768. For an in-depth discussion of Jehovah's relationship to Mt. Zaphon, see Richard J. Clifford, "The Temple and the Holy Mountain," in Truman G. Madsen, *Temple in Antiquity*.
76. See Drinkard, "North," 4:1136; and McKenzie, *Dictionary of the Bible*, 620.
77. See Boadt, "Ezekiel," 325.
78. Brown, "Book of Alma," 1:151.
79. This is not intended to imply that Hagoth and his people were necessarily wicked. Rather, the utilization of north at the conclusion of the book of Alma serves to highlight the transition of control of the city of Zarahemla from that of righteous leadership to unrighteousness rule.
80. See Ryken, Wilhoit, and Longman, *Dictionary of Biblical Imagery*, 500.
81. Cooper, *Encyclopaedia of Traditional Symbols*, 96. See Ryken, Wilhoit, and Longman, *Dictionary of Biblical Imagery*, 500, who added that "one might conclude that Jesus shows preference for the right as the hand that naturally gives alms when he tells the disciples, 'Do not let your left hand know what your right hand is doing' (Mt 6:3)."
82. Wilson, *Dictionary of Bible Types*, 255.
83. See Cowley, *Wilford Woodruff*, 481; and Pratt, in *Journal of Discourses*, 16:48.
84. Ryken, Wilhoit, and Longman, *Dictionary of Biblical Imagery*, 942.
85. See Cirlot, *Dictionary of Symbols*, 369; Cooper, *Encyclopaedia of Traditional Symbols*, 190; Drinkard, "West," 6:908; and Ryken, Wilhoit, and Longman, *Dictionary of Biblical Imagery*, 942.
86. See Conner, *Interpreting the Symbols and Types*, 63, 179; Drinkard, "West," 6:908; Myers, *Eerdmans Bible Dictionary*, 1054; Ryken, Wilhoit, and Longman, *Dictionary of Biblical Imagery*, 942; Todeschi, *Encyclopedia of Symbolism*, 284; and Unger, *Bible Dictionary*, 1165.
87. See Kidner, *Tyndale Old Testament Commentaries: Psalms 73–150*, 465; and Ryken, Wilhoit, and Longman, *Dictionary of Biblical Imagery*, 942. For examples, see Exodus 26:22 and Numbers 3:23.
88. Myers, *Eerdmans Bible Dictionary*, 1054. "The ancient Semitic orientation toward the east ('forward') meant that the west was 'behind' (Is 9:12). Thus *behind* is another designation for the west in the Bible, conjuring up notions of that which is to be discarded, irrelevant, lacking in priority and not requiring attention. . . . The Israelites literally turned their back on the west" (Ryken, Wilhoit, and Longman, *Dictionary of Biblical Imagery*, 942). For examples, see Deuteronomy 11:24; 34:2; Isaiah 9:12; Joel 2.20; Zechariah 14:8.
89. See Drinkard, "West," 6:908.

90. Merisums occur when an author mentions the extremes of some category or situation in order to imply that a totality of something is intended. Merisums encompass two opposites, and everything in between them. So, for example, Jeremiah speaks of all men knowing Christ, "from the least of them unto the greatest of them" (Jeremiah 31:34).
91. Smith, *Teachings of the Prophet Joseph Smith*, 132.
92. Smith, *Words of Joseph Smith*, 180–81. See Smith, *Teachings of the Prophet Joseph Smith*, 287.
93. Ryken, Wilhoit, and Longman, *Dictionary of Biblical Imagery*, 942.
94. Todeschi, *Encyclopedia of Symbolism*, 284.
95. Cooper, *Encyclopaedia of Traditional Symbols*, 59, 190.
96. See Cirlot, *Dictionary of Symbols*, 369.
97. See Hamlin, *Inheriting the Land*, 87–88.
98. See Hess, *Joshua*, 197.
99. See Boling and Wright, *Joshua*, 283.
100. Although many interpret the Hebrew word *Sinim* as referring to the Chinese, Hebraists reject the interpretation both linguistically and historically. Credible scholars have deemed the word translated *Sinim* as "unintelligible," and have indicated that the location referred to is unknown (see McKenzie, *Second Isaiah*, 107 note b; Knight, *Servant Theology*, 134; and Delitzsch, *Biblical Commentary on the Prophecies of Isaiah*, 2:266–68).
101. See Ryken, Wilhoit, and Longman, *Dictionary of Biblical Imagery*, 942.

NOTES TO CHAPTER 8: PEOPLE AS TYPES

1. In the case of Joseph of Egypt, his life was a highly detailed type of the life of Christ.
2. Connor, *Interpreting the Symbols and Types*, 107.
3. Thus there are scriptural figures whom biblical scholars perceive as having typologically significant lives in a detailed sense. However, there are also numerous figures in scripture whose lives seem typological or symbolic (in a Christocentric sense) only in general terms—but a detailed breakdown would nullify any such type. Examples of the latter include: Aaron as a high priest, and Christ as the "Great High Priest" (Exodus 28:1–4; Hebrews 5:4–6); Boaz as the kinsman-redeemer (or *goel*), and Christ as our *goel* (Ruth 2–4; Romans 8); Eliezer (meaning "God is my help") as the servant of Abraham who frees those in bondage, and Christ as the Great Servant of all who are in bondage (Genesis 15:2; 24:2; John 8:31–37); Job as the suffering saint, and Christ as the ultimate Suffering Saint (Job; Acts 17:3; James 5:10–11); Nehemiah as the governor or king who directs the rebuilding of the city of Jerusalem, and Christ as the Governor or King who will direct the restoration of Jerusalem or the building of a New Jerusalem (Nehemiah 4; Matthew 2:5–6; 3 Nephi 21:23); Samson as the

mighty deliverer and judge, and Christ as the Deliverer and Judge of all (Judges 13–16; 2 Peter 2:9).
4. See Matthews, "Jesus Christ in the Scriptures," 2:746.
5. The idea that Jesus and Lucifer were spirit brothers is not unique to LDS Christology (see Russell, *Lucifer*, 44, 48, 187–88; and Peterson and Ricks, *Offenders for a Word*, 149–51).
6. Augustine, *Trinity*, 4:17.
7. See Philo of Alexandria, "De Sacrificiis Abelis et Cain," 94.
8. See Smith and Cornwall, *Exhaustive Dictionary of Bible Names*, 2.
9. Ginzberg, *Legends of the Jews*, 1:107.
10. See Nibley, *Three Facsimiles from the Book of Abraham*, 75.
11. See *Book of Jasher*, 11:13–37; and Young, *Discourses of Brigham Young*, 106.
12. See Smith, *Answers to Gospel Questions*, 1:7; Romans 8:17.
13. See LDS Bible Dictionary, s.v. "Michael," 732; and Smith and Cornwall, *Exhaustive Dictionary of Bible Names*, 180.
14. Nibley renders one passage of "The Combat of Adam and Eve against Satan" as follows: "So Adam continued to make this sacrifice for the rest of his days. And God caused his word to be preached to Adam. On the fiftieth day [while] Adam [was] offering sacrifice as was his custom, Satan appeared in the form of a man and smote him in the side with a sharp stone even as Adam raised his arms in prayer. Eve tried to help him as blood and water flowed on the altar. 'God sent his word and revived Adam saying: Finish thy sacrifice, which is most pleasing to me. For even so will I be wounded and blood and water will come from my side; that will be the true Sacrifice, placed on the altar as a perfect offering.... And so God healed Adam'" (cited in *Enoch the Prophet*, 171–72). See Ginzberg, *Legends of the Jews*, 1:71, 89, 166, 285; 5:93 note 55, 116 note 108, 139 note 20, 190 note 56.
15. See Myers, *Eerdmans Bible Dictionary*, 336; and Smith and Cornwall, *Exhaustive Dictionary of Bible Names*, 70.
16. See Collins, "Enoch," 267.
17. See Genesis 22. The *Genesis Rabbah* 56:8 states that Isaac was thirty-seven when his father was commanded to sacrifice him. This figure is based on the fact that Sarah was ninety when Isaac was born and then she died thirty-seven years later at the age of 127 (Gen. 23:1). Thus, assuming that Sarah died shortly after the episode on Moriah, Isaac would have been somewhere between 35 and 37 years of age (see Hamilton, *Handbook on the Pentateuch*, 108; and McConkie, *Mortal Messiah*, 1:364).
18. See Martin-Achard, "Isaac," 3:469; and *Book of Jasher*, 23:49–56.
19. See Brown, Driver, and Briggs, *Hebrew and English Lexicon*, 687.
20. See Smith and Cornwall, *Exhaustive Dictionary of Bible Names*, 118; and Myers, *Eerdmans Bible Dictionary*, 535.
21. See Tuttle, in Conference Report, April 1958, 121; and Smith, *Answers to Gospel Questions*, 4:123.

22. See Smith, *Teachings of the Prophet Joseph Smith,* 181.
23. See Smith, *Words of Joseph Smith,* 28.
24. For a more thorough look at this type, see McConkie, *Gospel Symbolism,* 28–36; McConkie, *His Name Shall Be Joseph,* 78–79; and Read, *Unveiling Biblical Prophecy,* 32–35. Walter L. Wilson notes that some "forty-two different aspects of Christ may be seen" in the life of Joseph who was sold into Egypt (*Dictionary of Bible Types,* 241).
25. See Smith and Cornwall, *Exhaustive Dictionary of Bible Names,* 255–56.
26. Judah is the Hebrew equivalent of the Greek name Judas.
27. See Bitton, *Images of the Prophet Joseph Smith,* 76–77.
28. See Smith and Cornwall, *Exhaustive Dictionary of Bible Names,* 155.
29. Regarding the betrayers of the Prophet Joseph, Truman G. Madsen wrote: "To name a few: William McClellin, John C. Bennett, William Law, and to some degree Thomas B. Marsh. Up until the Nauvoo era every one of the Prophet's own counselors, with the sole exception of his brother Hyrum, either betrayed him, went astray, faltered, or failed in some way. Some, glorious to report, found their way back. Orson Hyde, not a member of the First Presidency but one of the Twelve, under oath endorsed terrible things said against the Church and the Prophet, of which he later repented. But many remained bitter in their opposition to the end. 'If it were not for a Brutus,' Joseph said in 1844, 'I might live as long as Caesar would have lived.' There was more than one! So, much enmity came from within and Joseph struggled as the revelation warned him he would: 'If thou art in perils among false brethren. . . .' " (*Joseph Smith the Prophet,* 53).
30. See Roberts, *Comprehensive History of the Church,* 2:200.
31. The Prophet was only thirty-eight years old when he was martyred.
32. The Savior was only approximately thirty-three years of age at the time of His crucifixion (see McConkie, *Mortal Messiah,* 4:418–19).
33. See Smith, *Teachings of the Prophet Joseph Smith,* 330.
34. Justin Martyr says that Joshua's name was changed from Oshea to "Jesus" specifically because Joshua was a type for Christ ("Dialogue with Trypho," 1:236).
35. See Brown, Driver, and Briggs, *Hebrew and English Lexicon,* 221.
36. See Thayer, *Greek-English Lexicon,* 300.
37. See Cowley, *Cowley's Talks on Doctrine,* 137.
38. See Ginzberg, *Legends of the Jews,* 3:400.
39. As evidence of the early development of Christian traditions regarding Christ's manifestation of gifts of the Spirit in his youth, see "First Gospel of the Infancy of Jesus Christ" and "Thomas' Gospel of the Infancy of Jesus Christ," in *Lost Books of the Bible,* 38–62. Although this author does not place much credence in the accounts in these documents, they nevertheless make the point that by the second century A.D. popular legends

Notes to Chapter 8: People

supported the idea that when Jesus was a child he had miraculous powers and numerous gifts of the Spirit.

40. See Madsen, "'Putting on the Names,'" 1:464.
41. For a good discussion of the many miracles and powers possessed by Jesus, see Matthews, *Miracles of Jesus*.
42. See Grant and Tracy, *Interpretation of the Bible*, 34; and McConkie, *Gospel Symbolism*, 154–57.
43. See Smith, *Teachings of the Prophet Joseph Smith*, 365.
44. See Ginzberg, *Legends of the Jews*, 2:264; 5:397 note 42.
45. Ginzberg records: "Jethro . . . made him the shepherd of his flocks. By the way he tended the sheep, God saw his fitness to be the shepherd of His people, for God never gives an exalted office to a man until He has tested him in little things. Thus Moses . . . [was] tried as [a shepherd] of flocks, and only after [he] had proved [his] ability as such, He gave [him] dominion over men" (*Legends of the Jews*, 2:300–301).
46. See Flavius Josephus, *Antiquities of the Jews*, book 4, chapter 8, verse 48; Clement of Alexandria, *Stromata*, book 6, chapter 15; Clement of Alexandria, *Fragments from Cassiodorus*, chapter two; and Ginzberg, *Legends of the Jews*, 6:166 note 960; 6:162 note 951.
47. See Brown, Driver, and Briggs, *Hebrew and English Lexicon*, 602; Smith and Cornwall, *Dictionary of Bible Names*, 184; and Petersen, *Moses*, 41.
48. See Propp, *Exodus 1–18*, 152–53.
49. See Mouritsen, "Is Christ the Redeemer of Other Worlds?" 31–32; Romney, "Jesus Christ: Lord of the Universe," 46–48; and Maxwell, *Not My Will, But Thine*, 51–52.
50. In her book *Unveiling Biblical Prophecy*, Lenet Hadley Read offers some interesting insights into the symbolic nature of the life and ministry of the prophet Noah (see pages 21–22).
51. See Ivins, in Conference Report, October 1914, 92; and McConkie, *Millennial Messiah*, 360.
52. See Smith, *Doctrines of Salvation*, 1:74.
53. See McConkie, *Millennial Messiah*, 696; and Lassetter, "Dispensations of the Gospel," 1:388–90.
54. See McConkie, "Preparation of Prophets," 74.
55. See Smith and Cornwall, *Dictionary of Bible Names*, 220.
56. See Clark, *Messages of the First Presidency*, 4:277.
57. See Smith, in Conference Report, October 1914, 130; and Mace, *Autobiography*, 197–98. See also McConkie, *Millennial Messiah*, 307–8; and Talmage, *Jesus the Christ*, 539–40.
58. As noted in chapter 6, the number twelve symbolizes or implies priesthood.
59. President Brigham Young taught: "Your endowment is, to receive all those ordinances in the house of the Lord, which are necessary for you, after you have departed this life, to enable you to walk back to the presence of the

Father, passing the angels who stand as sentinels, being enabled to give them the key words, the signs and tokens, pertaining to the holy Priesthood, and gain your eternal exaltation" (*Discourses of Brigham Young,* 416).

60. See Conner, *Interpreting the Symbols and Types,* 110; and Ryken, Wilhoit, and Longman, *Dictionary of Biblical Imagery,* 122.
61. For helpful insights into the symbolic nature of the Hosea-Gomer story, see Top, "Marriage of Hosea and Gomer," 223–39; and Jackson, "Marriage of Hosea and Jehovah's Covenant with Israel," 57–75.
62. See Smith and Cornwall, *Dictionary of Bible Names,* 110. The LDS Bible Dictionary indicates that the name Hosea and the name Joshua are two variant forms of the same Hebrew name. Their Greek equivalent is Jesus, and serves to establish the fact that, in the story of Hosea, the prophet stands as a type for Christ who unfailingly loves wayward Israel, represented by Gomer (see LDS Bible Dictionary, s.v. "Joshua," 717–18).
63. It is believed that Gomer was not a professional prostitute, but rather a Baal worshiper, and thus a participant in a fertility cult. Such being the case, her *adultery* was *idolatry,* as is the case with Israel when she breaks her covenants with Jehovah (see Sperry, *Voice of Israel's Prophets,* 280; Wood, "Hosea," 7:164–65; and Andersen and Freedman, *Hosea,* 157–58).
64. Such happened in Noah's day. It happened to the generations that followed Joseph of Egypt. It happened in the days of Jeremiah and Lehi. And it happened shortly after the gospel was restored in the meridian of times.
65. See Smith and Cornwall, *Dictionary of Bible Names,* 150–51.
66. See ibid., 166.
67. See ibid., 165.
68. For example, see Exodus 34:15–16; Leviticus 17:7; 20:6; Deuteronomy 31:16; 2 Chronicles 21:11, 13.
69. For comparisons between Esau and Jacob, and the law of Moses and the fulness of the gospel of Jesus Christ, see Tertullian, "An Answer to the Jews," chapter one, 3:151; Irenaeus, "Against Heresies," 1:493; 21:3; Cyprian of Carthage, "Treatise of Cyprian," treatise 12, book 1, verse 19, 5:512; and Read, *Unveiling Biblical Prophecy,* 29–30.
70. See Brown, in Conference Report, October 1963, 94.
71. "Periodically, throughout history, Satan has prevailed momentarily over the forces for good. In the meridian of times we find this evident as the universal apostasy came to pass, and those who followed the adversary *appeared* to have triumphed as the Church fled from the earth. This was not the case though, as the woman was taken and fed for a period of time so that when she returned there would be no stopping her from establishing truth and righteousness upon the earth forever" (Smith, *Book of Revelation,* 124). "Frustrated because he could not destroy the child [the political kingdom of God], the dragon turns on the woman [Church] herself, but she escapes by fleeing into the wilderness" (Draper, *Opening the Seven Seals,* 133).

Notes to Chapter 8: People

72. 2 Kings 19:21; Psalm 9:14; Song of Solomon 3:11; Isaiah 1:8; 3:16–17; 4:3–6; 10:32; 16:1; 37:22; 52:2; 62:11; Jeremiah 4:31; 6:2, 23; Lamentations 1:6; 2; 4:22; Micah 1:13; 4; Zephaniah 3:14; Zechariah 2:10; 9:9; Hebrews 12:22–24; 2 Nephi 3:16–17; 8:25; 14:4; 20:32; 3 Nephi 20:37; Moroni 10:31; D&C 124:11.
73. See Smith, *Doctrines of Salvation*, 3:86.
74. See Roberts, *Comprehensive History of the Church*, 3:16–17.
75. See Richards, "Temple Manifestations of the Spirit," 3:227.
76. See Anderson, "Oliver Cowdery," 1:339.
77. See Book of Commandments, 7:3.
78. See Roberts, *Comprehensive History of the Church*, 4:536.
79. See Smith and Cornwall, *Dictionary of Bible Names*, 5; and McConkie and Parry, *Guide to Scriptural Symbols*, 189.
80. See Smith, *Teachings of the Prophet Joseph Smith*, 345.
81. See Smith and Cornwall, *Dictionary of Bible Names*, 5; and McConkie and Parry, *Guide to Scriptural Symbols*, 12.
82. See Hamilton, *Handbook on the Pentateuch*, 108; McConkie, *Mormon Doctrine*, 1:364; and *Genesis Rabbah* 56:8.
83. See McConkie, *Mortal Messiah*, 3:312.
84. See Martin-Achard, "Isaac," 3:463. See also Genesis 17:17, note 17a (LDS edition of KJV); JST, Genesis 17:23.
85. See Clawson, in Conference Report, April 1918, 34.
86. See Ballard, in Conference Report, October 1910, 82.
87. The translation used in this comparison comes from John H. Sailhamer. This comparison is an adaption of one drawn by Sailhamer, who sees the parallel as more of a linguistic mirroring rather than the standard comparison of events and attributes. He wrote: "The account of Abraham's 'sojourn' in Egypt bears the stamp of having been intentionally shaped to parallel the later account of God's deliverance of Israel from Egypt (Gen 41–Ex 12). Both passages have a similar message as well. Thus here [Genesis 12], at the beginning of the narratives dealing with Abraham and his seed, we find an anticipation of the events that will occur at the end. As with other sections of the book, the parallels are striking" ("Genesis," 2:116–17). See Sailhamer, *Pentateuch as Narrative*, 141–43.
88. See Clark, "Abraham," 1:7–8; and Bitton, *Images of the Prophet Joseph Smith*, 70.
89. See Smith, *Teachings of the Prophet Joseph Smith*, 365.
90. See ibid., 382.
91. See Roberts, *Comprehensive History of the Church*, 2:235–36, 348–51.
92. The Book of Abraham in the Pearl of Great Price is scripture written by Abraham while he was in Egypt, "by his own hand, upon papyrus."
93. The Doctrine and Covenants consists primarily of revelations given to the Prophet Joseph.

94. Abraham, reared in a home steeped in apostasy, is himself the first of a family of prophets and righteous followers of God.
95. In New York, Ohio, Missouri, Illinois, and indirectly Utah, the Prophet Joseph started communities of Saints dedicated to the building up of Zion.
96. See Jubilees 11:16–17; and Charlesworth, *Old Testament Pseudepigrapha*, 2:79.
97. In New York, Ohio, Missouri, Illinois, and indirectly Utah.
98. See Smith and Cornwall, *Dictionary of Bible Names*, 70.
99. See Roberts, *Comprehensive History of the Church*, 2:18–22; Smith, *History of the Church*, 4:3–5; and Smith, *History of Joseph Smith by His Mother*, 226–29.
100. See Pratt, *Angel of the Prairies*, 21; and McConkie, *Mormon Doctrine*, 789.
101. See Thompson, "Study of the Political Involvements in the Career of Joseph Smith," 45–69; and Andrus, *Joseph Smith and World Government*.
102. Elder McConkie wrote: "It may well be that more people saw the Lord in Enoch's day than at any other time in the entire history of the earth, or that more people saw him than at all other times combined" (*Promised Messiah*, 598–99).
103. See ibid., 584.
104. See Bitton, *Images of the Prophet Joseph Smith*, 73–75.
105. See Smith, *Teachings of the Prophet Joseph Smith*, 304; and Bushman and Jessee, "Joseph Smith," 3:133.
106. See Welling, in Conference Report, October 1915, 18.
107. See Richards, "Memories of Carthage Jail," 299–300; Pratt, *Autobiography of Parley P. Pratt*, 392; and Tullidge, *Life of Joseph the Prophet*, 543–44.
108. Davis Bitton notes that while in Liberty Jail the Prophet Joseph Smith wrote, "I feel like Joseph in Egypt"—indicating, according to Bitton, that the parallels between the lives of the two prophets were evident in the mind of the seer of the Restoration (see Bitton, *Images of the Prophet Joseph Smith*, 71). See also McConkie, *Gospel Symbolism*, 36–43.
109. See Smith and Cornwall, *Dictionary of Bible Names*, 155; and McConkie, *Gospel Symbolism*, 38.
110. "When mistreated, he was inclined to 'get even' by offering the hospitality of his home. That involved Emma and her talents in cooking. Often he invited people with little warning—'If ye will not embrace our religion, accept our hospitality.'" (Madsen, *Joseph Smith the Prophet*, 31).
111. See *History of the Church*, 1:88, 91, 95; 3:63, 402, 462; 4:30, 364–65, 419–20, 489; 5:86–89, 100, 145, 155, 171–79, 204–6, 212, 220–21, 226–27, 231, 233–38, 240–45, 251, 299, 446–48, 460–65, 474, 476–78, 489, 492, 496–97, 500, 508, 513–15, 526, 532–38; 6:35, 67–68, 105, 139–40, 146, 218–19, 359, 394, 435, 453–55, 487, 510, 547, 561, 565, 567, 569, 587, 590, 592, 597; 7:11–12, 85, 97, 147, 172.
112. The Doctrine and Covenants, albeit only a sampling of this, is nevertheless strong evidence of the Prophet's prophetic gift.

Notes to Chapter 8: People 383

113. See "Joseph Smith and Trials," in Madsen, *Joseph Smith the Prophet*, 51–65, 152–59.
114. See Butler, "The 'Author' and the 'Finisher' of the Book of Mormon," 61–68; Holzapfel, "Mormon, the Man and the Message," 128; and Bitton, *Images of the Prophet Joseph Smith*, 61–65.
115. Smith, *History of Joseph Smith*, 67.
116. See ibid., 46.
117. See Madsen, *Joseph Smith the Prophet*, 44.
118. See Taylor, "Man, the Offspring of God," 17:374; and Madsen, *Joseph Smith the Prophet*, 44.
119. See Madsen, *Joseph Smith the Prophet*, 20; and Quincy, *Figures of the Past*, 380.
120. See Young, in *Journal of Discourses*, 19:39–40.
121. See Cannon, *Life of Joseph Smith the Prophet*, 498.
122. See ibid., 528.
123. See Smith, *Teachings of the Prophet Joseph Smith*, 258.
124. See Sill, *Upward Reach*, 250.
125. See Acts 7:30; Smith, *Doctrines of Salvation*, 2:233; and Ginzberg, *Legends of the Jews*, 5:404 note 69.
126. See Arrington, *Presidents of the Church*, 47–49.
127. See Whitney, *Saturday Night Thoughts*, 132–37; Exodus 2:15; Acts 7:21–29; and Petersen, *Moses*, 41.
128. See Rich, *Ensign to the Nations*, 190, 199–200; and Arrington, *Brigham Young*, 223–49.
129. See Allen and Leonard, *Story of the Latter-day Saints*, 198–215; and Berrett and Burton, *Readings in LDS Church History*, 2:89–124.
130. See Woodruff, *Discourses of Wilford Woodruff*, ix.
131. See Journal History, 23 February 1847; and Nibley, *Exodus to Greatness*, 329.
132. Brigham Young was responsible for the building of the Salt Lake, St. George, Manti, and Logan temples (see Arrington, *Presidents of the Church*, 146, 387, 393; and Nibley, *Presidents of the Church*, 52, 59–61).
133. In Exodus 2:21 we are informed that Moses married Zipporah the Midianite, who according to D&C 84:6–7 would have been a member of the Church. Indeed, it was her father who ordained Moses to the priesthood. In Numbers 12:1 Moses marries an Ethiopian or Cushite woman (named Tharbis), for which Aaron and Miriam chastize him—apparently because she is not an Israelite or a believer. Ancient sources indicate that this second wife was likely taken for political reasons (see Josephus, *Complete Works of Josephus*, 58; "Fragments from the Lost Writings of Irenaeus," 1:573; Ginzberg, *Legends of the Jews*, 2:286–89; 5:409 note 80; 6:90 note 488; 6:136 note 791; "Constitution of the Holy Apostles," 7:450; Hertz, *Pentateuch and Haftorahs*, 618; and Kraut, *Polygamy in the Bible*, 72–73).

134. See Ginzberg, *Legends of the Jews*, 5:404 note 69.
135. Brigham Young was an apostle for some forty-two years. At his death he was in his thirty-eighth year of presiding over either the Quorum of the Twelve or the Church.
136. See Reynolds and Sjodahl, *Commentary on the Book of Mormon*, 1:253; and Bitton, *Images of the Prophet Joseph Smith*, 71–73.
137. He is responsible for the Pentateuch or Torah, but felt very uncomfortable with his speaking abilities (see Exodus 4:10).
138. He is responsible for the Doctrine and Covenants, Pearl of Great Price, and Book of Mormon, and yet did not necessarily feel that his speaking ability was his greatest gift (see Smith, *History of the Church*, 6:478).
139. Nearly every chapter of the Book of Exodus depicts Moses as conversing with Jehovah.
140. See Jessee, "Kirtland Diary of Wilford Woodruff," 382.
141. See Reynolds and Sjodahl, *Commentary on the Book of Mormon*, 1:253.
142. See Smith, *Teachings of the Prophet Joseph Smith*, 255.
143. See ibid.
144. See ibid.
145. See Hartshorn, *Joseph Smith*, 2, 53; and Madsen, *Joseph Smith the Prophet*, 31, 45–46.
146. See McConkie, *Millennial Messiah*, 331–32.
147. See Roberts, *Outlines in Ecclesiastical History*, 295.
148. See Holzapfel, "Mormon, the Man and the Message," 128.
149. See Madsen, *Joseph Smith the Prophet*, 20; and Quincy, *Figures of the Past*, 380.
150. See Smith, *Teachings of the Prophet Joseph Smith*, 285; and "Nauvoo Neighbor," 20 December 1843, in Smith, *Words of Joseph Smith*, 260.
151. See the Doctrine and Covenants; and the collections of teachings of Joseph Smith: *Encyclopedia of Joseph Smith's Teachings; Teachings of the Prophet Joseph Smith; Words of Joseph Smith*, and *Discourses of the Prophet Joseph Smith*.
152. See Anderson, "Parallel Prophets," 12–17; and Bitton, *Images of the Prophet Joseph Smith*, 75–76.
153. The earliest known description of Paul's Damascus vision was penned some twenty-four years after the event took place.
154. The earliest known account of Joseph's First Vision was recorded twelve years after the event took place.
155. See Anderson, "Parallel Prophets," 14.
156. Paul is responsible for some fourteen New Testament epistles and letters, many of which are saturated in doctrinal teachings.
157. The Doctrine and Covenants is saturated with doctrinal teachings of the restored gospel.
158. See Anderson, "Parallel Prophets," 13.

Notes to Chapter 9: Names

159. See Smith, *Teachings of the Prophet Joseph Smith*, 371.
160. Richard Lloyd Anderson wrote: "Joseph Smith also proved his sincerity by sacrifice. Writing to the Church during unfair arrest attempts that kept him in hiding in and out of Nauvoo for months, he also looked back: 'The envy and wrath of man have been my common lot all the days of my life . . . and I feel, like Paul, to glory in tribulation.' (D&C 127:2.) Indeed, although the Prophet didn't summarize all his trials, any historian could easily take Paul's format and adapt it to Joseph Smith's life, as Joseph himself did in Liberty Jail in alluding to his lifetime burdens. (See D&C 122:5.) For instance, a number of times professing Christians leveled guns at him with the threat of death. Once he was beaten, tarred and feathered, and left unconscious. Twice he was endangered by stagecoach runaways when on the Lord's business. He took back roads and waded through swamps to escape his enemies. He endured years of inconvenient travel on land for the kingdom, as well as risking many steamboat journeys on waterways. He faced years of unjust legal harassment, which made his own home unsafe, and he was imprisoned for a long winter in a filthy jail on unverified charges. Through all, he maintained the responsibility of leading the Church, worrying, praying, and planning for the welfare of his family and his fellow Saints" ("Parallel Prophets," 17).
161. See Jones, "Martyrdom of Joseph Smith and His Brother Hyrum," 101.
162. See Forbush, *Fox's Book of Martyrs*, 4.
163. See Richards, "Memories of Carthage Jail," 299–300; Pratt, *Autobiography of Parley P. Pratt*, 392; and Tullidge, *Angel of the Prairies*, 543–44.
164. See Fontana, *Secret Language of Symbols*, 34; and Todeschi, *Encyclopedia of Symbolism*, 289.
165. See Nibley, "Law and the Atonement," in *Teachings of the Book of Mormon*, semester 1, lecture 17, 11.
166. Admittedly, the Prophet taught, "The devil has no power over us only as we permit him." But he also added, "The moment we revolt at anything which comes from God, the devil takes power" (*Teachings of the Prophet Joseph Smith*, 181). We have power only to destroy Satan's influence over us, but not his influence over this world and its many inhabitants. That power is vested only in God (see Taylor, *Government of God*, 95–98).

NOTES TO CHAPTER 9: NAMES AS SYMBOLS

1. See Thomasson, "What's in a Name?" 8.
2. Porter and Ricks, "Names in Antiquity," 1:513.
3. Madsen, "'Putting on the Names'" 1:458.
4. Other examples include employing David's name over a city (see 2 Samuel 12:28), seven women seeking the name of a man to take away their reproach (see Isaiah 4:1), and the name of God being placed over the nations (see Amos 9:12) and over Israel (see Isaiah 63:19) (see McConkie and Parry, *Guide to Scriptural Symbols*, 175).

5. Ryken, Wilhoit, and Longman, *Dictionary of Biblical Imagery*, 585. See Myers, *Eerdmans Bible Dictionary*, 747. Note a few examples of using someone's name: (a) in ministry (Deuteronomy 18:5; Matthew 18:5; Hebrews 6:10); (b) in battle (1 Samuel 17:45; 2 Chronicles 14:11; Psalm 20:5, 7; 44:5; 118:10–12); (c) when acting as a representative by "investiture of authority" (John 5:43; Romans 1:5; Colossians 3:17); (d) in a blessing or cursing (Deuteronomy 10:8; 2 Samuel 6:18; 2 Kings 2:24; Psalm 129:8; Isaiah 66:5); (e) in commanding (2 Thessalonians 3:6); (f) in speaking or prophesying (Exodus 5:23; 1 Kings 22:16; 1 Chronicles 21:19; Ezra 5:1; Jeremiah 20:9; Daniel 9:6; Acts 5:28; 9:29; James 5:10); (g) in casting out evil spirits (Luke 10:17; Acts 16:18); and (h) in performing an ordinance (Matthew 28:19; Acts 2:38; 8:16; 10:48; 19:5).
6. See Porter and Ricks, "Names in Antiquity," 512; Harris, "Book of Abraham Facsimiles," 270; Nibley, "On the Sacred and the Symbolic," 559; Ifrah, *Universal History of Numbers*, 214; Kidner, *Genesis*, 170; and Clifford and Murphy, "Genesis," 34.
7. Names connected with a physical characteristic might include Esau ("hairy"), Adin ("dainty" or "delicate"), Amasai ("burdensome"), and Korah ("bald").
8. Names describing personality or temperament might include Nabal ("fool"), Achar ("one who causes trouble"), Hanan ("compassionate," "merciful," or "gracious"), and Mithcah ("sweet").
9. "New names were frequently conferred upon individuals at the time of their enthronement. . . . In the Book of Mormon, all kings were to be called 'Nephi,' giving honor both to the original Nephi as well as to the new king (Jacob 1:11)" (Porter and Ricks, "Names in Antiquity," 1:507).
10. Names that indicate one's occupation might include Asa ("physician" or "healer"), Sophereth ("registrar" or "scribe"), and Machir ("salesman").
11. See Eakin, *Religion and Culture of Israel*, 70, 102; and Conner, *Interpreting the Symbols and Types*, 10. "Personal names served as miniature biographies, descriptions of character, testimonies or expressions of praise to God, reminders of significant events, and divine warning. In short, Bible names served as memorials, symbols, and prophecies" (McConkie, *Gospel Symbolism*, 173).
12. See Ryken, Wilhoit, and Longman, *Dictionary of Biblical Imagery*, 583. See also Farbridge, *Studies in Biblical and Semitic Symbolism*, 239–44; and McConkie and Parry, *Guide to Scriptural Symbols*, 113, 175. "In the cultures of the ancient Near East . . . the name of someone (or something) was perceived not as a mere abstraction, but as a real entity, 'the audible and spoken image of a person, which was taken to be his spiritual essence.' According to Philo of Alexandria, the name 'is like a shadow which accompanies the body.' Similarly, Origen viewed the name as the designation of the individual's essence" (Porter and Ricks, "Names in Antiquity," 1:501).
13. This is particularly the case with theophoric names. Israelite theophoric names begin or end with some form of *Yah* or *Jah* (for Yahweh [Jehovah]),

or El (for Elohim). They are compound words composed of a noun, pronoun, adjective, or verb combined with a name of God. When given to a person, they represent declarations about or expressions of petition to the Deity mentioned in the name. Parents would give their children theophoric names both to honor their God and in hope that the child would live a godly life. For additional details on theophoric names, see chapter 11 of this work.

14. See Ryken, Wilhoit, and Longman, *Dictionary of Biblical Imagery*, 583; and McConkie and Parry, *Guide to Scriptural Symbols*, 113, 175. "The majority of Israelite names, and ancient Semitic names in general, had a readily understandable meaning. That parents consciously chose a child's name is implied by the content of these names, many of which are translatable sentences" (Dana M. Pike, "Names," 682). See also Taylor, "Name, Names," 687. Names that indicated events surrounding the birth of a child included Haggai ("born on a day of a festival") and Peleg ("division"), who was born during the days when the earth was divided (1 Chronicles 1:19).

15. See Kidner, *Genesis*, 162; and Speiser, *Genesis*, 230. "Some children, such as Ishmael and Isaac, received a name by divine command, usually one with prophetic meaning (Solomon, Jesus, John) or even direct prophetic purpose (Isaiah's children, Is 7:3; 8:3, 18; Hosea's, Hos 1:4, 6, 9). The name Jacob (. . . 'let God protect') was given punningly to a child who at birth seized his elder twin's . . . 'heel,' and was later interpreted, by further wordplay, to explain his tendency to . . . 'supplant' (Gen 25:26; 27:36). When Jacob's name was extended to his posterity, these associations were not forgotten (Jer 9:4; Hos 12:3). Abigail's similar joke about her husband's name, Nabal, meaning 'worthless' or 'good-for-nothing' (1 Sam 25:25), has been taken unsmilingly by generations of commentators" (Ryken, Wilhoit, and Longman, *Dictionary of Biblical Imagery*, 583). See also McConkie and Parry, *Guide to Scriptural Symbols*, 175.

16. Ryken, Wilhoit, and Longman, *Dictionary of Biblical Imagery*, 583. See Porter and Ricks, "Names in Antiquity," 1:504, 507.

17. Smith and Cornwall, *Exhaustive Dictionary of Bible Names*, vii.

18. Porter and Ricks, "Names in Antiquity," 1:513.

19. Reynolds and Sjodahl, *Commentary on the Book of Mormon*, 6:75.

20. See McConkie and Parry, *Guide to Scriptural Symbols*, 113, 176.

21. Unfortunately, current editions of the Book of Mormon do not provide us with that same source. Notably, Reformed Egyptian is a lost language. Thus, the meaning of many Book of Mormon names has been lost. However, in recent years much has been done to draw attention to the Hebrew, Egyptian, and occasionally Greek words and names that appear in significant numbers in the Book of Mormon. What is available is illuminating and should be utilized.

22. I have found the following sources very valuable in my daily studies: Smith and Cornwall, *Exhaustive Dictionary of Bible Names*; Brown, Driver, and Briggs, *Hebrew and English Lexicon*; Thayer, *Greek-English Lexicon*; McConkie and Parry, "Symbols, Names, and Titles for Deity" and

"Symbolic and Theophoric Names," in *Guide to Scriptural Symbols*, 112–90; Nibley, "Proper Names in the Book of Mormon," 281–94; Nibley, "Men of the East," in *Lehi in the Desert, World of the Jaredites, There Were Jaredites*, 25–42; Nibley, *Teachings of the Book of Mormon*, semester 1, lecture 26, 1–13, and semester 1, lecture 27, 1–14; Hoskisson, "An Introduction to the Relevance of and a Methodology for a Study of the Proper Names of the Book of Mormon," 2:126–35; and Tvedtnes, "Phonemic Analysis of Nephite and Jaredite Proper Names," 1–8.

23. See Smith and Cornwall, *Exhaustive Dictionary of Bible Names*, 2.
24. Ginzberg, *Legends of the Jews*, 1:107.
25. See Nibley, "Near Eastern Background," 1:189–90.
26. Nibley, *Teachings of the Book of Mormon*, semester 1, lecture 26, 11. There is some disagreement as to the meaning of this name. For example, George Reynolds interprets it as meaning "a worker of Jehovah" (see *Story of the Book of Mormon*, 298). Smith and Cornwall interpret the name as meaning "great people" or "son of my people" (see *Exhaustive Dictionary of Bible Names*, 15).
27. See Brown, *Death of the Messiah*, 1:59; and Wilkins, "Barabbas," 1:607.
28. See Albright and Mann, *Matthew*, 126, 154; Fitzmyer, *Luke X–XXIV*, 920–21; and Mann, *Mark*, 253. Alternate translations include either "lord of the house" or "lord of the flies," but neither makes a great deal of sense (see Lewis, "Beelzebul," 1:638–39; and Smith and Cornwall, *Exhaustive Dictionary of Bible Names*, 35–36).
29. During the last year of his life, Caesar proclaimed his divinity. That being the case, the name *Caesar* (meaning "one cut out") may have reference to the dictator's belief that he was "cut out" in the image of his god.
30. Nibley, *Teachings of the Book of Mormon*, semester 1, lecture 26, 12. See also semester 2, lecture 30, 6.
31. See Nibley, *Ancient Documents and the Pearl of Great Price*, lecture 8, 12; and Nibley, *Teachings of the Book of Mormon*, semester 3, lecture 78, 262. Elsewhere Nibley interprets the word *Deseret* as meaning "hives of bees" (see *Teachings of the Book of Mormon*, semester 4, lecture 109, 253).
32. See Nibley, *Teachings of the Book of Mormon*, semester 1, lecture 26, 1; and semester 3, lecture 57, 15.
33. Nibley, *Ancient Documents and the Pearl of Great Price*, lecture 21, 4. See lecture 17, 12.
34. See Nibley, *Teachings of the Book of Mormon*, semester 1, lecture 26, 1.
35. See Moore, *Esther*, 20; and Humphreys, "Esther," 280.
36. See Smith and Cornwall, *Exhaustive Dictionary of Bible Names*, 74.
37. Ibid., 76.
38. See Bruce, *Paul*, 360; Johnson, *Sacra Pagina*, 414; and Braund, "Felix," 2:783.
39. See Green, "Festus, Porcius," 2:794.
40. See Gillman, "Fortunatus," 2:852; and Walls, "Fortunatus," 439.

Notes to Chapter 9: Names

41. See Smith and Cornwall, *Exhaustive Dictionary of Bible Names*, 79, 82.
42. See Nibley, *Teachings of the Book of Mormon*, semester 3, lecture 81, 292.
43. See ibid., semester 2, lecture 54, 9.
44. See Smith and Cornwall, *Exhaustive Dictionary of Bible Names*, 104.
45. See Brown, Driver, and Briggs, *Hebrew and English Lexicon*, 27.
46. McConkie, "Joseph Smith as Found in Ancient Manuscripts," 17. See McConkie, *Gospel Symbolism*, 193.
47. This author has always been struck with the emphasis that commentators place on the Hebrew of Isaiah 7:14. The point is often made that the Hebrew emphasizes how the mother of the Messiah shall give him the name Immanuel (see, for example, Young, *Book of Isaiah*, 1:289; and Parry, Parry, and Peterson, *Understanding Isaiah*, 76). That should not be taken to literally mean that Mary would name Jesus "Immanuel." On the contrary, the angel Gabriel commanded her to do otherwise (Matthew 1:21). But one will look in vain for any commentary concerning the Virgin Mary saying of Jesus, in so many words, "Look at my Son. He is God!" Did she bear witness to that effect? I believe that she did. Are such words recorded in scripture? Not with any degree of clarity. However, it appears that the point of the prophecy, as it pertains to her naming him Immanuel, is that she will testify in her words and actions that he was indeed the Son of God and not, as some assumed, the son of Joseph the carpenter. Mary's words and actions at the wedding at Cana seem to fulfill Isaiah's statement that she would name or call him Immanuel. For the most part, as evidence of her great faith in her Son, Mary provokes that first miracle of Jesus' mortal ministry and, in so doing, causes his disciples to "believe on him" (see John 2:1–11). Thus, she did in effect call his name Immanuel.
48. See Smith and Cornwall, *Exhaustive Dictionary of Bible Names*, 116.
49. See Clifford and Murphy, "Genesis," 22.
50. See Martin-Achard, "Isaac," 3:463.
51. The interpretation of Isaac as meaning "laughing" seems problematic for a number of reasons. The main problem is found in the fact that God, not Abraham, chooses this name for the child. If the name is accurately interpreted as "laughing," it would seem that God's intent would have to have been to "rub in the face" of Abraham and his wife their disbelief, an act which seems contrary to the nature of God. Two other possibilities are that the child would be "laughing" or happy, or perhaps God was saying to Sarah that although she had laughed in disbelief, now she would laugh with joy.
52. See Smith and Cornwall, *Exhaustive Dictionary of Bible Names*, 118.
53. Valletta, "Jared and His Brother," 307.
54. Smith and Cornwall, *Exhaustive Dictionary of Bible Names*, 155.
55. Ibid., 255–56.
56. See Nibley, *Teachings of the Book of Mormon*, semester 1, lecture 2, 9.
57. See MacKenzie, *Egyptian Myths and Legends*, 368; and Wells, *Nefertiti*, 126.

58. See Ryken, Wilhoit, and Longman, *Dictionary of Biblical Imagery*, 583.
59. McConkie, *Mormon Doctrine*, 744.
60. See Smith, *Teachings of the Prophet Joseph Smith*, 299–300; and Hinckley, *Teachings of Gordon B. Hinckley*, 114–15, 184.
61. Ginzberg, *Legends of the Jews*, 5:401 note 57.
62. See Brown, Driver, and Briggs, *Hebrew and English Lexicon*, 602; Smith and Cornwall, *Exhaustive Dictionary of Bible Names*, 184; and Petersen, *Moses*, 41.
63. See Propp, *Exodus 1–18*, 152–53.
64. See Nibley, *Prophetic Book of Mormon*, 397, 401.
65. Reynolds and Sjodahl, *Commentary on the Book of Mormon*, 3:145–46. See Reynolds, *Story of the Book of Mormon*, 297.
66. See Nibley, *Teachings of the Book of Mormon*, semester 2, lecture 47, 9.
67. Reynolds, *Story of the Book of Mormon*, 296.
68. See Pratt, *Key to the Science of Theology*, 15; Nibley, *Lehi in the Desert, World of the Jaredites, There Were Jaredites*, 165; and Nibley, *Mormonism and Early Christianity*, 366.
69. See Nibley, *Teachings of the Book of Mormon*, semester 1, lecture 26, 11.
70. Nibley, *Lehi in the Desert, World of the Jaredites, There Were Jaredites*, 344.
71. Nibley, *Teachings of the Book of Mormon*, semester 3, lecture 73, 97.
72. Ibid.
73. See ibid., 197; see also semester 1, lecture 2, 9; semester 2, lecture 54, 3.
74. See Edelman, "Saul," 5:990.
75. See Sperry, *Paul's Life and Letters*, 40.
76. See Robinson, *Life of Paul*, 78–79; and Edelman, "Saul," 5:990. The German theologian Adolf Deissmann believes that Paul was simply Saul's surname (see *Paul*, 89). This makes sense in light of the Prophet Joseph Smith's comment that Paul was "about 5 foot high" (Ehat and Cook, *Words of Joseph Smith*, 59). Similarly, the early Christian "Acts of Paul" states that the Apostle was "a man small of stature" (see Schneemelcher, *New Testament Apocrypha*, 2:354). See also "The Acts of Paul and Thecla," 1:7, in *Lost Books of the Bible*, 100). It is quite possible that "Paul" was the surname of a family for whom shortness was hereditary.
77. See Middleton, "Paul among the Prophets," 123.
78. Carlyon, *Guide to the Gods*, 291.
79. See Gillman, "Quartus," 5:583. If they were, indeed, brothers, then they were apparently also the sons of parents who had limited skills in the areas of creativity and name selection.
80. Nibley, *Teachings of the Book of Mormon*, semester 2, lecture 51, 10.
81. See Beck, "Rebekah," 5:629.
82. Nibley, *Teachings of the Book of Mormon*, semester 4, lecture 109, 252.
83. See Smith and Cornwall, *Exhaustive Dictionary of Bible Names*, 217.

Notes to Chapter 10: Animals

84. Reynolds, *Story of the Book of Mormon*, 296.
85. See Nibley, *Teachings of the Book of Mormon*, semester 1, lecture 26, 1, 8.
86. Smith and Cornwall, *Exhaustive Dictionary of Bible Names*, 239. See also McConkie, *Doctrinal New Testament Commentary*, 2:65.
87. Martin, "Tertullus," 6:391.
88. Josephus, *Complete Works of Josephus*, 418.
89. See Smith and Cornwall, *Exhaustive Dictionary of Bible Names*, 245.
90. See ibid., 228.
91. In Jeremiah 26 and Nehemiah 8 this name is spelled *Urijah*; nevertheless, it is the same name. See ibid., 251.
92. See Bedford, "Vaizatha," 6:781. See also Bedford, "Adalia," 1:61–62; and Moore, *Esther*, 87.
93. See Moore, *Esther*, 8; and McKenna, "Vashti," 6:785.
94. See Nibley, *Teachings of the Book of Mormon*, semester 1, lecture 11, 5; semester 2, lecture 50, 5; and semester 2, lecture 55, 3.
95. Nibley, *Teachings of the Book of Mormon*, semester 2, lecture 55, 3.

NOTES TO CHAPTER 10: ANIMALS AS SYMBOLS

1. Nibley renders one passage of "The Combat of Adam and Eve against Satan" as follows: "So Adam continued to make this sacrifice for the rest of his days. And God caused his word to be preached to Adam. On the fiftieth day [while] Adam [was] offering sacrifice as was his custom, Satan appeared in the form of a man and smote him in the side with a sharp stone even as Adam raised his arms in prayer. Eve tried to help him as blood and water flowed on the altar. 'God sent his word and revived Adam saying: *Finish thy sacrifice, which is most pleasing to me. For even so will I be wounded and blood and water will come from my side; that will be the true Sacrifice, placed on the altar as a perfect offering.* . . . And so God healed Adam'" (cited in *Enoch the Prophet*, 171–72). See Ginzberg, *Legends of the Jews*, 1:71, 89, 166, 285; 5:93 note 55, 116 note 108, 139 note 20, 190 note 56.

2. See Acts 10:28–48; see also Acts 11:1–10. One scholar noted, "The vision implied the abolition of the distinction between Jews and non-Jews" (Soler, "Dietary Prohibitions of the Hebrews," 30).

3. This is not to suggest that they felt it appropriate to ignore the regulations of the law of *kashrut* (or kosher). Rather, they simply understood that a metaphorical message underlay the temporal practice. One biblical scholar suggested that Peter's vision was an indication that animals deemed unclean for consumption symbolized "unclean men [or] Gentiles" (Munck, *Acts of Apostles*, 93). This position is a fairly common one. The Jewish scholar J. H. Kurtz noted that clean animals are figures of the chosen and holy people, and the unclean of the heathen (see *Sacrificial Worship of the Old Testament*, 28–29; and *Offerings, Sacrifices and Worship*,

28–29). Another wrote: "The vision which was given to Peter (Acts x.10ff.) was intended to teach him and the other apostles that the opinion of the Jews of that time, that the heathen, as such, were unclean, and must first be cleansed by circumcision to be received into the Christian Church, was an error and delusion; that, on the contrary, the whole creation of God was pure, and that the distinction between clean and unclean animals had first come by the fall of man into the pure and good creation of God" (Keil, *Manual of Biblical Archaeology*, 2:122 note 6).

4. See Brown, Driver, and Briggs, *Hebrew and English Lexicon*, 379.
5. See Botterweck and Ringgren, *Theological Dictionary of the Old Testament*, 5:331. See also Bulmer, "Uncleanliness of the Birds of Leviticus and Deuteronomy," 309–10.
6. See Botterweck and Ringgren, *Theological Dictionary of the Old Testament*, 5:337, 338–39; Stubblefield, "Mark 7:1–23 in Light of the First Century Understanding of Clean-Unclean," 2; and Isaiah 1:16; 6:5; Psalm 51:9; Ecclesiastes 9:2.
7. There is a common assumption that the animals were pronounced unclean because of the probability that they either carried or caused disease. Many commentaries on the books of Leviticus and Deuteronomy have given this very popular explanation. For example, see Childs, *Old Testament Theology in a Canonical Context*, 85; Fee and Stuart, *How to Read the Bible*, 161; Harrison, *Introduction to the Old Testament*, 390–91; and R. K. Yerkes, "Unclean Animals in Leviticus 11 and Deuteronomy 14," 27–28. Even some medieval sources encourage this strain of thought (see Maimonides, *Guide of the Perplexed*, 3:48; and Nachmanides, *Leviticus*, 136). Most within the Church have had the opportunity of sitting through a sacrament meeting talk or a gospel doctrine lesson on Leviticus 11 or Deuteronomy 14 in which the speaker or teacher described the kosher law as an "Old Testament version of the Word of Wisdom." For examples of this, see Skousen, *Third Thousand Years*, 347; Dummelow, *Commentary on the Holy Bible*, 92; and Bryan, *Cosmos, Chaos and the Kosher Mentality*, 148. The Hebrew simply does not allow for such an interpretation. The Hebrew word *tawhore* means the ceremonial cleanliness of animals, and not their physical purity, but *tawmay* implies ethical or religious uncleanliness in animals. This cannot be understood as physical filth or dirt (see Brown, Driver, and Briggs, *Hebrew and English Lexicon*, 373a, 379b; see also Kittel, *Theological Dictionary of the New Testament*, 3:416 note 15; Wilson, *Old Testament Word Studies*, 78; Neusner, *Idea of Purity in Ancient Judaism*, 1; Wouk, *This Is My God*, 103; and Grunfeld, *Jewish Dietary Laws*, 1:13, 31).
8. Of all of these sources, the General Epistle of Barnabas is perhaps the most detailed and most authoritative. In the early Church it held a prominent position in the Codex Sinaiticus and other early Christian compilations of the New Testament. It was not only read regularly in the worship services of the early Christian church, but it was quoted by notable early Christian figures such as Clement and Athanasius—and was considered orthodox

at least through the fourth century. To date it retains its position among the writings of the Apostolic Fathers. Although some in modernity look upon the text with condescension, in light of early Christian attitudes toward the document, such criticism seems unjustified and potentially naive. For background on the General Epistle of Barnabas, and its position of orthodoxy in the early Christian church, see Gaskill, "Touch Not the Unclean Thing," 89–94.

While all animal symbolism can be either positive or negative, this author has chosen to highlight the most common interpretation. For more information on this subject, see Gaskill, "Touch Not the Unclean Thing."

9. "General Epistle of Barnabas," 1:143; brackets in original.
10. Ibid. In some scripture passages, the eagle carries a more positive connotation (see Exodus 19:4; Psalm 103:5; Isaiah 40:31; Revelation 12:14).
11. "General Epistle of Barnabas," 1:143.
12. Cairns, Word and Presence, 245. "It states, Eternal will bring a nation against thee from afar, for, Vespasian and his son Titus came with a very large Roman army into the Land and captured all the fortified cities of Judea, and oppressed them greatly, as is known from the history books that they also captured the walls of Jerusalem and there remained only the Sanctuary and the wall of the Court. They [the besieged] ate the flesh of their sons and their daughters. And when the Sanctuary was also captured, then was fulfilled *and ye shall be plucked from off the Land*" (Nachmanides, *Deuteronomy*, 325–26). "This crowning horror of a long-continued siege actually took place during the siege of Samaria by the Syrians (2 K 6 $^{26-29}$), in the siege of Jerusalem by Nebuchadnezzar (Lam 4^{10}), and later in the final overthrow of Jerusalem by Titus, as recorded by Josephus in his 'Wars of the Jews.' . . . These words were fulfilled at the exile, and even more literally at the destruction of Jerusalem during the Roman supremacy. Since that time the Jews have been repeatedly persecuted and driven from one country to another" (Dummelow, *Commentary on the Holy Bible*, 135).
13. See "General Epistle of Barnabas," 1:143. Adam Clarke notes the "proverbial" nature of the eagle in this passage (Clarke, *Holy Bible with a Commentary and Critical Notes*, 1:813).
14. See Brown, Driver, and Briggs, *Hebrew and English Lexicon*, 676–77; and Kalland, "Deuteronomy," 3:177.
15. Cairns, *Word and Presence*, 246.
16. Kalland, "Deuteronomy," 3:174. See Thompson, *Deuteronomy*, 276. For an additional example of this category of symbolism, see "animals as types or symbols of Christ" in chapter 11 of this work.
17. According to J. C. Cooper, the camel, when swallowed, also stands as a symbol for disobedience (*Encyclopaedia of Traditional Symbols*, 56). Kevin Todeschi noted that in some cases the camel stands as a representation of spiritual death or spiritual starvation in the life of him whom the camel depicts (*Encyclopedia of Symbolism*, 24, 56). Both of these insights are appropriate for the Pharisees, in light of that which is given in Matthew

23. Sources, both modern and ancient, associate the camel with things such as immorality or adultery, disobedience, and personal apostasy.
18. See Achtemeier, *Harper's Bible Dictionary*, 349; and Carson, "Matthew," 8:480.
19. Yonge, *Works of Philo*, 627. See Winston, *Philo of Alexandria*, 284.
20. Ibid., 296.
21. Winston, *Philo of Alexandria*, 284.
22. See Douglas, *Purity and Danger*, 56; Wenham, "Theology of Unclean Food," 9–10; Kurtz, *Offerings, Sacrifices and Worship*, 28; and Kurtz, *Sacrificial Worship of the Old Testament*, 28.
23. See Douglas, *Purity and Danger*, 56. For examples of others who agree with Douglas, see Harrison, *Leviticus*, 128–29; Milgrom, *Leviticus*, 641–742; and Wenham, "Theology of Unclean Food," 6–15.
24. Douglas, *Purity and Danger*, 56.
25. For example, see Albright and Mann, *Matthew*, 280; Carson, "Matthew," 8:480; France, *Matthew*, 328–29; and Grieve, "Matthew," 720.
26. See Cooper, *Encyclopaedia of Traditional Symbols*, 68.
27. See Julien, *Mammoth Dictionary of Symbols*, 153; and Todeschi, *Encyclopedia of Symbolism*, 25, 108.
28. See Winston, *Philo of Alexandria*, 283–84; and Yonge, *Works of Philo*, 626–27.
29. See ibid.
30. See "General Epistle of Barnabas," 1:143.
31. See Carson, "Matthew," 8:330; Jeremias, *Parables of Jesus*, 226; and Jeremias, *Rediscovering the Parables*, 177.
32. Adam Clarke noted: "A proper distinction shall be made between those who served God, and those who served him not; for many shall doubtless be found who shall bear the *name* without the *nature* of Christ. By *picking out the good, and throwing away the bad*, ver. 48, is meant that separation which God shall make between false and true professors, casting the former into hell, and bringing the latter to heaven" (*Holy Bible with a Commentary and Critical Notes*, 5:151). Grieve wrote: "Not all who have heard the message of the Kingdom will be found worthy to enter it" ("Matthew," 713).
33. McConkie, *Mortal Messiah*, 2:266.
34. "General Epistle of Barnabas," 1:143.
35. In light of Matthew 13, verses 49 and 50, it would be hard to draw any other conclusion.
36. It seems quite clear that the "corruption" of fish described here is intended as a symbol.
37. Madsen, *Joseph Smith the Prophet*, 104.
38. See Cirlot, *Dictionary of Symbols*, 34, 150–51; Cooper, *Encyclopaedia of Traditional Symbols*, 124; Fairbairn, *Typology of Scripture*, 1:220; Hall,

Dictionary of Subjects and Symbols in Art, 231; Julien, *Mammoth Dictionary of Symbols*, 309; and Todeschi, *Encyclopedia of Symbolism*, 25, 192. See also 2 Corinthians 6:14–17.

39. See Cirlot, *Dictionary of Symbols*, 34, 66, 82–84, 104, 196, 331; Cooper, *Encyclopaedia of Traditional Symbols*, 26–27; Fontana, *Secret Language of Symbols*, 92, 167; Hall, *Dictionary of Subjects and Symbols in Art*, 54; Julien, *Mammoth Dictionary of Symbols*, 49–50; and Todeschi, *Encyclopedia of Symbolism*, 52.

40. See Cirlot, *Dictionary of Symbols*, 120, 195, 339; Cooper, *Encyclopaedia of Traditional Symbols*, 151; Fontana, *Secret Language of Symbols*, 91; Hall, *Dictionary of Subjects and Symbols in Art*, 105; Julien, *Mammoth Dictionary of Symbols*, 378; and Todeschi, *Encyclopedia of Symbolism*, 25, 157.

41. See "Sibylline Oracles," 303, note e2, in Charlesworth, *Old Testament Pseudepigrapha*, 1:467; Cirlot, *Dictionary of Symbols*, 239; Cooper, *Encyclopaedia of Traditional Symbols*, 94–95; Fontana, *Secret Language of Symbols*, 91; Hall, *Dictionary of Subjects and Symbols in Art*, 186; Henry, *Catholic Customs and Symbols*, 12, 21, 65, 147; Julien, *Mammoth Dictionary of Symbols*, 233; and Todeschi, *Encyclopedia of Symbolism*, 25, 157.

42. See Cooper, *Encyclopaedia of Traditional Symbols*, 74; Fairbairn, *Typology of Scripture*, 2:468–70; Fontana, *Secret Language of Symbols*, 166; Hall, *Dictionary of Subjects and Symbols in Art*, 139; Julien, *Mammoth Dictionary of Symbols*, 179–81; and Todeschi, *Encyclopedia of Symbolism*, 25, 121.

43. See ibid.

44. See "General Epistle of Barnabas," 1:144; Winston, *Philo of Alexandria*, 282; Wright, "Unclean and Clean (OT)," 6:739; and Yonge, *Works of Philo*, 626.

45. See "General Epistle of Barnabas," 1:144.

46. See Winston, *Philo of Alexandria*, 283; and Yonge, *Works of Philo*, 626.

47. Ibid.

48. Ibid.

49. See "General Epistle of Barnabas," 1:144.

50. Douglas, *Purity and Danger*, 47.

51. See Fee and Stuart, *How to Read the Bible*, 67. Note that the parallel passage to this, 2 Corinthians 6:14–17, is "traditionally . . . interpreted as forbidding marriage between a Christian and non-Christian." See also Clarke, *Holy Bible with a Commentary and Critical Notes*, 1:795; Furnish, *II Corinthians*, 371–72; and Goppelt, *Typos*, 147. Kruse indicates that the "Hebrew . . . on which our English versions are based contains a prohibition, not of yoking, but of breeding different species of animals" (*2 Corinthians*, 136). See also Harris, "2 Corinthians," 10:359–60; Newton, *Concept of Purity*, 111–12; and Scott, "II Corinthians," 853.

52. Yonge, *Works of Philo*, 636.

53. Eilberg-Schwartz shows that the ass is a common symbol in the East for "resident aliens," or those who are not of the covenant race, but live among them (*Savage in Judaism*, 126–28). Moses Maimonides drew this

same parallel in the 12th century when he indicated that the ox and ass in this verse were calculated to conjure up, in the mind of readers, kosher issues (see Cairns, *Word and Presence*, 196).

54. Paul employs the Greek word *akathartos*, which can imply ceremonial or moral impurity, as the Hebrew word *tawmay* does.
55. See Kimball, *Teachings of Spencer W. Kimball*, 247; and Hunter, *Teachings of Howard W. Hunter*, 111.
56. "Whether thy neighbor be thy brother or thy enemy, his property must be protected and restored." It is a God-given responsibility for Israel (Hertz, *Pentateuch and Haftorahs*, 842).
57. See Cooper, *Encyclopaedia of Traditional Symbols*, 166–67; Fontana, *Secret Language of Symbols*, 56, 78, 93; Ginzberg, *Legends of the Jews*, 1:358–59; 5:294; Julien, *Mammoth Dictionary of Symbols*, 329–30; Neusner, *Enchantments of Judaism*, 128; and Todeschi, *Encyclopedia of Symbolism*, 25, 200.
58. See Firmage, "Zoology," 6:1132; Lobban, "Pigs and Their Prohibition," 57; McConkie, *Mortal Messiah*, 3:249; Mackie, *Bible Manners and Customs*, 103; Von Rohr Sauer, "Cultic Role of the Pig in Ancient Times," 201; Simoons, *Eat Not This Flesh*, 20–22, 27; and Smith, *Religion of the Semites*, 218.
59. Farrar, *Life of Christ*, 326 note 1.
60. *Baba Kamma* 82b, cited in Morris, *Luke*, 264, and in Fitzmyer, *Luke I–IX*, 1088.
61. See Simoons, *Eat Not This Flesh*, 27.
62. Craddock, *Luke*, 187.
63. One biblical scholar points out that the prodigal's actions in becoming a swine herder indicate that he willingly gave up the practice of his former religion (see Browning, *Gospel According to Saint Luke*, 131).
64. Trench, *Notes on the Parables of Our Lord*, 141–42.
65. Cited in ibid., 142.
66. "His initial motive was not particularly lofty (the desire to be better fed)" (Morris, *Luke*, 265). "The motivation for his return was hunger," not sorrow for sins (Liefeld, "Luke," 8:984). It is interesting that the prodigal makes the decision to offer himself to his father as a servant, yet when he arrives home, his initial commitment is conspicuously absent from the text. Some commentators feel that the fact that he does not carry through with his promise indicates a lack of sincerity in his repentance (see Liefeld, "Luke," 8:984; and Morris, *Luke*, 265).
67. In the context of the prodigal's arrival, the father reminds his eldest son: "Son, thou art ever with me, and *all* that I have is thine" (Luke 15:31; emphasis added). President Joseph Fielding Smith wrote: "There is rejoicing in heaven over every sinner who repents; but those who are faithful and transgress not any of the commandments shall inherit 'all that the Father hath,' while those who might be sons, but through their 'riotous living' waste their inheritance, may come back through repentance to

salvation to be servants, not to inherit exaltation as sons" (*Way to Perfection*, 21–22; see also McConkie, *Mortal Messiah*, 3:253). See Maturin, *Parables of Our Lord*, 246–47, who notes that, as loving and willing to embrace his wayward son as the father was, the prodigal can never again be as he once was, and as his elder brother remained. In a similar vein, BYU professor Richard G. Ellsworth penned the following regarding the status of the prodigal son: "Through this parable Jesus points out that the repentance and forgiveness of the erring are not threats to those who have been faithful. What is it to them if the erring and the sinful are forgiven? There is no indication in the story that the erring one will have restored to him that which he has wasted and lost. The theme is not one of restoration but rather that of the consistency of the Lord's love, his ever-ready, dependable acceptance for all those who will finally, sincerely, come to him. True, the prodigal son is welcomed by a great feast, but this is not a gift to him; rather, it is a celebration of joy, for, as his father says, 'It is meet that we should make merry and be glad, for this thy brother was dead and is alive again, and was lost and is found'" ("Literary Artistry of the Parables of Jesus," 76–77). Of course, those who stray and return with truly broken hearts, fulfilling all the requirements the Church and the Lord place on them, can indeed come unto exaltation—a recurring message of comfort and hope from prophets both ancient and modern.

68. Holland, "Hands of the Fathers," 14–15. Similarly, Clement of Alexandria condemned those Christians who, like the prodigal, "abused the Father's gifts" and neglected "to raise [their] eyes aloft to what is true" rather than depending on their own strength and the things of this world ("Instructor," 2:239). The parable describes in simplicity what God is like: ever merciful and loving, even to those who have hurt him or are steeped in sin. According to Liefeld, "The central figure [of the parable], the father, remains constant in his love for both [of his sons]" ("Luke," 8:983). Fitzmyer writes, "Jesus in this parable lays down the fundamental principle of God's relation to sinful men: that God loves the sinner while he is still a sinner, *before* he repents" (*Luke I–IX*, 1086).

69. Williamson, *Mark*, 104. See Albright and Mann, *Matthew*, 101; Clarke, *Holy Bible with a Commentary and Critical Notes*, 5:303; Fitzmyer, *Luke I–IX*, 735, 737; Carson, "Matthew," 8:217; Wessel, "Mark," 8:657–59; Mann, *Mark*, 278 note 2, 279 note 11; Morris, *Luke*, 170; and Wood, "Mark," 687.

70. See Cole, *Mark*, 158; Fitzmyer, *Luke I–IX*, 738; Mann, *Mark*, 279; and Morris, *Luke*, 171. Each of these authors suggests that the name or title offered by the man possessed is likely suggestive of the Roman legion of Jesus' day, which consisted of some 6,000 soldiers. In other words, the man was possessed by numerous evil spirits. As R. Alan Cole stated, "This man of Gerasa was completely bound by Satan as he had never been by the chains and fetters imposed by humans" (*Mark*, 158).

71. Smith, *Words of Joseph Smith*, 60.

72. Some commentators acknowledge that the man was demonically possessed (see Liefeld, "Luke," 8:912; and Morris, *Luke*, 171), while others

insist that he was merely the victim of some sort of mental ailment (see Albright and Mann, *Matthew*, 101; Cole, *Mark*, 156; and Fitzmyer, *Luke I–IX*, 733). It is my belief, and the position implied by the symbolism, that the man was possessed, and that this story is, as Walter Liefeld (8:914) suggested, about "the problem of evil."

73. Clarke, *Holy Bible with a Commentary and Critical Notes*, 5:107.
74. Liefeld, "Luke," 8:914.
75. Fitzmyer, *Luke I–IX*, 734.
76. Kselman and Barre, "Psalms," 541. Fitzmyer notes that "it can denote the abode of the dead (see Ps 107:26; Rom 10:7) or the final prison of Satan and the demons (Rev 20:3). It is used often in the LXX [as] the symbol of chaos and disorder" (*Luke I–IX*, 739 note 31). C. S. Mann indicates that, in this pericope, the sea represents the "place of final punishment for demons" (*Mark*, 278–79). Edwin Firmage indicated that the sea was a symbol for the "repository of impurity" ("Zoology," 6:1132). "Jesus . . . effectively sends the demons back to their place: the primeval abyss, the depths of the sea. (Compare Luke 8:31, which makes this point more explicitly.)" (Williamson, *Mark*, 104). See Clarke, *Holy Bible with a Commentary and Critical Notes*, 5:420; Freyne, "Sea of Galilee," 2:900; Morris, *Luke*, 171; and Liefeld, "Luke," 8:913.
77. In other words, it is not coincidental that the episode about the man possessed follows immediately after the story of Jesus calming the sea in all three synoptic accounts.
78. Liefeld, "Luke," 8:912, 913.
79. See Wessel, "Mark," 8:658. Joseph Fitzmyer indicates that the action of the pigs gave a very visual demonstration of what those spirits who possessed this man could and would do to him (see *Luke I–IX*, 734).
80. Clarke, *Holy Bible with a Commentary and Critical Notes*, 5:107.
81. Roberts, *Comprehensive History of the Church*, 1:82–84.
82. This genre of symbolism is not foreign to the Book of Mormon, although it is less frequently seen therein. Passages such as Alma 5:57, 59; 3 Nephi 4:7; and Ether 9:18 all employ animal symbolism. However, unlike the Bible, the Book of Mormon seems less set on propagating symbols, and more set on teaching the truths behind those symbols. Numerous comments within the body of that book indicate that the Nephites understood the biblical symbols and what they represented, but their focus was on ensuring that their people did not become confused or miss the point of the symbols. Thus the Book of Mormon's tendency is to teach the truths rather than emphasize the symbols. See 2 Nephi 11:4; 25:24–30; Jacob 4:4–5; Mosiah 13:30–32.

NOTES TO CHAPTER 11: TYPES AND SYMBOLS OF CHRIST

1. Nephi uses the word *type* rather than *symbol*. A type is a symbol that is fulfilled by an ante-type; the type coming first, but its fulfillment coming at a

later time. An example would be the paschal lamb (as the type) and Jesus' sacrifice (as the ante-type). A symbol, however, is something that represents something else, potentially even something concurrently extant with the symbol.

2. Holland, *Christ and the New Covenant*, 159.
3. Habershon, *Study of the Types*, 35.
4. As examples: Augustine, *City of God*, book 16, chapter 43; Fairbairn, *Typology of Scripture;* Greidanus, *Preaching Christ;* Habershon, *Study of the Types;* Lee, "Truly All Things Testify of Him," 99–112; Lund, *Key to the Plan of Salvation*, 54–75; and McConkie, *Gospel Symbolism*, 28–36, 48–50, 151–53, 263.
5. See McConkie, *Gospel Symbolism*, 146–60; and Habershon, *Study of the Types*, 122–34, 165–74.
6. See Bitton, *Images of the Prophet Joseph Smith*, 76–77; and Gibbons, in Conference Report, April 1991, 39–42.
7. See Bennion, *Introduction to the Gospel*, 212; and Ballif, "Melchizedek Priesthood," 2:882–83.
8. The Hebrew word for Nod means literally "wandering."
9. See Fontana, *Secret Language of Symbols*, 34; and Todeschi, *Encyclopedia of Symbolism*, 289.
10. Nibley, *Teachings of the Book of Mormon*, semester 1, lecture 17, 11.
11. Admittedly, the Prophet taught: "The devil has no power over us only as we permit him." But he also added, "The moment we revolt at anything which comes from God, the devil takes power" (Smith, *Teachings of the Prophet Joseph Smith*, 181). We only have power to destroy Satan's influence over us, but not his influence over this world and its many inhabitants. That power is vested only in God (see Taylor, *Government of God*, 95–98).
12. Philo, "De Sacrificiis Abelis et Cain," 1:2, 94.
13. See Smith and Cornwall, *Exhaustive Dictionary of Bible Names*, 2.
14. Ginzberg, *Legends of the Jews*, 1:107.
15. See Matthews, "Jesus Christ in the Scriptures," 2:746.
16. The idea that Jesus and Lucifer were spirit brothers is not unique to LDS Christology. See Russell, *Lucifer*, 44, 48, 187–88; and Peterson and Ricks, *Offenders for a Word*, 149–51.
17. Augustine, *Trinity*, 4:17.
18. Cope, *Symbolism in the Bible and the Church*, 190, 199.
19. The Greek actually says vultures rather than eagles.
20. See Horton, "Joseph Smith—Matthew," 208; McConkie, *Mortal Messiah*, 3:438–39; McConkie, *Doctrinal New Testament Commentary*, 1:648; and Talmage, *Jesus the Christ*, 573 note h.
21. See Irenaeus, "Against Heresies," 1:478–79; 14:1.
22. Cited in Carson, "Matthew," 8:503. Contemporary biblical scholars

William F. Albright and C. S. Mann also acknowledge the possibility that the carcass represents "the Messiah in His death" (*Matthew*, 296).
23. See Freedman and Simons, *Midrash Rabbah*, 2:149–50.
24. Robinson, *Believing Christ*, 118–19.
25. See McConkie, *Millennial Messiah*, 352.
26. See "General Epistle of Barnabas," 1:143. See also Fairbairn, *Typology of Scripture*, 1:219; and Todeschi, *Encyclopedia of Symbolism*, 95.
27. See Smith, *Doctrines of Salvation*, 2:287–88.
28. McConkie, *Mortal Messiah*, 4:232 note 22. See McConkie, *New Witness for the Articles of Faith*, xiv.
29. Talmage, *Jesus the Christ*, 660–61.
30. Habershon, *Study of the Types*, 44.
31. The typology of the veil does not end there. See our discussion of the veil as clothing in chapter 4 of this work.
32. See Levine, *Numbers 1–20*, 421; Nachmanides, *Numbers*, 4:190; and Sakenfeld, *Journeying with God*, 104.
33. See discussion of the number twelve in chapter 6 of this work.
34. See Draper, *Opening the Seven Seals*, 46, 56, 83; and Smith, *Book of Revelation*, 48, 267, 288.
35. Since the tribe of Levi is traditionally not counted as part of the twelve tribes, some commentators assume that there must have been thirteen, rather than twelve rods (see, for example, Levine, *Numbers 1–20*, 422). However, this seems insufficient cause to call into question the text, which clearly states that there were twelve rods placed in the temple. It must be assumed that Ephraim and Manasseh were grouped under the tribe of Joseph in this particular episode.
36. Habershon, *Study of the Types*, 47. See "Constitution of the Holy Apostles," 7:442.
37. Habershon, *Study of the Types*, 47–48. See McConkie, *Gospel Symbolism*, 46, 59 note 1, 73; and McConkie and Parry, *Guide to Scriptural Symbols*, 94. Not only did the rod typify Christ's resurrection, but Aaron himself—when serving in the tabernacle—functioned as a type for Christ (see Habershon, *Study of the Types*, 25, 124; and McConkie, *Gospel Symbolism*, 250).
38. See Cogan and Tadmor, *II Kings*, 70.
39. See Dummelow, *Commentary on the Holy Bible*, 232; Walsh and Begg, "1–2 Kings," 176; and Wiseman, *1 and 2 Kings*, 209.
40. Buttrick, *Interpreter's Bible*, 3:215.
41. See Wiseman, *1 and 2 Kings*, 209; and Brown, Driver, and Briggs, *Hebrew and English Lexicon*, 981.
42. "The sea is a common symbol for chaos and death" (Kselman and Barre, "Psalms," 541). Water can "denote . . . the abode of the dead (see Ps 107:26; Rom 10:7) or the final prison of Satan and the demons (Rev 20:3). It is used often in the LXX [as] . . . the symbol of chaos and

disorder" (Fitzmyer, *Gospel According to Luke 1–19*, 739 note 31). It is the "place of final punishment for demons," according to C. S. Mann (*Mark*, 279). See Firmage, "Zoology," 6:1132; Williamson, *Mark*, 104; Clarke, *Holy Bible with a Commentary and Critical Notes*, 5:420; Freyne, "Sea of Galilee," 2:900; Morris, *Luke*, 171; and Liefeld, "Luke," 8:913.

43. Habershon, *Study of the Types*, 42. See John 12:23–24.
44. Both President Brigham Young and President Spencer W. Kimball taught that resurrection is a priesthood ordinance (see Brigham Young, 24 August 1872, in *Journal of Discourses*, 15:137–39; and *Church News*, "Conference Issues," 1970–1987, 12).
45. See Ryken, Wilhoit, and Longman, *Dictionary of Biblical Imagery*, 583.
46. See ibid.; and McConkie and Parry, *Guide to Scriptural Symbols*, 113, 175.
47. See McConkie and Parry, *Guide to Scriptural Symbols*, 113, 176.
48. Pike, "Theophoric Names," 4:1018.
49. *Tetragrammaton* is a Greek word that means literally "four letters." It is the four-letter Hebrew name for God, traditionally written YHWH.
50. See Pike, "Theophoric Names," 4:1018. It is worth noting that in the Book of Mormon there appear names that are technically theophoric, but which do not employ the root of either YHWH or El. In the biblical text such theophoric names are traditionally efforts to venerate pagan deities. In the Book of Mormon, however, they appear referential to Jehovah but also serve as evidence of a strong Egyptian influence. One prime example of this is the name Ammon, which means "the one who is not known, the secret one whom we can't name, whose name is not known to us." Ammon, Amon, or Amun was the great and universal god of the Egyptian empire. It was also the most common name among the Nephites. Anciently the name was frequently used in the building of other Egyptian names, Omni being a good example of this, as it means "he who belongs to Amon" (Nibley, *Lehi in the Desert, World of the Jaredites, There Were Jaredites*, 25; and Nibley, *Approach to the Book of Mormon*, 286). Elder McConkie wrote: "Since God revealed himself to Adam by certain names, we might suppose that those names, or variants of them, would be preserved among succeeding generations, even though people coming later developed false religions. It is, also, not uncommon for important names to be carried from one language to another by transliteration rather than translation. Hence, it is of more than passing interest to note that the Egyptians worshiped a deity, considered by them to be supreme, whose name bears a striking resemblance to that of the true God, as his name was recorded in the Adamic language. The Egyptian deity Ammon, or Amon, or Amen (who corresponds to Zeus of the Greeks and Jupiter of the Romans) was first worshiped as the local deity of Thebes; he was shown as a ramheaded god of life and reproduction. Later, united with the sun-god to become a supreme deity, he was known as Amen-Ra, with the other gods as his members or parts. It is also interesting to note that Amen, a transliterated word which is the same in Egyptian, Hebrew, Latin, Greek, Anglo-Saxon, and English, is one of the names of Christ. Speaking

to John on the isle of Patmos, our Lord said: 'These things saith the Amen, the faithful and true witness, the beginning of the creation of God.' (Rev. 3:14)" (*Mormon Doctrine,* 29–30; see Nibley, *Teachings of the Book of Mormon,* semester 1, lecture 7, 7; and semester 1, lecture 26, 11).

51. Pike, "Theophoric Names," 4:1019.
52. See Horsely, "Names, Double," 4:1016.
53. In their book *Guide to Scriptural Symbols* (175–88), McConkie and Parry offer a fairly extensive list of theophoric names.
54. See Romney, "Temples—The Gates to Heaven," 16.
55. His miracles include healing a bitter spring, dividing the waters of the river Jordan, providing water for the people and livestock to drink, multiplying a widow's oil and meal, raising a boy from the dead, curing Naaman of leprosy, purifying a poisonous batch of pottage, and causing an iron ax head to float.
56. LDS Bible Dictionary, s.v. "Israel," 708.
57. Smith, *Teachings of the Prophet Joseph Smith,* 365.
58. Lundwall, *Lectures on Faith,* 6:5–7.
59. See Peterson, "P. T. Barnum *Redivivus,*" 87. Equally inaccurate, but with good intent, was a statement in the 1970s comedy *Out of the Mouth of Babes.* In that short film one LDS child was asked the question, "Where does God live?" The six- or seven-year-old child responded, "God lives in colon." Although the child's response is also wrong, it is scarcely more ridiculous than the declaration that "God lives on the Star Base Planet Kolob."
60. See Skinner, "Book of Abraham," 16–22; McConkie, "Heavens Testify of Christ," 240; and McConkie, *Gospel Symbolism,* 7–8.
61. McConkie, "Heavens Testify of Christ," 243.
62. Regarding the meaning of the word *Kolob,* Hugh Nibley has written: "Joseph Smith's spelling [of Kolob] is also notable, since it is a rather good attempt to render the Sephardic sounds phonetically. . . . *Kolob* is the common Semitic word for star, but of unkommon [sic.] origin; its original meaning is usually taken to have been 'to glisten, be lustrous, bright,' though it also has the root meaning 'to be dispersed,' and refer to the source of something—a well or a spring. In Arabic it signifies 'a star, an asterism, a constellation.'" (*Three Facsimiles,* 71–72). Symbolically speaking, this linguistic definition of the word only serves to strengthen the argument that Kolob is a detailed representation of Christ.
63. See Read, *Unveiling Biblical Prophecy,* 44. By the metaphorical phrase "gather his heavensent nourishment," I do not intend to imply solely acceptance of the fulness of the Gospel of Jesus Christ—although that is the major symbolic representation. Specifically, any who have listened to and heeded the promptings of the light of Christ or the Holy Ghost are partakers of some portion of the "heavensent manna." When Christ returns, these people will be living at least a terrestrial law, if not celestial, and thus will abide the day of his coming. Those who refused to gather

manna in Moses' day died. Spiritually speaking, those who refuse to gather the "heavenly manna" in our day (whether by rejecting the fulness of the gospel when the Spirit witnesses of its truths, or by living contrary to the dictates of their conscience or the Spirit) die to the things of God, and will be destroyed at Christ's coming.

64. Hinckley, in Conference Report, April 1990, 69.
65. See the discussion regarding directions in chapter 7 of this work.
66. See McConkie, *Angels*, 59.
67. See McConkie, *Mormon Doctrine*, 702–3.
68. See Myers, *Eerdmans Bible Dictionary*, 924; Unger, *Bible Dictionary*, 996; Douglas, *New Bible Dictionary*, 1161; and McKenzie, *Dictionary of the Bible*, 789.
69. See Draper, *Opening the Seven Seals*, 121; Bullinger, *Number in Scripture*, 151; Smith, *Book of Revelation*, 288; and Johnston, *Numbers in the Bible*, 67. Curiously, one scholar interprets the Hebrew word for "seraph" as meaning spirits in a state much like that of the Holy Ghost (see Douglas, *New Bible Dictionary*, 1161).
70. See Fairbairn, *Typology of Scripture*, 1:227; see also 1:218, 221, 223.
71. See Myers, *Eerdmans Bible Dictionary*, 204.
72. See Unger, *Bible Dictionary*, 192; *Random House Webster's College Dictionary*, s.v., "cherub," 233; and Douglas, *New Bible Dictionary*, 208–9.
73. McConkie, *Gospel Symbolism*, 256. McConkie draws on D&C 132:19. See also McConkie, *Mormon Doctrine*, 192.
74. McConkie, *Angels*, 75. McConkie does indicate that cherubs "symbolize the presence of Jehovah" (ibid.), and that, to his mind, D&C 109:79 "infers that the name *seraphs* may apply to angels other than pre-mortal spirit children of the Eternal Father" (ibid., 76). See Douglas, *New Bible Dictionary*, 208.
75. Similarly, Alma wrote: "What does the scripture mean, which saith that God placed cherubim and a flaming sword on the east of the garden of Eden, lest our first parents should enter and partake of the fruit of the tree of life, and live forever? . . . There was a space granted unto man in which he might repent; therefore this life became a probationary state; a time to prepare to meet God; a time to prepare for that endless state which has been spoken of by us, which is after the resurrection of the dead" (see Alma 12:21–27).
76. See McConkie, *Gospel Symbolism*, 274. See also Cooper, *Encyclopaedia of Traditional Symbols*, 178. Joseph Fielding McConkie also noted that "the Tree of Life . . . contained the power of everlasting life" (*Gospel Symbolism*, 274).
77. Thomas, "Jacob's Allegory," 13.
78. Julien, *Mammoth Dictionary of Symbols*, 162. See Cirlot, *Dictionary of Symbols*, 347.
79. Black, "Behold, I Have Dreamed a Dream," 123 note 7.

80. See Fairbairn, *Typology of Scripture*, 2:208.
81. See Julien, *Mammoth Dictionary of Symbols*, 149–50.
82. See McConkie, *Gospel Symbolism*, 259. See also Cooper, *Encyclopaedia of Traditional Symbols*, 66–67; Todeschi, *Encyclopedia of Symbolism*, 108; and Fontana, *Secret Language of Symbols*, 139.
83. See Barth, *Ephesians 4–6*, 800; McConkie and Parry, *Guide to Scriptural Symbols*, 102; McConkie, *Gospel Symbolism*, 272–73; Cirlot, *Dictionary of Symbols*, 324; and Ephesians 6:17; Hebrews 4:12; Revelation 1:16; 19:15; 1 Nephi 21:2; D&C 6:2; 27:18.
84. See Cooper, *Encyclopaedia of Traditional Symbols*, 167; and Fontana, *Secret Language of Symbols*, 72.
85. See Todeschi, *Encyclopedia of Symbolism*, 250.
86. Bayley, *Lost Language of Symbolism*, 2:74.
87. Young, *Discourses of Brigham Young*, 416.
88. "Apocalypse of Daniel," 1:755–770; see chapters 13 and 14 of this "Apocalypse" in their entirety. See also Nibley, *Since Cumorah*, 155–56.
89. Stuy, *Collected Discourses*, vol. 5, 5 October 1896.
90. See Nibley, "Expanding Gospel," 12; Nibley, *Ancient Documents and the Pearl of Great Price*, lecture 6, 9; and Nibley, *Since Cumorah*, 155–56.
91. Nibley, *Ancient Documents and the Pearl of Great Price*, lecture 19, 3.
92. Brown, "Nag Hammadi Library," 260.
93. See Gordon, *Before the Bible*, 16–17, cited in Nibley, *Since Cumorah*, 155. The presence of such items in ancient, yet extracanonical, texts is a testament to the inspiration of the Prophet Joseph and his successor, President Brigham Young; these prophets would not have had access to these traditions, yet appropriately the tripartite messengers are central to the endowment story line.
94. Passages such as D&C 129:6–7 add to this concern; we are told that Satan and his hosts cannot fake physical touch, nor can spirits who have yet to be born into a body or who have died and are yet to be resurrected. Only resurrected or translated beings have the ability to have physical contact with mortals (see Smith, *Answers to Gospel Questions*, 2:44).
95. Cowley, *Talks on Doctrine*, 46. See Turner, "Doctrine of the Firstborn and Only Begotten," 96; Young, in *Journal of Discourses*, 6:224–25; McConkie, *Doctrinal New Testament Commentary*, 1:766; and McConkie, *Promised Messiah*, 114.
96. This appearance took place some time between May and June of 1829 (see Porter, "Restoration of the Priesthood," 1–12).
97. Addison Everett letter, cited in Oliver Boardman Huntington Journal.
98. Smith, *Words of Joseph Smith*, 8.
99. Andrew F. Ehat, "Temple Ordinances and the Succession Question," 256 note 86.
100. See Robinson, "God the Father," 2:548.

Notes to Chapter 11: Types of Christ

101. See Thayer, *Greek-English Lexicon*, 270; Smith and Cornwall, *Exhaustive Dictionary of Bible Names*, 257; and LDS Bible Dictionary, s.v. "Zebedee," 791.
102. See Filson, "Who Was the Beloved Disciple?" 83–88; Tenney, "Gospel of John," 9:140; and Titus, "Identity of the Beloved Disciple," 323–28.
103. See Welch, *Sermon at the Temple*, 14–83.
104. McConkie, *Mortal Messiah*, 3:186–87.
105. McConkie, *Promised Messiah*, 378, 453.

BIBLIOGRAPHY

ANCIENT SOURCES

"The Apocalypse of Daniel." In *The Old Testament Pseudepigrapha*, 1:755–70. Edited by James H. Charlesworth. 2 vols. New York: Doubleday, 1983.

Augustine. *City of God.* In *Great Books of the Western World*, 129 618. Edited by Robert Maynard Hutchins. Chicago: Encyclopaedia Britannica, 1982.

———. *On Christian Doctrine.* In *Great Books of the Western World*, 619–98. Edited by Robert Maynard Hutchins. Chicago: Encyclopaedia Britannica, 1982.

———. *Trinity, The.* Translated by Stephen McKenna. Washington: Catholic University of America Press, 1970.

The Book of Jasher. Salt Lake City: J. H. Parry and Company, 1887.

Bray, Gerald, ed. *Ancient Christian Commentary on Scripture: New Testament Volume 8, 1–2 Corinthians.* Downers Grove, Ill.: InterVarsity Press, 1999.

Charlesworth, James H., ed. *The Old Testament Pseudepigrapha.* 2 vols. Garden City, N.Y.: Doubleday, 1983.

Clement of Alexandria. "Fragments from Cassiodorus." In *The Ante-Nicene Fathers*, 2:569–77. Edited by Alexander Roberts and James Donaldson. 10 vols. Peabody, Mass.: Hendrickson Publishers, 1994.

———. "The Instructor." In *The Ante-Nicene Fathers*, 2:207–96. Edited by Alexander Roberts and James Donaldson. 10 vols. Peabody, Mass: Hendrickson Publishers, 1994.

———. "Stromata." In *The Ante-Nicene Fathers*, 2:299–567. Edited by Alexander Roberts and James Donaldson. 10 vols. Peabody, Mass.. Hendrickson Publishers, 1994.

"Constitution of the Holy Apostles." In *The Ante-Nicene Fathers*, 7:385–505. Edited by Alexander Roberts and James Donaldson. 10 vols. Peabody, Mass.: Hendrickson Publishers, 1994.

Cruse, C. F., trans. *Eusebius' Ecclesiastical History.* Peabody, Mass.: Hendrickson Publishers, 1998.

Cyprian of Carthage. "The Treatise of Cyprian." In *The Ante-Nicene Fathers*, 5:421–557. Edited by Alexander Roberts and James Donaldson. 10 vols. Peabody, Mass.: Hendrickson Publishers, 1994.

"Dialogue of the Savior." In *The Nag Hammadi Library in English*, 244–55. Edited by James M. Robinson. San Francisco: Harper and Row Publishers, 1988.

"The First Gospel of the Infancy of Jesus Christ." In *The Lost Books of the Bible*, 38–59. New York: Bell Publishing, 1979.

"Fragments from the Lost Writings of Irenaeus." In *The Ante-Nicene Fathers*, 1:568–78. Edited by Alexander Roberts and James Donaldson. 10 vols. Peabody, Mass.: Hendrickson Publishers, 1994.

Freedman, H., and M. Simons, eds. *The Midrash Rabbah*. London: Soncino Press, 1977.

"The General Epistle of Barnabas." In *The Ante-Nicene Fathers*, 1:133–49. Edited by Alexander Roberts and James Donaldson. 10 vols. Peabody, Mass: Hendrickson Publishers, 1994.

"The Gospel of Bartholomew." Cited in Hugh Nibley. *Mormonism and Early Christianity*, 49–50, 87. Provo, Utah: Foundation for Ancient Research and Mormon Studies, 1987.

Irenaeus. "Against Heresies." In *The Ante-Nicene Fathers*, 1:307–567. Edited by Alexander Roberts and James Donaldson. 10 vols. Peabody, Mass.: Hendrickson Publishers, 1994.

Josephus, Flavius. *The Complete Works of Josephus*. Translated by William Whiston. Grand Rapids, Mich.: Kregel Publications, 1981.

Justin Martyr. "Dialogue with Trypho." In *The Ante-Nicene Fathers*, 1:156–270. Edited by Alexander Roberts and James Donaldson. 10 vols. Peabody, Mass.: Hendrickson Publishers, 1994.

Maimonides, Moses. *Guide of the Perplexed*. Chicago: University of Chicago Press, 1963.

Migne, J. P., trans. "The Combat of Adam and Eve against Satan." In *Troisième et Dernière Encyclopédie Théologique*, 23:329–30. Paris: P. J. Migne, 1856. Cited in Hugh Nibley. *Enoch the Prophet*, 171–72. Provo, Utah: Foundation for Ancient Research and Mormon Studies, 1986.

Nachmanides, Ramban. *Commentary on the Torah*. Translated by Charles B. Chavel. 5 vols. New York: Shilo Publishing House, 1971–76.

Neusner, Jacob. *Genesis Rabbah*. 3 vols. Atlanta, Georgia: Scholars Press, 1985.

Origen. "De Principiis." In *The Ante-Nicene Fathers*, 4:239–382. Edited by Alexander Roberts and James Donaldson. 10 vols. Peabody, Mass.: Hendrickson Publishers, 1994.

———. "Homily on Leviticus." In Gilbert Cope, *Symbolism in the Bible and the Church*, 32. London: SCM Press, Ltd., 1959.

Philo of Alexandria. "De Sacrificiis Abelis et Cain." In *The Works of Philo: Complete and Unabridged*, 94–111. Translated by C. D. Yonge. Rev. ed. Peabody, Mass.: Hendrickson Publishers, 1997.

———. *The Works of Philo: Complete and Unabridged*. Translated by C. D. Yonge. Rev. ed. Peabody, Mass.: Hendrickson Publishers, 1997.

Plato: The Collected Dialogues. Translated by Edith Hamilton and Huntington Cairns. New Jersey: Princeton University Press, 1989.
Roberts, Alexander, and James Donaldson, eds. The Ante-Nicene Fathers. 10 vols. Peabody, Mass.: Hendrickson Publishers, 1994.
Robinson, James M., ed. The Nag Hammadi Library in English. San Francisco: Harper and Row Publishers, 1988.
Tertullian. "An Answer to the Jews." In The Ante-Nicene Fathers, 3:151–73. Edited by Alexander Roberts and James Donaldson. 10 vols. Peabody, Mass.: Hendrickson Publishers, 1994.
Thaumaturgus, Gregory. "Four Homilies." In The Ante-Nicene Fathers, 6:58–71. Edited by Alexander Roberts and James Donaldson. 10 vols. Peabody, Mass.: Hendrickson Publishers, 1994.
"Thomas' Gospel of the Infancy of Jesus Christ." In The Lost Books of the Bible, 60–62. New York: Bell Publishing, 1979.
Victorinus. "Commentary on the Apocalypse of the Blessed John." In The Ante-Nicene Fathers, 7:344–60. Edited by Alexander Roberts and James Donaldson. 10 vols. Peabody, Mass.: Hendrickson Publishers, 1994.
Winston, David A., trans. Philo of Alexandria: The Contemplative Life, The Giants, and Selections. New York: Paulist Press, 1981.

ARTICLES

Adams, Lisa Ramsey. "Eternal Progression." In Encyclopedia of Mormonism, 2:465–66. Edited by Daniel H. Ludlow. 4 vols. New York: Macmillan, 1992.
Alexander, Ralph. "Ezekiel." In The Expositor's Bible Commentary, 6:737–996. Edited by Frank E. Gaebelein. 12 vols. Grand Rapids, Mich.: Zondervan, 1976–92.
Alsup, John. "Typology." In The Anchor Bible Dictionary, 6:682–85. Edited by David Noel Freedman. 6 vols. New York: Doubleday, 1992.
Anderson, Richard Lloyd. "Oliver Cowdery." In Encyclopedia of Mormonism, 1:335–40. Edited by Daniel H. Ludlow. 4 vols. New York: Macmillan, 1992.
———. "Parallel Prophets: Paul and Joseph Smith." In Ensign, March 1985, 12–17.
Ballard, Melvin J. In Conference Report, October 1910, 78–85.
Ballif, Jae R. "Melchizedek Priesthood." In Encyclopedia of Mormonism, 2:882–85. Edited by Daniel H. Ludlow. 4 vols. New York: Macmillan, 1992.
Banwell, B. O. "Neck." In The New Bible Dictionary, 874. Edited by J. D. Douglass. Grand Rapids, Mich.: Eerdmans, 1971.
Barclay, William. "Great Themes of the New Testament." In The Expository Times 70 (1959): 292–96.

Barr, James. "Biblical Theology." In *Interpreter's Dictionary of the Bible.* Supplementary volume: 104–11. Nashville: Abingdon Press, 1976.
Beck, Astrid Billes. "Rebekah." In *The Anchor Bible Dictionary,* 5:629–30. Edited by David Noel Freedman. 6 vols. New York: Doubleday, 1992.
Bedford, Peter. "Adalia." In *The Anchor Bible Dictionary,* 1:61–62. Edited by David Noel Freedman. 6 vols. New York: Doubleday, 1992.
———. "Vaizatha." In *The Anchor Bible Dictionary,* 6:781. Edited by David Noel Freedman. 6 vols. New York: Doubleday, 1992.
Bennett, William Henry. "Number." In *Dictionary of the Bible,* 701–4. Edited by James Hastings. New York: Charles Scribner's Sons, 1963.
Berrett, Lamar C. "Endowment Houses." In *Encyclopedia of Mormonism,* 2:456. Edited by Daniel H. Ludlow. 4 vols. New York: Macmillan, 1992.
Bickmore, Barry. "Clearing Up Misconceptions," a review of Patrick Madrid, *Pope Fiction: Answers to 30 Myths and Misconceptions about the Papacy.* In *FARMS Review of Books* 13, no. 2 (2001): 197–99.
Birch, B. C. "Number." In *The International Standard Bible Encyclopedia,* 3:556–61. Edited by Geoffrey W. Bromiley. 4 vols. Grand Rapids, Mich.: Eerdmans, 1979.
Black, Susan Easton. "Behold, I Have Dreamed a Dream." In *The Book of Mormon: First Nephi, the Doctrinal Foundation,* 113–24. Edited by Monte S. Nyman and Charles D. Tate Jr. Provo, Utah: Religious Studies Center, Brigham Young University, 1988.
Boadt, Lawrence. "Ezekiel." In *The New Jerome Biblical Commentary,* 305–28. Edited by Raymond E. Brown, Joseph A. Fitzmyer, and Roland E. Murphy. Englewood Cliffs, N.J.: Prentice Hall, 1990.
Bowman, Raymond A., and Charles W. Gilkey. "The Book of Ezra and the Book of Nehemiah." In *The Interpreter's Bible,* 3:549–819. Edited by George Arthur Buttrick. 12 vols. Nashville: Abingdon Press, 1951–57.
Braund, David C. "Felix." In *The Anchor Bible Dictionary,* 2:783. Edited by David Noel Freedman. 6 vols. New York: Doubleday, 1992.
Brown, Cheryl. "Book of Mormon: Book of Alma." In *Encyclopedia of Mormonism,* 1:150–52. Edited by Daniel H. Ludlow. 4 vols. New York: Macmillan, 1992.
Brown, Hugh B. In Conference Report, October 1963, 85–89.
Brown, Raymond E., and Robert North. "Biblical Geography." In *The New Jerome Biblical Commentary,* 1175–95. Edited by Raymond E. Brown, Joseph A. Fitzmyer, and Roland E. Murphy. Englewood Cliffs, N.J.: Prentice Hall, 1990.
Brown, S. Kent. "The Nag Hammadi Library: A Mormon Perspective." In *Apocryphal Writings and the Latter-day Saints,* 260. Edited by C. Wilfred Griggs. Provo, Utah: Religious Studies Center, Brigham Young University, 1986.
Bulmer, Ralph. "The Uncleanliness of the Birds of Leviticus and Deuteronomy." In *Man* 24 (1989): 304–21.

Bushman, Richard L., and Dean C. Jessee. "Joseph Smith." In *Encyclopedia of Mormonism*, 3:1331–48. Edited by Daniel H. Ludlow. 4 vols. New York: Macmillan, 1992.

Butler, John M. "The 'Author' and the 'Finisher' of the Book of Mormon." In *The Book of Mormon: Fourth Nephi through Moroni, From Zion to Destruction*. Edited by Monte S. Nyman and Charles D. Tate Jr. Provo, Utah: Religious Studies Center, Brigham Young University, 1995, 61–68.

Buttrick, George A. "Symbol." In *The Interpreter's Dictionary of the Bible*, 4:472–76. Edited by George A. Buttrick. 4 vols. New York: Abingdon Press, 1962.

Cardwell, Kenneth. "The Fish on the Fire: John 21:9." In *The Expository Times* 102 (October 1990): 12–14.

Carson, D. A. "Matthew." In *The Expositor's Bible Commentary*, 8:1–599. Edited by Frank E. Gaebelein. 12 vols. Grand Rapids, Mich.: Zondervan, 1976–92.

Church News. "Conference Issues," 1970–87.

Clark, E. Douglas. "Abraham." In *Encyclopedia of Mormonism*, 1:7–8. Edited by Daniel H. Ludlow. 4 vols. New York: Macmillan, 1992.

Clawson, Rudger. In Conference Report, April 1918, 32–35.

Clifford, Richard J. "The Temple and the Holy Mountain." In *Temple in Antiquity*. Edited by Truman G. Madsen. Provo, Utah: Religious Studies Center, Brigham Young University, 1984.

———, and Roland E. Murphy. "Genesis." In *The New Jerome Biblical Commentary*, 8–43. Edited by Raymond E. Brown, Joseph A. Fitzmyer, and Roland E. Murphy. Englewood Cliffs, N.J.: Prentice Hall, 1990.

Cole, R. A. "Colours." In *The New Bible Dictionary*, 244. Edited by J. D. Douglas. Grand Rapids, Mich.: Eerdmans, 1971.

Collins, John J. "Enoch." In *Harper's Bible Dictionary*, 267. Edited by Paul J. Achtemeier. San Francisco: Harper Collins Publishers, 1985.

Compton, Todd. "The Handclasp and Embrace as Tokens of Recognition." In *By Study and Also by Faith: Essays in Honor of Hugh W. Nibley on the Occasion of His Eightieth Birthday, 27 March 1990*, 1:611–42. Edited by John M. Lundquist and Stephen D. Ricks. 2 vols. Provo, Utah: Foundation for Ancient Research and Mormon Studies, 1990.

———. "Symbolism." In *Encyclopedia of Mormonism*, 3:1428–30. Edited by Daniel H. Ludlow. 4 vols. New York: Macmillan, 1992.

———. "The Whole Token: Mystery Symbolism in Classical Recognition Drama." In *Epoche* 13 (1985): 1–81.

Cundall, Arthur E. "Judges." In *Tyndale Old Testament Commentaries: Judges and Ruth*, 7–215. Edited by Arthur E. Cundall and Leon Morris. Downers Grove, Ill.: InterVarsity Press, 1968.

Drinkard, Joel F. "Direction and Orientation." In *The Anchor Bible Dictionary*, 2:204. Edited by David Noel Freedman. 6 vols. New York: Doubleday, 1992.

———. "East." In *The Anchor Bible Dictionary*, 2:248. Edited by David Noel Freedman. 6 vols. New York: Doubleday, 1992.

———. "North." In *The Anchor Bible Dictionary*, 4:1135–36. Edited by David Noel Freedman. 6 vols. New York: Doubleday, 1992.

———. "Numbers." In *Harper's Bible Dictionary*, 711–12. Edited by Paul J. Achtemeier. San Francisco: Harper Collins Publishers, 1985.

———. "South." In *The Anchor Bible Dictionary*, 6:171. Edited by David Noel Freedman. 6 vols. New York: Doubleday, 1992.

———. "West." In *The Anchor Bible Dictionary*, 6:908. Edited by David Noel Freedman. 6 vols. New York: Doubleday, 1992.

Edelman, Diana V. "Saul." In *The Anchor Bible Dictionary*, 5:989–99. Edited by David Noel Freedman. 6 vols. New York: Doubleday, 1992.

Edwards, Douglas R. "Dress and Ornamentation." In *The Anchor Bible Dictionary*, 2:232–38. Edited by David Noel Freedman. 6 vols. New York: Doubleday, 1992.

Eichrodt, Walther. "Is Typological Exegesis an Appropriate Method?" In *Essays on Old Testament Hermeneutics*, 224–45. Edited by Claus Westermann. Richmond, Va.: John Knox Press, 1963.

Efird, James M. "Swaddling." In *Harper's Bible Dictionary*, 1001–2. Edited by Paul J. Achtemeier. San Francisco: Harper Collins Publishers, 1985.

Ellsworth, Richard G. "The Literary Artistry of the Parables of Jesus." In *A Symposium on the New Testament*, 74–77. Provo: Brigham Young University, 14–16 August 1980.

Emmet, Cyril W. "Head." In *Dictionary of the Bible*, 368. Edited by James Hastings. New York: Charles Scribner's Sons, 1963.

Everett, Addison. Letter to Oliver B. Huntington, 17 February 1881. Cited in Oliver Boardman Huntington Journal, #14, 31 January 1881 (backdated).

Ewing, W. "Hair." In *Dictionary of the Bible*, 359–60. Edited by James Hastings. New York: Charles Scribner's Sons, 1963.

———. "Nose, Nostrils." In *Dictionary of the Bible*, 701. Edited by James Hastings. New York: Charles Scribner's Sons, 1963.

Filson, Floyd V. "Who Was the Beloved Disciple?" In *Journal of Biblical Literature* 68, no. 2 (June 1949): 83–88.

Firmage, Edwin. "Zoology." In *The Anchor Bible Dictionary*, 6:1109–67. Edited by David Noel Freedman. 6 vols. New York: Doubleday, 1992.

Freyne, Sean. "The Sea of Galilee." In *The Anchor Bible Dictionary*, 2:899–901. Edited by David Noel Freedman. 6 vols. New York: Doubleday, 1992.

Friberg, Joran. "Numbers and Counting." In *The Anchor Bible Dictionary*, 4:1139–46. Edited by David Noel Freedman. 6 vols. New York: Doubleday, 1992.

Gibbons, Francis M. In Conference Report, April 1991, 39–42; or *Ensign*, May 1991, 32–33.

Gillman, John. "Fortunatus." In *The Anchor Bible Dictionary*, 2:852–53. Edited by David Noel Freedman. 6 vols. New York: Doubleday, 1992.

———. "Quartus." In *The Anchor Bible Dictionary*, 5:583. Edited by David Noel Freedman. 6 vols. New York: Doubleday, 1992.

Goff, Alan. "Boats, Beginnings, and Repetitions." In *Journal of Book of Mormon Studies*, 1, no. 1 (Fall 1992): 67–84.

Green, Joel B. "Festus, Porcius." In *The Anchor Bible Dictionary*, 2:794–95. Edited by David Noel Freedman. 6 vols. New York: Doubleday, 1992.

Grieve, Matthew. "Matthew." In *A Commentary on the Bible*, 700–723. Edited by Arthur S. Peake. New York: Thomas Nelson and Sons, 1919.

Grogan, Geoffrey W. "Isaiah." In *The Expositor's Bible Commentary*, 6:1–354. Edited by Frank E. Gaebelein. 12 vols. Grand Rapids, Mich.: Zondervan, 1976–92.

Harris, James R. "The Book of Abraham Facsimiles." In *Studies in Scripture, Vol. 2: The Pearl of Great Price*, 247–86. Edited by Robert L. Millet and Kent P. Jackson. Salt Lake City: Randall Book, 1985.

Harris, Murray J. "2 Corinthians." In *The Expositor's Bible Commentary*, 10:299–406. Edited by Frank E. Gaebelein. 12 vols. Grand Rapids, Mich.: Zondervan, 1976–92.

Hinckley, Gordon B. In Conference Report, April 1990, 65–69; or *Ensign*, May 1990, 49–52.

Holland, Jeffrey R. In Conference Report, April 1999, 15–19. Or *Ensign*, May 1999, 14–16.

———. "Of Souls, Symbols, and Sacraments." Brigham Young University devotional address, 12 January 1988.

Holzapfel, Richard Neitzel. "Mormon, the Man and the Message." In *The Book of Mormon: Fourth Nephi through Moroni, From Zion to Destruction*. Edited by Monte S. Nyman and Charles D. Tate Jr. Provo, Utah: Religious Studies Center, Brigham Young University, 1995, 117–31.

Horsely, G. H. R. "Names, Double." In *The Anchor Bible Dictionary*, 4:1011–17. Edited by David Noel Freedman. 6 vols. New York: Doubleday, 1992.

Horton, George, Jr. "Book of Mormon—Transmission from Translator to Printed Text." In *The Book of Mormon: The Keystone Scripture*, 237–55. Edited by Paul R. Cheesman. Provo, Utah: Religious Studies Center, Brigham Young University, 1988.

———. "Joseph Smith—Matthew: Profiting from Prophecy." In *The Pearl of Great Price: Revelations from God*, 197–212. Edited by H. Donl Peterson and Charles D. Tate Jr. Provo, Utah: Religious Studies Center, Brigham Young University, 1989.

Hoskisson, Paul Y. "An Introduction to the Relevance of and a Methodology for a Study of the Proper Names of the Book of Mormon." In *By Study and Also by Faith: Essays in Honor of Hugh W. Nibley on the Occasion of His Eightieth Birthday, 27 March 1990*, 2:126–35. Edited by John M. Lundquist and Stephen D. Ricks. 2 vols. Provo, Utah: Foundation for Ancient Research and Mormon Studies, 1990.

Humphreys, W. Lee. "Esther." In *Harper's Bible Dictionary*, 280–82. Edited by Paul J. Achtemeier. San Francisco: Harper Collins Publishers, 1985.

Hyatt, Philip J. "Dress." In *Dictionary of the Bible*, 222–25. Edited by James Hastings. New York: Charles Scribner's Sons, 1963.

Ivins, Anthony W. In Conference Report, October 1914, 91–96.

Jackson, Kent P. "The Marriage of Hosea and Jehovah's Covenant with Israel." In *Isaiah and the Prophets: Inspired Voices from the Old Testament*, 57–75. Edited by Monte S. Nyman. Provo, Utah: Religious Studies Center, Brigham Young University, 1984.

Jensen, Joseph, and William H. Irwin. "Isaiah 1–39." In *The New Jerome Biblical Commentary*, 229–48. Edited by Raymond E. Brown, Joseph A. Fitzmyer, and Roland E. Murphy. Englewood Cliffs, N.J.: Prentice Hall, 1990.

Jessee, Dean C. "The Kirtland Diary of Wilford Woodruff." In *BYU Studies* 12, no. 4 (1972): 365–99.

Jewett, Paul. "Concerning the Allegorical Interpretation of Scripture." In *Westminster Theological Journal*, 17 (1954): 1–20.

Johnson, Alan. "Revelation." In *The Expositor's Bible Commentary*, 12:397–603. Edited by Frank E. Gaebelein. 12 vols. Grand Rapids, Mich.: Zondervan, 1976–92.

Jones, Daniel. "The Martyrdom of Joseph Smith and His Brother Hyrum." In *BYU Studies* 24, no. 1 (Winter 1984): 78–109.

Jorgensen, Bruce W. "The Dark Way to the Tree: Typological Unity in the Book of Mormon." In *Literature of Belief: Sacred Scripture and Religious Experience*, 217–31. Edited by Neal E. Lambert. Provo, Utah: Religious Studies Center, Brigham Young University, 1981.

Kselman, John S., and Michael L. Barre. "Psalms." In *The New Jerome Biblical Commentary*, 523–52. Edited by Raymond E. Brown, Joseph A. Fitzmyer, and Roland E. Murphy. Englewood Cliffs, N.J.: Prentice Hall, 1990.

Lassetter, Courtney J. "Dispensations of the Gospel." In *Encyclopedia of Mormonism*, 1:388–90. Edited by Daniel H. Ludlow. 4 vols. New York: Macmillan, 1992.

Lategan, Bernard C. "Hermeneutics." In *The Anchor Bible Dictionary*, 3:150–54. Edited by David Noel Freedman. 6 vols. New York: Doubleday, 1992.

LDS Bible Dictionary. Salt Lake City: The Church of Jesus Christ of Latter-day Saints, 1979.

Lee, Harold B. *Feet Shod with the Preparation of the Gospel of Peace*, 2–7. Brigham Young University Speeches of the Year. Provo, Utah: Brigham Young University, 1954.

Lee, Robert England. "Truly All Things Testify of Him." In *The Lord of the Gospels: The 1990 Sperry Symposium on the New Testament*, 99–112. Edited by Bruce A. Van Orden and Brent L. Top. Salt Lake City: Deseret Book, 1991.

Lewis, Theodore J. "Beelzebul." In *The Anchor Bible Dictionary*, 1:638–40. Edited by David Noel Freedman. 6 vols. New York: Doubleday, 1992.

Liefeld, Walter L. "Luke." In *The Expositor's Bible Commentary*, 8:795–1059.

Edited by Frank E. Gaebelein. 12 vols. Grand Rapids, Mich.: Zondervan, 1976–92.

Lobban, Richard A., Jr. "Pigs and Their Prohibition." In *International Journal of Middle East Studies*, 26 (1994): 57–75.

Lund, Gerald N. "Understanding Scriptural Symbols." In *Ensign*, October 1986, 23–27.

Madsen, Truman G. "'Putting on the Names': A Jewish-Christian Legacy." In *By Study and Also by Faith: Essays in Honor of Hugh W. Nibley on the Occasion of His Eightieth Birthday, 27 March 1990*, 1:458–81. Edited by John M. Lundquist and Stephen D. Ricks. 2 vols. Provo, Utah: Foundation for Ancient Research and Mormon Studies, 1990.

Marshall, Evelyn T. "Garments." In *Encyclopedia of Mormonism*, 2:534–35. Edited by Daniel H. Ludlow. 4 vols. New York: Macmillan, 1992.

Martin, Thomas W. "Tertullus." In *The Anchor Bible Dictionary*, 6:391. Edited by David Noel Freedman. 6 vols. New York: Doubleday, 1992.

Martin-Achard, Robert. "Isaac." In *The Anchor Bible Dictionary*, 3:462–70. Edited by David Noel Freedman. 6 vols. New York: Doubleday, 1992.

Matthews, Robert J. "Jesus Christ in the Scriptures: Jesus Christ in the Bible." In *Encyclopedia of Mormonism*, 2:745–48. Edited by Daniel H. Ludlow. 4 vols. New York: Macmillan, 1992.

McConkie, Bruce R. "The Bible—A Sealed Book." In *Church Educational System Symposium*, Brigham Young University, 17 August 1984. Reprinted in *Doctrines of the Restoration: Sermons and Writings of Bruce R. McConkie*, 276–98. Edited by Mark L. McConkie. Salt Lake City: Bookcraft, 1989.

McConkie, Joseph Fielding. "The Heavens Testify of Christ." In *Studies in Scripture, Vol. 2: The Pearl of Great Price*, 235–45. Edited by Robert L. Millet and Kent P. Jackson. Salt Lake City: Randall Books, 1985.

———. "Joseph Smith as Found in Ancient Manuscripts." In *Isaiah and the Prophets: Inspired Voices from the Old Testament*, 11–30. Edited by Monte S. Nyman. Provo, Utah: Religious Studies Center, Brigham Young University, 1984.

———. "The Preparation of Prophets." In *The Pearl of Great Price: Revelations from God*, 73–90. Edited by H. Donl Peterson and Charles D. Tate Jr. Provo, Utah: Religious Studies Center, Brigham Young University, 1989.

McCurdy, J. F. "North Country, Land of the North." In *Dictionary of the Bible*, 701. Edited by James Hastings. New York: Charles Scribner's Sons, 1963.

McEleney, Neil J. "153 Great Fishes (John 21:11): Gematriacal Atbash." In *Biblica* 58, no. 3 (1977): 411–17.

McKenna, John. "Vashti." In *The Anchor Bible Dictionary*, 6:785. Edited by David Noel Freedman. 6 vols. New York: Doubleday, 1992.

Meyers, Carol. "Apron." In *The Anchor Bible Dictionary*, 1:318–19. Edited by David Noel Freedman. 6 vols. New York: Doubleday, 1992.

Middleton, Michael W. "Paul Among the Prophets: Obtaining a Crown." In *The Apostle Paul: His Life and His Testimony—The 23rd Annual Sidney B.*

Sperry Symposium, 110–31. Edited by Paul Y. Hoskisson. Salt Lake City: Deseret Book, 1994.

Millet, Robert L. "Alma 2." In *Encyclopedia of Mormonism*, 1:33–35. Edited by Daniel H. Ludlow. 4 vols. New York: Macmillan, 1992.

Mouritsen, Robert G. "I Have a Question: Is Christ the Redeemer of Other Worlds?" In *Ensign*, April 1976, 31–32.

Muirhead, L. A. "Numbers." In *Dictionary of the Apostolic Church*, 2:92–96. Edited by James Hastings. 2 vols. New York: Charles Scribner's Sons, 1915, 1918.

Nelson, Russell M. In Conference Report, April 1993, 49–53; or *Ensign*, May 1993, 38–41.

Nibley, Hugh. "Book of Mormon: Near Eastern Background." In *Encyclopedia of Mormonism*, 1:187–90. Edited by Daniel H. Ludlow. 4 vols. New York: Macmillan, 1992.

———. "Commencement Speech." Brigham Young University, 19 August 1983.

———. "Evangelium Quadraginta Dierum: The Forty-day Mission of Christ—The Forgotten Heritage." In *Mormonism and Early Christianity*, 10–44. Edited by Todd M. Compton and Stephen D. Ricks. Provo, Utah: Foundation for Ancient Research and Mormon Studies, 1987.

———. "The Expanding Gospel." In *BYU Studies* 7, no. 1 (Autumn 1965): 3–27.

———. "Men of the East." In *Lehi in the Desert, The World of the Jaredites, There Were Jaredites*, 25–42. Provo, Utah: Foundation for Ancient Research and Mormon Studies, 1988.

———. "On the Sacred and the Symbolic." In *Temples of the Ancient World*, 535–621. Edited by Donald W. Parry. Provo, Utah: Foundation for Ancient Research and Mormon Studies, 1994.

———. "Proper Names in the Book of Mormon." In *An Approach to the Book of Mormon*, 281–94. Provo, Utah: Foundation for Ancient Research and Mormon Studies, 1988.

Nyman, Monte S. "The Contribution of the JST to Understanding the Old Testament Prophets." In *The Joseph Smith Translation: The Restoration of Plain and Precious Things*, 121–45. Edited by Monte S. Nyman and Robert L. Millet. Provo, Utah: Religious Studies Center, Brigham Young University, 1985.

Ostler, Blake. "Clothed Upon: A Unique Aspect of Christian Antiquity." In *BYU Studies* 22, no. 1 (Winter 1982): 31–45.

Owen, O. T. "One Hundred and Fifty Three Fishes." In *The Expository Times* 100 (July 1989): 52–54.

Packer, Boyd K. In Conference Report, October 1984, 81–85; or *Ensign*, November 1984, 66–69.

Palmer, F. H. "Head." In *The New Bible Dictionary*, 508–9. Edited by J. D. Douglas. Grand Rapids, Mich.: Eerdmans, 1971.

Parry, Donald W. "Garden of Eden: Prototype Sanctuary." In *Temples of the*

Ancient World, 126–51. Edited by Donald W. Parry. Provo, Utah: Foundation for Ancient Research and Mormon Studies, 1994.

Peterson, Daniel C. "P. T. Barnum *Redivivus*." In *Review of Books on the Book of Mormon*, vol. 7, no. 2 (1995): 38–105. Edited by Daniel Peterson. Provo, Utah: Foundation for Ancient Research and Mormon Studies.

Pike, Dana M. "Names." In *Harper's Bible Dictionary*, 682–84. Edited by Paul J. Achtemeier. San Francisco: Harper Collins Publishers, 1985.

———. "Theophoric Names." In *The Anchor Bible Dictionary*, 4:1018–19. Edited by David Noel Freedman. 6 vols. New York: Doubleday, 1992.

Pope, M. H. "Number, Numbering, Numbers." In *The Interpreter's Dictionary of the Bible*, 3:561–67. Edited by George A. Buttrick. 4 vols. New York: Abingdon Press, 1962.

Porter, Bruce H., and Stephen D. Ricks. "Names in Antiquity: Old, New, and Hidden." In *By Study and Also by Faith: Essays in Honor of Hugh W. Nibley on the Occasion of His Eightieth Birthday, 27 March 1990*, 1:501–22. Edited by John M. Lundquist and Stephen D. Ricks. 2 vols. Provo, Utah: Foundation for Ancient Research and Mormon Studies, 1990.

Porter, Larry C. "The Restoration of the Priesthood." In *Brigham Young University Religious Studies Center Newsletter* 9, no. 3 (May 1995): 1–12.

Pratt, Orson. In *Journal of Discourses*, 3:344–54. 26 vols. London: Latter-day Saints' Book Depot, 1854–86.

Rad, Gerhard von. "Typological Interpretation of the Old Testament." In *Essays on Old Testament Hermeneutics*, 17–39. Edited by Claus Westermann. Richmond, Va.: John Knox Press, 1963.

Richards, Franklin D. "Memories of Carthage Jail." In *Contributor* 7, no. 8 (May 1886): 299–300.

———. "Temple Manifestations of the Spirit." In *Collected Discourses Delivered by President Wilford Woodruff, His Two Counselors, the Twelve Apostles, and Others*, 3:223–34. Compiled and edited by Brian H. Stuy. 5 vols. Burbank, Calif.: B. H. S. Publishing, 1987–92.

Rigdon, Sidney. "Perfection." In *Messenger and Advocate* 3 (November 1836): 406–8.

Robinson, Stephen E. "God the Father." In *Encyclopedia of Mormonism*, 2:548. Edited by Daniel H. Ludlow. 4 vols. New York: Macmillan, 1992.

Romeo, Joseph A. "Gematria and John 21:11—The Children of God." In *Journal of Biblical Literature* 97, no. 2 (1978): 263–64.

Romney, Marion G. "Jesus Christ: Lord of the Universe." In *Improvement Era*, November 1968, 46–48.

———. "Temples—The Gates to Heaven." In *Ensign*, March 1971, 12–16.

Ross, Allen P. "Proverbs." In *The Expositor's Bible Commentary*, 5:881–1134. Edited by Frank E. Gaebelein. 12 vols. Grand Rapids, Mich.: Zondervan, 1976–92.

Rust, Richard Dilworth, and Donald W. Parry. "Book of Mormon Literature."

In *Encyclopedia of Mormonism*, 1:181–85. Edited by Daniel H. Ludlow. 4 vols. New York: Macmillan, 1992.

Sailhamer, John H. "Genesis." In *The Expositor's Bible Commentary*, 2:1–284. Edited by Frank E. Gaebelein. 12 vols. Grand Rapids, Mich.: Zondervan, 1976–92.

Schweizer, R. Eduard. "Body." In *The Anchor Bible Dictionary*, 1:767–72. Edited by David Noel Freedman. 6 vols. New York: Doubleday, 1992.

Scott, Anderson C. "II Corinthians." In *A Commentary on the Bible*, 849–56. Edited by Arthur S. Peake. New York: Thomas Nelson and Sons, 1919.

Scott, Richard G. In Conference Report, October 1996, 100–104; or *Ensign*, November 1996, 73–75.

Segal, J. B. "Numerals in the Old Testament." In *Journal of Semitic Studies*, 10 (Spring 1965): 2–20.

Skinner, Andrew C. "The Book of Abraham: A Most Remarkable Book." In *Ensign*, March 1997, 16–22.

———. "Savior, Satan, and Serpent: The Duality of a Symbol in the Scriptures." In *The Disciple As Scholar: Essays on Scripture and the Ancient World, in Honor of Richard Lloyd Anderson*, 359–84. Edited by Stephen D. Ricks and Donald W. Parry. Provo, Utah: Foundation for Ancient Research and Mormon Studies, 2000.

Smith, Joseph Fielding. "Fall—Atonement—Resurrection—Sacrament." In *Charge to Religious Educators*, 124–28. 2d ed. Salt Lake City: The Church of Jesus Christ of Latter-day Saints, 1982.

Soler, Jean. "The Dietary Prohibitions of the Hebrews." In *New York Review of Books*, 14 June 1979, 24–30.

Taylor, John. "Man, the Offspring of God." In *Journal of Discourses*, 17:369–76.

Taylor, John. "Name, Names." In *Dictionary of the Bible*, 687–88. Edited by James Hastings. New York: Charles Scribner's Sons, 1963.

Tenney, Merrill C. "The Gospel of John." In *The Expositor's Bible Commentary*, 9:1–203. Edited by Frank E. Gaebelein. 12 vols. Grand Rapids, Mich.: Zondervan, 1976–92.

Thomas, M. Catherine. "Jacob's Allegory: The Mystery of Christ." In *The Allegory of the Olive Tree*, 11–20. Edited by Stephen D. Ricks and John W. Welch. Provo, Utah: Foundation for Ancient Research and Mormon Studies, 1994.

Thomasson, Gordon C. "What's in a Name? Book of Mormon Language, Names, and [Metonymic] Naming." In *Journal of Book of Mormon Studies* 3, no. 1 (Spring 1994): 1–27.

Titus, Eric L. "The Identity of the Beloved Disciple." In *Journal of Biblical Literature* 69, no. 4 (December 1950): 323–28.

Top, Brent L. "The Marriage of Hosea and Gomer." In *A Witness of Jesus Christ: The 1989 Sperry Symposium on the Old Testament*, 223–39. Edited by Richard D. Draper. Salt Lake City: Deseret Book, 1990.

Turner, Rodney. "The Doctrine of the Firstborn and Only Begotten." In *The*

Pearl of Great Price: Revelations from God, 91–117. Edited by H. Donl Peterson and Charles D. Tate Jr. Provo, Utah: Religious Studies Center, Brigham Young University, 1989.

———. "The Lamanite Mark." In *The Book of Mormon: Second Nephi, The Doctrinal Structure*, 133–57. Edited by Monte S. Nyman and Charles D. Tate Jr. Provo, Utah: Religious Studies Center, Brigham Young University, 1989.

Tuttle, A. Theodore. In Conference Report, April 1958, 120–21.

Tvedtnes, John. "A Phonemic Analysis of Nephite and Jaredite Proper Names." Provo, Utah: Foundation for Ancient Research and Mormon Studies, 1977.

———. "Priestly Clothing in Bible Times." In *Temples of the Ancient World*, 649–704. Edited by Donald W. Parry. Provo, Utah: Foundation for Ancient Research and Mormon Studies, 1994.

Valletta, Thomas R. "Jared and His Brother." In *The Book of Mormon: Fourth Nephi through Moroni, From Zion to Destruction*, 303–22. Edited by Monte S. Nyman and Charles D. Tate Jr. Provo, Utah: Religious Studies Center, Brigham Young University, 1995.

Vaner, William. "The Christian Use of Jewish Numerology." In *The Masters Seminary Journal* 8, no. 1 (Spring 1997): 47–59.

Von Rohr Sauer, A. "The Cultic Role of the Pig in Ancient Times." In *Memoriam P. Kahle*, 201–7. Edited by M. Black and G. Fohrer. Berlin: A. Topelmann, 1968.

Walls, A. F. "Fortunatus." In *The New Bible Dictionary*, 439. Edited by J. D. Douglas. Grand Rapids, Mich.: Eerdmans, 1971.

Walsh, Jerome T., and Christopher T. Begg. "1–2 Kings." In *The New Jerome Biblical Commentary*, 160–85. Edited by Raymond E. Brown, Joseph A. Fitzmyer, and Roland E. Murphy. Englewood Cliffs, N.J.: Prentice Hall, 1990.

Welling, Milton H. In Conference Report, October 1915, 17–19.

Wenham, Gordon J. "The Theology of Unclean Food." In *Evangelical Quarterly* 53 (1981): 6–15.

Wessel, Walter W. "Mark." In *The Expositor's Bible Commentary*, 8:601–793. Edited by Frank E. Gaebelein. 12 vols. Grand Rapids, Mich.: Zondervan, 1976–92.

Wilkins, Michael J. "Barabbas." In *The Anchor Bible Dictionary*, 1:607. Edited by David Noel Freedman. 6 vols. New York: Doubleday, 1992.

Wood, A. Skevington. "Ephesians." In *The Expositor's Bible Commentary*, 11:1–92. Edited by Frank E. Gaebelein. 12 vols. Grand Rapids, Mich.: Zondervan, 1976–92.

Wood, H. G. "Mark." In *A Commentary on the Bible*, 681–99. Edited by Arthur S. Peake. New York: Thomas Nelson and Sons, 1919.

Wood, Leon J. "Hosea." In *The Expositor's Bible Commentary*, 7:159–225. Edited by Frank E. Gaebelein. 12 vols. Grand Rapids, Mich.: Zondervan, 1976–92.

Wright, David. "Unclean and Clean (OT)." In *The Anchor Bible Dictionary*, 6:729–41. Edited by David Noel Freedman. 6 vols. New York: Doubleday, 1992.

Yamauchi, Edwin. "Ezra, Nehemiah." In *The Expositor's Bible Commentary*, 4:561–771. Edited by Frank E. Gaebelein. 12 vols. Grand Rapids, Mich.: Zondervan, 1976–92.

Yerkes, R. K. "The Unclean Animals in Leviticus 11 and Deuteronomy 14." In *Jewish Quarterly Review* 14 (1923–1924): 1–29.

Young, Brigham. "Increase of Saints." In *Journal of Discourses*, 15:135–39. 26 vols. London: Latter-day Saints' Book Depot, 1854–86.

———. "Trying to Be Saints." In *Journal of Discourses*, 19:36–45. 26 vols. London: Latter-day Saints' Book Depot, 1854–86.

Young, Lorenzo D. "The Lord's Providential Care." In *Journal of Discourses*, 6:222–26. 26 vols. London: Latter-day Saints' Book Depot, 1854–86.

Youngblood, Ronald F. "1 and 2 Samuel." In *The Expositor's Bible Commentary*, 3:551–1104. Edited by Frank E. Gaebelein. 12 vols. Grand Rapids, Mich.: Zondervan, 1976–92.

BOOKS

Achtemeier, Paul J., ed. *Harper's Bible Dictionary*. San Francisco: Harper Collins Publishers, 1985.

Albright, W. F., and C. S. Mann. *The Anchor Bible: Matthew*. New York: Doubleday, 1971.

Allen, James B., and Glen M. Leonard. *The Story of the Latter-day Saints*. Salt Lake City: Deseret Book, 1976.

Ali, Abdullah Yusuf, ed. *The Holy Qur'an: Text, Translation, and Commentary*. Elmhurst, N.Y.: Tahrike Tarsile Qur'an, 1987.

Althaus, Paul. *The Theology of Martin Luther*. Translated by Robert C. Schultz. Philadelphia: Fortress Press, 1966.

Andersen, Francis I., and David Noel Freedman. *The Anchor Bible: Hosea*. New York: Doubleday, 1980.

Anderson, Richard Lloyd. *Understanding Paul*. Salt Lake City: Deseret Book, 1983.

Andrus, Hyrum G. *Joseph Smith and World Government*. Salt Lake City: Deseret Book, 1958.

Arrington, Leonard J. *Brigham Young: American Moses*. New York: Alfred A. Knopf, 1985.

———. *The Presidents of the Church*. Salt Lake City: Deseret Book, 1986.

Baldwin, Joyce G. *Tyndale Old Testament Commentaries: Esther*. Downers Grove, Ill.: InterVarsity Press, 1984.

---. *Tyndale Old Testament Commentaries: Haggai, Zechariah, Malachi.* Downers Grove, Ill.: InterVarsity Press, 1972.

Barber, Allen H. *Celestial Symbols.* Bountiful, Utah: Horizon, 1997.

Barth, Markus. *The Anchor Bible: Ephesians 4–6.* New York: Doubleday, 1974.

Bayley, Harold. *The Lost Language of Symbolism: An Inquiry into the Origin of Certain Letters, Words, Names, Fairy-Tales, Folklore, and Mythologies.* 2 vols. New York: Carol Publishing, 1990, 1993.

Bennion, Lowell L. *An Introduction to the Gospel.* Salt Lake City: Deseret Sunday School Union Board, 1959.

Berrett, William J., and Alma P. Burton. *Readings in LDS Church History.* 3 vols. Salt Lake City: Deseret Book, 1953–58.

Bitton, Davis. *Images of the Prophet Joseph Smith.* Salt Lake City: Aspen Books, 1996.

Boling, Robert G., and G. Ernest Wright. *The Anchor Bible: Joshua.* New York: Doubleday, 1982.

A Book of Commandments: For the Government of the Church of Christ. Zion [Mo.]: W. W. Phelps and Co., 1833.

Books of Adam and Eve. In *Apocrypha and Pseudepigrapha of the Old Testament.* 2 vols. Edited by R. H. Charles. Oxford: Clarendon Press, 1973.

Botterweck, Johannes, and Helmer Ringgren, eds. *Theological Dictionary of the Old Testament.* 11 vols. Grand Rapids, Mich.: Eerdmans, 1986.

Bray, Raymond. *The Revelation Decoded.* N.p.: A World of Art Publishing, 1996.

Breneman, Mervin. *The New American Commentary: Ezra, Nehemiah, Esther.* N.p.: Broadman and Holman Publishers, 1993.

Brewster, Hoyt W. *Doctrine and Covenants Encyclopedia.* Salt Lake City: Bookcraft, 1988.

---. *Isaiah Plain and Simple: The Message of Isaiah in the Book of Mormon.* Salt Lake City: Deseret Book Company, 1995.

Bromiley, Geoffrey W., ed. *The International Standard Bible Encyclopedia.* Rev. ed. 4 vols. Grand Rapids, Mich.: Eerdmans, 1979–88.

Brough, R. Clayton. *The Lost Tribes.* Rev. ed. Bountiful, Utah: Horizon Publishers, 1992.

Brown, Francis, S. R. Driver, and Charles A. Briggs. *The Brown-Driver-Briggs Hebrew and English Lexicon.* Peabody, Mass.: Hendrickson Publishers, 1999.

---, eds. *A Hebrew and English Lexicon of the Old Testament.* New York: Oxford, 1968.

Brown, Matthew B. *The Gate of Heaven: Insights on the Doctrines and Symbols of the Temple.* American Fork, Utah: Covenant Communications, 1999.

---, and Paul Thomas Smith. *Symbols in Stone: Symbolism on the Early Temples of the Restoration.* American Fork, Utah: Covenant Communications, 1997.

Brown, Raymond E. *The Anchor Bible: The Gospel According to John, XIII–XXI.* New York: Doubleday, 1970.

———. *The Birth of the Messiah.* New York: Doubleday, 1977.

———. *The Death of the Messiah: From Gethsemane to the Grave.* 2 vols. New York: Doubleday, 1994.

———, Joseph A. Fitzmyer, and Roland E. Murphy, eds. *The New Jerome Biblical Commentary.* Englewood Cliffs, N.J.: Prentice Hall, 1990.

Browning, W. R. F. *The Gospel According to Saint Luke.* London: SMC Press, 1979.

Bruce, F. F. *Paul: Apostle of the Heart Set Free.* Grand Rapids, Mich.: Eerdmans, 1999.

Bryan, David. *Cosmos, Chaos and the Kosher Mentality.* Sheffield, England: Sheffield Academic Press, Ltd., 1995.

Bullinger, E. W. *Figures of Speech Used in the Bible.* Grand Rapids, Mich.: Baker Book House, 1987.

———. *Number in Scripture: Its Supernatural Design and Spiritual Significance.* Grand Rapids, Mich.: Kregel Publications, 1967.

Buttrick, George Arthur, ed. *The Interpreter's Bible.* 12 vols. New York: Abingdon Press, 1951–1957.

Cairns, Ian. *International Theological Commentary: Word and Presence—Deuteronomy.* Grand Rapids, Mich.: Eerdmans, 1992.

Cannon, George Q. *The Life of Joseph Smith the Prophet.* Salt Lake City: Deseret Book Company, 1986.

Carlyon, Richard, comp. *A Guide to the Gods.* New York: Quill, 1982.

Charles, John D. *Endowed from on High: Understanding the Symbols of the Endowment.* Bountiful, Utah: Horizon Publishers, 1997.

Cheesman, Paul R., ed. *The Book of Mormon: The Keystone Scripture.* Provo, Utah: Religious Studies Center, Brigham Young University, 1988.

Childs, Brevard S. *Old Testament Theology in a Canonical Context.* Philadelphia: Fortress Press, 1986.

Church, Leslie F., ed. *The NIV Matthew Henry Commentary in One Volume.* Grand Rapids, Mich.: Zondervan, 1992.

Cirlot, J. E. *A Dictionary of Symbols.* 2d ed. New York: Philosophical Library, 1971.

Clark, James R., comp. *Messages of the First Presidency of The Church of Jesus Christ of Latter-day Saints.* 6 vols. Salt Lake City: Bookcraft, 1965–75.

Clarke, Adam. *The Holy Bible Containing the Old and New Testaments . . . with a Commentary and Critical Notes.* 6 vols. New York: Methodist Book Concern, n.d.

Cogan, Mordechai, and Hayim Tadmor. *The Anchor Bible: II Kings.* New York: Doubleday, 1988.

Coggins, Richard J., and S. Paul Re'emi. *International Theological Commentary:*

Israel among the Nations—Nahum, Obadiah, Esther. Grand Rapids, Mich.: Eerdmans, 1985.

Cole, R. Alan. *Tyndale New Testament Commentaries: Mark.* Grand Rapids, Mich.: Eerdmans, 1997.

———. *Tyndale Old Testament Commentaries: Exodus.* Leicester: InterVarsity Press, 1973.

Comay, Joan. *Who's Who in the Old Testament, Together with the Apocrypha.* New York: Holt, Rinehart and Winston, 1971.

Conner, Kevin J. *Interpreting the Symbols and Types.* Portland, Ore.: City Bible Publishing, 1992.

Cooper, J. C. *An Illustrated Encyclopaedia of Traditional Symbols.* London: Thames and Hudson, 1995.

Cope, Gilbert. *Symbolism in the Bible and the Church.* London: SCM Press, Ltd., 1959.

Cowley, Matthias F. *Cowley's Talks on Doctrine.* Chattanooga, Tenn.: Ben E. Rich, 1902.

———. *Wilford Woodruff, Fourth President of The Church of Jesus Christ of Latter-day Saints, History of His Life and Labors.* Salt Lake City: Bookcraft, 1964.

Craddock, Fred B. *Interpretation: A Bible Commentary for Teaching and Preaching—Luke.* Louisville, Ky.: John Knox Press, 1973.

Dahood, Mitchell. *The Anchor Bible: Psalms I, 1–50.* New York: Doubleday, 1966.

———. *The Anchor Bible: Psalms III, 101–150.* New York: Doubleday, 1970.

Danielou, Jean. *The Bible and the Liturgy.* South Bend, Ind.: University of Notre Dame Press, 1956.

Dantzig, Tobias. *Number, the Language of Science.* New York: Macmillan, 1959.

Davidson, Richard M. *Typology in Scripture: A Study of Hermeneutical TYPOS Structures.* Berrien Springs, Mich.: Andrews University Press, 1981.

Davis, John J. *Biblical Numerology.* Grand Rapids, Mich.: Baker Book House, 2000.

Deissmann, Adolf. *Paul: A Study in Social and Religious History.* New York: Harper and Brothers Publishers, 1957.

de Lange, Nicholas. *Judaism.* Oxford: Oxford University Press, 1987.

Delitzsch, Franz. *Biblical Commentary on the Prophecies of Isaiah.* 3d ed. 2 vols. Grand Rapids, Mich.: Eerdmans, 1954.

Dixon, Jenna, ed. *The Senate Prayers of Peter Marshall.* Sandwich, Mass.: Billies, 1996.

Donaldson, Matthew R., comp. *The Restoration Study Bible.* 2 vols. Sacramento, Calif.: n.d.

Douglas, J. D., ed. *The New Bible Dictionary.* Grand Rapids, Mich.: Eerdmans, 1971.

Douglas, Mary. *Purity and Danger: An Analysis of Concepts of Pollution and Taboo.* Boston: Routledge and Kegan Paul, 1980.

Draper, Richard D. *Opening the Seven Seals: The Visions of John the Revelator.* Salt Lake City: Deseret Book Company, 1991.

Dummelow, J. R., ed. *A Commentary on the Holy Bible.* New York: Macmillan, 1936.

Eakin, Frank E., Jr. *The Religion and Culture of Israel: An Introduction to Old Testament Thought.* Boston: Allyn and Bacon, 1971.

Edwards, Jonathan. *Images or Shadows of Divine Things.* New Haven, Conn.: Yale University Press, 1948.

Ehat, Andrew F. "Joseph Smith's Introduction of Temple Ordinances and the 1844 Mormon Succession Question." Provo, Utah: Master's thesis, Brigham Young University, 1981.

Eilberg-Schwartz, H. *The Savage in Judaism.* Bloomington, Ind.: University of Indiana Press, 1990.

Elliott, John H. *The Anchor Bible: 1 Peter.* New York: Doubleday, 2000.

Ellis, Peter F. *The Genius of John: A Composition-Critical Commentary on the Fourth Gospel.* Collegeville, Minn.: The Liturgical Press, 1984.

Fairbairn, Patrick. *The Typology of Scripture.* Grand Rapids, Mich.: Kregel Publications, 1989.

Farbridge, Maurice, H. *Studies in Biblical and Semitic Symbolism.* London: Kegan Paul, Trench, Trubner and Co., Ltd., 1923.

Farrar, Frederic W. *History of Interpretation.* New York: Macmillan, 1886.

———. *The Life of Christ.* Portland, Ore.: Fountain Publications, 1964.

Fee, Gordon, and Douglas Stuart. *How to Read the Bible for All It's Worth.* 2d ed. Grand Rapids, Mich.: Zondervan, 1993.

Fitzmyer, Joseph A. *The Anchor Bible: The Gospel According to Luke I–IX.* New York: Doubleday, 1970.

———. *The Anchor Bible: The Gospel According to Luke X–XXV.* New York: Doubleday, 1985.

Fontana, David. *The Secret Language of Symbols: A Visual Key to Symbols and Their Meanings.* San Francisco: Chronicle Books, 1994.

Forbush, William Byron, ed. *Fox's Book of Martyrs.* Grand Rapids, Mich.: Zondervan, 1967.

Ford, J. Massyngberde. *The Anchor Bible: Revelation.* New York: Doubleday, 1975.

Foulkes, Francis. *Tyndale New Testament Commentaries: Ephesians.* Rev. ed. Grand Rapids, Mich.: Eerdmans, 1997.

France, R. T. *Tyndale New Testament Commentaries: Matthew.* Grand Rapids, Mich.: Eerdmans, 1997.

Freedman, David Noel, ed. *The Anchor Bible Dictionary.* 6 vols. New York: Doubleday, 1992.

Fretheim, Terrence. *Interpreting Biblical Texts: The Pentateuch.* Nashville: Abingdon Press, 1996.

Frye, Northrop. *Anatomy of Criticism: Four Essays*. Princeton, N.J.: Princeton University Press, 1957.

Furnish, Victor Paul. *The Anchor Bible: II Corinthians*. New York: Doubleday, 1984.

Gaebelein, Frank E., ed. *The Expositor's Bible Commentary*. 12 vols. Grand Rapids, Mich.: Zondervan, 1976–92.

Gaskill, Alonzo L. *"Touch Not the Unclean Thing": The Implications of Barnabian Kosher Typology for Biblical Exegesis*. Newburgh, Ind.: The University of Liverpool and Trinity Theological Seminary, 2000.

Ginzberg, Louis. *The Legends of the Jews*. 7 vols. Philadelphia: Jewish Publication Society of America, 1967–69.

Glassé, Cyril. *A Concise Encyclopedia of Islam*. San Francisco: Harper San Francisco, 1989.

Goppelt, Leonhard. *Typos: The Typological Interpretation of the Old Testament in the New*. Grand Rapids, Mich.: Eerdmans, 1982.

Gordon, Cyrus H. *Before the Bible*. New York: Harper, 1962. Cited in Hugh Nibley. *Since Cumorah*. Provo, Utah: Foundation for Ancient Research and Mormon Studies, 1988.

Gower, Ralph. *The New Manners and Customs of Bible Times*. Chicago: Moody Press, 1996.

Grant, Robert, and David Tracy. *A Short History of the Interpretation of the Bible*. 2d ed. Philadelphia: Fortress Press, 1984.

Greenberg, Moshe. *The Anchor Bible: Ezekiel 1–20*. New York: Doubleday, 1983.

Greidanus, Sidney. *Preaching Christ from the Old Testament: A Contemporary Hermeneutical Method*. Grand Rapids, Mich.: Eerdmans, 1999.

Grunfeld, Dayan I. *The Jewish Dietary Laws*. 3d ed. 2 vols. New York: Soncino Press, 1982.

Habershon, Ada R. *Study of the Types*. Grand Rapids, Mich.: Kregel Publications, 1974.

Hall, James. *Dictionary of Subjects and Symbols in Art*. New York: Harper and Row Publishers, 1979.

Hamilton, Victor P. *Handbook on the Pentateuch*. Grand Rapids, Mich.: Baker Book House, 1982.

Hamlin, E. John. *International Theological Commentary: At Risk in the Promised Land—Judges*. Grand Rapids, Mich.: Eerdmans, 1990.

———. *International Theological Commentary: Inheriting the Land—Joshua*. Grand Rapids, Mich.: Eerdmans, 1983.

Harrington, Daniel J., ed. *Sacra Pagina: The Acts of the Apostles*. Collegeville, Minn.: The Liturgical Press, 1992.

Harrison, R. K. *Introduction to the Old Testament*. Grand Rapids, Mich.: Eerdmans, 1969.

———. *Tyndale Old Testament Commentaries: Leviticus*. Leicester: InterVarsity Press, 1980.

Hart, Louis F., and Alexander A. Di Lella. *The Anchor Bible: The Book of Daniel.* New York: Doubleday, 1978.

Hartmann, A. *The Close Relationship between the Old Testament and the New.* Hamburg: N. P., 1831.

Hartshorn, Leon R. *Joseph Smith: Prophet of the Restoration.* Salt Lake City: Deseret Book, 1970.

——. *Put on the Whole Armor of God.* Salt Lake City: Deseret Book, 1979.

Hasel, Gerhard. *Old Testament Theology: Basic Issues in the Current Debate.* 2 vols. Grand Rapids, Mich.: Eerdmans, 1975.

Hastings, James, ed. *Dictionary of the Apostolic Church.* 2 vols. Edinburgh: T. and T. Clark, 1918.

——. *Dictionary of the Bible.* Rev. ed. New York: Charles Scribner's Sons, 1963.

Henry, Hugh T. *Catholic Customs and Symbols.* New York: Benziger Brothers, 1925.

Hertz, Joseph, ed. *The Pentateuch and Haftorahs.* 2d ed. London: Soncino Press, 1962.

Hess, Richard S. *Tyndale Old Testament Commentaries: Joshua.* Downers Grove, Ill.: InterVarsity Press, 1996.

Hill, Andrew E. *The Anchor Bible: Malachi.* New York: Doubleday, 1998.

Hinckley, Gordon B. *Teachings of Gordon B. Hinckley.* Salt Lake City: Deseret Book, 1997.

Hocking, David. *The Coming World Leader: Understanding the Book of Revelation.* Portland, Ore.: Multnomah Press, 1988.

Holland, Jeffrey R. *Christ and the New Covenant: The Messianic Message of the Book of Mormon.* Salt Lake City: Deseret Book, 1997.

Holzapfel, Richard Neitzel, and David Roth Seely. *My Father's House: Temple Worship and Symbolism in the New Testament.* Salt Lake City: Bookcraft, 1994.

Hunter, Howard W. *The Teachings of Howard W. Hunter.* Edited by Clyde J. Williams. Salt Lake City: Bookcraft, 1997.

Hunter, Milton R. *Pearl of Great Price Commentary.* Salt Lake City: Stevens and Wallis, 1951.

Ifrah, Georges. *The Universal History of Numbers: From Prehistory to the Invention of the Computer.* New York: John Wiley and Sons, 2000.

Isaacs, Ronald H. *The Jewish Book of Numbers.* New Jersey: Jason Aronson Inc., 1996.

Janzen, J. Gerald. *International Theological Commentary: Abraham and All the Families of the Earth—Genesis 12–50.* Grand Rapids, Mich.: Eerdmans, 1993.

Jeremias, Joachim. *The Parables of Jesus.* New York: Charles Scribner's Sons, 1963.

——. *Rediscovering the Parables.* New York: Charles Scribner's Sons, 1966.

Johnson, Luke Timothy. *The Anchor Bible: The First and Second Letters to Timothy*. New York: Doubleday, 2001.

———. *Sacra Pagina: The Acts of the Apostles*. Collegeville, Minn.: The Liturgical Press, 1992.

Johnston, Robert D. *Numbers in the Bible: God's Design in Biblical Numerology*. Grand Rapids, Mich.: Kregel Publications, 1990.

Journal of Discourses. 26 vols. Liverpool: Latter-day Saints' Book Depot, 1854–86.

Journal History of The Church of Jesus Christ of Latter-day Saints. Salt Lake City: Historical Department Archives, The Church of Jesus Christ of Latter-day Saints.

Julien, Nadia. *The Mammoth Dictionary of Symbols*. New York: Carroll and Graf Publishers, 1996.

Keil, C. F. *Manual of Biblical Archaeology*. 2 vols. Edinburgh: T. and T. Clark, 1888.

———, and F. Delitzsch. *Biblical Commentary on the Old Testament: The Prophecies of Isaiah*. 2 vols. Grand Rapids, Mich.: Eerdmans, 1954.

Kertzer, Morris N., and Lawrence A. Hoffman. *What Is a Jew?* New York: Collier Books, 1993.

Kidner, Derek. *Tyndale Old Testament Commentaries: Genesis*. Downers Grove, Ill.: InterVarsity Press, 1967.

———. *Tyndale Old Testament Commentaries: Psalms 1–72*. Downers Grove, Ill.: InterVarsity Press, 1973.

———. *Tyndale Old Testament Commentaries: Psalms 73–150*. Downers Grove, Ill.: InterVarsity Press, 1973.

Kimball, Spencer W. *Faith Precedes the Miracle*. Salt Lake City: Deseret Book, 1979.

———. *The Teachings of Spencer W. Kimball*. Edited by Edward L. Kimball. Salt Lake City: Bookcraft, 1982.

Kittel, Gerhard, ed. *Theological Dictionary of the New Testament*. 10 vols. Grand Rapids, Mich.: Eerdmans, 1965.

Klein, William W., Craig L. Blomberg, and Robert L. Hubbard Jr. *Introduction to Biblical Interpretation*. Dallas: Word Publishing, 1993.

Knight, George A. F. *International Theological Commentary: Servant Theology—Isaiah 40–55*. Grand Rapids, Mich.: Eerdmans, 1984.

Kraut, Ogden. *Polygamy in the Bible*. Salt Lake City: Pioneer Press, 1983.

Kruse, Colin. *Tyndale New Testament Commentaries: 2 Corinthians*. Leicester: InterVarsity Press, 1998.

Kurtz, J. H. *Offerings, Sacrifices and Worship in the Old Testament*. Peabody, Mass.: Hendrickson Publishers, 1998.

———. *Sacrificial Worship of the Old Testament*. Edinburgh: T. and T. Clark, 1863, and Grand Rapids, Mich.: Baker, 1980.

Lee, Harold B. *Stand Ye in Holy Places*. Salt Lake City: Deseret Book, 1974.

Levine, Baruch A. *The Anchor Bible: Numbers 1–20.* New York: Doubleday, 1993.

Locks, Gutman G. *The Spice of Torah—Gematria.* New York: Judaica Press, 1985.

Lost Books of the Bible, The. New York: Bell Publishing Company, 1979.

Ludlow, Daniel H., ed. *Encyclopedia of Mormonism.* 4 vols. New York: Macmillan, 1992.

Lund, Gerald N. *Jesus Christ, Key to the Plan of Salvation.* Salt Lake City: Deseret Book, 1991.

Lundbom, Jack R. *The Anchor Bible: Jeremiah 1–20.* New York: Doubleday, 1999.

Lundquist, John M., and Stephen D. Ricks, eds. *By Study and Also by Faith: Essays in Honor of Hugh W. Nibley on the Occasion of His Eightieth Birthday, 27 March 1990.* 2 vols. Provo, Utah: Foundation for Ancient Research and Mormon Studies, 1990.

Lundwall, N. B., comp. *Lectures on Faith.* Salt Lake City: Bookcraft, n.d.

Mace, Rebecca E. Howell. Wandle Mace, Autobiography. Provo, Utah: BYU Special Collection, n.d.

MacKenzie, Donald A. *Egyptian Myths and Legends.* New York: Gramercy Books, 1978.

Mackie, George M. *Bible Manners and Customs.* New York: Fleming H. Revell Company, n.d.

Madsen, Truman G. *Joseph Smith the Prophet.* Salt Lake City: Bookcraft, 1989.

Mann, C. S. *The Anchor Bible: Mark.* New York: Doubleday, 1986.

Marshall, I. Howard. *Tyndale New Testament Commentaries: Acts.* Grand Rapids, Mich.: InterVarsity Press, 1998.

Matthews, Robert J. *The Miracles of Jesus.* Provo, Utah: Brigham Young University, 1968.

Maturin, B. W. *The Parables of Our Lord.* Baltimore: The Carroll Press, 1951.

Maxwell, Neal A. *Look Back at Sodom.* Salt Lake City: Deseret Book, 1975.

———. *Not My Will, But Thine.* Salt Lake City: Bookcraft, 1988.

McBrien, Richard P., ed. *The Harper Collins Encyclopedia of Catholicism.* San Francisco: Harper San Francisco, 1995.

McConkie, Bruce R. *Doctrinal New Testament Commentary.* 3 vols. Salt Lake City: Bookcraft, 1987–88.

———. *Doctrines of the Restoration: Sermons and Writings of Bruce R. McConkie.* Edited by Mark L. McConkie. Salt Lake City: Bookcraft, 1998.

———. *The Millennial Messiah.* Salt Lake City: Deseret Book, 1982.

———. *Mormon Doctrine.* 2d ed. Salt Lake City: Bookcraft, 1979.

———. *The Mortal Messiah.* 4 vols. Salt Lake City: Deseret Book, 1980–81.

———. *A New Witness for the Articles of Faith.* Salt Lake City: Deseret Book, 1985.

McConkie, Joseph Fielding. *Gospel Symbolism.* Salt Lake City: Bookcraft, 1985.

――――. *His Name Shall Be Joseph: Ancient Prophecies of the Latter-day Seer.* Salt Lake City: Hawkes Publishing Co., 1980.

――――, and Donald W. Parry. *A Guide to Scriptural Symbols.* Salt Lake City: Bookcraft, 1990.

McConkie, Oscar W., Jr. *Angels.* Salt Lake City: Deseret Book, 1975.

McEachern, Alton H. *The Layman's Bible Book Commentary: Psalms.* Nashville: Broadman Press, 1981.

McKechnie, Jean L., ed. *Webster's New Twentieth Century Dictionary of the English Language Unabridged.* 2d ed. N.p.: Collins World, 1978.

McKenzie, John L. *The Anchor Bible: Second Isaiah.* New York: Doubleday, 1968.

――――. *Dictionary of the Bible.* Milwaukee: The Bruce Publishing Company, 1965.

Milgrom, Jacob. *The Anchor Bible: Leviticus 1–16, 17–22, and 23–27.* New York: Doubleday, 1991, 2000, 2001.

Moore, Carey A. *The Anchor Bible: Esther.* New York: Doubleday, 1971.

Morris, Leon. *The New International Commentary on the New Testament: The Gospel According to John.* Rev. ed. Grand Rapids, Mich.: Eerdmans, 1995.

――――. *Tyndale New Testament Commentaries: 1 Corinthians.* Rev. ed. Grand Rapids, Mich.: Eerdmans, 1998.

――――. *Tyndale New Testament Commentaries: Luke.* Grand Rapids, Mich.: Eerdmans, 1999.

――――. *Tyndale New Testament Commentaries: Revelation.* Rev. ed. Grand Rapids, Mich.: Eerdmans, 1999.

Motyer, J. Alec. *Isaiah: An Introduction and Commentary.* Leicester: InterVarsity Press, 1999.

――――. *Tyndale Old Testament Commentaries: Isaiah.* Leicester: InterVarsity Press, 1999.

Munck, Johannes. *The Anchor Bible: The Acts of the Apostles.* New York: Doubleday, 1967.

Myers, Allen C., ed. *The Eerdmans Bible Dictionary.* Grand Rapids, Mich.: Eerdmans, 1987.

Myers, Carol L., and Eric M. Myers. *The Anchor Bible: Haggai, Zechariah 1–8.* New York: Doubleday, 1987.

Neusner, Jacob. *The Enchantments of Judaism: Rites of Transformation from Birth through Death.* Atlanta, Ga.: Scholars Press, 1991.

――――. *The Idea of Purity in Ancient Judaism.* Leiden, The Netherlands: E. J. Brill, 1973.

Newton, Michael. *The Concept of Purity at Qumran and in the Letters of Paul.* Cambridge: Cambridge University Press, 1985.

Nibley, Hugh. *Ancient Documents and the Pearl of Great Price.* Provo, Utah: Foundation for Ancient Research and Mormon Studies, 1989.

———. *An Approach to the Book of Mormon.* Provo, Utah: Foundation for Ancient Research and Mormon Studies, 1988.

———. *Approaching Zion.* Provo, Utah: Foundation for Ancient Research and Mormon Studies, 1989.

———. *Enoch the Prophet.* Provo, Utah: Foundation for Ancient Research and Mormon Studies, 1986.

———. *Lehi in the Desert, The World of the Jaredites, There Were Jaredites.* Provo, Utah: Foundation for Ancient Research and Mormon Studies, 1988.

———. *The Message of the Joseph Smith Papyri: An Egyptian Endowment.* Salt Lake City: Deseret Book, 1976.

———. *Mormonism and Early Christianity.* Provo, Utah: Foundation for Ancient Research and Mormon Studies, 1987.

———. *The Prophetic Book of Mormon.* Provo, Utah: Foundation for Ancient Research and Mormon Studies, 1989.

———. *Since Cumorah.* Provo, Utah: Foundation for Ancient Research and Mormon Studies, 1988.

———. *Teachings of the Book of Mormon: Transcripts of Lectures Presented to an Honors Book of Mormon Class at Brigham Young University, 1988–1990.* 4 vols. Provo, Utah: Foundation for Ancient Research and Mormon Studies, 1988–90.

———. *Temple and Cosmos: Beyond This Ignorant Present.* Provo, Utah: Foundation for Ancient Research and Mormon Studies, 1992.

———. *The Three Facsimiles from the Book of Abraham.* Provo, Utah: Foundation for Ancient Research and Mormon Studies, 1980.

———. *The World and the Prophets.* Provo, Utah: Foundation for Ancient Research and Mormon Studies, 1987.

Nibley, Preston. *Exodus to Greatness: The Story of the Mormon Migration.* Salt Lake City: Deseret News Press, 1947.

———. *The Presidents of the Church. Revised and enlarged edition.* Salt Lake City: Deseret Book, 1974.

Nicoll, W. Robertson. *Expositor's Greek Testament.* 5 vols. Grand Rapids, Mich.: Eerdmans, 1983.

Nyman, Monte S., and Robert L. Millet, eds. *The Joseph Smith Translation: The Restoration of Plain and Precious Things.* Provo, Utah: Religious Studies Center, Brigham Young University, 1985.

Old Testament: Genesis–2 Samuel [Church Educational System student manual]. 2d ed. Salt Lake City: The Church of Jesus Christ of Latter-day Saints, 1981.

Orr, William F., and James Arthur Walther. *The Anchor Bible: 1 Corinthians.* New York: Doubleday, 1976.

Packer, Boyd K. *The Things of the Soul.* Salt Lake City: Deseret Book, 1996.

Parry, Donald W., Jay A. Parry, and Tina M. Peterson. *Understanding Isaiah.* Salt Lake City: Deseret Book, 1998.

Parry, Jay A., and Donald W. Parry. *Understanding the Book of Revelation.* Salt Lake City: Deseret Book, 1998.

Peake, Authur S., ed. *A Commentary on the Bible.* New York: Thomas Nelson and Sons, 1919.

Petersen, Mark E. *Moses: Man of Miracles.* Salt Lake City: Deseret Book, 1978.

Peterson, Daniel C., and Stephen D. Ricks. *Offenders for a Word: How Anti-Mormons Play Word Games to Attack the Latter-day Saints.* Salt Lake City: Aspen Books, 1992.

Pope, Marvin H. *The Anchor Bible: Song of Songs.* New York: Doubleday, 1977.

Pratt, Parley P. *The Angel of the Prairies: A Dream of the Future.* Salt Lake City: Deseret News Press, 1880.

———. *Autobiography of Parley P. Pratt.* Edited by Parley P. Pratt Jr. Salt Lake City: Deseret Book, 1985.

———. *Key to the Science of Theology.* 9th ed. Salt Lake City: Deseret Book, 1965.

Propp, William H. C. *The Anchor Bible: Exodus 1–18.* New York: Doubleday, 1999.

Pryor, John W. *John, Evangelist of the Covenant People.* Downers Grove, Ill.: InterVarsity Press, 1992.

Quincy, Josiah. *Figures of the Past.* Boston: Robert Brothers Publishers, 1883.

Rad, Gerhard von. *Old Testament Theology.* 2 vols. New York: Harper and Row, 1962.

Random House Webster's College Dictionary. Springfield, Mass.: Merriam-Webster Inc., 1996.

Rasmussen, Ellis T. *A Latter-day Saint Commentary on the Old Testament.* Salt Lake City: Deseret Book, 1993.

Read, Lenet Hadley. *Unveiling Biblical Prophecy: A Summary of Biblical Prophecy concerning Christ, the Apostasy, and Christ's Latter-day Church.* San Francisco: Latter-day Light Publications, 1990.

Rector, Hartman, and Connie Rector. *No More Strangers.* 4 vols. Salt Lake City: Bookcraft, 1971–90.

Reicke, Bo. *The Anchor Bible: The Epistles of James, Peter and Jude.* New York: Doubleday, 1964.

Rest, Friedrich. *Our Christian Symbols.* New York: The Pilgrim Press, 1987.

Reynolds, George. *The Story of the Book of Mormon.* 3d ed. Chicago: Henry C. Etten and Co., 1888.

———, and Janne M. Sjodahl. *Commentary on the Book of Mormon.* 7 vols. Edited and arranged by Philip C. Reynolds. Salt Lake City: Deseret Book, 1955–61.

Rich, Russell R. *Ensign to the Nations: A History of the LDS Church from 1846 to 1972.* Provo, Utah: BYU Press, 1974.

Richardson, Alan. *The Gospel According to St. John.* New York: Collier Books, 1962.

Ricoeur, Paul. *The Symbolism of Evil*. Boston: Beacon Press, 1969.

Roberts, B. H. *A Comprehensive History of the Church of Jesus Christ of Latter-day Saints*. 2d rev. ed. 7 vols. Salt Lake City: Deseret Book, 1978.

———. *New Witnesses for God*. Salt Lake City: The Deseret News, 1909.

———. *Outlines in Ecclesiastical History*. Salt Lake City: Deseret Book, 1979.

Robinson, Benjamin Willard. *The Life of Paul*. Chicago: University of Chicago Press, 1963.

Robinson, Stephen E. *Believing Christ*. Salt Lake City: Deseret Book, 1992.

Roth, Wolfgang. *Isaiah*. Atlanta: John Knox Press, 1988.

Roundy, S. B. "Record Book." Salt Lake City: Historical Department Archives, The Church of Jesus Christ of Latter-day Saints.

Russell, Jeffery Burton. *Lucifer: The Devil in the Middle Ages*. Ithaca, N.Y.: Cornell University Press, 1984.

Ryken, Leland. *How to Read the Bible as Literature*. Grand Rapids, Mich.: Zondervan, 1984.

———, James C. Wilhoit, and Tremper Longman III, eds. *Dictionary of Biblical Imagery*. Downers Grove, Ill.: InterVarsity Press, 1998.

Sabiers, Karl G. *Astounding New Discoveries*. Los Angeles: Robertson Publishing Company, 1941.

Sailhamer, John H. *The Pentateuch as Narrative: A Biblical-Theological Commentary*. Grand Rapids, Mich.: Zondervan, 1992.

Sakenfeld, Katharine Doob. *International Theological Commentary: Journeying with God—Numbers*. Grand Rapids, Mich.: Eerdmans, 1995.

Sarna, Nahum M., ed. *The JPS Torah Commentary: Exodus*. Philadelphia: Fortress Press, 1991.

Schneemelcher, Wilhelm, ed. *New Testament Apocrypha*. 2 vols. Philadelphia: Westminster Press, 1965.

Scott, E. F. *The Moffatt New Testament Commentary: The Epistles of Paul to the Colossians, to Philemon, and to the Ephesians*. London: Hodder and Stoughton, 1952.

Scott, R. B. Y. *The Anchor Bible: Proverbs, Ecclesiastes*. New York: Doubleday, 1965.

Sill, Sterling W. *The Upward Reach*. Salt Lake City: Bookcraft, 1962.

Simoons, Frederick J. *Eat Not This Flesh*. Madison, Wis.: University of Wisconsin Press, 1961.

Skousen, Royal, ed. *The Printer's Manuscript of the Book of Mormon: Typographical Facsimile of the Entire Text in Two Parts*. Provo, Utah: Foundation for Ancient Research and Mormon Studies, 2001.

Skousen, W. Cleon. *Isaiah Speaks to Modern Times*. Salt Lake City: Ensign Publishing Company, 1984.

———. *The Third Thousand Years*. Salt Lake City: Bookcraft, 1964.

Smith, Hyrum M., and Janne M. Sjodahl. *The Doctrine and Covenants Commentary*. Rev. ed. Salt Lake City: Deseret Book, 1978.

Smith, Joseph. *The Discourses of the Prophet Joseph Smith*. Edited by Alma P. Burton. 3d ed. Salt Lake City: Deseret Book, 1974.

———. *Encyclopedia of Joseph Smith's Teachings*. Edited by Larry E. Dahl and Donald Q. Cannon. Salt Lake City: Bookcraft, 1998.

———. *History of The Church of Jesus Christ of Latter-day Saints*. 7 vols. 2d rev. ed. Salt Lake City: Deseret Book, 1978.

———. *Teachings of the Prophet Joseph Smith*. Selected by Joseph Fielding Smith. Salt Lake City: Deseret Book, 1976.

———. *The Words of Joseph Smith: The Contemporary Accounts of the Nauvoo Discourses of the Prophet Joseph*. Edited by Andrew F. Ehat and Lyndon W. Cook. Provo, Utah: Religious Studies Center, Brigham Young University, 1980.

Smith, Joseph F. *Gospel Doctrine: Selections from the Sermons and Writings of Joseph F. Smith*. Salt Lake City: Bookcraft, 1998.

Smith, Joseph Fielding. *Answers to Gospel Questions*. Compiled by Joseph Fielding Smith Jr. 5 vols. Salt Lake City: Deseret Book, 1957-66.

———. *Doctrines of Salvation: Sermons and Writings of Joseph Fielding Smith*. Compiled by Bruce R. McConkie. 3 vols. Salt Lake City: Bookcraft, 1954-56.

———. *The Way to Perfection*. Salt Lake City: Genealogical Society of Utah, 1949.

Smith, Lucy Mack. *History of Joseph Smith by His Mother*. Salt Lake City: Bookcraft, 1954.

Smith, Mick. *The Book of Revelation: Plain, Pure, and Simple*. Salt Lake City: Bookcraft, 1998.

Smith, Stelman, and Judson Cornwall. *The Exhaustive Dictionary of Bible Names*. New Jersey: Bridge-Logos Publishing, 1998.

Smith, W. Robertson. *The Religion of the Semites*. New York: Meridian Books, 1956.

Smith, William. *A Dictionary of the Bible*. New York: John C. Winston Company, 1884.

———. *The New Bible Dictionary*. New York: Doubleday, 1979.

Speiser, E. A. *The Anchor Bible: Genesis*. New York: Doubleday, 1962.

Sperry, Sidney B. *Paul's Life and Letters*. Salt Lake City: Bookcraft, 1955.

———. *The Voice of Israel's Prophets*. Salt Lake City: Deseret Book, 1961.

Strong, James J. *The New Strong's Exhaustive Concordance of the Bible*. Nashville: Thomas Nelson Publishers, 1990.

Stubblefield, Jon Michael. "Mark 7:1-23 in Light of the First Century Understanding of Clean-Unclean." Ph.D. dissertation, Southern Baptist Theological Seminary. Ann Arbor: University Microfilms, 1975.

Stuy, Brian H., comp. and ed. *Collected Discourses Delivered by President Wilford Woodruff, His Two Counselors, the Twelve Apostles, and Others*. 5 vols. Burbank, Calif.: B. H. S. Publishing, 1987-92.

Talmage, James E. *The Articles of Faith*. Salt Lake City: Deseret Book, 1975.

———. *The House of the Lord*. Rev. ed. Salt Lake City: Deseret Book, 1971.

———. *Jesus the Christ: A Study of the Messiah and His Mission According to Holy Scriptures Both Ancient and Modern*. Salt Lake City: Deseret Book, 1979.

Tate, Charles D., Jr., ed. *The Book of Mormon: Fourth Nephi through Moroni, From Zion to Destruction*. Provo, Utah: Religious Studies Center, Brigham Young University, 1995.

Taylor, John. *The Gospel Kingdom: Selections from the Writings and Discourses of John Taylor*. Selected by G. Homer Durham. Salt Lake City: Bookcraft, 1987.

———. *The Government of God*. Liverpool: S. W. Richards, 1852.

———. *Mediation and Atonement*. Salt Lake City: Deseret News Company, 1882.

Taylor, John B. *Tyndale Old Testament Commentaries: Ezekiel*. Downers Grove, Ill.: InterVarsity Press, 1969.

Thayer, Joseph H. *Thayer's Greek-English Lexicon of the New Testament*. Peabody, Mass.: Hendrickson Publishers, 1999.

Thompson, Edward G. "A Study of the Political Involvement in the Career of Joseph Smith." Masters thesis. Provo, Utah: Brigham Young University, 1966.

Thompson, J. A. *Tyndale Old Testament Commentaries: Deuteronomy*. Downers Grove, Ill.: InterVarsity Press, 1974.

Todeschi, Kevin. *The Encyclopedia of Symbolism*. New York: The Berkley Publishing Group, 1995.

Trench, Richard Chenevix. *Notes on the Parables of Our Lord*. Grand Rapids, Mich.: Baker Book House, 1963.

Tresidder, Jack. *Symbols and Their Meanings*. London: Duncan Baird Publishers, 2000.

Tullidge, Edward W. *The Life of Joseph the Prophet*. New York: Privately published, 1878.

Unger, Merrill F. *Unger's Bible Dictionary*. Chicago: Moody Press, 1966.

Van Orden, Bruce A., and Brent L. Top, eds. *The Lord of the Gospels: The 1990 Sperry Symposium on the New Testament*. Salt Lake City: Deseret Book, 1991.

Vine, W. E. *An Expository Dictionary of New Testament Words*. New Jersey: Fleming H. Revell, 1966.

Virkler, Henry A. *Hermeneutics: Principles and Processes of Biblical Interpretation*. Grand Rapids, Mich.: Baker Book House, 1981.

Watch Tower Bible and Tract Society of Pennsylvania. *Aid to Bible Understanding*. New York: International Bible Students Association, 1971.

———. *Revelation: Its Grand Climax at Hand*. New York: International Bible Students Association, 1988.

Bibliography: Books

———. *You Can Live Forever in Paradise on Earth*. New York: International Bible Students Association, 1982.
Webster, Noah. *Noah Webster's First Edition [1828] of An American Dictionary of the English Language*. San Francisco: Foundation for American Christian Education, 1967.
Welch, John W. *The Sermon at the Temple, and the Sermon on the Mount*. Provo, Utah: The Foundation for Ancient Research and Mormon Studies, 1990.
Wells, Evelyn. *Nefertiti*. New York: Doubleday, 1964.
Wenham, Gordon J. *Tyndale Old Testament Commentaries: Numbers*. Downers Grove, Ill.: InterVarsity Press, 1981.
Westermann, Claus, ed. *Essays on Old Testament Hermeneutics*. Richmond, Va.: John Knox Press, 1963.
Wheeler, Marion, ed. *His Face: Images of Christ in Art*. New York: Chameleon Books, 1988.
Whitcomb, John S. *Esther: Triumph of God's Sovereignty*. Chicago: Moody Press, 1979.
Whitney, Orson F. *Saturday Night Thoughts*. Salt Lake City: Deseret News, 1921.
Widtsoe, John A. *Evidences and Reconciliations*. Bookcraft: Salt Lake City, 1960.
———. *Priesthood and Church Government in the Church of Jesus Christ of Latter-day Saints*. Salt Lake City: Deseret Book, 1961.
———. *A Rational Theology*. Salt Lake City: Deseret Book, 1937.
Wilcox, S. Michael. *House of Glory: Finding Personal Meaning in the Temple*. Salt Lake City: Deseret Book, 1995.
Williamson, Lamar, Jr. *Interpretation: A Bible Commentary for Teaching and Preaching—Mark*. Louisville, Ky.: John Knox Press, 1983.
Wilson, Walter L. *A Dictionary of Bible Types*. Peabody, Mass.: Hendrickson Publishers, 1999.
Wilson, William. *Old Testament Word Studies*. Grand Rapids, Mich.: Eerdmans, 1977.
Wiseman, Donald J. *Tyndale Old Testament Commentaries: 1 and 2 Kings*. Downers Grove, Ill.: InterVarsity Press, 1993.
Woodruff, Wilford W. *The Discourses of Wilford W. Woodruff*. Selected by G. Homer Durham. Salt Lake City: Bookcraft, 1969.
Wouk, Herman. *This Is My God*. New York: Dell Publishing Company, 1964.
Young, Brigham. *Discourses of Brigham Young*. Selected by John A. Widtsoe. Salt Lake City: Bookcraft, 1998.
Young, Edward J. *The Book of Isaiah*. 3 vols. Grand Rapids, Mich.: Eerdmans, 1997.
Zepp, Ira G., Jr. *A Muslim Primer*. Westminster, Md.: Wakefield Editions, 1992.

SCRIPTURE INDEX

OLD TESTAMENT

Genesis
1:4, p. 114
1:26, p. 141
1:26–27, p. 23
1:27, pp. 115, 175
2:2–3, p. 357
2:8, p. 152
2:10–14, p. 119
2:24, p. 113
3, p. 114
3:7, pp. 62, 64
3:15, p. 46
3:16, p. 128
3:21, pp. 64, 70
3:23–24, p. 151
3:24, p. 297
4:5–8 (JST), p. 243
4:8, p. 200
4:9, p. 259
4:15, p. 357
4:25, p. 190
5:1, p. 23
5:29, p. 189
6–9, p. 189
6:5, p. 48
6:15–16, p. 190
7, p. 283
7:1–2, p. 244
7:1–4, p. 189
7:2, pp. 115, 125, 244
7:2–4, p. 357
7:4, p. 190
7:12, p. 137
7:17–18, p. 190
9:4, p. 99
9:4–5, p. 29
9:6, p. 29
11:1, 6–7, p. 113
11:2–4, p. 170
11:4, 8, p. 220
11:9, p. 222
11:30, p. 177
11:31, p. 174
12, p. 381
12:1–9, p. 157
12:8, p. 286
12:10–12, p. 201
12:13, 15–20, p. 202
13:1, pp. 202, 203
13:2, 4, p. 203
13:3, p. 158
13:14, p. 149
14, p. 174
14:4, p. 137
14:14, pp. 148, 286
14:14–16, p. 142
14:15, p. 374
14:17–20 (JST), p. 184
14:18–20, p. 184
14:20, p. 142
14:26 (JST), pp. 183, 185
14:33–36 (JST), p. 185
15, p. 204
15:2, pp. 142, 376
15:4, p. 336
15:6, p. 173
16:1–4, p. 204
16:6, p. 229
16:7–12, p. 288
16:11, p. 221
17:4–20 (JST), p. 130
17:12, p. 130
17:15, p. 238
17:15–22, p. 177
17:17, pp. 230, 381
17:18, p. 174
17:19, p. 230
17:20, p. 288
18, p. 174
18–19, p. 203
18:3, p. 116
18:12, p. 230
18:20–33, p. 173
19, p. 12
21, p. 177
21:1–3, p. 200
21:14, p. 54

437

22, pp. 200, 377
22:2, pp. 178, 201
22:4, 6, 9, p. 178
22:8, p. 13
22:11, 13, p. 178
22:21, p. 232
23:1, p. 377
24, p. 193
24:2, pp. 142, 376
24:12–28, 58, p. 193
24:45–46, p. 54
24:69–70 (JST), p. 78
25:1, p. 204
25:23, pp. 179, 196, 336
25:25, p. 101
25:27, p. 179
25:29–34, pp. 179, 196, 197
25:30, p. 354
25:34, p. 196
27, p. 237
27:6–33, p. 196
27:17–33, 41–46, p. 197
27:37–41, p. 179
27:40, p. 53
28:10–19, p. 286
28:14, p. 149
29, pp. 125, 152
30:24, p. 221
32:28, p. 179
32:30, p. 222
33, p. 197
35:11, p. 66
35:12, p. 197
35:18, p. 220
37–46, p. 207
37:2–3, 5–10, 13, 26, p. 180
37:4–11, 18–20, 28, 36, 40–41, p. 207
37:24, pp. 181, 207
37:26–28, p. 181
37:29, p. 346

37:34, p. 74
39, p. 181
39:1, 7–20, p. 207
39:16–19, p. 181
41, p. 125
41–44, p. 87
41:45, pp. 180, 231
41:46, p. 181
41:54, p. 201
42–46, p. 207
42:24, p. 207
43:26–28, p. 181
43:30, p. 207
45, p. 181
45:5, 7, p. 181
45:14, p. 207
46:28, 31, 33, p. 201
46:29, p. 207
46:34, p. 202
47:1, 5–6, 27, p. 202
48:13–14, p. 165
48:14, p. 46
48:16, p. 220
49:8, p. 53
49:26, p. 46
50:29 (JST), p. 187
50:29–35 (JST), p. 186

Exodus

1, p. 186
2:10, pp. 212, 233
2:13–14, p. 186
2:14–15, p. 210
2:15, pp. 210, 212, 383
2:21, p. 383
3, p. 210
3:1, p. 210
3:4, p. 242
3:5, p. 75
4, pp. 187, 212
4:10, p. 384
4:10–17, pp. 199, 211
4:16, 29–31, p. 199
4:31, p. 53

5:3, p. 116
5:23, p. 386
7–10, p. 133
7–12, pp. 187, 212
7:9, p. 199
8:5, 16, p. 199
10:13, p. 154
11:1, p. 202
12, p. 270
12:5, p. 13
12:11, pp. 52, 75
12:15, 19, p. 125
12:31–33, p. 202
12:35, 38, p. 203
13:3, p. 187
13:9, 16, p. 39
14, pp. 187, 212
14:21, pp. 154, 155
15, p. 203
15:1–19, p. 188
15:20–27, p. 187
16, pp. 187, 295
16:22–30, p. 296
16:31, p. 295
17, p. 187
17:6, p. 283
17:9–10, 13, p. 183
17:12, p. 44
18, pp. 187, 211
19:4, pp. 57, 393
20–24, p. 187
20:21, p. 86
22:2–3, p. 29
23:17, p. 116
24:9–10, p. 199
24:9–11, p. 188
24:10, p. 351
24:18, p. 138
25:4, p. 100
25:10–13, 17–18, p. 93
25:31–32, p. 125
26:1, 14, p. 100
26:1, 31, 36, pp. 89, 96
26:22, p. 375

Scripture Index 439

27:2, p. 49
27:9, p. 104
28, p. 64
28:1–4, p. 376
28:2, 4, p. 341
28:4, 37, 39, p. 69
28:6, p. 104
28:9–12, 21, 29, p. 242
28:12, p. 55
28:33, p. 100
28:36–38, p. 39
29:1–9, p. 61
29:6, p. 69
29:7, p. 46
29:9, pp. 69, 74
29:19–21, 32–33, p. 100
30:19–21, p. 39
31–34, p. 187
31:10, p. 341
32:1–6, 21–25, p. 199
32:9, p. 52
32:30–32, p. 187
33, p. 211
33:5, p. 52
33:11, p. 23
33:17, p. 242
34:15–16, p. 380
34:24, p. 176
34:29, p. 49
36:24, p. 103
39–40, p. 199
39:7, p. 55
39:27, p. 74
39:28, p. 70
39:28, 31, p. 69
40, p. 199
40:12–15, p. 61

Leviticus
6:11, p. 61
7:12, 15, p. 222
8:7, pp. 69, 74
8:9, pp. 69, 70
8:12, p. 46
8:35, p. 130
9:1, p. 130
11, pp. 245, 256, 392
11:3, p. 257
11:7, p. 261
11:10, p. 255
11:29–31, p. 245
12:5, p. 29
13–14, pp. 41, 198
13:19, p. 102
14, pp. 35, 101, 126, 198
14:14, 17, p. 35
14:37, p. 102
15:19, 25, p. 29
16, p. 104
16:1–4, p. 61
16:4, pp. 69, 341
16:8–10, 26, p. 100
16:14, p. 126
17:7, p. 380
17:11, 14, p. 29
19:19, p. 342
19:32, p. 43
20:6, pp. 195, 380
21:10–15, p. 198
21:16–24, p. 329
22:27, p. 222

Numbers
4:8, p. 100
5:22, p. 336
6:5, 18, p. 42
6:24–26, p. 359
7, p. 188
8:7, p. 283
9:12, p. 13
11, p. 188
11:20, p. 53
12:1, pp. 212, 383
12:3, p. 188
13:16, pp. 183, 290
14:20–23, p. 138
15:35, p. 90
15:38, p. 351
16:1–3, p. 212
17:1–11, p. 281
19:2, pp. 102, 354
20:8, p. 199
21, p. 144
21:9, p. 143
22–24, p. 224
22:12, 20–35, p. 224
23:22, p. 49
27:4, p. 220
31:16, p. 224
34:24, p. 232

Deuteronomy
1:2, p. 134
2:5, p. 38
3:11, p. 235
3:25–28, p. 188
3:27, p. 149
4:29, p. 48
4:34, p. 28
6:4, p. 113
6:5, p. 48
6:8, p. 39
8:3, pp. 187, 295
9:18, pp. 138, 186
9:25, p. 138
10:8, p. 386
10:16, p. 48
11:11, p. 161
11:18, p. 39
11:24, pp. 38, 375
12:23, p. 29
14, pp. 245, 256, 392
14:6, p. 257
16:16, p. 116
17:6, p. 115
18:5, p. 386
19:15, p. 115
22:1, 4, 10, pp. 258, 259
22:9, p. 258
22:11, pp. 258, 342
25:3, p. 138
25:6–7, 10, p. 220

26:8, p. 28
28, p. 250
28:1–14, 49, 53–57, 64–65, p. 249
28:48, p. 53
29:5, p. 62
30:3, pp. 163, 170
31:16, p. 380
32:2, p. 161
32:11, p. 57–58
32:25, p. 43
33, p. 188
33:2, p. 157
33:12, p. 54
33:17, p. 49
34:1–4, p. 212
34:2, p. 375

JOSHUA
1:3, p. 38
2:18, 21, p. 99
3:14–17, p. 155
4:5, p. 54
5:15, p. 76
6, p. 137
6:2–4, 15, p. 126
8:13, p. 167
9:2, p. 113
9:15, p. 188
10:24, p. 53
19:27, p. 374

JUDGES
5:8, p. 68
7, p. 228
9:48, p. 54
11:18, p. 170
13–16, p. 377
16:15–21, pp. 43, 127

RUTH
1:20, p. 221
2–4, p. 376
4:1–8, p. 76
4:10, p. 220

1 SAMUEL
1, p. 290
1:20, p. 220
2:9, p. 37
3, p. 116
10:3, p. 286
11:7, p. 54
14:14, p. 54
14:45, p. 42
15:26–28, p. 73
16:3, p. 242
16:7, p. 48
16:11, p. 176
16:13, pp. 50, 176
17:4–7, p. 123
17:28, p. 48
17:40, p. 121
17:45, p. 386
17:46, pp. 46, 121
17:49–50, p. 176
18:11–12, p. 176
20:41, p. 158
24:4–20, p. 73
25:24, p. 39

2 SAMUEL
3:31, p. 350
6:6, p. 45
7:12–16, p. 176
8, p. 176
10:6, p. 53
11:11, p. 240
12:1–4, p. 330
12:30, p. 70
13:19, p. 46
14:7, p. 220
14:25–26, p. 41
15:30, pp. 46, 75
15:32, p. 46
16:11, p. 33
18:18, p. 220
21:10, p. 350
22:3, p. 49
22:9, p. 53
22:10, 39, p. 38
22:14, p. 55

1 KINGS
1:52, p. 42
3:26, p. 336
6:38, p. 137
7:1, p. 137
7:23–24, 26, pp. 116, 134
8:19, 54, p. 51
8:22, p. 29
11:4, p. 137
11:9–13, p. 114
17:21, p. 116
18, p. 287
18:3, p. 234
18:27, p. 226
18:34, p. 116
19:8, p. 367
19:12, p. 33
19:19, p. 72

2 KINGS
1:12–14, p. 51
2:2–3, p. 286
2:8, p. 73
2:24, p. 386
3:22, p. 102
5:6–9, p. 176
6:4–7, p. 282
6:7, p. 284
6:30, p. 350
10:15, p. 44
15, p. 198
19:1–2, p. 350
19:21, p. 381
19:28, p. 340
25:7, p. 134

1 CHRONICLES
7:16, p. 240
10:9–10, p. 46
11:44, p. 240
16:11, p. 290
21:19, p. 386
27:17, p. 232

Scripture Index

2 Chronicles
6:9, p. 66
6:12–13, p. 51
6:40, p. 33
7:14, p. 290
7:15, p. 33
21:15–19, p. 336
28:15, p. 75
29:30, p. 53
32:8, p. 28
32:21, p. 336
32:26, p. 48

Ezra
5:1, p. 386
9:3, pp. 41, 346

Nehemiah
4, p. 376
8, p. 391
8:4, p. 240
8:6, p. 53
9:29, pp. 52, 54

Esther
2:17, p. 70
2:22, p. 220
4:1, p. 74
4:1–4, p. 350
6:8, p. 96
8:15, pp. 90, 96
9:5–10, p. 240

Job
1:20, p. 46
7:1–2, p. 198
12:5, p. 37
13:28, p. 62
14:6, p. 198
15:32, p. 94
16:15, p. 350
17:9, p. 45
17:11, p. 47
18:17, p. 220
20:14, p. 336

23:10, p. 93
27:21, p. 154
30:18, p. 53
30:27, p. 336
30:28, p. 89
30:30, pp. 88, 89
36:10, p. 34
37:2–5, p. 55
37:9, 22, p. 374
41:20, p. 53

Psalms
2:7–8, p. 176
4:1, pp. 289, 290
9:14, p. 381
17:8, p. 58
18:2, p. 49
18:7–11, p. 105
18:8, p. 53
18:9, 11, p. 86–87
18:13, p. 55
20:5, 7, p. 386
22:14, p. 336
23:1–3, 6, p. 94
24:3–4, p. 45
26:10–11, p. 45
28:2, p. 29
30:11, p. 350
33:11, p. 47
34:15, p. 33
34:16, p. 220
35:13, p. 350
36:7, p. 58
36:11, p. 45
37:1–2, p. 94
40:12, p. 42
41:5, p. 220
44:5, p. 386
46:1, p. 287
49:11–12, p. 220
50:6, p. 286
51:7, p. 101
51:9, p. 392
52:8, p. 94
55:17, p. 359

57:1, p. 58
63:7, p. 58
69:4, p. 42
71:6, p. 336
75:6, p. 167
76:2, p. 184
83:4, p. 220
92:10, p. 50
97:2, p. 86
102:26, p. 62
103:5, p. 393
103:12, p. 167
104:2, pp. 77, 86
105:4, p. 290
107:3, p. 167
110:4, p. 184
112:4, p. 155
113:3, p. 168
115, p. 56
115:3–8, p. 56
118:6, p. 286
118:10–12, p. 386
118:26, p. 220
119:105, p. 38
121:3, p. 344
126:4, p. 158
129:8, p. 386
134:1–2, p. 29
139:8–10, p. 167
141:2, p. 29

Proverbs
1:15–16, p. 38
3, p. 126
4:1, p. 126
10:6, p. 46
10:7, p. 220
17:3, p. 93
17:4, p. 34
20:29, p. 43
23:2, p. 56
24:16, p. 126
25:2, p. 325
25:20, p. 62
26:11, p. 246

27:21, p. 93
30:20, p. 198

ECCLESIASTES
6:4, p. 220
9:13–16, p. 330
10:2, p. 165
12:13, p. 226

SONG OF SOLOMON
3:11, p. 381
4:1, p. 41
4:15–16, p. 159
5:4, p. 336
5:11, p. 41
6:5, p. 41

ISAIAH
1:8, p. 381
1:16, p. 392
1:18, pp. 101, 104, 105
1:21–23, p. 195
3–4, p. 127
3:16, p. 52
3:16–17, p. 381
3:24, p. 42
4:1, pp. 363, 364, 385
4:3–6, p. 381
5:1–7, p. 20
5:20, p. 86
5:27, p. 52
6:3, p. 359
6:5, p. 392
7:14, pp. 198, 229, 288, 389
7:20, p. 42
8:2, p. 240
8:8, pp. 58, 288
9:6, pp. 55, 185, 293
9:12, p. 375
10:5–16, p. 164
10:32, p. 381
11:5, p. 52
11:12, pp. 120, 149
11:14, p. 169

13, p. 21
13:12, p. 92
14, p. 21
14:12–13, p. 163
14:12–20, p. 233
14:13, p. 374
14:22, p. 220
14:31, p. 164
16:1, p. 381
16:11, p. 336
16:14, p. 198
20:2–4, pp. 13, 75
21:16, p. 198
22:6, p. 68
24:22, p. 181
25:7, p. 348
27:7–9, p. 154
30:30–31, p. 55
33:15, p. 35
37:1, p. 74
37:22, p. 381
40:31, p. 393
41:13, p. 287
43:6, p. 374
44:20, p. 48
45:3–4, p. 242
45:6, p. 168
48:19, p. 336
49:1, pp. 242, 336
49:12, pp. 167, 170
49:13, p. 153
50:9, p. 62
51:3, p. 290
51:6, 8, p. 62
52:2, p. 381
52:10, p. 28
53:2, p. 179
53:3, p. 197
53:7, p. 182
54:5, p. 194
56:5, p. 220
57:3–12, p. 198
59:17, p. 339
59:19, p. 168
60:1–3, p. 155

61:10, p. 73
62:5, p. 198
62:11, p. 381
63:1–3, p. 100
63:2, pp. 102, 354
63:11, p. 187
63:15, p. 336
63:19, p. 385
65:4, p. 261
65:15, p. 220
66:5, p. 386
66:17, p. 261

JEREMIAH
1:2, p. 137
1:13–16, pp. 163, 164
1:14–16, p. 164
3:3, p. 40
3:6–8, p. 194
3:6–11, p. 198
3:12, p. 163
3:14, p. 194
3:18, pp. 163, 374
4:6, pp. 163, 164
4:14, p. 47
4:19, p. 336
4:27–29, p. 89
4:31, p. 381
6:1, 22, pp. 163, 164
6:2, 23, p. 381
6:10, p. 33
7–8, p. 98
7:26, p. 52
7:29, p. 41
8:21, pp. 87, 89
9:26, p. 48
10:22, pp. 163, 164
11:16–17, p. 94
11:20, p. 48
13, p. 159
13:11, p. 52
13:19, p. 159
13:20, p. 163
14:2, p. 89

Scripture Index

16:15, pp. 163, 164, 374
17:7–8, p. 94
17:9, p. 48
18:1–4, p. 114
18:17, p. 154
20:9, p. 386
21:5, p. 28
23:5b, p. 21
23:8, pp. 163, 374
23:20, p. 47
25:3, p. 137
25:9, pp. 163, 164
25:26, p. 163
26, p. 391
26:20–23, p. 240
27:2, 8, p. 53
30:3, pp. 163, 170
31:4, p. 198
31:8, pp. 163, 374
31:34, p. 376
31:20, p. 336
32:17, p. 28
36:30, p. 133
40–42, p. 232
46:20, 24, p. 375
47:2, p. 375
48:37, p. 42
48:40, pp. 58, 250
49:22, pp. 58, 250
50:9, p. 164
50:15, p. 44
50:3, 9, 41–43, p. 375
51:11, p. 68
51:48, p. 375

Lamentations
1:6, p. 381
1:20, p. 336
2:11, p. 336
4:8, pp. 87, 88
4:22, p. 381
5:10, p. 88

Ezekiel
1–24, p. 287
1:4, p. 374
1:15–21, p. 333
1:18, p. 36
1:26, p. 89
3:17–19, p. 259
5:1–5, 12, p. 118
7:19, p. 336
9:4, p. 41
10:12, p. 36
10:19, p. 156
11:19, p. 48
11:22–23, p. 154
12:2, p. 34
16, p. 194
16:1–5, p. 347
16:10, p. 75
17:18, p. 44
18:31, p, 48
20:45–49, p. 160
21, p. 373
23:5–6, p. 195
23:6, p. 90
23:7, p. 351
23:34, p. 41
25–48, p. 287
26:7, p. 164
30:21, p. 76
33:3–6, p. 259
34:15–16, p. 76
36:25–26, p. 161
37:9, pp. 120, 149
37:17, p. 113
38:6, 15, p. 164
39:2–4, p. 164
43:1–2, 4, p. 156
43:2–5, p. 155
44:17–18, p. 70

Daniel
1, p. 286
2:19, 31 34, p. 20
2:30, p. 47
3, p. 286

4:33, p. 41
5:1–6, p. 51
5:7, 16, p. 97
5:27, p. 97
6, p. 286
6:10, p. 359
7:9, pp. 43, 61, 105
7:9–14, p. 293
7:21–25, p. 117
9:6, p. 386
10:6, p. 91
11:21–45, p. 164
12:7, p. 117

Hosea
1:2, p. 194
1:2–3, p. 13
2, pp. 194, 195
2:2–13, p. 195
3:1–3, p. 195
4, p. 195
8:1, p. 250
13:15, p. 154
14:8, p. 94

Joel
1, p. 289
2:2, p. 87
2:20, p. 375
3:17, 21, p. 23

Amos
9:9, pp. 163, 170
9:12, p. 385

Obadiah
1:21, p. 182

Jonah
3:4, p. 138
4:8–11, p. 154

Micah
1:8, p. 75
1:13, p. 381

Nahum
3:1–4, p. 195

Habakkuk
3:3, p. 373

Zephaniah
1:4, p. 220
1:15, p. 87
2:12, p. 164
3:14, p. 381

Haggai
1:11, p. 132

Zechariah
1:8, p. 102
1:17, p. 290
2:6, pp. 120, 164, 374
2:6–9, p. 164
2:10, p. 381
2:10–13, p. 23
3:3–5, p. 69
6:2, pp. 87, 99, 102
6:6, pp. 87, 164
6:8, p. 164
7:11, p. 34
7:14, pp. 163, 170
9:9, p. 381

13:6, p. 188
13:8–9, p. 118
14:1–5, p. 188
14:8, p. 119

Malachi
1:11, p. 168
3:14, p. 89
4:2, p. 59

Matthew
1–2, p. 184
1:21, p. 389
1:23, p. 198
1:26, p. 168
2, p. 186
2:1–2, pp. 153, 186
2:1–6, 16 (JST), p. 173
2:5–6, p. 376
2:12, p. 153
2:15, p. 187
3:1–4, p. 206
4:1–10, p. 186
4:1–11 (JST), p. 138
4:1–11, pp. 181, 190
4:2, p. 186
4:8 (JST), p. 186
4:17, pp. 184, 189
5–7, p. 187
5:8, p. 48
5:17, p. 196
5:29–30, p. 37
5:30, p. 45
5:35, p. 184
5:48, p. 183
6:22–23, p. 36

7:6, p. 260
7:13–14, p. 256
7:37 (JST), p. 180
8:1–4, p. 198
8:28–32, p. 263
9:18, p. 116
10:1–2, p. 185
10:1–4, pp. 134, 182, 188
10:4, p. 180
10:7–8, p. 198
10:25, p. 224
10:30, p. 42
11:28–29, p. 189
11:29, p. 188
12:24, p. 224
12:38–39, p. 251
12:39, p. 198
12:40, p. 333
13, pp. 5, 120, 256, 394
13:10–17, p. 7
13:15, pp. 33, 34
13:16, p. 34
13:24–30, p. 114
13:47–50, p. 255
13:48, p. 256

13:49–50, p. 394
14–15, p. 187
14:8, p. 206
14:25–32, p. 187
15:19, p. 48
16:4, p. 198
17:2, p. 105
18:5, p. 386
18:6, p. 53
18:8, p. 45
18:16, p. 115
18:21–22, p. 127
19:26, p. 287
20:2, p. 87
21:10, p. 295
21:34 (JST), p. 7
21:42, p. 47
21:42–46, p. 186
21:46, p. 182
22:1–10, p. 191
22:1–14, pp. 192, 256
22:40, p. 115
23, p. 393–94
23:1–4, p. 54
23:1–36, p. 250
23:21 (JST), p. 252
23:24, p. 250

23:27, p. 247
23:35, p. 291
23:37, p. 58
24, pp. 180, 188, 276
24:27 (JST), p. 168
24:27, p. 156
24:28 (JST), p. 276
24:28, p. 276
25:1–13, pp. 20, 121, 296
25:31–33, p. 114
26:15, p. 181
26:26–28, pp. 184, 278
26:37, p. 304
26:53, p. 135
26:59 (JST), p. 181
26:59–60, p. 182
27:3, p. 141
27:17–26, p. 224
27:29, p. 178
27:45, p. 87
27:46, pp. 127, 277
27:51, p. 279
28:3, pp. 61, 104
28:16–20, p. 188
28:19, p. 386

MARK
1:1, p. 190
1:11, p. 180
1:13, p. 186
1:40–45, pp. 50, 198
4:33–34, p. 13
5:1–13, pp. 260, 263
5:13, p. 283
5:25–43, p. 135
6, p. 187
6:7, p. 115
6:14–18, 25, p. 206
6:24–28, p. 46
7:21, p. 47
8:38, p. 198
9:3 (JST), p. 206
9:3, p. 105
9:23, p. 287

9:42, p. 53
9:43, p. 45
10:15, p. 198
12:10, p. 47
13:29, p. 168
14:22–24, p. 278
14:55–59, p. 182
15:22, pp. 178, 201
15:33, p. 87
15:37–39, p. 279
16:5, pp. 104, 105

LUKE
1, p. 291
1:11–19, p. 287
1:26–38, pp. 177, 189, 287
1:27, p. 198
2:7, pp. 76, 77, 182
2:12, 16, p. 77
2:25–35, p. 284
2:41–52 (JST), p. 183
2:46 (JST), p. 366
3:23, p. 181
4, p. 116
5:1–9, p. 51
6:13, p. 242
7:12–15, p. 116
8:26–33, p. 263
8:31, p. 398
9, p. 187
9:29, p. 105
9:62, p. 45
10:1, pp. 115, 188
10:5–6, p. 189
10:17, p. 386
11:1, p. 304
11:5–10, p. 330
11:51, p. 291
12:35, p. 52
13:1–5, p. 189
13:24, p. 256
13:29, p. 149
13:34, pp. 58, 77
14:12–14, p. 192

14:12–24, p. 191
15:5, p. 54
15:11–32, p. 260
15:22, p. 75
15:31, p. 396
16:19–31, p. 31
16:22, p. 174
17:2, p. 53
17:11–19, p. 198
17:17, p. 132
17:37, p. 276
18:1–9, p. 330
18:17, p. 198
20:17, p. 47
21:24, pp. 163, 170
22:19–20, p. 278
22:43, pp. 174, 178
22:44 (JST), pp. 30, 100
22:44, p. 99
22:48, p. 182
23:2, p. 225
23:28, 31, p. 95
23:33, p. 178
23:34, 43, 46, p. 127
23:44, p. 87
23:45, p. 279
24:39, p. 284

JOHN
1:1, pp. 288, 295
1:14, p. 185
1:21–28 (JST), p. 206
1:29, pp. 13, 196
2, p. 187
2:1–11, pp. 187, 389
2:12–14, p. 198
2:12–16, p. 174
2:19, 21, p. 19
3:5, p. 161
3:14, pp. 333, 369
3:15, p. 369
3:16, pp. 23, 174, 179, 200, 299, 304, 369
3:31, p. 197

4:1–3 (JST), p. 184
4:14, p. 159
4:35, p. 105
5:6–8, p. 161
5:19, pp. 177, 184
5:22, pp. 91, 187
5:25, 28, p. 55
5:43, p. 386
6, pp. 197
6:14, p. 182
6:31–35, p. 295
6:35, pp. 12, 161, 187, 295
6:42, p. 190
6:48, p. 12
6:53–54, p. 29
6:53–58, p. 278
7:5, p. 189
7:17, p. 193
7:37–39, pp. 120, 161, 283
8:12, p. 12, 86
8:17–18, p. 115
8:28, p. 177
8:31–37, p. 376
9:5, pp. 12, 86
10:1, p. 256
10:3, p. 242
10:11, pp. 172, 187, 274
10:12–13, p. 198
10:14, pp. 176, 180
11, p. 116
12:23–24, p. 401
13:5–14, p. 39
13:23, p. 304
14:6, pp. 156, 173, 183, 275
14:26, p. 25
14:27, pp. 185, 343
16:33, pp. 99, 185
17:12, pp. 200, 216, 272
18:15, p. 304
19, p. 97

19:2–3, p. 97
19:12, 15, p. 225
19:17, p. 178
19:23, p. 74
19:25–28, 30, p. 127
19:34, p. 175
20, p. 331
20:12, p. 104
21:21–23, p. 304

ACTS
1:3, p. 138
1:9, p. 188
1:10, p. 104
2:30, p. 52
2:38, p. 386
4:10–12, p. 194
4:11, p. 47
4:12, pp. 173, 290
5:28, p. 386
5:30, p. 197
5:34–39, p. 239
5:38–39, p. 228
7:21–29, p. 383
7:30, p. 383
7:51, pp. 33, 34, 52
7:54, p. 33
7:55–56, p. 238
7:55–58, p. 34
8:16, p. 386
9:15, p. 236
9:29, p. 386
10, pp. 116, 243
10:9–48, p. 244
10:25, p. 39
10:28–48, p. 391
10:38–48, p. 193
10:48, p. 386
11:1–10, p. 391
11:28–30, p. 225
13:9, p. 214
13:27, p. 181
16:18, p. 386
17:3, p. 376
17:28–29, p. 200

18:2, p. 225
18:9–10, p. 214
19:5, p. 386
21:28, p. 239
22:17–21, p. 214
23:11, p. 214
23:29, p. 239
24:1–2, p. 239
24:22, 26–27, p. 227
26:9–23, p. 214
27:12, p. 373
27:34, p. 42
28:23, p. 215
28:27, p. 33

ROMANS
1:4, p. 282
1:5, p. 386
1:24, p. 47
2:14, p. 47
2:29, p. 48
4:11, p. 173
5:5, p. 48
5:8, p. 178
5:14, pp. 3, 333
6:3–5, p. 129
6:17, p. 48
7:24, p. 235
8, p. 376
8:17, pp. 193, 197
9:10–13, p. 179
10:10, p. 47
12:5, p. 276
13:12, p. 65
14:11, p. 51
16:20, p. 38
16:23, p. 237

1 CORINTHIANS
2:10, p. 25
3:11, p. 103
4:17, p. 239
6:9–10, p. 191
10:1, p. 3
10:1–11, p. 12

11:2–13, p. 81
11:10, pp. 81, 82
11:14–15, p. 42
15, p. 214
15:21–22, pp. 3, 23
15:25–27, p. 176
15:27–28, p. 179
15:40–41, p. 92
15:45, p. 175
15:45–50, p. 114
15:52–54, p. 345
15:53, p. 364

2 CORINTHIANS
3:12–16, p. 80
3:14–18, p. 4
4:3, p. 80
4:4, p. 293
4:6, p. 183
6:7, p. 65
6:14–17, pp. 259, 395
10:4, p. 65
11:2–3, p. 198
11:24–28, p. 215
12:7, p. 236

GALATIANS
3:19 (JST), p. 186
3:29, p. 174
4:6, p. 47
4:22–26, p. 3

EPHESIANS
1:17–23, p. 47
3:17, p. 48
4:4–6, p. 113
4:10, p. 197
4:15, pp. 47, 175
5:20, p. 220
5:21, p. 79
5:22–25, pp. 78, 79
5:23, p. 47
6:6, p. 48
6:11–17, p. 65
6:14, pp. 52, 65

6:14–18, p. 122
6:15, pp. 37, 67
6:16, p. 67
6:17, pp. 68, 339, 344, 404

PHILIPPIANS
1:8, p. 336
2:1, p. 336
4:13, p. 176

COLOSSIANS
1:2, p. 364
1:15, p. 175
1:18, pp. 47, 276
2.10, p. 47
2:17, p. 3
3:12, pp. 236, 336
3:15, p. 48
3:17, p. 386
4:13, 15–16, p. 364

1 THESSALONIANS
5:8, p. 66

2 THESSALONIANS
3:6, p. 386

1 TIMOTHY
1:2, p. 239
2:5, pp. 71, 173, 187
5:19, p. 115
5:21, p. 82

2 TIMOTHY
4:3, p. 33
4:6, p. 215
4:8, p. 70

PHILEMON
1:7, 12, 20, p. 336

HEBREWS
1:3, pp. 175, 200, 293
1:11, p. 62

3:1, pp. 100, 185
4, p. 189
4:12, pp. 48, 344, 404
5:4–6, p. 376
5:10, p. 100
5:12, p. 198
6:10, p. 386
7, pp. 3, 184
7:1–2, p. 185
7:14–16, p. 184
8:1–5, p. 3
8:6–13, p. 114
9–10, p. 3
9:11, p. 185
9:13–14, p. 29
9:28, p. 174
10:1, p. 3
10:9, 16, 17, p. 114
10:19–22, p. 71
10:28, p. 115
11:30, p. 137
12:16, p. 354
12:22–24, p. 381
12:26, p. 55

JAMES
1:12, p. 70
3:9, p. 23
4:4, p. 198
4:8, p. 40
5:10, p. 386
5:10–11, p. 376

1 PETER
1:11, p. 25
1:20, p. 176
3:18–21, p. 129

1 JOHN
3:1–3, p. 71
5:1, p. 175

JUDE
1:13, p. 88
1:14, pp. 124–25, 177

REVELATION
1:4, pp. 127, 364
1:14, p. 43
1:15, p. 91
1:16, pp. 344, 404
2:7, pp. 105, 192
2:10, p. 70
2:14, p. 224
2:17, pp. 105, 161
2:18, p. 91
3:4, p. 105
3:4–5, pp. 72, 104, 345
3:5, p. 355
3:11, p. 70
3:14, p. 402
3:21, p. 183
4:4, p. 93
4:6–8, p. 36
4:8, pp. 58, 359
5:1, 5–6, p. 128
5:5, 8, p. 20
5:6, pp. 50, 178
6:2, pp. 105, 355
6:4, pp. 99, 102
6:5–6, p. 87
6:8, p. 94
6:11, pp. 61, 74, 104
6:12, p. 88
7:2, p. 153
7:4, p. 136
7:4–8, p. 110
7:9, pp. 61, 74
7:14, pp. 104, 355
8:7–12, p. 118
8:10–11, p. 283
11:3–14, p. 117
11:6, p. 283
11:15, pp. 180, 190
12–14, p. 147
12:1, pp. 20, 135, 332
12:1–4, p. 19
12:3, pp. 50, 102
12:3–4, pp. 99, 102, 217, 273
12:6, pp. 117, 197
12:9, pp. 217, 273
12:14, p. 393
13:1, p. 50
13:1–2, p. 19
13:16–14:1, p. 40
13:16–17, pp. 146, 148
13:18, pp. 111, 144, 145, 148
14:14, p. 105
14:20, p. 360
15:6, pp. 345, 355
16:12, p. 155
17:1–5, p. 98
17:4, pp. 101–2; 355
17:14, p. 293
18:23, p. 191
19:7–9, p. 191
19:8, pp. 74, 101, 104, 345
19:11–13, p. 100
19:11–14, p. 105
19:13, pp. 61, 353
19:15, p. 404
20:4, 13, p. 23
20:11, p. 105
21, p. 192
21–22, p. 114
21:2, p. 192
21:12–14, p. 135
21:21, pp. 93, 135
21:22, p. 345
22:1–2, pp. 119, 192
22:17, p. 192

BOOK OF MORMON

1 NEPHI
2:4, 11, p. 92
2:10, p. 232
2:16, p. 213
3:12, p. 91
3:29, p. 213
4:8–18, p. 91
4:17–18, p. 46
5:14, p. 208
5:18–19, p. 91
6, p. 213
7:1–5, p. 289
8:4, p. 88
8:10–11, p. 105
8:10–12, p. 4
8:19, p. 4
8:20, p. 67
10:4, p. 181
10:13, p. 113
11:8–23, p. 4
11:9–24, p. 298
11:21, p. 299
11:24, p. 39
11:35–36, pp. 4, 15
12:10–11, p. 355
12:14–19, p. 208
13, p. 98
13:15, pp. 86, 105
14:10, p. 114
15, p. 213
15:21–22, p. 4
16:10, p. 4
16:13, p. 158
17:4, p. 131
17:24, p. 187
19, p. 213
19:7, p. 337
19:8, p. 213
19:23, pp. 9, 18, 327, 333
21:12, p. 170

Scripture Index 449

21:13, p. 153
22, p. 213
22:10–11, p. 28
22:15–31, p. 189

2 Nephi

2:11, p. 176
2:25, pp. 64, 175
3:5, p. 208
3:9, p. 182
3:11, 15, p. 208
3:18, p. 211
4:17, p. 235
4:25, p. 59
4:34, p. 28
5, p. 213
5:21, pp. 86, 105
8:5, p. 28
9:9, pp. 217, 273
9:44, p. 36
10:14, p. 185
11, p. 213
11:4, pp. 3, 13, 269, 398
13:10, p. 192
15:20, 24, p. 99
17:14, pp. 198, 288
18:8, p. 288
19:20, p. 28
22:2, p. 287
23:12, p. 92
24:12–13, p. 163
24:12–14, p. 179
25–33, p. 213
25:24–30, p. 398
27:27, p. 86
28:30, p. 24
30:6, p. 86
31:7, p. 172
31:13, p. 71
32:8, p. 267

Jacob

1:11, p. 386
2:10, p. 36

2:13, p. 52
2:25, p. 52
3:9, p. 86
4:4–5, p. 398
4:5, 11, p. 23
4:16–17, p. 103
4:17, p. 47
5:30, pp. 163, 170
7, p. 238
7:10–11, p. 269
7:11, p. 283

Enos

1:13, p. 28

Omni

1:2, p. 235

Mosiah

1:12, p. 220
1:13, p. 198
1:17, p. 289
2:9, p. 33
2:41, p. 192
3:5–10, p. 186
3:7, pp. 31, 99
3:15, pp. 3, 333
3:18, p. 189
3:19, pp. 121, 166
4:16–26, p. 193
5:7, pp. 173, 174
5:8, pp. 47, 71
5:11, p. 220
5:12, 14, p. 242
5:13, pp. 47, 48
7:9, p. 234
7:31, p. 154
9:18, pp. 289, 290
10:5–8, p. 165
11:13–14, p. 165
11:25, p. 350
12:6, p. 154
12:21, p. 38
12:24, p. 28
13:10, p. 3

13:30–32, pp. 333, 398
13:32, p. 184
15:8, p. 99
15:9, p. 336
15:15–18, p. 38
16:14, p. 3
17:10, p. 29
18, p. 131
19, p. 228
23:3, p. 131
23:10, pp. 289, 290
24:13–14, p. 55
25:22–23, p. 128
26:23, p. 175
26:36, p. 220
27:31, pp. 36, 51
29:20, p. 28

Alma

1:24, p. 220
2, p. 153
2:35–38, p. 169
2:36–37, p. 167
2:37, p. 222
3:13–19, pp. 40, 102
5:19, p. 71
5:21, 24, p. 72
5:21–22, p. 29
5:33, 62, p. 191
5:34, p. 161
5:50, p. 185
5:53, p. 337
5:57, pp. 220, 398
5:59, p. 398
6:3, p. 220
6:7, p. 153
7:10, p. 198
7:10–13, pp. 55, 77
7:12, p. 336
8:3, p. 233
8:3–5, p. 169
8:6–10, p. 165
8–10, p. 169
11:40–41, p. 23
11:44, pp. 23, 42

12:7, p. 48
12:21, pp. 151, 297
12:21–27, p. 403
12:33–34, p. 23
13:5, p. 23
13:10–11, p. 191
13:11, pp. 104, 355
13:14–18, p. 3
13:16, p. 184
13:18, pp. 184, 185
13:19, p. 185
16:5, p. 223
17, p. 28
18:13, p. 237
18:16, p. 128
18:20, p. 47
19:6, pp. 86, 105
25:10, 15, p. 3
26:3, pp. 86, 105
26:11–12, p. 287
26:37, p. 336
30, p. 231
30:44, pp. 269, 270
30:52, p. 231
31:31–32, p. 290
33:19, p. 3
33:19–20, p. 143
34:8, p. 187
34:15, p. 336
34:33–34, p. 296
34:36, pp. 191, 355
37:38–40, p. 4
37:38–45, p. 3
38:9, p. 86
39:5, p. 253
40:23, p. 42
42:2, pp. 151, 297
42:23, p. 23
43:27, p. 170
44:4, p. 189
47:8, p. 47
49:10, p. 47
60:24, p. 47

60:33, p. 337
63:5, p. 165

HELAMAN

1:7–9, p. 235
1:22–23, p. 165
5:44, p. 343
6:10, p. 233
8:13–15, p. 143
8:27, p. 121
9:2, 4–5, 8–9, 19, 39, p. 122
13:11, p. 195
14:2, p. 121

3 NEPHI

3–4, p. 228
3:10, p. 228
3:11, p. 229
5:20, p. 208
7:8, p. 123
9:13, p. 195
9:22, pp. 55, 198
10:6, p. 195
11:1–7, p. 116
11:7, p. 274
11:37–38, p. 198
12:1, p. 134
13:22–23, p. 36
20:19, p. 50
20:22, p. 176
20:23, p. 182
25:2, p. 59
25:3, p. 38

MORMON

1:2, 5, 6, 15, p. 208
1:2–4, pp. 133, 208
1:3–4, p. 209
2, p. 209
2:1, p. 208
2:17–18, p. 133
2:18, p. 209

2:19, p. 210
5:6, p. 38
5:14, p. 194
5:15, p. 86
6, pp. 209, 366
6:6, p. 133
6:10, 12–15, p. 139
6:17, p. 209
7:5–7, p. 99
8:3, p. 209
8:10–11, p. 208

ETHER

1:1, p. 165
2:3, p. 226
2:24, p. 230
2:25, p. 231
3:1, p. 131
4:1, p. 190
6:12, p. 38
8–11, p. 161
8–15, pp. 160, 373
8:13–15, p. 57
9:18, p. 398
9:30–35, p. 160
10:4–7, p. 238
10:5, p. 54
10:19, p. 160
13:10, p. 355
13:11, p. 165
15:30, p. 46

MORONI

5:2, pp. 172, 274
6:7, p. 220
7:9, p. 48
8:16, p. 286
9:3–6, p. 209
9:26, p. 176
10:23, p. 176
10:30, p. 248
10:31, p. 381

DOCTRINE AND COVENANTS

1:14, p. 28
1:19, pp. 28, 289
1:38, pp. 213, 306
3:8, p. 28
4:4, p. 105
4:5, p. 37
5:22, p. 215
6:2, pp. 344, 404
6:6, p. 205
6:16, p. 47
6:21, p. 183
6:23, p. 343
6:28, pp. 115, 199
6:29–30, p. 215
7:3, p. 304
8:2, p. 47
8:6–9, p. 199
9:14, p. 42
10:5, p. 267
10:65, p. 77
10:70, p. 86
11:6, p. 205
11:21, p. 343
11:25, pp. 24, 333
12:6, p. 205
13, pp. 135, 199, 203
14:6, p. 205
15:2, p. 28
18:22, p. 184
18:25, p. 242
18:27, p. 134
19, p. 206
19:15–20, p. 184
19:18, p. 100
20:14, p. 70
20:21, p. 23
20:43, p. 304
20:59, p. 191
20:79, p. 29
20:83, p. 220
21:5, p. 213
27:2, p. 29
27:7, p. 206

27:15, p. 52
27:15–18, p. 65
27:16, pp. 65, 66, 67
27:16–18, p. 122
27:17, p. 67
27:18, pp. 68, 344, 404
28:1–4, p. 199
29:11, 42, p. 23
29:12, p. 61
29:25, p. 42
33:1, pp. 33, 47, 48
35:13–14, p. 28
35:14, pp. 38, 52
36:1–2, p. 44
36:8, p. 52
38:1, p. 297
38:4, p. 174
38:27, p. 113
39:8, p. 46
41:1, p. 293
42:6, p. 115
42:32–39, p. 205
43:21–22, p. 156
43:29, p. 23
45, p. 20
45:9, p. 120
45:24–25, pp. 163, 170
45:44, p. 177
45:51–53, pp. 181, 197
49:5, p. 23
52:37, p. 46
58:5, p. 47
59:3, p. 38
59:21, pp. 143, 262
63:32–34, p. 155
68:25, p. 347
68:27, p. 129
76, pp. 205, 214
76:13, p. 23
76:14, 23, p. 205
76:22–23, p. 213
76:22–24, p. 214
76:25, pp. 23, 179, 293

76:25–27, pp. 179, 233
76:25–29, p. 205
76:26, pp. 200, 216, 272
76:67, p. 177
76:70, 75–78, p. 331
76:110, p. 181
77:4, pp. 36, 57
77:9, p. 153
77:11, p. 136
78:1, 4, 9, p. 205
84:6–7, p. 383
84:14, pp. 185, 203
84:33–41, p. 347
84:38, pp. 57, 341
84:116, pp. 42, 289
85:6, p. 33
85:7, p. 336
88:6–13, p. 294
88:21, p. 187
88:25–27, p. 192
88:40, p. 334
88:67, p. 88
88:74, pp. 38, 45
88:104, pp. 35, 51
88:112–15, p. 179
93:21, pp. 177, 293
93:39, p. 85
99:3, p. 198
100:9–11, p. 211
101:9, pp. 33, 336
101:38, p. 290
101:90, p. 289
107:3–4, p. 184
107:43, p. 200
107:55, p. 175
107:83, p. 46
109:61, p. 88
109:76, p. 61
109:79, p. 403
110, pp. 203, 205
110:1–4, p. 199
110:1–10, p. 214

110:2, pp. 205, 213
110:3, p. 43
110:11, pp. 165, 212
115:4, p. 177
115:4–5, p. 120
121–122, p. 212
121:3–4, 45, p. 336
121:33, p. 28
121:36, p. 347
121:36–37, 39, 41–44, p. 78
122, p. 207
122:5, p. 385
122:6–7, p. 207
122:9, pp. 226, 286
124:21, 57, p. 46
124:38, p. 211
127:1–3, p. 203
127:2, pp. 182, 203, 214, 385
128, p. 205
128:3, p. 115

128:4, 24, pp. 103
128:17, p. 206
128:20, pp. 203, 302
128:22, p. 288
129, pp. 217, 274
129:6–7, p. 404
130:10, p. 105
130:11, p. 242
130:22, p. 304
132, p. 204
132:1–55, p. 204
132:7, p. 191
132:16–17, p. 352
132:17, p. 341
132:19, pp. 300, 403
132:20, p. 52
132:30, p. 66
132:45, p. 293
132:49, p. 210
133:25, p. 23
133:26–32, p. 165
133:34, p. 46

133:46–51, p. 100
133:48, pp. 100, 354
133:67, p. 28
133:69, p. 350
135, p. 182
135:1, pp. 88, 209
135:3, pp. 182, 209, 211
135:5, p. 72
135:6, p. 95
136, p. 211
136:36, p. 29
136:39, p. 209
137:1–3, p. 214
138:38, p. 185
138:41, pp. 173, 185, 189
138:42, p. 76
138:53–55, p. 293

PEARL OF GREAT PRICE

Moses

1:1, 11, p. 186
1:6, pp. 23, 185
1:8, pp. 186, 210
1:17, 33, p. 23
1:12–23, p. 186
1:26, p. 187
1:33, p. 30
2:1, 26–27, p. 23
3:7, p. 175
3:10, p. 119
3:18, p. 23
4:1, p. 23
4:2, p. 178
4:13, pp. 62, 342
4:21, p. 46
4:22, p. 128
4:27, p. 70

4:31, pp. 151, 297
5:4–8, p. 13
5:7–28, 33, 41, p. 271
5:11, p. 62
5:12–13, 25–27, 32–36, pp. 216, 273
5:17, pp. 172, 215, 271, 272, 274
5:18, pp. 215, 272
5:19–21, pp. 216, 272
5:20, pp. 172, 274
5:21, pp. 172, 216, 272, 274
5:24, pp. 200, 216, 217, 272, 273
5:26, 32, pp. 172, 274
5:27–28, 31, 37–39, 41, 51, pp. 217, 273
5:29, pp. 57, 340

5:40, pp. 217, 273, 274
6:3–4, p. 190
6:41, p. 372
6:42, p. 152
6:57, p. 224
6:63, pp. 4, 270
7:4, 16, 21, 69, p. 23
7:5–12, p. 165
7:13, 19–21, 23–26, 69, p. 205
7:18, pp. 113, 141, 205
7:27–38, p. 137
7:31, p. 31
7:49, p. 234
7:62–63, p. 177
8:1–3, 27, p. 189
8:2, p. 52
8:22, p. 48
8:22–30, p. 137

Scripture Index

ABRAHAM
1:5–17, p. 203
1:15, p. 174
1:29–30, p. 87
2:2–15, p. 87
2:6, 9–11, p. 203
2:9, p. 173
2:15, p. 174
3, p. 291
3:1, pp. 204, 294
3:2, pp. 177, 204, 293
3:3, pp. 185, 204, 291, 293
3:4, pp. 204, 293
3:9, p. 291
3:16, pp. 293, 294
3:15–19, p. 292
3:19, pp. 97, 177, 185
3:22, p. 185
3:22–23, pp. 175, 189, 203
3:24, pp. 175, 293, 294
3:27, pp. 55, 172, 178, 180, 185, 274
3:28, pp. 172, 216, 272, 274
5:10, p. 119
5:18, p. 113

JOSEPH SMITH—MATTHEW
1 (JS–M), p. 188
1:26, p. 168

JOSEPH SMITH—HISTORY
1:1, 46, p. 182
1:3, 27–54, p. 208
1:7, 16, pp. 208, 213
1:15, 30–32, p. 205
1:16, 25, 30, 44, 46, 49, p. 207
1:16–17, pp. 203, 204
1:16–20, p. 211
1:16–25, p. 214
1:20, p. 176
1:17, 23–25, 59, p. 213
1:24, pp. 205, 214
1:30–31, p. 345
1:35, 62, p. 204
1:66–67, p. 209
1.68–71, p. 199

ARTICLES OF FAITH
1:10, p. 189

SUBJECT INDEX

Aaron: as type for Oliver Cowdery, 199; staff of, 280–82; as type for Christ, 400 (n. 37)
Abel: as type for Christ, 172–73, 274–75; meaning of, 173, 223; Cain's envy toward, 271; as good shepherd, 275
Abraham: gematria in account of, 141–42; symbolism in story of, 157–58; as type for Christ, 173–74; as type for God the Father, 200–201; as type for Joseph of Egypt, 201–3; as type for Moses, 201–3; as type for Joseph Smith, 203–4; fulfillment of covenant with, 230; sojourn of, 381 (n. 87); book of, 381 (n. 92); background of, 382 (n. 94); as father of Isaac, 389 (n. 51)
Actions: typical, 13; hands as symbol of, 43–45
Adam: as type for Christ, 175; as type for God the Father, 200; Hebrew root of name, 335 (n. 17)
Adam and Eve: sinless condition of, before the Fall, 30; clothing of, 62–63, 70–72, 342 (n. 14), 345 (n. 54); fall of, 63, 151–52, 166; wisdom of, 63–64, 342 (n. 18); unselfishness of, 64; symbolism in account of, 151–52, 301–2; trials of, 271; expulsion of, from

Eden, 297–300; visited by messengers, 301; work of, 360 (n. 72); sacrificial offering of, 377 (n. 14), 391 (n. 1)
Adam-ondi-Ahman, definition of, 166
Adulterer, as type for idolatry, 198
Agency, 41; Adam and Eve's wise use of, 64; feet as symbols of, 67
Aha, meaning of, 223
Akish, symbolism regarding, 57
Albright, William F., on carcass as symbol, 399–400 (n. 22)
Allegory, 171, 330 (n. 16); definition of, 14
Ambrosiaster, 348 (n. 108); on veil as symbol, 81
Amlicites, willful disobedience of, 40
Ammon, meaning of, 223, 388 (n. 26), 401–2 (n. 50)
Amon, meaning of, 223, 388 (n. 26)
Analysis: historical and cultural, 16–17; other methods of, 17–18
Anderson, Richard Lloyd, on sacrifices made by Joseph Smith, 385 (n. 160)
Angels, 297–300; symbolism regarding, 58; white garments of, 104; ministering, 341 (n. 129)
Anger, nose as symbol of, 53
Animals: as symbols, 243, 245, 258; clean and unclean, 244, 277–78,

455

392 (n. 7); "creeping things," 245; as symbols (list), 307–12; symbolism of, in Peter's vision, 391–92 (nn. 2, 3); in Book of Mormon, 398 (n. 82)
Ante-type, 398–99 (n. 1)
Anti-Christ: symbolic representation of, 144; six hundred sixty-six as symbol of, 147; Korihor as, 231–32
Antitype, definition of, 11–12
Apocalypse of Daniel, 300–301
Apostasy, 195, 380 (n. 71); thirteen as symbol of, 136–37; symbolism for, 146, 194–95, 259, 284; west as symbol of, 169; fish without scales as symbol of, 246; of Pharisees, 393–94 (n. 17)
Apostles, Nephite, 366 (n. 155)
Apron: as symbol, 62–64, 372 (n. 22); priesthood significance of, 64; Hebrew word for, 342 (n. 11); significance of, 342 (n. 14)
Aquinas, Thomas, on literal and figurative meanings, 2
Archetype: definition of, 15; esoteric, 331 (n. 21)
Arm, symbolism of, 28–29; upraised, 29
Armor of God, 65, 68, 122, 339 (n. 89); 344 (n. 38)
Ashes, sackcloth and, 74
Ass, as symbol, 395–96 (n. 53)
Atonement: blood symbolic of, 29–31; cleansing power of, 35; Mosaic symbolism regarding, 49–50; symbolic representation of, 75, 101, 125, 143; sacrificial animals symbolic of, 243; story of Cain and Abel as symbol of, 275; universal nature of, 278
Attitude, neck as symbol of, 52–53
Augustine, Saint, on parable of prodigal son, 261
Authority, 271, 348 (n. 105); robe as symbol of, 72–73; veil as symbol of, 80–81; divine recognition of, 82; priesthood, 103, 135; twelve as symbol for, 134; fulness of, 136; investiture of, 386 (n. 5)
Axe head, story of, 282–84

Baal, 224; priests of, 226
Babel: Tower of, 170; meaning of, 222
Baby, as type for immaturity in gospel, 198
Balaam, meaning of, 224
Baptism: symbolism regarding, 90; eight as symbol of, 129; saving powers of, 130; symbolic clothing in, 341 (n. 7)
Baptismal font, symbolism regarding, 134
Barabbas, meaning of, 224
Barnabas, Epistle of, 392–93 (n. 8)
Bayley, Harold: on sword and fire, 299; on hand as symbol, 338 (nn. 70, 71); on caps as symbols, 344 (n. 49)
Beast: wings and eyes of the, 58; mark of the, 144, 146–47, 370–71 (n. 223); meaning of, 359 (n. 66)
Beelzebub, meaning of, 224, 388 (n. 28)
Behaviors, symbolic, 27
Benjamin, king, on symbolism in scriptures, 3
Benoni, meaning of, 220
Bethel, meaning of, 157–58, 286
Bethlehem, meaning of, 222
Bible: historical context of, 16–17; symbolism in, 326–27 (nn. 8, 11, 12); literal and figurative interpretation of, 330 (n. 13); understanding meaning of, 331 (nn. 26, 27, 29); versification of, 363 (n. 115)

Bible dictionaries, use of, 223
Bickmore, Barry, on erroneous gematria, 370 (n. 211)
Birds of prey, 247–50. See also Eagle
Birth, names as symbols of, 221
Bitton, Davis, on parallels between Joseph Smith and Joseph of Egypt, 382 (n. 108)
Black, 354 (n. 107); as symbol, 85–89
Black, Susan Easton, on tree of life, 298
Blasphemy, six hundred sixty-six as symbol of, 147
Blood: symbolism of, 29–31, 329 (n. 37), 336 (n. 37); as symbol of mortality, 31; representation of, 99
Blue: as symbol, 89–90, 350 (nn. 29–31), 350–51 (nn. 32, 34, 35, 40)
Body, 150; ancient symbols regarding, 27–28; as symbol, 334–35 (n. 4)
Body parts, as symbols (list), 313–15
Bondage, 340 (n. 110)
Book of Mormon: significance of number eight in, 131; names in, 235, 387 (n. 21), 401–2 (n. 50); as autobiography, 349 (n. 19); animal symbolism in, 398 (n. 82)
Bosom, as symbol, 31–32, 335 (n. 20)
Bowels, symbolism of, 32–33
Bows, symbolism of, 69
Brass: as symbol, 90–91; serpent, 3, 91, 143–44, 369 (n. 197)
Bread: Christ as, of life, 161; symbolism of, 294–95
Breast, as symbol, 31–32, 335 (n. 20)
Brewster, Hoyt Jr., on gospel of peace, 343–44 (n. 36)

Brown, Raymond, on swaddling clothes, 76–77
Brown, S. Kent, on messengers to Adam and Eve, 301
Bullinger, E. W.: on symbolic use of numbers in book of Revelation, 128; on significance of number eight, 130; on symbolism in scripture, 325 (n. 3); on ancient tabernacle, 365 (n. 132); on Canaanite names, 371 (n. 229)
Bulls, as symbols, 257
Burdens, shoulders as symbol of, 54–55

Caesar, meaning of, 225, 388 (n. 29)
Cain: symbolism regarding, 57; as symbol for Lucifer, 215–17, 272–74; counterfeit oaths and covenants of, 340 (n. 123)
Cain and Abel, symbolism in story of, 271–75
Cainan, land of, 372 (n. 23)
Calling and election made sure, 136
Calvin, John, on symbolism in parable of carcass and eagles, 276
Camels, as symbols, 250–53, 391–94 (n. 17)
Cana, symbolism in story of, 123
Caps and hats, symbolism of, 69–70, 344 (n. 49)
Carcass, symbolism of, 276, 399–400 (n. 22)
Catholic church, symbolism regarding, 145
Celestial kingdom, symbolic representation of, 92
Chaos: west as symbol of, 166; water as symbol of, 265
Chapter headings, scriptural, 21
Character, heart as symbol of, 48
Chastity: sash as symbol of, 74; veil as symbol of, 78

Chemish, meaning of, 225
Cherubim and flaming sword, meaning of, 403 (n. 75)
Cherubs, 297–300, 403 (n. 74)
Children, as type for innocence, 198
Choice and accountability, 37–39
Christ. *See* Jesus Christ
Church, ancient: symbolism regarding, 128; priesthood authority in, 135; marriage partners as types for, 192
Church, great and abominable, 98–99, 101–2
Church of Firstborn, 136
Church of Jesus Christ of Latter-day Saints, The: symbolism in, 4; New Jerusalem as type for, 191–92; less active members of, 259; unity among members of, 358 (n. 46)
Churches, seven, 364 (n. 121)
Circumcision, 130
Clarke, Adam: on righteousness as protection against evil spirits, 264; on true and false servants of God, 394 (n. 32)
Claudius, meaning of, 225
Cleanliness: inner, 72, 248; feet as symbol of, 39
Cleansing: ceremony, 101; water as symbol for, 265
Clement of Alexandria, on prodigal son, 397 (n. 68)
Clothing: spiritual significance of, 61; preservation of, 62; as symbol (list), 316–18; of Mosaic high priest, 102, 341 (n. 4), 342 (n. 10), 350 (n. 30); symbolic, in restored Church, 341 (n. 7); contrasting symbolism of, 355 (n. 111); white, 355 (nn. 112–14)
Cloven hoof, 257
Coat, seamless, 74

"Coats of skins," 70–72
Coldness, north as symbol of, 162
Cole, R. Alan, on possession by evil spirits, 397 (n. 70)
Color, 83; ancient descriptions of, 83–84; relationship to nature, 84; significance of, in scripture, 84–85; in Mosaic tabernacle, 89, 96, 100, 104; symbolism of (list), 315–16; interpretation of symbolism in, 348 (n. 4)
Commitment: hands as symbol of, 45; lack of, 198, 251–52
Compass, four points of, 149
Compassion, 277: bowels as symbol of, 32–33; swaddling clothes as symbol of, 77
Completeness, four as symbol of, 119
Completion: seven as symbol of, 124; nine as symbol of, 131
Concepts, abstract, 8–9
Consecration, 132
Cooper, J. C.: on symbolic meaning of robes, 72; on camel and gnat as symbols, 393–94 (n. 17)
Cope, Gilbert: on purpose of Bible, 326 (n. 9); on allegorization, 330 (n. 13); on understanding Bible, 331 (n. 27)
Countenance, darkening of, 86
Country, Gentile, 263
Courage, Daniel an example of, 225–26
Covenant making, symbolic representation of, 124
Covenant people, east symbolic of, 152–53
Covenants, 2; symbolic representation of, 76, 166; south as symbol of, 157, 159–60; names as symbols of, 221; Christocentric nature of, 306; knot as symbol of, 344 (n. 43)

Cowdery, Oliver, visit of Peter, James, and John to, 302–3
Cowley, Matthias F., on First Presidency as symbol of Godhead, 302
Creation: periods of, 124; numerology in, 357 (n. 26)
Cross, symbolism of, 7–8
Crown, as symbol, 69–70, 344 (n. 48)
Crucifixion, symbolism regarding, 279–80
Cud chewing, as symbol, 257
Cycle, complete, 133
Cyril of Jerusalem, on ancient ordinances, 341 (n. 5)

Daniel: symbolism in book of, 109, 225–26; meaning of, 225, 286
Darkness: and light, 85–86; north as symbol of, 162; symbolic representation of, 166, 349 (n. 19)
Daughters of Zion, as type for city of Jerusalem and inhabitants, 198
David: and Goliath, symbolism in account of, 121, 158, 352 (n. 84); as type for Christ, 176; city of, 385 (n. 4)
Davidson, Richard, on typology, 327 (n. 19)
Davis, John, on numerology, 112, 356 (n. 12)
Day of Atonement, 126; priestly clothing on, 104
Death: blood as symbol of, 29; swaddling clothes as symbol of, 77; black as symbol of, 85; red as symbol of, 99; rending of veil as type for, 280
Deception, symbolism pertaining to, 101–2, 245
Defeat, horns as symbol of, 49–50
Deficit, six as symbol of, 122

Deissmann, Adolf, 6; on gematria in Revelation, 144; on Paul's name, 390 (n. 7)
Deity, attributes of, 117, 303–4. *See also* Godhead
Delilah, meaning of, 226
Demons, chief of, 224
Deseret, meaning of, 226
Desires: eyes as symbol of, 36–37; forehead as symbol of, 39–41; heart as symbol of, 48
Destruction: symbolic representation of, 224; broad path to, 256
Determination, goat as symbol of, 257
Devil, west as kingdom of, 168
Direction(s): four, 149; significance of, 150; sense of, 150; symbolic use of, in temple, 170; as symbol (list), 318
Disbelief, symbol for, 86
Disobedience, 35; feet as symbol of, 37–38; possession by unclean spirits due to, 263–64
Disrespect, symbolic representation of, 337 (n. 46)
Divinity, light as symbol of, 85
Division, symbolic representation of, 114
Doctrine and Covenants, contents of, 381 (n. 93)
Dogs, symbolism of, 245–46
Double-mindedness, 40–41
Draper, Richard, on symbolic representation of punishment, 87

Eagle: as symbol, 246, 276, 278, 399 (n. 19); as symbol of scattering of Israel, 393 (n. 12)
Ears, symbolism of, 33–36, 56
East: symbolic meanings of, 150–57, 375 (n. 88); Hebrew words for, 151; as symbol of movement

toward God, 152; orientation toward, 162
East and west, 375 (n. 88); as symbol of totality, 167–68
Eden: paradisiacal condition of, 119; expulsion from, 297–300
Edwards, Jonathan, on typology, 333 (n. 45)
Eight, as symbol, 129–31, 365 (nn. 128, 129, 132–34)
Eight Witnesses, 93
Eisegesis, 325–26 (chap. 1, n. 1)
Eleazar, meaning of, 286–87
Eleven, as symbol, 133
Eliezer, gematria in account of, 141–42
Elijah: meaning of, 226, 286–87; fast of, 367 (n. 171)
Elisha: meaning of, 287; miracles performed by, 402 (n. 55)
Ellsworth, Richard G., on parable of prodigal son, 396–97 (n. 67)
Emotions: bowels as symbol of, 32–33; color and, 83
Endowment, temple. See Temple endowment
Enoch, 372 (n. 23), 382 (n. 102); gematria regarding, 125; vision of, 165; as type for Christ, 177; as type for Joseph Smith, 205
Enos, meaning of, 226
Ensign, gospel as, 120
Ephod, 64, 342 (n. 19)
Ephraim, symbolism in blessing of, 165
Esau: symbolism in story of, 101; and Jacob, as types for Judaism and Christianity, 196–97
Eschatology, definition of, 366 (n. 146)
Esther: clothing of, 90; meaning of, 227
Eternal judgment, symbolic representation of, 35–36
Eve, sorrow and conception of, multiplied, 128–29. See also Adam and Eve
Event: as type, 12; renaming as indication of, 221
Evil: closing ears to, 35; symbolism regarding, 65–66; black as symbol of, 85, 88; triumph of good over, 117–18; Goliath as symbol of, 123; west as symbol of, 166
Evil spirits, 264, 266–67, 397–98 (nn. 70, 72, 76, 77, 79); protection against, 264
Exaltation: loss of, 94; temple endowment and, 300
Exegesis, definition of, 325–26 (chap. 1, n. 1)
Extremes, in scriptural interpretation, 23–24
Eyes, as symbol, 35–37, 336 (n. 42)
Ezekiel: symbolism in book of, 109; meaning of, 287

Fairbairn, Patrick, on cherubs, 297
Faith: light as symbol of, 86; shield of, 344 (n. 38)
Fall, the, 166; consequences of the, 128–29; symbolism in account of, 151
Famine, black symbolic of, 87
Farbridge, Maurice: on symbolism in Eastern cultures, 5; on Samson, 337 (n. 62)
Farrar, Frederic W., on Jewish attitude toward swine, 261
Fear, knees as symbol of, 50–51
Fee, Gordon, on context of scriptures, 2
Feet: symbolism of, 37–39; as symbols of agency, 67; trampling under, 337 (n. 46)
Felix, meaning of, 227
Fertility, symbols of, 32–33
Festus, meaning of, 227
Fidelity, sash as symbol of, 74

Fig leaves: aprons of, 62; as symbol, 62, 342 (n. 14), 372 (n. 22)
Finality, nine as symbol of, 131–32
Fire, as symbol, 299
Firmage, Edwin, on sea as symbol, 360 (n. 75), 398 (n. 76)
First Presidency: as symbol, 302; heeding counsel of, 306
Fish: without scales, 246, 254; unclean, 253–54; division of good from bad, 254–55; bad, 255–56; as symbols, 394 (n. 36)
Fitzmyer, Joseph: on symbolism in story of possessed swine, 265; on swaddling clothes, 347 (n. 87)
Five, as symbol, 120–22
Flames, as symbols, 299
Food, misconceptions about healthfulness of, 245
Forehead, symbolism of, 39–41
Forgiveness, seventy times seven, 127
Fornication, rabbits as symbol of, 246
Fortunatus, meaning of, 227
Forty: symbolism of, 137–38; days, 367 (n. 171)
Forty-two, symbolism of, 138
Foundation, temple as a, 103
Fountain, symbolic meaning of, 158–59
Four, as symbol, 119–20, 360 (n. 74)
Fractions, symbolic use of, 118
Freedom, symbolism regarding, 75
Fulness, seven as symbol of, 124

Gabriel, meaning of, 287
Gain, personal, 247
Gamaliel, meaning of, 228
Garments: temple, 70–72; unspotted, 72; white, 104; holy, 341 (n. 4); ancient, 345 (n. 57)
Gematria, 139–48, 357 (n. 31), 369 (n. 199); definition of, 111, 139; regarding Enoch, 125; regarding number nine, 131–32; in account of Eliezer, 141–42; early use of, 139–40; systems of, 140; in accounts of Judas, 141; regarding Reformation, 145–46; as teaching tool, 148; erroneous, 370 (n. 211); in book of Revelation, 144, 370 (n. 222)
"Genre mistake," 18
Gentile nations, symbolism regarding, 163
Geographical completeness, four as symbol of, 119–20
Gethsemane, Christ's suffering in, 99, 278–79
Giddianhi, meaning of, 228–29
Gideon, meaning of, 228
Ginzberg, Louis, on Eve's naming of son, 223
Gloom, north as symbol of, 162
Glory, kingdoms of, 117
Gluttony: symbols of, 245; swine as symbol of, 260
Gnat: straining at, 250–51; as symbol, 252–53, 393–94 (n. 17)
Goats, as symbols, 256–57
God: man's relationship to, 47, 79, 92, 264; protection offered by, 54; armor of, 65, 122, 339 (n. 89); power of, 96; grace of, 120–21; judgments of, 132; wrath of, 132–33, 153–54, 164, 261–62; Abraham receives help from, 142; abode of, 154; glory of, 155–56; throne of, 350–51 (n. 32), 402 (n. 59); true and false servants of, 394 (n. 32); name of, 401 (n. 49)
God the Father, 200–201; characteristics of, 303–4
Godhead: three as symbol of, 115–16; First Presidency as symbol of, 302; characteristics

of, 303–4; Peter, James, and John as type for, 305
Godliness, 89; hair as symbol of, 43; east as symbol of, 151–53; three as symbol of, 300
God's care, hair as symbol of, 41–42
God's will: east as symbol for, 151–53; compliance to, 152; obedience to, 257
Gold, as symbol, 91–93, 352 (nn. 48, 50)
Goliath, symbolism in account of, 123
Goppelt, Leonhard, on interpretation of scripture, 327 (n. 15)
Gordon, Cyrus, on triads of officers, 301
Gospel, 21; as ensign, 120; Gentile nations to receive, 244; security connected with, 245; charting own course in, 254
Governance: head as symbol of, 47; twelve as symbol for, 134
Grace of God, five as symbol of, 120–21
Grant, Robert M., on hermeneutical interpretation, 18
Grasshoppers, as symbols, 246
Gratitude, lack of, 261–62
Great number, one thousand as symbol of, 139
Greed, symbols of, 56
Green: as symbol, 93–96, 352 (n. 56); negative connotations of, 94–95
Guilt, blood as symbol of, 29

Habershon, Ada, on colors as symbols, 348 (n. 4)
Hagar, meaning of, 229
Hagoth, 375 (n. 79); symbolism in account of, 165
Hair: as symbol, 41–43, 337–38 (n. 64); white, 43
Hands: as symbol, 43–45, 56, 338 (nn. 65, 66, 70, 71, 74); raised, 44; laying on of, 44; clean, 45; right and left, 338 (n. 66)
Hartshorn, Leon, on armor of God, 344 (n. 38)
Hats, symbolism of, 69–70
Head: Hebrew connotations of, 45–46; symbolism of, 45–47
Healing: symbolism in stories of, 135; of man with unclean spirits, 262–65
Health: hair as symbol of, 41–42; spiritual, 248
Heart: unclean, 40–41; desires of, 41; symbolism of, 46–49
Heathens, swine as symbol of, 261
Heaven, symbolism regarding, 89
Hebrew, knowledge of, 332 (n. 35)
Heidegger, Martin, on hermeneutics, 332–33 (n. 39)
Helaman: book of, 121–22; meaning of, 229
Helmet, symbolism of, 68
Henry, Matthew, on swaddling clothes, 77
Hermeneutics, 11, 18, 332–33 (n. 39)
Hezekiah, meaning of, 287
High priest, Mosaic: clothing of, 102, 341 (n. 4), 342 (n. 10), 350 (n. 30); as type for Christ, 104
Hinckley, Gordon B., on symbolism in temple, 296
Hireling, as type for uncommitted individual, 198
Holiness: hair as symbol of, 42; symbolic representation of, 104
Holland, Jeffrey R.: on Jesus Christ as exemplar, 262; on symbolism regarding Jesus Christ, 269
"Holy garments," 341 (n. 4)
Holy Ghost: seeking guidance of, 7, 18–19; symbols regarding, 50, 59; companionship of, 68–69; characteristics of, 303–4

Holy Land, symbolic representation of, 226
Hoof: cloven, 257; solid, 258
Hope, green as symbol of, 93
Horns: symbolism of, 49–50; satanic, 339 (n. 98)
Hosea and Gomer, as type for apostasy, 194–95, 380 (nn. 62, 63)
Humility: feet as symbol of, 39; sheep as symbols of, 257
Hypocrisy: dogs as symbols of, 245–46; swine as symbol of, 246, 260–61; modern examples of, 247–48; gnat and camel as examples of, 252–53
Hyrum, meaning of, 229

Ichabod, meaning of, 221
Idioms, symbolic nature of, 20–21
Idolatry, 198, 351 (n. 40)
Ill omen, thirteen as symbol of, 136
Image, definition of, 11
Imagery, 331 (n. 29); keys to understanding, 333 (n. 41)
Immanuel, meaning of, 229–30, 288, 389 (n. 47)
Immaturity, spiritual, 198
Immorality: rabbits as symbol of, 246; of Pharisees, 251
Imperfection, six as symbol of, 122
Incompleteness, symbols for, 58, 122
Increase, eternal, 352 (n. 60)
Indignation, nose as symbol of, 53
Inheritance, attitude toward, 261
Innocence, 198
Inspiration, 19, 24–25, 404 (n. 93); in interpreting book of Revelation, 147; essential to scripture interpretation, 332 (n. 35)
Institutions, typical, 12–13
Integrity, loins as symbol of, 52

Intent: direction as indicator of, 150; unrighteous, 255
Interpretation, responsible, 18–22
Interruption, numeric symbol for, 117
Intimacy, spiritual, 31–32
Invasion, north as symbol of, 164
Iranaeus, on carcass as type for Christ, 276
Isaac: as type for Christ, 177–78; meaning of, 230, 389 (n. 51); age of, at time of sacrifice experience, 377 (n. 17)
Isaiah: meaning of, 288; book of, 363–64 (n. 117)
Ishmael, meaning of, 220, 288–89
Isopsephy, definition of, 368 (n. 184)
Israel: symbol of three in ancient, 116–17; lost tribes of, 133, 163, 360 (n. 76), 374 (n. 72); twelve tribes of, 134, 280–82; symbolism in wandering of, 137–38; gathering of, 158, 169–70, 276, 374 (n. 71); "prostituting" of, 195; meaning of, 230, 289; idolatrous practices of, 351 (n. 40); scattering of, 393 (n. 12)

Jacob: symbolism in story of, 101, 125; as type for Christ, 179. See also Esau
James, characteristics of, 304
Jared, meaning of, 230
Jaredites, fall of the, 160–61, 373–74 (n. 56)
Jeremiah: use of north in writings of, 163; meaning of, 289
Jericho, symbolism in account of, 126, 137
Jerusalem: symbols for, 198, 347 (n. 85); siege of, 393 (n. 12)
Jesus Christ: symbolism regarding, 3, 71, 91, 111, 269–306,

326 (n. 8); use of parables, 7, 13–14; as focal point of scriptures, 25, 270; atonement of, 30–31, 99; second coming of, 35, 156, 168; humility of, 39; shoulders symbolic of, 55; birth and ministry of, 76–77, 115–16, 138; as bridegroom, 79; submission to, 79; as light of world, 85–86; as shepherd, 94; mockery of, by soldiers, 97; suffering in Gethsemane, 99, 278–79; high priest as type for, 104; resurrection of, 130–31; power and authority of, 134–35, 224; brass serpent as symbol for, 143; prophecies about, 156; as bread of life, 161; people as types for, 172–93, 376–77 (n. 3), 400 (n. 37); Abel symbolic of, 172–73, 274–75; taking name of, 219, 242; significance of name, 231, 364–65 (nn. 123, 133, 134), 389 (n. 47); followers of, 245; sheep as symbols of, 257; goat as symbol for, 257; as exemplar, 262; unclean spirits cast out by, 262–65; testimony of, 269–70; examples of scriptural types for, 270; Kolob as type for, 291–94; manna as type for, 295–96; characteristics of, 303–4; in temple at age twelve, 366 (n. 156); as spirit brother to Lucifer, 377 (n. 5), 399 (n. 16); age of, at Crucifixion, 378 (n. 32); traditional beliefs regarding, 378–79 (n. 39); miraculous powers of, 378–79 (n. 39); evil spirits cast out by, 397–98 (nn. 70, 72, 76, 77, 79)
Joel, meaning of, 289
John, characteristics of, 304
John the Baptist, as type for Joseph Smith, 206
Johnston, Robert, on numerology, 356 (n. 11)
Joseph of Egypt: symbolism in account of, 125, 133; meaning of, 221, 231; as type for Christ, 180–81, 201–3; as type for Joseph Smith, 206–7, 382 (n. 108)
Joseph Smith Translation: significance of veil in, 81; of story of gnats and camel, 252; of parable of carcass and eagles, 276
Joshua: symbolism in account of, 169; as type for Christ, 183; meaning of, 290, 378 (n. 34), 380 (n. 62)
Judas: symbolism in account of, 134; gematria in account of, 141
Judea, siege of, 393 (n. 12)
Judgment, 225–26; eternal, 35–36; divine, 86–88, 164; brass as symbol of, 91; nine as symbol of, 131, 366 (n. 140); symbols for, 360 (n. 74)
Julius Caesar, meaning of, 225
Justin Martyr, on Joshua's name, 378 (n. 34)

Kareah, meaning of, 232
Kemuel, meaning of, 232
Keys, priesthood, 303
Kimball, Spencer W.: on parable of ten virgins, 361–62 (n. 83); on resurrection as priesthood ordinance, 401 (n. 44)
Kinsman, ten as symbol for, 133
Knees, symbolism of, 27, 50–51
Knight, Newel, evil spirit cast out of, 266–67
Knots, as symbols, 69, 344 (n. 43)
Knowledge: eyes as symbol of, 36–37; heart as seat of, 46–47

Kolob: throne of God near, 291; as type for Jesus Christ, 291–94; misconceptions regarding, 402 (n. 59); meaning of, 402 (n. 62)
Korihor: meaning of, 231; as anti-Christ, 231–32
Kosher foods, 244–45, 248
Krutz, J. H., on symbolism in Old Testament, 327 (n. 20)

Laban, meaning of, 232
Lambs, as symbols, 256–57
Lameness, symbol for, 225
Language: symbolic representation of, 113; understanding ancient, 332 (n. 35)
Last days, prophecy regarding, 117
Law of consecration, 132
Law of Moses: symbolic numbers in, 116; symbolic representation of, 123; punishment under, 138; animals in, 244; clean and unclean animals defined in, 277–78
Leadership, head as symbol of, 46–47
Leah, meaning of, 238
Learning, 328–29 (n. 331)
Leaven, as symbol, 125
Lee, Harold B.: on traits of righteous man, 66–67; on armor of God, 68
Left: hand, 162–63; and north, similar meaning of, 374 (n. 67)
Lemuel, meaning of, 232
Lepers, cleansing ceremony for, 126; ten, 132; as type for sinfulness, 198
Letters and numbers, ancient use of, 139–40
Levi: staff of, 280–82; tribe of, 400 (n. 35)
Liahona, symbolic significance of, 3
Liefield, Walter, on man possessed by evil spirits, 397–98 (n. 72)

Life: blood as symbol of, 29; head as symbol of, 46; green as symbol of, 93; red as symbol of, 99; symbols of preservation of, 161
Light: eyes as symbol of, 36–37; as symbol of divinity, 85; and dark, symbolism of, 85–86, 349 (n. 19); as symbol of faith, 86; white as symbol of, 104; Hebrew word for, 345 (n. 54)
Linen, 345 (n. 57); breeches, 71
Linguistics, 21
Literary devices, 13–15
Loathing, nose as symbol of, 53
Locust, as symbol, 246, 251–52
Loins, as symbols, 51–52, 343 (n. 26)
Lot, symbolism in story of, 141–42
Love, thirteen as symbol of, 140–41
Lucifer, 215–17, 371 (n. 225); symbolism regarding, 163–64; meaning of, 232; Cain as symbol for, 272–74. *See also* Satan
Lust, goats as symbols of, 257

Madsen, Truman G., on betrayal of Joseph Smith, 378 (n. 29)
Man: fallen state of, 120–22; seven women to take hold of, 126–27; son of a, 224
Manasseh, symbolism in blessing of, 165
Mann, C. S.: on sea as symbol, 360 (n. 75), 398 (n. 76); on carcass as symbol, 399–400 (n. 22)
Manna: as type for Jesus Christ, 295–96; as symbol, 402–3 (n. 63)
Mantle (robe), as symbol of power and authority, 72–73
Mark of the beast, 144, 146–47, 370–71 (n. 223). *See also* Beast
Marriage: responsibilities of, 64; covenant, 69; as symbol of man's relationship to God, 78–79;

symbolic representation of, 113;
partners, as types, 192;
interfaith, 258–59, 395 (n. 51);
eternal, 300; plural, 127, 363–64
(n. 117)
Marshall, Peter: on small deeds, xii,
325 (n. 4)
Mary, symbolism regarding, 350
(n. 29)
Materialism, 160; gematria
regarding, 370 (n. 216)
McConkie, Bruce R.: on parables,
7; on literal meanings of
scriptures, 23; on name of Satan,
233; on diversity of Church
members, 255, on Christ's
suffering in Gethsemane, 279;
on seraphs and angels, 297; on
true order of prayer, 304–5; on
ordinances and symbolism,
306–7; on understanding
ancient languages, 332 (n. 35);
on parable of ten virgins, 361–62
(n. 83); on symbolism in "seven
women" verse in Isaiah, 363–64
(n. 117); on godliness of Enoch's
people, 382 (n. 102); on divine
origin of names, 401–2 (n. 50)
McConkie, Joseph Fielding: on
inspiration, 24; on trees as
symbols, 95; on meaning of
name Hyrum, 229; on cherubs
as protectors, 298; on symbolism
in scripture, 326 (n. 8); on
authorial awareness in scripture,
333–34 (n. 45); on truth, 334
(n. 47); on cherubs and seraphs,
403 (n. 74); on tree of life, 403
(n. 76)
McConkie, Oscar W. Jr., on
cherubs, 298
Meanings: literal and figurative, 2;
hidden, 148
Melchizedek, as type for Christ, 3,
183–85

Melchizedek Priesthood,
restoration of, 302–3
Melek, meaning of, 233
Merism, 167, 376 (n. 90)
Messengers, revelation received
through, 301, 303
Metaphor, definition of, 13
Mind, forehead as symbol of, 39–41
Ministering angels, 341 (n. 129)
Missionaries, as two witnesses, 115
Missionary work, 36–37; blessings
of, 38–39; symbols pertaining to,
105
Miter, symbolism of, 70
Modesty, veil as symbol of, 78
Moon, as symbol, 20, 331–32
Moral purity, silver as symbol of,
102–3
Mordecai, purple robe of, 96
Mormon: symbolism in story of,
133; as type for Joseph Smith,
208–10; meaning of, 233
Morris, Leon, on veil as symbol, 81
Mortality: blood as symbol of, 29,
31; imperfect nature of, 123;
symbols for, 224
Mosaic high priest, clothing of, 89,
100
Mosaic law: symbolism in, 2;
symbolic numbers in, 116;
symbolic representation of, 123;
animals in, 244; clean and
unclean animals defined in,
277–78
Mosaic tabernacle. *See* Tabernacle,
Mosaic
Moses, 137–38, 201–3; symbolic
use of numbers by, 107; as type
for Christ, 185–88; as type for
Brigham Young, 210–11; as type
for Joseph Smith, 211–12;
meaning of, 233; qualifications
of, 379 (n. 45); marriages of, 383
(n. 133); speaking abilities of,

384 (n. 137); characteristics of, 384 (n. 139)
Motif, 14–15
Mountain: as symbol, 337 (n. 48); holy, 375 (n. 75)
Mourning: hair as symbol of, 41–42; sackcloth as symbol of, 74, 346 (n. 69); black as symbol of, 88–89
Mouth, symbolism of, 56
Mulek, meaning of, 233
Mysteries, mistaken exploration of, 246

Name: significance of, 219, 242, 386 (nn. 11, 12), 387 (nn. 14, 15); as symbol of ownership, responsibility, 219–20; secret, 220; blotting out of, 220; new, 221, 285–86, 386 (n. 9); scriptural references to, 222; symbolism in, 284–86; theophoric, 285, 386–87 (n. 13); as symbol, 385 (n. 4), 386 (n. 5); connected with physical traits, 386 (n. 7); connected with personality, 386 (n. 8); as indicators of occupation, 386 (n. 10); given by divine command, 387 (n. 15); divine origin of Book of Mormon, 401–2 (n. 50)
Native Americans, symbolism of hand among, 44–45
Natural man, symbolism regarding, 165–66
Nature, relationship of color to, 84
Neck, symbolism of, 52–53
Nehemiah, meaning of, 290
Nelson, Russell M., 331 (n. 32)
Nephi: on scriptures as types, 3, 398–99 (n. 1); as type for Joseph Smith, 213; meaning of, 234
Nephites: symbolism in story of, 123; symbolism understood by, 333 (n. 43)
Nero, gematria regarding, 144
New beginnings, eight as symbol of, 129
New Jerusalem, as type, 191–92
New Testament, numerology in, 364–65 (n. 123)
Nibley, Hugh: on name Amon, 223; on meaning of Chemish, 225; on meaning of Enos, 226; on meaning of Omni, 235; on meaning of Rabbanah, 237; on meaning of Zoram, 241; on three messengers to Adam and Eve, 301; on symbolism of blood, 336 (n. 37); on counterfeit oaths and covenants of Cain, 340 (n. 123); on caps and hats, 344 (n. 49); on Book of Mormon as autobiography, 349 (n. 19); on white clothing, 355 (n. 114); on Adam and Eve's sacrificial offering, 377 (n. 14); on meaning of Kolob, 402 (n. 62)
Nimrod, meaning of, 234
Nine, as symbol, 131–32, 366 (n. 140)
Noah, 380 (n. 64); numeric symbolism in account of, 125; symbolism in story of, 129–30, 137; as type for Christ, 189–90; meaning of, 234; ministry of, 379 (n. 50)
Nod, meaning of, 399 (n. 8)
North: ancient connotations of, 162; Hebrew word for, 162; association of, with left hand, 162–63, 374 (n. 67); as symbol of evil, 164–65; as symbol, 373–74 (n. 56), 374 (n. 64)
Nose, symbolism of, 50, 53, 107, 110, 340 (n. 110)
Numbers: misconceptions about, 108–9; ancient use of, 108–9;

multiplication of, 110–11; repetition of, 111; symbolic and literal, 112, 123–24, 367 (n. 162); as symbols (list), 319–21
Numeric symbolism: in book of Revelation, 111, 117, 128, 362 (n. 96); in Mosaic tabernacle, 125, 361 (n. 81); in rituals, 126
Numerology, 356 (nn. 11, 12), 368 (nn. 181, 185); definition of, 107; history of, 109–10; categories of, 110–12, 368 (n. 188); in Old Testament, 356 (n. 12); in New Testament, 364–65 (n. 123); erroneous use of, 371 (n. 229)

Oaths: throat as symbol of, 57; and covenants, counterfeit, 340 (n. 123)
Obadiah, meaning of, 234
Obedience, ears as symbols of, 33–36
Offices, typical, 13
Offspring, loins as symbol of, 51–52
Og, meaning of, 234
Oil, as symbol of Holy Ghost, 50
Old Testament: typological approach to, 5; symbolism in, 327 (nn. 15, 20, 21); interpretation of symbolism in, 327–28 (n. 21); numerology in, 356 (n. 12)
Olive, as symbol, 352 (n. 64)
Oliver Cowdery, 199
Omni, meaning of, 235, 401–2 (n. 50)
Omniscience, eyes as symbols of, 36
One: as symbol, 112–14, 358 (n. 44); Hebrew words for, 113
Oneness: numeric symbol for, 113; symbolic representation of, 140–41
One thousand, symbolism of, 139

Opposition: symbolic representation of, 114; six as symbol of, 122
Oppression: neck as symbol of, 53; symbolic representation of, 144–45
Oppressors, names of, 144–45
Order, goat as symbol of, 257
Ordinances, priesthood, 135, 306–7, 341 (n. 5), 401 (n. 44)
Orientation, symbolism regarding, 149. See also Direction
Origen: on symbolism in scriptures, 2; on spiritual meaning of scripture, 327 (n. 12); on significance of names, 386 (n. 12)
Ostler, Blake, on ancient garments and temples, 345 (n. 57)
Ownership, name as symbol of, 219–20
Oxen, 256–57; twelve, symbolism of, 134

Paanchi, meaning of, 235
Packer, Boyd K., on recognizing truth, 25, 148, 334 (n. 46)
Parable, 5, 330 (nn. 12, 13, 15); Christ's use of, 7, 13–14; as extended simile, 14; of ten virgins, 121, 361–62 (n. 83); of prodigal son, 260–62, 396–97 (nn. 63, 66, 67, 68); misinterpretation of, 330 (n. 15)
Parenthood: unselfish nature of, 63–64; symbolism regarding, 77
Passover, 75
Paths, alternate, 256
Patience, oxen as symbols of, 257
Paul: on scriptural symbols, 3–4; on marriage relationship, 78–79; on woman's role, 80–81; as type for Joseph Smith, 214–15; meaning of, 236, 390 (nn. 7, 76); vision

of, 384 (n. 154); writings of, 384 (n. 156)
Peace, 343–44 (n. 36)
Peniel, meaning of, 222, 290
People, as generalized types for Christ, 376–77 (n. 3)
Pericope, 373 (n. 51); regarding sea, 398 (n. 76)
Personal revelation. *See* Revelation
Persons, typical, 12
Peter, vision of, 243–44, 391–92 (nn. 2, 3)
Peter, James, and John: as symbol, 300–306; restoration of Melchizedek Priesthood by, 302–3; as type for Godhead, 305; appear to Joseph Smith and Oliver Cowdery, 404 (n. 97)
Petrine revelation, 244
Pharaoh, meaning of, 236–37
Pharisees: denouncement of, 250–51; apostasy of, 393–94 (n. 17)
Philo of Alexandria: on symbolism, 2; on locust as symbol, 251; on cloven hoof, 257; on significance of names, 386 (n. 12)
Pig. *See* swine
Place, name of, 222
Plague(s): black as symbol of, 87; ten, 132–33, 366 (n. 145); east wind as symbol of, 153–54; sixth, 155
"Plates of brass," 91
Pledge, hand as symbol of, 44
Plunder, symbols for, 249–50
Plural marriage, 127, 363–64 (n. 117)
Poverty, symbolism regarding, 74–76
Power, 348 (n. 105); arm as symbol of, 28; horns as symbol of, 49–50; priesthood, 55–56, 110–11, 339 (n. 97); throat as symbol of, 55–57; wings as

symbol of, 58; robe as symbol of, 72–73; divine recognition of, 82; one thousand as symbol of, 139; oxen as symbols of, 257
Pratt, Orson, 364 (n. 118)
Prayer: symbolism of kneeling in, 27; veil and, 81–82; imperfection in, 122; Jesus Christ as exemplar in, 262; importance of, 264; unwillingness to offer, 266–67; the Lord's, 304; true order of, 304–5; Jewish, 358 (n. 45); symbolism of number three in, 359 (n. 62)
Preparation, symbols regarding, 67
Preparedness: loins as symbol of, 52; personal, 361–62 (n. 83), 402–3 (n. 63)
Priesthood: symbolism in ordination to, 3; robes of, 73–74; symbolic representation of, 110; twelve as symbol for, 134, 281, 339 (n. 97), 379 (n. 58); fulness of, 135; symbolism in, 271; keys, 303; signs and tokens of, 366–67 (n. 158); ordinances of, 135, 306–7, 341 (n. 5), 401 (n. 44)
Priesthood authority: symbolic representation of, 103; in ancient Church, 135
Priesthood bearers: cleanliness essential to, 39; symbolic representation of, 135
Priesthood power, 55–56, 110–11, 339 (n. 97)
Principles, abstract, 11
Priorities: forehead as symbol of, 40–41; heart as symbol of, 48
Prodigal son, parable of, 260–62, 396–97 (nn. 63, 66, 67, 68)
Prooftexting, 325–26 (chap. 1, n. 1)
Prophets: teachings of, 68–69; known by name, 242; guidance of, 248; responsibilities of, 270;

scripture interpretation by, 332 (n. 35)
Protection, 352 (n. 63); bosom as symbol of, 31–32; wings as symbol of, 57–58; against evil spirits, 264
Pruning vineyard, 95
Punishment, symbols of, 87
Purity, 198; symbols for, 27, 66, 104; gold as symbol of, 92–93
Purple: symbolism of, 96–99; robes of, 96, 97
Pythagoras, as "father of the symbolism of numbers," 110

Quartus, 390 (n. 79); meaning of, 237

Rabbanah, meaning of, 237
Rabbits, as symbols, 246
Rachel, meaning of, 238
Rain: south as symbol of, 157; as symbol, 158–59; as symbol of blessings, 161
Read, Lenet Hadley: on significance of number eight, 131; on ministry of Noah, 379 (n. 50)
Rebekah: as type for bride of Christ, 193; meaning of, 237–38
Rebellion: ears as symbols of, 34; thirteen as symbol of, 136–37; symbols of, 194, 247
Rebirth, eight as symbol of, 129
Red, as symbol, 99–102, 353–54 (n. 88)
Redemption, symbolic representation of, 102
Reformation, gematria regarding, 145–46
Refreshment, south as symbol of, 157
"Remnant theology," 118
Renaming, significance of, 221
Renewal, south as symbol of, 157
Repentance: sackcloth as symbol of, 74; complete, 126; symbolism regarding, 198; of prodigal son, 396–97 (nn. 67, 68)
Reproduction: two as symbol of, 115; symbolism of number seven in, 128
Reproductive organs, symbolism of, 51–52
Reproductive power, aprons as symbol of, 62–63
Responsibility: shoulders as symbol of, 54–55; covenant, 135; name as symbol of, 219–20
Resurrection, 9, 401 (n. 44); green as symbol of, 93; red as symbol of, 99; symbolic representation of, 120; of Christ, 130–31; eight as symbol of, 129; as priesthood ordinances, 401 (n. 44)
Revelation, 19; symbolism regarding, 90; silver as symbol of, 103
Revelation, book of, 109, 128; symbolism of eyes in, 36; symbolism of forehead in, 40–41; symbolism of beasts in, 58; color symbolism in, 88; numeric symbolism in, 111, 117, 128, 362 (n. 96); symbolism of fractions in, 118; 144,000 individuals in, 136; inspiration in interpreting, 147
Reverence: symbolic representation of, 38–39, 75–76; knees as symbol of, 50–51
Reward: green as symbol of, 94; purple as symbol of, 97
Reynolds, George: on name Melek, 233; on meaning of Nephi's name, 234; on Sarah's name, 238
Right hand, 375 (n. 81); association of south with, 157
Righteousness: symbolic representation of, 65–67, 104,

117–18, 255; commitment to, 126; enemies of, 169; as protection, 264; Samson's abandonment of, 337 (n. 62)
Riplakish, meaning of, 238
Robe of authority, 55
Robes, symbolism of, 72–74
Robinson, Stephen E., on Christ's compassion for sinner, 277
Rods, twelve, 400 (n. 35); symbolism of, 280–82
Royalty, symbolic representation of, 96
Ryken, Leland, on symbolism of veil, 80

Sabbath observance, 90
Sackcloth, as symbol, 74, 346 (n. 69)
Sacrament, symbolism regarding, 278
Sacrifice: power of, 49–50; Mosaic, significance of, 102; animal, 243; oxen as symbols of, 257; ancient, 367 (n. 170)
Sailhamer, John H., on Abraham's sojourn, 381 (n. 87)
Salvation, 352 (n. 63); helmet of, 339 (n. 89)
Samson: symbolism in story of, 43; numerical symbolism in account of, 127; strength of, 127, 337 (n. 62)
Samuel, meaning of, 220, 290
Samuel the Lamanite, prophecies of, 121
Sarah: meaning of, 238; as mother of Isaac, 389 (n. 51)
Sarai, meaning of, 238
Sash, symbolism of, 74
Satan, 3, 215–17; symbolic representation of, 56–57, 161, 163–64, 339 (n. 90), false promises of, 57; limitations of, 118–19, 404 (n. 9); west as

kingdom of, 168; name of, 233; goat as symbol of, 257; protection against, 264, 301, 344 (n. 38); influence of, 263, 385 (n. 166), 399 (n. 11); appears to Joseph Smith and Oliver Cowdery, 302–3, 404 (n. 96); temporary victory of, 380 (n. 71)
Saul, meaning of, 236
"Saved by water," 130
Scapegoat, symbolism of, 100–101
Scarlet: as symbol of war and bloodshed, 99–100; symbolism of, 101, 353–54 (nn. 87–88)
Scott, Richard G., on Adam and Eve, 63
Scripture: literal interpretation of, 1, 19, 23, 328 (n. 26); symbolic language in, 1–2, 3, 19, 325 (n. 3), 326 (n. 8), 328 (n. 26); as types, 3, 398–99 (n. 1); analysis of, 16–17; latter-day, 19–20; authors of, 21–22; ascribing mistaken meaning to, 22–23; extremes in interpretation, 23–24; historicity of, 23–24, 333 (n. 44); significance of clothing in, 61; understanding, 79–80; colors named in, 83–84; inspired authors of, 108–9; cultural background of, 326 (n. 4); spiritual meaning of, 327 (n. 12); inspiration in interpreting, 332 (n. 35); authorial awareness of, 333–34 (n. 45); numerology in, 356 (nn. 12, 14)
Scripture study, pitfalls to avoid in, 332 (n. 35)
Sea, 2; calming of the, 265; as symbol, 360 (n. 75), 398 (n. 76), 400–401 (n. 4)
Seals, seven, 127–28
Second Coming, 35, 156, 168; unrighteous consumed at time

of, 255–56; symbolism regarding, 402–3 (n. 63)
Secret combinations, 160; symbols pertaining to, 56–57
Security, bosom as symbol of, 31–32
Self-centeredness, swine as symbol of, 260
Self-deception, 247
Self-discipline, 37; hands as symbol of, 45; goat as symbol of, 257
Seraph, 297, 403 (n. 74); meaning of, 403 (n. 69)
Serpent, brass, 3, 91, 143–44, 369 (n. 197)
Serpents: poisonous, 160–61, 373–74 (n. 56); as symbols, 161
Service, symbols for, 259–60
Seth, as type for Christ, 190
Seven, 110, 123–29, 363 (n. 114); Hebrew meaning of, 124; as symbol of completeness, 128; churches, 364 (n. 121)
Seven women, possible symbolic interpretation of, 126–27, 363–64 (nn. 117, 119, 120)
Sheep, as symbols, 256–57
Shelem, meaning of, 222
Shema, 358 (n. 45)
Sherem, meaning of, 238
Shield, symbolism of, 68
Shoes: symbolism of, 67, 74–76; as symbols of uncleanness, 75
Shoulders, symbolism of, 54–55
Silver, symbolism of, 102–3
Simile, definition of, 13
Sin: blood symbolic of, 29–30; black as symbol of, 85
Sinfulness, state of, 198
Sinim, Hebrew meaning of, 376 (n. 100)
Sinners: double-minded, 40–41; goats as symbols of, 257
Six, 58, 122–23; as symbol of imperfection, 147–48
Six hundred and sixty-six, 139, 144–48, 369 (nn. 199, 200), 371 (n. 223)
Sjodahl, Janne M., on name Melek, 233
Skin: darkening of, 88; Hebrew word for, 345 (n. 54); light and dark, 349 (n. 19)
Sky, as symbol, 351 (n. 35)
Slavery, 340 (n. 110); symbolism regarding, 75
Smith, Hyrum: martyrdom of, 95; counsel to, 343 (n. 35)
Smith, Joseph, 203–15, 331 (n. 32); on interpretation of symbols, 19–20; martyrdom of, 95; on Second Coming, 156, 168; as type for Christ, 181–82; on Satan's influence, 263, 385 (n. 166), 399 (n. 11); casts evil spirit out of Newel Knight, 266–67; restoration of Melchizedek Priesthood to, 302–3; Satan appears to, 302–3, 404 (n. 96); on meaning of beast, 359 (n. 66); betrayers of, 378 (n. 29); likeness of, to Joseph of Egypt, 382 (n. 108); character of, 382 (nn. 110, 112); speaking abilities of, 384 (n. 138); first vision of, 384 (n. 154); writings of, 384 (n. 157); inspiration received by, 404 (n. 93); Peter, James, and John appear to, 404 (n. 97)
Smith, Joseph Fielding: on fall of Adam, 63; on parable of prodigal son, 396–97 (n. 67)
Smith, Mick, on meaning of number one, 358 (n. 44)
Socrates, 328–29 (n. 31)
Son, prodigal. *See* Prodigal son, parable of
Soothsayers, numerology practiced by ancient, 368 (n. 185)
Sorrow, west as symbol of, 166

Soul, heart as symbol of, 49
South: Hebrew word for, 157; as symbol, 157–61, 373–74 (n. 56); as symbol for covenant, 157, 159–60
Sperry, Sidney B., on Paul's name, 236
Spirits: unclean, 262–65; discernment of, 303; evil, 266–67, 397–98 (nn. 70, 72, 76, 77, 79)
Spiritual death, symbolism regarding, 265
Spiritual development, purple as symbol of, 97
Spirituality, 361–62 (n. 83)
Spiritual perfection, seven as symbol of, 124
Spouse, unfaithful, as symbol of apostasy, 194
Stability, symbols for, 149, 254
Staff, blooming of, 280–82
Stephen: martyrdom of, 33–34; meaning of, 238–39
Sticks, twelve, 400 (n. 35); symbolism of, 280–82
Strait and narrow path, avoidance of, 256
Strength: arm as symbol of, 28; horns as symbol of, 49–50; wings as symbol of, 58–59; of Samson, 127, 337 (n. 62)
Stuart, Douglas, on context of scriptures, 2
Study guides, 21
Subjection, feet as symbol of, 38
Submission: arms as symbol of, 28–29; knees as symbol of, 50–51; veil as symbol of, 78
Submit, Greek word for, 347 (n. 95)
Sun: symbolic representation of, 92, 169; setting of, 166–67; rising and setting of, 167–68; and moon, as symbols, 331–32 (n. 33)

Superabundance, eight as symbol of, 365 (n. 129)
Supplication, hand as symbol of, 44–45
Swaddling clothes, as symbol, 76–77, 347 (nn. 85, 87)
Swine: as symbol, 246, 260–65, 398 (n. 79); unclean spirits cast into, 262–65; as symbol of Gentile land, 263; as example of power of evil, 265
Sword, as symbol, 68–69, 299–300, 403 (n. 75)
Symbol, definition of, 11, 329 (n. 4)
Symbolic numbers: origin of, 112; common, 123–24. See also Numbers
Symbolism: scriptural, 1–3, 19, 325 (n. 3), 326 (n. 8), 328 (n. 26); Topical Guide listings on, 4; definition of, 6, 326 (n. 2); reasons for using, 6–9; as universal language, 7; power of, 7–8; multiple interpretations of, 8, 24–25; abstract concepts represented by, 8–9; interpretation of, 11; literary, 15; connotations and denotations of, 19; consistency in meanings of, 20; unintentional, 22; errors in interpretation of, 22–25; misunderstandings about, 80; study of, 325 (n. 5); LDS, 327 (n. 17); Christocentric, 327–28 (n. 21); significance of, 331 (nn. 29, 33), ancient use of, 333 (n. 40); numeric, 367–68 (n. 179)
Symbols, miscellaneous (list), 321–23
Sympathy, bowels as symbol of, 32–33

Tabernacle, ancient, 365 (n. 132)
Tabernacle, Mosaic, 49, 70,

365 (n. 132); use of color in, 89, 96, 100, 104; curtains of, 100; foundations of, 102–3; symbolic use of numbers in, 125, 361 (n. 81); gate of, 156; symbolism in, 350 (n. 31)
"Table of shewbread," covering of, 100
Talmage, James E.: on the Fall, 151–52; on Christ's suffering in Gethsemane, 279
Taylor, John, 364 (n. 118); on symbolism of bow knot, 69; on symbolic meaning of pruning vineyard, 95
Temperament, nose as symbol of, 53
Temple: symbolic elements of, 27, 75, 102–3, 296, 342 (n. 14), 345 (nn. 57, 58); symbolic clothing in, 61, 341 (n. 7); Israelite, 64; veil of, 80, 280; Eden as first, 119–20; symbolism of number five in, 121; east gate of, 156; symbolic use of directions in, 170
Temple clothing, 347 (n. 92); symbolic meaning of, 70–72, 345 (nn. 57, 58)
Temple endowment, 366–67 (n. 158), 379–80 (n. 59); purpose of, 300; symbolism in, 306
Temple garment, 70–72
Temptation, symbols regarding, 67–68
Ten, as symbol, 132–33, 366 (n. 147)
Ten virgins, parable of, 121, 361–62 (n. 83)
Tertullus, meaning of, 239
Testaments, two, 115
Testimony: two as symbol of, 115; regarding Jesus Christ, 269–70
Tetragrammaton, meaning of, 401 (n. 49)

Thaumaturgus, Gregory, on swaddling clothes, 77
Theudas, meaning of, 239
"Third part," as symbol, 118–19, 359–60 (n. 69)
Thirteen, as symbol, 110, 136–37, 140–41
Thirty, significance of, 141
Thomas, M. Catherine, on tree of life as symbol, 298
Thoughts, forehead as symbol of, 39–41
Thousand, one, symbolism of, 139
Three: symbolism of, 115–17, 359 (n. 62); as symbol of godliness, 300
Three and one-half, as symbol, 117–19, 359 (n. 65)
Three hundred and fifty-eight, symbolism of, 143–44
Throat, as symbol, 55–57
Time: arresting of normal course of, 117; division of, 117, 122–23; imperfect nature of, 123
Timothy, meaning of, 239
Tithing, law of, 132
Toes, animals with multiple, 258
Tongue, naughty, 34
Totality: four as symbol of, 119; seven as symbol of, 124
Transfiguration, symbolism pertaining to, 105
Tree, as symbol, 95–96, 342 (n. 14)
Tree of life, 403 (n. 76); as scriptural motif, 15; fruit of, 105; symbolism of, 298–300
Triads of officers, 301
Tribe, ten as symbol for, 133
Truth: symbolism in harmony with, 21, 65–66; clarity of, 25, 334 (n. 46), 398 (n. 82); acceptance of, 35–36; symbolism regarding, 65–66; mockery of, 97–99, 101–2; recognizing, 148
Twelve: symbolic meaning of, 72,

134–36, 281, 339 (n. 97), 379
  (n. 58); Apostles, 134
Twenty-six, significance of, 141
Two, as symbol, 114–15, 358 (n. 47)
Type: definition of, 11–12, 329
  (n. 4); comparison of, to symbol,
  11–12; classes of, 12–13;
  erroneous interpretation of,
  24–25; brass serpent as, 143–44
Types, people as (list), 171–217
Typology, 171, 327 (n. 19), 330
  (n. 16), 333 (n. 45)

Ulam, meaning of, 240
Uncleanliness: symbolic
  representation of, 29–30;
  Hebrew word for, 244
Unity: symbols of, 112–13, 140–41;
  among Church members, 358
  (n. 46)
Uriah, meaning of, 240, 391 (n. 91)
Uzzah, 339 (n. 81)
Uzzia, meaning of, 240

Vajezatha, meaning of, 240–41
Vaniah, meaning of, 241
Vashti, meaning of, 241
Veil, 348 (nn. 105–7); of temple,
  71, 80, 280; symbolism of, 78,
  80–82, 400 (n. 31); mistaken
  ideas regarding, 78–79; as
  symbol of unbelief, 79–80;
  rending of, 280; as symbol in
  modern times, 347 (n. 92)
Victorinus, on symbolism of seven
  women, 364 (n. 120)
Victory: head as symbol of, 46;
  horns as symbol of, 49–50
Virgin, as type for purity, 198
Virginity: sash as symbol of, 74;
  symbolic representation of, 104
Virgins, parable of ten, 121, 361–62
  (n. 83)
Virkler, Henry A., on symbols and
  types, 329 (n. 4)

von Rad, Gerhard, on
  interpretation of scriptures, 18
Vultures, as symbols, 246, 399
  (n. 19)

War in heaven, 359–60 (n. 69);
  Satan's limitations in, 118–19
Warrior, name representing, 223
Washing, as symbol, 334 (n. 3)
Water: as symbol, 20, 360 (n. 75),
  400–401 (n. 42); muddy, 254;
  scriptural connotations of, 265
Weakness: knees as symbol of, 51;
  preying upon others', 246
Wealth: symbolic representation of,
  92, 96; unrighteous pursuit of,
  247
Week, symbolic of completeness,
  124
West: negative symbolic images of,
  166–67; as symbol, 166–70, 375
  (n. 88); Hebrew words for, 167
White: as symbol, 103–5, 354
  (n. 107); stone, symbolic
  meaning of, 105; negative
  connotations of, 355 (n. 110);
  clothing, 355 (nn. 112–14)
"Whited sepulchers," 247
Whole, ten symbolic of a unit
  within the, 132
Wickedness, 160–61; temporary
  triumph of, 359 (n. 65)
Will: heart as symbol of, 48; throat
  as symbol of, 55–57
Wind, east, 153–54
Winds, four, 120
Wings, symbolism of, 57–59
Wisdom: hair as symbol of, 43; gold
  as symbol of, 92–93
Wise Men, symbolism in account
  of, 153
Witnesses, two or three, 114–15
Woman, symbol for, 158–59
Women: role of, 80–81, 347
  (nn. 94, 95), 363–64 (n. 117);

seven, significance of, 126–27, 363–64 (nn. 117, 119, 120); worldly, 127
Woodruff, Wilford, on messengers from God, 301
Word: refusal to hear, 34; sword as symbol of, 299–300; obtaining the, 343 (n. 35)
Words, 332 (n. 34); and numbers, 357 (n. 20)
Work, of Adam and Eve, 360 (n. 72)
World: overcoming, 78, 245; history of, 127–28
Worldliness, symbolism for, 92, 146, 359 (n. 66)
Worship, symbolic representation of, 38–39
Wrath of God, 164
Wrong choice, left hand symbolic of, 163

Yahweh's glory, east as symbol of, 155

Yoke, as symbol of responsibility, 54
Yom Kippur, symbolic ceremony during, 100–101. *See also* Day of Atonement
"You shall sell," gematria regarding, 370 (n. 216)
Young, Brigham, 210–11; on temple endowment, 300, 366–67 (n. 158), 379–80 (n. 59); as Apostle, 384 (n. 135); on resurrection as priesthood ordinance, 401 (n. 44); inspiration received by, 404 (n. 93)
Youth, immoral behavior of, 247

Zacharias, meaning of, 290–91
Zebach Shelem, meaning of, 222
Zedekiah, symbolism in story of, 133–34
Zion: symbolic representation of, 140–41; redemption of, 158; building up of, 382 (n. 95)
Zoram, meaning of, 241